FEMINIST
THOUGHT

FOURTH EDITION

FEMINIST THOUGHT

A MORE COMPREHENSIVE INTRODUCTION

Rosemarie Tong

University of North Carolina, Charlotte

With a special contribution by Tina Fernandes Botts,
University of North Carolina, Charlotte

WESTVIEW PRESS

A Member of the Perseus Books Group

Westview Press was founded in 1975 in Boulder, Colorado, by notable publisher and intellectual Fred Praeger. Westview Press continues to publish scholarly titles and high-quality undergraduate- and graduate-level textbooks in core social science disciplines. With books developed, written, and edited with the needs of serious nonfiction readers, professors, and students in mind, Westview Press honors its long history of publishing books that matter.

Published by Westview Press,
A Member of the Perseus Books Group

Westview Press books are available at special discounts for bulk purchases in the United States by corporations, institutions, and other organizations. For more information, please contact the Special Markets Department at the Perseus Books Group, 2300 Chestnut Street, Suite 200, Philadelphia, PA 19103, or call (800) 810-4145, ext. 5000, or e-mail special.markets@perseusbooks.com.

Set in 11 point Adobe Garamond Pro

Library of Congress Cataloging-in-Publication Data

Tong, Rosemarie.
    Feminist thought : a more comprehensive introduction / Rosemarie Tong, University of North Carolina, Charlotte ; with a special contribution by Tina Fernandes Botts, University of North Carolina, Charlotte.—Fourth Edition.
        pages   cm
    Includes bibliographical references and index.
    ISBN 978-0-8133-4841-4 (paperback)—ISBN 978-0-8133-4842-1 (e-book)
1. Feminist theory. I. Title.
HQ1206.T65 2013
305.4201—dc23   2013005323

10 9 8 7 6 5 4 3 2 1

Contents

Preface

It has been a real pleasure working on the fourth edition of *Feminist Thought*—an ongoing project in which I never lose interest. Although I didn't alter the chapters on liberal, radical, and Marxist feminism in any substantial way, I did combine the third edition's chapters on psychoanalytic feminism and care-focused feminism. In doing so, I sharpened my thoughts on this material. I also decided to resurrect a section on existentialist feminism from the second edition of my book and combine it with the chapter on postmodern feminism. The result is a much fuller chapter on two demanding approaches to feminist thought. Thanks to my talented colleague, Tina Fernandes Botts, the chapter on multicultural and global feminism in the third edition has been replaced by an enriched chapter entitled "Women of Color Feminisms." Moreover, the chapter on ecofeminism has several new sections. Especially important is the new material on vegetarian/vegan feminism. Finally, the book now has a conclusion, a refreshed bibliography, and questions for discussion at the end of each chapter.

I feel good about the current configuration of *Feminist Thought*. Of all my writings, this book best represents who I am as a philosopher, a feminist, and a woman. I do hope readers find this edition of *Feminist Thought* useful for themselves and their students. As always, this book is meant as a launching pad for others' feminist thoughts.

Acknowledgments

The older I get, the more intensely I realize how dependent I am on others' help. First, I owe much to my talented colleague, Tina Fernandes Botts, a philosopher and lawyer, who brought new life to the chapter now called "Women of Color Feminisms." Tina's remarkable insights added depth and breadth to a chapter I knew was in need of an overhaul. I know that readers of the fourth addition will benefit from Tina's innovative work. I would also like to thank Tina for tightening the arguments throughout the book and for adding other new sections where necessary. And, of course, I want to thank Ada Fung, my ever-ready editor at Westview Press. Others I wish to acknowledge at Perseus are Cathleen Tetro, publisher; Priscilla McGeehon, editorial director; Brooke Maddaford, development editor; and Stephen Pinto, editorial assistant. I'd also like to thank my project editor, Annie Lenth, for shepherding my project through the production process, and my copyeditor, Iris Bass, for perfecting my manuscript. I also want to thank the anonymous reviewers for stimulating me to improve the third edition of *Feminist Thought,* and my graduate student, Melissa Wilson, for drafting the section on vegetarian feminism, and helping with the discussion questions and bibliography. Finally, it is important to me to emphasize that without the expert assistance of my longtime typist and researcher, Lisa Singleton, this book would not be ready for the presses. Lisa typed my many revisions of each chapter not only patiently but with a measure of good cheer. I am very grateful to Lisa for all of her hard work, dedication, professionalism, and support.

As readers can tell, many people helped me during the past year or so. Without their assistance, I'd still be looking at the proverbial blank slate, wondering what to do and how to accomplish it. Truly, we are interdependent creatures, who need one another to survive and thrive.

Introduction

The Diversity of Feminist Thinking

Since writing my first introduction to feminist thought twenty-four years ago, I have become increasingly convinced that feminist thought resists categorization into tidy schools of thought. *Interdisciplinary, intersectional,* and *interlocking* are the kind of adjectives that best describe the way we feminists think. There is an exhilaration in the way we move from one idea to the next, revising our thoughts in midstream. Yet despite the very real problems that come with trying to categorize the thought of an incredibly diverse and large array of feminist thinkers, feminist thought is old enough to have a history complete with a set of labels: liberal, radical, Marxist/socialist, psychoanalytic, care-focused, existentialist, postmodern, women of color, global, postcolonial, transnational, and ecofeminist. To be sure, this list of labels is incomplete and highly contestable. Indeed, it probably does not capture the full range of feminism's intellectual and political commitments to women. Yet, feminist thought's traditional labels still remain serviceable. They signal to the public that feminism is not a monolithic ideology and that all feminists do not think alike. The labels also help mark the number of different approaches, perspectives, and frameworks that a variety of feminists have used to shape both their explanations for women's oppression and their proposed solutions for its elimination.

Because so much of contemporary feminist theory reacts against traditional liberal feminism, liberalism is as good a place as any to begin a survey of feminist thought. This perspective received its classic formulation in Mary Wollstonecraft's *A Vindication of the Rights of Woman*,[1] John Stuart Mill's "The

1

Subjection of Women,"[2] and the nineteenth-century women's suffrage move-ment. Its main thrust, an emphasis still felt in such groups as the National Or-ganization of Women (NOW), is that female subordination is rooted in a set of customary and legal constraints that blocks women's entrance to and success in the so-called public world. To the extent that society holds the false belief that women are, by nature, less intellectually and physically capable than men, it tends to discriminate against women in the academy, the forum, and the mar-ketplace. As liberal feminists see it, this discrimination against women is unfair. Women should have as much chance to succeed in the public realm as men do. Gender justice, insist liberal feminists, requires us, first, to make the rules of the game fair and, second, to ensure that none of the runners in the race for society's goods and services is systematically disadvantaged.

But is the liberal feminist program robust enough to undo women's op-pression? Radical feminists think not. They claim the patriarchal system is characterized by power, dominance, hierarchy, and competition. It cannot be reformed but only ripped out, root and branch. It is not just patriarchy's legal and political structures that must be overturned on the way to women's liber-ation. Its social and cultural institutions (especially the family and organized religion) must also be thoroughly transformed.

As in the past, I remain impressed by the diverse modalities of thinking that count as "radical feminist thought." Although all radical feminists focus on sex, gender, and reproduction as the loci for the development of feminist thought,[3] some of them favor so-called androgyny, stress the pleasures of sex (be it heterosexual, lesbian, or autoerotic), and view as unalloyed bless-ings for women not only the old reproduction-controlling technologies but also the new reproduction-assisting technologies. In contrast, other radical feminists reject androgyny; emphasize the dangers of sex, especially hetero-sexual sex; and regard as harmful to women the new reproduction-assisting technologies and, for the most part, the old reproduction-controlling tech-nologies. As in the third edition of my book, I sort this varied array of radical feminist thinkers into two groups: *radical-libertarian feminists* and *radical-cultural feminists*.[4]

With respect to gender-related issues, radical-libertarian feminists usually reason that if, to their own detriment, men are required to exhibit masculine characteristics only, and if, to their own detriment, women are required to exhibit feminine characteristics only, then the solution to this harmful state of affairs is to *permit* all human beings to be androgynous—to exhibit a full range of masculine *and* feminine qualities. Men should be permitted to ex-plore their feminine dimensions; and women, their masculine ones. No hu-man being should be forbidden the sense of wholeness that comes from combining his or her masculine and feminine sides.

Disagreeing with radical-libertarian feminists that a turn to androgyny is a liberation strategy for women, radical-cultural feminists argue against this move in one of three ways. Some antiandrogynists maintain the problem is not femininity in and of itself, but the low value that patriarchy assigns to feminine qualities (e.g., "gentleness, modesty, humility, supportiveness, empathy, compassionateness, tenderness, nurturance, intuitiveness, sensitivity, unselfishness"), and the high value it assigns to masculine qualities (e.g., "assertiveness, aggressiveness, hardiness, rationality or the ability to think logically, abstractly and analytically, ability to control emotion").[5] They claim that if society can learn to value "feminine" traits as much as "masculine" traits, women's oppression will be a bad memory. Other antiandrogynists object, insisting femininity *is* the problem because it has been constructed by men for patriarchal purposes. To be liberated, women must reject femininity as it has been constructed for them and give it an entirely new meaning. Femininity should no longer be understood as those traits that deviate from masculinity. On the contrary, femininity should be understood as a way of being that needs no reference point external to it. Still other antiandrogynists, reverting to a "nature theory," argue that despite patriarchy's imposition of a false, or inauthentic, *feminine* nature upon women, many women have nonetheless rebelled against it, unearthing their true, or authentic, *female* nature instead. Full personal freedom for a woman consists, then, in her ability to renounce her false feminine self in favor of her true female self.

As difficult as it is to fully reflect the gamut of radical feminist thought on gender, it is even more difficult to do so with respect to sexuality. Radical-libertarian feminists argue that no specific kind of sexual experience should be prescribed as *the* best kind for women.[6] Every woman should be encouraged to experiment sexually with herself, with other women, and with men. Although heterosexuality can be dangerous for women within a patriarchal society, women must nonetheless feel free to follow the lead of their own desires, embracing men if that is their choice.

Radical-cultural feminists disagree. They stress that through pornography, prostitution, sexual harassment, rape, and woman battering,[7] through foot binding, suttee, purdah, clitoridectomy, witch burning, and gynecology,[8] men have controlled women's sexuality for male pleasure. Thus, to become liberated, women must escape the confines of heterosexuality and create a distinct female sexuality through celibacy, autoeroticism, or lesbianism.[9] Only alone, or with other women, can women discover the true pleasure of sex.

Radical feminist thought is as diverse on issues related to reproduction as it is on matters related to sexuality. Radical-libertarian feminists claim biological motherhood drains women physically and psychologically.[10] Women should be free, they say, to use the old reproduction-controlling technologies and the new reproduction-assisting technologies on their own terms—to prevent or terminate unwanted pregnancies or, alternatively, to have children when they want them (pre- or postmenopausally), how they want them (in their own womb or that of another woman), and with whom they want them (a man, a woman, or alone). Some radical-libertarian feminists go further than this, however. They look forward to the day when ectogenesis (extracorporeal gestation in an artificial uterus) entirely replaces the natural process of pregnancy. In contrast to radical-libertarian feminists, radical-cultural feminists claim biological motherhood is the ultimate source of woman's power.[11] It is women who determine whether the human species continues—whether there is life or no life. Women must guard and celebrate this life-giving power, for without it, men will have even less respect and use for women than they have now.[12]

Somewhat unconvinced by the liberal and radical feminist agendas for women's liberation, Marxist and socialist feminists claim it is impossible for anyone, especially women, to achieve true freedom in a class-based society, where the wealth produced by the powerless many ends up in the hands of the powerful few. With Friedrich Engels,[13] Marxist and socialist feminists insist women's oppression originated in the introduction of private property, an institution that obliterated whatever equality of community humans had previously enjoyed. Private ownership of the means of production by relatively few persons, originally all male, inaugurated a class system whose contemporary manifestations are corporate capitalism and imperialism. Reflection on this state of affairs suggests that capitalism itself, not just the larger social rules that privilege men over women, is the cause of women's oppression. If all women—rather than just the "exceptional" ones—are ever to be liberated, the capitalist system must be replaced by a socialist system in which the means of production belong to everyone. No longer economically dependent on men, women will be just as free as men.

Socialist feminists agree with Marxist feminists that *capitalism* is the source of women's oppression, and with radical feminists that *patriarchy* is the source of women's oppression. Therefore, the way to end women's oppression, in socialist feminists' estimation, is to kill the two-headed beast of capitalist patriarchy or patriarchal capitalism (take your pick). Motivated by this goal, socialist feminists seek to develop theories that explain the relationship between capitalism and patriarchy.

During the first stage of theory development, socialist feminists offered several "two-system" explanations of women's oppression. Among these two-system theories were those forwarded by Juliet Mitchell and Alison Jaggar. In *Woman's Estate,* Mitchell claimed that women's condition is determined not only by the structures of production (as Marxist feminists think), but also by the structures of reproduction and sexuality (as radical feminists believe), and the socialization of children (as liberal feminists argue).[14] She stressed that women's status and function in all of these structures must change if women are to achieve full liberation. Still, in the final analysis, Mitchell gave the edge to capitalism over patriarchy as women's worst enemy.

Like Mitchell, Alison Jaggar attempted to achieve a synthesis between Marxist and radical feminist thought. Acknowledging that all feminist perspectives recognize the conflicting demands made on women as wives, mothers, daughters, lovers, and workers,[15] Jaggar insisted that socialist feminism is unique because of its concerted effort to interrelate the myriad forms of women's oppression. She used the unifying concept of alienation to explain how, under capitalism, everything (work, sex, play) and everyone (family members and friends) that could be a source of women's integration as persons, becomes instead a cause of their disintegration. Together with Mitchell, Jaggar insisted there are only complex explanations for women's subordination. Yet, in contrast to Mitchell, she named patriarchy rather than capitalism as the worst evil visited on women.

After Mitchell and Jaggar, another group of socialist feminists aimed to develop new explanations of women's oppression that did not in any way pinpoint capitalism or patriarchy as the *primary* source of women's limited well-being and freedom. Iris Marion Young and Heidi Hartmann constructed explanations for women's oppression that viewed capitalism and patriarchy as interactive to the point of full symbiosis. To a greater or lesser extent, these thinkers addressed the question of whether capitalism could survive the death of patriarchy, or vice versa. Although the nuances of their theories were difficult to grasp, Young and Hartmann—like their predecessors Mitchell and Jaggar—pushed feminists to address issues related to women's unpaid, underpaid, or disvalued work.

To the degree that liberal, radical, and Marxist-socialist feminists focus on the macrocosm (patriarchy or capitalism) in their respective explanations of women's oppression, psychoanalytic and care-focused feminists are most at home in the microcosm of the individual. They claim the roots of women's oppression are embedded deep in the female psyche. Initially, psychoanalytic feminists focused on Sigmund Freud's work, looking within it for a better understanding of sexuality's role in the oppression of women. According to Freud, in the so-called pre-Oedipal stage, all infants are symbiotically attached to their mothers, whom they perceive as omnipotent. The mother-infant relationship is an ambivalent one, however: sometimes mothers give too much—their presence is overwhelming—but other times mothers give too little—their absence disappoints.

The pre-Oedipal stage ends with the so-called Oedipal complex, the process by which the boy gives up his first love object, the mother, to escape castration at the hands of the father. As a result of submitting his id (desires) to the super-ego (collective social conscience), the boy is fully integrated into culture. To-gether with his father, he will rule over nature and woman, both of whom supposedly contain a similarly irrational power. In contrast to the boy, the girl, who has no penis to lose, separates slowly from her first love object, the mother. As a result, the girl's integration into culture is incomplete. She exists at the periphery, or margin, of culture as the one who does not rule but is ruled, largely because, as Dorothy Dinnerstein suggested, she fears her own power.[16]

Because the Oedipus complex is the root of male rule, or patriarchy, some psychoanalytic feminists speculate that the complex is nothing more than the product of men's imagination—a psychic trap that everyone, especially women, should try to escape. Others object that unless we are prepared for reentry into a chaotic state of nature, we must accept some version of the Oedipus complex as the experience that integrates the individual into soci-ety. In accepting *some* version of the Oedipus complex, Sherry Ortner noted, we need not accept the *Freudian* version, according to which the qualities of authority, autonomy, and universalism are labeled male, whereas love, depen-dence, and particularism are labeled female.[17] These labels, meant to privi-lege that which is male over that which is female, are not essential to the Oedipus complex. Rather, they are simply the consequences of a child's actual experience with men and women. As Ortner saw it, dual parenting (as recommended also by Dorothy Dinnerstein and Nancy Chodorow) and dual participation in the workforce would change the gender valences of the Oedipus complex.[18] Authority, autonomy, and universalism would no longer be the exclusive property of men; love, dependence, and particularism would no longer be the exclusive property of women.

Not sure that dual parenting and dual participation in the workforce were up to changing the gender valences of the Oedipal complex, a new generation of psychoanalytic feminists turned to theorists such as Jacques Lacan for more insights into the psychosexual dramas that produce "man" and "woman," the "feminine" and the "masculine," the "heterosexual" and the "lesbian," and so forth. Formidable theorists such as Luce Irigaray and Julia Kristeva claimed that feminists had spent too much time focusing on the Oedipal realm and not nearly enough time on the prelinguistic, pre-Oedipal domain. Often re-ferred to as the Imaginary, this is the domain infants are supposed to leave behind so they can enter the Symbolic order, the realm of language, rules, and regimes: civilization. But, asked Irigaray and Kristeva, why should women abandon the Imaginary so they can be oppressed, suppressed, and repressed in patriarchy's Symbolic order? Why not instead stay in the Imaginary, and relish the joy of being different from men? Why not remain identified with one's first love, the mother, and develop with her new ways of speaking and writing, of constituting one's subjectivity, that do not lead to women's oppression? Why lead life on men's terms at all?

In the third edition of this book, I decided not to discuss such theorists as Carol Gilligan and Nel Noddings alongside psychoanalytic feminists. I have now changed my thinking and choose to discuss care-focused feminists (sometimes referred to as gender feminists or cultural feminists) in the same chapter as psychoanalytic feminists. What fundamentally joins psychoanalytic and care-focused feminists is their common interest in the differences that distinguish the female psyche from the male psyche. However, unlike psychoanalytic feminists, care-focused feminists do not emphasize boys' and girls' *psychosexual* development. Instead they stress boys' and girls' *psychomoral* development.

Another feature that distinguishes care-focused feminists from psychoanalytic feminists is (obviously) their focus on the nature and practice of care. More than any other group of feminist thinkers, care-focused feminists are interested in understanding why, to a greater or lesser degree, women are usually associated with the emotions and the body, and men with reason and the mind. On a related note, care-focused feminists seek to understand why women as a group are usually linked with interdependence, community, and connection, whereas men as a group are usually linked with independence, selfhood, and autonomy. These thinkers offer a variety of explanations for *why* societies divide realities into things "feminine" and things "masculine." But whatever their explanation for men's and women's differing gender identities and behaviors, care-focused feminists regard women's hypothetically greater capacities for care as a human strength, so much so that they sometimes privilege feminist approaches to an ethics of care over the reigning ethics of justice in the Western world. In addition, care-focused feminists provide insightful explanations for why women as a group disproportionately shoulder the burden of care in virtually all societies, and why men as a group do not routinely engage in caring practices. Finally, care-focused feminists provide plans and policies for reducing women's burden of care so that women have as much time and energy as men have to develop themselves as full persons.

Another change made in this fourth edition is adding a section on existentialist feminism to the chapter on postmodern feminism. Looking into women's psyches more deeply than do even psychoanalytic and care-focused feminists, Simone de Beauvoir provided an ontological-existential explanation for women's oppression. In *The Second Sex,* one of the key theoretical texts of twentieth-century feminism,[19] she argued that woman is oppressed by virtue of her otherness. Woman is the other because she is not-man. While man is the free, self-determining being who defines the meaning of his existence; woman is the other, the object whose meaning is determined for her. If woman is to become a self, a subject, she must, like man, transcend the definitions, labels, and essences limiting her existence. She must make herself be whoever she wants to be.

Postmodern feminists take de Beauvoir's understanding of otherness and turn it on its head. Woman is still the other; however, rather than interpreting this condition as something to be rejected, postmodern feminists embrace it. They claim woman's otherness enables individual women to stand back and criticize the norms, values, and practices that the dominant male culture (patriarchy) seeks to impose on everyone, particularly those who live on its periphery. Thus, otherness, for all of its associations with being excluded, shunned, unwanted, abandoned, and marginalized, has its advantages. It is a way of existing that allows for change and difference. Women are not unitary selves, essences to be defined and then ossified. On the contrary, women are free spirits.

Of all the changes I have made to this edition, perhaps the greatest occur in the chapter now entitled "Women of Color Feminisms." Formerly entitled "Multicultural, Global, and Postcolonial Feminism" and now coauthored with my colleague, Tina Fernandes Botts, who lives the experience of being a woman of color in philosophy and feminism, the revised chapter has the twin goals of (1) better highlighting the uniqueness of the feminist experiences of various kinds of women of color in the United States, and (2) better highlighting that the primary focus of all three forms of feminism on the world stage (global, postcolonial, and transnational), is improving the quality of life of women of color. Accordingly, the revised chapter has been divided into two main parts: "Women of Color Feminisms in the United States" and "Feminisms on the World Stage."

In the first part, each of the experiences of five different types of women of color feminisms in the United States is treated on its own terms: African American/Black feminism, Mixed Race feminism, Latin American/Latina feminism, Asian American feminism, and Indigenous feminism. We changed the label "multicultural feminism" to "women of color feminisms" and broke down the first part of the chapter into separate units so as to better respect the unique experiences of oppression of each of these historically oppressed groups and to give voice and respect to each of their distinctive vantage points. At the same time, we understand the groups of women in this part of the chapter to have in common the experience of having been racialized (assigned a race) inside of the history and ongoing presence of racial hierarchy that permeates the culture of the United States. At least in this sense, the experiences of oppression and patriarchy of women of color in the United States are importantly different from those of their mainstream (white) sisters, and we think it is important to continue to interrogate this reality for as long as it continues.

In the second part, global, postcolonial, and transnational feminisms are examined, all of which we understand as related but distinctive approaches to worldwide feminist concerns. Viewed along a continuum beginning with global feminism, moving into postcolonial feminism, and then into transnational feminism, a shift in ideological vantage point can be observed from such notions as universal human rights and global coalitions (global feminism) to a focus on the specific, situated needs of different groups of women of color in developing nations (postcolonial feminism), to full-blown critiques of the possibility of global or transnational feminist engagement rooted in gaps understood to exist between the ways in which these two different approaches to worldwide feminism address subalternity, voice, agency, and representation.

Of all of the approaches to feminism, ecofeminism may offer the broadest and also the most demanding conception of the self's relationship to the other. According to ecofeminism, we are connected not only to one another but also to the nonhuman world: animal and even vegetative. Accordingly, ecofeminism entails the view that we do not sufficiently acknowledge our responsibilities to the nonhuman world. As a result, we do things like deplete the world's natural resources with our machines, pollute the environment with our toxic fumes, and stockpile arms centers with tools of total destruction. In so doing, we delude ourselves that we are controlling nature and enhancing ourselves, when in point of fact, as ecofeminist Ynestra King has stated, nature is already rebelling.[20] Ecofeminists insist that the only way not to destroy ourselves is to strengthen our relationships with the nonhuman world.

Clearly, it is a major challenge to contemporary feminism to reconcile the pressures for diversity and difference with those for integration and commonality. Fortunately, contemporary feminists do not shrink from this challenge. It seems that each year, we better understand the reasons why women worldwide are the "second sex" and how to change this state of affairs. In this fourth edition of my book, I have tried to discuss the weaknesses as well as the strengths of each of the feminist perspectives presented here. In so doing, I have aimed not so much at neutrality as I have at respect and delight, as each feminist perspective has made a rich and lasting contribution to feminist thought. At the end of this book, readers looking for one winning view will be disappointed. Although all feminist perspectives cannot be equally correct, there is no need here for a definitive final say. Instead there is always room for growth, improvement, reconsideration, and expansion for true feminist thinkers. This breathing space helps keep us free from the authoritarian trap of having to know it all.

Liberal Feminism

Liberalism, the school of political thought from which liberal feminism has evolved, is in the process of reconceptualizing, reconsidering, and restructuring itself.[1] Because this transformation is well under way, it is difficult to determine the precise status of liberal feminist thought. Therefore, if we wish to gauge the accuracy of Susan Wendell's provocative claim that liberal feminism has largely outgrown its original base,[2] we must first understand the assumptions of both classical and welfare liberalism. It may turn out that liberal feminists are "liberal" only in some ways.

Conceptual Roots of Liberal Feminist Thought and Action

In *Feminist Politics and Human Nature*,[3] Alison Jaggar observed that liberal political thought generally locates our uniqueness as human persons in our capacity for rationality. The belief that reason distinguishes us from other animals is, however, relatively uninformative, so liberals have attempted to define reason in various ways, stressing either its *moral* aspects or its *prudential* aspects. When reason is defined as the ability to comprehend the rational principles of morality, then the value of individual autonomy is stressed. In contrast, when reason is defined as the ability to determine the best means to achieve some desired end, then the value of self-fulfillment is stressed.[4]

Whether liberals define reason largely in moral or prudential terms, they nevertheless concur that a just society allows individuals to exercise their autonomy and to fulfill themselves. Liberals claim that the "right" must be given priority over the "good."[5] In other words, our entire system of individual rights is justified because these rights constitute a framework within which we can all choose our own separate goods, provided we do not deprive others of theirs. Such a priority defends religious freedom, for example, neither on the grounds that it will increase the general welfare nor on the grounds that a godly life is inherently worthier than a godless one, but simply on the grounds that people have a right to practice or not practice their own brand of spirituality. The same holds for all those rights we generally identify as fundamental.

The proviso that the right takes priority over the good complicates the construction of a just society. For if it is true, as most liberals claim, that resources are limited and each individual, even when restrained by altruism,[6] has an interest in securing as many available resources as possible, then it will be a challenge to create political, economic, and social institutions that maximize the individual's freedom without jeopardizing the community's welfare.

When it comes to state interventions in the private sphere (family or domestic society),[7] liberals agree that the less we see of Big Brother in our bedrooms, bathrooms, kitchens, recreation rooms, and nurseries, the better. We all need places where we can, among family and friends, shed our public personae and be our "real" selves. When it comes to state intervention in the public sphere (civil or political society),[8] however, a difference of opinion emerges between so-called classical, or libertarian, liberals on the one hand, and so-called welfare, or egalitarian, liberals on the other.[9]

Classical liberals think the state should confine itself to protecting civil liberties (e.g., property rights, voting rights, freedom of speech, freedom of religion, freedom of association). They also think that, instead of interfering with the free market, the state should simply provide everyone with an equal opportunity to determine his or her own accumulations within that market. In contrast, welfare liberals believe the state should focus on economic disparities as well as civil liberties. As they see it, individuals enter the market with differences based on initial advantage, inherent talent, and sheer luck. At times, these differences are so great that some individuals cannot take their fair share of what the market has to offer unless some adjustments are made to offset their liabilities. Because of this perceived state of affairs, welfare liberals call for government interventions in the economy, such as legal services, school loans, food stamps, low-cost housing, Medicaid, Medicare, Social Security, and Temporary Assistance for Needy Families (TANF), so that the market does not perpetuate or otherwise solidify huge inequalities.

Although both classical-liberal and welfare-liberal streams of thought appear in liberal feminist thought, most contemporary liberal feminists seem to favor welfare liberalism. In fact, when Susan Wendell (not herself a liberal feminist) described contemporary liberal feminist thought, she stressed it is "committed to major economic re-organization and considerable redistribution of wealth, since one of the modern political goals most closely associated with liberal feminism is equality of opportunity, which would undoubtedly require and lead to both."[10] Very few, if any, contemporary liberal feminists favor the elimination of government-funded safety nets for society's most vulnerable members.

Because it is nearly impossible to discuss all liberal feminist thinkers, movements, and organizations in a single book, I have decided to focus only on Mary Wollstonecraft, John Stuart Mill, Harriet Taylor (Mill), the women's suffragists in the United States, Betty Friedan, and the National Organization for Women. My aim is to construct a convincing argument that, for all its shortcomings, the overall goal of liberal feminism is the worthy one of creating "a just and compassionate society in which freedom flourishes,"[11] or, in Martha Nussbaum's words, a society in which each person is recognized as having "a course from birth to death that is not precisely the same as that of any other person; that each person is one and not more than one, that each feels pain in his or her own body, that the food given to A does not arrive in the stomach of B."[12] Only in a society where women can perceive themselves as unique, special persons can women thrive equally well as men.

Eighteenth-Century Thought: Equal Education

Mary Wollstonecraft wrote at a time (1759–1799) when the economic and social position of European women was in decline. Up until the eighteenth century, productive work (work that generated an income from which a family could live) had been done in and around the family home by women as well as men. But then the forces of industrial capitalism began to draw labor out of the private home and into the public workplace. At first, this industrialization moved slowly and unevenly, making its strongest impact on married, bourgeois women. These women were the first to find themselves left at home with little productive work to do. Married to relatively wealthy professional and entrepreneurial men, these women had no incentive to work outside the home or, if they had several servants, even inside it.[13]

In reading Wollstonecraft's *A Vindication of the Rights of Woman,*[14] we see how affluence worked against these eighteenth-century, married, bourgeois women. Wollstonecraft compared such "privileged" women to members of "the feathered race," birds that are confined to cages and that have nothing to do but preen themselves and "stalk with mock majesty from perch to perch."[15] Middle-class ladies were, in Wollstonecraft's estimation, "kept" women who sacrificed health, liberty, and virtue for whatever prestige, pleasure, and power their husbands could provide. Because these women were not allowed to exercise outdoors lest they tan their lily white skin, they lacked healthy bodies. Because they were not permitted to make their own decisions, they lacked liberty.

And because they were discouraged from developing their powers of reason—given that a great premium was placed on indulging self and gratifying others, especially men and children—they lacked virtue.

Although Wollstonecraft did not use terms such as "socially constructed gender roles," she denied that women are, by nature, more pleasure seeking and pleasure giving than men. She reasoned that if they were confined to the same cages that trap women, men would develop the same flawed characters.[16] Denied the chance to develop their rational powers, to become moral persons with concerns, causes, and commitments beyond personal pleasure, men, like women, would become overly "emotional," a term Wollstonecraft tended to associate with hypersensitivity, extreme narcissism, and excessive self-indulgence.

Given her generally negative assessment of emotion and the extraordinarily high premium she placed on reason as the capacity distinguishing human beings from animals, it is no wonder Wollstonecraft abhorred Jean-Jacques Rousseau's *Emile*.[17] In this classic of educational philosophy, Rousseau portrayed the development of rationality as the most important educational goal for boys, but not for girls. Rousseau was committed to sexual dimorphism, the view that "rational man" is the perfect complement for "emotional woman," and vice versa.[18] As he saw it, men should be educated in such virtues as courage, temperance, justice, and fortitude, whereas women should be educated in such virtues as patience, docility, good humor, and flexibility. Thus, Rousseau's ideal male student, Emile, studies the humanities, the social sciences, and the natural sciences, whereas Rousseau's ideal female student, Sophie, dabbles in music, art, fiction, and poetry while refining her homemaking skills. Rousseau hoped sharpening Emile's mental capacities and limiting Sophie's would make Emile a self-governing citizen and a dutiful paterfamilias; and Sophie, an understanding, responsive wife and a caring, loving mother.

Wollstonecraft agreed with Rousseau's projections for Emile but not with his projections for Sophie. Drawing upon her familiarity with middle-class ladies, she predicted that, fed a steady diet of "novels, music, poetry, and gallantry," Sophie would become a detriment rather than a complement to her husband, a creature of bad sensibility rather than good sense.[19] Her hormones surging, her passions erupting, her emotions churning, Sophie would show no practical sense in performing her wifely and, especially, motherly duties.

Wollstonecraft's cure for Sophie was to provide her, like Emile, with the kind of education that permits people to develop their rational and moral capacities, their full human potential. At times, Wollstonecraft constructed her argument in favor of educational parity in utilitarian terms. She claimed that unlike emotional and dependent women, who routinely shirk their domestic duties and indulge their carnal desires, rational and independent women will tend to be "observant daughters," "affectionate sisters," "faithful wives," and "reasonable mothers."[20] The truly educated woman will be a major contributor to society's welfare. Rather than wasting her time and energy on idle entertainments, she will manage her household—especially her children—"properly."[21] But it would be a mistake to think that most of Wollstonecraft's arguments for educational parity were utilitarian. On the contrary, her overall line of reasoning in *A Vindication of the Rights of Woman* was remarkably similar to Immanuel Kant's overall line of reasoning in the *Groundwork of the Metaphysic of Morals*—namely, that unless a person acts autonomously, he or she acts as less than a fully human person.[22] Wollstonecraft insisted if rationality is the capacity distinguishing human beings from animals, then unless females are mere animals (a description most men do not apply to their own mothers, wives, and daughters), women as well as men have this capacity. Thus, society owes girls the same education that it owes boys, simply because all human beings deserve an equal chance to develop their rational and moral capacities so they can achieve full personhood.

Repeatedly, Wollstonecraft celebrated reason, usually at the expense of emotion. As Jane Roland Martin said, "In making her case for the rights of women . . . [Wollstonecraft] presents us with an ideal of female education that gives pride of place to traits traditionally associated with males at the expense of others traditionally associated with females."[23] It did not occur to Wollstonecraft to question the value of these traditional male traits. Nor did it occur to her to blame children's lack of virtue on their absentee fathers, who should be summoned, in her view, only when "chastisement" is necessary.[24] On the contrary, she simply assumed traditional male traits were "good," and women—not men—were the ones who were rationally and morally deficient.

Throughout the pages of *A Vindication of the Rights of Woman*, Wollstonecraft urged women to become autonomous decision makers; but beyond insisting that the path to autonomy goes through the academy, she provided women with little concrete guidance.[25] Although Wollstonecraft toyed with the idea that women's autonomy might depend on women's economic and political independence from men, in the end she decided *well-educated* women did not need to be economically self-sufficient or politically active in order to be autonomous. In fact, Wollstonecraft dismissed the woman's suffrage movement as a waste of time, as in her estimation, the whole system of legal representation was merely a "convenient handle for despotism."[26]

Despite the limitations of her analysis, Wollstonecraft did present a vision of a woman strong in mind and body, a person who is not a slave to her passions, her husband, or her children. For Wollstonecraft, the ideal woman is less interested in fulfilling herself—if by self-fulfillment is meant any sort of pandering to duty-distracting desires—than in exercising self-control.[27] To liberate herself from the oppressive roles of emotional cripple, petty shrew, and narcissistic sex object, a woman must obey the commands of reason and discharge her wifely and motherly duties faithfully.

What Wollstonecraft most wanted for women is personhood. She claimed that a woman should not be reduced to the "toy of man, his rattle," which "must jingle in his ears whenever, dismissing reason, he chooses to be amused."[28] In other words, a woman is not a "mere means," or instrument, to one or more man's pleasure or happiness. Rather, she is an "end-in-herself," a rational agent whose dignity consists in having the capacity for self-determination.[29] To treat someone as a mere means is to treat her as less than a person, as someone who exists not for herself but as an appendage to someone else. So, for example, if a husband treats his wife as no more than a pretty indoor plant, he treats her as an object that he nurtures merely as a means to his own delight. Similarly, if a woman lets herself be so treated, she lets herself be treated in ways that do not accord with her status as a full human person. Rather than assuming responsibility for her own development and growing into a mighty redwood, she forsakes her freedom and lets others shape her into a stunted bonsai tree. No woman, insisted Wollstonecraft, should permit such violence to be done to her.

Nineteenth-Century Thought: Equal Liberty

Writing approximately one hundred years later, John Stuart Mill and Harriet Taylor (Mill) joined Wollstonecraft in celebrating rationality. But they conceived of rationality not only morally, as autonomous decision making, but also prudentially, as calculative reason, or using your head to get what you want. That their understanding of rationality should differ from that of Wollstonecraft is not surprising. Unlike Wollstonecraft, both Mill and Taylor claimed the ordinary way to maximize aggregate utility (happiness/pleasure) is to permit individuals to pursue their desires, provided the individuals do not hinder or obstruct each other in the process. Mill and Taylor also departed from Wollstonecraft in insisting that if society is to achieve sexual equality, or gender justice, then society must provide women with the same political rights and economic opportunities as well as the same education that men enjoy.

Like Mary Wollstonecraft, who twice attempted suicide, refused marriage until late in life, and had a child out of wedlock, John Stuart Mill and Harriet Taylor led fairly unconventional lives. They met in 1830, when Harriet Taylor was already married to John Taylor and was the mother of two sons (a third child, Helen, would be born later). Harriet Taylor and Mill were immediately attracted to each other, both intellectually and emotionally. They carried on a close, supposedly platonic relationship for twenty years, until the death of John Taylor, whereupon they married. During the years before John Taylor's death, Harriet Taylor and Mill routinely saw each other for dinner and frequently spent weekends together along the English coast. John Taylor agreed to this arrangement in return for the "external formality" of Harriet's residing "as his wife in his house."[30]

Due to their unorthodox bargain with John Taylor, Harriet Taylor and Mill found the time to author, separately and conjointly, several essays on sexual equality. Scholars generally agree that Taylor and Mill coauthored "Early Essays on Marriage and Divorce" (1832), that Taylor wrote the "Enfranchisement of Women" (1851), and that Mill wrote "The Subjection of Women" (1869). The question of these works' authorship is significant because Taylor's views sometimes diverged from Mill's.

Given their personal situation, Mill and Taylor's focus on topics such as marriage and divorce is not surprising. Confident in their relationship, Mill and Taylor did not feel they had to agree with each other about how to serve women's and children's best interests. Because she accepted the traditional view that maternal ties are stronger than paternal ones, Taylor simply assumed the mother would be the one to rear the children to adulthood in the event of divorce. Thus, she cautioned women to have few children. In contrast, Mill urged couples to marry late, have children late, and live in extended families or communelike situations so as to minimize divorce's disrupting effects on children's lives.[31]

Although Taylor, unlike Mill, did not contest traditional assumptions about male and female child-rearing roles, she did contest traditional assumptions about women's supposed preference for marriage and motherhood over a career or occupation. Mill contended that even after women were fully educated and totally enfranchised, most of them would *choose* to remain in the private realm, where their primary function would be to "adorn and beautify" rather than to "support" life.[32] In contrast, in "Enfranchisement of Women," Taylor argued that women needed to do more than read books and cast ballots; they also needed to be *partners* with men "in the labors and gains, risks and remunerations of productive industry."[33] Thus, Taylor predicted that if society gave women a bona fide choice between devoting their lives "to one *animal* function and its consequence"[34] on the one hand, and writing great books, discovering new worlds, and building mighty empires on the other, many women would be only too happy to leave "home, sweet home" behind them.

Whereas the foregoing passages from "Enfranchisement" suggest Taylor believed a woman had to choose between housewifery and mothering on the one hand and working outside the home on the other, some other passages indicate she believed a woman had a third option: namely, adding a career or an occupation to her domestic and maternal roles and responsibilities. In fact, Taylor claimed a married woman cannot be her husband's true equal unless she has the confidence and sense of entitlement that come from contributing "materially to the support of the family."[35] Decidedly unimpressed by Mill's 1832 argument that women's economic equality would depress the economy and subsequently lower wages,[36] Taylor wrote instead: "Even if every woman, as matters now stand, had a claim on some man for support, how infinitely preferable is it that part of the income should be of the woman's earning, even if the aggregate sum were but little increased by it, rather than that she should be compelled to stand aside in order that men may be the sole earners, and the sole dispensers of what is earned."[37] In short, to be partners rather than servants of their husbands, wives must earn an income outside the home.

In further explaining her view that married as well as single women should work, Taylor admitted that married women, especially if they had children, would need domestic help. Realizing that women cannot both work full-time outside the home and full-time inside the home without exhausting themselves, Taylor conceded that working women with children would need a "panoply of domestic servants" to help ease their burdens.[38] In critic Zillah Eisenstein's estimation, Taylor's words revealed her privileged status. Circa 1850, only upper-middle-class women such as Taylor could afford to hire a slew of household workers.[39] Thus, Taylor, a product of class privilege, offered rich women a way to "have it all" without offering poor women the same. Never did she wonder who would be taking care of the families of the women they hired. Would these lower-class domestic workers be able to find women poorer than themselves to care for their children? Or would their children simply have to fend for themselves?

Like Wollstonecraft, Taylor wrote not so much to *all* women as to a certain privileged class of married women. Nonetheless, her writings helped smooth the entrance of many poor as well as rich women into the public world. So, too, did Mill's. He argued in "The Subjection of Women" that if women's rational powers were recognized as equal to men's, then society would reap significant benefits: public-spirited citizens for society itself, intellectually stimulating spouses for husbands, a doubling of the "mass of mental faculties available for the higher service of humanity," and a multitude of very happy women.[40] Although Mill's case for the liberation of women did not depend on his ability to prove that *all* women can do anything men can do, it did depend on his ability to demonstrate that *some* women can do anything men can do.[41] Unlike Wollstonecraft, who put no "great stress on the example of a few women who, from having received a masculine education, have acquired courage and resolution,"[42] Mill used the life stories of exceptional women to strengthen his claim that male-female differences are not absolute but instead are differences of average. The average woman's inability to do something the average man can do, said Mill, does not justify a law or taboo barring all women from attempting that thing.[43]

Mill also made the point that even *if* all women are worse than all men at something, this still does not justify forbidding women from trying to do that thing, for "what women by nature cannot do, it is quite superfluous to forbid them from doing. What they can do, but not so well as the men who are their competitors, competition suffices to exclude them from."[44] Although Mill believed women would fare quite well in any competitions with men, he conceded that occasionally a biological sex difference might tip the scales in favor of male competitors. Like Wollstonecraft, however, he denied the existence of general intellectual or moral differences between men and women: "I do not know a more signal instance of the blindness with which the world, including the herd of studious men, ignore and pass over all the influences of social circumstances, than their silly depreciation of the intellectual, and silly panegyrics on the moral, nature of women."[45]

Also like Wollstonecraft earlier, Mill claimed that society's *ethical* double standard hurts women. He thought many of the "virtues" extolled in women are, in fact, character traits that impede women's progress toward personhood. This is as true for an ostensibly negative trait (helplessness) as for an ostensibly positive trait (unselfishness). Mill suggested that because women's concerns were confined to the private realm, women were preoccupied with their own interests and those of their immediate families. As a result of this state of affairs, women's unselfishness tended to take the form of extended egoism. Women's charity typically began and ended at home. They spared no effort to further the interests of their loved ones, but they showed marked disinterest in the commonweal.

As described above, women's family-oriented "unselfishness" was not the humanitarian unselfishness Mill espoused. He treasured the unselfishness that motivates people to take into account the good of society as a whole as well as the good of the individual person or small family unit. Mill believed that if women were given the same liberties men enjoy, and if women were taught to value the good of the whole, then women would develop genuine unselfishness. This belief explains Mill's passionate pleas for women's suffrage. He thought that when citizens vote, they feel obligated to cast their ballots in a way that benefits all of society and not just themselves and their loved ones.[46] Whether Mill was naive to think that citizens are inherently public-spirited is, of course, debatable.

Overall, Mill went further than Wollstonecraft did in challenging men's alleged intellectual superiority. Stressing that men's and women's intellectual abilities are of the same *kind,* Wollstonecraft nonetheless entertained the thought that women might not be able to attain the same *degree* of knowledge that men could attain.[47] Mill expressed no such reservation. He insisted intellectual achievement gaps between men and women were simply the result of men's more thorough education and privileged position. In fact, Mill was so eager to establish that men are not intellectually superior to women that he tended to err in the opposite direction, by valorizing women's attention to details, use of concrete examples, and intuitiveness as a superior form of knowledge not often found in men.[48]

Unlike Taylor, and despite his high regard for women's intellectual abilities, Mill assumed most women would continue to choose family over career even under ideal circumstances—with marriage a free contract between real equals, legal separation and divorce easily available to wives, and jobs open to women living outside the husband-wife relationship. He also assumed that women's choice of family over career was entirely voluntary and that such a choice involved women consenting to put their other interests in life on the back burner until their children were adults: "Like a man when he chooses a profession, so, when a woman marries, it may in general be understood that she makes choice of the management of a household, and the bringing up of a family, as the first call upon her exertions, during as many years of her life as may be required for the purpose; and that she renounces not all other objects and occupations, but all which are not consistent with the requirements of this."[49] Mill's words attested to his apparent belief that ultimately, women, more than men, are responsible for maintaining family life. However enlightened his general views about women were, Mill could not overcome the belief that she who bears the children is the person best suited to rear them.

As noted, Taylor disagreed with Mill that truly liberated women would be willing to stay at home to rear their children to adulthood. Yet, like Mill, Taylor was fundamentally a reformist, not a revolutionary. To be sure, by inviting married women with children as well as single women to work outside the home, Taylor did challenge the traditional division of labor where the man earns the money and the woman manages its use. But Taylor's challenge to this aspect of the status quo did not go far enough. For example, it did not occur to her that if wives were to work full-time outside the home like their husbands, then husbands would have to parent alongside their wives and share domestic duties equally with them. Otherwise women would have to work a "double duty" or, if rich enough, hire other women to do *their* housework and childcare.

Nineteenth-Century Action: The Suffrage

Both John Stuart Mill and Harriet Taylor Mill believed women needed suffrage in order to become men's equals. They claimed the vote gives people the power not only to express their own political views but also to challenge those systems, structures, and attitudes that contribute to their own and/or others' oppression. Thus, it is not surprising that the nineteenth-century US women's rights movement, including the woman suffrage movement, was tied to the abolitionist movement, though not always in ways that successfully married gender and race concerns.[50]

When white men and women began to work in earnest for the abolition of slavery, it soon became clear to female abolitionists that male abolitionists were reluctant to link the women's rights movement with the slaves' rights movement. Noting it was difficult for them to view women as oppressed as slaves (or was it just *male* slaves?), male abolitionists persuaded female abolitionists to disassociate women's liberty struggles from slaves' liberty struggles. Indeed, male abolitionists even convinced famed feminist orator Lucy Stone to lecture on abolition instead of women's rights whenever her audience size was noticeably large.[51]

Convinced their male counterparts would reward them for being team players, the US women who attended the 1840 World Anti-Slavery Convention in London thought that women would play a major role at the meeting. Nothing could have proved less true. Not even Lucretia Mott and Elizabeth Cady Stanton, two of the most prominent leaders of the US women's rights movement, were allowed to speak at the meeting. Angered by the way in which the men at the convention had silenced women, Mott and Stanton vowed to hold a women's rights convention upon their return to the United States. Eight years later, in 1848, three hundred women and men met in Seneca Falls, New York, and produced a Declaration of Sentiments and twelve resolutions. Modeled on the Declaration of Independence, the Declaration of Sentiments stressed the issues Mill and Taylor had emphasized in England, particularly the need for reforms in marriage, divorce, property, and child custody laws. The twelve resolutions emphasized women's rights to express themselves in public—to speak out on the burning issues of the day, especially "in regard to the great subjects of morals and religion," which women were supposedly more qualified to address than men.[52] The only one of the twelve resolutions the Seneca Falls Convention did not unanimously endorse was Resolution Nine, Susan B. Anthony's Woman's Suffrage Resolution: "Resolved, that it is the duty of the women of this country to secure to themselves their sacred right to the franchise."[53] Many convention delegates were reluctant to press such an "extreme" demand for fear that all of their demands would be rejected. Still, with the help of abolitionist Frederick Douglass, Resolution Nine did manage to pass.

Assessing the Seneca Falls Convention from the vantage point of the twentieth century, critics observe that, with the exception of Lucretia Mott's hastily added resolution to secure for women "an equal participation with men in the various trades, professions, and commerce,"[54] the nineteenth-century meeting failed to address class concerns, such as those that troubled underpaid white female mill and factory workers. Moreover, the convention rendered black women nearly invisible. In the same way that the abolitionist movement had focused on the rights of black *men,* the nineteenth-century women's rights movement focused on the rights of mostly privileged *white* women. Neither white women nor white men seemed to notice much about black women.

Despite these slights, many working-class white women and black women did nonetheless contribute to the nineteenth-century women's rights movement. In fact, some black women were exceptionally gifted feminist orators. For example, Sojourner Truth delivered her often quoted speech on behalf of women at an 1851 women's rights convention in Akron, Ohio. Responding to a group of male hecklers, who taunted that it was ludicrous for (white) women to desire the vote because they could not even step over a puddle or get into a horse carriage without male assistance, Sojourner Truth pointed out that no man had ever extended such help to her. Demanding that audience look at her black body, Sojourner Truth proclaimed that her "womanhood," her "female nature," had never prevented her from working, acting, and yes, speaking like a man: "I have ploughed, and planted, and gathered into barns and no man could head me! And ain't I a woman? I could work as much and eat as much as a man—when I could get it—and bear the lash as well! And ain't I a woman? I have borne thirteen children and seen them most all sold off to slavery, and when I cried out with my mother's grief, none but Jesus heard me! And ain't I a woman?"[55]

As the fates would have it, the Civil War began just as the women's rights movement was gaining momentum. Seeing in this tragic war their best opportunity to free the slaves, male abolitionists again asked female abolitionists to put women's causes on the back burner, which they reluctantly did. But the end of the Civil War did not bring women's liberation with it, and feminists increasingly found themselves at odds with recently emancipated black men. Concerned that women's rights would again be lost in the struggle to secure black (men's) rights, the male as well as female delegates to an 1866 national women's rights convention decided to establish an Equal Rights Association. Co-chaired by Frederick Douglass and Elizabeth Cady Stanton, the association had as its announced purpose the unification of the black (men's) and woman suffrage struggles. There is considerable evidence, however, that Stanton and some of her co-workers actually "perceived the organization as a means to ensure that Black men would not receive the franchise unless and until white women were also its recipients."[56] Unmoved by Douglass's and Truth's observation that on account of their extreme vulnerability, black men needed the vote even more than women did, Anthony and Stanton were among those who successfully argued for the dissolution of the Equal Rights Association for fear that the association might indeed endorse the passage of the Fifteenth Amendment, which enfranchised black men but not women.

Upon the dissolution of the Equal Rights Association, Anthony and Stanton established the National Woman Suffrage Association. At approximately the same time, Lucy Stone, who had some serious philosophical disagreements with Stanton and especially Anthony about the role of organized religion in women's oppression, founded the American Woman Suffrage Association. Henceforward, the US women's rights movement would be split in two.

In the main, the National Woman Suffrage Association forwarded a revolutionary feminist agenda for women, whereas the American Woman Suffrage Association pushed a reformist feminist agenda. Most American women gravitated toward the more moderate American Woman Suffrage Association. By the time these two associations merged in 1890 to form the National American Woman Suffrage Association, the wide-ranging, vociferous women's rights movement of the early nineteenth century had been transformed into the single-issue, relatively tame woman's suffrage movement of the late nineteenth century. From 1890 until 1920, when the Nineteenth Amendment was passed, the National American Woman Suffrage Association confined almost all of its activities to gaining the vote for women. Victorious after fifty-two years of concerted struggle, many of the exhausted suffragists chose to believe that simply by gaining the vote, women had become men's equals.[57]

Twentieth-Century Action: Equal Rights

For nearly forty years after the passage of the Nineteenth Amendment, feminists went about their work relatively quietly in the United States. Then, around 1960, a rebellious generation of feminists loudly proclaimed as fact what the suffragists Stanton and Anthony had always suspected: To be fully liberated, women need economic opportunities and sexual freedoms as well as civil liberties. Like their grandmothers, some of these young women pushed a reformist, liberal agenda, whereas others forwarded a more revolutionary, radical program of action.

By the mid-1960s, most liberal feminists had joined an emerging women's *rights* group, such as the National Organization for Women (NOW), the National Women's Political Caucus (NWPC), or the Women's Equity Action League (WEAL). The general purpose of these groups was to improve women's status "by applying legal, social, and other pressures upon institutions ranging from the Bell Telephone Company to television networks to the major political parties."[58] In contrast, most radical feminists had banded together in one or another women's *liberation* groups. Much smaller and more personally focused than the liberal women's rights groups, these radical women's liberation groups aimed to increase women's consciousness about women's oppression. The groups' spirit was that of the revolutionary new left, whose goal was not to *reform* what they regarded as an elitist, capitalistic, competitive, individualistic system, but to *replace* it with an egalitarian, socialistic, cooperative, communitarian, sisterhood-is-powerful system. Among the largest of these radical women's liberation groups were the Women's International Terrorist Conspiracy from Hell (WITCH), the Redstockings, the Feminists, and the New York Radical Feminists. Although Maren Lockwood Carden correctly noted in her 1974 book, *The New Feminist Movement,* that the ideological contrasts between the women's rights and women's liberation groups of the 1960s had blurred by the mid-1970s,[59] women's rights groups still remained less revolutionary than women's liberation groups.

Because this chapter is about *liberal* feminists, I reserve discussion of radical women's liberation groups to Chapter 2. Here I concentrate on the history of twentieth-century liberal *women's rights* groups and their activities, most of which have been in the area of legislation. Between the passage of the Nineteenth Amendment and the advent of the second wave of US feminism during the 1960s, only two official feminist groups—the National Woman's Party and the National Federation of Business and Professional Women's Clubs—promulgated women's rights. Despite their efforts, however, discrimination against women did not end, largely because the importance of women's rights had not yet been impressed on the consciousness (and conscience) of the bulk of the US population. This state of affairs changed with the eruption of the civil rights movement. Sensitized to the myriad ways in which US systems, structures, and laws oppressed blacks, those active in or at least sympathetic toward the civil rights movement were able to see analogies between discrimination against blacks and discrimination against women. In 1961, President John F. Kennedy established the Commission on the Status of Women, which produced much new data about women and resulted in the formation of the Citizens' Advisory Council, various state commissions on the status of women, and the passage of the Equal Pay Act. When Congress passed the 1964 Civil Rights Act—amended with the Title VII provision to prohibit discrimination on the basis of *sex* as well as race, color, religion, or national origin by private employers, employment agencies, and unions—a woman shouted from the congressional gallery, "We made it! God bless America!"[60] Unfortunately, this woman's jubilation and that of women in general was short-lived; the courts were reluctant to enforce Title VII's "sex amendment." Feeling betrayed by the system, women's joy turned to anger, an anger that feminist activists used to mobilize women to fight for their civil rights with the same passion blacks had fought for theirs.

Among these feminist activists was Betty Friedan, a feminist theorist and activist. Friedan reflected on how she and some of her associates had reacted to the courts' refusal to take Title VII's "sex amendment" seriously: "The absolute necessity for a civil rights movement for women had reached such a point of subterranean explosive urgency by 1966, that it only took a few of us to get together to ignite the spark—and it spread like a nuclear chain reaction."[61] The "spark" to which Friedan pointed was the formation of the National Organization for Women (NOW) by Friedan, Rev. Pauli Murray, the first African American female Episcopal priest, and Shirley Chisholm, the first African American to run for president of the United States of America. NOW was the first explicitly feminist group in the United States in the twentieth century to challenge sex discrimination in all spheres of life: social, political, economic, and personal. After considerable behind-the-scenes maneuvering, Friedan—then viewed as a home-breaker because of her controversial book *The Feminine Mystique* (see the next section for discussion)—was elected NOW's first president in 1966 by its three hundred charter members, male and female.

Although NOW's first members included radical and conservative feminists as well as liberal feminists, it quickly became clear that NOW's essential identity and agenda were fundamentally liberal. For example, the aim of NOW's 1967 Bill of Rights for Women was to secure for women the same rights men have. NOW demanded the following for women:

I. That the US Congress immediately pass the Equal Rights Amendment to the Constitution to provide that "Equality of rights under the law shall not be denied or abridged by the United States or by any State on account of sex," and that such then be immediately ratified by the several States.

II. That equal employment opportunity be guaranteed to all women, as well as men, by insisting that the Equal Employment Opportunity Commission enforces the prohibitions against racial discrimination.

III. That women be protected by law to ensure their rights to return to their jobs within a reasonable time after childbirth without the loss of seniority or other accrued benefits, and be paid maternity leave as a form of social security and/or employee benefit.

IV. Immediate revision of tax laws to permit the deduction of home and child-care expenses for working parents.

V. That child-care facilities be established by law on the same basis as parks, libraries, and public schools, adequate to the needs of children from the pre-school years through adolescence, as a community resource to be used by all citizens from all income levels.

VI. That the right of women to be educated to their full potential equally with men be secured by Federal and State legislation, eliminating all discrimination and segregation by sex, written and unwritten, at all levels of education, including colleges, graduate and professional schools, loans and fellowships, and Federal and State training programs such as the Job Corps.

VII. The right of women in poverty to secure job training, housing, and family allowances on equal terms with men, but without prejudice to a parent's right to remain at home to care for his or her children; revision of welfare legislation and poverty programs which deny women dignity, privacy, and self-respect.

VIII. The right of women to control their own reproductive lives by removing from the penal code laws limiting access to contraceptive information and devices, and by repealing penal laws governing abortion.[62]

NOW's list of demands pleased the organization's liberal members but made both its conservative and radical members angry, albeit for different reasons. Whereas conservative members objected to the push for permissive contraception and abortion laws, radical members were angered by NOW's failure to support women's sexual rights, particularly the right to choose between heterosexual, bisexual, and lesbian lifestyles. Missing from NOW's 1967 Bill of Rights was any mention of important women's issues such as domestic violence, rape, sexual harassment, and pornography.[63]

Although Friedan acknowledged that "the sex-role debate . . . cannot be avoided if equal opportunity in employment, education and civil rights are ever to mean more than paper rights,"[64] she still insisted "that the gut issues of this revolution involve employment and education and new social institutions and not sexual fantasy."[65] Worried that NOW would change its traditional liberal focus to a more radical one, Friedan was among those who most strongly opposed public support of lesbianism by NOW. Allegedly, she termed NOW's lesbian members a "lavender menace,"[66] because, as she saw it, they alienated mainstream society from feminists in general.

Friedan's concerns about the "lavender menace" notwithstanding, NOW eventually endorsed four resolutions forwarded by the "lavender menace," the Gay Liberation Front and Radicalesbians. The resolutions, presented at NOW's 1970 Congress to Unite Women, read:

1. Women's Liberation is a lesbian plot.
2. Whenever the label lesbian is used against the movement collectively or against women individually, it is to be affirmed, not denied.

3. In all discussions of birth control, homosexuality must be included as a legitimate method of contraception.
4. All sex education curricula must include lesbianism as a valid, legitimate form of sexual expression and love.[67]

Moreover, NOW began to stress that its aim was to serve not only the women most likely to survive and thrive in the system but any woman who believed women's rights should be equal to men's. The organization's points of focus started to rapidly evolve throughout the 1980s, 1990s, and 2000s. For example, NOW's first Lesbian Rights Conference was held in 1984; its first Global Feminist Conference, in 1992; its first Women of Color and Allies Summit, in 1998; and its first Women with Disabilities and Allies Summit, in 2003.[68] During the same period of time NOW's leadership also began to change. More women of color and more lesbians, bisexual, transsexual, and transgender women joined NOW and contributed to its direction. As a result of these positive changes, NOW, which celebrated its fortieth anniversary in 2006, is less likely to be perceived as a white, heterosexual women's organization than as an organization that welcomes all women.

NOW's greater attention to women's differences has led it to make more modest claims about its constituency. Its members no longer claim to know what all women want but only what *specific* groups of women need. Increasingly, the intellectual energies of NOW as well as other women's rights groups have become focused on the so-called sameness-difference debate: Is gender equality best achieved by stressing women's oneness as a gender or their diversity as individuals; likewise, the similarities between women and men or the differences between them? To this day, the many answers to these basic questions continue to shape and reshape NOW's political agenda.

Twentieth-Century Thought: Sameness Versus Difference

It is instructive to reflect upon Betty Friedan's career as a writer, not only because of her identification with NOW, but also because of her own evolution as a thinker who first took it for granted that all women are the same as men and who then came to quite a different conclusion. Like most contemporary liberal feminists, Friedan gradually accepted both the *radical* feminist critique that liberal feminists are prone to co-optation by the "male establishment" and the *conservative* feminist critique that liberal feminists are out of touch with the bulk of US women who hold the institutions of marriage, motherhood, and the family in high regard. When she wrote her 1963 classic, *The*

Feminine Mystique,[69] Friedan seemed oblivious to any other perspectives than those of white, middle-class, heterosexual, educated women who found the traditional roles of wife and mother unsatisfying. She wrote that in lieu of more meaningful goals, these women spent too much time cleaning their already tidy homes, improving their already attractive appearance, and indulging their already spoiled children.[70] Focusing on this unappealing picture of family life in affluent US suburbs, Friedan concluded that contemporary women needed to find meaningful work in the full-time, public workforce. Wives' and mothers' partial absence from home would enable husbands and children to become more self-sufficient people, capable of cooking their own meals and doing their own laundry.[71]

Although Friedan had little patience for obsequious wives and doting mothers, she did not, as some critics thought, demand women *sacrifice* marriage and motherhood for a high-powered career. On the contrary, she believed a woman could have a loving family as well: "The assumption of your own identity, equality, and even political power does not mean you stop needing to love, and be loved by, a man, or that you stop caring for your own kids."[72] In Friedan's estimation, the error in the feminine mystique was not that it *valued* marriage and motherhood but that it *overvalued* these two institutions. To think that a woman who is a wife and mother has no time for a full-time, professional career is to limit her development as a full human person, said Friedan. As soon as a woman sees housework for what it is— something to get out of the way, to be done "quickly and efficiently"—and sees marriage and motherhood for what it is, a part of her life but not all of it, she will find plenty of time and energy to develop her total self in "creative work" outside the home.[73] With just a bit of help, any woman, like any man, can meet all of her personal obligations and thereby become free to assume significant roles and responsibilities in the public world, reasoned Friedan.

In critics' estimation, *The Feminine Mystique* explained well enough why marriage and motherhood are not enough for a certain kind of woman. But as the critics saw it, the book failed to address a host of issues deeper than "the problem that has no name"—Friedan's tag for the dissatisfaction supposedly felt by suburban, white, educated, middle-class, heterosexual housewives in the United States. In particular, *The Feminine Mystique* misjudged just how difficult it would be for even privileged women to combine a career with marriage and motherhood unless major structural changes were made both within and outside the family. Like Wollstonecraft, Taylor, and Mill before her, Friedan sent women out into the public realm without summoning men into the private domain to pick up their fair share of the slack.

By the time she wrote *The Second Stage,*[74] about twenty years after *The Feminine Mystique,* Friedan had come to see that her critics were right. Often it is very difficult for a woman to combine marriage, motherhood, and full-time work outside the home. Observing the ways in which some members of her daughter's generation ran themselves ragged in the name of feminism—trying to be full-time career women as well as full-time housewives and mothers—Friedan concluded that 1980s "superwomen" were no less oppressed (albeit for different reasons) than their 1960s "stay-at-home" mothers had been. Increasingly, she urged feminists to ask themselves whether women either can or should try to meet not simply one but two standards of perfection: the one set in the workplace by traditional men, who had wives to take care of all their nonworkplace needs, and the one set in the home by traditional women, whose whole sense of worth, power, and mastery came from being ideal housewives and mothers.[75]

Friedan's own answer to the question she posed was that women needed to stop trying both to "do it all" and to "be it all." She insisted, however, that the proper cure for the superwoman syndrome was not simply to renounce love in favor of work, or vice versa. On the contrary, said Friedan, women who chose either work or love often told her they regretted their decision. For example, one woman who renounced marriage and motherhood for a full-time career confessed to Friedan, "I was the first woman in management here. I gave everything to the job. It was exciting at first, breaking in where women never were before. Now it's just a job. But it's the devastating loneliness that's the worst. I can't *stand* coming back to this apartment alone every night. I'd like a house, maybe a garden. Maybe I should have a kid, even without a father. At least then I'd have a family. There has to be some better way to live."[76] Another woman who made the opposite choice, forsaking job for family, admitted to Friedan:

> It makes me mad—makes me feel like a child—when I have to ask my husband for money. My mother was always dependent on my father and so fearful of life. She is lost now without him. It frightens me, the thought of being dependent like my mother, though I have a very happy marriage. I get so upset, listening to battered wives on television, women with no options. It improves your sense of self-worth when you don't depend on your husband for everything good in life, when you can get it for yourself. I'm trying so hard to treat my daughter equally with my son. I don't want her to have the fears that paralyzed my mother and that I've always had to fight. I want her to have real options.[77]

Rather than despairing over these and other women's choices, Friedan used them as talking points to convince 1980s feminists to move from what she termed first-stage feminism to what she labeled second-stage feminism.

She noted this new form of feminism would require women to work with men to escape the excesses of the *feminist* mystique, "which denied the core of women's personhood that is fulfilled through love, nurture, home" as well as the excesses of the *feminine* mystique, "which defined women solely in terms of their relation to men as wives, mothers and homemakers."[78] Together, women and men might be able to develop the kind of social values, leadership styles, and institutional structures needed to permit both sexes to achieve fulfillment in the public and private world alike.

Friedan's program for reigniting the women's movement was, as we shall see, vulnerable to several attacks. For example, it inadequately challenged the assumption that women are "responsible for the private life of their family members."[79] Zillah Eisenstein criticized Friedan's support of so-called flextime (an arrangement that permits employees to set their starting and leaving hours): "It is never clear whether this arrangement is supposed to ease women's double burden (of family and work) or significantly restructure *who* is responsible for childcare and *how* this responsibility is carried out."[80] Suspecting that women rather than men would use flextime to mesh their workday with their children's school day, Eisenstein worried that flextime would give employers yet another reason to devalue female employees as less committed to their work than male employees.

In all fairness to Friedan, however, she did explicitly mention in *The Second Stage* (written after Eisenstein's critique of Friedan) that when an arrangement such as flextime is described as a structural change permitting mothers to better care for their children, the wrongheaded idea that home and family are *women's* sole responsibility rather than *women's and men's* joint responsibility is reinforced.[81] Unlike the Friedan of *The Feminine Mystique,* the Friedan of *The Second Stage* seemed quite aware that unless women's assimilation into the public world is coupled with the simultaneous assimilation of men into the private world, women will always have to work harder than men. Although Friedan conceded that most men might not be ready, willing, or able to embrace the "househusband" role, she nonetheless insisted it is just as important for men to develop their private and personal selves as it is for women to develop their public and social selves. Men who realize this also realize women's liberation is men's liberation. A man does not have to be "just a breadwinner"[82] or just a runner in the rat race. Like his wife, he, too, can be an active participant in the thick web of familial and friendship relationships he and she weave together.[83]

In some ways, the difference between the Friedan of *The Feminine Mystique* and the Friedan of *The Second Stage* is the difference between a feminist who believes women need to be the *same* as men to be equal to men and a feminist who believes women can be men's equal, provided society values the "feminine" as much as the "masculine." The overall message of *The Feminine Mystique* was that women's liberation hinged on women's becoming like men. Friedan peppered the pages of *The Feminine Mystique* with such comments as: "If an able American woman does not use her human energy and ability in some meaningful pursuit (which necessarily means competition, for there is competition in every serious pursuit of our society), she will fritter away her energy in neurotic symptoms, or unproductive exercise, or destructive 'love,'" and "Perhaps men may live longer in America when women carry more of the burden of the battle with the world instead of being a burden themselves. I think their wasted energy will continue to be destructive to their husbands, to their children, and to themselves until it is used in their own battle with the world."[84] In the book, Frieden put forth that to be a full human being is, in short, to think and act like a man.

Eighteen years after the publication of *The Feminine Mystique*, Friedan's message to women had substantially changed. In *The Second Stage*, she described as *culturally feminine* the so-called beta styles of thinking and acting, which emphasize "fluidity, flexibility and interpersonal sensitivity," and as *culturally masculine* the so-called alpha styles of thinking and acting, which stress "hierarchical, authoritarian, strictly task-oriented leadership based on instrumental, technological rationality."[85] Rather than offering 1980s women the same advice she had offered 1960s women—namely, minimize your feminine, beta tendencies and maximize your masculine, alpha tendencies—Friedan counseled 1980s women to embrace feminine, beta styles. Having convinced herself that women did not need to deny their differences from men to achieve equality with men, Friedan urged 1980s women to stop "aping the accepted dominant Alpha mode of established movements and organizations" and start using their "Beta intuitions" to solve the social, political, and economic problems that threaten humankind.[86] The challenge of the second stage of feminism, insisted Friedan, was for women (and men) to replace the "win-or-lose, do-or-die method of the hunter or the warrior" with the kind of thinking "women developed in the past as they dealt on a day-to-day basis with small problems and relationships in the family, mostly without thinking about it in the abstract."[87] Only then would the world's citizens realize their very survival depends on replacing competitive strategies with cooperative initiatives.

Given the foregoing analysis, it is not surprising that Friedan later claimed gender-specific laws rather than general-neutral laws are better able to secure equality between the sexes. In 1986, she joined a coalition supporting a California law requiring employers to grant as much as four months' unpaid leave to women disabled by pregnancy or childbirth. In taking this stand, she alienated the NOW members who believed that to treat men and women equally should mean to treat them in the same way: If men should not receive special treatment on account of their sex, then neither should women. According to Friedan, this line of reasoning, which she herself pressed in the 1960s, is misguided. It asks the law to treat women as "male clones," when in fact "there has to be a concept of equality that takes into account that women are the ones who have the babies."[88]

If the Friedan of the 1980s is right, then the task of liberal feminists is to determine not what liberty and equality are for abstract, rational persons but what liberty and equality are for concrete men and women. To be sure, this is a difficult task. Among others, Rosalind Rosenberg advised liberal feminists, "If women as a group are allowed special benefits, you open up the group to charges that it is inferior. But, if we deny all differences, as the women's movement has so often done, you deflect attention from the disadvantages women labor under."[89] Rosenberg's cautionary words raise many questions. Is there really a way to treat women and men both *differently* and *equally* without falling into some version of the pernicious separate-but-equal approach that characterized race relations in the United States until the early 1960s? Or should liberal feminists work toward the elimination of male/female differences as the first step toward true equality? If so, should women become like men so as to be equal with men? Or should men become like women so as to be equal with women? Or finally, should both men and women become androgynous, each person combining the same "correct" blend of positive masculine and feminine characteristics, so as to be equal with every other person?

To the degree that *The Feminine Mystique* advised women to become like men, *The Second Stage* urged women to be like women. But *The Second Stage* did more than this. It also encouraged men and women alike to work toward an androgynous future in which all human beings manifest both traditionally masculine and traditionally feminine traits. Once she decided that androgyny was in all human beings' best interests, Friedan stayed committed to her vision. Indeed, she devoted many pages of her third major book, *The Fountain of Age,* to singing androgyny's praises. Specifically, she urged aging alpha men to develop their passive, nurturing, or contemplative feminine qualities, and aging beta women to develop their bold, assertive, commanding, or adventurous masculine qualities.[90] Insisting that people over fifty should explore their "other side"—whether masculine or feminine—Friedan noted that women over fifty who go back to school or work or who become actively engaged in the public world report the fifty-plus years as being the best ones of their lives. Similarly, men over fifty who start focusing on the quality of their personal relationships and interior lives report a similar kind of satisfaction in older age. Unfortunately, added Friedan, the number of men who age well is far smaller than the number of women who age well. In our society, there are simply more opportunities for older women to develop their masculine traits than there are for older men to develop their feminine traits. If a man has neglected his wife and children for years because he has made work his first priority, by the time he is ready to attend to his personal relationships, these relationships may be extremely troubled. As a result, he may decide to seek a new wife with whom to have a second family—*repeating* the activities of his youth in the hope of "getting it right" this time. Worried about the left-behind "old wife" and "first family," Friedan urged aging men to find ways of loving and working that *differed* from the ways they loved and worked as twenty-, thirty-, or forty-year-olds.

The overall message of *The Fountain of Age* is that the people most likely to grow, change, and become more fully themselves as they age are precisely those people who move beyond polarized sex roles and creatively develop whichever side of themselves they neglected to develop as young men and women. In short, the happiest and most vital old men and women are androgynous persons.

The more she focused on the idea of androgyny, the more Friedan seemed to move toward humanism and away from feminism, however. Increasingly, she described *feminist* "sexual politics" as the "no-win battle of women as a whole sex, oppressed victims, against men as a whole sex, the oppressors."[91] In addition, she urged women to join with men to create a "new [human] politics that must emerge beyond reaction."[92] Eventually, Friedan claimed that because "human wholeness" is the true "promise of feminism," feminists should move beyond a focus on *women's* issues (issues related to women's reproductive and sexual roles, rights, and responsibilities) to work with men on "the concrete, practical, everyday problems of living, working and loving as equal persons."[93]

In a shift that appears to be more than mere coincidence, NOW's focus has also moved in the "human" direction suggested by Friedan, a trend that has brought NOW and its first president under concerted attack by radical feminists in particular. In contrast to Friedan and many liberal members of NOW, radical feminists doubt feminism can move beyond "women's issues" and still remain *feminism*. They claim that as long as our culture's understanding of what it means to be a human being remains androcentric (male-centered), it is premature for feminists to become humanists.

To be sure, Friedan was not the first liberal feminist who found humanism attractive. In their own distinct ways, Wollstonecraft, Taylor, and Mill each wanted *personhood*, full membership in the human community for women. The hypothesis that the ends and aims of feminism may, after all, be identical with those of humanism is a controversial one but worth keeping in mind as we consider recent trends in liberal feminism.

Contemporary Directions in Liberal Feminism

Betty Friedan is just one of thousands of women who may be classified as liberal feminists. As Zillah Eisenstein noted, Elizabeth Holtzman, Bella Abzug, Eleanor Smeal, Pat Schroeder, and Patsy Mink are liberal feminists, as are many other leaders and members of NOW and the Women's Equity Action League.[94] Although these women are sometimes divided on specific issues related to women, they do agree that the single most important goal of women's liberation is sexual equality, or, as it is sometimes termed, gender justice.

Liberal feminists wish to free women from oppressive gender roles—that is, from those roles used as excuses or justifications for giving women a lesser place, or no place at all, in the academy, the forum, and the marketplace. These feminists stress that patriarchal society conflates *sex* and *gender*,[95] deeming appropriate for women only those jobs associated with the traditional feminine personality. Thus, in the United States, for example, women are pushed into such jobs as nursing, teaching, and childcare, while they are steered away from jobs in business, science, technology, engineering, and mathematics. In addition, legislation specifically barring women from such "masculine" jobs as mining and firefighting or preventing women from working the night shift or overtime is not exactly a distant memory. To be sure, de jure gender discrimination in the workplace is relatively rare nowadays. But de facto gender discrimination in the workplace remains all too prevalent. Faced with a choice between male or female candidates for certain jobs, many employers still prefer to hire men for particularly demanding positions on the grounds that women are more likely than men to let their family responsibilities interfere with their job commitment and performance.

It is sometimes argued that men, no less than women, are also the victims of de facto gender discrimination—that even if the law has always favored men (or at least white men) other vehicles of social control have not. Thus, men's liberation activists complain about parents who never hire male babysitters and about nursery schools that prefer to fill their staff positions with women. Although liberal feminists sympathize with men who find it difficult to pursue child-centered careers because of de facto gender discrimination, they still think the kind of de facto gender discrimination men experience is not nearly as systematic as the kind that women experience. Society remains structured in ways that favor men and disfavor women in the competitive race for power, prestige, and money. The fact that, as of 2012, US women still earned only seventy-seven cents for every dollar men earned is not an accident.[96] Although women sometimes earn less than men because they choose to work less hard or fewer hours than men do, more often, women's salaries are lower than men's because society expects women to make their families their first priority. If a dual-career couple has a child, an aging parent, or an ailing relative in need of care, chances are that the female member of the couple will be the person who slows down or gives up her career to lend a helping hand.

In their discussions of the structural and attitudinal impediments to women's progress, contemporary liberal feminists often disagree about how to handle these hurdles. There are two types of liberal feminists: classical and welfare. Like classical liberals in general, classical liberal feminists favor limited government and a free market. They also view political and legal rights as particularly important. Freedom of expression, religion, and conscience play a major role in the psyches of classical liberal feminists. In contrast, welfare liberal feminists are like welfare liberals in general. Welfare liberals think government should provide citizens, especially underprivileged ones, with housing, education, health care, and social security. Moreover, they think the market should be limited by means of significant taxes and curbs on profits. For welfare liberal feminists, social and economic rights are the condition of possibility for the exercise of political and legal rights.

One way to better understand the difference between classical liberal feminists and welfare liberal feminists is to focus on a concrete issue, such as affirmative action policy. Classical liberal feminists believe that after discriminatory laws and policies have been removed from the books, thereby formally enabling women to compete equally with men, not much else can be done about "birds of a feather flocking together"—about male senior professors, for example, being more favorably disposed toward a male candidate for a faculty promotion than toward an equally qualified female candidate. In contrast, welfare liberal feminists urge society to break up that "old flock (gang) of mine," especially when failure to make feathers fly results in significant gender asymmetries with respect to the rank of full professor, for example. One typical late 1990s study found that "only one in eight women has attained full rank compared to nearly nine out of ten men.[97] The same study found that in engineering, nearly three in five men become full professors, whereas only one in five women become full professors. In view of such statistics, feminists advocate that female applicants to both schools and jobs either be (1) selected over *equally* qualified white male applicants (so-called affirmative action) or, more controversially, (2) selected over *better*-qualified white male applicants, provided the female applicants are still able to perform adequately (so-called preferential treatment).[98] Welfare liberal feminists insist that to the degree such policies are viewed as temporary, they do not constitute reverse discrimination. As soon as men and women have equal social status and economic clout, there will be no need for either affirmative action or preferential treatment policies. Indeed, when women achieve de facto as well as de jure equality with men, policies advantaging women over men would be unfair.

We may think the only meaningful liberal feminist approaches to combating gender discrimination are the classical and welfare approaches, both of which rely heavily on legal remedies. But as noted earlier, in the analysis of Betty Friedan's writings, another approach to combating gender discrimination uses the ideal of androgyny to counteract society's traditional tendency to value masculine traits or men more than feminine traits or women. If society encouraged everyone to develop both positive masculine and positive feminine traits, then no one would have reason to think less of women than of men. Discrimination on the bases of gender and biological sex would cease.

Clearly, discussions of sex differences, gender roles, and androgyny have helped focus liberal feminists' drive toward liberty, equality, and fairness for all. According to Jane English, such terms as *sex roles* and *gender traits* denote "the patterns of behavior which the two sexes are socialized, encouraged, or coerced into adopting, ranging from 'sex-appropriate' personalities to interests and professions."[99] Boys are instructed to be masculine; girls, to be feminine. Psychologists, anthropologists, and sociologists tend to define the "masculine" and "feminine" in terms of prevailing cultural stereotypes, which are influenced by racial, class, and ethnic factors. Thus, to be masculine in middle-class, white, Anglo-Saxon, Protestant United States is, among other things, to be rational, ambitious, and independent, and to be feminine is, among other things, to be emotional, nurturant, and dependent. To be sure, even within this segment of the population, exceptions to the rule will be found. Some biological males will manifest feminine gender traits, and some biological females will manifest masculine gender traits. But these individuals will be deemed exceptional or deviant. No matter what group of people (e.g., working-class Italian Catholics) is under scrutiny, then, gender-role stereotyping will limit the individual's possibilities for development as a unique self. The woman who displays characteristics her social group regards as masculine will be viewed as less than a *real* woman; the man who shows so-called feminine traits will be considered less than a *real* man.[100]

To liberate women and men from the culturally constructed cages of masculinity and femininity, many liberal feminists besides Betty Friedan advocate the formation of androgynous personalities.[101] Some liberal feminists favor monoandrogyny—the development of an ideal personality type that embodies the best of prevailing masculine and feminine gender traits.[102] According to psychologist Sandra Bem, the monoandrogynous person possesses a full complement of traditional female qualities—nurturance, compassion, tenderness, sensitivity, affiliation, cooperativeness—along with a full complement of traditional male qualities—aggressiveness, leadership, initiative, competitiveness.[103] (Recall that this list of traditional qualities probably needs to be modified, depending on the racial, class, and ethnic characteristics of the group under consideration.) Other liberal feminists resist monoandrogyny and instead advocate polyandrogyny—the development of multiple personality types, some of which are totally masculine; others, totally feminine; and still others, a mixture.[104] Whether liberal feminists espouse monoandrogyny or polyandrogyny, however, they tend to agree a person's biological sex should not determine his or her psychological and social gender.

Critiques of Liberal Feminism

In recent years, nonliberal feminists have increasingly dismissed liberal feminists. These critics claim that the main tenets of liberal feminist thought (i.e., all human persons are rational and free, share fundamental rights, and are equal) do not necessarily advance all women's interests. At best, they advance the interests of only certain kinds of women—namely, privileged women who, because of their privilege, think and act like men. Because the critiques leveled against liberal feminism are quite harsh, we need to carefully assess their merit.

Critique One: Reason, Freedom, and Autonomy Are Not As Good As They Sound

In *Feminist Politics and Human Nature,* Alison Jaggar formulated a powerful critique of liberal feminism. She claimed that the rational, free, and autonomous self that liberals favor is not neutral between the sexes. On the contrary, it is a "male" self.

Realizing that not everyone would understand why a rational, free, and autonomous self is "male," Jaggar carefully defended her point. She first noted that because liberals, including liberal feminists, locate human beings' "specialness" in human rationality and autonomy, liberals are so-called normative dualists— thinkers committed to the view that the functions and activities of the mind are somehow better than those of the body.[105] Eating, drinking, excreting, sleeping, and reproducing are not, according to this view, quintessential human activities, because members of most other animal species also engage in them. Instead, what sets human beings apart from the rest of animal creation is their capacity to think, reason, calculate, deliberate, and comprehend.

Jaggar then speculated that because of the original sexual division of labor, mental activities and functions were increasingly emphasized over bodily activities and functions in Western liberal thought. Given men's distance from nature, their undemanding reproductive and domestic roles, and the amount of time they were consequently able to spend cultivating the life of the mind, men tended to devalue the body, regarding it as a protective shell whose contours had little to do with their self-definition. In contrast, given women's close ties to nature, their heavy reproductive and domestic roles, and the amount of time they consequently had to spend caring for people's bodies, women tended to value the body, viewing it as essential to their personal identity. Because men took over the field of philosophy early on, observed Jaggar, men's way of seeing themselves came to dominate Western culture's collective pool of ideas about human nature. As a result, all liberals, male or female, nonfeminist or feminist, tend to accept as truth the priority of the mental over the bodily, even when their own daily experiences contradict this belief.

Liberal feminists' adherence to some version of normative dualism is problematic for feminism, according to Jaggar, not only because normative dualism leads to a devaluation of bodily activities and functions but also because it usually leads to both political solipsism and political skepticism. (Political solipsism is the belief that the rational, autonomous person is essentially isolated, with needs and interests separate from, and even in opposition to, those of every other individual. Political skepticism is the belief that the fundamental questions of political philosophy—what constitutes human well-being and fulfillment, and what are the means to attain it?—have no shared answer.) Thus, the result of valuing the mind over the body and the independence of the self from others is the creation of a politics that puts an extraordinary premium on liberty—on the rational, autonomous, independent, self-determining, isolated, and separated person's ability to think, do, and be whatever he or she deems worthy.[106]

Jaggar criticized political solipsism on empirical grounds, noting it makes little sense to think of individuals as somehow existing prior to the formation of community through some sort of contract. She observed, for example, that any pregnant woman knows a child is related to others (at least to her) even before it is born. The baby does not—indeed could not—exist as a lonely atom prior to subsequent entrance into the human community. Human infants are born helpless and require great care for many years. She explained that because this care cannot be adequately provided by a single adult, humans live in social groups that cooperatively bring offspring to maturity: "Human interdependence is . . . necessitated by human biology, and the assumption of individual self-sufficiency is plausible only if one ignores human biology."[107] Thus, Jaggar insisted, liberal political theorists need to explain not how and why isolated individuals come together but how and why communities dissolve. Competition, not cooperation, is the anomaly.

To add force to her empirical argument, Jaggar observed that political solipsism makes no sense conceptually. Here she invoked Naomi Scheman's point that political solipsism requires belief in abstract individualism.[108] The abstract individual is one whose emotions, beliefs, abilities, and interests can supposedly be articulated and understood without any reference whatsoever to social context. Kant's person is this type of abstract individual—a pure reason unaffected/uninfected by either the empirical-psychological ego or the empirical-biological body. However, Kant's philosophy notwithstanding, said Scheman, we are not *abstract* individuals. We are instead *concrete* individuals able to identify certain of our physiological sensations as ones of sorrow, for example, only because we are "embedded in a social web of interpretation that serves to give meaning"[109] to our twitches and twinges, our moans and groans, our squealing and screaming. Apart from this interpretative grid, we are literally *self-less*—that is, our very identities are determined by our socially constituted wants and desires. We are, fundamentally, the selves our communities create, an observation that challenges the US myth of the self-sufficient individual.

Political skepticism collapses together with political solipsism, according to Jaggar, for political skepticism also depends on an overly abstract and individualistic conception of the self. In contrast to the liberals or liberal feminists who insist the state should refrain from privileging any one conception of human well-being over another, Jaggar argued that the state should serve as more than a traffic cop who, without commenting on drivers' stated destinations, merely makes sure their cars do not collide. Whether we like it or not, she said, human biology and psychology dictate a set of basic human needs, and societies that treat these basic needs as optional cannot expect to survive, let alone to thrive. Thus, said Jaggar, the state must do more than keep traffic moving; it must also block off certain roads even if some individuals want to travel down them.

Defenders of liberal feminism challenge Jaggar's and Scheman's critique of liberal feminism on the grounds that the liberalism of liberal *feminists* is not the same as the liberalism of liberal *nonfeminists*. In what she termed a qualified defense of liberal feminism, Susan Wendell stressed that liberal feminists are not fundamentally committed either to separating the rational from the emotional or to valuing the former over the latter. On the contrary, they seem fully aware that reason and emotion, mind and body, are "equally necessary to human survival and the richness of human experience."[110] Indeed, observed Wendell, if liberal feminists lacked a conception of the self as an *integrated* whole, we would be hard pressed to explain their tendency to view androgyny as a positive state of affairs. For the most part, liberal feminists want their sons to develop a wide range of emotional responses and domestic skills as much as they want their daughters to develop an equally wide range of rational capacities and professional talents. Complete human beings are *both* rational and emotional. Thus, Wendell urged critics to read liberal feminist texts more sympathetically, as "a philosophically better kind of liberalism"[111] and to overcome the misconception that "[a] commitment to the value of individuals and their self-development, or even to the ethical priority of individuals over groups," is automatically a commitment "to narcissism or egoism or to the belief that one's own most important characteristics are somehow independent of one's relationships with other people."[112] Just because a woman refuses to spend her whole day nurturing her family does not mean she is more selfish than a man who, in the name of professional duty, may spend no time with his family. A person is selfish only when he or she takes more than his or her fair share of a resource: money, time, or even something intangible such as love.

Critique Two: Women as Men?

Jean Bethke Elshtain, a communitarian political theorist, is even more critical of liberal feminism than Alison Jaggar is. Like Jaggar, Elshtain claimed liberal feminists are wrong to emphasize individual interests, rights, and personal freedom over the common good, obligations, and social commitment, because "there is no way to create real communities out of an aggregate of 'freely' choosing adults."[113] In addition, more so than Jaggar, Elshtain castigated liberal feminists for putting an apparently high premium on so-called male values. She accused the Friedan of the 1960s—and, to a lesser extent, Wollstonecraft, Mill, and Taylor—of equating male being with human being, "manly" virtue with human virtue. In her critique "Why Can't a Woman Be More like a Man?" Elshtain identified what she considered liberal feminism's three major flaws: (1) claiming women *can* become like men if they set their minds to it; (2) claiming most women *want* to become like men; and (3) claiming all women *should* want to become like men, to aspire to masculine values.

With respect to the first claim, that women *can* become like men, Elshtain pointed to the general liberal feminist belief that male-female differences are the products of culture rather than biology, of nurture rather than nature. She claimed liberal feminists refuse to entertain the possibility that some sex differences are biologically determined, for fear that affirmative answers could be used to justify the repression, suppression, and oppression of women. For this reason, many liberal feminists have, in Elshtain's estimation, become "excessive environmentalists," people who believe that gender identities are the nearly exclusive product of socialization, changeable at society's will.[114]

Although she wanted to avoid both the reactionary position of contemporary sociobiologists, according to whom biology is indeed destiny, and the sentimental speculations of some nineteenth- and twentieth-century feminists—according to whom women are, by nature, morally better than men[115]—Elshtain claimed that society cannot erase long-standing male-female differences without inflicting violence on people. Unless we wish to do what Plato suggested in *The Republic,* namely, banish everyone over the age of twelve and begin an intensive program of centrally controlled and uniform socialization from infancy onward, we cannot hope, said Elshtain, to eliminate gender differences between men and women in just a few generations. In sum, women *cannot* be like men unless we are prepared to commit ourselves to the kind of social engineering and behavior modification that is incompatible with the spirit, if not also the letter, of liberal law.[116]

Liberal feminism also has a tendency, claimed Elshtain, to overestimate the number of women who want to be like men. She dismissed the view that any woman who wants more than anything else to be a wife and mother is a benighted and befuddled victim of patriarchal "false consciousness." Patriarchy, in Elshtain's estimation, is simply not powerful enough to make mush out of millions of women's minds. If it were, feminists would be unable to provide a cogent explanation for the emergence of feminist "true consciousness" out of pervasive patriarchal socialization. Elshtain observed that liberal feminists' attempt to reduce "wifing" and "mothering" to mere "roles" is misguided:

> Mothering is *not* a "role" on par with being a file clerk, a scientist, or a member of the air force. Mothering is a complicated, rich, ambivalent, vexing, joyous activity that is biological, natural, social, symbolic, and emotional. It carries profoundly resonant emotional and sexual imperatives. A tendency to downplay the differences that pertain between, say, mothering and holding a job, not only drains our private relations of much of their significance, but also oversimplifies what can and should be done to alter things for women, who are frequently urged to change roles to solve their problems.[117]

If, after investing years of physical and emotional energy in being a wife and mother, a woman is told she made the wrong choice, that she could have done something "significant" with her life instead, her reaction is not likely to be a positive one. It is one thing to tell a person he or she should try a new hairstyle; it is quite another to advise a person to get a more meaningful destiny.

Finally, as Elshtain saw it, liberal feminists are wrong to sing "a paean of praise to what Americans themselves call the 'rat race,'"[118] to tell women they *should* absorb traditional masculine values. Articles written for women about dressing for success, making it in a man's world, being careful not to cry in public, avoiding intimate friendships, being assertive, and playing hardball serve only to erode what may, according to Elshtain, ultimately be the best about women: their learned ability to create and sustain community through involvement with friends and family. Woman ought to resist membership in the "rat race" culture. Rather than encouraging one another to mimic the traditional behavior of successful men, who spend a minimum of time at home and a maximum of time at the office, women ought to work toward the kind of society in which men as well as women have as much time for friends and family as for business associates and professional colleagues.

Although she came close here to forwarding the problematic thesis that every wife and mother is the Virgin Mary in disguise, Elshtain insisted maternal thinking "need not and must not descend into the sentimentalization that vitiated much Suffragist discourse."[119] Fearing that full participation in the public sphere would threaten female virtue, the suffragists reasoned "the vote" was a way for women to reform the evil, deceitful, and ugly public realm without ever having to leave the supposed goodness, truth, and beauty of the private realm. As Elshtain saw it, had the suffragists not constructed a false polarity between male vice and female virtue, between the "evil" public world and the "good" private world, they might have marched into the public world, demanding it absorb the virtues and values of the private world from which they had come.[120]

In assessing Elshtain's critique of liberal feminism, 1990s liberal feminists observed that although Elshtain's critique applied to Friedan's *The Feminine Mystique* (1963), it did not apply to Friedan's *The Second Stage* (1981). More generally, 1990s liberal feminists found several reasons to fault Elshtain's communitarian line of thought. In particular, they saw her as embracing an "overly romanticized view of a traditional community, where the status quo is not only given but often embraced"[121] and where, therefore, women's traditional roles remain largely unchanged even if supposedly more valued by society as a whole. They also saw her as accepting the values of a community without critically examining its exclusionary potentialities or asking what kind of communities constitute an environment in which women can thrive.

Critique Three: Racism, Classism, and Heterosexism

Feminist critics of liberal feminism fault it not only for espousing a male ontology of self and an individualist politics but also for being only or mainly focused on the interests of white, middle-class, heterosexual women. Although liberal feminists accept this criticism as a just and fair one, they nonetheless note in their own defense that they have come a long way since the nineteenth century when, for example, they largely ignored black women's concerns. Nowadays, the situation is quite different. Liberal feminists are very attentive to how a woman's race affects her views on any number of topics, including fairly mundane ones such as housework.

We will recall that because Friedan addressed a largely white, middle-class, and well-educated group of women in *The Feminist Mystique,* it made sense for her to describe the housewife role as oppressive. After all, her primary audience did suffer from the kind of psychological problems people experience when they are underchallenged and restricted to repeatedly performing the same routine tasks. But as Angela Davis commented, the house-wife role tends to be experienced as liberating rather than oppressive by a significant number of black women.[122] Indeed, stressed Davis, many black women, particularly poor ones, would be only too happy to trade their problems for the "problem that has no name." They would embrace white, middle-class, suburban life enthusiastically, happy to have plenty of time to lavish on their families and themselves.

Liberal feminists' increased stress on issues of race has prompted an increasing number of minority women to join and become active in liberal feminist organizations. For example, largely because NOW has allied itself with minority organizations devoted to welfare reform, civil rights, immigration policy, apartheid, and migrant worker and tribal issues, by 1992, minority women constituted 30 percent of NOW's leadership and 10 percent of its staff.[123] Unlike nineteenth-century liberal feminists, today's liberal feminists no longer mistakenly contrast women's rights with blacks' rights, implying that black women are neither "real women" nor "real blacks" but some sort of hybrid creatures whose rights are of little concern to either white women or black men.

In addition to racism, classism previously existed to a marked degree within liberal feminism, largely because the women who initially led the women's rights movement were mainly from the upper middle class. Seemingly oblivious to the social and economic privileges of the women whom she addressed in *The Feminine Mystique,* Friedan simply assumed all or most women were supported by men and therefore worked for other than *financial* reasons. Later, when she came into increased contact with single mothers trying to support their families on meager wages or paltry welfare benefits, Friedan realized just how hard life can be for a poor urban woman working in a factory, as opposed to a wealthy suburban woman driving to a PTA meeting. Thus, in *The Second Stage,* Friedan tried to address some of the economic concerns of working women. Nevertheless, her primary audience remained the daughters of the housewives she had tried to liberate in the 1960s: well-educated, financially comfortable, working mothers whom she wished to rescue from the hardships of the so-called double day. In the final analysis, *The Second Stage* is a book for middle-class professional women (and men) much more than a text for working-class people. It envisions a society in which men and women assume equal burdens and experience equal benefits in both the public and the private worlds. But it fails to ask whether a capitalist society can afford to develop ideal work and family conditions for *all* of its members or only for the "best and brightest"—that is, for those professionals and quasi professionals who are already well enough off to take advantage of joint appointments, parental leaves, the mommy track, flex-time, leaves of absence, and so on.

Similarly, Friedan's *The Fountain of Age* (1993) is directed more toward relatively well-to-do and healthy old people than relatively poor and frail old people. Although Friedan's anecdotes about people remaking their lives after the age of sixty are inspiring, they are, as one commentator noted, mostly tales about "life-long achievers with uncommon financial resources"[124] who are continuing to do in their "golden years" what they did in their younger years. The experience of this group of people is to be contrasted with US cit-izens whose work years have worn them out physically and psychologically and who find it extremely difficult to survive, let alone thrive, on a small, fixed income. As such people age, especially if they are infirm, their main en-emy is not "self-image." On the contrary, it is "unsafe neighborhoods, un-manageable stairs, tight budgets and isolation."[125] To be sure, Friedan noted the plight of aging, infirm US citizens in *The Fountain of Age* and recom-mended a variety of concrete ways (e.g., home care and community support) to ameliorate their situation. Yet she failed to address society's *general unwill-ingness* to allocate time, money, and love to old people who act old and need more than what some consider their fair share of society's resources. Indeed, by emphasizing the importance of remaining "vital" in old age, Friedan may have inadvertently helped widen the gap between advantaged and disadvan-taged old people.

Finally, in addition to racism and classism, heterosexism has posed prob-lems for liberal feminists. When lesbians working within the women's rights movement decided publicly to avow their sexual identity, the leadership and membership of organizations such as NOW disagreed about how actively and officially the organization should support gay rights. As already described, Friedan was among the feminists who feared that a vocal and visible lesbian constituency might further alienate the public from "women's rights" causes. Friedan's successor in office, Aileen Hernandez, was embarrassed by her pre-decessor's lukewarm support for lesbians, however. Upon accepting the presi-dency of NOW in 1970, Hernandez issued a strong statement in support of lesbians: "[NOW does] not prescribe a sexual preference test for applicants. We ask only that those who join NOW commit themselves to work for full equality for women and that they do so in the context that the struggle in which we are engaged is part of the total struggle to free all persons to develop their full humanity. . . . [W]e need to free *all* our sisters from the shackles of a society which insists on viewing us in terms of sex."[126] Lesbians, no less than heterosexual women, insisted Hernandez, have sexual rights.

To be sure, not all of NOW's membership applauded Hernandez's views. Specifically, conservative members complained that "gay rights" was not a bona fide woman's issue. Radical members of NOW countered that if anyone knew what a real *woman's* issue was, it was the lesbian: she who puts women, not men, at the center of her private as well as public life. The battle between these two groups in NOW escalated to such a degree it threatened NOW's existence for a year or so before the organization officially proclaimed lesbian rights as a NOW issue. In 1990, NOW manifested its support of lesbians in a particularly visible way: It elected Patricia Ireland, an open bisexual, as its president. It is important to stress, however, that even today NOW supports lesbianism as a personal sexual preference—as a lifestyle or partner choice some women make—rather than as a political statement about the best way to achieve women's liberation. Liberal feminists do not claim that women must orient all of their sexual desires toward women and away from men or that all women must love women more than they love men. The claim is instead that men as well as women must treat each other as equals, as persons equally worthy of love.

Conclusion

One way to react to the limitations of liberal feminism is to dismiss it as a bourgeois, white movement. In essence, this is precisely what Ellen Willis did in her 1975 article "The Conservatism of *Ms.*," which faulted *Ms.* magazine, the most widely recognized publication of liberal feminism, for imposing a pseudofeminist "party line." After describing this line at length, Willis noted its overall message was a denial of women's pressing need to overthrow patriarchy and capitalism and an affirmation of women's supposed ability to make it in the "system." Whatever *Ms.* has to offer women, insisted Willis, it is not feminism:

> At best, *Ms.*'s self-improvement, individual-liberation philosophy is relevant only to an elite; basically it is an updated women's magazine fantasy. Instead of the sexy chick or the perfect homemaker, we now have a new image to live up to: the liberated woman. This fantasy, misrepresented as feminism, misleads some women, convinces others that "women's lib" has nothing to do with them, and plays into the hands of those who oppose any real change in women's condition.[127]

Willis's criticism may have been on target at the time, but *Ms.* has changed since the mid-1970s. Its editors have featured articles that show, for example, how classism, racism, and heterosexism intersect with sexism, thereby doubling, tripling, and even quadrupling the oppression of some women. Specifically, it has investigative reporting issues on such topics as overseas sweatshops, sex marketing, and global human rights.[128] Moreover, liberal feminists have, with few exceptions,[129] moved away from their traditional belief that any woman who wants to can liberate herself "individually" by "throwing off" her conditioning and "unilaterally" rejecting "femininity."[130] They now believe that achieving even a modest goal such as "creating equal employment opportunity for women" calls for much more than the effort of individual women; it will require the effort of a whole society committed to "giving girls and boys the same early education and ending sex prejudice, which in turn will require major redistribution of resources and vast changes in consciousness."[131] Sexual equality cannot be achieved through individual women's willpower alone. Also necessary are major alterations in people's deepest social and psychological structures.

In a 2002 article entitled "Essentialist Challenges to Liberal Feminism," Ruth E. Groenhout argued that feminists who are not liberal feminists should reconsider their wholesale rejection of liberalism. Specifically, she suggested that, properly interpreted, the liberal view of human nature is not quite as bad as Jaggar and Elshtain portrayed it. As Groenhout understands it, the liberal picture of human nature contains "a crucial aspect of the feminist analysis of the wrongness of sexist oppression."[132]

> Sexual oppression, and social systems that perpetuate sexual oppression, are morally evil because they limit or deny women's capacity to reflect on and determine their own lives. Sexism also causes immeasurable harm to people, and its consequences are a part of the evil it causes, but sexism would be wrong even if it did not result in either impoverishment or sexualized violence against women. It is wrong, ultimately, because it treats some humans as less than human and limits their freedom to take responsibility for their own lives.[133]

Another philosopher who has recently defended liberal feminism is Martha Nussbaum. According to Anne Phillips, Nussbaum correctly identified the three main criticisms nonliberal feminists have leveled against liberalism, and therefore, liberal feminism: (1) Liberalism is too "individualistic"; (2) liberalism's conception of equality is too "abstract and formal"; and (3) liberalism overemphasizes the role of reason in human life to the neglect of emotion.[134] Nussbaum argued that liberalism is individualistic, but in the right sort of way. It is incorrect, said Nussbaum, to view such liberal thinkers as Kant, Mill, Hume, Smith, and Rawls as pushing for "normative egoism"; that is, the view that it is "always best to promote the satisfaction of one's own self-interest."[135] Regarding the individual as the basic unit for the construction of society, continued Nussbaum, is a good thing for women and other oppressed people. The collective—be it the state or the family—should not subsume the individual to its ends, purposes, or goal. Rather, people should be recognized as separate selves that are "hungry and joyful and loving and needy one by one, however closely [they] may embrace one another."[136] The philosopher Immanuel Kant was right to insist that each individual be regarded as an "end" in himself/herself, rather than as a mere means to someone else's ends.[137] Seeing herself as a subject to be respectfully and fairly treated is, according to Nussbaum, a source of empowerment for a woman who has only been used to serve men's and children's interests. The ability to single one's self out of one's relationships is important to one's sense of self as being unique and worthy of other's consideration.

With respect to liberalism's penchant for "abstractness" at the peril of "concreteness," Nussbaum conceded that some liberals have been guilty of forwarding a merely formal view of equality of opportunity that assumes, for example, that if a woman is not barred from pursuing a job or an educational slot, she has as much chance as a man to secure her goal. In Nussbaum's estimation, many women need much more than a set of laws that permit them to seek their chosen path in life. They also need the material means to do so. Defending her "capabilities" approach to equality, Nussbaum noted that "liberals standardly grant that the equality of opportunity that individuals have a right to demand from their governments has material prerequisites, and that these prerequisites may vary depending on one's situation in society."[138]

Nussbaum also defended liberalism against another version of the charge of abstractness; namely, that liberalism supposedly abstracts the individual from his/her social and historical differences, as if one's community were not constitutive of one's self-identity. Nussbaum asserted that liberals do understand how particular contexts shape individuals. Nonetheless, they also stress "that the core of rational and moral personhood is something [however "abstract"] all human beings share."[139] Moreover, said Nussbaum, the idea that all human beings share a common core, irrespective of their historical and social circumstances, is

> an idea that the women of the world badly need to vindicate their equality and to argue for change. It is the disparity between humanity and its social deformation that gives rise to claims of justice. And the communitarian vision of persons, in which we are at heart and essentially what our traditions have made us, is a vision that leaves reduced scope for feminist critique.[140]

In addition to defending liberalism against "abstractness," Nussbaum defended it from the charge that it is hyperrational to the detriment of the emotions. She claimed that at least Aristotle, Rousseau, Adam Smith, and even

John Stuart Mill have plenty for room for the emotions in their philosophies. More significantly, Nussbaum asserted that emotion is not the polar opposite of reason. Indeed, when they are rightly expressed, emotions are highly cognitive. There is a place for example, for anger, which should be expressed at the sight of injustice. The emotions motivate, convey, and embody our ethical assessments of the goodness/badness, rightness/wrongness of certain situations or relationships.

Such thinkers as Groenhut and Nussbaum remind us that for all the ways liberal feminism may have gone wrong for women, it has done some things very right for women along the way. Women owe to liberal feminists many of the civil, educational, occupational, and reproductive rights they currently enjoy. They also owe to liberal feminists the ability to walk confidently in the public domain, claiming it is no less their territory than men's. Perhaps enough time has passed for feminists critical of liberal feminism to reconsider their dismissal of it. Certainly, enough time has passed for the states to ratify the Equal Rights Amendment or, if that fails, to give a hearing to the yet-unsubmitted Constitutional Equality Amendment (CEA), according to which:

1. Women and men shall have equal rights throughout the United States and every place and entity subject to its jurisdiction; through this article, the subordination of women to men is abolished;
2. All persons shall have equal rights and privileges without discrimination on account of sex, race, sexual orientation, marital status, ethnicity, national origin, color or indigence;
3. This article prohibits pregnancy discrimination and guarantees the absolute right of a woman to make her own reproductive decisions including the termination of pregnancy;
4. This article prohibits discrimination based upon characteristics unique to or stereotypes about any class protected under this article. This article also prohibits discrimination through the use of any facially neutral criteria which have a disparate impact based on membership in a class protected under this article.
5. This article does not preclude any law, program or activity that would remedy the effects of discrimination and that is closely related to achieving such remedial purposes;
6. This article shall be interpreted under the highest standard of judicial review;
7. The United States and the several states shall guarantee the implementation and enforcement of this article.[141]

Although it is important not to burden the Constitution with unnecessary amendments, liberal feminists seem right to insist that some amendment, such as the CEA, is very important. Women's status has indeed improved over the last century, but it is still not high enough. Good is not good enough.

Questions for Discussion

1. In what ways does liberal feminism aim to promote rights over goods?
2. What are some practical ways in which women may achieve a balance of public and private pursuits? Consider various groups of women (single mothers, racial minorities, married women, lesbians, economically disadvantaged women, etc.).
3. Were nineteenth-century feminists right in agreeing to put on the back burner their own cause to focus on the abolition movement, or do you believe both causes could have been pursued concurrently without detriment to each other?
4. Is there value in attaining legal equality (e.g., the right to vote) when social equality is still lagging?
5. Has there been a historic need for men to be liberated from their traditional roles, even if relatively uncommunicated? Does combining the idea of men's liberation with that of women's liberation helpfully progress a discussion of humanism, or needlessly distract from women's issues?
6. Discuss specific examples in which the cognitive nature of emotions is demonstrated.

Radical Feminism

Libertarian and Cultural Perspectives

As we noted in Chapter 1, the 1960s and 1970s feminists who belonged to women's rights groups, such as the National Organization for Women, believed they could achieve gender equality by reforming the "system"—by working to eliminate discriminatory educational, legal, and economic policies.[1] Achieving equal rights for women was the paramount goal of these reformers, and the fundamental tenets of liberal political philosophy were a comfortable fit for these reformers. But not all 1960s and 1970s feminists wanted to find a place for women in the "system." The feminists who formed groups such as the Redstockings, the Feminists, New York Radical Women, and New York Feminists perceived themselves as revolutionaries rather than reformers. New York Radical Women (NYRW) refused to join the 1968 Jeannette Rankin Brigade peace march in Washington, DC, a large gathering of women's groups united to oppose the Vietnam War, because it was only a *reaction* to those who governed patriarchal America. NYRW felt that by appealing to Congress, the Brigade was keeping its "traditional passive role of reacting to men instead of gaining real political power.[2] Interestingly, this group of revolutionary feminists was the same one that protested the 1968 Miss America Pageant, calling it a "cattle auction" and tossing bras, girdles, *Playboy* magazines, mops, and other items that represented women's oppression into a trash can.[3] Similarly, Redstockings (a neologism combining the term *bluestocking*, a negative term for brainy women, with *red*, for its close linkage to the revolutionary left) engaged in proactive activism. It was famous for its "speakouts" and street theater dramatizations on the issue of abortion rights.[4]

Referring to themselves as "radical feminists" these groups of revolutionary feminists introduced to women the practice of consciousness-raising. Women came together in small groups and shared with each other their personal experiences *as women*. They discovered that their individual experiences were not unique to them but widely shared by many women. According to Valerie Bryson, consciousness-raising showed how the trauma of a woman who had been raped or who had had to resort to an illegal abortion seemed to be linked to the experiences of the wife whose husband refused to do his share of housework, appeared never to have heard of the female orgasm, or sulked if she went out for the evening; the secretary whose boss insisted that she wear "feminine" clothes, expected her to "be nice" to important clients, or viewed her as the office coffee maker; and the female student whose professors expected her to do less well and refused requests to study female writers or even traded good grades for sexual favors.[5]

Empowered by the realization that women's fates were profoundly linked, radical feminists proclaimed that "the personal is political" and that all women are "sisters." They insisted that men's control of women's sexual and reproductive lives and women's self-identity, self-respect, and self-esteem is the most fundamental of all the oppressions human beings visit on each other.

The claim that women's oppression *as women* is more fundamental than other forms of human oppression is difficult to unpack. According to Alison Jaggar and Paula Rothenberg, it can be interpreted to mean one or more of five things:

1. That women were, historically, the first oppressed group.
2. That women's oppression is the most widespread form of oppression, existing in virtually every known society.
3. That women's oppression is the form of oppression hardest to eradicate and cannot be removed by other social changes, such as the abolition of class society.
4. That women's oppression causes the most suffering to its victims, qualitatively as well as quantitatively, although the suffering may often go unrecognized because of the sexist prejudices of both the oppressors and the victims.
5. That women's oppression . . . provides a conceptual model for understanding all other forms of oppression.[6]

But just because radical feminists agreed in principle that sexism is the first, most widespread, or deepest form of human oppression did not mean they also agreed about the nature and function of this pernicious ism or the best way to eliminate it. On the contrary, radical feminists split into two basic camps—*radical-libertarian feminists* and *radical-cultural feminists*—and depending on their camp, these feminists voiced very different views about how to fight sexism.

Radical-libertarian feminists claimed that an exclusively feminine gender identity is likely to limit women's development as full human persons. Thus, they encouraged women to become androgynous persons, that is, persons who embody both (good) masculine and (good) feminine characteristics or, more controversially, any potpourri of masculine and feminine characteristics, good or bad, that strikes their fancy. Among the first radical-libertarian feminists to celebrate androgynous women was Joreen Freeman. She wrote, "What is disturbing about a Bitch is that she is androgynous. She incorporates within herself qualities defined as 'masculine' as well as 'feminine.' A Bitch is blatant, direct, arrogant, at times egoistic. She has no liking for the indirect, subtle, mysterious ways of the 'eternal feminine.' She disdains the vicarious life deemed natural to women because she wants to live a life of her own."[7] In other words, a "Bitch" does not want to limit herself to being a sweet girl with little in the way of power. Instead, she wants to embrace as part of her gender identity those masculine characteristics that permit her to lead life on her own terms.

Freeman's views did not go unchallenged. Among others, Alice Echols rejected as wrongheaded Freeman's celebration of the Bitch. She said that Freeman's Bitch was far too masculine to constitute a role model for women. Still, Echols credited Freeman for expressing radical-libertarian feminists' desire to free women from the constraints of female biology. Just because a woman is biologically a female does not mean she is destined to exhibit only feminine characteristics. Women can be masculine as well as feminine.[8] They can choose their gender roles and identities, mixing and matching them at will.

Later, after the shock value of Freeman's rhetoric had dissipated, some radical feminists began to have second thoughts about the wisdom of women's striving to be androgynous persons. As they saw it, a Bitch was not a full human person but only a woman who had embraced some of the worst features of masculinity. According to Echols, this group of radical feminists, soon labeled radical-cultural feminists, replaced the goal of androgyny with a summons to affirm women's essential "femaleness."[9] Far from believing, as radical-libertarian feminists did, that women should exhibit both masculine and feminine traits and behaviors, radical-cultural feminists expressed the view that it is better for women to be strictly female/feminine. Women, they said, should not try to be like men. On the contrary, they should try to be more like women, emphasizing the values and virtues culturally associated with women ("interdependence, community, connection, sharing, emotion, body, trust, absence of hierarchy, nature, immanence, process, joy, peace and life") and de-emphasizing the values and virtues culturally associated with men ("independence, autonomy, intellect, will, wariness, hierarchy, domination, culture, transcendence, product, asceticism, war and death").[10] Moreover, and in the ideal, women should appreciate that, despite cultural variations among themselves, all women share one and the same female nature,[11] and the less influence men have on this nature, the better.[12] Indeed, some radical-cultural feminists thought that women's essential nature was better than men's and that women ought to govern men, thereby putting themselves into opposition to liberal feminists who advocated sexual equality.

To be certain, like any other conceivable classification of radical feminists, the libertarian-cultural distinction is subject to criticism. Yet, in my estimation, this particular distinction helps explain not only why some radical feminists embrace the concept of androgyny and others eschew it, but also why some radical feminists view sex and reproduction as oppressive, even dangerous for women, whereas others view sex and reproduction as liberating, even empowering for women. As we shall see throughout this chapter, radical feminists are not afraid to take exception to each other's views.

Libertarian and Cultural Views on the Sex/Gender System

To appreciate radical-libertarian and radical-cultural feminist views on androgyny in greater detail, it is useful first to understand the so-called sex/gender system. According to radical-libertarian feminist Gayle Rubin, the sex/gender system is a "set of arrangements by which a society transforms biological sexuality into products of human activity."[13] So, for example, patriarchal society uses certain facts about male and female biology (chromosomes, anatomy, hormones) as the basis for constructing a set of masculine and feminine gender identities and behaviors that serve to empower men and disempower women. In the process of accomplishing this task, patriarchal society convinces itself its cultural constructions are somehow "natural" and therefore that people's "normality" depends on their ability to display whatever gender identities and behaviors are culturally linked with their biological sex.

Among others, radical-libertarian feminists rejected patriarchal society's assumption there is a necessary connection between one's sex (male or female) and one's gender (masculine or feminine). Instead, they claimed that gender is separable from sex and that patriarchal society uses rigid gender roles to keep women passive ("affectionate, obedient, responsive to sympathy and approval, cheerful, kind and friendly") and men active ("tenacious, aggressive, curious, ambitious, planful, responsible, original and competitive").[14] They claimed the way for women to dispel men's wrongful power over women is for both sexes first to recognize women are no more destined to be passive than men are destined to be active, and then to develop whatever combination of feminine and masculine traits best reflects their individually unique personality.

Some Libertarian Views on Gender

Millett's Sexual Politics

Among other prominent radical-libertarian feminists, Kate Millett insisted that the roots of women's oppression are buried deep in patriarchy's sex/gender system. In *Sexual Politics* (1970), she claimed the male-female sex relationship is the paradigm for all *power* relationships: "Social caste supersedes all other forms of inegalitarianism: racial, political, or economic, and unless the clinging to male supremacy as a birthright is finally forgone, all systems of oppression will continue to function simply by virtue of their logical and emotional mandate in the primary human situation."[15] Because male control of the public and private worlds maintains patriarchy, male control must be eliminated if women are to be liberated. But this is no easy task. To eliminate male control, men and women have to eliminate gender—specifically, sexual status, role, and temperament—as it has been constructed under patriarchy.

Patriarchal ideology exaggerates biological differences between men and women, making certain that men always have the dominant, or masculine, roles and women always have the subordinate, or feminine, ones. This ideology is so powerful, said Millett, that men are usually able to secure the apparent consent of the very women they oppress. Men do this through institutions, such as the academy, the church, and the family, each of which justifies and reinforces women's subordination to men, resulting in most women's internalization of a sense of inferiority to men. Should a woman refuse to accept patriarchal ideology by casting off her femininity—that is, her submissiveness/subordination—men will use coercion to accomplish what conditioning has failed to achieve. Intimidation is everywhere in patriarchy, according to Millett. The streetwise woman realizes that if she wants to survive in patriarchy, she had better act feminine, or else she may be subjected to "a variety of cruelties and barbarities."[16]

Millett stressed that despite men's continual attempts to condition and coerce all women, many women have proved uncontrollable. During the 1800s, for example, US women's resistance to men's power took several forms, including the women's movement inaugurated in 1848 at Seneca Falls, New York. As noted in Chapter 1, this spirited movement helped women gain many important legal, political, and economic liberties and equalities. Nevertheless, the women's movement of the 1800s failed to liberate women fully, because it did not adequately challenge the sex/gender system at its deepest roots. As a result, twentieth-century patriarchal forces regained some of the ground they had lost from nineteenth-century feminist activists.

Millett singled out authors D. H. Lawrence, Henry Miller, and Norman Mailer as some of the most articulate leaders of patriarchy's 1930–1960 assault on feminist ideas. She claimed that readers typically took Lawrence's, Miller's, and Mailer's *descriptions* of relationships in which women are sexually humiliated and abused by men as *prescriptions* for ideal sexual conduct. Millett considered this view of heterosexual relationships to be pornographic, and that pornography often functions in much the same way as advertising does. The perfectly slim bodies of the models who grace the covers of *Vogue* become standards for average women. Nobody has to articulate an explicit law, "Thou shalt mold thine lumpen body in the image of one of America's top models." Women simply know what is expected of them, what it means to be beautiful. In the same way, women exposed to pornographic authors simply know what is expected of them, what it means to be a sexually exciting person as opposed to a sexually prissy person.

In addition to these literary pornographers, Millett identified two other patriarchal groups—neo-Freudian psychologists and Parsonian sociologists—as leading the assault on feminists. Although Sigmund Freud's openness about sexuality, his willingness to talk about what people do or do not do in the bedroom, initially appeared as a progressive step toward better, more various, and more liberating sexual relations, Millett claimed Freud's disciples used his writings to "rationalize the invidious relationship between the sexes, to ratify traditional roles, and to validate temperamental differences."[17] In a similar vein, the followers of Talcott Parsons, an eminent sociologist, used his writings to argue that distinctions between masculine and feminine traits are biological/natural rather than social/cultural, and that without rigid gender dimorphism, society could not function as well as it does now. Convinced that gender identities and behaviors are not "an arbitrary imposition on an infinitely plastic biological base," but "an adjustment to the real biological differences between the sexes," Parsons's disciples confidently asserted that women's subordination to men is natural.[18]

Rather than concluding her discussion of patriarchal reactionaries on a despairing note, however, Millett ended it on an optimistic one. In the late 1970s, women were, she believed, regrouping their forces. Aware of their nineteenth-century predecessors' mistakes, these twentieth-century feminists were determined not to repeat history. Millett observed in contemporary feminism a determined effort to destroy the sex/gender system—the basic source of women's oppression—and to create a new androgynous society in which men and women are equals at every level of existence.[19] Interesting and important,

Millett noted that the only way to create this ideal society would require women to temporarily separate from men so that both men and women could better appreciate the value of women. Apparently, an androgynous society is one in which both sexes value female worth as much as male worth.

Firestone's The Dialectic of Sex

Like Millett, Shulamith Firestone, another radical-libertarian feminist, claimed the material basis for the sexual/political ideology of female submission and male domination was rooted in the reproductive roles of men and women. Firestone, however, believed Millett's solution to this problem—the elimination of the sexual double standard that permits men but not women to experiment with sex, and the inauguration of a dual-parenting system that gives fathers and mothers equal child-rearing responsibilities—was inadequate. It would, in her estimation, take far more than such modest reforms in the sex/gender system to free women's (and men's) sexuality from the biological imperatives of procreation and to liberate women's (and men's) personalities from the socially constructed and rigid constraints of femininity and masculinity. In fact, said Firestone, it would take a major biological and social revolution to effect this kind of human liberation: Artificial (ex utero) reproduction would need to replace natural (in utero) reproduction, and so-called intentional families, whose members *chose* each other for reasons of friendship or even simple convenience, would need to replace the traditional biological family constituted in and through its members' genetic connections to one another.

Firestone maintained that with the end of the biological family would come the breakup of the Oedipal family situation that prohibits, among other things, parent-child incest. No longer would there be concerns about so-called inbreeding as people reverted to their natural "polymorphous perversity"[20] and again delighted in all types of sexual behavior. Genital sex, so important for the purposes of biological sex, would become just one kind of sexual experience—and a relatively unimportant one—as people rediscovered the erotic pleasures of their oral and anal cavities and engaged in sexual relations with members of the same as well as the opposite sex.

Firestone claimed that as soon as both men and women were truly free to engage in polymorphous, perverse sex, it would no longer be necessary for men to display only masculine identities and behaviors and for women to display only feminine ones. Freed from their gender roles at the level of biology (i.e., reproduction), women would no longer have to be passive, receptive, and vulnerable, sending out "signals" to men to dominate, possess, and penetrate them so as to keep the wheels of human procreation spinning. Instead, men and women would be encouraged to mix and match feminine and masculine traits and behaviors in whatever combination they wished. As a result, not only would individuals evolve into androgynous persons, but society as a whole would become androgynous. As Firestone saw it, the biological division of the sexes for the purpose of procreation had created not only a false dichotomy between masculinity and femininity, but also an invidious cultural split between the sciences and the arts.

Firestone believed we associate science and technology with men and the humanities and the arts with women. Thus, the "masculine response" to reality is the "technological response": "objective, logical, extroverted, realistic, concerned with the conscious mind (the ego), rational, mechanical, pragmatic and down-to-earth, stable."[21] In contrast, the "feminine response" to reality is the "aesthetic response": "subjective, intuitive, introverted, wishful, dreamy or fantastic, concerned with the subconscious (the *id*), emotional, even temperamental (hysterical)."[22] Only when the aforementioned biological revolution eliminates the need for maintaining rigid lines between male and female, masculine and feminine, will we be able to bridge the gap between the sciences and the arts. Androgynous persons will find themselves living in an androgynous society in which the categories of the technological and the aesthetic, together with the categories of the masculine and the feminine, will have disappeared through what Firestone termed "a mutual cancellation—a matter-antimatter explosion, ending with a poof!"[23] At last, claimed Firestone, the male Technological Mode would be able to "produce in actuality what the female Aesthetic Mode had envisioned," namely, a world in which we use our knowledge to create not hell but heaven on earth—a world in which men no longer have to toil by the sweat of their brow to survive and in which women no longer have to bear children in pain and travail.[24]

Some Cultural Views on Gender

Marilyn French

Because Marilyn French attributes male-female differences more to biology (nature) than to socialization (nurture), and because she seems to think traditional feminine traits are somehow better than traditional masculine traits, I view her as more of a radical-cultural feminist than a radical-libertarian feminist. Like Millett and Firestone fifteen years earlier, French claimed men's oppression of women leads logically to other systems of human domination. If it is possible to justify men's domination of women, it is possible to justify all forms of domination. "Stratification of men above women," wrote French, "leads in time to stratification of classes: an elite rules over people perceived as 'closer to nature,' savage, bestial, animalistic."[25]

Because French believed sexism is the model for all other isms, including racism and classism, she sought to explain the differences between sexism's enslaving ideology of "power-over" others and an alternative, nonsexist liberating ideology of "pleasure-with" others. Examining the origins of patriarchy, French concluded early humans lived in harmony with nature. They saw themselves as small parts of a larger whole into which they had to fit if they wanted to survive. Considering evidence from primates and the world's remaining "simple societies," French speculated that the first human societies were probably matricentric (mother centered), for it was the mother who more than likely played the primary role in the group's survival-oriented activities of bonding, sharing, and harmonious participation in nature. Nature was friend, and as sustainer of nature and reproducer of life, woman was also friend.[26] French also speculated that as the human population grew, food inevitably became scarce. No longer experiencing nature as a generous mother, humans decided to take matters into their own hands. They developed techniques to free themselves from the whims of nature. They drilled, dug, and plowed nature for its bounty. The more control humans gained over nature, however, the more they separated themselves from it physically and psychologically. French claimed that because a "distance had opened up between humans and their environment as a result of increasing controls exercised over nature," humans became alienated from nature.[27] Alienation, defined by French as a profound sense of separation, aroused "hostility," which in turn led to "fear" and finally to "enmity." It is not surprising, then, that these negative feelings intensified men's desire to control not only nature but also women, whom they associated with nature on account of their role in reproduction.[28]

Out of men's desire to control the woman/nature dyad was born patriarchy, a hierarchical system that values having power over as many people as possible. Originally developed to ensure the human community's survival, the desire for power over others rapidly became, under patriarchy, a value cultivated simply for the experience of being the person in charge, the lawgiver, the boss, number one in the pecking order. French speculated that untempered by cooperation, patriarchal competition would inevitably lead to unbridled human conflict.[29]

Intent on sparing the world conflict—particularly as it could, in these times, escalate into a nuclear holocaust—French claimed that feminine values must be reintegrated into the masculine society created by a patriarchal ideology. If we want to survive the twenty-first century, said French, we must treasure in our lives and actions "love and compassion and sharing and nutritiveness [*sic*] equally with control and structure, possessiveness and status,"[30] Were we to take this last assertion at face value, we could easily infer that, for French, the best society is an androgynous one in which both men and women embrace the historically feminine values of love, compassion, sharing, and nurturance just as eagerly as they embrace the historically masculine values of control, structure, possessiveness, and status. Yet a closer reading of French suggests she actually esteemed feminine values *more* than masculine values and that any time she affirmed a masculine value, she did so only because she had subjected it to what Joyce Trebilcot termed a "feminist reconceiving"[31]—that is, a linguistic reinterpretation of a concept that involves changing its descriptive meaning, the evaluative meaning, or both.[32] According to French, most of her linguistic reinterpretations of masculine values involved changing their descriptive rather than evaluative meaning. For example, French did not claim that the masculine value of so-called structure is *bad* in and of itself. Instead, she argued that structure, understood as a system or an organization, is *good* provided it serves to connect rather than disconnect people.[33]

Because of her obvious dislike for the *masculine* version of power over others, French claimed the androgynous person must strike a balance between pleasure with others and a *feminine* version of power over others she labeled "power-to" do for others. French emphasized it is good for us to have power as well as pleasure in our lives, provided our power manifests itself not as the desire to destroy (power over others) but as the desire to create (power to do for others). Conceding we may never be able to completely eliminate our desire to be "top dog," French nonetheless insisted it is possible for us to curb our competitive drives and to cultivate instead our cooperative capacities.

Mary Daly

Even more than Millett, Firestone, and French, radical-cultural feminist Mary Daly analyzed traditional understandings of gender. Although Daly began her intellectual journey in *Beyond God the Father: Toward a Philosophy of Women's Liberation* (1973) with a plea for androgyny, she ultimately rejected the terms "masculine" and "feminine" as hopelessly befuddled products of patriarchy. Her term-transforming travels through *Gyn/Ecology* ended in *Pure Lust,* a spirited defense of "wild," "lusty," and "wandering" women—women who no longer desire to be androgynous and who prefer to identify themselves as radical lesbian feminist separatists.

In *Beyond God the Father,* her first major work, Daly focused on God as the paradigm for all patriarchs, arguing that unless God is dislodged from both men's and women's consciousness, women will never be empowered as full persons.[34] She repeatedly claimed that if anyone ever had a power-over-others complex, it is the transcendent God who appears in Judaism, Islam, and especially Christianity. This God is so remote and aloof that he dwells in a place beyond earth, suggesting that power over others inevitably leads to separation from others. A transcendent God, observed Daly, is a God who thinks in terms of I-it, subject-object, or self-other relationships. Furthermore, what is most alien to this transcendent God, this total being, is the natural world he called into existence out of total nothingness. Thus, women, who are associated with nature on account of their reproductive powers, play the role of object/other against both God's and men's role of subject/self.

Because the old transcendent God rejected women, Daly wished to replace him with a new, immanent God. An immanent God thinks in terms of I-thou, subject-subject, or self-self relationships and is thoroughly identified with the natural world in which he/she/it abides, she said. Thus, women are equal to men before this God, whom Daly described as Be-ing.[35]

One of the main ways in which I-it thinking is reflected in patriarchal society, said Daly, is through the institution of rigid masculine and feminine gender roles, polarizing the human community into two groups. Because men collectively perceive and define women as the second sex, each man becomes an I, or a self, and each woman becomes an it, or another. One way, then, to overcome I-it thinking, and the transcendent God who thinks I-it thoughts, is to break down gender dimorphism by constructing an androgynous person who is neither "I" nor "it" but beyond both forms of existence.

Significantly, Daly's concept of androgyny in *Beyond God the Father* requires the rejection of both the pluralist model of androgyny, according to which men and women have separate but supposedly equal and complementary traits, and the assimilation model of androgyny, according to which women and men exhibit feminine as well as masculine traits.[36] As she saw it, both of these models of androgyny were deficient because neither of them asked whether the traditional concepts of masculinity and femininity are worth preserving.

Although Daly's concerns about using the terms *masculinity* and *femininity* were similar to those previously raised by French, she proposed to handle these terms in a different way than French had. Whereas French seemed interested in reinterpreting traditional masculine traits, Daly focused exclusively on reinterpreting traditional feminine traits. Daly insisted that positive feminine traits such as love, compassion, sharing, and nurturance must be carefully distinguished from their pathological excesses, the sort of masochistic feminine "virtues" for which they are frequently mistaken. For example, loving ordinarily is good, but under patriarchy, loving can become, for women, a form of total self-sacrifice or martyrdom. Thus, Daly argued that the construction of the truly androgynous person cannot and must not begin until women say no to the values of the "morality of victimization." Out of this no, said Daly, will come a yes to the values of the "ethics of personhood."[37] By refusing to be the other, by becoming selves with needs, wants, and interests of their own, women will end the game of man as master and woman as slave.

In *Beyond God the Father,* Daly observed what she described as the Unholy Trinity of Rape, Genocide, and War combining in their one patriarchal person the legions of sexism, racism, and classism. In *Gyn/Ecology: The Metaethics of Radical Feminism,* she articulated this claim more fully, arguing that this Unholy Trinity, this single patriarchal person, has but one essential message: necrophilia, defined as "obsession with and usually erotic attraction toward and stimulation by corpses, typically evidenced by overt acts (as copulation with a corpse)."[38] Whereas Daly emphasized in *Beyond God the Father* that women cannot thrive as long as they subscribe to the morality of victimization, she stressed in *Gyn/Ecology* that women cannot even survive as long as they remain in patriarchy. Not only are men out to twist women's minds, but they are also out to destroy women's bodies through such practices as Hindu suttee, Chinese foot binding, African female circumcision, European witch burning, and Western gynecology.[39]

In *Gyn/Ecology,* Daly decided to reject several concepts she had used in *Beyond God the Father.* Among these concepts was androgyny, a concept that she came to view as twisted, as idealizing someone like "John Travolta and Farrah Fawcett-Majors Scotch-taped together."[40] The more Daly reflected on the traditional understanding of femininity, the more convinced she became that women should not strive to be "feminine." She claimed that because patriarchy had constructed both the positive feminine qualities of nurturance, compassion, and gentleness and the negative feminine qualities of pettiness, jealousy, and vanity, women should reject the seemingly "good" aspects of femininity as well as the obviously "bad" ones. They are all "man-made constructs" shaped for the purposes of trapping women deep in the prison of patriarchy.[41]

Stripped of their *femininity,* women would be revealed in their original (prepatriarchal) *female* power and beauty, insisted Daly. Daly used Jerzy Kosinski's image of a painted bird to detail the differences between "false femininity" and "true femaleness." Kosinski tells the tale of a keeper who imprisons a natural, plain-looking bird simply by painting its feathers with a glittering color. Eventually, the bird is destroyed by her painted "friends," the victims of their jealousy. Reversing Kosinski's image, Daly claimed when it comes to women, it is not the artificial, painted birds (whom Daly looks upon as tamed, domesticated, feminized females), but the natural, plain-looking birds (whom Daly calls "wild females") who suffer. For Daly, painted birds are the women who permit "Daddy" to deck them out in splendor, to "cosmetize" and perfume them, to girdle and corset them. They are the women whom "Daddy" dispatches to destroy real, natural women: that is, the women who refuse to be what the patriarchs want them to be, who insist on being themselves no matter what, and who peel patriarchal paint off their minds and bodies.[42] In Daly's words, the "painted bird functions in the anti-process of double-crossing her sisters, polluting them with poisonous paint."[43] The real, natural woman, in contrast, is "attacked by the mutants of her own kind, the man-made women."[44]

For Daly, flying is the antidote to being painted. The real, natural woman does not take off patriarchal paint only to become vulnerable. Rather, she "takes off." She "sends the paint flying back into the eyes of the soul-slayers"; she "soars . . . out of the circle of Father Time" and flies "off the clock into other dimensions."[45] She flies free of "mutant fembirds," the women who have permitted themselves to be constructed by patriarchy. She also flies free of the power of patriarchal language and therefore patriarchal values.

Daly is a transvaluator of values. She claimed that with respect to women, she whom the patriarch calls evil is in fact good, whereas she whom the patriarch calls good is in fact bad. Providing a dictionary of new language in the last section of *Gyn/Ecology*, Daly invited "hags," "spinsters," and "haggard heretics" to "unspook" traditional language and their old feminine selves by "*spinning*" for themselves a new, unconventional language and new female selves. Daly insisted that *women* should decide who women want to be. For example, if women want to be hags instead of bathing beauties, then so be it. It is for women to decide whether being a hag is good or bad. Explained Daly:

> *Hag* is from an Old English word meaning "harpy, witch." Webster's gives as the first and "archaic" meaning of *hag*: "a female demon: FURY, HARPY." It also formerly meant: "an evil or frightening spirit." (Lest this sound too negative, we should ask the relevant questions: "Evil" by whose definition? "Frightening" to whom?) A third archaic definition of *hag* is "nightmare." (The important question is: Whose nightmare?) *Hag* is also defined as "an ugly or evil-looking old woman." But this, considering the source, may be considered a compliment. For the beauty of strong, creative women is "ugly" by misogynistic standards of "beauty." The look of female-identified women is "evil" to those who fear us. As for "old," ageism is a feature of phallic society. For women who have transvalued this, a Crone is one who should be an example of strength, courage, and wisdom.[46]

By the time she wrote the last page of *Gyn/Ecology*, Daly had completely replaced the ideal of the androgynous person with the ideal of the "wild female" who dwells beyond masculinity and femininity. To become whole, a woman needs to strip away the false identity—femininity—patriarchy has constructed for her. Then and only then will she experience herself as the self she would have been had she lived her life in a matriarchy rather than a patriarchy.

In *Pure Lust: Elemental Feminist Philosophy,* Daly continued her transvaluation of values. In this book about woman's power, Daly extended French's analysis of power-to. It is this power men have fed on, making women grow thin, weak, frail, even anorexic. To grow strong, women must resist the trap of androgyny. Utterly dependent on their God-given helpmates, patriarchs offer women androgyny in a last-ditch effort to keep women by their side: "Come, join forces with us. Masculinity and femininity together!" Women should not, said Daly, be deceived by these inviting words, which are simply a ploy on the part of men to appropriate for themselves whatever is best about women. Men have gradually realized it is in their own (but not women's) best interests to become androgynous persons, because their maleness has so little to offer them. For example, at the end of the film *Tootsie,* after the lead character's male identity has been disclosed (Dustin Hoffman had been posing as a female television star named Dorothy), he tells Julie, a woman he had befriended in his incarnation as Dorothy, that he actually *is* Dorothy. Daly commented, "The message clearly is one of cannibalistic androgynous maleness. Little Dustin, whom Julie had loved but rejected because she believed he was a woman, incorporates the best of womanhood—like Dionysus and Jesus before him."[47] Men want to be androgynous so that they can subsume or even consume all that is female, draining women's energies into their bodies and minds. Instead of submitting to the gynocidal process of androgyny, women must, said Daly, spin new, powerful self-understandings, remaining radically apart from men, reserving their energies for their own pursuits.

What is most impressive about *Pure Lust* is Daly's ability to provide new meanings, simultaneously prescriptive and descriptive, for terms. The term *lust* is a case in point. Daly wrote, "The usual meaning of *lust* within the lecherous state of patriarchy is well known. It means 'sexual desire, especially of a violent self-indulgent character: lechery, lasciviousness.'"[48] Lust, then, is evil, said Daly, but only because we live in a society with a slave morality, which resents women. If we lived instead in a nonpatriarchal society, continued Daly, *lust* would have good meanings such as "vigor," "fertility," "craving," "eagerness," and "enthusiasm."[49] Thus, the lusty women of *Pure Lust* are the wild females of *Gyn/Ecology,* the undomesticated women who refuse to be governed by the rules of men's "sadosociety," which is "formed/framed by statues of studs, degrees of drones, canons of cocks, fixations of fixers, precepts of prickers, regulations of rakes and rippers . . . bore-ocracy."[50]

The Daly of *Pure Lust* had no use for what she regarded as the petrified language of patriarchy, referring to it only with the aim of redefining, reinterpreting, or reclaiming its terms. *Pure Lust* transvaluated what counts as moral virtue and moral vice for women. In particular, the book showed how patriarchal forces deprived natural women of bona fide passions, substituting for these true passions a collection of "plastic" and "potted" ones: a set of inauthentic, counterfeit emotions created for artificial women.

According to Daly, plastic passions, such as guilt, anxiety, depression, hostility, bitterness, resentment, frustration, boredom, resignation, and fulfillment, are no substitute for genuine passions, such as love, desire, joy, hate, aversion, sorrow, hope, despair, fear, and anger. Whereas genuine passions spur women to meaningful action, plastic passions enervate women. In Daly's estimation, the plastic passion of fulfillment, for example, is not to be confused with the genuine passion of joy. Fulfillment is simply the "therapeutized perversion" of joy. A fulfilled woman is "filled full," "finished," "fixed" just the way patriarchy likes her. Because she is so "totaled," she cannot live the "e-motion of joy." She lacks the energy to move or act purposely.[51] *Fulfillment,* said Daly, is just another term for Betty Friedan's "problem that has no name"[52]—having a comfortable home, a successful husband, a wonderful child, but no joy.

Like plastic passions, potted passions are also a poor substitute for genuine passions, in Daly's estimation. Although potted passions are in many ways more real than plastic passions, they are not nearly as grand as genuine passions. To appreciate Daly's point, we may view a genuine passion as a live evergreen out in the woods, a potted passion as a decked-out but cut (and hence, dying) Christmas tree, and a plastic passion as an artificial Christmas tree. The genuine passion of love, for example, is a life-transforming emotion, but when it is either potted or packaged and then sold as "romance," women are duped into settling for love's illusion rather than its reality.[53] There is, of course, something tragic about settling for so little when there is so much to be had. Thus, Daly hoped the words in *Pure Lust* would help women liberate themselves from the pots and plastic molds blocking their volcanic genuine passions.

Sexuality, Male Domination, and Female Subordination

Radical-libertarian and radical-cultural feminists have very different ideas not only about gender but also about sexuality.[54] Among the feminists who have written insightfully on this difference is Ann Ferguson. Unfortunately for my purposes, Ferguson and I use different terms to express what I think are essentially the same ideas. To avoid an unnecessarily confusing discussion of Ferguson's work, I substitute my terms *radical-libertarian* and *radical-cultural* for her terms *libertarian* and *radical.*

According to Ferguson, radical-libertarian feminists' views on sexuality are as follows:

1. Heterosexual as well as other sexual practices are characterized by repression. The norms of patriarchal bourgeois sexuality repress the sexual desires and pleasures of everyone by stigmatizing sexual minorities, thereby keeping the majority "pure" and under control.
2. Feminists should repudiate any theoretical analyses, legal restrictions, or moral judgements that stigmatize sexual minorities and thus restrict the freedom of all.
3. As feminists we should reclaim control over female sexuality by demanding the right to practice whatever gives us pleasure and satisfaction.
4. The ideal sexual relationship is between fully consenting, equal partners who negotiate to maximize one another's sexual pleasure and satisfaction by any means they choose.[55]

In contrast, radical-cultural feminists' views on sexuality are as follows:

1. Heterosexual sexual relations generally are characterized by an ideology of sexual objectification (men as subjects/masters; women as objects/slaves) that supports male sexual violence against women.
2. Feminists should repudiate any sexual practice that supports or normalizes male sexual violence.
3. As feminists we should reclaim control over female sexuality by developing a concern with our own sexual priorities, which differ from men's—that is, more concern with intimacy and less with performance.
4. The ideal sexual relationship is between fully consenting, equal partners who are emotionally involved and do not participate in polarized roles.[56]

Radical-libertarian feminists challenged theories of sexuality that separated supposedly good, normal, legitimate, healthy sexual practices from supposedly bad, abnormal, illegitimate, unhealthy sexual practices.[57] These feminists urged women to experiment with different kinds of sex and not to confine themselves to a limited range of sexual experiences.[58]

Among the most forceful and articulate spokespersons for radical-libertarian-feminist ideology in the 1970s was Gayle Rubin. She claimed that contemporary society remains uncomfortable with any form of sex that is not between married, heterosexual couples intent on procreating children.[59] It represses—indeed punishes—to a greater or lesser extent unmarried heterosexuals who engage in casual sex for pleasure, bisexuals, homosexuals, lesbians, transsexuals, transvestites, fetishists, sadomasochists, sex workers, and "those whose eroticism crosses transgenerational boundaries."[60] As a result of this state of affairs, many people deny themselves the joys of sex, said Rubin. Wanting to let people have a good time, so to speak, Rubin urged feminists to lead a campaign to stop viewing sex in terms "of sins, disease, neurosis, pathology, decadence, pollution or the decline and fall of empires."[61] For Rubin, all sex was good; no judgments should be made about the rightness or wrongness of any form of sex, including lesbian sadomasochism. Indeed, Rubin, as a student of gay male leather subculture, in 1978 coformed Samois, the first-known lesbian SM group.[62]

Not surprisingly, radical-libertarian feminists' views on sexuality were not uniformly accepted by one and all. Rejecting Rubin's celebration of all forms of sexuality, radical-cultural feminists insisted that, in a patriarchal society, it was feminists' responsibility to make judgments about one form of sexuality in particular: namely, sex between men and women. Radical-cultural feminists equated heterosexuality as they experienced it with "male sexuality," that is, "driven, irresponsible, genitally-oriented and potentially lethal"[63] sexuality. They contrasted this "male sexuality" with "female sexuality," that is "muted, diffuse, interpersonally-oriented, and benign"[64] sexuality. In radical-cultural feminists' estimation, because men want "power and orgasm" in sex and women want "reciprocity and intimacy" in sex,[65] the only kind of sex that is *unambiguously good* for women is monogamous lesbianism.[66] Women must understand, they said, that patriarchal heterosexuality is an institution bent on sapping women's emotional energies and keeping women perpetually dissatisfied with themselves. It must be destroyed so that women can fully live.[67]

The Pornography Debate

Women's different reactions to pornography, or their use of it in their lives, dramatically highlight the general differences between radical-libertarian feminists and radical-cultural feminists on sexual matters. Radical-libertarian feminists urged women to use pornography to overcome their fears about sex, to arouse sexual desires, and to generate sexual fantasies.[68] These feminists claimed that women should feel free to view and enjoy all sorts of pornography, including violent pornography. Some radical-libertarian feminists even invited women to engage in rape fantasies in which men "had their way" with women in bed. There is a difference between an actual rape and a rape fantasy, insisted the most "libertarian" members of the radical-libertarian feminist camp. The same woman who derives sexual pleasure from *playing* Scarlett O'Hara–Rhett Butler sex games with her boyfriend would protest loudly were he *actually* to attempt to rape her. Just because a woman wants to explore whether power games are part of what makes sex "sexy" for her does not mean she wants to serve as an object for male violence in real life.[69] Rather than stubbornly insisting that pornographic representations of men sexually dominating women somehow harm women in real life, said radical-libertarian feminists, feminists should engage in an entirely open-minded and nondefensive examination of pornography, saving their venom for real rapists.

Ironically, radical-libertarian feminists' defense of pornography served to increase, not decrease, radical-cultural feminists' opposition to it. Radical-cultural feminists stressed that sexuality and gender *are* the products of the same oppressive social forces. There is no difference between gender discrimination against women in the boardroom and the sexual objectification of women in the bedroom. In both instances, the harm done to women is about men's power over women. Pornography is nothing more than patriarchal propaganda about women's "proper" role as man's servant, helpmate, caretaker, and plaything, according to radical-cultural feminists. Whereas men exist for themselves, women exist for men. Men are subjects; women are objects, they said.

Radical-cultural feminists insisted that with rare exception, pornography harms women. First, it encourages men to behave in sexually harmful ways toward women (e.g., sexual harassment, rape, domestic violence). Second, it defames women as persons who have so little regard for themselves that they actively seek or passively accept sexual abuse. And third, it leads men not only to think less of women as human beings but also to treat them as second-class citizens unworthy of the same due process and equal treatment men enjoy.

Unable to prove that exposure to pornographic representations directly causes men either to harm women's bodies or to defame women's characters, radical-cultural feminists sought protection for women in antidiscrimination laws. They followed the lead of Andrea Dworkin and Catharine MacKinnon, who defined pornography as "the graphic sexually explicit subordination of women through pictures or words that also includes women dehumanized as sexual objects, things, or commodities; enjoying pain or humiliation or rape; being tied up, cut up, mutilated, bruised, or physically hurt; in postures of sexual submission or servility or display; reduced to body parts, penetrated by objects or animals, or presented in scenarios of degradation, injury, torture; shown as filthy or inferior; bleeding, bruised, or hurt in a context that makes these conditions sexual."[70]

Radical-cultural feminists claimed that sexuality is the primary locus of male power in which women-harming gender relations are constructed.[71] They also claimed that because pornographers systematically depict women as less fully human and, therefore, less deserving of respect and good treatment than men, pornographers can and ought to be viewed as agents of sexual discrimination, guilty of violating women's civil rights. For this reason, any woman—or man, child, or transsexual used in the place of a woman—should be granted a legal cause of action against a particular pornographer or pornographic business if she is coerced into a pornographic performance, has pornography forced on her, or has been assaulted or attacked because of a particular piece of pornography. Further, any woman should be able to bring civil suit against traffickers in pornography, on behalf of all women.[72] Emptying the pockets of pornographers is the best way for feminists to fight the misogynistic ideology pornographers willingly spread.

Although radical-cultural feminists, under the leadership of MacKinnon and Dworkin, were initially successful in their attempt to have antipornography ordinances passed in Minneapolis and Indianapolis, a coalition of radical-libertarian and liberal feminists called the Feminist Anti-Censorship Taskforce (FACT) joined nonfeminist free-speech advocates to work against MacKinnon and Dworkin's 1980s legislation. Largely because of FACT's efforts, the US Supreme Court eventually declared the Minneapolis and Indianapolis antipornography ordinances unconstitutional.[73] During the period that FACT worked to defeat MacKinnon and Dworkin's legislation, its membership insisted such phrases as "sexually explicit subordination of women" have no context-free, fixed meaning.[74]

FACT referred to the film *Swept Away* to show just how difficult it is to decide whether a particular scene or set of scenes depicts the sexually explicit subordination of women. In the movie, an attractive, upper-class woman and a brawny, working-class man are shown, during the first half of the film, as *class* antagonists and then, during the second half of the film, as *sexual* antagonists, when they are stranded on an island and the man exacts his revenge on the woman by repeatedly raping her. Initially, she resists him, but gradually she falls in love with him, and eventually, he with her.

Because scenes in *Swept Away* clearly present the woman character as enjoying her own sexual humiliation, the film falls under a radical-cultural feminist definition of pornography and could have been suppressed, pending the outcome of a civil suit brought against its creators, manufacturers, and distributors. According to FACT, however, such suppression would have represented censorship of the worst sort because the film challenged viewers to think seriously about precisely what does and does not constitute the sexually explicit subordination of women. Critical and popular opinion of the film varied, ranging from admiration to repulsion. Whereas the reviewer for *Ms.* wrote that "'Swept Away' comes to grips with the 'war' between the sexes better than anything" she had ever read or seen, the reviewer for the *Progressive* stated he did not know what was "more distasteful about the film—its slavish adherence to the barroom credo that what all women really want is to be beaten, to be shown who's boss, or the readiness with which it has been accepted by the critics."[75] FACT emphasized if two film critics can see the images and hear the words of *Swept Away* so differently, then contextual factors, such as the critics' own sexual fantasies and erotic impulses, must ultimately explain their divergent interpretations. What looks like the sexually explicit subordination of a woman to a radical-cultural feminist may, as far as the woman herself is concerned, be the height of sexual pleasure.

Shocked by radical-libertarian feminists' seeming acceptance of women's sexual abuse, radical-cultural feminists accused radical-libertarian feminists of false consciousness, of buying the "bill of goods" men are only too eager to sell women. Bitter debates about sexuality broke out between radical-libertarian and radical-cultural feminists, reaching fever pitch at the 1982 Barnard College sexuality conference. A coalition of radical-libertarian feminists, including lesbian practitioners of sadomasochism and butch-femme relationships, bisexuals, workers in the sex industry (prostitutes, porn models, exotic dancers), and heterosexual women eager to defend the pleasures of sex between consenting men and women, accused radical-cultural feminists of prudery. To this charge, radical-cultural feminists responded they were not prudes. On the contrary, they were *truly* free women who could tell the difference between "erotica," where the term denotes sexually explicit depictions and descriptions of women being integrated, constituted, or focused during loving or at least life-affirming sexual encounters, and "thanatica," where the term denotes sexually explicit depictions and descriptions of women being disintegrated, dismembered, or disoriented during hate-filled or even death-driven sexual encounters.

Radical-libertarian feminists faulted radical-cultural feminists for presenting "vanilla" sex—gentle, touchy-feely, side-by-side (no one on the top or the bottom) sex—as the only kind of sex that is good for women. Why, asked radical-libertarian feminists, should we limit women, or men for that matter, to a particular "flavor" of sex? If women are given free rein, some may choose vanilla sex, but others may prefer "rocky-road" sex—encounters where pain punctuates pleasure, for example. No woman should be told that if she wants to be a *true* feminist, then she must limit herself to only certain sorts of sexual encounters. After all, if women's sexuality is as "absent" as Catharine MacKinnon herself has claimed,[76] then it is premature for anyone, including radical-cultural feminists, to fill the vacuum with only their own ideas. Better that all sorts of women offer diverse descriptions of what they find truly pleasurable. To this line of reasoning, radical-cultural feminists again retorted that radical-libertarian feminists were not *true* feminists but deluded pawns of patriarchy who had willfully closed their ears to pornography's women-hating message. Before too long, the Barnard conference collapsed, as the gulf between radical-libertarian and radical-cultural feminists widened.

Over thirty years have passed since the Barnard conference and the Feminist Sex War that shut it down midstream. Interestingly, the debate about feminist sex continues, with radical-libertarian feminist generally having the upper hand at this time. Consider a typical, late 2005 blog generated by Kae-Lyn called "Feminist Porn: Sex, Consent, and Getting Off." KaeLyn states:

> I have talked to many feminist women who struggle to balance what really happens behind closed doors and what they feel the bedroom politics of a "good feminist" should be. Enjoying BDSM, strap-on sex and sex toys, genderplay, rape and incest taboo, mainstream pornography, and other "deviant" sexual taboos with a consensual partner does not make a "bad feminist" or a hypocrite. To the contrary, feminism is what gave me permission to love sex, with myself and with others, to embrace my sexual orientations, and find out what turns me on . . . How is that not feminist?[77]

Of the ninety-nine people who participated in the blog, most of them agreed to a greater or lesser degree with KaeLyn.[78] For example, #48, Ashley, said radical-cultural feminists can be "judgmental," offering a "negative take on bdsm and kink." Not agreeing with what radical-cultural feminists say about sex within patriarchy, she concludes her posting to the blog with the following statement:

> Sometimes recognizing power dynamics and playing with them/challenging them is a lot more radical than pretending that sex is (or should be) all Enya, clouds and puppy dog tails.[79]

Noticeably, almost half of the bloggers also talked about sex workers in a sympathetic way, rather than condemning them as the dupes of patriarchy. Decriminalizing prostitution and providing more and different work opportunities for poor women who said they would rather work as sex workers than as clerks in a grocery store were mentioned over twenty times.[80] The overall tenor of the blog exchange was civil, respectful, and thoughtful, rather than warlike. Still, even if the feminist sex wars of the 1970s are over, young feminists continue to raise questions about how consensual their sexual activities and preferences are.

The Lesbianism Controversy

Another topic that divided radical-libertarian feminists from radical-cultural feminists was lesbianism, particularly "separatist" lesbianism. Lesbianism fully surfaced as an issue within the women's movement during the 1970s. Ironically, at the Second Congress to Unite Women, a group of women wearing T-shirts emblazoned LAVENDER MENACE staged a protest. The organizers of the conference had anticipated trouble due to the publication of Anne Koedt's provocative essay "The Myth of the Vaginal Orgasm." In this essay, Koedt claimed many women believe the orgasms they feel during heterosexual intercourse are vaginally caused, when in fact they are clitorally stimulated. Koedt also claimed that many men fear "becom[ing] sexually expendable if the clitoris is substituted for the vagina as the center of pleasure for women."[81] Viewing men's fear of "sexual expendability" as alarmist, Koedt noted that even if all women recognized they did not *need* men as sexual partners for *physiological* reasons, many women would still select men as sexual partners for *psychological* reasons.[82]

Radical-libertarian feminists interpreted Koedt as justifying women's engagement in noncompulsory (freely chosen) heterosexuality. Since a woman does not *need* a male body to achieve sexual pleasure, she does not have to engage in sexual relations with a man unless *she* wants to. In contrast to radical-libertarian feminists, radical-cultural feminists interpreted Koedt as implying that as there is no physiological reason for a woman to have sex with a man, there is no *feminist* psychological reason for a woman to *want* to have sex with a man. Indeed, there are only *nonfeminist* psychological reasons for a woman to want to have sex with a man.[83] Therefore, if a woman wants to be a *true* feminist, she must become a lesbian. She must do what comes "naturally," thereby freeing her own consciousness from the false idea that she is deviant, abnormal, sick, crazy, or bad because she enjoys sex with women, not with men.

For a time, the radical-cultural feminists' interpretation of Koedt's essay predominated in feminist circles, so much so that many heterosexual feminists felt deviant, abnormal, sick, crazy, or bad if they wanted to have sex with men. Deirdre English, a radical-libertarian feminist, reported she found it "fascinating and almost funny"[84] that so many heterosexual feminists "seemed to accept the idea that heterosexuality meant cooperating in their own oppression and that there was something wrong with being sexually turned on to men. How many times have I heard this? 'Well, unfortunately, I'm not a lesbian but I wish I was, maybe I will be.'"[85] The so-called political lesbian was born: a woman who does not find herself erotically attracted to women but who tries as hard as possible to be women-oriented. Commented Charlotte Bunch:

As long as straight women see lesbianism as a bedroom issue, they hold back the development of politics and strategies that would put an end to male supremacy and they give men an excuse for not dealing with their sexism . . . Lesbianism is the key to liberation and only women who cut their ties to male privilege can be trusted to remain serious in the struggle against male dominance. Those who remain tied to men, individually or in political theory, cannot always put women first.[86]

Bunch's quote, said Bat-Ami Bar On, presents lesbianism, first and foremost, as a political stance: as the leader in the battle against male patriarchy.[87]

Radical-libertarian feminists agreed with radical-cultural feminists that heterosexuality is a flawed institution that has harmed many women. Still, radical libertarians insisted it would be just as wrong for radical-cultural feminists to impose lesbianism on women as it had been for patriarchy to impose heterosexuality on women.[88] Men's having sex with women is not, in and of itself, bad for women, in radical-libertarian feminists' estimation. Rather, what is bad for women is men's having sex with women in a particular way: "fucking for a minute and a half and pulling out."[89] Women can and do find pleasure in sex with men, when men make women's sexual satisfaction just as important as their own sexual satisfaction, said radical-libertarian feminists.

Radical-libertarian feminists also stressed that individual men, as bad as they could be, were not women's primary oppressors. On the contrary, women's main enemy was the patriarchal system, the product of centuries of male privilege, priority, and prerogative. Thus, unlike those radical-cultural feminists who urged women to stop relating to men on all levels beginning with the *sexual,* radical-libertarian feminists did not press for a separatist agenda. On the contrary, radical-libertarian feminists urged women to confront individual men about their chauvinistic attitudes and behaviors in an effort to get men freely to renounce the unfair privileges patriarchy had bestowed upon them.[90] These feminists recalled that even Women's International Terrorist Conspiracy from Hell (WITCH), one of the most militant feminist groups in the 1960s, had not urged women to renounce men or heterosexuality entirely, but to relate to men only on gynocentric terms:

WITCH lives and laughs in every woman. She is the free part of each of us, beneath the shy smiles, the acquiescence to absurd male domination, the make-up or flesh-suffocating clothing our sick society demands. There is no "joining" WITCH. If you are a woman and dare to look within yourself, you are a Witch. You make your own rules. You are free and beautiful. You can be invisible or evident in how you choose to make your Witch-self known. You can form your own Coven of sister Witches (thirteen is a cozy number for a group) and do your own actions.

You are pledged to free our brothers from oppression and stereotyped sexual roles (whether they like it or not) as well as ourselves. You are a Witch by saying aloud, "I am a Witch" three times, and *thinking about that.* You are a Witch by being female, untamed, angry, joyous, and immortal.[91]

Thus, twenty-first-century women, like women in the 1960s, do not have to live together on the fringes of society or to have sex only with one another to be liberated, according to today's radical-libertarian feminists. Freedom comes to women as the result of women's giving one another the power of self-definition and the energy to rebel continually against any individual man, group of men, or patriarchal institution seeking to disempower or otherwise weaken women. Still, twenty-first-century women should not, according to today's radical-cultural feminists, simply assume that women have the power to overcome the forces of patriarchy easily. They point to Adrienne Rich's 1980s article "Compulsory Heterosexuality and Lesbian Existence," in which Rich argued that male power has suppressed female sexuality in eight ways: (1) by denying women their own sexuality; (2) by forcing male sexuality upon women; (3) by controlling women's reproductive capacities; (4) by controlling or "robbing" women of their children; (5) by confining women physically and/or limiting their movement; (6) by using women as virtual commodities in certain "male transactions;" (7) by "cramp[ing] [women's] creativeness;" and by (8) limiting or withholding women's access to large areas of social knowledge and culture.[92] Although women's sexuality has in many ways been liberated from patriarchy's control, in many ways it has not. One does not have to look far to run across the practice of clitoridectomy; rejection of lesbians; rape; women-beating; incest; nonconsensual participation in the so-called sex-industry; problems in women's gaining access to contraception, abortion, and even proper sex education; purdah, nonconsensual veilings, arranged marriages for monetary and/or status reasons; restrictions on midwives; downgrading of women-directed art and music; illiteracy; paucity of women in science, technology, engineering, math, and other [lucrative] male professions; and so forth. Men are not necessarily conspiring with one another to keep women down, but the power of the institution of compulsory heterosexuality, and certainly of unreflective heterosexuality, persists.

Reproduction, Men, and Women

Not only do radical-libertarian and radical-cultural feminists have different views about sex, but they also have different ideas about reproduction.

Whereas radical-libertarian feminists believe women should substitute artificial for natural modes of reproduction, radical-cultural feminists believe it is in women's best interests to procreate naturally. As we shall see, radical-libertarian feminists are convinced the less women are involved in reproduction, the more time and energy women will have to engage in society's productive processes. In contrast, radical-cultural feminists are convinced the ultimate source of women's power rests in their power to gestate new life. To take this power from a woman is to take away her trump card and to leave her with an empty hand, entirely vulnerable to men's power.

Natural Reproduction:
The Site of Women's Oppression

Firestone's *The Dialectic of Sex*.   In *The Dialectic of Sex,* Shulamith Firestone claimed that patriarchy, the systematic subordination of women, is rooted in the biological inequality of the sexes. Her reflections on women's reproductive role led her to a feminist revision of the materialist theory of history offered by Karl Marx and Friedrich Engels. So focused were Marx and Engels on economic class struggle as the driving force of history that they paid scant attention to what Firestone termed "sex class." Firestone proposed to make up for this oversight by developing a feminist version of historical materialism in which sex class, rather than economic class, is the central concept.

To appreciate Firestone's co-optation of Marxist method, we have only to contrast her definition of *historical materialism* with Engels's definition of *historical materialism,* which is "that view of the course of history which seeks the ultimate cause and great moving power of all historical events in the economic development of society, in the changes of the modes of production and exchange, in the consequent division of society into distinct classes, and in the struggles of these classes against one another."[93] Firestone reformulated his definition as follows:

> Historical materialism is that view of the course of history which seeks the ultimate cause and the great moving power of all historical events in the dialectic of sex: the division of society into two distinct biological classes for procreative reproduction, and the struggles of these classes with one another; in the changes in the modes of marriage, reproduction and child care created by these struggles; in the connected development of other physically-differentiated classes (castes); and in the first division of labor based on sex which developed into the (economic-cultural) class system.[94]

In other words, for Firestone, relations of reproduction, rather than those of production, are the driving forces in history. The original class distinction is rooted in men's and women's differing reproductive roles; economic and racial class differences are derivatives of sex class differences.

In much the same way that Marx concluded workers' liberation requires an economic revolution, Firestone concluded women's liberation requires a biological revolution.[95] Like the proletariat who must seize the means of *production* to eliminate the economic class system, women must seize control of the means of *reproduction* to eliminate the sexual class system. Just as the ultimate goal of the communist revolution is, in a classless society, to obliterate class distinctions, the ultimate goal of the feminist revolution is, in an androgynous society, to obliterate sexual distinctions. As soon as technology overcomes the biological limits of natural reproduction, said Firestone, the biological fact that some persons have wombs and others have penises will "no longer matter culturally."[96] Sexual intercourse will no longer be necessary for human reproduction. Eggs and sperm will be combined in vitro, and embryos will be gestated outside of women's bodies.

No matter how much educational, legal, and political equality women achieve and no matter how many women enter public industry, Firestone insisted that nothing fundamental will change for women as long as natural reproduction remains the rule; and artificial or assisted reproduction, the exception. Natural reproduction is neither in women's best interests nor in those of the children so reproduced. The joy of giving birth—invoked so frequently in this society—is a patriarchal myth. In fact, pregnancy is "barbaric," and natural childbirth is "at best necessary and tolerable"; and at worst, "like shitting a pumpkin."[97] Moreover, said Firestone, natural reproduction is the root of further evils, especially the vice of possessiveness that generates feelings of hostility and jealousy among human beings. Engels's *Origin of the Family, Private Property, and the State* was incomplete not so much because he failed adequately to explain why men became the producers of surplus value, said Firestone, but because he failed adequately to explain *why* men wish so intensely to pass *their* property on to *their* biological children. The vice of possessiveness—the favoring of one child over another on account of the child's being the product of one's own ovum or sperm—is precisely what must be overcome if humans are to put an end to divisive hierarchies.

Piercy's *Woman on the Edge of Time*.   Firestone's last point was developed by Marge Piercy in her science fiction novel *Woman on the Edge of Time*.[98] Piercy set the story of her utopia within the tale of Connie Ramos's tragic life. Connie is a late-twentieth-century, middle-aged, lower-class Chicana with a history of what society regards as "mental illness" and "violent behavior."

Connie has been trying desperately to support herself and her daughter, Angelina, on a pittance. One day, when she is near the point of exhaustion, Connie loses her temper and hits Angelina too hard. As a result of this one outburst, the courts judge Connie an unfit mother and take her beloved daughter away from her. Depressed and despondent, angry and agitated, Connie is committed by her family to a mental hospital, where she is selected as a human research subject for brain-control experiments. Just when things can get no worse, Connie is psychically transported by a woman named Luciente to a future world called Mattapoisett—a world in which women are not defined in terms of reproductive functions and in which both men and women delight in rearing children. In Mattapoisett, there are neither men nor women; rather, everyone is a "per" (short for *person*).

What makes Piercy's futuristic world imaginable is artificial reproduction. In Mattapoisett, babies are born from the "brooder." Female ova, fertilized in vitro with male sperm selected for a full range of racial, ethnic, and personality types, are gestated in an artificial placenta. Unable to comprehend why Mattapoisett women have rejected the experience that meant the most to her—physically gestating, birthing, and nursing an offspring—Connie is initially repelled by the brooder. She sees the embryos "all in a sluggish row . . . like fish in the aquarium."[99] Not only does she regard these embryos as less than human, she pities them because no woman loves them enough to carry them in her own womb and, bleeding and sweating, bring them into the world.

Eventually, Connie learns from Luciente that the women of Mattapoisett did not easily give up natural reproduction for artificial reproduction. They did so only when they realized natural reproduction was the ultimate cause of all isms, including sexism: "It was part of women's long revolution. When we were breaking all the old hierarchies. Finally there was the one thing we had to give up too, the only power we ever had, in return for no power for anyone. The original production: the power to give birth. Cause as long as we were biologically enchained, we'd never be equal. And males never would be humanized to be loving and tender. So we all became mothers. Every child has three. To break the nuclear bonding."[100] Thus, as a result of women's giving up their monopoly on the power to give birth, the original paradigm for power relations was destroyed, and all residents of Mattapoisett found themselves in a position to reconstitute human relationships in ways that defied the hierarchical ideas of better-worse, higher-lower, stronger-weaker, and especially dominant-submissive.

Piercy's utopia is more radical than a Marxist utopia because the family is eliminated as a biological as well as an economic unit. Individuals possess neither private property nor their own children. No one has his or her own genetic child. Children are not viewed as the possessions of their biological mothers and fathers, to be brought into this world in their parents' image and likeness and reared according to their idiosyncratic values. Rather, children are viewed as precious human resources for the entire community, to be treasured on account of their uniqueness. Each child is reared by three co-mothers (one man and two women or two men and one woman), who are assisted by "kidbinders," a group of individuals who excel at mothering Mattapoisett's children. Child-rearing is a communal effort, with each child having access to large-group experiences at childcare centers and small-group experiences in the separate dwellings of each of his or her co-mothers.[101]

Connie initially doubts that Mattapoisett's system for begetting, bearing, and rearing children is all it is touted to be. She wonders whether co-mothers and kidbinders really love the children they rear. But gradually, she decides a biological relationship is not essential to good parenting. Indeed, she eventually agrees that artificial reproduction is superior to natural reproduction because it results in a truly nurturing and unselfish mode of mothering, totally separated from ambivalent feelings of resentment and guilt and always freely chosen.

Natural Reproduction:
The Site of Women's Liberation

Marge Piercy critiqued.   As nicely as Piercy reformulated some of Firestone's more controversial ideas, radical-cultural feminists nonetheless challenged her views as well as Firestone's. Claiming that most women continue to view their life-giving abilities as empowering and enjoyable, radical-cultural feminists dismissed Mattapoisett as a social ideal that is both implausible and unintelligible to today's women. Women should not give up biological motherhood for ex utero gestation, not now, not ever.

Radical-cultural feminists insisted Mattapoisett is an implausible social ideal for today's women because women's oppression is not likely to end if women give up the only source of men's dependence on them: "Technological reproduction," said Azizah al-Hibri, "does not equalize the natural reproductive power structure—it *inverts* it. It appropriates the reproductive power from women and places it in the hands of men who now control both the sperm and the reproductive technology that could make it indispensable. . . . It 'liberates' them from their 'humiliating dependency' on women in order to propagate."[102] That is, far from liberating women, reproductive technology further consolidates men's power over women; it gives them the ability to have children without women's aid.

In addition to being an implausible social ideal for today's women, Mattapoisett is, in the estimation of radical-cultural feminists, also an unintelligible social ideal to today's women. Even though some women use other women's eggs and wombs to procreate and some women adopt other women's children, society continues to define a mother as someone who is genetically, gestationally, and socially related to the children she rears with or without a spouse or partner. Indeed, most women who go to infertility clinics do so because they want Connie's experience of carrying a child for nine months "heavy under their hearts," bearing a baby "in blood," and nursing a child.[103] Thus, there is no way for women to decide in the abstract whether they should deprive themselves of a very meaningful present experience for a future experience they might or might not find equally meaningful.

Firestone et al. critiqued.   Having dismissed Piercy's "utopia" as an implausible and unintelligible world for today's women, radical-cultural feminists proceeded to criticize Firestone's master plan to achieve women's liberation as a blueprint for women's further enslavement. They claimed women's oppression was caused not by female biology in and of itself, but by men's jealousy of women's reproductive abilities and subsequent desire to seize control of female biology through scientific and technological means.[104]

Viewing natural reproduction through the lens of male alienation from the gestational process and female immersion in it, radical-cultural feminist Mary O'Brien noted that until the introduction of artificial reproduction, the "reproductive consciousness" of a man differed from that of a woman in at least three ways. First, the woman experienced the process of procreation as one continuous movement taking place *within* her body, whereas the man experienced this same process as a discontinuous movement taking place *outside* his body. After the act of sexual intercourse, through which he impregnated the woman, the man had no other procreative function. Second, the woman, not the man, necessarily performed the fundamental *labor* of reproduction—pregnancy and birthing. At most, the man could attend childbirth classes with the woman and try to imagine what being pregnant and giving birth feel like. Third, the woman's connection to her child was certain—she knew, at the moment of birth, the child was flesh of her flesh. In contrast, the man's connection to the child was uncertain; he could never be absolutely sure, even at the moment of birth, whether the child was in fact genetically related to him. For all he knew, the child was the genetic progeny of some other man.[105]

In radical-cultural feminists' estimation, men's alienation from natural reproduction helps explain why men have played a smaller role in the life of the "product" of natural reproduction than women have. It also helps explain why men have sought to limit women's reproductive powers. In *Of Woman Born,* Adrienne Rich noted men realize patriarchy cannot survive unless men are able to control women's power to *bring* or *not bring* life into the world. Rich described how men took the birthing process into their own hands. Male obstetricians replaced female midwives, substituting their "hands of iron" (obstetrical forceps) for midwives' hands of flesh (female hands sensitive to the female anatomy).[106] In addition, Rich cataloged the ways in which male physicians wrote the rules not only for giving birth but also for being pregnant. Male experts told women how to act during pregnancy—when to eat, sleep, exercise, have sex, and the like. In some instances, males even dictated to women how to feel during childbirth. The overall effect of men's intrusion into the birthing process was to confuse women, because men's "rules" for women's pregnancies often clashed with women's "intuitions" about what was best for their bodies, psyches, and babies. For example, when a woman and physician disagreed about whether she needed a cesarean section to deliver her baby, a woman did not know whether to trust the *authority* of her physician or the *experience,* the sensations, of her own body.

To the degree they were deprived of control over their pregnancies, said Rich, women experienced pregnancy as a mere event, as something that simply happened to them. Indeed, confessed Rich, she herself felt out of control and alienated during her pregnancy:

> When I try to return to the body of the young woman of twenty-six, pregnant for the first time, who fled from the physical knowledge of her pregnancy and at the same time from her intellect and vocation, I realize that I was effectively alienated from my real body and my real spirit by the institution—not the fact—of motherhood. This institution—the foundation of human society as we know it—allowed me only certain views, certain expectations, whether embodied in the booklet in my obstetrician's waiting room, the novels I had read, my mother-in-law's approval, my memories of my own mother, the *Sistine Madonna* or she of the Michelangelo *Pietà,* the floating notion that a woman pregnant is a woman calm in her fulfillment or, simply, a woman waiting.[107]

Rich concluded that if they reclaimed their pregnancies from the authorities, women would no longer have to sit passively waiting for their physicians to deliver their babies to them. Instead, women would actually direct the childbirth process, experiencing its pleasures as well as its pains. In Rich's estimation, childbirth does not have to feel like "shitting a pumpkin."[108] On the contrary, it can feel a great deal more exhilarating and certainly far less dehumanizing.

Rich's concerns about the ways in which patriarchal authorities have used medical science to control women's reproductive powers reached new heights in the works of Andrea Dworkin, Margaret Atwood, Gena Corea, and Robyn Rowland. Dworkin claimed infertility experts have joined gynecologists and obstetricians to seize control of women's reproductive powers once and for all. She said artificial reproduction is patriarchy's attempt to guarantee that women's procreative experience is just as alienating as men's.[109] With the introduction of in vitro fertilization and the use of surrogate mothers, a woman's experience of bringing a child into the world becomes discontinuous, especially if her only contribution to this process is the donation of her egg. Moreover, the woman who relies on artificial reproduction to procreate can no longer be certain that the child born to her is indeed *her* genetic child. For all she knows, the embryo transplanted into her womb is not her embryo but the embryo of someone else. Finally, should scientists develop an artificial placenta, women's "labor" would no longer be needed to complete the procreative process. Speculating that patriarchal society might view a reproductively useless woman as somebody good only for sex work or domestic work, Dworkin urged women to resist the further development of reproductive technology.

Concerns such as Dworkin's are one of the inspirations for Margaret Atwood's *The Handmaid's Tale*,[110] a work of feminist science fiction in stark contrast to Marge Piercy's *Woman on the Edge of Time*. In the Republic of Gilead, Atwood's dystopia, women are reduced to one of four functions. There are the Marthas, or domestics; the Wives, or social secretaries and functionaries; the Jezebels, or sex prostitutes; and the Handmaids, or reproductive prostitutes. One of the most degrading Gileadean practices, from a woman's perspective, is a ritualistic form of sexual intercourse in which the so-called Commander pretends to have sex with his Wife. The Wife, who is infertile, lies down on a bed with her legs spread open. The Wife's Handmaid, one of the few fertile women in Gilead, puts her head between the spread legs of the Wife. Then the Commander engages in sexual intercourse with the Handmaid. If the Handmaid gets pregnant, the Commander and his Wife lay claim to the child she is gestating. Adding to the oddity of this arrangement is the fact that on the day the Handmaid gives birth to the child, the Wife simulates labor pains, as other Wives and Handmaids in Gilead gather round the Wife and her Handmaid in a rare moment of "female bonding."

After one such birth day, the central character, Offred—whose name literally means "to be of Fred"—recalls better times and speaks in her mind to her mother, who had been a feminist leader: "Can you hear me? You wanted a woman's culture. Well, now there is one. It isn't what you meant, but it exists. Be thankful for small mercies."[111] Of course, they are *very* small mercies, for with the exception of birth days—those rare occasions when a Handmaid manages to produce a child—women have little contact with one another.

The Marthas, Wives, Jezebels, and Handmaids are segregated from one another, and the contact women do have—even within an assigned class—is largely silent, for women are permitted to speak to one another only when absolutely necessary.

Like Dworkin and Atwood, Gena Corea was suspicious of what the new reproductive technologies and their concomitant social arrangements promise women. Corea claimed if men control the new reproductive technologies, men will use them not to empower women but to further empower themselves. To reinforce her point, she drew provocative analogies between Count Dracula and Robert Edwards, one of the codevelopers of in vitro fertilization. Corea suggested that just as Dracula never had enough blood to drink, Edwards never had enough eggs to use in experiments. Indeed, Edwards routinely attended the hysterectomies his colleagues performed, for the sole purpose of collecting the eggs they discarded after the surgeries.[112] Fearing that male infertility experts such as Edwards do not have women's best interests at heart, Corea ended her essay "Egg Snatchers" with the question, "Why are [men] splitting the functions of motherhood into smaller parts? Does that reduce the power of the mother and her claim to the child? ('I only gave the egg. I am not the real mother.' 'I only loaned my uterus. I am not the real mother.' 'I only raised the child. I am not the real mother.')"[113]

Agreeing with Dworkin, Atwood, and Corea that the new reproductive technologies will simply increase men's control over women, Robyn Rowland, another radical-cultural feminist, pointed to the work of microbiologist John Postgate as an example of the form this new power over women might take. In an interview with Rowland, Postgate, who wanted to control the size of the human population, proposed the development of a "manchild pill," which would ensure the conception of boys. Girls would become scarce and the birthrate would inevitably plunge. Postgate conceded that under such circumstances, men would probably start to fight one another for the sexual and reproductive services of society's few remaining women. Women would need to be sequestered for their own good while society developed rules for a system of male access to them.[114]

As if a vision of a future world in which the term *trophy wife* denotes an even uglier reality than it does now is not bad enough, Rowland imagined an even worse scenario: a world in which only a few superovulating women are permitted to exist, a world in which eggs are taken from women, frozen, and inseminated in vitro for transfer into artificial placentas. The replacement of women's childbearing capacity by male-controlled technology would, she said, leave women entirely vulnerable, "without a product" with which "to bargain" with men: "For the history of 'mankind' women have been seen in terms of their value as childbearers. We have to ask, if that last power is taken and controlled by men, what role is envisaged for women in the new world?"[115]

Unlike radical-libertarian feminists, radical-cultural feminists urged women not to forsake their power to bring new life into the world. Only oppressive forms of power need to be forsaken, and according to radical-cultural feminists, women's reproductive powers are anything but oppressive. On the contrary, women's life-giving capacities are the paradigm for the ability of people to connect with one another in a caring, supportive relationship.

Interestingly, contemporary radical-libertarian feminists and many contemporary schools of feminist thought continue to debate the wisdom of women using reproductive technology. On the positive side, many feminists argue that an increasing number of women are heading as well as using fertility clinics. To them, assisted reproduction does not seem like a bid for men to get power over women. Rather, it seems like an opportunity for women to seize control of whatever reproductive capacities they may have and to use the help of others to produce a child they may really want.[116] Pro–assisted reproduction champions point, for example, to lesbian couples who use in vitro fertilization (IVF) so that the egg of one member of the lesbian couple can get fertilized by donor sperm and the other member of the lesbian couple can gestate the resulting embryo. Due to this complicated technological process, both members of the lesbian couple can lay claim to having a biological connection to their child.[117]

In response to contemporary radical-libertarian feminists, radical-cultural feminists point out that many women feel compelled to use IVF, for example, so that they can have a baby no matter the risk to their health.[118] They also point out that young women are coaxed into freezing their eggs while in their twenties so that they can get pregnant in their early forties.[119] As egg freezing and postmenopausal pregnancy get normalized, say these radical-cultural feminists, women's bodies will increasingly have to do technology's bidding. There will be nothing "natural" left about the reproductive process.

Radical-Libertarian and Radical-Cultural Views on Mothering

Although commentators do not always make adequate distinctions between biological and social motherhood, these two dimensions of mothering need to be distinguished. If we accept Alison Jaggar's extension of the term *mothering* to "any relationship in which one individual nurtures and cares for another,"[120] then a person does not need to be a biological mother to be a social mother. Nevertheless, patriarchal society teaches its members that the woman who bears a child is best suited to rear him or her. In viewing this tenet as one that often places unreasonable demands on women's bodies and energies, radical-libertarian feminists have tended to make strong arguments against biological motherhood. Not surprisingly, many radical-cultural feminists have challenged these arguments, insisting no woman should, in an act of unreflective defiance against patriarchy, deprive herself of the satisfaction that comes from not only bearing a child but also playing a major role in his or her personal development. As we shall see, the arguments on both sides of this debate are powerful.

The Case Against Biological Motherhood

There are at least two versions of the radical-libertarian feminist case against biological motherhood: a weaker, more general version offered by Ann Oakley, and a stronger, more specific version offered by Shulamith Firestone. As Oakley saw it, biological motherhood is a myth based on the threefold belief that "all women need to be mothers, all mothers need their children, all children need their mothers."[121]

The first assertion, that all women need to be mothers, gains its credibility, according to Oakley, from the ways in which girls are socialized and from popular psychoanalytic theory that provides "pseudo-scientific backing" for this process of socialization. If parents did not give their daughters dolls; if the schools, the churches, and the media did not stress the wonders of biological motherhood; if psychiatrists, psychologists, and physicians did not do everything in their power to transform "abnormal" girls (i.e., "masculine" girls, who do not want to be mothers) into "normal" girls (i.e., "feminine" girls, who do want to be mothers), then girls would not grow into women who *need* to mother to have a sense of self-worth. For Oakley, women's supposed need to mother "owes nothing" to women's "possession of ovaries and wombs" and everything to the way in which women are socially and culturally conditioned to be mothers.[122]

The second assertion, that mothers need their children, is based on the belief that unless a woman's "maternal instinct" is satisfied, she will become increasingly frustrated. In Oakley's view, there is no such thing as maternal instinct. Women do not naturally experience a desire to have a biological child, and there are no hormonally based drives that "irresistibly draw the mother to her child in the tropistic fashion of the moth drawn to the flame"[123] during and after pregnancy. To support her contention that the "instinct" for mothering is learned, Oakley pointed to a study in which 150 first-time mothers were observed. Few of these women knew how to breast-feed, and those who did had seen either their own mother or some other female relative nurse a baby. Additionally, Oakley noted that most women who abuse or neglect their children were themselves abused or neglected as children. Never having seen another woman mother properly, these women never learned the behavior repertoire society associates with adequate mothering. Mothers, in short, are not born; they are made.[124]

The third assertion, that children need their mothers, is, according to Oakley, the most oppressive feature of the myth of biological motherhood. Oakley noted that this assertion contains three assumptions unnecessarily tying women to children: first, that children's mothering needs are best met by their biological mother; second, that children, especially young children, need the care of their biological mother much more than the care of anyone else, including their biological father; and third, that children need *one* nurturant caretaker (preferably the biological mother), not many.[125]

As Oakley saw it, each of these three assumptions (in support of the assertion children need their mother) is false. First, social mothers are just as effective as biological mothers. Studies have shown, claimed Oakley, that adopted children are at least as well adjusted as nonadopted children.[126] Second, children do not need their biological mother more than children need their biological father. Men, no less than women, can play the major role in their children's upbringing. What children need are adults with whom to establish intimate relationships—trustworthy and dependable persons who provide children with consistent care and discipline. Finally, one-on-one child-rearing is not necessarily better than collective socialization or "multiple mothering." Children reared in Israeli kibbutzim, for example, are just as happy, intelligent, emotionally mature, and socially adept as children reared exclusively by their biological mothers in US suburbs.[127]

In Oakley's estimation, being a biological mother is not a natural need of women, any more than being reared by their biological mother is a natural need of children. Therefore, she concluded, biological motherhood is a social construction, a myth with an oppressive purpose. Not wanting to be accused of selfishness and even abnormality, women who would be happier not having children at all become mothers reluctantly; and women who would be happier sharing their child-rearing responsibilities with one or more nurturant adults make of mothering an exclusive and twenty-four-hour-a-day job. No wonder, said Oakley, so many mothers are unhappy—an unhappiness made all the worse because society looks with disfavor on any mother who expresses dissatisfaction with her all-consuming maternal role.

Although Shulamith Firestone's negative assessment of biological motherhood did not substantively differ from Oakley's, it was harsher in tone. In *The Dialectic of Sex,* Firestone suggested the desire to bear and rear children is less the result of an "authentic liking" for children and more a "displacement" of ego-extension needs. For a man, a child is a way to immortalize his name, property, class, and ethnic identification; for a woman, a child is a way to justify her homebound existence as absolutely meaningful. At times, a father's need for immortality or a mother's need for meaning becomes pathological. When this happens, said Firestone, the less-than-perfect child inevitably suffers.[128]

Firestone believed that if adults, especially women, did not feel they had a duty to have children, they might discover in themselves an *authentic* desire to live in close association with children. People do not need to be biological parents to lead child-centered lives, said Firestone. Ten or more adults could agree, for example, to live with three or four children for as long as the children needed a stable family structure. During their years together, the people in this household would relate not as parents and children but as older and younger friends. Firestone did not think adults have a natural desire to be any closer to children than this kind of household arrangement permits. Instead, she believed adults have been socialized to view biological reproduction as life's raison d'être because without this grandiose sense of mission and destiny, the pains of childbearing and the burdens of child-rearing would have proved overwhelming. Now that technology promises to liberate the human species from the burdens of reproductive responsibility, Firestone predicted women will no longer want to bear children in pain and travail or rear children endlessly and self-sacrificially. Rather, women and men will want to spend some, though by no means most, of their time and energy with and on children.[129]

The Case for Biological Motherhood

Although radical-cultural feminist Adrienne Rich agreed with some of Firestone's analysis, she criticized Firestone for condemning biological motherhood "without taking full account of what the experience of biological pregnancy and birth might be in a wholly different political and emotional context."[130] Throughout *Of Woman Born,* Rich sharply distinguished between biological motherhood understood as "the *potential relationship* of any woman to her powers of reproduction and to children" and biological motherhood understood as "the *institution,* which aims at ensuring that that potential—and all women—shall remain under male control."[131] As Rich saw it, there is a world of difference between *women's* deciding who, how, when, and where to mother and *men's* making these decisions for women.

Rich agreed with Firestone that biological motherhood, as it has been institutionalized under patriarchy, is definitely something from which women should be liberated. If success is measured in terms of patriarchy's ability to determine not only women's gender behavior but also their gender identity through "force, direct pressure . . . ritual, tradition, law and language, customs, etiquette, education, and the division of labor," then *institutionalized* biological motherhood is one of patriarchy's overwhelming successes.[132] Men have convinced women that unless a woman is a mother, she is not really a woman, said Rich. Indeed, until relatively recently, the forces of patriarchy convinced most women that mothering is their one and only job. This view of women's role is very restricting. It blocks women's access to the public realm of culture, and it fails to acknowledge women's right to have and to fulfill their own wants and needs. Good mothers are not supposed to have any personal friends or plans unrelated to those of their families. They are supposed to be on the job twenty-four hours a day and love every minute of it. Ironically, observed Rich, it is just this expectation that causes many women to act in anything but "motherly" ways. The constant needs of a child can tax a mother's patience and, with no relief from the child's father or any other adult, make her feel angry, frustrated, and bitter:

> I remember being uprooted from already meager sleep to answer a childish nightmare, pull up a blanket, warm a consoling bottle, lead a half-asleep child to the toilet. I remember going back to bed starkly awake, brittle with anger, knowing that my broken sleep would make the next day hell, that there would be more nightmares; more need for consolation, because out of my weariness I would rage at those children for no reason.[133]

Rich's point was not that mothers do not love their children but that no person can be expected to remain always cheerful and kind unless the person's own physical and psychological needs are satisfactorily met.

Rich also argued eloquently that the *institution* of biological motherhood prevents women from rearing their children as women think they should be reared. She recounted squabbles with her own husband about the best way to raise their two sons. She also recalled mothering his way even though she knew full well that father did not always know best. Under patriarchy, she wrote, most men have demanded sons for the wrong reasons: "as heirs, field-hands, cannon-fodder, feeders of machinery, images and extensions of themselves; their immortality."[134] What is worse, most husbands have demanded their wives help them raise their sons to be "real men"—that is, "macho" or hyperaggressive and supercompetitive men. Rich happily recalled a seashore vacation she spent with her two boys, but without her husband. While vacationing alone, she and her children lived spontaneously for several weeks, ignoring most of the established rules of patriarchy. They ate the wrong food at the wrong time. They stayed up past the proper bedtime. They wore the wrong clothes. They giggled at silly jokes. Through all of these "trespasses" against the rules of the father, they were enormously happy. Indeed, suggested Rich, were fathers told they do *not* know best, then mothers would find child-rearing energizing rather than enervating, joyful rather than miserable.

According to Rich, Firestone was wrong to argue that female biology is necessarily limiting and that the only way to liberate women from this limitation is through reproductive technology. In a patriarchal society, the solution to the pains of childbearing is not reproductive technology but for a woman to ride with, not against, her body. A woman must not reject her body before she has had a chance to use it as she thinks best. Likewise, the solution to the impositions of child-rearing in a patriarchal society is not the renunciation of children; the solution is for every woman to rear children feminist style.

Genetics, Gestational, and Rearing Connections

The attention of radical-cultural feminists and radical-libertarian feminists has recently centered on surrogate, or contracted, motherhood—an arrangement in which a third party is hired and usually paid to bear a child who will be reared by someone else.[135] The birth mother (the woman whose gestational services have been contracted) is either the full biological mother of the child (both the genetic and the gestational mother) or the gestational but not the genetic mother of the child.

In general, radical-cultural feminists oppose contracted motherhood on the grounds it creates destructive divisions among women. One such division is between economically privileged women and economically disadvantaged women. The privileged can hire the disadvantaged to meet the former's reproductive needs, adding gestational services to the child-rearing services poor women traditionally have provided to rich women. The second division is one Gena Corea envisioned, namely, among child-begetters, child-bearers, and child-rearers. According to Corea, reproduction is currently being segmented and specialized as if it were simply a mode of production. In the future, no one woman will beget, bear, and rear a child. Rather, genetically superior women will beget embryos in vitro; strong-bodied women will bear these test-tube babies to term; and sweet-tempered women will rear these newborns from infancy to adulthood.[136] As a result of this division of labor, a dystopia similar to the one Atwood described in *The Handmaid's Tale* could actually come into existence, complete with divisive female-female relationships. No woman was whole in Gilead; all individual women were reduced to parts or aspects of the monolith, Woman.

In addition to lamenting the ways in which contracted motherhood might harm women's relationships to each other and to their children, radical-cultural feminists bemoan its rooting of parental rights either in persons' *genetic* contribution to the procreative process or in persons' professed *intention* to rear children. Basing parental rights exclusively on genetic contribution means if a surrogate mother is genetically unrelated to the child in her womb, she has no parental rights to it after it is born. Only if she is the genetic as well as the gestational mother of the child does she have grounds for claiming parental rights to it—rights that have to be balanced against those of the child's genetic father. In contrast, basing parental rights exclusively on one or more persons' professed intention to rear the child implies that because the surrogate mother has expressed no such intentions, she has no grounds for claiming parental rights to the child even if she is genetically related to the child.

According to radical-cultural feminists, men have reason to base all parental rights on either genes or intentions. After all, until the time a man takes an active part in the rearing of his child, the only kind of relationship he can have with his child is a genetic or an intentional one. Unlike his wife or other female partner, he cannot experience the kind of relationship a pregnant woman can experience with her child. For this reason, observe radical-cultural feminists, patriarchal society unfairly dismisses the gestational relationship as unimportant, as a mere biological event with no special parental meaning. But the truth of the matter, continue radical-cultural feminists, is that the gestational connection is of extraordinary importance. It is the child's gestator who proves through her concrete actions, some of which may cause her inconvenience and even pain, that she is *actually* committed to the child's well-being. As radical-cultural feminists see it, when parental claims are in question, the kind of *lived commitment* a gestational parent has to a child should count at least as much as the kind of *contemplated commitment* a genetic or an intentional parent has to a child.

Radical-libertarian feminists disagree with radical-cultural feminists' assessment of contracted motherhood, arguing that contracted motherhood arrangements, if handled properly, can bring women closer together rather than drive them farther apart. These feminists note some contracted mothers and commissioning couples live near each other so they can *all* share in the rearing of the child whom they have collaboratively reproduced.[137] Thus, contracted motherhood need not be viewed as the male-directed and male-manipulated specialization and segmentation of the female reproductive process but as women getting together (as in the case of the postmenopausal South African mother who carried her daughter's in vitro fetus to term) to achieve, in unison, something they could not achieve without each other's help.[138] As long as women control collaborative-reproduction arrangements, contracted motherhood increases rather than decreases women's reproductive freedom, in radical-libertarian feminists' estimation.

Believing it does women a disservice to overstate the importance of the gestational connection, radical-libertarian feminists object to the radical-cultural feminist position on contracted motherhood for two reasons. First, if women want men to spend as much time caring for children as women now do, then women should not repeatedly remind men of women's *special* connection to infants. Doing so implies that women are more suited to parenting tasks than men are. Second, if women want to protect their bodily integrity from the forces of state coercion, then women should not stress the symbiotic nature of the maternal-fetal connection. Increasingly aware of pregnant women's power to affect the well-being of their fetuses during the gestational process, society is more and more eager to control the pregnancies of "bad gestators." If a pregnant woman harms her fetus by drinking large quantities of alcohol or using illicit drugs, concerned citizens will urge that she be treated, voluntarily or involuntarily, for her addictions. Should treatment fail, many of these same citizens will become more aggressive in their demands; they will recommend that the state punish the "bad gestator" for negligently, recklessly, or intentionally engaging in life-style behavior resulting in serious, largely irreparable damage to her future child. Society will brand such a woman as a "fetal abuser" or "fetal neglecter." For this reason, if no other, radical-libertarian feminists believe the less that women emphasize how "special" the mother-fetus relationship is, the better served will women's interests be.

Critiques of Radical-Libertarian and Radical-Cultural Feminism: Beyond Polarization

In many ways, radical-libertarian and radical-cultural feminists are each other's best critics, but they are certainly not each other's only critics. Nonradical feminists have directed much in the way of criticism against both the "libertarian" and the "cultural" wings of radical feminist thought. For example, in the estimation of socialist feminist Ann Ferguson, both radical-libertarian and radical-cultural feminist perspectives on sexuality fail on account of their *ahistoricity*. There is, she said, no one universal "function" for human sexuality, whether it is conceived as the emotional intimacy of radical-cultural feminists or the sheer physical pleasure of radical libertarian feminists.[139] Thus, radical-cultural feminists are wrong to insist on an *essential* female sexuality as women's real (that is, beyond-history's-grip) sexuality. Ferguson observed that her own lesbianism is no more based on the fact that her "original," or first, sexual object was her mother than on the fact that her second sexual object was her father. Rather, what explains her current way of loving is "first, the historical and social contexts in my teenage years which allowed me to develop a first physical love relationship with a woman; and, second, the existence of a strong self-identified lesbian-feminist oppositional culture today which allowed me to turn toward women again from an adult life hitherto exclusively heterosexual."[140] Ferguson speculated that had she grown up in a more restricted sexual environment or in a less feminist era, she probably would not have *wanted* to have lesbian lovers. After all, she said, "One's sexual objects are defined by the social contexts in which one's *ongoing* gender identity is constructed in relation to one's peers."[141]

Like radical-cultural feminists, radical-libertarian feminists are guilty of ahistoricism, in Ferguson's estimation, but in a different way. Radical-libertarian feminists seem to think that a woman is always able to give free or true consent. Thus, radical-libertarian feminist Gayle Rubin claimed if a woman experiences herself *as* consenting to heterosexual or lesbian sadomasochism or bondage and domination, then she *is* consenting to these practices. No one has a right to criticize her as a "victim of false consciousness," a person who fails to realize that were she truly a man's equal, she would have nothing to do with any form of sexuality that eroticizes dominance-and-subordination relationships. But in Ferguson's estimation, depending on this woman's "social context," the woman may in fact be a "victim of false consciousness." The "freedom" of an economically dependent housewife to consent to S/M sex with her husband must be challenged; so, too, must the "freedom" of a teenage prostitute to consent to sex with a man far older and richer than she.[142]

Issues of real versus apparent consent arise just as frequently in the reproductive arena as they do in the sexual realm. Radical-libertarian feminists, such as Firestone and Rubin, would probably accept as a *real* choice a woman's decision to sell her gestational services. No doubt they would view such a decision as helping to erode the institution of biological motherhood, which maintains that she who bears a child should rear the child not only because she is best suited for this task but also because she wants to do so. Because a surrogate mother is prepared to walk away from the child she has gestated for the "right price," she debunks the "myth" of biological motherhood. But in Ferguson's estimation, it is debatable whether all surrogate mothers choose money over the product of their gestational labor. Depending on a woman's social circumstances, her consent to surrender the child she has gestated to the couple who contracted for it may not be truly free. Since most surrogate mothers are less advantaged than their clients, the surrogates might easily be driven to sell one of the few things they have that patriarchal society values: their reproductive services. To say women choose to do this might simply be to say that when women are forced to choose between being poor and being exploited, they may choose being exploited as the lesser of two evils.

Conclusion

Assuming such socialist feminists as Ferguson are correct to stress that women's sexual and reproductive desires, needs, behaviors, and identities are largely the product of the time and place that women occupy in history, these feminists are also right to argue that (1) neither heterosexuality nor lesbianism is either inherently pleasurable or inherently dangerous for women; and (2) neither natural reproduction nor artificial reproduction is either inherently empowering or inherently disempowering for women. All radical feminists, whether libertarian or cultural, should ask themselves what kind of sexual and reproductive practices people would adopt in a society in which all economic, political, and kinship systems were structured to create equality between men and women and as far as possible between adults and children. In such an egalitarian world, would men and women engage in "male breadwinner/female housewife sex prostitution," or would they instead develop forms of egalitarian heterosexuality seldom imagined, let alone practiced, in our very unequal, patriarchal world? Would some lesbians continue to engage in S/M and butch-femme relationships, or would all lesbians find themselves turned off by such practices? Would there be "man-boy" love (pederasty) or "parent-child" love (incest)? Would women use more or less in the way of contraceptives? Would couples contract for gestational mothers' services, or would they instead prefer to adopt children? Would there be more or fewer children? Would most people choose to reproduce "artificially," or would they instead choose to reproduce the "old-fashioned," natural way?

What is common to the kind of questions just posed, is that the answers they yield will be lived in the future world that feminists *imagine* and not, for the most part, in the present world feminists *experience.* For now, feminists should seek to develop an approach to sexuality and reproduction that permits women to understand both the pleasures and the dangers of sex, and the liberating and enslaving aspects of reproduction. The one-sided approaches of the past have turned out to be part of the problem of human oppression, rather than a remedy for it. The sooner these either/or approaches to sexuality and reproduction are replaced with both/and approaches, the sooner will men and women stop playing the destructive game of male domination and female subordination.[143]

Questions for Discussion

1. Discuss the helpfulness of understanding the totality of oppressive human suffering in lieu of women's oppression. Could there be ways in which positing a hierarchical order of human suffering is harmful?

2. Compare and contrast examples of how Marilyn French's concepts of "power-over" and "power-to" may function in government, business, social life, and within the home.

3. Is orthodox religion generally incompatible with radical feminism? Why or why not? Is religion the core problem, or could the historical interpretation and implementation of religion be the larger issue?

4. Is there anything problematic with believing technology is the solution to ending women's oppression? Does this minimize sociopolitical and individual responsibility? Imagine a world in which technology has erased biological differences. Would this technologically advanced society necessarily embrace sexual equality?

5. Compare and contrast the benefits and drawbacks of both traditional one-on-one child-rearing and the "multiple mothering" Ann Oakley posed. Is bloodline ever morally relevant when considering maternal and/or paternal responsibilities?

6. What kind of social and political policies would you recommend adopting in a society in which all economic, political, and kinship systems were egalitarian?

Marxist and Socialist Feminism
Classical and Contemporary

Although it is possible to distinguish between Marxist and socialist feminist thought, it is quite difficult to do so. The differences between these two schools of thought seem more a matter of emphasis than of substance. Classical Marxist feminists work within the conceptual terrain laid out by Marx, Engels, Lenin, and other nineteenth-century thinkers. They regard classism rather than sexism as the fundamental cause of women's oppression. In contrast, socialist feminists are not certain that classism is women's worst or only enemy. They write in view of Russia's twentieth-century failure to achieve socialism's ultimate goal—namely, the replacement of class oppression and antagonism with "an association, in which the free development of each is the condition for the free development of all."[1] Post-1917 Communism in the Soviet Union and later in the so-called Eastern Bloc was not true socialism but simply a new form of human exploitation and oppression. Women's lives under Communism, particularly during the Stalin years (1929–1953), were not manifestly better than women's lives under capitalism. Women's move into the productive workplace had not made them men's equals either there or at home. For these reasons and related ones, socialist feminists decided to move beyond relying on class as the sole category for understanding women's subordination to men. Increasingly, they tried "to understand women's subordination in a coherent and systematic way that integrates class and sex, as well as other aspects of identity such as race/ethnicity or sexual orientation."[2]

Some Marxist Concepts and Theories

To appreciate the differences between classical Marxist and contemporary socialist feminism, we need to understand the Marxist concept of human nature. As noted in Chapter 1, liberals believe that several characteristics distinguish human beings from other animals. These characteristics include a set of abilities, such as the capacity for rationality and the use of language; a set of practices, such as religion, art, and science; and a set of attitude and behavior patterns, such as competitiveness and the tendency to put oneself over others. Marxists reject the liberal conception of human nature, claiming instead that what makes us different from other animals is our ability to produce our means of subsistence. We are what we are because of what we do—specifically, what we do to meet our basic needs through productive activities such as fishing, farming, and building. Unlike bees, beavers, and ants, whose activities are governed by instinct and which cannot willfully change themselves, we create ourselves in the process of intentionally transforming and manipulating nature.[3]

For the liberal, the ideas, thoughts, and values of individuals account for change over time. For the Marxist, material forces—the production and reproduction of social life—are the prime movers in history. In laying out a full explanation of how change takes place over time, an explanation usually termed *historical materialism,* Marx stated, "The mode of production of material life conditions the general process of social, political, and intellectual life. It is not the consciousness of men that determines their existence, but their social existence that determines their consciousness."[4] In other words, Marx believed a society's total mode of production—that is, its forces of production (the raw materials, tools, and workers that actually produce goods) plus its relations of production (the ways in which production is organized)—generates a superstructure (a layer of legal, political, and social ideas) that in turn reinforces the mode of production. Adding to Marx's point, Richard Schmitt later emphasized that the statement "human beings create themselves" is not to be read as "men and women, as *individuals,* make themselves what they are," but instead as "men and women, through production *collectively,* create a society that, in turn, shapes them."[5] So, for example, people in the United States think in certain ways about liberty, equality, and freedom *because* their mode of production is capitalist.

Like Marxists in general, Marxist and socialist feminists claim that social existence determines consciousness. For them, the observation that "women's work is never done" is more than an aphorism; it is a description of the nature of woman's work. Always on call, women form a conception of themselves they would not have if their roles in the family and the workplace did not keep them socially and economically subordinate to men. Thus, Marxist and socialist feminists believe we need to analyze the links between women's work status and women's self-image to understand the unique character of *women's* oppression.[6]

The Marxist Theory of Economics

To the degree Marxist and socialist feminists believe women's work shapes women's thoughts and thus "female nature," these thinkers also believe capitalism is a system of power relations as well as exchange relations. When capitalism is viewed as a system of exchange relations, it is described as a commodity or market society in which everything, including one's own labor power, has a price and all transactions are fundamentally exchange transactions. But when capitalism is viewed instead as a system of power relations, it is described as a society in which every kind of transactional relation is fundamentally exploitative. Thus, depending on one's emphasis, the worker-employer relationship can be looked at as either an exchange relationship in which items of equivalent value are freely traded—labor for wages—or as a workplace struggle in which the employer, who has superior power, takes advantage of workers in any number of ways.

Whereas liberals view capitalism as a system of voluntary exchange relations, Marxists and socialists view capitalism as a system of exploitative power relations. According to Marx, the value of any commodity is determined by the amount of labor, or actual expenditure of human energy and intelligence, necessary to produce it.[7] To be more precise, the value of any commodity is equal to the *direct* labor incorporated in the commodity by workers, plus the *indirect* labor stored in workers' artificial appendages—the tools and machines made by the direct labor of their predecessors.[8] Because all commodities are worth exactly the labor necessary to produce them and because workers' labor power (capacity for work) is a commodity that can be bought and sold, the value of workers' labor power is exactly the cost of whatever it takes (food, clothing, shelter) to maintain them throughout the workday. But there is a difference between what employers pay workers for their mere *capacity* to work (labor power) and the value that workers actually create when they put their work capacity to use in producing commodities.[9] Marx termed this difference "surplus value," and from it employers derive their profits. Thus, capitalism is an exploitative system because employers pay workers only for their labor power, without also paying workers for the human energy they expend and the intelligence they transfer into the commodities they produce.[10]

At this point in an analysis of Marxist economic thought, it seems reasonable to ask how employers get workers to labor for more hours than are necessary to produce the value of their subsistence, especially when workers receive no compensation for this extra work. The answer to this query is, as Marx explained in *Capital*, a simple one: Employers have a monopoly on the means of production, including factories, tools, land, means of transportation, and means of communication. Workers are forced to choose between being exploited and having no work at all. It is a liberal fiction that workers freely sign mutually beneficial contractual agreements with their employers. Capitalism is just as much a system of power relations as it is one of exchange relations. Workers are free to contract with employers only in the sense that employers do not hold a gun to their heads when they sign on the dotted line.

Interestingly, there is another, less discussed reason why employers are able to exploit workers under capitalism. According to Marx, capitalist ideologies lead workers and employers to focus on capitalism's surface structure of exchange relations.[11] As a result of this ideological ploy, which Marx called the "fetishism of commodities," workers gradually convince themselves that even though their money is very hard earned, there is nothing inherently wrong with the specific exchange relationships into which they have entered, because life, in all its dimensions, is simply one colossal system of exchange relations.

That liberal ideologies, typically spawned in capitalist economics, present practices such as prostitution and surrogate motherhood as contractual exercises of free choice, then, is no accident, according to Marxist and socialist feminists. The liberal ideologies claim that women become prostitutes and surrogate mothers because they *prefer* these jobs over other available jobs. But, as Marxist and socialist feminists see it, when a poor, illiterate, unskilled woman chooses to sell her sexual or reproductive services, chances are her choice is more coerced than free. After all, if one has little else of value to sell besides one's body, one's leverage in the marketplace is quite limited.

The Marxist Theory of Society

Like the Marxist analysis of power, the Marxist analysis of class has provided both Marxist and socialist feminists with some of the conceptual tools necessary to understand women's oppression. Marx observed that every political economy—the primitive communal state, the slave epoch, the precapitalist society, and the bourgeois society—contains the seeds of its own destruction. Thus, according to Marx, there are within capitalism enough internal contradictions to generate a class division dramatic enough to overwhelm the very system that produced it. Specifically, there exist many poor and propertyless workers. These workers live very modestly, receiving subsistence wages for their exhausting labor while their employers live in luxury. When both these groups of people, the haves and the have-nots, become conscious of themselves *as* classes, said Marx, class struggle ensues and ultimately topples the system that produced these classes.[12] It is important to emphasize the dynamic nature of class. Classes do not simply appear. They are slowly and often painstakingly formed by similarly situated people who share the same wants and needs. According to Marx, people who belong to any class initially have no more unity than do "potatoes in a sack of potatoes.[13] But through a long and complex process of struggling together about issues of local and later national interest to them, a group of people gradually becomes a unity, a true class. Because class unity is difficult to achieve, its importance cannot be overstated, said Marx. As soon as a group of people is fully conscious of itself as a class, it has a better chance of achieving its fundamental goals. There is power in group awareness.

Class consciousness is, in the Marxist framework, the opposite of false consciousness, a state of mind that impedes the creation and maintenance of true class unity. False consciousness causes exploited people to believe they are as free to act and speak as their exploiters are. The bourgeoisie is especially adept at fooling the proletariat. For this reason, Marxists discredit egalitarian, or welfare, liberalism, for example, as a ruling-class ideology that tricks workers into believing their employers actually care about them. As Marxists see it, fringe benefits such as generous health-care plans or paid maternity leave are not gifts employers generously bestow on workers, but a means to pull the wool over workers' eyes. Grateful for the benefits their employers give them, workers minimize their own hardships and suffering. Like the ruling class, the workers begin to perceive the status quo as the best possible world for workers and employers alike. The more benefits employers give their workers, the less likely those workers will form a class capable of recognizing their true needs as human beings.

Because Marxist and socialist feminists wish to view women as a collectivity, Marxist teachings on class and class consciousness play a large role in Marxist and socialist feminist thought. Much debate within the Marxist and socialist feminist community has centered on the following question: Do women per se constitute a class? Given that some women are wives, daughters, friends, and lovers of *bourgeois* men, whereas other women are the wives, daughters, friends, and lovers of *proletarian* men, it would appear women do not constitute a single class in the strict Marxist sense. Yet, bourgeois and proletarian women's domestic experiences, for example, may bear enough similarities to motivate unifying struggles such as the 1970s wages-for-housework campaign (see page 106). Thus, many Marxist and socialist feminists believe women can gain a consciousness of themselves as a *class* of workers by insisting, for example, that domestic work be recognized as real work, that is, productive work. The observation that wives and mothers usually love the people for whom they work does not mean that cooking, cleaning, and childcare are not productive work. At most it means wives' and mothers' working conditions are better than those of people who work for employers they dislike.[14]

By keeping the Marxist conceptions of class and class consciousness in mind, we can understand another concept that often plays a role in Marxist and socialist feminist thought: alienation. Like many Marxist terms, the term *alienation* is extraordinarily difficult to define simply. In *Karl Marx,* Allen Wood suggested we are alienated "if we either experience our lives as meaningless or ourselves as worthless, or else are capable of sustaining a sense of meaning and self-worth only with the help of illusions about ourselves or our condition."[15] Robert Heilbroner added that alienation is a profoundly fragmenting experience. Things or persons that are or should be connected in some significant way are instead viewed as separate. As Heilbroner saw it, this sense of fragmentation and meaninglessness is particularly strong under capitalism.

As a result of invidious class distinctions, as well as the highly specialized and highly segmented nature of the work process, human existence loses its unity and wholeness in four basic ways. First, workers are alienated from the *product* of their labor. Not only do workers have no say in what commodities they will or will not produce, but the fruits of their labor are snatched from them. Therefore, the satisfaction of determining when, where, how, and to whom these commodities will be sold is denied the workers. What should partially express and constitute their being-as-workers confronts them as a thing apart, a thing alien.[16]

Second, workers are alienated from *themselves* because when work is experienced as something unpleasant to be gotten through as quickly as possible, it is deadening. When the potential source of workers' humanization becomes the actual source of their dehumanization, workers may undergo a major psychological crisis. They start feeling like hamsters on a hamster wheel, going nowhere.

Third, workers are alienated from *other human beings* because the structure of the capitalist economy encourages and even forces workers to see one another as competitors for jobs and promotions. When the source of workers' solidarity (other workers experienced as cooperators, friends, people to be with) becomes instead the source of their isolation (other workers experienced as competitors, enemies, people to avoid), workers become disidentified with one another, losing an opportunity to add joy and meaning to their lives.

Fourth, workers are alienated from *nature* because the kind of work they do and the conditions under which they do it make them see nature as an obstacle to their survival. This negative perception of nature sets up an opposition where, in fact, a connectedness should exist—the connectedness among all elements in nature. The elimination of this type of alienation, entailing a return to a humane kind of work environment, is yet another important justification for the overthrow of capitalism.[17]

Building on the idea that in a capitalist society, human relations take on an alienated nature in which "the individual only feels himself or herself when detached from others,"[18] Ann Foreman claimed this state of affairs is worse for women than it is for men:

> The man exists in the social world of business and industry as well as in the family and therefore is able to express himself in these different spheres. For the woman, however, her place is within the home. Men's objectification within industry, through the expropriation of the product of their labour, takes the form of alienation. But the effect of alienation on the lives and consciousness of women takes an even more oppressive form. Men seek relief from their alienation through their relations with women; for women there is no relief. For these intimate relations are the very ones that are essential structures of her oppression.[19]

As Foreman saw it, women's alienation is profoundly disturbing because women experience themselves not as selves but as others. All too often, said Foreman, a woman's sense of self is entirely dependent on her family's and friends' appreciation of her. If they express loving feelings toward her, she will be happy, but if they fail to give her even a thank-you, she will be sad. Thus, Marxist and socialist feminists aim to create a world in which women can experience themselves as whole persons, as integrated rather than fragmented beings, as people who can be happy even when they are unable to make their families and friends happy.

The Marxist Theory of Politics

Like the Marxist theories of economics and society, the Marxist theory of politics offers Marxist and socialist feminists insights to help liberate women from the forces that oppress them. As noted previously, class struggle takes a certain form within the workplace because the interests of the employers are not those of the workers. Whereas it is in the employers' interests to use whatever tactics may be necessary (harassment, firing, violence) to get workers to work ever more effectively and efficiently for less wages than their work is worth, it is in the workers' interests to use whatever countertactics may be necessary (sick time, coffee breaks, strikes) to limit the extent to which their labor power is used to produce sheer profit for their employers.

The relatively small and everyday class conflicts occurring within the capitalist workplace serve as preliminaries to the full-fledged, large-scale class struggles that Marx envisioned. As noted earlier, Marx predicted that as workers become increasingly aware of their common exploitation and alienation, they will achieve class consciousness. United, the workers will be able to fight their employers for control over the means of production (e.g., the nation's factories). If the workers manage to win this fight, Marx claimed that a highly committed, politically savvy, well-trained group of revolutionaries would subsequently emerge from the workers' ranks. Marx termed this special group of workers the "vanguard" of the full-scale revolution for which he hoped. More than anything else, Marx desired to replace capitalism with socialism, a nonexploitative, nonalienating political economy through which communism, "the complete and conscious return of man himself as a social, that is, human being,"[20] could come into existence.

Under capitalism, Marx suggested, people are largely free to *do* what they want to do within the confines of the system, but they have little say in determining the confines themselves. "Personality," said Marx, "is conditioned and determined by quite definite class relationships."[21] Decades later, Richard Schmitt elaborated on Marx's powerful quote:

> In as much as persons do certain jobs in society, they tend to acquire certain character traits, interests, habits, and so on. Without such adaptations to the demands of their particular occupations, they would not be able to do a great job. A capitalist who cannot bear to win in competition, or to outsmart someone, will not be a capitalist for long. A worker who is unwilling to take orders will not work very often. In this way we are shaped by the work environment, and this fact limits personal freedom for it limits what we can choose to be.[22]

In contrast to the persons living under capitalism, persons living under communism are free not only to *do* but also to *be* what they want, because they have the power to see clearly and change the system that shapes them.

If we read between these lines, we can appreciate another of Marxism's major appeals to Marxist and socialist feminists. It promises to reconstitute human nature in ways that preclude all the pernicious dichotomies that have made slaves of some and masters of others. Marxism also promises to make people free, a promise women would like to see someone keep. There is, after all, something very liberating about the idea of women and men constructing together the social structures and social roles that will permit both genders to realize their full human potential.

The Marxist Theory of Family Relations

Although the fathers of Marxism did not take women's oppression nearly as seriously as they did workers' oppression, some of them did offer explanations for why women are oppressed qua women. With the apparent blessing of Marx, Engels wrote *The Origin of the Family, Private Property, and the State* (1845), in which he showed how changes in the material conditions of people affect the organization of their family relations. He argued that before the family, or structured conjugal relations, there existed a primitive state of "promiscuous intercourse."[23] In this early state, every woman was fair game for every man, and vice versa. All were essentially married to all. In the process of natural selection, suggested Engels, various kinds of blood relatives were gradually excluded from consideration as eligible marriage partners.[24] As fewer and fewer women in the tribal group became available to any given man, individual men began to put forcible claims on individual women as their possessions. As a result, the pairing family, in which one man is married to one woman, came into existence.

Noting that when a man took a woman, he came to live in *her* household, Engels interpreted this state of affairs as a sign of women's economic power. Because women's work was vital for the tribe's survival and because women produced most of the material goods (e.g., bedding, clothing, cookware, tools) that could be passed on to future generations, Engels concluded that early pairing societies were probably matrilineal, with inheritance and lines of descent traced through the mother.[25] Later, Engels speculated that pairing societies may have been not merely matrilineal societies but also matriarchal societies in which women ruled at the political, social, and economic levels.[26] But his main and less debatable point remained that whatever power women had in past times, it was rooted in their position in the household, at that time the center of production.[27] Only if the site of production changed would women lose their advantaged position.[28] As it turned out, said Engels, a site change did occur. The "domestication of animals and the breeding of herds" outside the household led to an entirely new source of wealth for the human community.[29] Somehow, men gained control of the tribe's animals (Engels did not tell us why or how),[30] and the male-female power balance shifted in favor of men, as men learned to produce more than enough animals to meet the tribe's needs for milk and meat.

Surplus animals constituted an accumulation of wealth that men used as a means of exchange between tribes. Possessing more than enough of a valuable socioeconomic good, men found themselves increasingly preoccupied with the issue of property inheritance. Directed through the mother's line, property inheritance was originally a minor matter of the bequest of a "house, clothing, crude ornaments and the tools for obtaining and preparing food— boats, weapons and domestic utensils of the simplest kinds."[31] As production outside the household began to outstrip production within it, the traditional sexual division of labor between men and women, which had supposedly arisen out of the physiological differences between the sexes—specifically, the sex act[32]—took on new social meanings. As men's work and production grew in importance, not only did the value of women's work and production decrease, but the status of women within society decreased. Because men now possessed things more valuable than the things women possessed and because men, for some unexplained reason, suddenly wanted *their own* biological children to get *their* possessions, men exerted enormous pressure to convert society from a matrilineal one into a patrilineal one. As Engels phrased it, mother right had "to be overthrown, and overthrown it was."[33]

Engels presented the "overthrow of mother right" as "the world-historic defeat of the female sex."[34] Having produced and staked a claim to wealth, men took control of the household, reducing women to the "slaves" of men's carnal desire and "mere instrument[s] for the production of [men's] children."[35] In this new familial order, said Engels, the husband ruled by virtue of his economic power: "He is the bourgeois and the wife represents the proletariat."[36] Engels believed men's power over women is rooted in the fact that men, not women, control private property. The oppression of women will cease only with the dissolution of the institution of private property.

The emergence of private property and the shift to patrilineage also explained, for Engels, the transition to the monogamous family. Before the advent of technologies such as in vitro fertilization, it was always possible to identify the biological mother of a child. If the child came out of a woman's body, the child was the biological product of her egg and some man's sperm. In contrast, before the development of DNA testing to establish biological paternity, the identity of a biological father was uncertain because a woman could have been impregnated by a man other than her husband. Thus, to secure their wives' marital fidelity, men imposed the institution of heterosexual monogamy on women, the purpose of which was, according to Engels, to provide a vehicle for the guaranteed transfer of a father's private property to his biological children. Male dominance, in the forms of patrilineage and patriarchy, is simply the result of the class division between the propertied man and the propertyless woman. Engels commented that monogamy was "the first form of the family to be based not on natural but on economic conditions."[37] In his estimation, the monogamous family is the product not of love and commitment but of power plays and economic exigencies.

Because Engels viewed monogamous marriage as an economic institution that has nothing to do with love and everything to do with the transfer of private property, he insisted that if wives are to be emancipated from their husbands, women must first become economically independent of men. He stressed that the first presupposition for the emancipation of women is "the reintroduction of the entire female sex into public industry," and the second is the socialization of housework and child-rearing.[38] Remarkably, Engels believed that proletarian women experience less oppression than do bourgeois women. As he saw it, the bourgeois family consists of a relationship between a husband and a wife in which the husband agrees to support his wife provided that she promises to remain sexually faithful to him and to reproduce only his legitimate heirs. "This marriage of convenience," observed Engels, "often enough turns into the crassest prostitution—sometimes on both sides, but much more generally on the part of the wife, who differs from the ordinary courtesan only in that she does not hire out her body, like a wage-worker, on piecework, but sells it into slavery once and for all."[39]

In contrast to the bourgeois marriage, the proletarian marriage is not, in Engels's estimation, a mode of prostitution, because the material conditions of the proletarian family differ substantially from those of the bourgeois family. Not only is the proletariat's lack of private property significant in removing the primary male incentive for monogamy—namely, the reproduction of legitimate heirs for one's property—but the general employment of proletarian women as workers outside the home also leads to a measure of equality between husband and wife. This equality, according to Engels, provides the foundation of true "sex-love." In addition to these differences, the household authority of the proletarian husband, unlike that of the bourgeois husband, is not likely to receive the full support of the legal establishment. For all these reasons, Engels concluded that with the exception of "residual brutality" (spouse abuse), all "the material foundations of male dominance had ceased to exist" in the proletarian home.[40]

Classical Marxist Feminism: General Reflections

Affirming the ideas of Marx and Engels, classical Marxist feminists tried to use a class analysis rather than a gender analysis to explain women's oppression. A particularly good example of classical Marxist feminism appeared in Evelyn Reed's "Women: Caste, Class, or Oppressed Sex?"[41] Stressing that the same capitalist economic forces and social relations that "brought about the oppression of one class by another, one race by another, and one nation by another"[42] also brought about the oppression of one sex by another, Reed resisted the view that women's oppression *as women* is the worst kind of oppression for *all* women. Although Reed agreed that relative to men, women occupy a subordinate position in a patriarchal or male-dominated society, she did not think that all women were equally oppressed by men or that no women were guilty of oppressing other women. On the contrary, she thought bourgeois women were capable of oppressing both proletarian men and women. In a capitalist system, money is most often power.

Not found in Reed is any manifesto urging all women to band together to wage a "caste war" against all men.[43] Rather, she encourages oppressed women to join oppressed men in a "class war" against their common capitalist oppressors, female and male. Reed thought it was misguided to insist that all women, simply by virtue of possessing two X chromosomes, belong to the same class. On the contrary, she maintained that "women, like men are a multiclass sex."[44] Specifically, proletarian women have little in common with bourgeois women, who are the economic, social, and political as well as sexual partners of the bourgeois men to whom they are linked. Bourgeois women are not united with proletarian women but with bourgeois men "in defense of private property, profiteering, militarism, racism—and the exploitation of other women."[45]

Clearly, Reed believed that the primary enemy of at least proletarian women is not patriarchy, but first and foremost, capitalism. Optimistic about male-female relations in a postcapitalist society, Reed maintained that "far from being eternal, woman's subjection and the bitter hostility between the sexes are no more than a few thousand years old. They were produced by the drastic social changes which brought the family, private property, and the state into existence."[46] With the end of capitalist male-female relationships, both sexes will thrive in a communist society that enables all its members to cooperate with one another in communities of care.

Women's Labor after the 1917 Communist Revolution in Russia

During the 1917 Communist Revolution and for several years afterward, Reed's brand of optimism seemed well founded. Women were invited to enter the productive workforce to supposedly find in it the beginnings of their full human liberation. With economic independence would come the possibility of women's developing self-confidence and viewing themselves as makers of meaningful human history. Unfortunately, things did not turn out so well for postrevolution Soviet women. On the contrary! Rather than finding in the workplace meaningful, high-waged work, most women found dronelike, exhausting work that was typically less valued than men's work.[47] Not wanting to jeopardize Communist plans to totally destroy capitalism, most Marxist feminists kept quiet about their workplace situation in public. However, in private they complained about such workplace disadvantages as (1) the relegation of most women to low-status "women's work" (i.e., secretarial work; rote factory work; and service work, including jobs related to cooking, cleaning, and caring for the basic needs of the young, the old, and the infirm); (2) the creation of "female professions" and "male professions"; (3) the payment of lower wages to women than the wages paid to men; and (4) the treatment of women as a "colossal reserve of labor forces" to use or not use, depending on the state's need for workers.[48]

Unable to find in strict Marxist theory an explanation for why, on the average, women were not faring as well as men in the productive workforce, some Marxist feminists turned their attention to the work women did in the domestic realm—work that men typically did not do. Trying to explain why women were saddled with their families' domestic work, whether or not the women worked in the productive workforce, Margaret Benston defined women as that class of people "responsible for the production of simple use-values in those activities associated with the house and family."[49] As she saw it, women must break out of this class to be liberated, but they cannot do so unless their domestic labor is socialized:

> Women, particularly married women with children, who work outside the home simply do two jobs; their participation in the labor force is only allowed if they continue to fulfill their first responsibility in the home. . . . Equal access to jobs outside the home, while one of the preconditions for women's liberation, will not in itself be sufficient to give equality for women; as long as work in the home remains a matter of private production and is the responsibility of women, they will simply carry a double work-load.[50]

To bring women into the productive workforce without simultaneously socializing the jobs of cooking, cleaning, and childcare is to make women's oppressed condition even worse, claimed Benston. To be sure, she conceded, the socialization of domestic work might lead to women doing the same sorts of "female" work outside the home as they do inside the home. But the simple fact that women will be doing this "female" work *outside* their own home for wages over which they have control can be viewed as an advancement for women, insisted Benston.

The Wages-for-Housework Campaign

Agreeing with Benston that in a socialist society, it might be necessary to socialize domestic work to achieve full liberation for women, Mariarosa Dalla
Costa and Selma James nonetheless argued that in a capitalist society, the
best way (or at least the most efficient way) for women to achieve economic
parity with men might not be for women to enter the productive workforce
and for domestic labor to be socialized, but instead for women to stay at
home and demand wages for the "real work"—that is, productive work—
they did there. Unlike most classical Marxist feminist thinkers, Dalla Costa
and James claimed that women's work *inside* the home generates surplus
value.[51] They reasoned that women's domestic work is the necessary condition for all other labor, from which, in turn, surplus value is extracted. By
providing not only food and clothes but also emotional comfort to current
(and future) workers, women keep the cogs of the capitalist machine running. Therefore, argued Dalla Costa and James, men's employers should pay
women wages for the housework they do.[52] Let housewives get the cash that
would otherwise fatten employers' wallets.[53]

Acknowledging that domestic labor could be viewed as productive work,
most Marxist feminists nonetheless concluded that paying women wages for
housework was neither as feasible nor as desirable as Dalla Costa and James
seemed to think. Paying women to do housework was not feasible, in their
estimation, for several reasons. First, if employers were required to pay housewives wages for housework, the employers would probably pay those housewives' husbands lower wages. Under such circumstances, the total capitalist
profit margin would remain high, and the material conditions of workers
would not improve. Second, not all or not even most women in advanced capitalist economies are stay-at-home domestic workers. Many married women as
well as married men work outside the home, as do many single men and
women. Would employers be required to pay all their workers' wages for their
at-home domestic work? If so, would employers have any way to monitor the
quantity and quality of their workers' domestic labor? Third, if small companies as well as major corporations were required to pay all their workers for domestic work, most small companies would probably go out of business. Back
in 1972, the height of the wages-for-housework campaign, the Chase Manhat-
tan Bank estimated that "for her average 100-hour workweek, the housewife
should be paid $257.53."[54] In that same year, noted Ann Crittenden Scott,
"White males had average incomes of $172 a week; white females had average
incomes of $108 a week."[55] By 2011, nearly forty years later, annual median
earnings in the United States for women per week were $684 per week, and for
men per week were $832.[56] Add to these median wages the wages for domestic

labor done by employees in their own homes, and there is no question that most small or even large companies could not sustain such a hit. Indeed, even if wages for domestic labor were paid at the median rate of $9.32 per hour for, say, a forty-hour domestic work week, each employee's salary would need to be topped off with over $19,393 annually.[57]

Clearly, it does not seem feasible to pay anyone, including wives, girl-friends, mothers, and daughters, wages for housework. But even if it were feasible to do so, would it be desirable? Many Marxist and other feminists in the 1970s were not confident that wages for housework would liberate women. Carol Lopate, among others, argued that paying women for house-work would have the net effect of keeping women isolated in their own homes with few opportunities to do anything other than routinized and rep-etitious work:

> The decrease in house size and the mechanization of housework have meant that the housewife is potentially left with much greater leisure time; however, she is often kept busy buying, using, and repairing devices which are theoretically geared toward saving her time. Moreover, the trivial, man-ufactured tasks which many of these technological aids perform are hardly a source of satisfaction for housewives. Max-Pacs may give "perfect coffee every time," but even a compliment about her coffee can offer little more than fleeting satisfaction to the housewife. Finally, schools, nurseries, day care, and television have taken from mothers much of their responsibility for the socialization of their children.[58]

Moreover, and even more important, paying women wages for domestic work would give women little impetus to work outside the household. As a result, the traditional sexual division of labor would be strengthened. Men would feel no pressure to do "women's work," and women would have little incentive to do "men's work."[59] One thinks here of the stereotyped stay-at-home "supermom" who is at the beck and call of her children to shuttle them to and from multiple sports events, club meetings, parties, mall visits, and the like. Many women try to derive meaning from making things happen for their children.

Contemporary Socialist Feminism: General Reflections

The more Marxist feminists realized that, like everyone else, they had unre-flectively assumed that domestic work is *women's* work, the more it concerned them that the advent of Communist/socialist societies had not resulted in the socialization of this work. Rather than there being an approximately equal number of men and women doing domestic work for wages, it was business as usual. That is, women continued to do domestic work in the home "for free," whether or not they had a paid job outside the home. Unable to explain in exclusively economic terms why domestic work is viewed as women's work in socialist as well as capitalist societies, many Marxist feminists concluded that domestic work is assigned to women in all societies simply because all women belong to the same sex class—namely, the second (female) sex, which exists to serve the first (male) sex.

The Marxist feminists who decided that women's sex class as well as economic class plays a role in women's oppression began to refer to themselves as socialist feminists or materialist feminists. One of the initial goals of this evolving group of feminist theorists was to develop a theory powerful enough to explain the complex ways in which capitalism and patriarchy allied to oppress women. The result of this effort was, as might be predicted, not a unitary theory, but a variety of theories that sorted themselves into two types: (1) two-system explanations of women's oppression and (2) interactive-system explanations of women's oppression.

Two-System Explanations of Women's Oppression

Two-system explanations of women's oppression typically combine a Marxist feminist account of class power with a radical feminist account of sex power.[60] Some two-system explanations adhere to the Marxist base-superstructure model that views economics as "the fundamental motor of social relations"[61] shaping the form of society, including its ideologies and psychologies. These explanations claim that, at root, women have more to fear from capitalist forces than from patriarchal forces.[62] In contrast, other two-system explanations are less committed to the Marxist base-superstructure model. They imply that patriarchy, not capitalism, may be women's ultimate worst enemy.

Juliet Mitchell.   In the early 1970s, Juliet Mitchell sketched a plausible two-system explanation of women's oppression. In *Woman's Estate,* she abandoned the classical Marxist feminist position according to which a woman's condition is simply a function of her relation to capital, of whether she is part of the productive workforce. In place of this monocausal explanation for women's oppression, she suggested women's status and function are multiply determined by their role in not only production but also reproduction, the socialization of children, and sexuality. "The error of the old Marxist way," she said, "was to see the other three elements as reducible to the economic; hence the call for the entry into production was accompanied by the purely abstract slogan of the abolition of the family. Economic demands are still *primary,* but must be accompanied by coherent policies for the other three elements (reproduction, sexuality and socialization), policies which at particular junctures may take over the primary role in immediate action."[63]

In attempting to determine which of these elements most oppressed 1970s US women, Mitchell concluded that US women had not made enough progress in the areas of production, reproduction, and the socialization of children. She noted that even though women are just as physically and psychologically qualified for high-paying, prestigious jobs as men are, employers continued to confine women to low-paying, low-status jobs.[64] Moreover, said Mitchell, despite the widespread availability of safe, effective, and inexpensive reproduction-controlling technologies, women often failed or refused to use them. As a result, the causal chain of "maternity—family—absence from production and public life—sexual inequality" continued to bind women to their subordinate status. Furthermore, although 1970s US women had far fewer children than US women did at the turn of the century, the modern women spent no less time socializing them.[65] In fact, the pressures to be a perfect mother, always attentive to every physical and psychological need of her children, seemed to be increasing.

Interestingly, like radical-libertarian feminists, Mitchell thought 1970s US women had made major progress in the area of sexuality. She claimed that unlike previous generations, 1970s US women felt free to express their sexual desires publicly and to present themselves as sexual beings. Still, Mitchell acknowledged that pushed to its extreme, women's newly won sexual liberation could mutate into a form of sexual oppression. Whereas turn-of-the-century US society condemned sexually active women as "wanton whores," 1970s US society tended to celebrate them as "sex experimenters" or healthy role models for sexually repressed women to emulate. Commenting on this state of affairs, Mitchell observed that too much sex, like too little sex, can be oppressive.[66] Women can be made to feel that something is wrong with them if they are not sexually active or sexually preoccupied.

Mitchell speculated that patriarchal ideology, which views women as lovers, wives, and mothers rather than as workers, is *almost* as responsible for women's position in society as capitalist economics is. She claimed that even if a Marxist revolution destroyed the family as an economic unit, it would not thereby make women men's equals *automatically.* Because of the ways in which patriarchal ideology has constructed men's and women's psyches, women would probably continue to remain subordinate to men until their minds and men's minds had been liberated from the idea that women are somehow less valuable than men.

Alison Jaggar.   Like Mitchell, Alison Jaggar provided a two-system explanation of women's oppression. But in the final analysis, instead of identifying capitalism as the primary cause of women's low status, she reserved this "honor" for patriarchy. Capitalism oppresses women as *workers,* but patriarchy oppresses women as *women,* an oppression that affects women's identity as well as activity. A woman is always a woman, even when she is not working. Rejecting the classical Marxist doctrine that a person has to participate directly in the capitalist relations of production to be considered truly alienated, Jaggar claimed, as did Foreman (see page 99), that all women, no matter their work role, are alienated in ways that men are not.[67]

Jaggar organized her discussion of women's alienation under the headings of sexuality, motherhood, and intellectuality. In the same way wageworkers may be alienated from the product(s) on which they work, women, viewed simply as women, may be alienated from the "product(s)" on which they typically work—their bodies. Women may insist that they diet, exercise, and dress only to please themselves, but in reality they most likely shape and adorn their flesh primarily for the pleasure of men. Moreover, women do not have final or total say about when, where, how, or by whom their bodies will be used, because their bodies can be suddenly appropriated from them through acts ranging from the "male gaze" to sexual harassment to rape. Likewise, to the same degree that wageworkers can be gradually alienated from themselves—their bodies beginning to feel like things, mere machines from which labor power is extracted—women can be gradually alienated from themselves. To the degree that women work on their bodies—shaving their underarms, slimming their thighs and augmenting their breasts, painting their nails and coloring their hair—they may start to experience their bodies as objects or commodities. Finally, just as many wageworkers are in competition with one another for their employers' approbation and rewards, many women are in competition with one another for men's approbation and reward.[68]

Motherhood, continued Jaggar, may also be an alienating experience for women, especially when mostly or exclusively men decide the policies and laws that regulate women's reproductive choices. For example, in societies that use children's labor power nearly as much as adults' labor power, women may be pressured to bear as many children as physically possible. In contrast, in societies that view children as an economic burden for parents to support, women may be discouraged from having large families. Indeed, women may be pressured or even forced to use contraception, be sterilized, or have an abortion.[69]

In the same way that women may be alienated from the *product* of their reproductive labor, said Jaggar, women may be alienated from the *process* of their reproductive labor. Obstetricians may try to take control of the birthing process, performing medically unnecessary cesarean sections or anesthetizing women about to deliver against their wishes. Moreover, as the new reproductive technologies develop, an increasing number of women may be alienated from both the product and the process of reproduction in even more dramatic ways. For instance, in vitro fertilization makes possible gestational surrogacy. With this technology, a woman can have one or more of her eggs surgically removed, fertilized in vitro with her partner's sperm, and then transferred into the womb of another woman for gestation. The woman who gestates the child contracts to return the child to the couple for rearing. Raising the same type of concerns that some radical-cultural feminists raised about gestational surrogacy, Jaggar claimed that such arrangements do not do full justice to the gestational mother in particular. By virtue of her reproductive work, the embryo is shaped into a viable human infant to which she may be emotionally as well as physically bonded. Should not this circumstance give her some parental claim to the child, even though she did not provide the "raw material," the egg, for the child?[70]

Child-rearing, like childbearing, may also be an alienating experience for women when scientific experts (most of whom are men) take charge of it, stressed Jaggar.[71] As she saw it, the pressures on mothers are enormous because, with virtually no assistance, they are supposed to execute every edict issued by child-rearing authorities, some of whom have never experienced the daily demands of child rearing. Echoing the thoughts of Adrienne Rich in *Of Woman Born*, Jaggar explained how contemporary child-rearing practices may ultimately alienate or estrange mothers from their children: The extreme mutual dependence of mother and child encourages the mother to define the child primarily with reference to her own needs for meaning, love, and social recognition. She sees the child as her product, as something that should improve her life and that often instead stands against her, as something of supreme value, whose life is viewed as more important than hers by antiabortionists, for example. The social relations of contemporary motherhood often make it impossible for her to see the child as part of a larger community to which both the child and she belong.[72]

One of the saddest features of a mother's possible alienation from her children, then, is that her inability to see her children as persons may be matched only by their inability to see her as a person. Alluding to Dorothy Dinnerstein and some other psychoanalytic feminists, Jaggar described how some children turn on their mother, blaming her for everything that goes wrong in their lives: "I'm a failure because you, my mother, loved me too much/too little." In addition to separating mothers from their children, the conditions of contemporary motherhood can drive wedges between mothers and fathers, said Jaggar. All too often, a domestic dispute begins with a father's laying down the law for the kids and a mother's defying its terms. Furthermore, the standards governing proper mothering sometimes impede the growth of genuine friendships between women, as mothers compete to rear the "perfect child"[73]—that is, the well-mannered, multitalented, physically attractive, achievement-oriented boy or girl whose photograph appears on every other page of the yearbook.

Finally, said Jaggar, not only may many women be alienated from their own sexuality and from the product and process of motherhood, but they may also be alienated from their own intellectual capacities. Many women feel so unsure of themselves that they hesitate to express their ideas in public, for fear their thoughts are not worth expressing; they remain silent when they should loudly voice their opinion. Worse, when women do express their thoughts forcefully and with passion, their ideas are often rejected as irrational or the product of mere emotion. To the extent men set the terms of thought and discourse, suggested Jaggar, women cannot be at ease in the world of theory.[74]

Jaggar concluded that although the overthrow of capitalism might end women's as well as men's exploitation in the productive workforce, it would not end women's alienation from everything and everyone, especially themselves.[75] Only the overthrow of patriarchy would enable women to become full persons.

Interactive-System Explanations of Women's Oppression

In contrast to two-system explanations, which, as we have just noted, tended to identify either class or sex as the primary source of women's oppression, interactive-system explanations strove to present capitalism and patriarchy as two co-equal partners colluding in a variety of ways to oppress women. Interactive-system thinkers included Iris Marion Young, Heidi Hartmann, and Sylvia Walby. To a greater or lesser extent, these contemporary socialist feminists used such terms as "capitalist patriarchy" or "patriarchal capitalism" in their work. Trying hard never to view one system as more fundamental than another to women's oppression, these feminists wanted to stress the interdependency of capitalism and patriarchy.

Iris Marion Young.   According to Iris Marion Young, as long as classical Marxist feminists try to use class as their central category of analysis, they will not be able to explain why women in socialist countries are often just as oppressed as women in capitalist countries. Precisely because class is a gender-blind category, said Young, it cannot provide an adequate explanation for women's specific oppression. Only a gender-sighted category such as the "sexual division of labor" has the conceptual power to do this.

Young reasoned that whereas class analysis looks at the system of production as a whole, focusing on the means and relations of production in the most general terms possible, a sexual division-of-labor analysis pays attention to the characteristics of the individual people who do the producing in society. In other words, a class analysis calls only for a general discussion of the respective roles of the bourgeoisie and the proletariat, whereas a sexual division-of-labor analysis requires a detailed discussion of who gives the orders and who takes them, who does the stimulating work and who does the drudge work, who works more hours and who works less hours, and who gets paid relatively high wages and who gets paid relatively low wages. Therefore, as compared with a class analysis, a sexual division-of-labor analysis can better explain why women usually take the orders, do the drudge jobs, work part-time, and get paid relatively low wages, whereas men usually give the orders, do the stimulating jobs, work full-time, and get paid relatively high wages.

Because she believed that capitalism and patriarchy are necessarily linked, Young insisted that a sexual division-of-labor analysis is a total substitute for, not a mere supplement to, class analysis. We do not need one theory (Marxism) to explain *gender-neutral capitalism* and another theory (feminism) to explain *gender-biased patriarchy,* said Young. Rather, we need a single theory—a socialist feminist theory—able to explain *gender-biased* (i.e., *patriarchal*) *capitalism.* *"My thesis,"* wrote Young, *"is that marginalization of women and thereby our functioning as a secondary labor force is an essential and fundamental characteristic of capitalism."*[76]

Young's thesis is a controversial one, a major departure from the more traditional Marxist view that workers, be they male or female, are interchangeable. She argued that capitalism is very much aware of its workers' gender and, I may add, race and ethnicity. Because a large reserve of unemployed workers is necessary to keep wages low and to meet unanticipated demands for increased supplies of goods and services, capitalism has both implicit and explicit criteria for determining who will constitute its primary, employed workforce and who will act as its secondary, unemployed workforce. For a variety of reasons, not the least being a well-entrenched gender division of labor, capitalism's criteria identify men as "primary" workforce material and women as "secondary." Because women are needed at home in a way men are not—or so *patriarchy* believes—men are freer to work outside the home than women are.

Under capitalism as it exists today, women experience patriarchy as unequal wages for equal work, sexual harassment on the job, uncompensated domestic work, and the pernicious dynamics of the public-private split. Earlier generations of women also experienced patriarchy, but they lived it differently, depending on the dynamics of the reigning economic system. As with class society, reasoned Young, patriarchy should not be considered a system *separate* from capitalism just because it existed *first*. In fact, class and gender structures are so intertwined that neither one actually precedes the other. A feudal system of gender relations accompanied a feudal system of class arrangements, and the social relations of class and gender grew up together and evolved over time into the forms we now know (e.g., the capitalist nuclear family). To say gender relations are independent of class relations is to ignore how history works.

Heidi Hartmann.   Reinforcing Young's analysis, Heidi Hartmann noted that a strict class analysis leaves largely unexplained why women rather than men play the subordinate and submissive roles in both the workplace and the home. To understand not only workers' relation to capital but also women's relation to men, said Hartmann, a feminist analysis of patriarchy must be integrated with a Marxist analysis of capitalism. In her estimation, the partnership between patriarchy and capitalism is complex because patriarchy's interests in women are not always the same as capitalism's interests in women. In the nineteenth century, for example, proletarian men wanted proletarian women to stay at home, where women could "personally service" men.[77] In contrast, bourgeois men wanted proletarian women to work for next to nothing in the productive workforce. The bourgeoisie presented this option to proletarian women as an opportunity to earn "pin money" to supplement their men's puny take-home pay. Only if all men—be they proletarian or bourgeoisie—could find some mutually agreeable way to handle this particular "woman question" could the interests of patriarchy and capitalism be harmonized.

    To some degree, this harmony was achieved when bourgeois men agreed to pay proletarian men a family wage large enough to permit them to keep their wives and children at home, said Hartmann. Bourgeois men struck this bargain with proletarian men because the bourgeois men decided that, all things considered, (1) stay-at-home housewives would produce and maintain healthier, happier, and therefore more productive male workers than working wives would, and (2) women and children could always be persuaded at a later date to enter the workforce for low wages should male workers demand high wages. For a time, this arrangement worked well enough, but over time, the size of the family wage shrank and many proletarian men could no longer pay all their family's bills. Consequently, many proletarian women decided to enter the workforce not to earn "pin money," but to earn enough money to help their male partners support the family's true living costs.[78] Regrettably, these women typically came home to male partners who had little or no interest in helping with domestic work. Hartmann concluded that women were in a no-win situation when it came to work-related issues. Everywhere women turned, the sexual division of labor disadvantaged them. The only possible hope for women was to fight capitalism and patriarchy simultaneously. These two systems are simply two heads of the same beast: capitalist patriarchy.

Women's Labor Issues

The preceding discussion suggests that the distinctions some socialist feminists make between two-system explanations and interactive-system explanations for women's oppression are somewhat forced and probably of more theoretical than practical interest to the average woman. Yet the relevance of contemporary socialist feminism's overall message for women cannot be overstated. Worldwide, women's oppression is strongly related to the fact that women's work, be it at home or outside the home, is still unpaid, underpaid, or disvalued, a state of affairs that largely explains women's lower status and power nearly everywhere.

Although much more could be said about women's domestic work than we have discussed, suffice it to say that according to a 2010 United Nations Development Programme (UNDP), "The omission of unpaid care work from national accounts leads to sizeable undercounts in all countries. By applying the wage rate of a general household worker to the number of hours that people spend on housework, the United Nations Research Institute for Social Development estimates that the omissions equal 10 to 39 percent of GDP. Incorporating unpaid work in national accounts would better reflect the realities of time use, especially for women."[79] Whether they live in developing or developed nations, socialist or capitalist nations, women still do the majority of unpaid work in the home, even when they also do full-time or part-time paid work outside the home. At present, US women do 25.9 hours of domestic work a week, whereas US men do 16.8 hours of domestic work a week. Moreover, US women do 3.9 hours of childcare a week, whereas US men do 1.8 hours of childcare a week. When these hours are added to US working women's 40-hour-a-week shift, it seems clear that women are working nearly a "double day." Add to this workload the amount of hours women caring for elderly relatives expend, typically 21.9 hours a week, and one begins to wonder for how long women can keep up this kind of pace.[80]

Although contemporary socialist feminists continue to bemoan the fact that women do too much work for free in the home, they have increasingly turned their attention to how little women are paid for the work they do outside the home. In particular, contemporary socialist feminists have focused on the gender pay gap and the often oppressive nature of women's work in the so-called global factory. To ignore these issues in this chapter would be to play into the unfortunate impression that just because "communism" has failed, and the former Soviet Union has been dismantled, all types of Marxist and socialist feminism are no longer needed. On the contrary, said Nancy Holmstrom:

> Today, the socialist feminist project is more pressing than ever. . . . The brutal economic realities of globalization impact everyone across the globe—but women are affected disproportionately. Displaced by economic changes, women bear a greater burden of labor throughout the world as social services have been cut, whether in response to structural adjustment plans in the third world or to so-called welfare reform in the United States. Women have been forced to migrate, are subject to trafficking, and are the proletarians of the newly industrializing countries. On top of all this they continue to be subject to sexual violence and in much of the world are not allowed to control their own processes of reproduction. How should we understand these phenomena and, more importantly, how do we go about changing them? Feminist theory that is lost in theoretical abstractions or that depreciates economic realities will be useless for this purpose. Feminism that speaks of women's oppression and its injustice but fails to address capitalism will be of little help in ending women's oppression. . . . Socialist feminism is the approach with the greatest capacity to illuminate the exploitation and oppression of most of the women of the world.[81]

Gender Pay Gap

Most, though not all, nations have a gender pay gap, in the estimation of Shawn Meghan Burn. Japan has a particularly egregious one. In 2011, Japanese women between the ages of thirty and thirty-four earn only 69 percent of Japanese men's wages.[82] Interestingly, the situation is dramatically different in Sweden, where women earn approximately 83 percent of men's wages.[83] In the United States, women earned 81 percent of men's wages in 2010. On average, women's median weekly wages in 2010 totaled $669 compared to men's median earnings of $824.[84] There is, however, data to support the claim that US women's most recent wage gains are in some measure the result of US men's wage losses.[85]

Some of the most frequently cited reasons for the gender pay gap are (1) the concentration of women in low-paying, female-dominated jobs; (2) the high percentage of women who work part-time rather than full-time; and (3) outright wage discrimination against women. Worldwide, women tend to engage in service work (teaching, nursing, childcare, eldercare), clerical work, agricultural work (picking fruit), and light industrial work (producing clothes, shoes, toys, and electronic devices), while men tend to engage in heavy industrial work, transportation work, management, administration, and policy work.[86]

Although US women have gained some access to high-paying, male-dominated jobs like legal occupations in recent years, their numbers in these occupations remain relatively small. A 2011 report from the US Bureau of Labor Statistics, for example, shows that only 31.9 percent of lawyers are women.[87] Also worrisome is that despite a significant increase in the number of women in such major professions as business and health care, women in these professions continue to hit the "glass ceiling," that is, "the invisible but effective barrier which prevents women from moving beyond a certain point on the promotion ladder."[88] For example, in the United States, women chief executive officers, especially in the Fortune 500 companies, are relatively few. An October 2011 *USA Today* article touted the "record high" eighteen female CEOs scheduled to run Fortune 500 companies by January 2012.[89] However, the number of women in less lucrative and prestigious jobs, such as human resources and accounting, are legion.[90] Similarly, it is no accident that just 33.8 percent of physicians and surgeons are female.[91] Nor is it an accident that female registered nurses comprise 91.1 percent of the total number of nurses in the United States.[92] Another notable statistic, once again related to the area of legal services, reveals that US women are more likely to be paralegals than are US men. Indeed, in the United States, women make up 84.3 percent of all paralegals and legal assistants.[93] Add to all these statistics the fact that men make up 75 percent of those occupied in computer and mathematical occupations, and over 94 percent of all mechanical engineers,[94] and one must conclude that women's presence in high-paying, high-status occupations and professions in the United States remains limited.

Beyond US women's relative lack of presence in certain high-paying jobs,[95] another explanation for the gender pay gap is women's tendency to limit the time they devote to work in the productive workforce. Far more women than men work part-time,[96] and far more women than men leave the productive workforce for months or even years to tend to family matters.[97] Thus, over time, women earn less than men, simply because women work fewer hours and years than men typically do.

As tempting as it may be to explain part of the current gender pay gap in terms of women's decision to work less hours or years in the paid workforce, this explanation does not address the question contemporary socialist feminists have since forcefully ask: Namely, *why* is it that *women* limit their paid work outside the home in ways that men do not? Is it because women do not want to work long hours outside the home? Or is it because women view the money they earn as luxury money they can forsake? Or is it because women think it is their responsibility rather than men's to take time off work to rear their children properly or to take care of their sick relatives and aging parents, or to do both?

One of the most disturbing aspects of the gender pay gap is that even when women work full-time, stay in the workforce, and do the same jobs that men do, women's wages often lag behind men's.[98] Clearly, this state of affairs requires not only a "capitalist" explanation (women are paid less because their wages are viewed as secondary wages), but also a "patriarchal" explanation: Women are paid less simply because they are *women*, a very disturbing thought to say the least.

when full time

In addition to not answering the question why women, rather than men, limit their time in the workforce, the human-capital approach does not explain why many employers prefer to hire women as part-timers. Could it be that female part-time workers, who, by the way, are usually not entitled to employer-paid benefit packages, can be easily motivated to work longer hours than they should? Acculturated to help out in a pinch, women who work part-time may work longer and harder than their contract specifies, simply because they do not want to let other people down.

women do more P2-time bc more motivated

Feminist solutions to the gender pay gap are various, depending on which aspects of the gap are put under the microscope or require the most attention. Liberal feminists prefer the remedy of equal pay for equal work. They invoke legislation such as the US 1963 Equal Pay Act, which mandates that women's pay should be equal to men's when their positions are equal.[99] Although the Equal Pay Act sounds like an ideal tool for US women to use, it may not be. Equal Pay Act civil suits put the burden of proof on the shoulders of the plaintiff. She has to prove that her work position is the same as that of a comparable male employee. Such proof might be relatively easy to secure in some lines of work such as mail carrier or flight attendant, but it is far harder to secure in a profession such as law, where different labels such as "associate," "assistant," and "partner" can be used to make two virtually identical positions sound quite different.[100] Moreover, the usefulness of the Equal Pay Act as a reference point for gender-based civil suits seems predicated on women's gaining access to slots in male-dominated jobs or professions. The act does little, if anything, to question the sexual division of labor per se, that is, to question why the kind of work men typically do tends to be valued more than the kind of work women typically do.

Viewing liberal feminists' preference for an equal-pay-for-equal-work remedy for the gender pay gap as a capitulation to the view that women have to be like men (in this instance, work like men) to be valued like men, many contemporary socialist feminists have joined with many radical-cultural feminists to endorse a comparable-worth remedy for the gender pay gap. As they see it, a comparable-worth remedy for the gender pay gap is an opportunity not only to secure better wages for women but also to force society to reconsider why it pays some people so much; and others, so little.[101]

Many social scientists are convinced that as long as women remain in traditionally female-dominated jobs and, more significantly, as long as society continues to assign less value to female-dominated jobs than to male-dominated jobs, the gender pay gap is likely to persist. We need to ask ourselves why in 2011 in the United States, social workers—over 80 percent of which were female—earned $798 weekly,[102] whereas construction managers, 93 percent of which were male, earned $1,325 weekly.[103] Do such pay differentials exist because supervising homebuilders is so much more physically, psychologically, and intellectually demanding than is counseling troubled people? Or do they exist simply because most construction managers are men and most social workers are women?

Convinced that gender considerations factor into how much or how little workers are paid, comparable-worth advocates demand that employers evaluate their employees *objectively* by assigning "worth points" to the four components found in most jobs: (1) "knowledge and skills," or the total amount of information or dexterity needed to perform the job; (2) "mental demands," or the extent to which the job requires decision making; (3) "accountability," or the amount of supervision the job entails; and (4) "working conditions," such as how physically safe the job is.[104] When Norman D. Willis and Associates used this index to establish the worth points for various jobs performed in the state of Washington in the 1980s, they found the following disparities: "A Food Service I, at 93 points, earned an average salary of $472 per month, while a Delivery Truck Driver I, at 94 points, earned $792; a Clerical Supervisor III, at 305 points, earned an average of $794. A Nurse Practitioner II, at 385 points, had average earnings of $832, the same as those of a Boiler Operator, with only 144 points. A Homemaker I, with 198 points and an average salary of $462, had the lowest earnings of all evaluated jobs."[105] After reflecting on the Willis and Associates study, a federal court judge in Tacoma ruled that the state was in violation of Title VII of the 1964 Civil Rights Act, which prohibits discrimination by type of employment and level of compensation, and should eliminate pay gaps within its systems.[106]

On the average, contemporary socialist feminists support a comparable-worth approach to further reducing the gender wage pay gap, for two reasons—one having to do with addressing the feminization of poverty, and the other with addressing the valuation of different kinds of work. Because 41 percent of all births occur by poor single women[107] and because women are the primary recipients of food stamps, legal aid, and Medicaid, if wage-earning women in female-dominated jobs were paid what their jobs are worth, these women might be able to support themselves and their families adequately without being forced, in one way or another, to attach themselves to men as a source of desperately needed income. In addition to seeing comparable worth as a way to alleviate women's poverty, contemporary socialist feminists see it as a way to highlight the arbitrariness of societal determinations about what kind of work counts as "worthy" work. According to Teresa Amott and Julie Matthaei, for example, we need to ask ourselves questions such as the following one:

> Why should those whose jobs give them the most opportunity to develop and use their abilities also be paid the most? The traditional argument—that higher pay must be offered as an incentive for workers to gain skills and training—is contradicted by the fact that our highly paid jobs attract many more workers than employers demand. And given unequal access to education and training, a hierarchical pay scheme becomes a mechanism for the intergenerational transmission of wealth privilege, with its historically-linked racism, sexism, and classism.[108]

Clearly, the comparable-worth remedy for the gender pay gap has more potential to destabilize capitalist forces than does the equal-pay-for-equal-work remedy for the gender pay gap. The question is whether consumerism writ large has made it all too difficult for a sufficient number of people to challenge the status quo.

Women's Work in the Global Market

In recent years, contemporary socialist feminists have sought to move beyond analyzing the gender pay gap in developed nations to discussing the working conditions of women in developing nations. The forces of so-called globalization—described by the World Bank as the "growing integration of economies and societies around the world"[109]—have resulted in the creation of very large, profit-driven multinational corporations. Most of these multinationals have as their point of origin one or more developed nations and as their point of destination one or more developing nations. Interestingly, multinationals in developing nations prefer to hire women not only because so many women need work but also because their manual dexterity and docility make them ideal sweatshop workers.

To better understand how much profit, say, a US multinational may make by moving its plants to a developing nation, we need read only some late 1990s statistics compiled by Shawn Meghan Burn:

The *maquiladoras* of Mexico's border towns are but one example of women in the global factory. There, over 2,000 multinational corporations have drawn over a half million workers, two-thirds of them women, who get paid between $3.75 and $4.50 a day. In El Salvador, women employees of the Taiwanese *maquilador* Mandarin are forced to work shifts of 12 to 21 hours during which they are seldom allowed bathroom breaks; they are paid about 18 cents per shirt, which is later sold for $20 each. Mandarin makes clothes for the Gap, J. Crew, and Eddie Bauer.

In Haiti, women sewing clothing at Disney's contract plants are paid 6 cents for every $19.99 *101 Dalmatians* outfit they sew; they make 33 cents an hour. Meanwhile, Disney makes record profits and could easily pay workers a living wage for less than one half of 1 percent of the sales price of one outfit. In Vietnam, 90 percent of Nike's workers are females between the ages of 15 and 28. Nike's labor for a pair of basketball shoes (which retail for $149.50) costs Nike $1.50, 1 percent of the retail price.[110]

The executives of US multinationals defend such low wages on the grounds that the wages are higher than those the workers would otherwise receive. Another argument is that the wages the multinationals pay are, at least, a living wage—that is, a wage sufficient to meet the subsistence needs of a family. But such claims, particularly the second one, are not always true. Other statistics compiled by Burn revealed, for example, that in the 1990s, Nicaraguan sweatshop workers earned in the range of $55 to $75 a month—less than half of the $165 a month their families needed to meet their most basic needs.[111] To be sure, some multinationals do pay their workers—female and male—living wages, but such multinationals seem to be more the exception rather than the rule.

Disturbed by the situation just described, contemporary socialist feminists have recently taken a lead in trying to improve not only pay but working conditions in sweatshops. Some of the strategies they have used involve the unionization of workers (even more difficult to achieve in today's developing nations than it was in the early days of union organizing in the United States) and consumer boycotts of sweatshop imports.[112]

Another phenomenon that concerns not only contemporary socialist feminists, but also other "brands" of feminists is the number of women who migrate from poor nations to do care work in rich nations. Specifically, rich nations are increasingly in need of people to provide them with "affordable" eldercare work. For example, in the United States, most eldercare workers who do home-based care are either native-born women of color or female migrant workers from all over the world. Interestingly, Ron Hoppe, a founder of WorldWide HealthStaff Associates, points out that Americans are not much interested in working for his company, which cannot pay its workers any more than fast-food businesses do. Most of the people, continues Hoppe, who seem willing to work for him are migrants, many of who come from caring [sic] cultures and all of whom are accustomed to work long hours for less money than Americans are.[113]

Relying on migrant women to do low-paid care work seems to be the order of the day, all things considered. No matter how poor a nation is, if there is a nation poorer than it, then that nation may be a source for female caregivers willing to work for very low wages. Not surprisingly, nations high up on the economic ladder see little or no reason not to rely on poor nations to supply them with care workers. For example, in the United Kingdom, 35 percent of the nurses who work in the eldercare environment are migrants and most of them work for low wages. In London, more than 60 percent of the people who do eldercare work are migrants.[114] These workers are nearly exclusively women, and they come from Zimbabwe, Poland, Nigeria, the Philippines, and India. Their employers like their "work ethic" and their "warmth, respect, empathy, trust, and patience in the care relationship."[115] They also like the fact that they are willing to work for wages that native-born eldercare workers find outrageously low.

As in the United Kingdom, in Taiwan there is an exceptionally high demand for migrant care workers. Since the early 1980s, significant numbers of undocumented migrant women have worked in Taiwanese households[116] thereby enabling Taiwanese women in the paid workforce to keep their jobs. Comments Pei-Chia Lan, "The filial duty of serving aging parents is transferred first from the son to the daughter-in-law (a gender transfer); later, it is outsourced to migrant care workers (a market transfer)."[117] As a result of citizens' pressure, the Taiwanese government has decided to document large numbers of migrant care workers. Specifically, in 1992, Taiwan started to grant work permits to "domestic caretakers" who agreed to care for severely ill or disabled people, children under the age of twelve, or elders over the age of seventy.[118] Moreover, it began to describe the importation of care workers from the Philippines and Indonesia in particular "as a solution to the growing demand for paid care work among both nuclear households and the aging population."[119]

In addition to taking advantage of female migrant care workers' willingness to work for low wages, rich nations often fail to acknowledge the deficits of care they are creating in poor nations. Families of female migrant care workers experience a loss in care for them. Women leave their children and/or their elderly parents behind, to be cared for in makeshift ways. They do this to send handsome remittances back home so that their families can gradually have a better quality of life.[120] But we must ask whether it is really fair to de-is it fair?

prive these families of their main caregivers so that people in advantaged nations can live a comfortable life in an intact family. We must also ask whether it is fair, for example, for rich nations to drain poor nations of their professional caregivers—their doctors and nurses—so that they (the people in rich nations) have ample care. Rich nations are notorious for poaching poor nations' physicians and nurses, so much so that they threaten to weaken the fragile health-care systems of some of the nations from whom they poach.[121]

Critiques of Marxist and Socialist Feminism

Given women's distinctly unprivileged position in the workplace, it is somewhat difficult to understand why, beginning in the 1970s, many feminists, including some Marxist feminists, abandoned *materialist* explanations of women's oppression. They turned instead to *psychological* explanations for women's oppression, explanations that could answer the question why women's status remains low irrespective of the political and economic character of the society in which they live. For example, the same Juliet Mitchell who wrote *Woman's Estate* in 1971 wrote *Psychoanalysis and Feminism* several years later.[122] In the later book, Mitchell claimed that the causes of women's oppression are ultimately buried deep in the human psyche.

Mitchell rejected liberal feminists' claim that social reforms aimed at giving women more educational and occupational opportunities will make women men's equals. Women's suffrage, coeducational studies, and affirmative action policies might change the way "femininity" is expressed, but these practices could not, in her view, significantly change the overall status of women. Likewise, Mitchell rejected the claim of radical-cultural feminists that reproductive technology is the key to women's liberation, because, as she saw it, a purely biological solution cannot resolve an essentially psychological problem. Finally, Mitchell rejected the claim of classic Marxist feminists that an economic revolution aimed at overthrowing capitalism will make men and women full partners. Just because women enter the productive workforce to labor side by side with men does not mean women will return home in the evening arm in arm with men. Mitchell observed that even Mao Zedong admitted that "despite collective work, egalitarian legislation, social care of children, etc., it was too soon for the Chinese really, deeply and irrevocably to have changed their *attitudes* towards women."[123] As Mitchell saw it, attitudes toward women will never really change as long as both female and male psychology are dominated by the phallic symbol. Thus, patriarchy and capitalism must be overthrown if society is to be truly humanized.[124]

Interestingly, the publication of *Psychoanalysis and Feminism* coincided with the first few issues of *m/f,* a journal devoted to questioning the bipolar opposition between masculinity and femininity. Launched in 1978, the first editorial of this British journal provided a strong statement of both dissatis-faction with classical Marxist models and the move toward cultural analysis. The editors placed themselves firmly within Marxism, expressing a wish to engage with class politics, but were explicitly critical of *materialist* explana-tions of women's oppression. Psychoanalysis was seen by the editors as essen-tial to an understanding of gendered subjectivity. So, too, was discourse, the language used to interpret women's identity and activity. Their next editorial questioned the very category "women," suggesting that there is no unity to "women," or to "women's oppression," and that differing discourses simply constructed varying definitions of "women."[125] Thus began the deconstruc-tion of "women" and the ascendancy of postmodern feminism, a type of fem-inism we will consider in Chapter 5.

Conclusion

As understandable as it was for many feminists to look under materialist sur-faces to find deeper cultural explanations for women's oppression, it was probably a mistake for them to reject materialist explanations outright. Stevi Jackson recently made a plea for a return to materialism—a plea that may rescue contemporary socialist feminism from undeserved neglect:

> A materialist analysis is as relevant now as it ever was. While accepting that traditional Marxists had little to say about gender divisions, that one theory cannot explain the whole of human life, the method of analysis Marx left us remains useful. There are good reasons why materialist per-spectives remain necessary to grapple with the complexities of a postcolo-nial world, with the intersections of gender, ethnicity, and nationality. It seems evident that the material foundations and consequences of institu-tionalized racism, the heritage of centuries of slavery, colonialism and im-perialism and the continued international division of labour are at least as important as culturally constituted difference. We live our lives now within a global system characterised by extremely stark material inequali-ties. Even within Western nations the material oppression suffered by women has not gone away, and for many women the situation is worsen-ing as a result of unemployment and cuts in welfare provision. Inter-sections between class, gender, and racism are clearly important here, too, and need to be pursued in terms of structural patterning of inequality as well as multilayered identities. The continued vitality of approaches which deal with such inequalities is crucial for feminist politics and theory.[126]

However exciting it may be for contemporary socialist feminists to probe women's psyche from time to time, the fundamental goal of these feminists still remains constant: to encourage women everywhere to unite in whatever ways they can to oppose structures of oppression, inequality, and injustice.

Questions for Discussion

1. Discuss some tangible examples of ways in which human beings "create themselves" through collective production. How does the capitalist mode of production impact women's historical and modern experiences?
2. In the Marxist sense, do you believe women constitute a class? Weigh the similarities and differences between bourgeois and proletarian women. Consider the benefits and drawbacks of viewing all women as belonging to a single class.
3. Explain the four Marxist forms of alienation. How are women alienated? Examine forms of alienation involving women's self-concept, relationships, careers, and political representation.
4. What were the concerns raised by women laborers post–Communist Revolution? What were the concerns of those women involved with the wages-for-housework campaign? How were the difficulties with implementing material solutions to their issues complementary?
5. Compare and contrast two-system explanations of women's oppression with interactive-system explanations. Do you feel one theory is more advantageous than the other? Why or why not?
6. Speculate on the sexual division of labor. Why do you think male-dominated careers tend to be valued more (monetarily, and arguably socially) than female-dominated careers? Could the "worth point" system resolve such disparities, or is such a system still subjective? In what other ways might arbitrary valuation of work be mediated?

4

Psychoanalytic and Care-Focused Feminism

Liberal, radical (libertarian and cultural), and Marxist/socialist feminists offer us explanations and solutions for women's oppression that are rooted either in society's political and economic structures or in human beings' sexual and reproductive relationships, roles, and practices. Liberal feminists claim that providing women with the same rights and opportunities men enjoy may be enough to eliminate gender inequity. Radical feminists think otherwise. They insist that if gender equity is our goal, we must first examine men's and women's sexual and reproductive rights and responsibilities. Only then will we understand fully why systems that foster male domination and female subordination are so persistent and prevalent. Radical-libertarian feminists claim that women need to be liberated not only from the burdens of natural reproduction and biological motherhood but also from the restrictions of a sexual double standard that gives men sexual freedoms women are typically denied. Radical-cultural feminists disagree. They claim that the source of women's power is rooted in women's unique reproductive role. All children are born of women; without women, *no* children would be born. Radical-cultural feminists also stress that male sexual behavior is not worthy of women's emulation, because men frequently use sex as an instrument of control and domination rather than of love and bonding. Finally, Marxist and socialist feminists hypothesize that unless capitalist economic structures are destroyed, people will continue to be divided into two oppositional classes—the haves and the have-nots—with women, more than men, finding themselves in the ranks of the have-nots.

In contrast to liberal, radical (libertarian and cultural), and Marxist/socialist feminists, psychoanalytic and care-focused feminists maintain that the fundamental explanation for women's way of acting is rooted deep in women's psyche, specifically, in women's way of thinking about themselves as women. Relying on Freudian constructs such as the pre-Oedipal stage and the Oedipal stage (discussed on pages 131–150) and/or on Lacanian constructs, such as the Symbolic order (discussed on pages 143–145), psychoanalytic feminists claim that gender identity, and hence gender inequity, is rooted in a series of infantile and early childhood experiences. These experiences, most of which are accessible to us only through psychoanalysis, are, in the estimation of psychoanalytic feminists, the cause of individuals' viewing themselves in masculine or feminine terms, of thinking of themselves as boys or girls. Moreover, these same experiences are the cause of society's privileging things "masculine" over things "feminine." Hypothesizing that in a nonpatriarchal society, masculinity and femininity would be both differently constructed and valued, psychoanalytic feminists recommend that we work toward such a society by altering our early infantile childhood experiences or, more radically, by transforming the linguistic structures that cause us to think of ourselves as men or women.

Related in several ways to psychoanalytic feminists are many care-focused feminists. However, unlike psychoanalytic feminists who focus on pre-Oedipal and Oedipal themes, care-focused feminists closely examine the virtues and values associated with femininity and especially mothering/parenting. Although care-focused feminists, as well as psychoanalytic feminists, probe women's psyches, care-focused feminists, such as Carol Gilligan, Nel Noddings, Virginia Held, and Eva Kittay, also pursue the relationship between women's and men's psychology and morality. They ask whether feminine caring or masculine justice is the best path to human goodness and whether the key to all human beings' liberation is to embrace the values and virtues traditionally associated with women.

Psychoanalytic Feminism: Focus on Freud

By no means was Sigmund Freud a feminist, yet psychoanalytic feminists have found in his writings clues about how to better understand the causes and consequences of women's oppression. Freud's theories about psychosexual development disturbed his late-nineteenth-century Viennese contemporaries not so much because he addressed traditionally taboo topics (e.g., homosexuality, sadism, masochism, and oral and anal sex), but because he theorized that all sexual "aberrations," "variations," and "perversions" are simply stages in the development of *normal* human sexuality.[1] According to Freud, children go through distinct psychosexual developmental stages, and their gender identity as adults is the result of how well or badly they have weathered this process.

Masculinity and femininity are, in other words, the product of sexual matura-
tion. If boys develop "normally" (i.e., typically), they will end up as men who
display expected masculine traits; if women develop "normally," they will end
up as women who display expected feminine traits.

The theoretical bases for Freud's views on the relationship between sex
and gender are found in *Three Contributions to the Theory of Sexuality*. In this
work, Freud laid out his theory of psychosexual development in detail. Because adults in Freud's time equated sexual activity with reproductive genital
sexuality (heterosexual intercourse), adults thought children were sexless.
Dismissing this view of children's sexualities as naive, Freud argued that far
from being without sexual interests, children engage in all sorts of sexual behavior. He claimed that children's sexuality is "polymorphous perverse"—
that insofar as the infant is concerned, her or his entire body, especially its
orifices and appendages, is sexual terrain. The infant moves from this type of
"perverse" sexuality to "normal" heterosexual genital sexuality by passing
through several stages. During the *oral* stage, the infant receives pleasure
from sucking her or his mother's breast or her or his own thumb. During the
anal stage, the two- or three-year-old child enjoys the sensations associated
with controlling the expulsion of her or his feces. During the *phallic* stage,
the three- or four-year-old child discovers that the genitals are a source of
pleasure, and either resolves or fails to resolve the so-called Oedipus complex. Around age six, the child ceases to display overt sexuality and begins a
period of latency that ends at around puberty, when the young person enters
the *genital* stage characterized by a resurgence of sexual impulses. If all goes
normally during this stage, the young person's libido (defined by Freud as
undifferentiated sexual energy) will be directed outward, away from autoerotic and homoerotic stimulation and toward a member of the opposite sex.

Freud stressed that the critical moment in the psychosexual drama here described occurs when the child tries to successfully resolve the Oedipus complex. He claimed that the fact that only boys have penises fundamentally
affects the way in which boys and girls undergo psychosexual development.
The boy's Oedipus complex stems from his natural attachment to his mother,
for it is she who nurtures him. Because of the boy's feelings toward his
mother, he wants to possess her—to have sexual intercourse with her—and to
kill his father, the rival for his mother's attentions. Freud added, however, that
the boy's hatred of his father is modulated by his coexisting love for his father.
Because the boy wants his father to love him, he competes with his mother for
his father's affections, experiencing increased antagonism toward her. Nevertheless, despite his increased antagonism toward his mother, the boy still
wishes to possess her and would attempt to take her from his father were it
not for his fear of being punished by his father. Supposedly, having seen either

his mother or some other female naked, the boy speculates that these creatures without penises must have been castrated, by his father, no less. Shaken by this thought, the boy fears his father will castrate him, too, should he dare to act on his desire for his mother. Therefore, the boy distances himself from his mother, a painful process that propels him into a period of sexual latency that will not surface again until the time of puberty.[2]

During the period of sexual latency, the boy begins to develop what Freud called a superego. To the degree the superego is the son's internalization of his father's values, it is a patriarchal, social conscience. The boy who successfully resolves the Oedipus complex develops a particularly strong superego. In the course of giving up mother love (albeit out of fear of castration), he learns how to defer to the authority of his father. The boy waits his turn for his own woman, temporarily subordinating his id (instincts) to his superego (the voice of social constraints). Were it not for the trauma of the Oedipus complex and his fear of castration, the boy would fail to mature into a man ready, willing, and able at the appropriate time to claim the torch of civilization from his father.

The female experience of the Oedipus complex is dramatically different from the male experience, in Freud's estimation. As Freud assumes is the case with boys, the girl's first love object is her mother. But unlike the typical boy, whose love object will supposedly remain a woman throughout his life, the typical girl has to switch from desiring a woman to desiring a man—at first her father and later, other men who take the place of the father. According to Freud, the transition from a female to a male love object begins when the girl realizes she does not have a penis, that she is castrated: "They [girls] notice the penis of a brother or playmate, strikingly visible and of large proportions, at once recognize it as the superior counterpart of their own small and inconspicuous organ (the clitoris), and from that time forward they fall a victim to envy for the penis."[3]

Supposedly preoccupied by her "deficiency," the girl somehow discovers her mother also lacks a penis. Distraught by the sight of her mother, the girl looks to her father to make good the deficiency she shares with her mother. She does not turn away from her mother without feeling an incredible sense of loss, however. Freud claimed that like any person who loses a love object, the girl will somehow try to become the abandoned love object. Thus, the girl tries to take her mother's place with her father. As a result, the girl comes to hate her mother not only because of her mother's supposedly inferior state of being but also because her mother is a rival for the father's affections. At first the girl desires to have her father's penis, but gradually she begins to desire something even more precious—a baby, which for her is the ultimate penis substitute.[4]

Freud theorized that it is much more difficult for the girl than the boy to achieve normal adult sexuality, precisely because the girl has to stop loving a woman (her mother)[5] and start loving a man (her father). This total switch in love object requires the girl to derive sexual pleasure from the "feminine" vagina instead of the "masculine" clitoris.[6] Freud further theorized that before the phallic stage, the girl has active sexual aims. Like the boy, she wants to take sexual possession of her mother, but with her clitoris. If the girl goes through the phallic stage successfully, said Freud, she will enter the stage of latency without this desire, and when genital sensitivity reappears at puberty, she will no longer long to use her clitoris actively. Instead, the girl will be content to use it passively for autoerotic masturbation or as a part of foreplay preparatory to heterosexual intercourse. But because the clitoris is not easy to desensitize, continued Freud, there is always the possibility the girl will either regress into the active clitoral stage (or arguably, become a lesbian) or, exhausted from suppressing her clitoris, give up on sexuality altogether.

The long-term negative consequences of penis envy and rejection of the mother go beyond possible frigidity for the girl. Freud thought the girl's difficult passage through the Oedipus complex scars her with several undesirable gender traits as she grows toward womanhood. First, she becomes *narcissistic* as she switches from active to passive sexual aims. Girls, said Freud, seek not so much to love as to be loved; the more beautiful a girl is, the more she expects and demands to be loved. Second, she becomes *vain*. As a compensation for her original lack of a penis, the girl focuses on her total physical appearance, as if her general "good looks" could somehow make up for her penile deficiency. Finally, the girl becomes a victim of an exaggerated sense of *shame*. It is, said Freud, not uncommon for girls to be so embarrassed by the sight of their "castrated" bodies that they insist on dressing and undressing under their bedsheets.[7]

As bad as female narcissism, vanity, and shame are, Freud suggested these character flaws in women are small in comparison to those that most account for women's inferiority as a sex. As discussed earlier, the boy's fear of castration enables him to resolve his Oedipus complex successfully, to submit himself fully to the father's law. In contrast, because the girl has no such fear—since she literally has nothing to lose—she moves through the Oedipus complex slowly, resisting the father's laws indefinitely.[8] That the girl is spared the threat of castration is, said Freud, a mixed blessing, for only by being pushed, albeit out of fear, to fully internalize the father's values can an individual develop a strong superego, which holds in check the animalistic urges of the id, the force that rules one's unconscious. As women remain resistant to the father's laws, women are supposedly less obedient than men to the civilizing forces of the superego. Ultimately, female moral inferiority is traceable to girls' lack of a penis. Because they do not have to worry about being castrated, girls are not nearly as motivated as boys supposedly are to become obedient rule followers whose "head" controls their "heart."

Feminist Critiques and Appropriations of Freud

Because penis envy and related ideas paint such an unflattering portrait of women, many feminists were and still are angered by traditional Freudian theory. In the 1970s, feminists with otherwise widely different agendas—for example, Betty Friedan,[9] Shulamith Firestone,[10] and Kate Millett[11]—made Freud a common target. They argued women's social position and powerlessness relative to men had little to do with female biology and much to do with the social construction of femininity. In contrast, other 1970s feminists, including Dorothy Dinnerstein and Nancy Chodorow, strove to reinterpret Freud's texts. Dinnerstein and Chodorow in particular maintained that by focusing less on the Oedipal stage and more on the pre-Oedipal stage of psychosexual development, they could provide a better account of sexuality and gender than Freud did. Many of society's views about women's inferiority and men's superiority, said Dinnerstein and Chodorow, are traceable to women's doing all or most of the mothering work in society. Were men to mother just as much as women do, boys and girls would grow up differently. They would realize that neither sex is inferior or superior to the other, and that both sexes merit equal respect.

Dorothy Dinnerstein: The Mermaid and the Minotaur

According to Dinnerstein, our culture's gender arrangements strongly influence how men and women conceive of themselves and each other, and the resulting portrait is not pretty. In it, women are depicted as "mermaids" and men as "minotaurs." Dinnerstein wrote, "The treacherous mermaid, seductive and impenetrable female representative of the dark and magic underwater world from which our life comes and in which we cannot live, lures voyagers to their doom. The fearsome minotaur, gigantic and eternally infantile offspring of a mother's unnatural lust, male representative of mindless, greedy power, insatiably devours live human flesh."[12]

Because Dinnerstein found this portrait ugly, she sought to explain why we continue to paint it over and over again, albeit in different hues. The answer to our pathological need to make monsters of ourselves is buried, she speculated, deep in our psychosexual development, in the pre-Oedipal stage. The infant's relationship with her or his mother is profoundly symbiotic because the infant is initially incapable of distinguishing between herself or himself and the mother. Because the maternal body is the infant's first encounter with the material or physical universe, the infant experiences the mother's body as a symbol of an unreliable and unpredictable universe. The mother is the source of pleasure but also of pain for the infant, who is never certain whether the mother will meet his or her physical and psychological needs. As a result, the infant grows up feeling very ambivalent toward mother figures (women) and what they represent (the material/physical universe, or nature).

Not wanting to reexperience utter dependence on an all-powerful force, men seek to control both women and nature, to exert power over them. Fearing the power of the mother within themselves, women concomitantly seek to be controlled by men. Men's need to control women and women's need to be controlled by men tragically leads, said Dinnerstein, to a *mis*shapen set of gender arrangements, which together constitute a paradigm for destructive human relations in general.

Dinnerstein pointed to men's greater sexual possessiveness as the first characteristic of currently skewed gender relationships. Men hope to overcome their past inability to totally control their mothers by trying to totally control their wives or girlfriends. Given men's intense desire to control women, when a woman is unfaithful to a man, the man feels the same despair he felt upon realizing his mother had a self separate from his own, a self whose will often conflicted with his. This refelt sense of despair, said Dinnerstein, explains men's violent reactions to their wives' or girlfriends' "infidelities," ranging from extramarital affairs with male lovers to pajama parties with female friends.

Curiously, although many women accept men's sexual possessiveness of women as some sort of right, women do not generally claim the same right for themselves. Dinnerstein explained this asymmetry as follows: Because a woman fears the power of the mother within herself, she is always in search of a man who can control her. But because a man does not represent "mother" to her in the way she represents "mother" to him, she needs him less than he needs her. No matter how deep the symbiosis she achieves with him, it will not equal the kind of symbiosis she had with her mother in the past or that she could have with another woman/mother now or in the future. Consequently, if a man leaves a woman, she will not feel the same intensity of grief she felt when her original mother left her.[13]

Muted female erotic impulsivity is the second mark of current gender arrangements, according to Dinnerstein. A muted female eroticism is one oriented exclusively toward male pleasure. Through sexual intercourse, the woman seeks to satisfy the man, and whatever pleasure she experiences is experienced vicariously as delight in his satisfaction. Her own sexual wants and needs must go unattended, for were she to insist on their fulfillment, she and the man would be in for a shock. They would both reexperience the rage they felt as infants when they first recognized their mothers as independent selves who had lives and interests of their own. Moreover, were she to let her partner totally satisfy her, the woman would feel enormous guilt for having abandoned her primary love object (mother and women) for a secondary love object (father and men). Better to deprive herself of sexual pleasure, she senses, than suffer the pangs of conscience.[14]

This guilt on the part of women contributes to the third feature of the current gender relations identified by Dinnerstein: the idea that sexual excitement and personal sentiment must be tied together for women but not for men. Because of the guilt she feels about abandoning her mother, a woman refuses to allow herself even vicarious pleasure in sex unless the relationship is infused with the same type of all-encompassing love that existed between her and her mother. To feel good about a sexual liaison, a woman must believe the relationship underlying it is like the one she initially had with her mother: deep, binding, and strong. Only such a sexual liaison can possibly justify her rejection of her mother. To forsake total symbiosis with her mother for a one-night stand with a man, for example, is to settle for a superficial intimacy that cannot approximate the deep intimacy of the mother-child relationship.

In contrast to women, men are notorious for their ability to separate sex from intense emotional commitment, according to Dinnerstein. This ability is also rooted in the mother-infant relationship, especially in the loss of the illusion of infant omnipotence. In the male-female sexual relationship, the man feels especially vulnerable because a woman "can reinvoke in him the unqualified, boundless, helpless passion of infancy."[15] Depending on how much a man needs to be in charge of his destiny, he will be threatened by the overwhelming powers of sexual passion. Once again, he will fear being overwhelmed by a woman able to shatter his ego by withdrawing herself from him. Thus, he will seek to remain in control of the sexual act, distancing himself from the woman with whom he is being intimate.

Dinnerstein claimed the fourth hallmark of current gender arrangements is that a woman is viewed as an "it," whereas a man is seen as an "I." Because the child encounters a woman before the child is able to distinguish an "I" (center of self-interested sentience and perception) from an "it" (an impersonal force of nature), Dinnerstein speculated that the child initially perceives its mother not as a person but as an object. In contrast, because the father usually plays a small role in an infant's upbringing, taking on a larger part in his child's life only after the child has made the I-it distinction, the child has less difficulty recognizing him as an "I," not an "it." Apparently, children perceive their fathers, but not their mothers, as persons with lives of their own. Dinnerstein also hypothesized that human beings fear the power of an "it" more than the power of an "I." In her estimation, this state of affairs explains why "it-like" female power, in the private or public realm, is ultimately more threatening to both men and women than male power. Thus, not only do men feel a need to control women, but women also feel a need to be controlled by men.[16]

The fifth characteristic of current gender arrangements is rooted in our general ambivalence toward the flesh, according to Dinnerstein. We hate the flesh because it limits our control and because we know it will ultimately die, yet we love it because it gives us pleasure. Our general ambivalence toward the body is, however, intensified in the case of women. On the one hand, women's bodies are powerful because they represent the forces of life; on the other hand, women's bodies are disgusting because they bleed and ooze. Because men's bodies do not carry as much symbolic baggage as women's do, men can imagine their own bodies to be largely free of the impurities and problems associated with women's bodies. Rather unfairly, men dispel any remaining ambivalence they may have about the male body by displacing their fears of the flesh onto the female body. The denigration of the female body as dirty, foul, and sinful causes women to deny their bodily core of self-respect, which then deprives women of the ability to reject confidently the negative feelings projected onto their bodies. As a result, many women come to hate their bodies and to punish them in many ways.[17] Bulimia, anorexia, and over-eating may at least in part be attributed to women's "flesh" problems.

Dinnerstein observed that the final characteristic of current gender arrangements is the tacit agreement between men and women that men should go out into the public sphere and women should stay behind within the private sphere. Women funnel their energies into symbiosis and personal relationships, eschewing enterprise for fear of putting power back into the hands of women, while men make enterprise their be all and end all, avoiding symbiosis and personal relationships for fear of losing control. Regrettably, the terms of this bargain permit both men and women to remain perpetual children, said Dinnerstein. Rather than taking responsibility for themselves and their world, men and women continue to play the kind of sex and gender games they should have stopped playing generations ago.

As Dinnerstein saw it, our destructive gender arrangements are the direct result of women's nearly exclusive role in child-rearing and our subsequent tendency to blame women for everything wrong about ourselves, especially that we are limited beings destined to err, decay, and die. We blame mother/woman for our limitations, speculated Dinnerstein, because it is mother/woman who most likely presides when we skin our knees, break our toys, get the flu, or flunk our exams. Dinnerstein insisted we must stop blaming mother/women for the human condition if we want to overcome our destructive gender arrangements—a set of relationships symptomatic of our increasing inability to deal with each one another and our world.

Ultimately, Dinnerstein's solution to the scapegoating of women was to propose a dual-parenting system. She believed that such a system would, for example, help us overcome our ambivalence about enterprise. All people, but especially men, tend to use world building as a defense against death, said Dinnerstein. Indeed, the wonders of civilization can be read as the tragic testimony of a species that strives to achieve the good, the true, and the beautiful, knowing full well everyone and everything are doomed to disintegration. Given his traditional role as world builder, society has not permitted man to express reservations about the ultimate worth of his worldly projects. But because of her traditional role as mother goddess—the "wise one" who is not easily deceived by the pomp and circumstance of civilization—society has given woman some license to articulate her misgivings about civilization. Indeed, said Dinnerstein, women often play the role of court jesters, poking fun at the games men play; women's irreverence serves to release the tension that ripples through the world of enterprise. As a result, things never seem bad enough for us to change the course of history dramatically. But, observed Dinnerstein, dual world building and dual childrearing would enable all of us to see just how bad the world situation is. Because men and women would have an *equal* role in world building as well as childrearing, women would no longer be able to play the role of court jesters. With nowhere to hide, not even in laughter, both sexes would be required to put aside their games to reshape a fundamentally misshapen world.[18]

Nancy Chodorow: The Reproduction of Mothering

Less interested in sexual relationships than Dinnerstein, Nancy Chodorow wondered why women *want* to mother even when they do not have to do so.[19] Rejecting Freud's idea that for women, babies are substitutes for penises, Chodorow found the answer to her question in a reconsideration of the pre-Oedipal stage of human psychosexual development. She pointed to the different "object-relational" experiences infants have with their mothers. According to Chodorow, the infant boy's pre-Oedipal relationship with his mother is sexually charged in a way that it is not for the infant girl. Feeling a sexual current between himself and his mother, the infant boy senses his mother's body is not like his body. As he enters the Oedipal stage, the growing boy senses how much of a problem his mother's otherness is. He cannot remain attached to her (i.e., overwhelmingly in love with her) without risking his father's wrath. Not willing to take this risk, the son separates from his mother. What

makes this process of separation less painful for the son than it might otherwise be is his dawning realization that power and prestige are to be had
through identification with men—in this case, the father. The boy's increasing
contempt for women supposedly helps him define himself in opposition to
the female sex his mother represents.[20]

In contrast to the mother-son pre-Oedipal relationship, the mother-
daughter pre-Oedipal relationship is characterized by what Chodorow termed
"prolonged symbiosis" and "narcissistic over-identification." Because both the
daughter and the mother are female, the infant girl's sense of gender and self
is continuous with that of her mother. During the Oedipal stage, however, the
mother-daughter symbiosis is weakened as the growing girl begins to desire
what her father symbolizes: the autonomy and independence that characterizes a subjectivity, or an "I," on the one hand and the ability to sexually satisfy
a woman—in this case, her mother—on the other. Thus, as Chodorow interpreted it, penis envy arises for the girl both because the penis symbolizes male
power *and* because it is the sexual organ that apparently satisfies her mother:
"Every step of the way . . . a girl develops her relationship to her father while
looking back at her mother—to see if her mother is envious, to make sure she
is in fact separate, to see if she is really independent. Her turn to her father is
both an attack on her mother and an expression of love for her."[21]

Although most girls do finally transfer their primary love from a female to
a male object, Chodorow suggested this transfer of love is never complete.
Whether a girl develops into a heterosexual woman or not, she will probably
find her strongest emotional connections with other women. Thus the pre-
Oedipal mother-daughter relationship provides a reference point for female
friendships and lesbian relationships: The original mother-daughter symbiosis
is never totally severed.[22]

Chodorow theorized that the psychosexual development of boys and girls
has several social implications. The boy's separateness from his mother is the
cause of his limited ability to relate deeply to others; this emotional deficiency, however, prepares him well for work in the public sphere, which values single-minded efficiency, a "survival-of-the-fittest" mentality, and the
ability to distance oneself from others so as to assess them objectively and
dispassionately.[23] In contrast, the girl's connectedness to her mother is the
cause of her ability to relate to others, to weave intimate and intricate human
connections—the kind of relationships that hold the private sphere together.
Unfortunately, this very ability is also what makes it difficult for a girl to create a place for herself in the public world. Precisely because women develop
permeable ego boundaries, women will tend to merge their own interests
with the interests of others, making the identification and pursuit of any independent interests discomfiting.

Because of her view that women's capacity for relatedness is overdeveloped, and men's, underdeveloped; and that men's capacity for separateness is overdeveloped, and women's, underdeveloped, Chodorow, like Dinnerstein, hypothesized that a dual-parenting system would eliminate these asymmetries. Were children reared by both their mother and their father, boys and girls would grow up equally capable of merging and separating, of valuing their relationships with others and taking pride in their autonomy. More specifically, dual-parented children would realize both men and women are self-interested as well as other-directed.[24] Finally, dual-parented children would no longer view the home as women's domain and the workplace as men's domain. On the contrary, they would grow up thinking that all human beings should spend some of their time out in the world working and the rest of it at home with their families and friends.

Critiques of Dinnerstein and Chodorow

Feminists critics challenged Dinnerstein and Chodorow for three reasons. First, they faulted these two theorists for claiming that the root causes of women's oppression are psychological rather than social.[25] According to Dinnerstein and Chodorow, our legal, political, economic, and cultural systems would be dramatically different if women did not want or need to mother. Women are not mothers because law, politics, economics, or culture has forced them to be mothers; rather, women are mothers because they want or need to be mothers. Feminist critics of Dinnerstein and Chodorow countered that woman's want or need to mother is caused not by psychological states of mind but by material conditions—that is, by specific social conditions, such as men's typically higher pay in the public labor force. In a society that gives far greater economic rewards to men than to women, it makes sense for women to convince themselves they *like* staying at home with their children. Women would stop wanting and needing to mother if social conditions were such that women were paid as much as or more than men in the public labor force, for example.

Second, feminist critics objected to what they perceived as both Dinnerstein's and Chodorow's failure to appreciate the diverse forms family structure takes. In particular, they faulted Dinnerstein and Chodorow for explaining the pre-Oedipal and Oedipal stages solely in terms of the structures of the two-parent, heterosexual family and for failing to explain it in terms of differently structured families. There are, after all, many sorts of family structures, ranging from single-parent structures to blended-family and extended-family structures. Moreover, sometimes a child's parents are both female, as when a lesbian couple rears the child; or sometimes a child's parents are both male, as when a gay couple rears him or her. If the Oedipus complex is indeed universal, richer accounts of how it plays out in different family structures must be provided. By focusing on the two-parent, heterosexual family structure, Dinnerstein and Chodorow missed an opportunity to formulate a *fully* feminist psychoanalytic theory.

Third, feminist critics objected to Dinnerstein's and Chodorow's preferred solution for women's oppression, the creation and maintenance of a dual-parenting system. Jean Bethke Elshtain, for example, singled out Dinnerstein for especially strong words. Dinnerstein, said Elshtain, believed women have less of a need to control things and people than men have. As a result of their special symbiotic relationships to their mothers, girls supposedly grow up to be nurturant, affectionate, and caring persons who are "less avid than men as hunters and killers, as penetrators of Mother Nature's secrets, plunderers of her treasure, outwitters of her constraints."[26] If this observation indeed applies to how women's psychology is shaped, asked Elshtain, what will happen to women's positive qualities when women spend as much time in the public realm as men currently do? Absolutely nothing, responded Dinnerstein. Women will remain caring, compassionate, and considerate, "even as they gain public roles, authority, power."[27] Not satisfied by Dinnerstein's response, Elshtain asked why we should assume that men are capable of developing good feminine qualities in the private realm, but not also assume that women are capable of developing bad masculine qualities in the public realm? If men can become more nurturant by taking care of their babies, then it seems women can become more aggressive by doing battle in the nation's boardrooms, courtrooms, and hospitals. In sum, observed Elshtain, Dinnerstein failed to ask herself what will be lost as well as gained for men and women in a dual-parenting/dual-working system.

Another feminist critic, Janice Raymond, offered a critique of dual parenting that applied equally well to Dinnerstein and Chodorow. Raymond observed that dual parenting *seems* like a reasonable way to transform distorted gender relations. After all, if Dinnerstein is right that "male absence from child rearing" is leading the world to nuclear war and ecological chaos, then by all means let fathers spend as much time in the nursery as mothers do. However, warned Raymond, to insist dual parenting is *the* solution to the human malaise is to elevate men again to the status of "saviors." Men's rapid insertion into the nursery, unaccompanied by women's rapid promotion in the work world, threatens to give men even more power than they now have—personal and psychic power within the family as well as political and economic power outside the family. Additionally, to present dual parenting as the solution to all our gender woes is again to neglect "gyn-affection," or woman-to-woman attraction and interaction.[28] Specifically, dual parenting, as presented by Dinnerstein and Chodorow, does not in any way compare and contrast lesbian households in which one women stays at home and the other goes to work, with lesbian households in which neither woman is the primary parent or primary worker.

As Raymond saw it, that *women* mainly mother is not the problem. Rather, the real problem is that women mother when, where, and how *men* want them to. Girls are taught to direct their love away from women and toward men. Girls see their mothers loving their fathers in a special way—so special that girls surmise men must be worthy of a love that women themselves do not deserve. Raymond speculated that were girls to see their mothers loving other women in an equally special way, girls would grow up with more positive feelings about themselves and other women. Despite their mutual claim that female bonds are stronger and deeper than male bonds, observed Raymond, neither Dinnerstein nor Chodorow envisioned powerful and strong women joining together in communities of care—communities supportive enough to give women as well as children the kind of love they would not otherwise find.[29] Women do not need men to help them mother.

Adding force to Raymond's critique of Dinnerstein and Chodorow were the words of Adrienne Rich. Rich observed that both Dinnerstein and Chodorow accepted without question the assumption that men are the appropriate object of women's sexual love and emotional energy. Specifically, she commented that both Dinnerstein and Chodorow are "stuck . . . trying to reform a man-made institution—compulsory heterosexuality—as if, despite profound emotional impulses and complementarities drawing women toward women, there is a mystical/biological heterosexual inclination, a 'preference' or 'choice' that draws women toward men."[30] Rich found it particularly puzzling that neither Dinnerstein nor Chodorow, both of whom focused on the pre-Oedipal stage, where mother love reigns supreme, thought to reject the institution of compulsory heterosexuality. Lesbianism rather than heterosexuality would seem to be "normal" for women. Why on earth, then, do girls decide to trade the fulfilling intensity of pre-Oedipal mother love for Oedipal father love? That seems the appropriate question for feminists to ask, in Rich's estimation.

Juliet Mitchell: Psychoanalysis and Feminism

Although Juliet Mitchell did not share Dinnerstein's and Chodorow's interest in dual parenting, she, too, sought to use the feminist ideas buried in Freud's views on the unconscious.[31] As Mitchell understood Freud's theory, it is not some simpleminded enunciation of the slogan "Biology is destiny." On the contrary, his theory demonstrates how social beings emerge from merely biological ones. Psychosexual development is a process of the "social interpretation" of biology, *not* the inexorable manifestation of biological destiny.[32]

Although Freud studied psychosexual development among a specific group of people (the petite bourgeoisie of nineteenth-century Vienna), said Mitchell, his analysis is applicable to psychosexual development among any group of people. However, continued Mitchell, it is important to separate the particular emphases of Freud's analysis, its incidental features, from its general parameters, its essence. There are, after all, certain things about nineteenth-century Viennese, petit bourgeois psychosexual development that are unique to it—that do not apply, for example, to twenty-first-century American, working-class psychosexual development, or to twenty-first-century Chinese, upper-class psychosexual development. Still, contemporary American and Chinese biological families, like the Viennese biological family, seem to play out the family drama Freud names the Oedipal situation.[33]

When Mitchell agreed with Freud that the Oedipal situation is universal, she meant that without some sort of prohibition on incest, human society is an impossibility. According to anthropologist Claude Lévi-Strauss, on whose work Mitchell relied, if sexual relations are permitted within the biological family, there will be no impetus for the biological family to form reproductive alliances between itself and other biological families to create the expanded network we call "society"[34] and to add to the genetic diversity of humankind.

As Lévi-Strauss explained, the incest taboo is the impetus that, by forbidding sexual relations within the biological family, forces people to form other, larger, social organizations. Of course, a mere ban on sexual intercourse within biological families is not enough. There must also be some way to facilitate sexual intercourse between biological families. Lévi-Strauss claimed this facilitation takes the form of an exchange system between biological families—specifically, the exchange of women from one group of men to another.[35] Because a woman is forbidden by the incest taboo from marrying her brother or father, the men in her biological family will push her to marry a man they select outside of the biological family. According to Lévi-Strauss, this male-controlled exchange of women constitutes humans' "decisive break" with the beasts. Moreover, added Mitchell, men's exchange of women rather than vice versa accounts for the *patriarchal* character of human society.[36]

Feminist Critiques of Mitchell

Mitchell's feminist critics found much of her analysis useful, but they remain unconvinced by it. They asked Mitchell why *women* rather than *men* are exchanged and why the *father* rather than the *mother* has power over the family. Mitchell sought the answers to these questions in Freud's *Totem and Taboo*, in which he described the primal murder of an original mythical father. The totem is the symbol of the father, and associated with it are two taboos, one against destruction of the totem and one against incest. In the myth, a group of brothers bands together to kill the feared and envied father—feared because of his power, envied because of his harem of women. After their act of patricide, the brothers, feeling very guilty about what they have done and not knowing quite what to substitute for the law of the father, eventually reestablish the father's two taboos. Freud commented that whereas the brothers' reinscription of the *totem* taboo is "founded wholly on emotional motives," their reinscription of the *incest* taboo is founded on a practical as well as an emotional basis.

> Sexual desires do not unite men but divide them. Although the brothers had banded together in order to overcome their father, they were all one another's rivals in regard to the women. Each of them would have wished, like his father, to have all women to himself. The new organization would have collapsed in a struggle of all against all, for none of them was of such overmastering strength as to be able to take on his father's part with success. Thus the brothers had no alternative, if they were to live together, but—not, perhaps, until they had passed through many dangerous crises—to institute the law against incest, by which they all alike renounced the women whom they desired and who had been their chief motive for dispatching their father.[37]

In sum, the brothers must refrain from incest; only then can patriarchy, in which they have a vested interest, thrive.

Although Mitchell's feminist critics dismissed the myth of the primal crime as a mere *myth,* Mitchell countered that the myth is an extraordinarily powerful one that speaks loudly to the collective human unconscious. The figure of the father stands for the desire of human beings to be transcendent, to assert their will, to be somehow in control of their lives. The father (and here Mitchell was borrowing from Jacques Lacan, discussed on page 143) is "he who is ultimately capable of saying 'I am who I am.'"[38] The father represents success in the so-called Symbolic order. He is disentangled from confusions and struggles. He is clear-thinking, farseeing, and powerful. Because he can say, "I am who I am," he can name things for what he wants them to be. Yet, however seductive the image of the transcendent father and the omnipotent patriarch may be, the image is also the source of women's oppression, conceded Mitchell. To the degree that the successful resolution of the Oedipus complex leads to patriarchy as well as civilization, continued Mitchell, it needs to be reinterpreted. There must be some way to explain psychosexual development that does not purchase civilization at women's expense.[39]

Responding in part to Mitchell's challenge, Sherry Ortner, a noted feminist anthropologist and theorist, made the following observation: "The Oedipus complex is part of a theory of the development of the person. It is powerful, and significantly, an eminently dialectical theory: the person evolves through a process of struggle with and ultimate supersession . . . of symbolic figures of love, desire, and authority. As a general structure (without gender valences attached to the particular figures), there seems no need to dispose of (and . . . probably no possibility of disposing of) this process."[40] Ortner theorized that because gender valences are historical accretions, they can be changed, and with their change, the Oedipal process can be freed from its current patriarchal agenda.[41] In other words, according to Ortner, there is no law that "maleness" and "femaleness" must be understood in only one way, or that "maleness" must be privileged over "femaleness."

In developing her argument, Ortner insisted that labeling authority, autonomy, and universalism as "male" and love, dependence, and particularism as "female" is not essential to the Oedipus complex. Gender valences are simply the consequences of a child's experiences with men and women. A society changes children's *ideas* about "maleness" and "femaleness" by changing children's experiences with men and women. Does this mean, then, that the implementation of Dinnerstein's and Chodorow's system of dual parenting would, after all, be enough to effect a different telling of the Oedipal tale? Or must society undergo a more radical social transformation than this one to eliminate the gender valences that favor one sex over the other? Must we, for example, enter Marge Piercy's Mattapoisett, a fictional world in which children are gestated ex utero and reared by three co-mothers (two men and one woman, or two women and one man)?[42] The possibilities for social transformation in general and for family structure in particular would seem to be many, each one requiring a different telling of the Oedipal tale.

With greater or lesser success, Chodorow, Dinnerstein, and Mitchell challenged a strict Freudian account of psychosocial development. They tried to provide explanations for psychosexual development that would help rather than hinder women's liberation. Still, this trio of later psychoanalytic feminists did not go far enough. They did not emphasize, as some other later psychoanalytic feminists would, that to understand why we construct men/maleness/masculinity and women/femaleness/femininity the way we do, we may not simply take as gospel a general theory of the psyche. Commented Chris Weedon:

If we assume that subjectivity is discursively produced in social institutions and processes, there is no pre-given reason why we should privilege sexual relations above other forms of social relations as constitutive of identity. There may, of course, be historically specific reasons for doing this in a particular analysis, but they will not be universal. Furthermore, if we are concerned specifically with the question of sexual identity, then psychoanalysis itself must be looked at as one discourse among many which has been influential in constituting inherently patriarchal norms of sexuality.[43]

Weedon's point is this: If we think, for example, that we can change current psychosocial identity by instituting a practice such as dual parenting, then we can also change current psychosexual identity, albeit differently, by instituting an alternative practice such as single parenting. As Weedon stated it, "Discourse constitutes rather than reflects meaning."[44] Everyday practice precedes the formulation of general theory.

Observations such as Weedon's partly explain why, in recent years, a new generation of psychoanalytic feminists, including Luce Irigaray and Julia Kristeva, have found French psychoanalyst Jacques Lacan's reinterpretation of Freud so useful. For Lacan, anatomy is not destiny; rather, language is destiny. Therefore, to the degree that language can be changed, destiny can be changed.

Psychoanalytic Feminism: Focus on Lacan

Building upon structural anthropologist Claude Lévi-Strauss's contention that every society is regulated by a series of interrelated signs, roles, and rituals, Jacques Lacan termed this series the "Symbolic order."[45] For a child to function adequately within society, he or she must be incorporated into the Symbolic order by undergoing three stages of psychosexual development.[46] In the first, or pre-Oedipal, phase—termed the "Imaginary" by Lacan—an infant is completely unaware of her or his own ego boundaries. In fact, the infant has no sense of where the mother's body ends and her or his own body begins. As far as the infant is concerned, he or she and the mother are one. Moreover, during this stage of development, the infant is neither feminine nor masculine but possibly either, because the infant has yet to acquire language.

In the second, or mirror, phase (also part of the Imaginary), the infant thinks the image of herself or himself, as reflected through the "mirror" of the mother's gaze, is her or his real self. According to Lacan, this is a normal stage in self-development. Before the infant can see herself or himself as a self, the infant must see herself or himself as seen by the mother—that is, as an other.[47] Lacan claimed that the process of infantile self-discovery serves as a paradigm for all subsequent relations; the self always discovers more about itself through the eyes of the other.

The third, or Oedipal, phase, in Lacan's scheme of things, includes a period of growing estrangement between the mother and the maturing child. Unlike the infant, the child does not view herself or himself as a unity; rather, the child regards the mother as the other—someone to whom the child must communicate his or her wishes and, therefore, someone who, due to the limitations of language, can never truly fulfill those wishes. During the Oedipal phase proper, the already weakened mother-child relationship is further eroded by the intervention of the father.[48] Fearing *symbolic* castration, the child separates from the mother in return for a medium (language) through which the child can maintain some connection with the mother—the original, never-to-be-had-again source of total gratification.[49]

Like Freud, Lacan maintained that boys experience the splitting from the mother differently than do girls. In the Oedipal phase, the boy rejects identification with his mother, eschewing the undifferentiated and silent state of the womb, and bonds with his anatomically similar father, who represents the Symbolic order, the word. Through identification with his father, the boy not only enters into subjecthood and individuality, but also internalizes the dominant order, the rules of society. In contrast, because of her anatomy, the girl cannot wholly identify with her father in the psychosexual drama. Nor can she totally disidentify with her mother. As a result, the girl cannot fully accept and internalize the Symbolic order.

From this situation, we can draw one of two conclusions. On the one hand, we can conclude that women are virtually excluded from the Symbolic order. On the other hand, we can conclude that women are repressed within the Symbolic order, forced into it unwillingly. A man with a predilection for contradictions, Lacan seemed to draw both of these conclusions. He thought that because women cannot totally internalize the "law of the father," this law must be imposed on them from the outside. Women are given the same words men are given: masculine words. These words cannot express what women *feel,* however; masculine words can express only what men *think* women feel. Lacking feminine words, women must either babble outside the Symbolic order or remain silent within it.

Thus far, it seems Lacan was not any more able than Freud was to find a comfortable place for women within his framework. Because women cannot completely resolve the Oedipal complex, they remain strangers in the Symbolic order, largely unknown because of their phallic wordlessness. Lacan speculated that were society to try to do the impossible—to know women—society would have to begin its inquiry at the pre-Oedipal level of the sexual pleasure (*jouissance*) of women. But like women, their *jouissance* cannot be known, because it can be neither thought nor spoken in the phallic language of the fathers. It leads a repressed existence at the margins of the Symbolic order, seeking a nonphallic language capable of thinking and speaking it. Were women's *jouissance* to find the words to express itself, it would burst the Symbolic order and the order's major prop, patriarchy.

Feminist Appropriations of Lacan's Thought

Luce Irigaray.   Although French psychoanalyst Luce Irigaray found much of value in Lacanian (and, for that matter, Freudian) thought, her overall aim was to liberate what she termed "feminine" philosophical thought from what she termed "masculine" philosophical thought. We will recall that, in Lacan, the Imaginary is the prelinguistic, pre-Oedipal domain in which the child initially mistakes herself or himself for her or his own mirror image. When the child realizes that the mirror image is distinct from his or her own real self, the child enters the Symbolic order. In this realm, the child is able to assert herself or himself as an "I" in language, a distinct subjectivity, separate from other subjectivities. Like Lacan, Irigaray drew contrasts between the Imaginary and the Symbolic order, but unlike Lacan, Irigaray claimed there is *within* the Imaginary a male/masculine imaginary and a female/feminine imaginary.[50] In other words, for Irigaray, the psyche is never bisexual, but always either male/masculine or female/feminine.

For Lacan, the Imaginary is a prison within which the infant is the captive of illusory images. After successfully completing the Oedipal phase, boys are liberated from the Imaginary and enter the Symbolic order, the realm of language and selfhood. Because they never completely resolve the Oedipal phase, however, girls either remain behind in the Imaginary or they enter the Symbolic order mute. In opposition to Lacan, Irigaray refused to bemoan this state of affairs. Instead, she viewed women's total existence in the Imaginary or wordlessness in the Symbolic order as two situations full of untapped possibilities for both women and society.

Irigaray noted that, at present, anything we know about the Imaginary and women, including women's sexual desire, we know from a male point of view. In other words, the only kind of woman we know is the "masculine feminine," the phallic feminine, woman as man sees her. But, said Irigaray, there is another kind of woman to know, the "feminine feminine," woman as women see her.[51] This woman must not be defined, however, through any statement definitively asserting what the true "feminine" is. Defining *woman* in any one way will re-create the phallic feminine: "To claim that the feminine can be expressed in the form of a concept is to allow oneself to be caught up again in a system of 'masculine' representations, in which women are trapped in a system or meaning which serves the auto-affection of the (masculine) subject."[52] What obstructs the progression of women's thought out of the Imaginary is the concept of sameness, the thought product of masculine narcissism and singularity.

Irigaray used the word *speculum* (a concave mirroring medical instrument used in vaginal examinations) to capture the nature and function of the idea of sameness in Western philosophy and psychoanalysis. "Specularization," commented Toril Moi, "suggests not only the mirror-image that comes from the visual penetration of the speculum inside the vagina," but also "the necessity of postulating a subject that is capable of reflecting on its own being."[53] Because of narcissistic philosophical "specularization"—which is epitomized in the medieval description of God as thought thinking thought—masculine discourse has never been able to understand woman, or the feminine, as anything other than a reflection of man, or the masculine. Therefore, it is impossible to think the "feminine feminine" within the structures of patriarchal thought. When men look at women, they see not women but reflections of the image and likeness of men.

In her study of Western philosophy and psychoanalysis, Irigaray found sameness everywhere. Her analysis of sameness in Freud's theory was particularly important because she used it to criticize his theory of female sexuality. Freud saw the little girl as a deficiency or negativity, as a "little man" without a penis. He suppressed the notion of difference, characterizing the feminine as a lack: Woman is a reflection of man, the same as a man except in her sexuality. Female sexuality, because it does not mirror male sexuality, is an absence, or lack, of the male's sexuality. Where woman does not reflect man, she does not exist and, stressed Irigaray, will never exist until the Oedipus complex is exploded.[54]

Irigaray claimed that if women want to experience themselves as something other than "waste" or "excess" in the little structured margins of man's world, they should take three steps of action.[55] First, women should create a female language, eschewing gender-neutral language as forcefully as they eschew male language. Not only is the search for "neutrality" pointless (because no one is really neutral about anything), claimed Irigaray, but it is also morally misguided. Trying to hide the identity of the speaker from the reader/listener is cowardly. Stressing that women will not find liberation in objectivity, Irigaray noted that "neither *I* nor *you,* nor *we* appears in the language of science."[56] Science forbids the "subjective," often because it wishes to mask the identities of its agents. Distressed by the unwillingness of science—and, for that matter, traditional Western philosophy and psychoanalysis—to take responsibility for its own words and deeds, Irigaray urged women to find the courage to speak in the active voice, avoiding at all costs the false security and ultimate inauthenticity of the passive voice.

Second, women should create a female sexuality. Irigaray contrasted the singularity that the male sexual organ implies with the multiplicity the female sexual organs imply. In particular, she localized the feminine voice in the labia, "two lips" that reveal woman to be neither one nor two. Woman is not two, because the labia belong to a single woman's body, "which keeps woman in touch with herself, but without any possibility of distinguishing what is touching from what is touched."[57] However, woman is not one, either, because the labia represent a woman's multiple and diffuse (nonphallic) sexuality: "So woman does not have a sex organ? She has at least two of them, but they are not identifiable as ones. Indeed, she has many more. Her sexuality is always at least double, goes even further; it is plural."[58]

Irigaray did not simply contrast the plural, circular, and aimless vaginal/clitoral libidinal economy of women with the singular, linear, and teleological phallic libidinal economy of men. She also argued that the expression of these libidinal economies is not restricted to sexuality but instead extends to all forms of human expression, including social structures. Just as the penetration of the penis prevents the lips from touching, so the phallic unity of the Symbolic order represses the multiplicity of female sexuality. Thus, patriarchy is the social manifestation of masculine libidinal economy and will remain the order of the day until the repressed "feminine feminine" is set free. Women can unshackle this potentiality, however, through lesbian and autoerotic practice. As women explore the multifaceted terrain of the female body, they can learn to think thoughts, speak words, and do deeds powerful enough to displace the phallus.

Third, in their efforts to be themselves, women should mime the mimes men have imposed on women. Women should take men's images of women and reflect them back to men in magnified proportions. Through miming, women can "*undo* the effects of phallocentric discourse simply by *overdoing* them."[59] For example, if men view women as sex objects, fetishizing women's breasts in particular, then women should pump up their breasts as big as possible and walk into church on Sunday, their breasts fully exposed in all their naked glory, as if to say, "Here, boys; we know what is on your minds. So look. See if we care." To be sure, conceded Irigaray, miming is not without its perils. The distinction between miming the patriarchal definition of woman so as to subvert it and merely fulfilling this definition is not clear. In their attempts to "overdo" the definition of woman, women may inadvertently be drawn back into it. Nevertheless, despite this risk, women should take every opportunity to raise a ruckus in the Symbolic order.

From the preceding discussion, there is clearly a tension between Irigaray's conviction that we must finally end the process of labeling and categorizing, on the one hand, and her competing conviction that we cannot help but engage in this process, on the other hand.[60] Because Irigaray dared to express both of these convictions, sometimes in the same breath, her critics described her as self-contradictory. Rather than feeling embarrassed by the ambiguities and ambivalence in her writing, however, Irigaray took increasing pleasure in them. For Irigaray, self-contradiction is a form of rebellion against the logical consistency required by phallocentrism: "'She' is indefinitely other in herself. This is doubtless why she is said to be whimsical, incomprehensible, agitated, capricious . . . not to mention her language, in which 'she' sets off in all directions leaving 'him' unable to discern the coherence of any meaning. Hers are contradictory words, somewhat mad from the standpoint of reason, inaudible for whoever listens to them with ready-made grids, with a fully elaborated code in hand."[61] Refusing to be pinned down even by her own theory, Irigaray vowed to liberate her life from the phallocentric concepts that would squeeze its multiple meanings—its exciting differences—into boring sameness.

Julia Kristeva.   Like Irigaray, psychoanalytic feminist Julia Kristeva relied on Lacan's work. She largely accepted Lacan's identification of the pre-Oedipal stage with the Imaginary (see pages 143–144). She also largely accepted his identification of the Oedipal and post-Oedipal stages with the Symbolic order. However, Kristeva added to Lacan's account a further complexity. She claimed that a certain modality of language, termed by her the "semiotic," is the exclusive modality of language in the pre-Oedipal period, whereas another modality of language, termed by her the "symbolic," is the dominant though not exclusive modality of language in the Oedipal and post-Oedipal stages. Furthermore, she associated the semiotic with maternal/poetic language and the symbolic with paternal/logical language. As Kristeva saw it, when the child enters the Symbolic order as described by Lacan, the child brings with himself or herself some of the language of the Imaginary. However, most of the language of the Imaginary is left behind, because it is fundamentally at odds with the Symbolic order. Thus, for Kristeva, the semiotic exists both inside and outside the Symbolic order, whereas for Lacan, it presumably exists only outside the Symbolic order.[62]

Further explaining the semiotic-symbolic distinction, Kristeva claimed that the symbolic modality of language is that aspect of meaning-making that permits us to make rational arguments; it produces linear, rational, objective, and grammatical writing. In contrast to the symbolic modality of language, the semiotic modality of language is that aspect of meaning-making that permits us to express feelings. It is, as Kelly Oliver has noted, "the drives as they make their way into signification."[63] The semiotic produces circular, emotional, subjective, and rule-breaking writing. Kristeva believed that a liberated person is someone able to play not only in the space *between* the pre-Oedipal Imaginary and the post-Oedipal Symbolic order but also in the space between the semiotic and symbolic aspects of meaning-making *inside* the Symbolic order.[64] In other words, she claimed that the liberated person can move freely between the "feminine" and the "masculine," chaos and order, revolution and the status quo.

Unlike Irigaray, Kristeva resisted identification of the "feminine" with biological women and the "masculine" with biological men. She maintained that when the child enters the Symbolic order, he or she may identify with either the mother or the father. Depending on the choice the child makes, the child will be more or less "feminine" or "masculine." Thus, men can exist and write in a "feminine" mode, and women can exist and write in a "masculine" mode. Perhaps most interesting and controversial is Kristeva's claim that the "feminine" writings of men have more revolutionary potential than those of women. Culture is more upset when a man speaks like a woman than when a woman speaks like a man, said Kristeva. As Oliver put it, Kristeva thought that "whereas in males an identification with the maternal semiotic is revolutionary because it breaks with traditional conceptions of sexual difference, for females an identification with the maternal does not break traditional conceptions of sexual difference."[65]

Kristeva's main emphasis was on difference in general rather than *sexual* difference in particular. Rejecting traditional accounts of two binary sexes, of two opposed *gender identities,* Kristeva admitted that there are, nonetheless, male and female *sexual differences.* Like Dinnerstein and Chodorow, Kristeva located the beginnings of sexual difference in the child's relation to the mother; but in Kristeva's version of this relationship, a child's sexual identity is specifically formed through a struggle to separate from the mother's body. The male does this not by rejecting his mother's body but by "abjecting" it, that is, reconceiving it as an object that represents everything that is disgusting about being a human being (excrement, blood, mucus).[66] In contrast, the more the female identifies with her mother's body, the more trouble she has rejecting or abjecting it. To the degree that the rejected or abjected maternal body is associated with women per se, women are grouped with society's "misfits"— the Jews, Gypsies, homosexuals, deformed, diseased—an identification that would, contrary to what Kristeva has said elsewhere, motivate women, far more than men, to be revolutionaries.

In Dorothy Leland's estimation, Kristeva's resolution of the Oedipal tale is particularly disturbing because it offers women only three "options"—none entirely good—to avoid psychosis.[67] The first option, which Kristeva considered undesirable for women, is total father-identification. According to Kristeva, Electra, who has her mother, Clytemnestra, killed so as to "avenge her father," is the perfect example of a totally father-identified woman.[68] Clytemnestra must be punished, indeed eliminated, because she has dared to take a lover, thereby exposing to the world her *jouissance* (instinctual pleasure), a *jouissance* that the patriarchal order forbids. By having her mother killed, Electra expresses her hate not only of her mother's *jouissance* but also of her own *jouissance*. Electra's expression of mother-hate/self-hate "perpetuates the patriarchal social/symbolic order," said Leland.[69]

The second option for women, which Kristeva also considered undesirable, is total mother-identification. Because she largely accepted Lacan's view that to become civilized, the child must repress both its *jouissance* and its symbiotic relation to the mother, Kristeva viewed total mother-identification as condemning women to "forever remain in a sulk in the face of history, politics, and social affairs."[70] In other words, the price of total mother-identification is not being permitted to be an adult.

The third option for women, which Kristeva considered desirable, is to avoid both total father-identification and total mother-identification:

> Let us refuse both extremes. Let us know that an ostensibly masculine, paternal identification . . . is necessary in order to have a voice in the chapter of politics and history . . . [But] let us right away be wary of the premium on narcissism that such an integration can carry; let us reject the development of a "homologous" woman [i.e., an Electra] who is finally capable and virile; and let us rather act on the socio-politico-historical stage as her negative: that is, act first with all those who refuse and "swim against the tide"—all who rebel against the existing relations of production and reproduction. But let us not take the role of Revolutionary either, whether male or female: let us on the contrary refuse all roles to summon [a] truth outside time, a truth that is neither true nor false, that cannot be fitted into the order of speech and social symbolism.[71]

By "truth," Kristeva meant the semiotic modality of language, said Leland.[72] Yet Kristeva did not view as desirable the total replacement of the symbolic modality of language in the Symbolic order with the semiotic modality of language. Any attempt to totally substitute the symbolic with the semiotic would, in her estimation, destroy the Symbolic order and, with it, civilization. Everyone would be propelled back into the pre-Oedipal stage, or the Imaginary. Permanent existence in this stage is nothing more or less than psychosis, according to Kristeva. Thus, the specific course of action Kristeva recommended for women who did not want to go crazy was to engage in an "impossible dialectic," a "permanent alienation" between the semiotic ("maternal" *jouissance*) and the Symbolic ("paternal" power or law).[73]

Reflecting on Kristeva's recommendation to women, Leland and many other critics of psychoanalytic feminism cannot help but think that women must have more options than the ones noted here. Some of these critics suggest that gender need not be interpreted in terms of masculinity or femininity only, and that sexuality need not be interpreted in terms of maleness or femaleness only. There are multiple genders and multiple sexualities.[74] Other of these critics suggest instead that psychoanalytic feminists develop an entirely non-Freudian/non-Lacanian account of psychosexual development—an account that permits women as well as men to be civilized without assigning either sex to "second sex" status. The merits of this suggestion are obvious. Unfortunately, psychoanalytic feminists have not been able to find in the Western tradition a more convincing psychosexual tale to tell than some version of the Oedipal tale. Whether there are better psychosexual tales told in non-Western traditions is, therefore, an avenue for feminist speculation and exploration.

Bridges Between Psychoanalytic and Care-Focused Feminists

Like psychoanalytic feminists, care-focused feminists are interested in the differences that distinguish the female psyche from the male psyche. However, unlike psychoanalytic feminists, care-focused feminists do not emphasize boys' and girls' psycho*sexual* development. If they stress any aspect of children's development in particular, it is what I would term boys' and girls' psycho*moral* development. According to care-focused feminists, boys and girls grow up into men and women with gender-specific values and virtues that serve to empower men and disempower women in a patriarchal society. Thus, one question to ask is whether women's liberation will be best served by women adopting male values and virtues, by men adopting female values and virtues, or by everyone adopting a mix of both female and male values and virtues. If the answer to this crucial question is that men and women should share a morality encompassing an equal mix of female and male virtues and values, then how should this morality be inculcated in boys and girls? Is dual parenting the best means to achieve the end of gender equity in everything, including the practice of morality? Or do care-focused feminists propose another means to achieve this worthy goal?

The Roots of Care-Focused Feminism:
Carol Gilligan and Nel Noddings

Carol Gilligan's Ethics of Care

In her groundbreaking book *In a Different Voice,* moral psychologist Carol Gilligan noted that men's emphasis on separation and autonomy leads them to develop a style of moral reasoning that stresses justice, fairness, and rights.[75] In contrast, women's emphasis on connections and relationships leads them to develop a style of moral reasoning that stresses the wants, needs, and interests of particular people. In addition to making this point, Gilligan claimed that because most experts in moral development theory have used *male* norms as opposed to *human* norms to measure women's as well as men's moral development, the experts have mistakenly concluded women are less morally developed than men. Deeply disturbed by this negative assessment of women, Gilligan set out to prove that not women, but the standards used to judge women's growth as moral persons, must be changed.[76]

In articulating her position that women are no less morally developed than men, Gilligan singled out her former mentor, Harvard's Lawrence Kohlberg, for particular criticism. According to Kohlberg, moral development consists of a six-stage process through which a child must pass to become a fully functioning moral agent. Stage One is "the punishment and obedience orientation." To avoid the "stick" of punishment or receive the "carrot" of a reward, the young child does as he or she is told. Stage Two is "the instrumental relativist orientation." Based on a limited principle of reciprocity ("you scratch my back and I'll scratch yours"), the young child does what meets others' needs, but only if his or her own needs are thereby met. Stage Three is "the interpersonal concordance or 'good boy–nice girl' orientation." The maturing child conforms to prevailing moral norms so as to secure the approbation of other people. Stage Four is "the 'law and order' orientation." The maturing child begins to do his or her duty, show respect for authority, and maintain the given social order for its own sake. Stage Five is "the social-contract legalistic orientation." The young adult adopts an essentially utilitarian moral point of view according to which individuals are permitted to do as they please, provided they refrain from harming other people in the process. Stage Six is "the universal ethical principle orientation." The adult adopts an essentially Kantian moral point of view that provides a moral perspective universal enough to serve as a critique of any conventional morality. The adult is no longer ruled by self-interest, the opinion of others, or the force of legal convention, but by self-legislated and self-imposed universal principles such as justice, reciprocity, and respect for the dignity of human persons.[77]

Gilligan took exception to Kohlberg's sixfold scale not because she regarded it as entirely without merit but because girls and women tested on it rarely got past Stage Three, the good-boy/nice-girl stage. Fearing that people would interpret this test result as confirming Freud's view that women are less moral than men, Gilligan set out to prove that women's low scores on Kohlberg's test were undeserved. She hypothesized that women did poorly on Kohlberg's scale because of its flawed design. It was, in her estimation, a test constructed to measure *men's* method of moral reasoning, as if men's way of moral reasoning was the standard of human moral reasoning. As a result of the scale's faulty construction, women who did not morally reason like men did poorly on it. Gilligan claimed the solution to this state of affairs was not to construct a test to measure *women's* method of moral reasoning, as if women's way of moral reasoning was the standard of human moral reasoning. Rather, the solution was to develop a test that could accurately measure both men's and women's moral development. Neither men nor women should be viewed as the morally inferior sex.

Eager to understand more about how women reason toward a moral decision, Gilligan conducted an empirical study of twenty-nine pregnant women. Each of these women was deciding whether to abort her fetus. Gilligan interviewed these women as they were working through their decision and sometimes after they had done so. She eventually concluded that no matter their age, social class, marital status, or ethnic background, each of these women manifested a way of thinking about moral matters that differed markedly from that of the men tested on Kohlberg's moral development scale. Rather than approaching the abortion decision analytically as if they were scientists trying to determine whose rights weigh more—the fetus's or the woman's— the women in Gilligan's study approached the abortion decision as a human relations problem. They worried about how their decision would affect not only the fetus but also themselves in connection to their partners, parents, friends, and so on, and they moved back and forth between three levels of moral reasoning as they sought to make moral sense of their abortion decision. Gilligan noted that the women who failed to come fully to terms with their abortion decision remained stuck either in Level One moral reasoning, in which the moral agent overemphasizes her own interests, or in Level Two moral reasoning, in which the moral agent overemphasizes others' interests. In contrast, the women who engaged in Level Three moral reasoning, in which the moral agents strike a balance between their own interests and those of others, appeared most at peace with their abortion decision.[78]

Importantly, in Gilligan's estimation women's style of moral reasoning is no better or worse than men's. It is simply different. Moreover, stressed Gilligan, although a woman or a man might, as an individual or as a member of a group, typically engage in a certain style of moral reasoning, fully developed moral agents are likely to display a marked ability to speak the languages of care and justice equally well. Had Gilligan stopped her research on moral development with this observation, we could confidently conclude that, for her, the *morally androgynous* person is the paradigm moral agent. However, after writing *In a Different Voice*, Gilligan hinted that the ideal moral thinker might after all be more inclined to an ethics of care than an ethics of justice. In her anthology *Mapping the Moral Domain*, she expressed concern that a high percentage of today's adolescents "tend[ed] to characterize care-focused solutions or inclusive problem-solving strategies as utopian or outdated."[79] Gilligan worried that because our culture overvalues scientific, objective, and rational thinking, teachers urge students to use only their head and not also their heart in moral deliberation. Challenging the wisdom of this pedagogical approach, Gilligan claimed that in many ways, young children who have not been schooled to suppress their feelings seem *more* moral than adults. Precisely because of their strong attachments to family members and friends, young children seem not only really to care about the feelings, wants, needs, and interests of those to whom they are related but also to act upon these sentiments. That girls are more likely than boys to grow into adults who continue to respond to other people's need to be loved and appreciated is probably not a sign of women's moral weakness, then, but of women's moral strength.

Nel Noddings's Ethics of Care

Like Gilligan, care-focused feminist Nel Noddings claimed that women and men speak different moral languages and that our culture favors a "masculine" ethics of justice over a "feminine" ethics of care. Although women can speak the language of justice as well as men can, said Noddings, this language is not women's native moral tongue. Indeed, women seem to enter the moral realm through a "different door" than men do, focusing less on "principles and propositions" and "terms such as justification, fairness, and justice" and more on "human caring and the memory of caring and being cared for."[80] As a result, women's style of moral reasoning is far less abstract and far more concrete than men's. For example, said Noddings, when faced with a decision about further medical treatment for her dying child, a mother is not likely to approach this intensely personal decision as she would approach an extremely difficult math problem. On the contrary, as she struggles to determine what is in her child's best interest, a mother will consult her personal ideals, feelings, and impressions.[81] She will not let her child suffer unnecessary pain for no good reason; she will do what her "heart" tells her "head" to do.

Ethics, insisted Noddings, is about particular relations, where a "relation" means "a set of ordered pairs generated by some rule that describes the affect—or subjective experience—of the members."[82] When all goes well, the cared-for person actively *receives* the caring deeds of the one caring, spontaneously sharing her or his aspirations, appraisals, and accomplishments with the one caring. Caring is not simply a matter of feeling favorably disposed toward humankind in general, of being concerned about people with whom we have no concrete connections. There is, said Noddings, a fundamental difference between the kind of care a mother gives her child and the kind of care a well-off American philanthropist gives a starving Somali child she or he has never met. Real care requires an active encounter with specific individuals; it cannot be accomplished through good intentions alone.

Noddings stressed the universality of the caring attitude underpinning her ethics. Caring is a defining feature of human beings, at least as important as their capacity for rationality. A child's memories of caring, for example, are not memories peculiar to him or her alone, said Noddings. On the contrary, virtually all human beings have such memories. Indeed, Noddings went so far as to claim "that the impulse to act in behalf of the present other is itself innate. It lies latent in each of us, awaiting gradual development in a succession of caring relations."[83]

Because our memories of caring and being cared for can fade, Noddings emphasized that we must use education to enhance our natural tendency to care. She noted our initial experiences of care come easily. We act from a *natural* caring that impels us to help others because we *want* to: "The relation of natural caring will be identified as the human condition that we, consciously or unconsciously, perceive as 'good.' It is that condition toward which we long and strive, and it is our longing for caring—to be in that special relation—that provides the motivation for us to be moral. We want to be *moral* in order to remain in the caring relation and to enhance the ideal of ourselves as one-caring."[84] The little boy helps his exhausted mother fold the laundry simply because she is his mother, claimed Noddings. He wants to be connected to her and to have her recognize him as her helper. Later, when he is an adolescent, his childhood memories both of caring *for* his mother and being cared for *by* his mother flood over him "as a feeling—as an 'I must.'"[85] In remembrance of his little-boy sentiments, he may choose to be late for a party so that he can help his mother instead. In such a circumstance, *natural* caring morphs into *ethical* caring, a deliberate, critical, and reflective extension of *natural* caring.

We should note that Noddings did not describe moral development as the process of *replacing* natural caring with ethical caring. Although ethical caring requires efforts that natural caring does not, Noddings disagreed with philosopher Immanuel Kant's view that doing things because we *ought* to do them is necessarily better than doing things because we *want* to do them. In contrast to Kant, Noddings argued our "oughts" build on our "wants":

> Recognizing that ethical caring requires an effort that is not needed in natural caring does not commit us to a position that elevates ethical caring over natural caring. Kant has identified the ethical with that which is done out of duty and not out of love, and that distinction in itself seems right. But an ethic built on caring strives to maintain the caring attitude and is thus dependent upon, and not superior to, natural caring. The source of ethical behavior is, then, in twin sentiments—one that feels directly for the other and one that feels for and with that best self, who may accept and sustain the initial feeling rather than reject it.[86]

Morality is not about affirming others' needs through the process of denying one's own interests. Rather, morality is about affirming one's own interests through the process of affirming others' needs. When we act morally (engage in ethical caring), we act to fulfill our "fundamental and natural desire to be and to remain related."[87] We meet others' needs not because inclination impels us to do so, or because reason forces us to do so, but because we choose reflectively to do so.

In addition to her book on caring, Noddings wrote a book on evil, in which she claimed women are more capable of withstanding evil than men are. According to Noddings, women's understanding of evil is concrete, whereas men's understanding of evil is abstract. For women, an evil event is a harmful event, something that hurts someone in particular. For men, an evil event is a rule-breaking event—a violation of God's commandments or the state's laws. Wanting to replace the abstract *idea* of evil as sin, guilt, impurity, and fault with the concrete *experience* of evil as "that which harms or threatens harm,"[88] Noddings insisted that eliminating evil is not about punishing sinners. Rather, it is about reducing the kind of pain, separation, and helplessness infants typically feel. Evil is isolation in one's hour of need, and the way to overcome isolation is through relationship.

In her attempt to further elucidate the differences between the "masculine" idea of evil and the "feminine" experience of evil, Noddings interpreted a story Doris Lessing told in *The Diary of a Good Neighbor*. In Lessing's story, Jane, a middle-aged, highly successful novelist and magazine editor, tries to alleviate the suffering of Maudie, a physically unattractive, lower-class, ninety-year-old woman. Several female nurses and nurse aides assist Jane's efforts. In contrast to the male physician, who views Maudie as a "case," these women view

Maudie as a unique individual who needs their help to fight the infirmities of old age and the ravages of disease. Reflecting on the women ministering to Maudie, Noddings noted none of them found abstract "meaning" in their patient's suffering. Nor did any of them speak of "God's will," as if Maudie's suffering were the price she had to pay for her "sins." On the contrary, they simply worked "to relieve her pain, alleviate her loneliness, and preserve—as nearly as they [could]—her autonomy." For Maudie's female healers, evil is "the deliberate or negligent failure" to help someone whose body is racked with pain, whose spirit is in anguish, or whose dignity as a person is in jeopardy.[89]

Noddings realized we cannot *eliminate* all evil, because it stems foremost from a separation of ourselves from other human beings, from an objectification of those around us. We can only *reduce* evil by accepting and combating our own penchant for it. Suppose, said Noddings, your child was going to be killed in one hour unless you found her, and standing before you was a man who knew where she was but would not tell you. Would you be able and willing to torture the information out of him? Noddings admitted she, for one, would be up to this "challenge."[90] Yet she asked herself whether this one exception to her rule of "do no evil" would lead her to make a series of exceptions, the sum total of which would negate the very rule upon which she had built her own morality.

For an answer to this disturbing question, Noddings turned to a story in Simon Wiesenthal's novel *The Sunflower.* Here, a young Jewish man, who turns out to be Simon himself, comes to the bedside of a dying Nazi named Karl. Guilt ridden because of his role in the Holocaust, Karl beseeches Simon to forgive him. Simon experiences feelings of both pity and repugnance toward Karl. After several minutes pass, however, Simon leaves without saying a word of forgiveness to him. He asks his readers to plumb their own souls and answer the question, "What would you have done in my place?"

In her reflections on Simon's story, Noddings implied that, had she been in Simon's place, she would have forgiven Karl. She claimed that because Simon viewed himself *symbolically,* as a representative of the Jewish people, he could not see the situation that confronted him *relationally.* In other words, Simon could not see the dying Nazi as an individual human being begging his forgiveness. Instead, Simon could see only Nazis in general: they who, as a group, had caused unforgivable harm to Jews in general. Commented Noddings: "Seeing each other and ourselves as symbols, is part of what sustains our capacity to inflict suffering."[91] In Noddings's estimation, Simon added to rather than subtracted from the world's evil when he refused to forgive Karl. She pointed out that even if Simon could only have yelled or screamed at Karl, a relationship of sorts might have been established between them:

"Then gradually each might have seen the full horror of their situation. They both might have seen that the possibility of perpetrating unspeakable crimes lay in Simon as well as in Karl and that the possibility and thus the responsibility to resist lay also in both."[92]

Critiques of Gilligan and Noddings

Critiques of Gilligan.   Much criticism has been directed at Gilligan's methodology.[93] Some critics claimed that Gilligan's empirical data was too thin to support the weighty generalizations she made about men's and women's supposedly different moral voices.[94] They emphasized that although most of the women in Gilligan's study made reference to their husbands, boyfriends, lovers, and fathers, Gilligan failed to ask these men about their views on abortion. Had she chosen to interview the men populating the background of her study, said the critics, Gilligan might have produced a more convincing study about men's and women's allegedly different styles of moral reasoning. Then again, continued the critics, she might have instead produced a study showing that men and women actually reason quite *similarly* about matters such as abortion. Such a study result would have had dramatic consequences for Gilligan, however. Indeed, it would have required Gilligan to rethink her views about women's supposed ethics of care and men's supposed ethics of justice.

As hard as it was for Gilligan to address critics of her methodology, it was even more difficult for her to address critics who claimed that even if women *are* better carers than men (for whatever reasons), it may still be epistemically, ethically, and politically unwise to advertise this state of affairs. Linking women with caring may promote the view that women care by nature, or the view that because women can and have cared, they should always care, no matter the cost to themselves.

Among the critics who worried about the negative consequences of associating women too closely with the values of care was Sandra Lee Bartky. In *Femininity and Domination,* Bartky sought to determine whether women's experience of feeding men's egos and tending men's wounds ultimately disempowers or empowers women. By way of example, she noted that the kind of "emotional work" female flight attendants (and I may add more recently male flight attendants) typically do often leads "to self-estrangement, an inability to identify one's own emotional states, even to drug abuse or alcoholism."[95] To pay a person to be "relentlessly cheerful"[96]—to smile at even the most verbally abusive and unreasonably demanding passengers—means paying a person to feign a certain set of emotions, said Bartky. A person can pretend to be happy only so many times before the person forgets how it feels to be genuinely or authentically happy.

Admitting that the kind of emotional work female flight attendants typically do for passengers is somewhat different from the kind of emotional work wives typically do for their husbands, Bartky noted that many wives find the experience of caring for their husbands empowering. The better caregiver a wife is, the more she may regard herself as the pillar without whom her husband would crumble. But, cautioned Bartky, *subjective feelings* of empowerment are not the same as the *objective reality* of actually having power. Women's androcentric emotional work probably harms women far more than it benefits them in the long run. According to Bartky, caring women reinforce men's status through a variety of "bodily displays," including "the sympathetic cocking of the head; the forward inclination of the body; the frequent smiling; the urging, through appropriate vocalizations, that the man continue his recital, hence, that he may continue to commandeer the woman's time and attention." Men do not accord women similar status, however, and because they do not, said Bartky, women's care of men amounts to "a collective genuflection by women to men, an affirmation of male importance that is unreciprocated."[97]

In Bartky's estimation, the epistemic and ethical consequences of women's unreciprocated care of men are most worrisome. The more emotional support a woman gives a man, the more she will tend to see things as he sees them. She will participate in *his* projects, share *his* friends, rejoice in *his* successes, and feel badly about *his* failures. But women do not need yet another reason to lose their sense of self or to doubt their own vision of reality and version of the truth. Men's and women's interests are not identical in a patriarchal society, and it is important for women to realize this.

For reasons related to Bartky's concerns about any ethics of care, philosopher Bill Puka singled out Gilligan's ethics of care for special criticism. He claimed care can be interpreted in two ways: (1) in Gilligan's way, "as a general orientation toward moral problems (interpersonal problems) and a track of moral development"; or (2) in his way, "as a sexist service orientation, prominent in the patriarchal socialization, social conventions, and roles of many cultures."[98] Those who interpret care as Gilligan did will trace women's moral development through the three levels presented earlier in this chapter. In contrast, those who interpret care as Puka did will view these supposed levels of moral development as coping mechanisms women use defensively in a patriarchal world structured to work against their best interests.

Not only was Gilligan criticized for overestimating the value of an ethics of care, she was criticized for underappreciating the value of an ethics of justice. For example, philosopher Brian Barry dismissed Gilligan's ethics of care "as an invitation to dispense with morality and replace it with nepotism, favoritism, and injustice."[99] Indeed, Barry went so far as to claim that care-focused women "would have to be excluded from all public responsibilities [because] it would be impossible to trust them to carry out public duties conscientiously."[100]

Less harsh than Barry's criticism of Gilligan's ethics of care were those criticisms that faulted her simply for not better explaining the relationship between care and justice.[101] For example, feminist philosopher Marilyn Friedman said that justice is relevant to care in at least three ways. First, if we view a personal relationship as a "miniature social system which provides valued mutual intimacy, support, and concern for those who are involved,"[102] we will fault relationships in which one person is the main "giver" and the other the main "taker." Regrettably, continued Friedman, many heterosexual relationships are deficient in just such a way. Women often serve men's physical and psychological needs and wants with little or no reciprocation for their caregiving acts. At some point, said Friedman, women must take men to task and demand, as a matter of justice, reciprocation. It is not fair for one person in a relationship to shoulder the lion's portion of the burden of care, while the other lounges in the security of being well cared for.

Second, noted Friedman, personal relationships create "special vulnerabilities to harm."[103] When someone who supposedly cares about us harms us, we may feel especially hurt or violated. An injustice perpetrated in the context of a caring relationship, said Friedman, is in many ways far worse than an injustice perpetrated outside such a context. For example, rape by an acquaintance may inflict deeper psychological wounds than rape by a stranger, because a "date rapist" takes advantage of the victim's trust.

Third, stressed Friedman, if we focus on our closest relationships, especially our familial relationships, we will discover they are fraught with the potential for myriad injustices. Should Mom and Dad give their son privileges they are not willing to give their daughter? Should Mr. and Mrs. Jones pay for their parents' nursing home expenses, or should they instead pay for their children's college education? Should Mr. Smith give up an excellent job so that he can move with Ms. Chang, who has a mediocre job, to a city where she will have an excellent job but he will have only a mediocre one? Unassisted by notions of justice, care cannot adequately address these questions, insisted Friedman. Despite Friedman's valid point about the interaction between justice and care, in fairness to Gilligan, they should have properly credited her for also exploring this interaction in several of her writings. Initially, Gilligan offered a care-justice convergence theory. She claimed that, properly practiced, care and justice *converge* in the realization that just as inequality adversely affects both parties in an unequal relationship, so, too, violence is destructive for everyone involved. This dialogue between fairness and care not only provides a better understanding of relations between the sexes but also gives rise to a more comprehensive portrayal of adult work and family relationships.[104]

But later, Gilligan replaced her care-justice convergence theory with a care-justice gestalt theory. Like an ambiguous drawing that may be seen either as a duck or as a rabbit, a moral drama may be framed either in terms of justice or in terms of care, she said. Although these two perspectives never completely and finally converge, they are not usually diametrically opposed polarities, stressed Gilligan. Most individuals are able to interpret a moral drama first from one of these perspectives and then from the other, even if a few individuals lack this perspectival skill. In the same way that some individuals can see only the duck *or* only the rabbit in an ambiguous "duck-rabbit" drawing, some individuals can view moral issues only through the lens of care *or* only through the lens of justice.[105]

Critiques of Noddings.   In some ways, Noddings met with even more criticism than Gilligan did. Although some of the criticisms directed against Noddings echoed those directed against Gilligan, others were unique to Noddings's work. For example, Sarah Lucia Hoagland focused on Noddings's seeming preoccupation with unequal relationships in which one person depends on the other for care.[106] As Hoagland saw it, the overall picture Noddings draws is that of the one-caring consistently giving and the cared-for consistently taking. In fact, said Hoagland, Noddings occasionally implies that the cared-for has *no* obligation to the one-caring over and beyond being a unique self: "The cared-for is free to be more fully himself in the caring relation. Indeed, this being himself, this willing and unselfconscious revealing of self, is his major contribution to the relation. This is his tribute to the one-caring."[107] Such a "tribute" to the one-caring is sad, said Hoagland. A unidirectional mode of caring does little to teach the cared-for about the burdens of the one-caring, and it does even less to teach the one-caring about the legitimacy of her or his own needs.

Hoagland also faulted Noddings for claiming that some type of "ethical diminishment" is almost always the consequence of breaking a relationship, even an abusive one. Hoagland was particularly disturbed by the following passage in Noddings's *Caring*:

> While I must not kill in obedience to law or principle, I may not, either, refuse to kill in obedience to principle. To remain one-caring, I might have to kill. Consider the case of a woman who kills her sleeping husband. Under most circumstances, the one-caring would judge such an act wrong. It violates the very possibility of caring for the husband. But as she hears how the husband abused his wife and children, about the fear

with which the woman lived, about the past efforts to solve the problem legally, the one-caring revises her judgment. The jury finds the woman not guilty by reason of an extenuated self-defense. The one-caring finds her ethical, but under the guidance of a sadly diminished ethical ideal. The woman has behaved in the only way she found open to protect herself and her children and, thus, she has behaved in accord with the current vision of herself as one-caring. But what a horrible vision! She is now one-who-has-killed once and who would not kill again, and never again simply one who would not kill.[108]

Angered by Noddings's words, Hoagland asserted that "ethical diminishment" is not the fate of the woman described. On the contrary, ethical empowerment is her fate. The abused woman has finally found the moral strength to exchange a disempowering and false ethical "ideal" for an empowering and true ethical ideal. An ethics that keeps the one-caring in a destructive relationship is not a *good* ethics, said Hoagland. If a wife is told that ending a relationship with an abusive husband may damage her moral self-image, this woman's guilt, coupled with fear of reprisal on the man's part, may cause her to stay in a relationship that may ultimately destroy her. Unlike Noddings, Hoagland refused to say anything at all negative about women who end abusive relationships: "I must be able to assess any relationship for abuse/oppression and withdraw if I find it to be so. I feel no guilt, I have grown, I have learned something. I understand my part in the relationship. I separate. I will not be there again. Far from diminishing my ethical self, I am enhancing it."[109] There are times in life when ethics demands we not care, insisted Hoagland.

To Hoagland's objections, Noddings replied that there is a difference between caring for others on the one hand and self-destruction on the other. Simple common sense dictates that "if caring is to be maintained, clearly, the one-caring must be maintained."[110] Still, continued Noddings, there are a variety of ways to maintain the one-caring, including ones that may permit the person to preserve her or his ethical ideal "undiminished." Not every abusive marital relationship has to terminate with a divorce decree, a prison sentence for the abuser, or an act of preemptive self-defense, claimed Noddings. A bad relationship may yet be salvaged through appropriate and creative forms of intervention:

Women in abusive relations need others to support them—to care for them. One of the best forms of support would be to surround the abusive husband with loving models who would not tolerate abuse in their presence and would strongly disapprove of it whenever it occurred in their absence. Such models could support and re-educate the woman as well, helping her to understand her own self-worth. Too often, everyone withdraws from both the abuser and the sufferer.[111]

But, replied Noddings' critics, even if some flawed relationships can be salvaged, some relationships are so bad they defy redemption and must be ended. In Fyodor Dostoyevsky's *The Brothers Karamazov,* there is a terrifying section in which Ivan shrieks that he does not want to dwell in a "heaven" in which a cruelly murdered child, his mother, and his murderer embrace in a hug of cosmic reconciliation. This scene illustrates the assertion by Noddings's critics that there is a final limit on caring. Some things are so evil that they must not be forgiven.

Maternal Ethics and the Ethics of Care

Despite the critics' serious reservations about invoking the mother-infant or parent-child relationship as the paradigm for caring human relationships, care-focused feminists nonetheless continued to claim that the concepts, metaphors, and images associated with such relationships are precisely the ones to use. Among these "maternal thinkers" were Sara Ruddick, Virginia Held, and Eva Kittay. Interestingly, all three of those thinkers viewed caring not only as an other-directed psychological attitude of attentiveness but also as a practice, work, or labor. Caring is about having a certain sort of mind-set, but it is also about assisting those in need of care. Moreover, another thread that tied Ruddick's, Held's, and Kittay's thought together was their insistence that caring practice, work, or labor should be performed in the public domain as well as the private realm.

Sara Ruddick

Sara Ruddick identified the ways in which mothering is both cultural and biological; that is, mothering is an activity that men as well as women *can* do, even though as a result of their historic experiences, women now do it better. Ruddick observed that although biology destines women to bear children, it does not destine women to rear them. Nevertheless, because of a complex interaction between women's childbearing capacities on the one hand and patriarchal society's child-rearing needs on the other, child-rearing became women's work. As a result of this state of affairs, most women, though by no means all women, developed what Ruddick termed "maternal practice."[112]

Ruddick claimed society should not trivialize maternal practice. Like any human practice, it requires special abilities and particular ways of thinking and acting: "The agents of maternal practice, acting in response to demands of their children, acquire a conceptual scheme—a vocabulary and logic of connections—through which they order and express the facts and values of their practice. . . . There is a unity of reflection, judgment, and emotion. This unity I call 'maternal thinking.'"[113]

Ruddick rejected the notion that maternal thinking is merely an emotional, irrational display of love that comes naturally to women. Instead she presented it as a type of learned thought. Like all modes of human thinking, maternal thinking has its own logic and interests, specifically, the preservation, growth, and acceptability of one's children.[114]

According to Ruddick, preserving the life of a child is the "constitutive maternal act."[115] Infants are totally vulnerable. They simply will not survive unless their caretakers feed, clothe, and shelter them. Ruddick gave the example of Julie, an exhausted young mother with a very demanding infant. Having reached her physical and psychological limits, Julie pictures herself killing her baby daughter. Horrified by her thought, Julie spends the night riding a city bus, her baby in her arms. She reasons that, as long as they remain in the public eye, her baby will be safe.[116]

Ruddick told Julie's story to stress how difficult it is for some mothers to meet their children's basic needs. Not every mother grows so run-down and desperate that she has to take steps to ensure that she will not kill her child. But even under relatively ideal circumstances, most mothers do have days when they find mothering too difficult. To preserve their children on these bad days, said Ruddick, mothers need to cultivate the intellectual virtue of scrutiny and the moral virtues of humility and cheerfulness.[117]

The second dimension of Ruddick's maternal practice is *fostering* children's growth. A good mother does not impose an already written script on her children. She does not insist her children meet unrealistic standards of abstract perfection. Instead, a good mother tells her children "maternal stories"—that is, realistic, compassionate, and "delightful" stories[118] that help her children reflect on the persons they have been, are, and might someday be. Faced with a stubborn daughter, for example, a mother should help her daughter understand why stubbornness is a character defect and how the girl could transform her stubbornness into the virtue of proper self-determination. A mother should help her children grow not only in physical size and mental intelligence but also in virtue. People become stubborn for reasons. They get tired of having to do things other people's way. Therefore, when they get the opportunity to resist, they fight back by digging in their heels and doing things their own way, no matter how disastrous the consequences may be. Self-awareness of this human tendency can help children understand why a modus operandi of perpetual stubbornness does not make good sense, and why it may be best to do things other people's way from time to time.

The third and final dimension of Ruddick's maternal practice is *training*. Mothers work hard to socialize their children, to transform them into law-abiding citizens who adhere to societal norms. But good mothers do not want their children to become mindless "conformists." Mothers may, for example, refuse to fit their children's vulnerable bodies into military uniforms, or diet them into designer jeans, or dress them for success in the so-called dog-eat-dog world. In a patriarchal society—that is, overly competitive, hierarchical, and individualistic—mothers may find themselves caught between the demands of patriarchy, on the one hand, and their own inner conviction that many of these demands are dehumanizing, on the other. If a mother trains her son to be a "winner," he may become both the chief executive officer of a large firm and a very mean-spirited human being. In contrast, if she refuses to teach her son the "ways of the world," he may become both a very nice guy and someone who is labeled a loser. On almost a daily basis mothers must decide, said Ruddick, when and when not to let their own personal values guide their child-rearing practices. Ruddick added that mothers should not make these decisions by themselves; ideally, they should make them together with their children. If children adopt their mothers' values unquestioningly, their "training" will never be completed.[119] External compliance with others' values is an inadequate substitute for learning how to choose one's own values and living in conformity to them.

Clearly, maternal practice is a complex activity. Overall, it is guided by what Ruddick termed the metavirtue of "attentive love." This metavirtue, which is at once cognitive and affective, rational and emotional, enables mothers to "really look" at their children and not be shocked, horrified, or appalled by what they see.[120] Indeed, among the several characteristics that distinguish maternal thinkers from nonmaternal thinkers is the utter realism of maternal thinkers, emphasized Ruddick. A mother who loves her children inattentively lets her fantasies blind her. She does not see her children as they actually are. Rather, she sees her children as they could perhaps be: the fulfillment of her dreams. In contrast to these mothers, mothers who love their children attentively accept their children for who they are, working within their physical and psychological limits.

Virginia Held

Approaching maternal practice from a somewhat different perspective than Ruddick, Virginia Held maintained that morality is not unitary. Rather, said Held, there are multiple moral approaches designed to fit certain sets of relationships and activities in the public and private realms. Some of these moral approaches, closely related to the value of justice, are likely to be of particular use in the legal and economic realms. In contrast, other moral approaches are tightly linked to the value of care and are likely to be of special help in the realms of childcare, health care, and education. Held insisted each of these two types of moral approaches should be recognized by the other as particularly valuable in its own sphere of influence *and* generally necessary in the other. Society should recognize that the moral approaches designed to govern family disputes are just as socially necessary as the moral approaches fashioned to negotiate international treaties.[121]

Held's point about multiple moral approaches merits careful consideration. At least in the Western world, moral approaches generated in, from, and for private relations have not usually been recognized as fully *moral* approaches. Rather, they have been viewed as merely private matters not warranting serious moral scrutiny. Held pointed out that all too often, traditional ethicists have assumed that bona fide moral issues take root in one sphere only, the public sphere. She claimed this assumption was wrongheaded. Experiences need not unfold in a bustling marketplace or a contentious courtroom to merit moral analysis. On the contrary, they may just as easily arise in a nursery or around the dinner table. In other words, Held maintained that what makes an experience worthy of moral analysis is not *where* it occurs but *how* it occurs. If moral experience is "the experience of consciously choosing, of voluntarily accepting or rejecting, of willingly approving or disapproving, of living with these choices, and above all of acting and of living with these actions and their outcomes,"[122] then such an experience can as easily occur in one's bedroom as in one's office. Therefore, any adequate moral theory must address filial, parental, spousal, and friendship relations as well as physician-patient, lawyer-client, and seller-buyer relations. In the grand scheme of moral concerns, women's struggles and striving in the private realm count as much as do men's struggles in the public realm.

Held stressed that traditional ethicists view contractual relations as the primary model for human interaction, justifying a human relationship as moral to the degree that it serves the separate interests of individual rational contractors. Yet life is about more than conflict, competition, and controversy— about getting what one wants. It is, as mothering persons know, also about cooperation, consensus, and community—about meeting other people's needs. Held speculated that were the relationship between a mothering person and a child, rather than the relationship between two rational contractors, the paradigm for good human relationships, society might look very different:

> Instead of seeing law and government or the economy as the central and appropriate determinants of society, an ethics of care might see bringing up children and fostering trust between members of the society as the most important concerns of all. Other arrangements might then be evalu-

ated in terms of how well or badly they contribute to the flourishing of children and the health of social relations that would certainly require a radical restructuring of society. Just imagine reversing the salaries of business executives and childcare workers.[123]

Held conceded, however, that the kinds of relationships that exist between mothering persons and children can be just as oppressive—indeed, even *more* oppressive—than the relationships that exist between two rational contractors. For example, it is sometimes harder to recognize and handle abuses of power in a parent-child relationship than in an employer-employee relationship.[124] Moreover, it takes greater moral skill to address questions of justice and rights in the domain of the family than it does in the workplace. One cannot quit a family as easily as one quits a job, nor should one, said Held.[125]

Like principles, relationships can be evaluated as good, bad, or somewhere between good and bad. Relationships that are entirely bad should be quit, but relationships that have more good dimensions than bad aspects should be given at least a chance to survive. Premature or unreflective severance of them is not warranted.

Unlike some maternal thinkers, Held believed that men as well as women can be mothering persons. Just because men cannot bear children does not mean that they cannot rear children. Men and women can—indeed should—appropriate the moral outlook of caregivers. Leaving caregiving alone to inattentive women produces boys with personalities "in which the inclination toward combat is overdeveloped and the capacity to feel for others is stunted."[126] Because bellicose, unfeeling *boys* usually mature into bellicose, unfeeling *men,* Held claimed that human survival may depend on our ability to reorganize the way we parent. For starters, equal parenting, based on men's and women's "equal respect" for each other's "equal rights to choose how to live their lives," should become the order of the day.[127]

So important are care and mothering to our world, said Held, that we must, as a society, cultivate the emotions necessary for their practice. Emotions, particularly sensitivity to the feelings of others, are essential to the practice of care and mothering/parenting. They are part of what makes a relationship good in a particular situation. Held noted that going through the motions of a caring activity "without any of the appropriate feelings" is not actually engaging in the practice of care. People who "are thoroughly unaware of what others are feeling and thinking, and grossly unable to read the moods and intentions of others" cannot truly care, said Held. They must be taught to care. Thus, it is not enough for schools to develop students' rational capacities—their powers of critical thinking. Schools must also develop students' emotional capacities—their powers of sympathy, empathy, and imagination.[128]

Eva Feder Kittay

One of the latest additions to the ranks of care-focused feminists who focus on the mother-child and similar relationships is Eva Feder Kittay. She described herself as among those feminist thinkers who "have begun to formulate a moral theory and a politics grounded in the maternal relation, the paradigm of a relation of care."[129] Yet, because Kittay did not want to be accused of bolstering either the essentialist view that women are by nature mothers or the mythical view that all mothers are good mothers, she used the terms "dependency relations" and "dependency workers" instead of "maternal relations" and "mothers" in her work.

For Kittay, the paradigm dependency worker is a close relative or friend who assumes daily responsibility for a dependent's survival. A dependency worker can be either male or female, according to Kittay, but because of a variety of socioeconomic, cultural, and biological factors, most societies have assigned dependency work to their female members. Kittay theorized that the dependency worker's labor is characterized by intimate and caring connections to the dependent. She also speculated that, typically, the dependency worker suffers negative personal or professional consequences, or both, as a result of doing the essential work she or he does.

Closely related to the paradigm case of a dependency worker, said Kittay, is the worker who is paid, often quite modestly, to care for an unrelated person, but who views her job as much more than a mere job. Kittay provided an example of such a dependency worker from her own life: namely, Peggy, the woman who has cared for her severely developmentally disabled daughter, Sesha, for over a quarter of a century and to whom Kittay has distributed many of her motherly tasks. Without Peggy's help, said Kittay, Sesha would not have done nearly as well as she has, and Kittay and her husband would not have done nearly so well in their professional careers. On the contrary, most of their energies, particularly Kittay's, would have been devoted to caring for Sesha.[130]

Unlike the subject of traditional equality theory, Kittay's dependency worker is not an independent, self-interested, and fully autonomous agent. On the contrary, she is, in Kittay's estimation, a transparent self, that is, "a self through whom the needs of another are discerned, a self that, when it looks to its own needs, it first sees the needs of another."[131] As Kittay saw it, to the degree that the dependent needs the help of the dependency worker, to that degree is the dependency worker obligated to the dependent.

Kittay's explanation for the dependency worker's obligations to the dependent resembled the one Robert Goodin offered in his book *Protecting the Vulnerable*.[132] According to Goodin, "The moral basis of special relations between individuals arises from the vulnerability of one party to the actions of another."[133] For example, a mother has an obligation to care for her infant because she is "*the* individual best situated, or exclusively situated to meet the needs of the dependent."[134] The source of a mother's moral obligation to her infant is not in the *rights* of the dependent as a person, but in the *relationship* that exists between one in need and one who is situated to meet the need. The defining characteristic of this largely socially constructed relationship is that it is not usually *chosen* but already *given* in the ties of family, the dynamics of friendship, or the obligations of employment.

The fact that a relationship is given to the dependency worker, however, does not mean that the dependency worker is necessarily wrong to break the relationship. Kittay disagreed with Goodin when he refused to absolve a slave from his "obligations" to a master who becomes so ill that he cannot survive without the slave's help. The master's fragile condition is the slave's one chance for freedom. Is the slave obligated to stay and take care of his master, who will most likely die if left unattended? Goodin argued yes. As he saw it, if a vulnerability arises in a relationship, the moral worth of the relationship is not relevant to the existence of the obligation.[135] Kittay argued no. As she saw it, the relationship that was given to the slave was a "relationship" that society should not have constructed. The relationship's coerciveness cancels out the obligations that human vulnerability ordinarily creates.

Interestingly, Kittay believed that others' obligations to dependency workers are at least as weighty as dependency workers' obligations to their dependents. Her rationale for this claim was rooted in the image of her mother, who used to sit down to dinner after serving her and her father and proclaim, "After all, *I'm* also a mother's child."[136] Kittay claimed that embedded in this statement is the fundamental source of human equality. Dependency workers and dependents exist together in a "nested set of reciprocal relations and obligations."[137] This web of human connections is governed by a principle Kittay termed "doulia." "Just as we have required care to survive and thrive, so we need to provide conditions that allow others—including those who do the work of caring—to receive the care they need to survive and thrive"[138] Interestingly, the term *doula,* from which the term *doulia* is derived, is from the Greek term meaning "slave" or "servant." However, in Kittay's work, the term *doula* is appropriated and redirected to mean a caregiver who cares for those who care for others.[139] So, for example, a doula cares for a mother so that the mother has energy to care for her infant. She, the mother and the infant are nested in a set of interdependent relationships. Thus because everyone is some mother's child, it is only fair that someone should take care of dependency workers and their dependents.[140]

For Kittay, a theory of justice that is not infused with a theory of care will never produce equality. People in John Rawls's hypothetical world subscribe to two principles of justice. The first principle claims that each person is to have an equal right to the most extensive total system of equal basic liberties compatible with a similar system of liberty for all. The second principle argues that social and economic inequalities are to be arranged so that they are both (a) to the greatest benefit of the least advantaged, and (b) attached to offices and positions open to all under conditions of fair and equal opportunity.[141] But people in Kittay's actual world subscribe to more than these two principles of justice. They also call for a third principle of social responsibility for care that Kittay articulates as follows: "To each according to his or her need for care, from each according to his or her capacity for care, and such support from social institutions as to make available resources and opportunities to those providing care, so that all be adequately attended in relations that are sustaining."[142]

Conclusion

What is enormously appealing about the writings of care-focused feminists is how they mesh with many of our ordinary intuitions about sexual behavior, mothering, and moral conduct. Many a woman has found in *The Mermaid and the Minotaur, The Reproduction of Mothering, Psychoanalysis and Feminism, In a Different Voice,* and *Caring* persuasive explanations for her need to love and be loved, for her willingness to give up a high-powered career for an intimate family life, for her willingness to forgive and to forget male abuse and neglect, and for her tendency to give too much and take too little.

To be sure, psychoanalytic explanations for women's oppression do not provide a total explanation for female subordination. Legal, political, and economic institutions and structures must also be taken into account. Nevertheless, to free herself from what is holding her back, a woman must do more than fight for her rights as a citizen; she must also probe the depths of her psyche to exorcise the original primal father from it. Only then will she have the space to think herself anew and become who she has the power to be.

Similarly, gender identity explanations for women's oppression are problematic. In expressing concern about the dangers of care, Gilligan's critics echo Elizabeth Cady Stanton's nineteenth-century admonition that given society's tendency to take advantage of women, it is vital that women make self-development rather than other-directed self-sacrifice their first priority.[143] Still, it is important not to overemphasize the problems of patriarchy. Whatever weaknesses care-focused feminist ethics of care may have, there are serious problems with women's abandoning all of their nurturant activities. The world would be a much worse place tomorrow than it is today were women suddenly to stop meeting the physical and psychological needs to those who depend on them. Just because men and children have more or less routinely taken advantage of some women's willingness to serve them does not mean every woman's caring actions should be contemptuously dismissed as yet another instance of women's "pathological masochism" or "passivity."[144] Care can be rescued from the patriarchal structures that would misuse or abuse it. If it is to be rescued, however, we need to recognize the differences between what Sheila Mullett terms "distortions of caring" on the one hand and "undistorted caring" on the other.[145]

According to Mullett, a person cannot truly care for someone if she or he is economically, socially, or psychologically forced to do so. Thus, genuine or fully authentic caring cannot occur under patriarchal conditions characterized by male domination and female subordination. Only under conditions of sexual equality and freedom can women care for men without men in any way diminishing, disempowering, or disregarding women. Until such conditions are achieved, women must care cautiously, asking themselves whether the kind of caring in which they are engaged:

1. Fulfills the one caring
2. Calls upon the unique and particular individuality of the one caring
3. Is not produced by a person in a role because of gender, with one gender engaging in nurturing behavior and the other engaging in instrumental behavior
4. Is reciprocated with caring, and not merely with the satisfaction of seeing the ones cared for flourishing and pursuing other projects
5. Takes place with the framework of consciousness-raising practice and conversation[146]

Care can be freely given only when the one caring is not taken for granted. As long as men demand and expect caring from women, both sexes will fail to actualize their moral potential. Neither men nor women will be able to care authentically.

Questions for Discussion

1. Discuss the ways in which historic Freudian psychoanalysis constructs such as "penis envy" and "rejection of the mother" contribute to a generally unflattering societal portrait of women.
2. Consider Dinnerstein's dual-parenting and dual–world building solution to current skewed gender arrangements. How might such a solution repair such grievances as the imbalance within male-female sexual relationships, the objectification and control of women, and the disproportionate number of women constrained to the private sphere and men to the public?

3. Provide examples of the feminist Lacanian notion that because both men and women are only provided with a masculine vocabulary (lacking adequate avenues for feminine expression), women therefore either must remain silent within the Symbolic order or babble outside of it. Explore illustrations from both private and public life. How could Irigaray's suggestion to create a female language help alleviate these situations?

4. How is the relationship between care and justice complementary? In what ways are an ethics of care and an ethics justice at odds? In what ways are they connected?

5. What conditions should be present within healthy caretaking/dependency relationships? Assess both personal and paid relationships. If the caretaker is receiving monetary remuneration for the role, does this lessen society's obligation to protect the caretaker's psychological and emotional well-being?

5

Existentialist and Postmodern Feminism

Shortly before Simone de Beauvoir died, Margaret A. Simons and Jessica Benjamin interviewed her for the journal *Feminist Studies*. In their background commentary, Simons and Benjamin commented on the significance of de Beauvoir's major theoretical work, *The Second Sex*:

> De Beauvoir's analysis of women's oppression in *The Second Sex* is open to many criticisms for its idealism—her focus on myths and images and her lack of practical strategies for liberation; for its ethnocentrism and androcentric view—her tendency to generalize from the experience of European bourgeois women, with a resulting emphasis on women's historic ineffectiveness. Still, we have no theoretical source of comparable sweep that stimulates us to analyze and relentlessly question our situation as women in so many domains—literature, religion, politics, work, education, motherhood, and sexuality. As contemporary theorists explore the issues raised in *The Second Sex,* we can see that in a sense all feminist dialogue entails a dialogue with Simone de Beauvoir. And a discussion with her can be a way of locating ourselves within our feminist past, present, and future.[1]

Written in 1958, yet still sounding contemporary, *The Second Sex* has clearly achieved the status of a classic in feminist thought. Thus, no introduction to feminist thought would be nearly complete without a discussion of this work, which has elucidated the significance of woman's otherness in existentialist terms.

Over the years there have been questions about the precise relationship between de Beauvoir's *Second Sex* and Jean-Paul Sartre's *Being and Nothingness*.

The first and ultimately mistaken view is that *The Second Sex* is simply an application of *Being and Nothingness* to women's specific situation. To be sure, Sartre and de Beauvoir were on-and-off lovers for many years and, initially, Sartre was de Beauvoir's teacher. However, by the time they both became well-known authors, de Beauvoir was anything but Sartre's student. On the contrary, she was his intellectual companion and at times his teacher.[2] Still, there are enough existentialist links between de Beauvoir and Sartre to warrant a brief overview of Sartre's thought.

Sartre's *Being and Nothingness*: A Backdrop to *The Second Sex*

Sartre popularized a body of ideas rooted in the philosophies of G. W. F. Hegel, Edmund Husserl, and Martin Heidegger. Chief among these ideas was Hegel's description of the psyche as "self-alienated spirit." Hegel saw consciousness presiding in a divided arena. On the one side resides the observing ego; on the other side lives the immanent self, or the observed ego.[3] Sartre made this distinction between the observer and the observed by dividing being into two parts: being-in-itself (*en-soi*) and being-for-itself (*pour-soi*). Being-in-itself refers to the repetitive, material existence humans share with animals, vegetables, and minerals; being-for-itself refers to the moving, conscious existence human beings share with one another.[4]

The distinction between being-in-itself and being-for-itself is useful in an analysis of the human person to the degree we associate being-in-itself with the body. The body has constant and objective being. As it can be seen, touched, heard, smelled, and tasted, the body is the perceived. In contrast, the perceiver—the entity that does the seeing, touching, hearing, smelling, and tasting—is not itself a perceptible object but, according to Sartre, still has a certain kind of being: being-for-itself. To appreciate being-for-itself fully, picture someone who is momentarily conscious of the fingers on her hand. Her "I" is identified with her fingers because they are, after all, *her* fingers, not anyone else's. However, her "I" is also distinct from her fingers because she is at the same time more than, or other than, her fingers. According to Sartre, what separates one's "I"—one's consciousness or one's mind—from one's body is, paradoxically, nothing (literally, *no-thing*, or nothingness).

To the first two kinds of being, Sartre added a third, being-for-others. Sartre sometimes described this mode of being *positively* as *Mitsein*, a communal "being-with." More frequently, however, he described it *negatively*, as involving "a personal conflict as each For-itself seeks to recover its own Being by directly or indirectly making an object out of the other."[5] Because each being-for-itself establishes itself as a subject, as a self, precisely by defining other beings as objects, as others, the action of consciousness sets up a system of fundamentally conflictual social relations. Thus, the process of self-definition is one of seeking power over other beings: "While I attempt to free myself from the hold of the Other, the Other is trying to free himself from mine; while I seek to enslave the Other, the Other seeks to enslave me. . . . Descriptions of concrete behavior must be seen within the perspective of conflict."[6] In establishing its self *as* a self, each self describes and prescribes roles for the other. Moreover, each subject conceives of itself of transcendent and free and views the other as immanent and enslaved.

Freedom, the distinguishing characteristic of a self, is, according to Sartre, more of a burden than a blessing. It is a burden because so long as a person is conscious, there is no relief from the freedom to choose and affirm. There are no answers in life, just questions. Worse, there is no such thing as *human nature,* an essence common to all human persons, determining what a person ought to be. Rather, there is only a *human condition,* into which all persons are thrown equally and without self-definition. Existence, said Sartre, precedes essence. In other words, we exist only as amorphous, living organisms until we create separate and essential identities for ourselves through conscious action—through making choices, coming to decisions, reaffirming old purposes and projects, or affirming new ones.

Sartre saw an intimate connection between his conception of freedom—so different from either the liberal or the Marxist—and his conception of nothingness.[7] He insisted that because nothing compels us to act in any one way, we are absolutely free. Our future is totally open; none of the blanks have been filled in for us. However, as we start filling in the blanks, we are overcome with a sense not so much of finding ourselves as of losing ourselves. When we elect one possibility for ourselves, we simultaneously annihilate others. We buy the future at the cost of our past, a cost that burdens our psyche. If we insist we do not experience any of the psychic burdens—dread, anguish, nausea—he described, Sartre will accuse us of "bad faith," a state of being akin to self-deception, false consciousness, or delusion.

Sartre analyzed several types of bad faith, the most typical being hiding oneself in a *role* that seems to leave one no room for choice. For example, anyone who has ever been to a premier French restaurant has probably met "the waiter," Sartre's exemplar of robust role-playing.[8] Everything about the quintessential French waiter is highly stylized. He will present the wine list with the requisite flourish; he will grimace if the diner selects the wrong combination of courses; and he will behave in an overly solicitous manner should the diner's soup arrive lukewarm. The waiter acts in these ways not only because his job depends on it but also because his role-playing helps him avoid the fundamental uncertainties and ambiguities of human existence. As noted, all conscious beings, or beings-for-themselves, are without essence or defini-tion. They must define themselves through the mutually related processes of decision-making and action-taking. In contrast, all nonconscious beings, or beings-in-themselves, are *massif* ("solid"). In other words, they are what they are. Conscious beings supposedly yearn for the safe, uncomplicated state of nonconscious beings. The questions that afflict conscious beings, the possibil-ities that haunts conscious beings, summoning them to decide who they want to be. Thus, the aim of bad faith is to escape this awful condition of continu-ous choosing. The waiter tries to become his role so he no longer has choices to make about his being.

Another mode of bad faith occurs when we pretend we are thinglike, that we are just a body or object in the world that we can observe. Sartre used the example of a young woman's dating an old man who desires sex with her. To preserve the particular excitement of the occasion—such as, "I have been no-ticed by this man . . . how interesting I must be"—the woman wards off her dawning realization she has a decision to make about whether to sleep with him. Each time her companion makes a leading statement—for example, "I find you so attractive"—she attempts to "disarm" the phrase of its sexual im-plications. She is controlling the situation quite well, until the man takes her hand. The moment of decision has come. To leave the hand there is to "en-gage herself" in the flirtation; to withdraw the hand is to ruin the evening. But then bad faith comes to the woman's rescue. She leaves her hand in the man's hands, but "she does not notice that she is leaving it."[9] She achieves this state of nonconsciousness, of oblivion, of thinghood by engaging her com-panion in lofty intellectual and spiritual conversation, thereby achieving the separation of her soul from her body. "The hand," said Sartre, "rests inert be-tween the warm hands of her companion—neither consenting nor resisting—a thing."[10] By divorcing herself from her hand, the woman masks from herself that she is a free subject, not a determined object.

The problem with trying to live in bad faith is twofold. First, no matter how hard the conscious subject tries to live in bad faith, in the final analysis complete bad faith is an ontological impossibility. *Pour-soi*, the conscious subject, cannot be *en-soi*, the nonconscious object. Only death, the fore-closure of all possibilities, permits the conscious subject to escape freedom once and for all. Second, no matter how the conscious subject tries to excuse or justify it, bad faith is an ethical horror. If freedom has any meaning, it is in taking responsibility for one's actions, in realizing there is always room for some sort of choice, no matter how constricted one's circumstances.

Sartre had no patience with Freudians who would destroy the ethical project by permitting people to hide from their responsibility in the so-called unconscious. For Sartre, not only our decisions and actions, but also our feelings, are conscious. We use our emotions to work magic tricks. When our lives get too difficult to handle, we consciously work ourselves up into a rage or down into a depression. We then use these emotional extremes as excuses for our unreadiness and unwillingness to cope with life. Similarly, said Sartre, if manic-depressives or obsessive-compulsives cannot explain their afflictions, it is because they are repressing these explanations. Where Freud spoke of unconscious wishes unconsciously repressed, Sartre spoke of falsehoods, of people refusing to admit what they know are ultimately the reasons or explanations for their actions.[11]

Of all Sartre's categories, being-for-others is probably the most suited for a feminist analysis. According to Sartre, human relations are variations on two basic themes of conflict between rival consciousnesses, between self and others. First, there is love, which is essentially masochistic. Second, there are indifference, desire, and hate, which are essentially sadistic.[12]

Fools that we are, most of us start out with very grand ideas about love, about harmonizing the self and the other, said Sartre. The quest for love, we believe, is our attempt to be one with the other. This attempt is similar to the Christian mystic's effort to become one with God without forsaking his or her unique personal identity. Mystical union, we believe, is a very mysterious state. The mystic is at one and the same time himself or herself *and* God. It is this mysterious state we wish to create for ourselves. At the physical level, such union without absorption would mean my lover, for example, would live my body as he simultaneously lives his own. My lover would know my body in such a way he would erase all separation between us without depriving either of us of our quality of otherness. Similarly, at the psychological level, such union without absorption would mean my lover would know my mind and still not rob me of my identity or lose his own.

According to Sartre, such union without absorption is an impossible dream. We live in a very nonmystical world. There is no possibility of harmony, or union, between the self and the other; the self's need for total freedom is too absolute to be shared. Our attempts at love—at union without absorption—will always deteriorate to mutual possession or to mutual objectification. Exhausted by the struggle to maintain our subjectivity and freedom but still desiring a relationship (albeit one that is literally self-destructive) with the other, we may be led to masochism, the prospect of losing our subjectivity altogether in that of the other, who is now invited to treat us as a mere object.

Masochism is, for Sartre, not the perversion of love but its essential consequence. Through pain and humiliation, we hope to erase our subjectivity, to actually become the object that the other, the torturer, perceives as us. Our suffering may seem to testify we have no choice in the matter; however, as Sartre explained, this is a delusion. To be masochists, we must *choose* to apprehend ourselves as objects. Thus, as a flight from subjectivity, masochism is a dead end. The more we try to reduce ourselves to mere objects, the more we became aware of ourselves as subjectivities who are attempting this reduction.[13]

Defeated in our attempt to exist either as lovers or as failed lovers (masochists), we may be driven to indifference-desire or sadism-hate, the attempt to defy the freedom of the other. Our defiance begins quietly with indifference, a form of what Sartre called "blindness," or the nonrecognition of the subjectivity of others. Blind, we make no attempt to apprehend the other as anything but an object: "I scarcely notice [others]; I act as if I were alone in the world."[14] This solipsism is ego building, for it allows us to overlook that we are determined by others, shaped by the look of those others among whom we strut. When we are indifferent to others, we pretend they do not exist, that they cannot define us or are indifferent to others, that they do not exist, that they cannot define us or pigeonhole us. Nevertheless, what occurs even without our acknowledgment still, in fact, occurs: There *are* others in whose eyes we are objects. What we refuse to recognize, then, may at any moment intrude upon us. The other may at any moment direct at us an altogether human look, and we may receive it. "Brief and terrifying flashes of illumination," said Sartre, may rip through the shroud of our indifference, forcing us to recognize the subjectivity and freedom of the other.[15]

Receiving the look of the other ruins our attempt at total indifference, at times so much so that we come to desire the other sexually. To desire the other sexually is to want the other as mere flesh, as total object. There is, said Sartre, something sadistic about this desire. But no sooner do we possess the other as body than we discover it was not the other as body but the other as self we desired: "To be sure, I can grasp the Other, grab hold of him, knock him down. I can, providing I have the power, compel him to perform this or that act, to say certain words. But everything happens as if I wished to get hold of a man who runs away and leaves only his coat in my hands. It is the coat, it is the outer shell which I possess. I shall never get hold of more than a body, a psychic object in the midst of the world."[16] Just when we think we are about to triumph over the other—just when the other's consciousness as well as flesh seems ready to yield to us—the other may look us in the eye and make of us an object. By reestablishing itself as a subject, insisted Sartre, the other frustrates our attempt at sadism.

Unable to eliminate the threat or independence of the other even through sadism, our only recourse is hate—the wish for the death of the other. We want to wipe out forever the self who has, by looking at us as the other, threatened our freedom. If we feel we have been ridiculous or evil or cowardly in the other's consciousness, we may wish to wipe out the embarrassment by destroying that consciousness. Sartre pointed out that hatred of a particular other is, in reality, hatred of all others. If we wish not to be a self-for-others, logically we should have to annihilate all others. But hate is also futile, for even if all others ceased to exist, the memory of their looks would live on forever in our consciousness, inseparable from whatever ideas we might try to form about ourselves. So even our last resource does not suffice. "Hate does not enable us to get out of the circle. It simply represents the final attempt, the attempt of despair. After the failure of this attempt nothing remains for the for-itself except to re-enter the circle and allow itself to be infinitely tossed."[17]

Simone de Beauvoir's Existentialism for Women

In adopting the ontological and ethical language of existentialism, de Beauvoir observed that men named "man" the self; and "woman," the other. If the other is a threat to the self, then woman is a threat to man. Therefore, if man wishes to remain free, he must subordinate woman to him. To be sure, gender oppression is not the only form of oppression. Far from it. Blacks know what it is to be oppressed by whites, and the poor know what it is to be oppressed by the rich. Nonetheless, insisted Dorothy Kaufmann McCall, women's oppression by men is unique for two reasons. "First, unlike the oppression of race and class, the oppression of woman is not a contingent historical fact, an event in time which has sometimes been contested or reversed. Woman has always been subordinate to man. Second, women have internalized the alien point of view that man is the essential, woman the inessential.[18]

Destiny and History of Women

A good way to test de Beauvoir's characterization of woman's oppression as unique is to ponder her analysis of how woman became the other. In the first three chapters of *The Second Sex,* which she entitled "The Data of Biology," "The Psychoanalytic Point of View," and "The Point of View of Historical Materialism," de Beauvoir discussed how woman became not only different and separate from man but also inferior to him. She claimed that although biologists, Freudian psychoanalysts, and Marxist economists helped illuminate the reasons for woman's "otherness," existentialist philosophers provided the best explanation for it.

De Beauvoir noted that biology provides society with facts, which society then interprets to suit its own ends. For example, biology describes the respective reproductive roles of males and females:

The sperm, through which the life of the male is transcended in another, at the same instant becomes a stranger to him and separates from his body, so that the male recovers his individuality intact at the moment when he transcends it. The egg, on the contrary begins to separate from the female body when, fully matured, it emerges from the follicle and falls into the oviduct; but if fertilized by a gamete from outside, it becomes attached again through implantation in the uterus. First violated, the female is then alienated—she becomes, in part, another than herself.[19]

Although these reproductive "facts" might explain why it is oftentimes harder for a woman to become and remain a self, especially if she has a child, in de Beauvoir's estimation they in no way prove the societal myth than women's capacity for selfhood is somehow intrinsically less than men's.

De Beauvoir repeatedly observed that although biological and physiological facts about woman—such as her primary role in reproduction relative to man's secondary role, her physical weakness relative to man's physical strength, and her inactive role in heterosexual intercourse relative to man's active role—are true enough, how much value we attach to these facts is up to us as social beings. She wrote:

The enslavement of the female to the species and the limitations of her various powers are extremely important facts; the body of woman is one of the essential elements in her situations in the world. But that body is not enough to define her as woman; there is no true living reality except as manifested by the conscious individual through activities and in the bosom of a society. Biology is not enough to give an answer to the question that is before us: why is woman the Other?[20]

In other words, because woman is being-for-herself as well as being-in-itself, we must look for causes and reasons beyond those suggested by female biology and physiology to fully explain why society has selected *woman* to play the role of the other.

When de Beauvoir looked beyond biology to psychology, especially psychoanalysis, for a better explanation of woman's otherness, she was disappointed. According to de Beauvoir, traditional Freudians all tell essentially the same story about woman: She is a creature who must struggle between her "viriloid" and her "feminine" tendencies, the first expressed through clitoral eroticism, the second through vaginal eroticism. To win this battle—to become "normal"—woman must overcome her "viriloid" tendencies and transfer her love from a woman to a man. Although de Beauvoir conceded Freud's genius—which, for her, consisted in his having forwarded the bold idea that sexuality is the ultimate explanation for the human condition—she nevertheless rejected this notion as simplistic:

> There is no need of taking sexuality as an irreducible datum, for there is in the existent a more original "quest of being," of which sexuality is only one of the aspects. The psychoanalysts hold that the primary truth regarding man [*sic*] is his relation with his own body and with the bodies of his fellows in the group; but man [*sic*] has a primordial interest in the substance of the natural world which surrounds him and which he tries to discover in work, in play, and in all the experiences of the "dynamic imagination." Man [*sic*] aspires to be at one concretely with the whole world apprehended in all possible ways. To work the earth, to dig a hole, are activities as original as the embrace, as coition, and they deceive themselves who see here no more than sexual symbols.[21]

In other words, civilization cannot be explained merely as the product of repressed or sublimated sexual impulses. Civilization is more complicated than this, and so are the relations between men and women.

In particular, de Beauvoir viewed Freud's explanation for woman's otherness as incomplete. She faulted Freudians for teaching that women's low social status relative to men is due simply to women's lack of the penis. Anticipating by decades a central tenet of the US woman's movement, de Beauvoir refused to concede it is women's anatomy that consigns women to second-class personhood and citizenship. Women "envy" those who possess a penis, said de Beauvoir, not because they want a penis per se but because they desire the material and psychological privileges society accords to penis possessors. The social status of men is not to be traced to certain features of the male anatomy; rather, the "prestige of the penis" is to be explained "by the sovereignty of the father." Women are the other not because they lack penises but because they lack power.[22]

Finally, de Beauvoir considered the Marxist explanation for why woman is the other and found it as unsatisfying as Freud's. Engels contended that from the beginning of time women performed *en-soi*–like tasks, such as cooking, cleaning, and child-rearing; whereas men performed *pour-soi*–like tasks, such as hunting and fighting, most of which involve the use of tools to subdue the world. As a result of this particular division of labor, men seized the means of production; they became the "bourgeois" and women became the "proletariat." Capitalism favors this state of affairs as it does not have to pay women for the work they do in the home. The "system" gets women's housework for free. Thus, men will remain the "bourgeois" and women the "proletariat" until capitalism is overthrown and the means of production are owned equally by men and women. Then and only then, said Engels, will work be divided not on the basis of individuals' gender but on the basis of individuals' ability, readiness, and willingness to perform certain jobs.

Disagreeing with Engels, de Beauvoir insisted a move from capitalism to socialism would not automatically change the relations between men and women. Women are just as likely to remain the other in a socialist society as in a capitalist society, for the roots of women's oppression are more than economic; they are ontological. Thus, de Beauvoir stressed: "If the human consciousness had not included . . . an original aspiration to dominate the Other, the invention of the bronze tool could not have caused the oppression of woman."[23] Women's liberation requires far more than the elimination of the institution of private property; it requires nothing less than the elimination of men's desire to control women—a very radical feminist notion.

Unsatisfied by the traditional biological, psychological, and economic explanations of women's oppression, de Beauvoir sought a deeper explanation for why men named man the self and woman the other. She speculated that in perceiving themselves as subjects capable of risking their lives in combat, men perceived women as objects, capable only of giving life. "It is not in giving life but risking life," said de Beauvoir, "that man is raised above the animal; that is why superiority has been accorded in humanity not to the sex that brings forth but to that which kills."[24] In addition, de Beauvoir surmised there was probably another, even more basic explanation for men's relegation of woman to the sphere of otherness. She observed that as soon as man asserted himself "as subject and free being, the idea of the Other [arose]"[25]—specifically, the idea of *woman* as the other. Woman became for man everything man was not, an alien power that man had best control, lest woman become the self and man the other.

Myths About Woman

As civilization developed, men discovered they could control women by creating myths about woman: her irrationality, complexity, and opaqueness. Throughout her analysis of men's myths about woman, de Beauvoir emphasized that each man is in search of the ideal woman—that is, the woman who can make him whole. But because men's basic needs are so similar, their ideal women tend to look the same. Literature attests to this fact, said de Beauvoir. Over and over again, men claim that self-sacrificial women— women who will stand by them and, if necessary, give up their very lives for them—are ideal women.[26]

In addition to idealizing/idolizing the self-sacrificial woman, man's myths about woman betray a fundamental ambivalence about her nature. In words anticipating those of psychoanalytic feminist Dorothy Dinnerstein and ecofeminist Susan Griffin, de Beauvoir described the ways in which men connect nature to women. Like nature, woman reminds men of both life and death. At one and the same time, woman is innocent angel and guilty demon. Because her natural body reminds man he is subject to disease, disintegration, death, and decay, man delights in her artificial body. Feathered and furred, powdered and perfumed, the "animal crudity" of women (her "odor") is hidden from man in his flight from carnality and the mortality to which her body points.[27]

If woman could simply scoff at the image of her "ideal," then the situation would not be so perilous for her. But woman is unable to do so because man has the power to control her—to use her for his own purposes no matter the cost she has to pay. Honoré de Balzac, said de Beauvoir, summarized man's attitude toward woman when he wrote:

> Pay no attention to her murmurs, her cries, her pains; *nature has made for our use* and for bearing everything: children, sorrows, blows and pains inflicted by man. Do not accuse yourself of hardness. In all the codes of so-called civilized nations, man has written the laws that ranged woman's destiny under his bloody epigraph: "*Vae victic!* Woe to the weak!"[28]

Finally, what makes the myth of woman so terrible is that many women come to internalize it as an accurate reflection of what it means to be woman.

Woman's Lived-Experience[29]

Unlike Sartre, de Beauvoir specified social roles as the primary mechanisms the self, or subject uses to control the other, or object. She labeled woman's tragic acceptance of her own otherness the feminine "mystery," which passes from generation to generation through the socialization of girls. De Beauvoir spoke from her own experience—that of a bourgeois French girl growing up between two world wars. She claimed girls recognize their bodily differences from boys very early on. With puberty, with the swelling of their breasts, and with the beginning of their menstrual flow, girls accept and internalize as shameful and inferior their otherness. This otherness is cemented, said de Beauvoir, in the institutions of marriage and motherhood.

As de Beauvoir saw it, the role of wife blocks women's freedom. Although de Beauvoir believed men and women are capable of deep love, she claimed the institution of marriage ruins couples' relationships. It transforms freely given feelings into mandatory duties and shrilly asserted rights. Marriage is a form of slavery, said de Beauvoir. It gives women (at least French bourgeois women) little more than "gilded mediocrity lacking ambition and passion, aimless days indefinitely repeated, life that slips away gently toward death without questioning its purpose."[30] Marriage offers women contentment, tranquility, and security, but is also robs women of the chance to be great. In return for their freedom, women are given "happiness." Gradually, women learn how to settle for less:

> It is not without some regret that she shuts behind her the doors of her new home; when she was a girl, the whole countryside was her homeland; the forests were hers. Now she is confined to a restricted space; Nature is reduced to the dimensions of a potted geranium; walls cut off the horizon. But she is going to set about overcoming these limitations. In the form of more or less expensive bric-a-brac she has exotic countries and past time; she has her husband representing human society; and she has her child, who gives her the entire future in portable form.[31]

If the role of wife limits women's self-development, the role of mother does so even more.[32] Although de Beauvoir conceded *rearing* a child to adulthood can be existentially engaging, she insisted *bearing* a child is not an action but a mere event. De Beauvoir stressed the ways in which pregnancy alienates a woman from herself, making it difficult for her to chart, unencumbered, the course of her destiny. Like radical-libertarian feminist Shulamith Firestone, de Beauvoir questioned the supposed joys of pregnancy, observing that even women who want to have children seem to have a tough time of it. Also like Firestone, de Beauvoir worried about the way in which the mother-child relationship is so easily distorted. At first the child seems to liberate the mother from her object status because she "obtains in her child what man seeks in woman: an other, coming nature and mind, who is to be both prey and *double*."[33] As time goes on, however, the child becomes a demanding tyrant—a toddler, an adolescent, an adult, a conscious subject who, by looking at the mother, can turn her into an object, into a machine for cooking, cleaning, caring, giving, and especially sacrificing. Reduced to an object, the mother, not unexpectedly, begins to view and to use her child as an object, as something that can make up for her lacks.

It is clear that "wifing" and "mothering" are, in de Beauvoir's estimation, two feminine roles that limit woman's freedom, but so, too, is the role of "career" woman, as Betty Friedan discussed late in life (see pages 28–29). De Beauvoir stressed a career woman can no more escape the cage of femininity than a wife and mother can. Indeed, in some ways, the career woman is in a worse situation than the stay-at-home wife and mother because she is at all times and places expected to be and act like a woman. In other words, a career woman is expected to add to her professional duties those "duties" implied in her "femininity," by which society seems to mean a certain sort of pleasing appearance. As a result, she develops an internal conflict between her professional and feminine interests. If the career woman devotes herself to her professional interests so much so that she neglects her appearance, she will see herself as falling very short of the standards set by beautiful women. Others will find fault with her hair, teeth, nails, complexion, figure, and clothes. Distressed by her lack of good looks and sex appeal, the career woman will be tempted to cut her workday short so she has more time for beauty treatments. If she reallocates her time in this fashion, however, the career woman will soon find herself playing second fiddle to the career man who, unlike her, is not required to cultivate narcissism as a virtue.[34]

Although all women engage in feminine role-playing, according to de Beauvoir, three kinds of women play the role of "woman" to the hilt. They are the prostitute, the narcissist, and the mystic. De Beauvoir's analysis of the prostitute was complex. On the one hand, the prostitute is a paradigm for woman as the other, as object, as the exploited one; on the other hand, the prostitute, like the man who purchases her services, is a self, a subject, an exploiter. She prostitutes herself, suggested de Beauvoir, not simply for the money but for the homage men pay to her "otherness." Unlike men's wives and girlfriends, prostitutes get something for yielding their bodies to men's dreams: "wealth, and fame."[35]

Conceding that the so-called streetwalker often sells her body because it is the only thing she has to sell, de Beauvoir stressed that in contrast the so-called call girl, the hetaera, who regards her whole self as capital, usually has the upper hand in a relationship.[36] Men need her more than she needs them. De Beauvoir's point seems to be that even if the hetaera, like the wife and the mother, cannot escape being the other, at least she is able to use her otherness to her own personal advantage. (As disturbing as I find de Beauvoir's account and as much as I want to resist it, I am reminded of a former colleague of mine, a brilliant and beautiful woman from the developing world, who used her "otherness" to capture the imagination of many of my male colleagues. At one point she said to me, "I make them pay for my otherness." And pay they did, for she had a way of trivializing and humiliating them both as men and as intellectuals.)

A feminine role even more problematic than the prostitute is the narcissist. De Beauvoir claimed that woman's narcissism results from her otherness. Woman is frustrated as a subject because she is not allowed to engage in self-defining activity and because her feminine activities are not fulfilling.[37] Woman then becomes her own object of importance. Believing herself to be an object—a belief confirmed by most everyone around her—she is fascinated by, and perhaps even fixated on, her own image: face, body, clothes. The sense of being a subject and object simultaneously is, of course, illusory. Nevertheless, the narcissist somehow believes that *she* is the impossible synthesis of being-for-itself and being-in-itself.[38]

Probably the most problematic feminine role in *The Second Sex* is the mystic who seeks to be the supreme object of a supreme subject. The mystic, wrote de Beauvoir, confuses God with man and man with God. She speaks of divine beings as if they were human beings, and she speaks of men as if they were gods. What the mystic seeks in divine love, said de Beauvoir, is "first of all what the *amoureuse* seeks in that of man: the exaltation of her narcissism: this sovereign gaze fixed attentively, amorously, upon her is a miraculous godsend."[39] The mystic does not pursue transcendence through God. Instead, she seeks to be possessed supremely by a God who would have no other woman before him. What the mystic wants from God is the exaltation of her objecthood.

In reflecting upon her descriptions of the wife, the mother, the career woman, the prostitute, the narcissist, and the mystic, de Beauvoir concluded these roles are not fundamentally of woman's own making. Not permitted to be a maker herself, woman, said de Beauvoir, has been constructed by man, by his structures and institutions. But because woman, like man, has no essence, she need not continue to be what man has made her to be. Woman can deconstruct herself. She can be a subject, engage in positive action in society, and redefine or abolish her roles as wife, mother, career woman, prostitute, narcissist, and mystic. Way before feminist postmodernists said so, de Beauvoir insisted woman can create her own self because there is no essence of eternal femininity prescribing a ready-made identity for her. All that is holding woman back from self-creation is society—a patriarchy that is, in de Beauvoir's estimation, reaching its end.[40] Woman, like man, is a subject rather than an object; she is no more being-in-itself than man is. Woman, like man, is being-for-itself, and it is high time for woman as well as man to recognize this fact.

There are, of course, no easy ways for woman to escape what de Beauvoir repeatedly described as woman's immanence—the limits, definitions, and roles that society, propriety, and men have imposed on her. Nevertheless, if woman wants to cease being the second sex, the other, she must overcome the forces of circumstances; she must have her say and her way as much as man does. On the way to transcendence, there are, said de Beauvoir, four strategies women can employ.

First, like Marxist-socialist feminists, de Beauvoir said women can go to work. To be sure, de Beauvoir recognized that work in a capitalist patriarchy can be oppressive and exploitative, particularly when it results in women's working a double day: one shift in the office or factory and one shift at home. Nonetheless, de Beauvoir insisted no matter how taxing or tiring a woman's job is, it still opens up possibilities for her that she would otherwise lack. By working outside the home alongside men, woman "regains her transcendence"; she "concretely affirms her status as subject, as someone who is actively charting the course of her destiny."[41]

Second, women can become intellectuals, members of the vanguard of change for women. Intellectual activity is, after all, the activity of one who thinks, looks, and defines, not the nonactivity of one who is thought about, looked at, and defined. De Beauvoir encouraged women to study writers such as Emily Brontë, Virginia Woolf, and Katherine Mansfield, who took themselves seriously enough as writers to probe death, life, and suffering.[42]

Third, women can work toward a socialist transformation of society. Like Sartre, de Beauvoir held out hope for an end to the subject-object, self-other conflict among human beings in general and between men and women in particular. In *Being and Nothingness,* Sartre added a footnote to his conclusion that all attempts at love or union are bound to lapse into either masochism or sadism. Sartre explained his "considerations do not exclude the possibility of an ethics of deliverance and salvation. But this can be achieved only after a radical conversion which we cannot discuss here."[43] The radical conversion he had in mind is a Marxist revolution. The struggle between one human being and another, which in *Being and Nothingness* arose from a psychological necessity derived from the nature of consciousness itself, became in Sartre's *Critique of Dialectical Reason,* a struggle between workers and capitalists caused not by psychological but by economic necessity. Sartre implied that if all people had adequate food, clothing, and shelter, they might be able to overcome the psychological barriers separating them. Love might be possible after all.

Like Sartre, de Beauvoir believed one of the keys to women's liberation is economic, a point she emphasized in her discussion of the independent woman. De Beauvoir reminded women that their circumstances will, of course, limit their efforts to define themselves. Just as a sculptor's creativity is limited by the marble block at hand, a woman's freedom is limited by the size of her bank account, for example. If a woman wants to be all that she can possibly be, she must help create the kind of society that will provide her with the material support to transcend her present limits.

Finally, to transcend their limits, women can refuse to internalize their otherness—that is, to identify themselves through the eyes of the dominant group in society. To accept the role of the other, said de Beauvoir, is to accept being an object. It is, as Josephine Donovan wrote, "to deny the subject-self that is autonomous and creative" and risk the kind of "madness and schizophrenia" that results from "engaging in a perpetual lie."[44] On the one hand, woman's *in-authentic* self lives as the "object-self" seen by the male world; on the other hand, woman's *authentic* self lives as a "withdrawn-invisible self—invisible at times even to oneself."[45] As a result, woman's person is split.

According to Donovan, Meredith Tax's analysis of women's "splitness" is particularly insightful. Tax described a woman who is forced to put up with men's catcalls and whistles as she walks down a public street. In such a situation, the woman has but two choices: "Either she remains sensitive and vulnerable to the pain; or she shuts it outs by saying, 'It's only my body they are talking about. It doesn't affect me. They know nothing about me.' Whatever the process, the solution is a split between the mind and the body."[46] Reinforcing Tax's analysis, Sandra Lee Bartky observed that the phenomenon of catcalling or whistling demonstrates just how pervasive women's objectification is in our society. No matter where they go, women can't seem to escape men's eyes.

In an attempt to further elucidate how the "gaze of the Other" petrifies women's self into an object, Bartky speculated that in our society the other that is internalized in women takes a particular form; it is the other created by the "fashion-beauty complex." Women are, she said, "resented everywhere with images of perfect female beauty—at the drugstore cosmetics display, the supermarket magazine counter, on television";[47] and it is these images women internalize, mercilessly measuring their imperfect bodies against the supposedly perfect bodies of high fashion. What women in our society—indeed in any society in which cosmetics and fashion exist—fail to realize, said Bartky, is something de Beauvoir knew only too well. De Beauvoir asserted that "costumes and styles are often devoted to cutting off the feminine body from any possible transcendence."[48] The mobility of the foot-bound or high-heeled woman is limited; the dexterity of the long-fingernailed or bejeweled woman is impeded. Women are so busy attending to their deficient bodies they have no times to improve their minds. Thus, the only way for a woman to become a self in a society such as ours is for her to *free* her self from her body, to refuse to fritter away her time at the beauty salon, when she could be engaged in some sort of creative or service-oriented project.

Critiques of Existentialist Feminism: A Communitarian Critique of Existentialist Feminism

Jean Bethke Elshtain faulted de Beauvoir's *Second Sex* for three reasons. She noted for one that the book was not accessible to the majority of women. "Immanence" and "transcendence," "essence" and "existence," "being-for-itself" and "being-in-itself" are ideas that do not arise directly out of ordinary women's lived experience but are abstractions that emerge from the philosopher's armchair speculations. De Beauvoir's technical words, said Elshtain, are more likely to "pummel" less formally educated women into agreeing with her than to persuade them they are indeed the second sex.[49]

Elshtain also strongly objected to de Beauvoir's treatment of the body, especially the female body. She claimed de Beauvoir presents all bodies, but particularly female bodies, as negative: unfortunate, insignificant, dirty, shameful, burdensome, inherently alienating. Elshtain speculated de Beauvoir's general distrust of the body was rooted in her existentialist anxieties about the carnality and mortality of the flesh. The body is a problem within the existentialist framework insofar as it is a stubborn and unavoidable object limiting the freedom of each conscious subject. De Beauvoir recorded in her memoirs her own war against the flesh: her squashed sexual urges, her attempts to do without sleep, her sense of horror as she relentlessly aged.[50] Because the slow disintegration of the body signals the coming of death—the end of consciousness, of freedom, of subjectivity—existentialists such as de Beauvoir have little desire to celebrate a body that represents to them the forces of death.

De Beauvoir's general distrust of the body, claimed Elshtain, became a very particular mistrust of the *female* body. According to de Beauvoir, woman's reproductive capacities rob her of her personhood. In contrast, a man's reproductive capacities do not threaten his personhood. After sexual intercourse, the man remains exactly as he was before sexual intercourse. But if fertilization takes place after sexual intercourse, a woman is no longer the same person she was before: "Ensnared by nature, the pregnant woman is plant and animal, a stock-pile of colloids, an incubator, an egg; she scares children proud of their young, straight bodies and makes young people titter contemptuously because she is a human being, a conscious and free individual, who has become life's passing instrument."[51] In focusing on this passage and others like it, Elshtain commented that de Beauvoir's description of pregnancy is profoundly alienating to the majority of pregnant women, most of whom view their "swelling with child" positively. One does not win many converts to feminism by claiming pregnant women are akin to vegetables.

Last, Elshtain criticized de Beauvoir for celebrating largely male norms. All of de Beauvoir's complaints about woman's character as passive, submissive, and immanent translate into a valorization of man's character as active, dominant, and transcendent. The denigration of woman's body arises from the elevation of man's mind. The deploring of woman's association with nature contrasts with the admiration of man's construction of culture. Thus, de Beauvoir prescribed women to achieve freedom by rejecting their bodies and connections to nature. As Elshtain saw it, de Beauvoir's prescription for women's oppression was flawed. To ask women to give up their female identity without considering the ramifications of trading in sisterhood for brotherhood or even personhood, said Elshtain, is irresponsible.[52]

Responses to Critiques of de Beauvoir

The critics of de Beauvoir invite us to ponder whether it is more liberating to think of woman as the product of a cultural construction or instead to think of woman as the result of a natural arrangement. They also invite us to wonder whether the realm of transcendence is better, worse, or simply different than the realm of immanence. Finally, they invite us to consider, as others already have, whether women's liberation requires women to reject the "feminine" entirely or to embrace it yet more wholeheartedly.

Despite the force of Elshtain's critique and critiques like it, much can and has been said in defense of de Beauvoir's existentialist feminism.[53] De Beauvoir is, admittedly, a challenging, even intimidating feminist thinker. But just because she spoke in her own voice—that of a highly educated, bourgeois, French woman—does not mean her words cannot speak to women whose life circumstances depart dramatically from her own.

De Beauvoir was dismayed when some of her supposedly nonsexist friends—for example, the existentialist Albert Camus—met the publication of *The Second Sex* coldly, rejecting it as a simpleminded assault upon masculinity.[54] She was also disheartened by the chilly response of the local Communist Party, which regarded her book as yet another trivial catalogue of female complaints intended to distract women from genuine class struggle.[55] To be sure, de Beauvoir also had her supporters; twenty-two thousand copies of *The Second Sex* were sold in the first week following its publication. However, what pleased de Beauvoir the most, according to one of her biographers, were the letters she received from grateful women of *every social class* whose lives had changed in positive directions after reading her reflections. Whether de Beauvoir's prose is difficult to read or not, these women found in her book a liberating message addressed to them in particular.[56]

The assertion that de Beauvoir was hostile to the body, especially to the female body, is one for which ample textual evidence exists. When de Beauvoir observed women have within their bodies a "hostile element"—namely, "the species gnawing at their vitals"—her words evoked feelings of fear, weakness, and disgust.[57] Nevertheless, despite her valorization of the mind over the body, de Beauvoir's rejection of the body was less virulent than Sartre's rejection of the body. In fact, de Beauvoir told Sartre that his attitude toward the body, especially the emotions, was *too* inflexible: "I criticized Sartre for regarding his body as a mere bundle of striated muscles, and for having cut it out of his emotional world. If you gave way to tears or nerves or seasickness, he said, you were simply being weak. I, on the other hand, claimed that stomach and tear ducts, indeed the head itself, were all subject to irresistible forces on occasion."[58]

To be sure, de Beauvoir's concession that "it's good to demand that a woman should not be made to feel degraded by, let's say, her monthly periods; that a woman refuse to be made to feel ridiculous because of her pregnancy; that a woman be able to be proud of her body, and her feminine sexuality"[59] does not mean that, after all, she really did love the body in general and the female body in particular. On the contrary, when informed that like many French feminists, many US feminists, especially radical feminists made woman's body the centerpiece of their feminism, de Beauvoir commented that she was opposed to any privileging of a special female way of being.

> There is no reason at all to fall into some wild narcissism, and build, on the basis of these givens, a system which would be the culture and the life of women. I don't think that women should repress their givens. She has the perfect right to be proud of being a woman, just as man is also proud of his sex. After all, he has the right to be proud of it, under the condition, however, that he does not deprive others of the right to a similar pride. Everyone can be happy with her or his body. But one should not make this body the center of the universe.[60]

As de Beauvoir saw it, the problem with making woman's body the linchpin of women's liberation is that it mistakes a biological fact for a social fact. Woman's body—as wonderful as it is—should not prescribe, or mandate, a definite mode of existence for all women. Rather, each woman should shape a unique mode of existence for herself.

Postmodern Feminism

Some of postmodern feminism's roots are found in the work of Simone de Beauvoir, who, as we just noted, phrased the fundamental question of feminist theory as, "Why is woman the *second* sex?" Rephrased in postmodern terms, the question becomes, "Why is woman the other?" why does woman remain earthbound, immanent and determined, as she watches man fly off into the realm of transcendence, the zone of freedom? De Beauvoir's answer to these questions may or may not prove convincing, but no reader of *The*

Second Sex can turn to its last page without concluding that to be "second," or "other," is not the best way for a person to be.

Postmodern feminists take de Beauvoir's understanding of otherness and turn it on its head. Woman is still the other, but rather than interpreting this condition as something to be transcended, postmodern feminists proclaim its advantages. The condition of otherness enables women to stand back and criticize the norms, values, and practices that the dominant culture (patriarchy) seeks to impose on everyone, including those who live on the periphery—in this case, women. Thus, otherness, for all of its associations with oppression and inferiority, is much more than an oppressed condition. It is also a way of being, thinking, and speaking allowing for openness, plurality, diversity, and differences.

Like postmodernists in general, postmodern feminists reject phallogocentric thought; that is, thought ordered around an absolute word (*logos*) that is "male" in style (hence the reference to the phallus). In addition, postmodern feminists reject any mode of thought, including feminist thought that aims to provide a single explanation for why women are oppressed or the steps *all* women must take to achieve liberation. To be sure, postmodern feminists' refusal to develop an overarching explanation and solution for women's oppression poses major problems for feminist theory. Yet this refusal also adds needed fuel to the feminist fires of plurality, multiplicity, and difference. Postmodern feminists invite women to become the kind of "feminists" they want to be. There is, in their estimation, no single formula for being a true feminist, but there are, nonetheless, ways that women can come together to effect social change. Thus, it is important to examine the roots of postmodern feminism to better see how postmodern feminists have shaped these roots into a tree, branches, and leaves of their own.

Postmodernism/Postmodern Feminism: Keynotes

In a moment of exasperation, Judith Butler (discussed in more detail on page 201) said she was tired of thinkers who include in the category "postmodern" any type of philosophical thought that is not modern (*modern* usually means the kind of philosophical thought that characterized the eighteenth-century European Enlightenment or Age of Reason):

> A number of positions are ascribed to postmodernism, as if it were the kind of thing that could be the bearer of a set of positions. . . . These characterizations are variously imputed to postmodernism or poststructuralism, which are conflated with each other and sometimes conflated with deconstruction, and sometimes understood as an indiscriminate assem-

blage of French feminism, deconstruction, Lacanian psychoanalysis, Foucaultian analysis, Rorty's conversationalism and cultural studies.[61]

Butler's point was that many critics of postmodernism/postmodern feminism are guilty of not doing their homework. They try to "colonize and domesticate" a wide variety of emerging modes of philosophical thought under what she termed the "sign of the same."[62] Rather than actually reading the writings of postmodernists/postmodern feminists closely, these critics prefer to dismiss them as variations on the same theme.

Butler's point is well taken. Yet, despite the diversity in postmodern/postmodern feminist thought, it is still possible to claim that a large number of postmodern feminists take their intellectual cues not only from existentialists, such as Simone de Beauvoir, but also from deconstructionists, such as Jacques Derrida, and poststructuralists, such as Michel Foucault. Although I could have discussed any number of postmodern feminists in this chapter, I have selected only two for detailed discussion.[63] First, I focus on Hélène Cixous and the influence of Jacques Derrida's writings on her thought. Second, I focus on Judith Butler and the influence of Michel Foucault's theories on her thought. To be sure, Cixous and Butler are simply representative postmodern feminists, which is a very large and eclectic class. My decision to focus on these two thinkers is mainly a matter of preference, but it is also part of a plan to identify points of resonance between them. It may, after all, be useful to maintain the category "postmodern feminism," if only to begin a fruitful discussion with other schools of feminist thought.

Before launching into a discussion of Jacques Derrida and Hélène Cixous, it may be well to consider postmodernism's position on the general map of Western philosophy. One of the easiest ways to understand postmodernism is to list the modernist (Enlightenment) beliefs it rejects. Jane Flax has provided a particularly good summary of the Enlightenment's main tenets, including the following:

1. There is a "stable, coherent self" that can know how and why it thinks the way it does.
2. Through its rational powers (reason), the self can gain "objective, reliable, and universal knowledge."
3. The knowledge that reason acquires is true; that is, it "represent[s] something real and unchanging (universal) about our minds and the structure of the natural world."
4. Reason has "transcendental and universal qualities"; that is, somehow reason exists independently of us viewed as historical beings situated in specific times and places.

5. Reason, freedom, and autonomy are interconnected in very complex ways. For example, if I am fully free, I will voluntarily obey the laws reason imposes on me. I will not rebel against the laws that bind me and all rational beings.
6. Power does not trump reason. On the contrary. Claims to power (authority) are grounded in reason. Therefore, when truth conflicts with power, reason steps in and decides the controversy in favor of truth.
7. The exemplar for all true knowledge is science understood as the "right use of reason." Science is neutral and objective in its methodology, and because this is so, it can utilize the laws of nature for our benefit.
8. Language, the tool we use to communicate the knowledge science produces, represents the real world that our rational minds observe. There is an isomorphic correspondence between word and thing. For example, the word "dog" corresponds to the entity, dog. Objects are not constructed by means of words or social conventions. Once perceived by our rational minds, objects are simply acknowledged by us through words.[64]

Enlightenment (modern) thought as summarized by Flax remains the kind of thought that is still operative in most Westerners' everyday lives. But, as postmodernists see it, most Westerners are living in a state of denial. The "Enlightenment world" is a figment of a certain kind of imagination. There is neither a stable self nor rational powers capable of yielding universal knowledge. Truth is whatever power proclaims it to be. Freedom is the power to do as one pleases, however irrational or nonbeneficial one's actions may be judged. Science is no more objective than politics or ethics, both of which are subjective, contextual, historical, contingent, and almost always deployed to serve self-interest. And language does not represent reality, because there is no reality for it to signify. On the contrary, language constructs reality—a reality that depends on words for its existence.

Jacques Derrida

Like Jacques Lacan, whose work was discussed in Chapter 4, Jacques Derrida focused much of his work on the mechanisms of the Symbolic order; that is, the series of interrelated signs, roles, and rituals a child must internalize to be able to function adequately in society. The more a child submits to the linguistic rules of society, the more those rules will be inscribed in his or her unconscious. In other words, the Symbolic order regulates society through the regulation of individuals; As long as individuals speak the language of the Symbolic order—internalizing its gender, race, and class norms—society will reproduce itself in fairly constant forms.

Derrida sought to liberate thinking from the assumption of singularity—that is, the view that one single truth or essence, a "transcendental signifier," exists, in and of itself, as a giver of meaning. He did this by using the techniques of a philosophical method often referred to as *deconstruction*. Deconstruction is a deliberate attempt to open or subject a literary, philosophical, or political text to several interpretations, some of which may contradict each other. According to Derrida, our understanding of any word—say, *cat*—does not depend on the "metaphysical presence" (existence/reality) of either any particular cat or the idea of cat/catness in general. Rather it depends on other words—on a very long chain of "signifiers" that refer to nothing over and beyond themselves.[65]

In an attempt to explain Derrida's deconstructionist views, most commentators focus on his concept of difference (which he spells *différance* instead of *différence,* the ordinary French spelling of the English word *difference*). Prior to the emergence of postmodern thought, structuralists insisted that so-called binary oppositions produce meaning in language. In other words, structuralists claimed our understanding of the term *masculine,* for example, depends on our understanding of the term *feminine,* and vice versa. Derrida disagreed with this reigning view. As he saw it, language is achieved through the free play of myriad signifiers. Bipolar thought must be resisted whenever it manifests itself.

Toril Moi clarified Derrida's understanding of "playful" signifiers by pointing to structuralist Ferdinand de Saussure's concept of the phoneme, "defined as the smallest differential—and therefore signifying—unit in language."[66] No one phoneme, say, *b,* has any meaning in and of itself, said Moi. On the contrary, the only reason *b* signifies anything is that it is different from *h* and numerous other phonemes. Likewise, the only reason the word *bat* means anything in English is that it can be contrasted with such words as *cat, hat,* and the myriad other words that constitute the English language. The word *bat* achieves its meaning by continually deferring its meaning to other English words. It never gets to rest safe and secure in the comfort of an actual bat or the idea of batness-in-itself. Nor does it come into permanent existence by virtue of the intent of some particular author who defines its meaning once and for all. Rather, the word *bat* becomes temporarily meaningful only when an author lets it come to the fore by suppressing other words that may, in turn, be selected over it by other authors. No phoneme, word, sentence, paragraph, article, book, has a final meaning. Thus, thinking is nothing more than continually producing new readings of texts.[67] Language and reality are variable and shifting, missing each other in an ever-flowing flux of words, according to Derrida. Words do not stand for things, for pieces of reality. Rather, reality eludes language, and language refuses to be pinned down or limited by reality.

Hélène Cixous

Although no single thinker is *behind* Hélène Cixous's complex thought, she found Derrida's concept of *différance* (defined by Moi as the "open-ended play between the presence of one signifier and the absence of others")[68] and his rejection of binary thought very useful. Cixous is primarily a novelist experimenting with literary style. In applying Derrida's notion of *différance* to writing, she contrasted feminine writing (*l'écriture féminine*) with masculine writing (*littérature*). Viewed within a psychoanalytic framework, masculine writing is rooted in a man's genital and libidinal economy, which is emblemized by the phallus. For a variety of sociocultural reasons, masculine writing has reigned supreme over feminine writing. In the words of Ann Rosalind Jones, man (white, European, and ruling class) has claimed, "I am the unified, self-controlled center of the universe. The rest of the world, which I define as the Other, has meaning only in relation to me, as man/father, possessor of the phallus."[69]

Cixous objected to masculine writing and thinking because they are cast in binary oppositions. Man has unnecessarily segmented reality by coupling concepts and terms in pairs of polar opposites, one of which is always privileged over the other. In her essay "Sorties," Cixous listed some of these dichotomous pairs:

> Activity/Passivity
> Sun/Moon
> Culture/Nature
> Day/Night
> Thought has always worked through opposition.
> Speaking/Writing
> Parole/Écriture
> High/Low
> Through dual, hierarchical oppositions.[70]

According to Cixous, each of these dichotomies finds its inspiration in the dyad man-woman. Man is associated with all that is active, cultural, light, high, or generally positive, whereas woman is associated with all that is passive, natural, dark, low, or generally negative. Moreover, the first term in the dyad man-woman is the term from which the second departs or deviates. Man is the self; woman is the other. Thus, woman exists in man's world on his terms. She is either the other for man, or she is unthought. After man is done thinking about woman, "what is left of her is unthinkable, unthought."[71]

Cixous challenged women to write themselves out of the world *men* constructed for women. She urged women to put themselves—the unthinkable/

unthought—into words. The kind of writing Cixous identified as woman's own—marking, scratching, scribbling, jotting down—connotes movements that, once again, bring to mind Heraclitus's ever-changing river. In contrast, the kind of writing Cixous associated with man composes the bulk of the so-called accumulated wisdom of humankind. Stamped with the official seal of social approval, masculine writing is too weighted down to move or change.

For Cixous, feminine writing is not merely a new style of writing; it is "the very possibility of change, the space that can serve as a springboard for subversive thought, the precursory movement of a transformation of social and cultural standards."[72] By developing feminine writing, women can, she insisted, change the way the Western world thinks, speaks, and acts. This is no easy task, however. Trying to write the nonexistent into existence, to "foresee the unforeseeable," may, after all, strain women writers to the breaking point.[73]

In further distinguishing woman's writing from man's, Cixous drew many connections between male sexuality and masculine writing and female sexuality and feminine writing. Male sexuality, which centers on what Cixous called the "big dick," is ultimately boring in its pointedness and singularity.[74] Like male sexuality, masculine writing, which Cixous usually termed phallogocentric writing, is also ultimately boring. Men write the same old things with their "little pocket signifier"—the trio of penis/phallus/pen.[75] Fearing the multiplicity and chaos that exist outside their Symbolic order, men always write in black ink, carefully containing their thoughts in a sharply defined and rigidly imposed structure.

In contrast, female sexuality is anything but boring. Cixous wrote in no uncertain terms:

> Almost everything is yet to be written by women about femininity: about their sexuality, that is, its infinite and mobile complexity; about their eroticization, sudden turn-ons of a certain minuscule-immense area of their bodies; not about destiny, but about the adventure of such and such a drive, about trips, crossings, trudges, abrupt and gradual awakenings, discoveries of a zone at once timorous and soon to be forthright.[76]

Like female sexuality, feminine writing is open and multiple, varied and rhythmic, full of pleasures and, more important, full of possibilities. When a woman writes, said Cixous, she writes in "white ink," letting her words flow freely where she wishes them to go: "Her writing can only keep going, without ever inscribing or discerning contours. . . . She lets the other language speak—the language of 1,000 tongues which knows neither enclosure nor death. . . . Her language does not contain, it carries; it does not hold back, it makes possible."[77]

Running through Cixous's writing are an optimism and a joy lacking in Derrida, for whom logocentrism is inevitable. Cixous insisted women writers have the ability to lead the Western world out of the dichotomous conceptual order that causes it to think, speak, and act in terms of someone who is dominant and someone else who is submissive. If woman explores her body "with its thousand and one thresholds of order," said Cixous, she "will make the old single-grooved mother tongue reverberate with more than one language."[78] The id, implied Cixous, is the source of all desires. "Oral drive, anal drive, vocal drive—all these drives are our strengths, and among them is the gestation drive—just like the desire to write: a desire to live self from within, a desire for the swollen body, for language, for blood."[79]

Michel Foucault

Michel Foucault agreed with Derrida and Cixous that "we should not view the subject as the knowing, willing, autonomous, self-critical or 'transcendental' subject of Kantian discourse."[80] Rather, we should understand the subject—that is, the individual person—as the product or effect of a variety of power relations manifested through a plurality of discourses. Understanding what Foucault means by power and power relations is no easy task, however. He said: "Power is not an institution, and not a structure; neither is it a certain strength we are endowed with; [rather] it is the name that one attributes to a complex strategical situation in a particular society."[81] Seeking to elucidate Foucault's understanding of power, Philip Barker claimed that power, as presented by Foucault, has the following features:

1. Power is coextensive with the social body;
2. relations of power are interwoven with other kinds of relations: production, kinship, family, sexuality;
3. power does not take the sole form of prohibition and punishment, but is multiple in form;
4. interconnections of power delineate general conditions of domination organized in a more or less coherent and unitary strategy;
5. power relations serve because they are capable of being utilised in a wide range of strategies;
6. there are no relations of power without possible resistances.[82]

We find ourselves the objects of multiple power relations and social discourses about sanity, sexuality, and violence, for example, and we experience ourselves as being controlled by these relations and discourses, as having to be obedient to them.

Discourse about sexuality is a primary site of power in contemporary society, according to Foucault. What society says about legitimate and taboo types of sexuality shapes the sexual behavior of individual persons.[83] We are, said Foucault, literally "policed" by society's discourse about sexuality.[84] Policed, I confess my sexual fantasies and hang-ups to my psychiatrist; I seek forgiveness for my sexual sins by exposing them to my priest; I report my whereabouts to my parole officer, if I bear the label of "sexual predator"; I reveal my sexual fantasies to my lover. In turn, these authorities judge me in one way or another. I take their judgments to heart, internalize them, and then regulate myself in terms of them. Madan Sarup commented that in Foucault's view, "complex differential power relationships extend to every aspect of our social, cultural, and political lives, involving all manner of (often contradictory) 'subject-positions,' and securing our assent not so much by the threat of punitive measures as by persuading us to internalize the norms and values that prevail within the social order."[85]

Foucault frequently claimed that as sexual subjects, we are the object of a set of intersecting power relations and discourses that inscribe themselves on our bodies and cause us to recognize ourselves in certain ways. Often, we are unaware of the social forces that have constituted our sexual subjectivity. For this reason, we operate on the unquestioning assumption that our subjectivity is our own. Thus, it is the role of critical thinkers to help us challenge the ways in which power relations and discourses have constituted our subjectivity, particularly our sexual subjectivity so that we can somehow reconstitute it.[86] Foucault claimed that he did not conduct his analyses "to say: this is how things are, look how trapped you are."[87] Rather, he conducted them to permit others to help us transform our realities.

To better appreciate how power relations and discourses shape our subjectivities, sexualities, and bodies, we may look at a specific example. A variety of feminist thinkers, including many postmodern feminist thinkers, have expressed disapproval of cosmetic surgery for the purpose of women's beautification. In particular, Kathryn Pauly Morgan, Naomi Wolf, and Debra Gimlin have argued that cosmetic surgery is a negative and harmful aspect of Western culture and is something that generally runs counter to the feminist stance on the female body. For Morgan, cosmetic surgery is "primarily self-imposed surveillance of the body under patriarchal power . . . a form of colonization of women's bodies."[88] She claimed that cosmetic surgery is required for women in ways that it is not required for men:

> As cosmetic surgery becomes increasingly normalized through the concept of female "make over" that is translated into columns and articles in the print media or made into nationwide television shows directed at female

viewers, as the "success stories" are invited on the talk shows along with their "makers," and as surgically transformed women enter the Miss America pageants, women who refuse to submit to the knives and to the needles, to the anesthetics and the bandages, will come to be seen as deviant in one way or another. Women who refuse to use these technologies are already becoming stigmatized as "unliberated," not caring about their appearance (a sign of disturbed gender identity and low self-esteem according to various health-care professionals), as "refusing to be all that they could be" or as "granola-heads."[89]

If this is not discourse at work, then what is?

Like Morgan, Wolf claimed that cosmetic surgery is an example of "institutionalized forms of power working in concert to force women into extreme beauty practices."[90] Wolf postulated that women's desire to be beautiful (and the forms that this desire takes) is "the result of nothing more exalted than the need in today's power structure, economy, and culture to mount a counter-offensive against women." Women's beauty, said Wolf, serves as the foundation of women's identity and leaves them "vulnerable to outside approval." Regarding cosmetic surgery in particular, Wolf claimed that a market for it has been created for surgeons to make money, but, more generally, for the powers-that-be to keep women politically, economically, and socially stagnated. Because women are forced to focus on their perceived flaws, their supposed ugliness, they have little time to focus on far more important issues.[91]

Adding yet more force to Morgan's and Wolf's essentially Foucaultian analysis of cosmetic surgery, Debra Gimlin observed that "cosmetic surgery is not about controlling one's own body but is instead an activity so extreme, so invasive that it can only be interpreted as subjugation."[92] On a more general note, discussing women's overall beauty regime in the United States, Sandra Lee Bartky made these observations:

> Women are no longer required to be chaste or modest, to restrict their sphere of activity to the home, or even to realize their properly feminine destiny in maternity. Normative femininity [that is, the rules for being a good woman] is coming more and more to be centered on women's body—not its duties and obligations or even its capacity to bear children, but its sexuality, more precisely, its presumed heterosexuality and its appearance. . . . The woman who checks her makeup half a dozen times a day to see if her foundation has caked or her mascara has run, who worries that the wind or the rain may spoil her hairdo, who looks frequently to see if her stockings have bagged at the ankle, or who, feeling fat, monitors everything she eats, has become, just as surely as the inmate of

Panopticon, a self-policing subject, a self committed to a relentless self-surveillance. This self-surveillance is a form of obedience to patriarchy.[93]

The question then becomes one of resistance. How can women disobey the "rule of the Father"? By refusing to submit to the knife? By using cosmetic surgery to deliberately make themselves ugly rather than beautiful?

Judith Butler

Although Judith Butler is influenced by many thinkers, she is certainly influenced by Freud, Derrida, and Foucault. In *Gender Trouble,* Butler challenged the general view that sex, gender, and sexuality constitute a seamless web such that if a person is biologically female (XX chromosomes), she will display feminine traits and desire men as her sexual partners. Instead, Butler claimed that there is no necessary connection between a person's sex and a person's gender. Indeed, she went further than this. Butler said that "sex, by definition, will be shown to have been gender all along."[94] She agreed with Simone de Beauvoir that one is not born a woman; one becomes a woman.[95]

But what does it mean to become a woman? Do I choose to become a woman? Or do the kind of discursive powers about which Foucault spoke determine that I become a woman? Butler claimed that there is no preexisting "I" that chooses its gender. Rather, in Foucaultian fashion, she stated that "to choose a gender is to interpret received gender norms in a way that organizes them anew. Less a radical act of creation, gender is a tacit project to renew one's cultural history in one's own terms. This is not a prescriptive task we must endeavor to do, but one in which we have been endeavoring all along."[96] Within the discursive territory of heterosexuality, said Butler, not only is gender constructed, but so, too, is sex constructed. I find myself in the territory of heterosexuality and start constructing both my sexual and gender identity through my actions.

Although most feminists have always thought *gender* is constructed, until relatively recently, few have also thought *sex* is constructed. But then Butler, among others, started to reflect on the identities of intersexed persons. Their sex is ambiguous and may be oriented in either male or female directions. Gender and sex, said Butler, are more like verbs than nouns. But my actions are limited. I am not permitted to construct my gender and sex willy-nilly, according to Butler. I am controlled by the scripts society writes about people's sex and gender. It takes considerable imagination and fortitude to alter these scripts.

In an attempt to rewrite the scripts that control them, many readers of Butler focused on her discussion of gender and sex as identities one chooses to perform. They mistakenly understood her to mean that gender and sex were wide-open categories and that individual subjects were free to choose any "sex" or "gender" they chose to enact. These readers failed to realize how limited their options were. Sara Salin attempted to explain these limitations:

> In Butler's scheme of things, if you decided to ignore the expectations and the constraints imposed by your peers, colleagues, etc. by "putting on a gender," which for some reason would upset those people who have authority over you or whose approval you require, you could not simply reinvent your metaphorical gender wardrobe or acquire an entirely new one (and even if you could do that, you would obviously be limited by what was available in the shops). Rather, you would have to alter the clothes you already have in order to signal that you are not wearing them in a "conventional" way—by ripping them or sewing sequins on them or wearing them back to front or upside-down. In other words, your choice of gender is curtailed, as is your choice of subversion—which might make it seem as though, what you are doing is not "choosing" or "subverting" your gender at all.[97]

I can cross-dress, I can undergo a sex change operation, I can act on my primary homosexual desire. But I remain in society's boy-girl grid.

Realizing that many of her readers were not understanding the nuances of her thought, Butler sought to distinguish between the concept of *performance* and her concept of *performativity*. She relied on the work of analytic philosopher John Austin to help her. Austin made a distinction between constative utterances or perlocutionary acts, on the one hand, and performative utterances or illuctionary acts, on the other.[98] Constative utterances or perlocutionary acts simply report and describe something, whereas performative utterances or illuctionary acts actually make what is being said happen. For example, a perlocutionary statement or act is an observational statement, such as, "Today is a windy day" or "My dress is blue." In contrast, an illuctionary statement or act is a power statement, such as, "I take you to be my wife" in the context of a wedding ceremony. Saying these words literally makes you a husband. Similarly, commented Salin, in Butler's scheme of things: "When the doctor or nurse declares 'It's a girl/boy,' they are not simply reporting on what they see . . . , they are actually assigning a sex and a gender to a body that can have no existence outside discourse."[99] In other words, to be in this world, one must fit into one of these categories. There would need to be a whole other way of classifying individuals to get out of the girl-boy game entirely. To get her point across, Butler referred to a cartoon strip in which an infant is proclaimed to be neither a boy nor a girl but a lesbian. She did this, said Salin, to introduce the idea that it might "be possible to designate or confer identity on the basis of an alternative set of discursively constituted attributes."[100] But a "possibility" is just that. Most interpreters of Butler think that her bottom line is pessimistic: that, at least in our lifetime, it is highly unlikely that we will be liberated from the gender games that preoccupy us and the hierarchical systems that entrap us. Butler's penultimate pessimism about transforming society prompted critic Martha Nussbaum to observe:

> Thus the one place for agency in a world constrained by hierarchy is in the small opportunities we have to oppose gender roles every time they take shape. When I find myself doing femaleness, I can turn it around, poke fun at it, do it a little bit differently. Such reactive and parodic performances in Butler's view, never destabilize the larger system. . . . Just as actors with a bad script can subvert it by delivering the bad lines oddly, so too with gender: the script remains bad, but the actors have a tiny bit of freedom.[101]

Convinced that Butler's thought in particular is no more than jargon for an elite group of feminists and other social critics, Nussbaum trivialized Butler's ideas about resistance. She claimed that Butler's advice to feminists—namely, that the best they can do is to make fun of the institution of sex-gender that constrains women (and men)—is akin to someone's advising abolitionists that the best they can do is to roll their eyes at the master-slave hierarchy that weakens slaves' bodies and crushes slaves' spirits.[102] But, continued Nussbaum, in the nineteenth century, US abolitionists did far more than roll their eyes at slavery. They fought with every ounce of their energy to achieve freedom for the slaves. Resistance to injustice is not a matter of personal sniping. It is a matter of public outrage.

Nussbaum's other disagreement with Butler is that Butler seems to reduce resistance to "jabbing" at one's oppressors. Indeed, in Nussbaum's estimation, Butler delights in the role of being oppressed. Specifically, Nussbaum claimed that the central thesis of Butler's book *The Psychic Life of Power* is "that we all eroticize the power structures that oppress us, and can thus find sexual pleasure only within their confines."[103] In other words, real social change "would so uproot our psyches that it would make sexual satisfaction impossible."[104] We would be forced to give up our sexual pacifiers if we were to engage in bona fide social revolution, and, above all, we do not want to lose what personally "turns us on." Nussbaum found this conclusion about ourselves truly sad. She asserted that personal sexual pleasure is not our raison d'être. Rather, doing good for others is the purpose of our lives: "Life . . . offers many scripts for resistance that do not focus narcissistically on personal self-preservation. Such scripts involve feminists (and others of course) in building laws and institutions without much concern for how a woman displays her own body and its gendered nature: in short, they involve working for others who are suffering."[105]

Written in 1999, Nussbaum's critique of Butler was very harsh and conceivably based on some misunderstanding of Butler's full views on matters related to social resistance and personal satisfaction. In her 1994 book, *Undoing Gender,* Butler insisted that she does not think "theory is sufficient for social and political transformation."[106] In fact, she claimed,

> [Something] besides theory must take place, such as interventions at social and political levels that involve actions, sustained labor, and institutionalized practice, which are not quite the same as exercise of theory. I would add, however, that in all of these practices, theory is presupposed. We are all, in the very act of social transformation, lay philosophers, presupposing a vision of the world, of what is right, of what is just, of what is abhorrent, of what human action is and can be, of what constitutes the necessary and sufficient conditions of life.[107]

Butler may have indeed believed this all along, but it may have taken the strong words of such critics as Nussbaum to prompt her to develop her thought in more applied and accessible directions. Such developments in Butler's thinking are a testimony to the resilience of feminist thought, an encouraging sign that it is far from stopping dead in its tracks.

Critiques of Postmodern Feminism

Nussbaum is not the only critic who bemoaned what she perceived as the unnecessarily dense style of postmodern feminism. In 1998, Judith Butler received the first prize in the annual Bad Writing Contest for the following sentence:

> The move from a structuralist account in which capital is understood to structure social relations in relatively homologous ways to a view of hegemony in which power relations are subject to repetition, convergence, and rearticulation brought the question of temporality into the thinking of structure, and marked a shift from a form of Althusserian theory that takes structural totalities as theoretical objects to one in which the insights into the contingent possibility of structure inaugurate a renewed conception of hegemony as bound up with the contingent sites and strategies of the rearticulation of power.[108]

Reacting strongly against the accusation that her writing style is too arcane, Butler protested that "accessible" and "common sense" scholarly work is not likely to demand critical thinking. According to Gary A. Olson and Lynn Worsham, for Butler, "being a critical intellectual means constantly interrogating our assumptions, continually calling into question, not necessarily to do away with what is being questioned but, rather, to discover, for example, how terms might assume new meanings in new contexts."[109] Clearly, if I may use the word, there is dispute about how illuminating or not postmodern feminist writers are. Other critics are not particularly disturbed by the opacity of postmodern feminist texts. Instead, they fault postmodern feminists for taking the "wrong" side not only in the so-called sameness-difference debate—are women essentially the same as men or fundamentally different from men?—but also in the so-called antiessentialism-essentialism debate—is woman's "nature" "plastic" (mutable, ever changing, always becoming something different, in Heraclitean flux) or "fixed" (immutable, unchangeable, always remaining the same, in Parmidean status)? Is *gender* ("femininity") an organic outgrowth of sex ("femaleness"), an arbitrary cultural imposition on sex or, more radically, a determinant of sex?

In an article entitled "Sexual Difference and the Problem of Essentialism," Elizabeth Grosz noted that in the past, so-called egalitarian feminists such as Simone de Beauvoir, Betty Friedan, Eva Figes, Kate Millett, Shulamith Firestone, and Germaine Greer promulgated the view that there is nothing distinctive about woman's nature. Women's subordinate status is the result not of biological nature but of cultural construction and can, therefore, be changed. In other words, stressed Grosz, egalitarian feminists maintained "that the 'raw materials' of socialization are fundamentally the same for both sexes: each has analogous biological or natural potential, which is unequally developed because the social roles imposed on the two sexes are unequal. If social roles could be readjusted or radically restructured, if the two sexes could be resocialized, they could be rendered equal. The differences between the sexes would be no more significant than the differences between the individuals."[110] Women can be "unfeminine"; men can be "unmasculine."

In their attempts to delink sex and gender, observed Grosz, egalitarian feminists made several mistakes. First, egalitarian feminists took "male achievements, values and standards as the norms to which women should aspire."[111] But why, in the name of equality, did they urge women to become men and not men to become women? Did they not value women's ways as much as men's? Second, they minimized women's specific needs and interests, including those that arise from "women's corporeality and sexuality."[112] In erasing women's bodies—women's reproductive and sexual identities—said

Grosz, egalitarian feminists also erased the visible signs of women's oppression as women and therefore women's concrete rallying points for justice between the sexes. As a result, women's struggle for gender justice became a mere moment in the struggle for human justice, and feminism receded into the bowels of humanism.

Sketching the contrast between egalitarian feminists on the one hand and so-called difference feminists on the other, Grosz implied that the latter feminists sought to prevent feminism's devolution into humanism and woman's (re)absorption into man. Difference feminists, especially postmodern feminists, celebrated women's bodies, reproductive rhythms, and sexual organs. Women and men are different and women have no interest in forsaking their differences, they said. Women do not want the right to be the *same* as men. Rather, women want the right to be as *free* as men—to construct themselves apart from, not in opposition to, men; to be opposite of men yet to be themselves.[113] Thus, Grosz claimed that as she understood the postmodern feminist idea of difference, it is a notion that, among other things,

> resists the homogenization of separate political struggles—insofar as it implies not only women's differences from men, and from each other; but also women's differences from other oppressed groups. It is not at all clear that, for example, struggles against racism will necessarily be politically allied with women's struggles or, conversely, that feminism will overcome forms of racist domination. This, or course, does not preclude the existence of common interests shared by various oppressed groups, and thus the possibility of alliances over specific issues; it simply means that these alliances have no prior necessity.[114]

Woman is not to be subsumed into man or vice versa, and feminism is not to be viewed as humanism dressed in a skirt.

Grosz's interpretation of the postmodern feminist understanding of differences is far more sympathetic than that of other readers. Whereas Grosz argued that difference feminists see difference "not as difference from a pre-given norm but as pure difference, difference itself, difference with no identity,"[115] critics of postmodern feminism claim that if the truth be told, difference feminists use the term *difference* in an "essentialist" way. To say that difference feminists are "essentialist," however, is to say that unlike more "enlightened" or "politically correct" feminists, difference feminists are incapable of "carefully holding apart the poles of sex and gender,"[116] of femaleness and femininity.

Rejecting the label of "essentialist," most postmodern feminists maintain that in their writings they *do* attempt to distinguish between "(1) women as biological and social entities and (2) the 'female,' 'feminine' or 'other,' where

'female' stands metaphorically for the genuinely other in a relation of difference (as in the system consciousness/unconsciousness) rather than opposition."[117] In other words, postmodern feminists insist that they describe
woman's nature "not as some sort of 'thing-in-itself' to which all the 'sensible
properties' of 'woman's nature' actually cling but as the 'totality of the properties, constituent elements,'"[118] and so on, without which it would be impossible consistently and coherently to refer to "woman's nature" at all.

Explaining that difference feminists are "nominalists" as opposed to "real-
ists," Teresa de Lauretis stated that as the majority of difference feminists see it,

> the "essence" of woman is more like the essence of the triangle than the
> essence of the thing-in-itself: it is the specific properties of (e.g., a female-
> sexed body), qualities (a disposition to nurturance, a certain relation to
> the body, etc.), or necessary attributes (e.g., the experience of femaleness,
> of living in the world as female) that women have developed or have been
> bound to historically, in their differently patriarchal sociocultural con-
> texts, which makes them women, and not men. One may prefer one tri-
> angle, one definition of women and/or feminism, to another and, within
> her particular conditions and possibilities of existence, struggle to define
> the triangle's existence, struggle to define the triangle she wants or wants
> to be—feminists do want differently.[119]

Just as we have no access to a triangle as it exists in itself but only to the enormous variety of particular triangles we can conceive of, we have no access to
woman as she exists in herself. Yet in the same way we can recognize a triangle, we know a woman when we see one.

De Lauretis stressed that like feminist realism/essentialism, feminist nom-
inalism/postmodernism, too, is problematic. Whereas the former implies
that all women must be the same, the latter suggests that women have nothing in common and therefore no basis for collaborative political action. In de
Lauretis's estimation, however, there is a way to avoid both the pitfalls of realism and pitfalls of nominalism, a way suggested in the notion of "woman
as position."[120] In becoming feminists, said de Lauretis, women assume a position, a point of view or perspective termed "gender," from which "to interpret or (re)construct values and meanings."[121] Proceeding from their specific
socio-historical locations—their concrete interests—feminist women *consciously* use the category of "gender" to forge political alliances aimed at increasing each other's freedom and well-being at particular places and times.
For de Lauretis, the (female) sex/(feminine) gender relationship is such that
gender is neither an unproblematic procession from biologically determined
sex, nor an unproblematic procession from biologically determined sex, nor

an imaginary construct that is purely arbitrary. Rather, gender is the "product and process of a number of social technologies" that "create a matrix of differences and cross any number of languages."[122] Gender points to a conception of women as neither already unified nor inseparably divided but as multiple and therefore *capable* of unifying and dividing at will. Furthermore, said de Lauretis, if postmodern feminists wish to remain "feminist," they must in some way privilege the category of gender so that women have some ground to stand on when they come together to improve their "estate."[123] Political action requires a platform—some sort of launching pad.

Conclusion

Despite all the criticisms raised against existentialist feminism and postmodern feminism, they remain two of the most challenging developments in contemporary feminist thought. Although existentialist and postmodern feminists have distinctive agendas, they share certain tendencies such as an appreciation for the possibilities latent in nothingness, absence, the marginal, the peripheral, the repressed, the other, the Second Sex. Moreover, they share a common desire to rethink Woman/women as the relationship between sex and difference, identity, power, and meaning. Still, existentialist feminists and postmodern feminists part ways at a deeply conceptual level. For de Beauvoir, binary and oppositional thinking is the way to think: self/other, man/woman, transcendence/immanence. In contrast, postmodern feminists, such as Cixous and Butler, resist binary thinking as impeding genuine thought.

Moreover, postmodern feminists desire to think nonbinary, nonoppositional thoughts, the kind that may have existed before the Bible says Adam was given the power to name the animals, to determine the beginning and ends of things: "And out of the ground the Lord God formed every beast of the field, and every fowl of the air; and brought them unto Adam to see what he would call them—and whatsoever Adam called every living creature, that was the name thereof."[124] We can imagine this original state prior to Adam's purported intrusion either as a Taoist undifferentiated "uncarved block,"[125] as a Lacanian imaginary, as a Kristevian abject, or as any number of disordered conditions—the point being that there was, in the beginning, *no word* but only myriad voices waiting for time and space to interpret their meaning.

Whether women can, by breaking the silence, by speaking and writing, help overcome binary opposition, phallocentrism, and logocentrism, is not certain. What is certain, however, is that the time has come for a new conceptual order. Bent upon achieving unity, we human beings have excluded, ostracized, and alienated so-called abnormal, deviant, and marginal people. As a result of this policy of exclusion, the human community has been impoverished. It seems, then, that men as well as women have much to gain by joining a variety of postmodern feminists in their celebration of multiplicity. Yet as Christine di Stefano emphasized, women may also have something to lose in their embrace of the enriching differences of race, class, sexual preference, ethnicity, culture, age, religion, and so on: they may lose themselves.[126] For the time being, it might be wise for women to heed di Stefano's caution: For women, whatever their differences,

> gender is basic in ways that we have yet to fully understand, . . . it functions as "a difference that makes a difference," even as it can no longer claim the legitimating mantle of *the* difference. The figure of the shrinking woman may perhaps be best appreciated and utilized as an aporia within contemporary theory: as a recurring paradox, question, dead end, or blind spot to which we must repeatedly return, because to ignore her altogether is to risk forgetting and thereby losing what is left of her.[127]

Women exist *as* women; at least I know I exist, and "ain't I a woman?"

Even Judith Butler admits, in the end, that she is a woman. Pressed to identify as a man or a woman at a lecture she was delivering, Butler said "'I *am* a woman'—although I accompanied my affirmation with a certain bewildered laughter."[128] She claimed:

> There is no circumventing the categorical violence of naming "women" or "men." Wittig, in her early years, wanted us not to use these terms anymore. She even wanted to change hospital practices, questioning why it is necessary to name a child a "boy" or a "girl" when it comes into the world . . . She also thought that we should not accept the given terms for anatomy, so that if asked if you have a vagina, for instance, you just say, "No." She felt that this would be a form of radical resistance to how vernacular language structures the body in ways that prepare it for heterosexual reproduction. There is a necessary violence that must be committed in the act of naming. I was probably more Wittigian in that way at the time that I wrote *Gender Trouble.* I now think, "Sure, you say it; you must say it; you use that language; you become dirtied by the language; you know you're lying; you know it's false, but you do use it." And you live with the consequences of this catachresis, this use of a term to describe something in a radically improper way.[129]

In the admission that one is, after all, a woman may be the condition of women speaking out on issues that matter to them and human beings in general.

Questions for Discussion

1. Analyze past and current examples that many women internalize "the myth of women." Consider incidences relevant to men's concept of the "ideal woman," ambivalence about women's nature, and the resulting subjugation of women throughout various spheres of life.

2. In what ways do the women role-playing within one of de Beauvoir's female archetypes (the mother, the wife, the career woman, the prostitute, the narcissist, and the mystic) ultimately diminish the female experience? How may women transcend these roles and emancipate themselves from being "the second sex"?

3. Is being "the other" always a negative thing? Reflect upon postmodern feminism's proposition that otherness is much more than simply an oppressed condition. Do you agree or disagree?

4. Who are some female writers using what Cixous calls "white ink"? Research such feminine authors online. Compare and contrast their "white ink" writing style with the "black ink" style of their masculine counterparts. What characteristics of "white ink" stand out in particular?

5. Butler says society writes so as to control sex and gender. Cite examples of the "scripts" Can we ever escape the boy-girl grid? How? Do you share Nussbaum's suggestion that an alternative focus on the alleviation of suffering is the more productive means by which to transform society? Why or why not?

6. What does de Lauretis mean when she suggests feminists embrace the notion of "woman as position"? How might such a proposal bridge theoretical gaps between egalitarian and difference feminists? Is gender enough to unify an entire movement, or are women too diverse a population?

Women of Color Feminisms

By Rosemarie Tong and Tina Fernandes Botts

If there is any concept unifying women of color feminisms, it is the concept that particular women's experiences differ and that to accurately and respectfully treat these differing experiences, it is necessary to describe them on the terms of the women themselves. Recognizing this unifying concept, my colleague Rosemarie Tong has generously asked me, a woman of color feminist and a philosopher, to work with her to update this chapter of her comprehensive text on feminist thought. I am honored to do that for her and for her readers. To strike a balance between including the distinctive voices of different women of color in this revised chapter, and preserving Rosie's previous work on global and postcolonial feminism, Rosie and I have divided this chapter into two sections: "Women of Color Feminisms in the United States" and "Women of Color Feminisms on the World Stage: Global, Postcolonial, and Transnational Feminisms." Although we recognize that, like all attempts at conceptual categorization, this attempt is somewhat arbitrary, the reader should note that we have divided the chapter in this way to accomplish two objectives: First, we would like to highlight and explore the unique perspectives of various groups of women of color in the United States, as the feminist experience in the United States is our own lived experience and therefore the one with which we are arguably able to speak with the most epistemic authority. Second, we understand global, postcolonial, and transnational feminisms to be related but distinguishable approaches to feminist challenges for women of color on the world stage. It is our hope that by treating them together in one section, we can illuminate both the similarities and differences between the theories as they appear to us at this time. We recognize that feminisms on the

211

world stage include the concerns of women other than women of color, but we do see women of color (alternatively known as subaltern women, Southern women, Third World women, or women in developing nations) as the primary focus of world feminisms. I would like to add that it is clear to me that although my status as a woman of color feminist may provide me more insight into the issues and perspectives treated in this chapter than a feminist of exclusively European descent, I am acutely aware that I am not able to speak on behalf of all feminists of color. I will say, however, that I have done my best to correctly characterize the perspectives of each of the feminist thinkers selected for inclusion in this chapter, while acknowledging that there are both theoretical and practical barriers between any attempt in that regard and the final product. —Tina Fernandes Botts

From Multiculturalism to Intersectionality

The term *of color* is ambiguous. For some, it simply means "nonwhite."[1] For others, the term has important sociological, historical, and political implications. For this second group, the term *of color* operates to stress the commonality of experience of groups of persons (across a variety of cultural and ethnic backgrounds) who have been racialized (that is, assigned a nonwhite race) inside Western cultural hegemony. The experience of being racialized includes, among other things, the experience of having one's non-Western culture devalued; the experience of having what W. E. B. DuBois called "double consciousness";[2] the experience of being pressured to assimilate to the dominant (white) culture; the experience of being denied access to "white privilege";[3] the experience of being expected to be more competent (e.g., in school, at work) than persons who have not been racialized, only to be perpetually considered not as competent; and being otherwise marginalized, oppressed, or subjugated by virtue of being a member of one or more (nonwhite) "racial" or ethnic groups. To be a person *of color*, in other words, means living in a constant state of vigilance regarding when and where the fact of one's having been racialized might pop up and operate as a barrier to the liberal ideal of the autonomous self. It also means, however, claiming one's unique cultural heritage and being willing to proudly and openly oppose white cultural hegemony when it presents itself as operating in opposition to that cultural heritage. The term *women of color* is meant to signify persons who have had the female experience within this group of persons, an experience understood as consisting of being oppressed both as a person of color and as a woman.

During the heyday of "multiculturalism" (roughly between the early to mid-1970s and the late 1990s), understood generally as a political and intellectual movement that called for public institutions to better recognize the unique collective social identities of certain historically oppressed groups in the United States, the term *women of color* fell in and out of favor among feminists. Originally, the term had a unifying effect, but later on, the term took on negative connotations and began to represent an attempt on the part of whites to lump all nonwhite women together, as if the differences between the various groups of nonwhite women, and the differences between their experiences of oppression and patriarchy, were inconsequential. Feminism has only just recently reappropriated the term *women of color* to capture both the similarity of experience attendant to being racialized within Euro-centric cultural imperialism (no matter what the nonwhite race ascribed) and also to capture the unique experiences of oppression and patriarchy of the different varieties of women of color. Of course, it would be impossible to create an exhaustive list of these individual group experiences, particularly because, as women of color feminisms highlight in the concept of "intersectionality," many women of color belong to not one but multiple historically oppressed subgroups. So, in this chapter, we have attempted to treat what seem to us at this time to be the main subgroups of women of color feminisms, while begging the pardon of any subgroup that has not been treated specifically here. For any such subgroup, we welcome suggestions for inclusion of your experiences and points of view in subsequent editions of this text. By way of clarification, however, readers should note that in this chapter, the term *women of color* is meant to capture both that the experience of being racialized is what links together all women of color, and that each and every subgroup has its own unique feminist experience.

For many women of color, mainstream feminism (in all of its forms, but particularly first- and second-wave feminism) fails to take their experiences and their perspectives on "the woman question" seriously and on their own terms. Operating as if every woman's experience is the same as the experiences of those women who have benefited from birth and continue to benefit on a daily basis from white privilege, mainstream feminism, on this view, is deeply deficient in its failure to adequately acknowledge, contemplate, and address the experiences and concerns of women of color. For example, many second-wave feminists write as if all women are white (as well as middle-class, heterosexual, and well educated). In 1998's *Inessential Woman: Problems of Exclusion in Feminist Thought,* Elizabeth Spelman explained what she saw as the reasons for this puzzling phenomenon.[4] Many (white) feminist theorists, particularly liberal feminists, in their desire to prove that women are men's full equals, wrote Spelman, stress women's sameness to one another as well as women's sameness to men, rather than their differences from one another and men. These theorists, said Spelman, fail to realize that it is possible to oppress people by ignoring their differences.

Moreover, to stress the sameness of all women is no guarantee against hierarchical ranking, on Spelman's view, if what one says is true of all women is only true or characteristic of some women. When Elizabeth Stanton said that (white) women should get the vote before Africans, Chinese, Germans, and Irish should, she obviously was relying on a concept of "woman" that blinded her to the experience of oppression of the female members of these groups.[5] Spelman urged feminist theorists to resist the impulse to gloss over women's differences, as if there exists some sort of universal "woman" into whom all of women's autobiographical differences flow and dissolve. Spelman observed:

> If . . . I believe that the woman in every woman is a woman just like me, and if I also assume that there is no difference between being white and being a woman, then seeing another woman "as a woman" will involve seeing her as fundamentally like the woman I am. In other words, the womanness underneath [the skin of the woman of color] is a white woman's [womanness].[6]

No wonder, said Spelman, so many women of color reject feminist thought. They regard it as white women's way of thinking. Feminist thought, stressed Spelman, must take the differences among women seriously; it cannot claim all women are white women down deep inside.

Women of color feminisms take seriously the differences among women, particularly their differing experiences of oppression. For women of color, in other words, not only is the female experience constituted by encounter with patriarchy but also by encounter with racial oppression. The lived experience of women of color, on this view, is such that the point at which patriarchy ends and racial oppression begins is altogether unclear. Instead, each woman of color is a site of multiple forms of oppression that operate upon her simultaneously, creating a new form of oppression such that the whole experience of oppression is an entirely different animal than the sum of its parts. The idea that women of color are living sites of multiple forms of oppression (i.e., at a minimum, discrimination on the basis of race and discrimination on the basis of gender) is a key theme in women of color feminisms.

Early work on the connections between multiple forms of oppression was done by Angela Davis,[7] the Combahee River Collective,[8] and Audre Lorde,[9] among others. Then, in 1991, Kimberlé Crenshaw coined the term *intersectionality* to highlight the ways in which existing institutional structures are set up in such a way as to be inhospitable to addressing the unique needs of women of color.[10] Crenshaw's point was that these institutions acknowledge racial discrimination and gender discrimination, but not the unique kind of discrimination experienced by women of color as a consequence of how racial and gender discrimination intersect in their lived experience. This is the case, for Crenshaw, in part because "women of color are situated within at least two subordinated groups that frequently pursue conflicting political agendas."[11] Antiracist discourse has failed to address the intersections of race and gender, for Crenshaw, because it fails to interrogate patriarchy, resulting in the reinforcement of the subordination of women. Mainstream feminist discourse has also failed women of color because its resistance strategies often replicate and reinforce (or at a minimum simply ignore) the subordination of people of color. Patricia Hill Collins has described the concept of intersectionality as follows:

> Intersectionality refers to particular forms of intersecting oppressions, for example, intersections of race and gender, or of sexuality and nation. Intersectional paradigms remind us that oppression cannot be reduced to one fundamental type, and that oppressions work together in producing injustice.[12]

Through the concept of intersectionality, then, women of color feminisms highlight that oppression is socio-historically situated and multidimensional, and that, to be effective, the solutions to the problems taken up by feminism will resist simplistic analysis but will instead be as complex as the women who experience them.

From the perspective of women of color feminisms, another problem with mainstream (white) feminist thought is that when it attempts to include the thoughts and experiences of women of color in its theorizing, it tends to lump the theorizing of all women of color together, as if the world of women were divided between white (official, central, "universal") feminism and all of those *other* (unorthodox, tangential, "biased") feminisms. Often subsuming the thought of all women of color under the heading "multicultural feminism," mainstream feminism tends to gloss over the unique experiences and viewpoints of different groups of feminists of color, such as African American/Black feminists, Latina feminists, Asian feminists, and Indigenous feminists, losing the power and the message of each of these feminist expressions in the process.[13] In this fourth edition of *Feminist Thought*, we are attempting to take steps toward correcting that error in mainstream feminist theory by treating each, unique area of women of color feminisms individually and on its own terms. What follows is a sampling of those areas.

Women of Color Feminisms in the United States

African American/Black Feminism

At the heart of women of color feminisms in the United States is African American/Black feminism. As a distinctive feminist presence, African American/ Black feminism goes as far back as first-wave feminism. At the center of the demand for female equality in America from the start were such women as Sojourner Truth, Anna Julia Cooper, and Ida Wells-Barnett. Truth articulated the key idea in African American/Black feminism that the experiences of African American/Black women are both the same as and different from the experiences of white American women. Anna Julia Cooper's 1892 book, *A Voice from the South: By a Woman from the South,* articulated the view that African American/Black women should be self-determined and act as moral leaders for the purpose of uplifting the African American/Black community.[14] Ida Wells-Barnett, who was the editor of a newspaper and published several writings of her own, was a member with W. E. B. DuBois of the Niagara Movement, was a founding member of the NAACP, and was a lifelong activist in the antilynching crusade.[15] Each of these women (and countless others) articulated and exemplified the (arguably) distinctively African American/ Black feminist mind-set that being a woman and being powerless are not necessarily coextensive. Through the way they lived their lives, these women problematized the mainstream notion of what it meant to be a woman (white, powerless, frail, irrational, ineffectual, etc.). In other words, African American/ Black feminism has from the beginning sought to accomplish one of mainstream feminism's ostensible goals: the deconstruction of stereotypical notions of what it means to be a woman. In the second wave, this aspect of African American/Black feminism emerged in the work of bell hooks, Audre Lorde, and others who chose to highlight that *even within the bounds of African American/Black feminism,* there are a multiplicity of vantage points, even further problematizing the stereotypical notion of what it means to be a woman.[16]

African American/Black feminism can be understood to begin with Sojourner Truth (née Isabella Baumfree). Born into slavery in approximately 1797, Truth arguably planted the seeds of distinctively African American/ Black feminist thought when she famously asked during the height of first-wave feminism, "Ain't I a woman?"[17] Truth escaped from slavery in 1826 and ultimately became a noted abolitionist and women's rights activist. Taking the stage to speak at the Women's Convention in Akron, Ohio, in 1851 just three years after the Women's Rights Convention in Seneca Falls, New York, Truth articulated the complex nature of what it meant to be a woman in America by highlighting two cornerstone ideas of African American/Black feminism—that, (1) lest anyone forget, African American/Black women are women; and (2) the experiences of African American/Black women are different from the experiences of pampered, middle-class white women. Truth stated:

> That man over there says that women need to be helped into carriages, and lifted over ditches, and to have the best place everywhere. Nobody ever helps me into carriages, or over mud-puddles, or gives me any best place! Look at me! Look at my arm! I have ploughed and planted, and gathered into barns, and no man could head me! Ain't I a woman?[18]

In other words, the experiences of African American/Black women in America are both the same as and different from the experiences of white women.[19] Truth's enigmatic words engage what later became a core issue in late twentieth-century and early twenty-first-century feminism: the issue of how to understand the female experience and feminism in such a way as to generate solidarity (universality of vision) and therefore power, while accommodating the wide variety of experiences of women of different racial and ethnic backgrounds, socioeconomic levels, sexualities, and histories of oppression (particularities of experience).

Key to Truth's distinctively African American/Black feminism is her experience of herself as being powerful, not powerless. This self-concept can be discerned in a comment made by Truth in 1853, as set down by Harriet Beecher Stowe:

> Sisters, I a'n't clear what you'd be after. Ef women want any rights more'n dey's got, why don't dey jes' take 'em, and not be talkin' about it?[20]

Women should seize their rights, emphasized Truth, not beg for them. Action is the path to women's liberation, not talk. Articulating a similar sentiment at a convention in 1878, Truth stated:

> If women would live as they ought to, they would get their rights as they went along.[21]

Truth's statements articulated again and again her sentiment that, from her perspective, (white) women's barrier to true power and equality was not outside of themselves, but inside. To her, white women seemed to think that to become powerful, they needed the permission of (white) men, but from Truth's perspective, if you want power, you take it. You don't ask permission to take it.[22]

The willingness of Truth, an African American/Black woman, to alienate the affections of those in power (white men) in pursuit of equality versus the seeming unwillingness of white women to do so, arguably gets to the heart of the difference between the African American/Black female experience and the white one, even in contemporary times. From the perspective of many African American/Black feminists, because white women marry white men—that is, because they sleep with the enemy—a large part of their access to power is through their association with white men. If white women alienate white men, they lose most of their access to power, they lose the "white privilege" they have as a consequence of their association with white men.[23] This reality creates a (political) barrier between African American/Black feminists and white women in two ways. First, white women are perceived by many African American/Black feminists as less committed to true equality than African American/Black feminists are, causing African American/Black feminists to break off from (white) feminism to create their own movement(s),[24] and second, white women are perceived by many African American/Black feminists as untrustworthy, due to white women's perceived willingness to sacrifice their sisters of color so as to maintain the modicum of "white privilege" afforded to them through their association with white men. Many root the divide between white feminists and feminists of color in the ways in which white women's silence on issues unique to women of color endorses the power of white men.[25]

Truth also articulated early on another theme in African American/Black feminism: a theme that later became known as intersectionality, or the view, as described by contemporary critical race theorist Kimberlé Crenshaw, that oppression operates simultaneously along a variety of avenues with the result that the oppression associated with being female is inseparable, at least for women of color, from the oppression associated with being ascribed a "race" with an inferior social status, such as "black," by society.[26] Truth's work as both an abolitionist and a women's rights activist often gave her opportunities to express versions of this view. Just after the civil war, for example, it appeared that black men would get the vote but women would not. The dominant position among African American supporters of women's rights was that it was more important for African American men to get the vote than for women to get the vote. Truth refused to choose sides. However, on behalf of African American women, Truth argued that African American women needed the vote because, without it, they would not be protected from African American *men*.

The idea that the experiences of oppression of African American women are different from the experiences of mainstream (middle-class, white) women, was taken up during the second wave by such thinkers as Audre Lorde and bell hooks. hooks pointed out, for example, that for African American women, racism and classism contributed as much to their oppression as did sexism. None of these forms of oppression can be eliminated before the elimination of any other, she asserted.[27]

Setting the stage for much African American/Black feminist scholarship to come, hooks also engaged the issue of the hypersexualization of the black female body on the part of mainstream culture, a culture steeped, according to hooks, in white supremacy. hooks claimed that mainstream culture caused large numbers of black women to react in one of two extreme ways: either to become overly modest prudes, obsessed with matters of bodily cleanliness and purity, or to capitalize on their purported sexiness.[28] Instead of internalizing these negative and stereotypical images of hypersexualized black femaleness, hooks urged black women to expunge from their minds these images so as to be free to esteem themselves, that is, to be proud of themselves and joyous about being black women.

Audre Lorde articulated the theme in African American/Black feminism that the experiences of African American women are different from those of mainstream (white) women, and that the examination of these different experiences brings something unique to the table of feminist inquiry, when she famously stated:

> Those of us who stand outside the circle of this society's definition of acceptable women; those of us who have been forged in the crucibles of difference . . . know that survival is not an academic skill. It is learning how to stand alone, unpopular and sometime reviled. . . . It is learning how to take our differences and make them strengths. For the master's tools will never dismantle the master's house.[29]

Lorde's point was that mere tolerance of the difference in experience that African American women bring to the table of feminism is insufficient to overcome the oppression that African American women face. Rather, for real change to occur, difference must be respected, affirmatively valued, and "seen as a fund of necessary polarities between which our creativity can spark like a dialectic."[30] Indeed, for Lorde, "difference is that raw and powerful connection from which our personal power is forged."[31] Weary from explaining her black woman's experience to white audiences, Lorde urged black women to stop explaining their difference from white women and to demand instead that white women start explaining *their* difference. Lorde's points are well taken. Difference, after all, is necessarily adjudged from a particular vantage point according to which sameness has already been defined.

The theme of the uniqueness of the oppression experienced by African American women was later reiterated by Patricia Hill Collins.[32] For Collins, in the United States, black women's oppression was systematized and structured along three interdependent dimensions: economic, political, and ideological. The *economic* dimension relegates black women to service occupations; the *political* dimension denies to black women the privileges and rights routinely extended to whites, including the very important right to an equal education; and the *ideological* dimension imposes a set of "controlling images" (e.g., mammies, Jezebels, breeders, smiling Aunt Jemimas, and the ubiquitous prostitutes and welfare mothers of contemporary popular culture) on black women, serving to justify as well as explain whites' treatment of black women. These negative, stereotypical images, Collins pointed out, have been fundamental to black women's oppression.[33] Collins theorized the ideological dimension was more powerful than either the economic or political dimension in maintaining black women's oppression. She emphasized that "race, class, and gender oppression could not continue without powerful ideological justification for their existence."[34] For this reason, Collins urged black feminists to release themselves from demeaning and degrading white stereotypes about them.

One example of the ways in which the experience of oppression of African American/black women differs from that of white women is in terms of the degree of agency (e.g., autonomy and control over their own bodies) each group is understood to have. For example, in the United States, accessible sterilization has generally proved to be a blessing for well-educated, economically privileged, white women but not for poor women, particularly poor African American women. Specifically, in the 1960s gynecologists followed what was known as the unofficial "rule of 120," which precluded the sterilization of a woman unless her age times the number of her living children equaled 120 or more.[35] Physicians followed this rule religiously when it came to white, middle-class, married women, but not when it came to any other woman; that is, not for African American women, poor women, single women, or women who fell into two or more of these groups. In some Southern US states, sterilization of indigent African American women was so common that the procedures were irreverently referred to as "Mississippi appendectomies."[36] More recently, but in the same spirit, some US legislators have drafted policies and laws linking the welfare eligibility of African American women to their willingness to use the contraceptive Norplant. In the estimation of these lawmakers, unless indigent African American women agree to use this long-term contraceptive implant, they and their children should be denied Aid to Families with Dependent Children.[37]

In the past ten years or so, African American/Black feminism has been recharged and given new vigor with the addition of several African American women into the discipline of academic philosophy. Almost all of them feminists, the thirty or so African American women philosophers in existence (out of a total of approximately eleven thousand professional philosophers) in the United States teach and write about the degree to which the discipline of philosophy—Western culture's bastion of high intellectualism—inherently, disturbingly, and consistently discredits and degrades the perspectives and experiences of persons of color, particularly women. Through its insistence on a kind of universalist thinking that delegitimizes the particularity of experience of women and marginalized racial and ethnic minority groups, the discipline of philosophy systematically reinforces the epistemological and ontological denigration of the African American female experience, and as a result, of African American women themselves. Donna-Dale Marcano, Kathryn Gines, and Kristie Dotson, to name a few, call for a revision of the philosophical canon so as to better accommodate this experience, as well as a call to bring philosophy up to speed with all of the other disciplines in the humanities and social sciences on the topics of race and ethnicity. Specifically, these African American women philosophers seek to establish and have formally acknowledged the role played by race and racism in perpetuating the domination, subjugation, and epistemological delegitimization of women of color.[38]

The universalist perspective so cherished by the discipline of philosophy—particularly in English-based contexts—is revealed by these feminists to be not so universal. No vantage point is free from "situatedness," say these feminists. In fact, say these feminists, what philosophy takes as a universal perspective is as deeply biased in favor of the interests of white, property-owning males, to the disadvantage of anyone not fitting that particular description.[39] The lesson for feminism is clear: The link between epistemological delegitimization and the patriarchal oppression of women—already well established in feminist theory—is further strengthened when the women in question are women of color.

Mixed Race Feminism

Mixed Race feminism is a category of feminist thought we ascribe here to women in the United States who self-identify both as racially mixed and feminist. Mixed Race feminists spend much time challenging what is known as the "black/white binary," or the worldview that entails two distinct but intertwined prevailing sentiments in the United States, namely (1) that there exist in the world what are known as distinctive, clearly definable, objective races of human beings; and (2) that there are two main races, white and black.[40]

Adrian Piper, for example, problematized the wedding in American culture of phenotypical traits (observable, physical features) and presumed "genetic" race, and/or between phenotypical traits and racial identity. Piper described her complex family genealogy as follows:

Our first European-American ancestor landed in Ipswich, Massachusetts, in 1620 from Sussex; another in Jamestown, Virginia, in 1675 from London; and another in Philadelphia, Pennsylvania, in 1751, from Hamburg. Yet another was the first in our family to graduate from my own graduate institution in 1778. My great-great-grandmother from Madagascar, by way of Louisiana, is the known African ancestor on my father's side, as my great-great-grandfather from the Ibo of Nigeria is the known African ancestor on my mother's, whose family has resided in Jamaica for three centuries.[41]

As someone who is perceived as black or white, depending on the circumstances, Piper described her situation as, more often than not, a no-win situation. Many black people were suspicious of her, demanding that she prove her "blackness" to them—a blackness she treasured and happened to claim as her primary and chosen identity. Even worse, some white people castigated her for "fooling" them into thinking that she was all white or for using her black genes to her advantage, as she did when she identified herself as African American instead of Caucasian on a demographic form to increase her chances of gaining admission to a prestigious graduate program.

Building on Piper's analysis, but making a different point, Naomi Zack claimed that the "one-drop" rule, according to which a person is black if he or she has any percentage of "black blood" in his or her ancestry, can play itself out in a variety of ways.[42] In such a nation as the United States, where, in the past, many white slave owners had children by black slaves, millions of people who currently regard themselves as white are actually black according to the "one-drop" rule. Similarly, many people who look black and identify themselves as black may in fact be genetically more white than black. The category of race, like the categories of gender and class, is not neat and tidy. In fact, it is very messy and increasingly difficult to use coherently.[43]

Taking Piper's and Zack's ideas further, Linda Martin Alcoff agreed that bodily markings are of a superficial nature and that racial categories have fluid borders. What counts as black in the United States may not count as black in another nation, stressed Alcoff. She noted that "the meanings of both race and such things as skin color or hair texture are mediated by language, religions, nationality, and culture, to produce a racialized identity."[44] Alcoff provided several excellent examples for her observation, including the following:

In the Dominican Republic, "black" is defined as Haitian, and dark-skinned Dominicans do not self-identify as black but as dark Indians or mestizos. Coming to the United States, Dominicans "become" black by the dominant US standards. Under apartheid in South Africa, numbers

of people would petition the government every year to change their official racial classification, resulting in odd official announcements from the
Home Affairs Minister that, for example, this year "nine whites became
colored, 506 colored became white, two whites became Malay . . . 40 coloreds became black, 666 blacks became colored, 87 coloreds became
Indian. . . ."[45]

In providing the above examples, Alcoff's point was not that people often
misidentify an individual as black when he or she is in fact white, but that "race
does not stand alone."[46] On the contrary, race and ethnicity are socially constructed and deconstructed. Moreover, when it is possible to do so, some individuals choose their race or ethnicity depending on their own priorities and
values or those of the society in which they live. It is telling, for example, that
in the South African example Alcoff provided, no whites applied to be black.

For Alcoff, however, the fact that race and ethnicity are fluid categories
does not mean that these categories are meaningless. Although all African
Americans, for example, are not essentially the same, sharing precisely the
same "set of characteristics, . . . set of political interests, and . . . historical
identity," said Alcoff, it is not accurate to say "that race is no more real than
phlogiston or witchcraft."[47] On the contrary, race is very real; it is intensely
present in such societies as the United States. As Alcoff described it, race "is a
structure of contemporary perception, . . . tacit, almost hidden from view,
and thus almost [but not quite] immune from critical reflection."[48] For Alcoff, this observation is particularly true of people who classify themselves as
white but do not reflect on what white identity is.

Tina Fernandes Botts is a mixed race feminist and a philosopher who ap-
preciates the perspectives of Piper, Zack, and Alcoff all too well. Understanding herself to operate in the tradition of these thinkers and as including in her
work what she understands as a key theme in all Mixed Race feminist thinking (the idea of the complexity of the human experience), Fernandes Botts has
written about the lived experience of mixed race persons within the particular
cultural context of the United States at different points in the country's history. Emphasizing both the biological unreality and the very real social reality
of race in US culture, Fernandes Botts has emphasized the historicity of racial
identity and the degree to which it is created by dynamics of oppression.

That monoracial identity is socially constructed does not preclude the possibility that monoracial identity is nevertheless socially *real.* The same is
true of multiracial identity. . . . The grander philosophical point is that in
some sense, everything is socially constructed. We agree as a group that
something is real and so it becomes real. We use it as if it were real and live

with it as if it were real, so that at a certain point, the argument can be made that there is nothing with which we interact on a daily basis that is any more or less real than the concept of race. At the point at which everything is equally socially real (or nonreal), biological reality is quite irrelevant. The fact is that our society operates as if race were real. This includes monoracial identity, biracial identity, and multiracial identity. It is also the case that some racial identities are associated with a history of oppression.[49]

In other work, Fernandes Botts has utilized insights from philosophical hermeneutics to examine the relationship between racial identity formation and gender identity formation. While acknowledging the role of intentional, performative choice in personal identity, Fernandes Botts has at the same time located a powerful source of both racial and gender identity formation in institutionalized oppression.[50]

Jennifer Lisa Vest is a feminist and philosopher who writes about the experience of her having African American, indigenous, and European ancestry. Expressing her philosophical ideas poetically through a medium she calls "philopoetics," Vest writes in her poem "Names," for example, about the various names that have been attributed to so-called black Indians (indigenous populations of mixed race) and at the same time highlights the role of oppression in identity formation:

> Before Jackson / Before rabid flesh-hunting Carolinians came / We were fluid and raceless / Ibo, Dahomey, Ga Fon, Hausa, Yoruba / We were Ewe and Dogon / farmers teaching hunters / clans expanding / We were Mikasukee, Tallahassee, Muskogee / allies and kinfolk / Before they called us / Mulatto, Mestizo / Mustee, Negro / Stolen property / Creek.[51]

Mixed Race feminists bring to the table of feminist theorizing a call for the recognition of the complexity of the human experience and of the limiting power of the experience of being racialized in America. They simultaneously, and either directly or indirectly, call for the recognition of the complexity of being gendered female as well. Mixed Race feminists highlight the role of systems of domination and subordination in racial identity formation, and in the process provide further fodder for a recognition of the complexity of both the female experience and the answer(s) to the "woman question."

Latin American/Latina Feminism

Sharing much overlap with both African American/Black feminism and Mixed Race feminism, Latin American/Latina feminism nevertheless has distinctive themes and insights. Latin American/Latina feminism shares with African American/Black feminism a call for recognition of the alterity (otherness) and uniqueness of the distinctive experiences of women of color, particularly as distinct from the experiences of mainstream (white, Western, or Euro-centric) feminists. Latin American/Latina feminism shares with Mixed Race feminism a concern with the concepts of racial and cultural mixedness, an interest in the implications of that mixedness for feminist projects, and a call for recognition of the complexity of the human experience. On its own terms, Latin American/Latina feminism, however, is primarily concerned with cross-cultural dialogue and the extent to which such dialogue is limited by differing levels of power of the parties to the conversation.

For example, Ofelia Schutte engaged the concept of otherness that all women of color experience in the United States through examining communication barriers that arise in cross-cultural exchanges and dialogues. For Schutte, the confrontation with alterity that occurs in cross-cultural exchanges involves a decentering of the self that "allows us to reach new ethical, aesthetic, and political ground."[52] But when these cross-cultural exchanges or dialogues are marked by differentials of power (as in attempts at dialogue between dominant and subaltern cultures), the result is "cross-cultural incommensurability."[53]

In *Borderlands/La Frontera,* Gloria Anzaldúa examines alterity and cross-cultural dialogue through inquiring into the condition of three groups of women: Latin American women in Latin American culture, Latin American women in white American culture, and lesbians in heterosexual culture. Describing such women as living a life of alienation and isolation, the women are conveyed as prisoners inside of cultural narratives not of their own making. To highlight the sense of disconnection and internal conflict experienced by such women, Anzaldúa's writing uses many different forms of the Spanish and English languages, creating a sense in the reader of the kind of disjunction and disharmony that, for Anzaldúa, characterizes the Latin American feminist experience.[54]

Similarly, Maria Lugones highlighted that although Latin American women in the United States have to participate in the Anglo world, Anglo women in the United States do not have to participate in the Latin American world. An Anglo woman can go to a Latin American neighborhood for a church festival, for example, and if she finds the rituals and music overwhelming, she can simply get in her car, drive home, and forget the evening. There is no way, however, that a Latin American woman can escape Anglo culture so easily, for the dominant white culture sets the basic parameters for her survival as a member of one of its minority groups. Still, Lugones's work highlights the agency of Latin American women through pointing out that although Western society views the Latin American woman as a woman of color, in her own home among her family and friends, she perceives herself *as herself*.[55]

Asian American Feminism

Asian American feminism shares with African American/Black feminism, Mixed Race feminism, and Latina feminism a sense of having been marginalized within feminism itself, as well as a sense of the experience of having been racialized as nonwhite within the broader culture of the United States. In *Partly Colored*, Leslie Bow wrote of the Asian American experience in the segregated south, and of how the African American experience of having been subjected to legalized segregation framed the experience of oppression of Asians during the Jim Crow era. The legacy of segregation (of African Americans), wrote Bow, to this day frames race relations in the United States, both as a matter of differential access to rights and as a struggle between black and white.[56] Since Asians, during the Jim Crow era, were construed as a "third race" inside America's black/white binary, they were neither white nor nonwhite, but "situated in between" racial categories in the United States, a kind of other's other, "partly colored," very much like indigenous Americans and mestizos. One insight Bow gleaned from the Asian American experience (in the segregated South) is:

> Race only becomes intelligible as a problem to be remedied by the state—it is only visible—through acts of discrimination antithetical to our notions of democratic universalism.[57]

Bow identified Asian Americans (as well as indigenous Americans and mestizos) as "interstitial populations," or populations *between* the primary racial categories understood to exist in the United States (black and white), who share many of the experiences of the persons of mixed race mentioned earlier in this chapter. Among other insights arising out of the "interstitial" racial status of Asians in the segregated South, for Bow, were those into the construction of difference generally, including gender difference. The legacy of the segregated South and the "racial anomalies" it produced, within its entrenched black/white binary, is a "productive site for understanding the investments that underlie a given system of relations; what is unaccommodated becomes a site of contested interpretation."[58] In this way, the Asian American experience can be understood as a force for the destruction of hierarchy:

> The interstices between black and white forces established perspectives and definitions into disorientation. The racially interstitial can represent

the physical manifestation of the law's instability, its epistemological limit, the point of interpellation's excess.[59]

However, said Bow, the Asian American immigration experience is often used to reproduce a dominant narrative of post–civil rights movement racial representation—a "progressive chronology of racial uplift that buttresses a liberal vision of ethnic incorporation"—rather than as a force for the destruction of hierarchy.[60] Examining the question of how the interstitial racial status of Asian Americans was sustained within the binary caste system containing only "Negroes" and "whites" in the segregated South, Bow noted that this interstitial racial status was simply not sustained. Instead, the racial status of Asian Americans underwent a "shift in status from colored to white, in the course of one generation."[61] Citing an influential study conducted on the Chinese in Mississippi in the mid-twentieth century, Bow pointed out that although the Supreme Court ruling in *Gum v. Rice* had formally established the Chinese as colored in 1927, by 1967, the Chinese were "card-carrying white people."[62] Among other proof, there was the "W" on their driver's licenses. So, in response to the black-white binary of the segregated South, rather than its destroying racial hierarchy, the racial status of Asian Americans can be understood to have become productive of that hierarchy, according to Bow. Asian Americans became a part of what has been called the "colonial sandwich": Europeans at the top, Asians in the middle, and Africans at the bottom.[63] The lessons for feminism are clear. "The space between the social enactment of identity and its idealization," wrote Bow, "reveals the structures that consolidate social power in its multiple manifestations."[64] Although racial intersitiality *can* theoretically operate in the service of dismantling hierarchy, in practice it often does not, the Asian American experience being a case in point.

Mitsuye Yamada made a similar point (the difference between theory and practice), this time as regards the feminist ideal and its reality. While noting that Asian American women need white feminist leaders ("the women who coordinate programs, direct women's buildings, and edit women's publications throughout the country") to accomplish political objectives that are important to them, she was dismayed that she often found her white feminist audiences responding to her as though they had "never known an Asian Pacific woman who [was] other than the passive, sweet, etc., stereotype of the 'Oriental' woman." Yamada remarked upon the difference between the general agreement among feminists on feminism as an *ideal* (a belief in equality for women, an agreement that all women should know what it means to be a woman in society, that all women should understand the "historical and psychological" forces that have shaped their thoughts, and that all women should understand how these forces determine the directions of their lives), and the reality that feminism marginalizes the issues that are important to women of color.[65]

This is a problem for feminism, according to Yamada, because "a movement that fights sexism in the social structure must deal with racism."[66] In response, many Asian Pacific women involved in radical politics have moved *not* into the upper echelons of women's organizations, but into groups active in promoting ethnic identity. These women can be found in ethnic studies programs in universities, ethnic theater groups, or ethnic community agencies. However, "this doesn't mean," stressed Yamada, that "[Asian Pacific women] have placed our loyalties on the side of ethnicity over womanhood."[67] She continued, "The two are not at war with one another; we shouldn't have to sign a 'loyalty oath' favoring one over the other."[68] Invoking one of the central problems of women of color feminisms (that women of color are intersectional sites of multiple forms of oppression), Yamada noted, "However, women of color are often made to feel that we must make a choice between [loyalty to race/ethnicity and loyalty to womanhood]."[69] Pointedly, Yamada explained:

> As a woman of color in a white society *and* as a woman in a patriarchal society, what is personal to me is political.[70]

Yamada expressed the frustration experienced by many women of color feminists when she stated,

> These [connections between different forms of oppression] are connections we expected our white sisters to see. . . . They should be able to see that political views held by women of color are often misconstrued as being personal rather than ideological. Views critical of the system held by an "out group" are often seen as expressions of personal angers against the dominant society. (If they hate it so much here, why don't they go back?)[71]

Indigenous Feminism

The Women of All Red Nations (WARN) was formed in the mid-1970s as a spin-off organization from the American Indian Movement (AIM).[72] Unhappy with the mostly supporting roles offered to women in AIM, indigenous women formed WARN to address issues facing indigenous women, such as reproductive rights, land treaties, and the Native American Rights Fund.[73] WARN was an anomaly as, historically, a fundamental theoretical divide has been commonly understood to exist between mainstream feminism and Indigenous feminists. Insight into this fundamental divide can be gleaned from examination of the work of Paula Gunn Allen.

In "Kochinnenako in Academe: Three Approaches to Interpreting a Kres Indian Tale," Allen analyzed what are known as Yellow Woman ("Kochinnenako") stories, the female-centered stories of the Keres of Laguna tribe and Acoma Pueblos tribe in New Mexico who paint their faces yellow—the color of women and also the color of corn—on certain ceremonial occasions.[74] Allen compared three different interpretations of the Kochinnenako story "Sha-ah-cock and Miochin or the Battle of the Seasons": a traditional Keres interpretation, a "modern feminist"/mainstream/Euro-centric interpretation, and a "feminist-tribal" interpretation. In the process, Allen highlighted some of the key components of the theoretical divide between mainstream (white) feminists and Indigenous feminists. One key component is the different assumptions about what it means to be a woman in the different approaches.

In the traditional Keres interpretation, the female will is central to the story. In the "modern feminist"/mainstream/Euro-centric interpretation (which entails "the Western romantic view of the Indian, and the usual antipatriarchal bias that characterizes the feminist analysis"), the woman has low status in the culture, is unhappy in her marriage, and thinks her husband is "cold and disagreeable, and she cannot love him."[75] Tacked on to the "modern feminist" (mainstream, liberal feminist) account of the story, Allen described the "radical feminist" account, which reads the story through the eyes of racism and the resistance to oppression. Allen summarized the "modern feminist"/"radical feminist" interpretations as containing two assumptions: first, that women are essentially powerless, and second, that conflict is basic to human existence; but neither of these assumptions is contained in Keres thought, says Allen. Whereas "modern feminism" sees the Yellow Woman's marriage in the story as an institution developed to establish and maintain male supremacy, from the Keres perspective, Yellow Woman's agency is central both to her marriage and to the story. Allen wrote,

> The contexts of Anglo-European and Keres Indian life differ so greatly in virtually every assumption about the nature of reality, society, ethics, female roles, and the sacred importance of seasonal change that simply telling a Keres tale within an Anglo-European narrative context creates a dizzying series of false impressions and unanswerable (perhaps even unposable) questions.[76]

Western (technological, industrialized) minds cannot adequately interpret tribal materials, said Allen, because they "see the world in ways that are alien to tribal understandings."[77] In particular, whereas tribal peoples see their world in a "unified-field fashion" and their literature is "accretive and fluid," mainstream (white) perception is masculinist and "single-focused," and its literature is linear and fixed. But, most important for the purposes of this chapter, whereas from a mainstream perspective (whether "modern" or "radical"), woman is a victim, from a tribal perspective, she is both an agent and an empowerer of change. If Allen was on to something, then Indigenous feminism exists in an orthogonal relationship to the continuum in Euro-centric feminism between the liberal and radical forms, offering instead a third alternative in which the very concept of what it means to be a woman is dramatically challenged. In traditional indigenous culture undiluted by Western influences, woman is not powerless but powerful: "Agency," Allen wrote, "is Kochinnenako's ritual role [in the story]; it is through her ritual agency that the orderly, harmonious transfer of primacy between Summer and Winter people is accomplished."[78] Also, because the "modern feminist" version of the story presents the Yellow Woman/Kochinnenako in a Euro-centric light (as a powerless victim), the very act of interpreting Yellow Women stories through Euro-centric eyes "will provide a tribally conscious feminist with an interesting example of how colonization works, however consciously or unconsciously, to misinform both the colonized and the colonizer" in ways that negatively alter the self-perception of the indigenous woman.[79] Allen hinted that the relationships between indigenous men and women became "severely disordered" as a result, leading to "frightening" levels of wife-abuse, rape, and battery of women in recent years.[80]

Although the relationship between feminism and indigenous women has been historically rocky, in recent years there has been a flurry of scholarship on the topic of Indigenous feminism. All recent works emphasizes the necessity of recognizing the feminism of indigenous women as unique and as a phenomenon entirely separate from mainstream, Euro-centric feminism. A representative piece is "From the 'F' Word to Indigenous/Feminisms," by Luana Ross, which opens as follows (quoting Kate Shanley):

> Just as sovereignty cannot be granted but must be recognized as an inherent right to self-determination, so Indian feminism must also be recognized as powerful in its own terms, in its own right.[81]

The piece provides a succinct account of recent thinking in Indigenous feminism, highlighting the work of key indigenous thinkers such as Beatrice Medicine, an anthropologist, who was a charter member of the American Indian Women's Service League in Seattle in 1954. Although Medicine did not specifically define her work as feminist, the work provided some of the earliest studies of indigenous women *through the eyes of an indigenous woman* and presented a new image of indigenous women as strong and capable.[82] Kate Shanley was one of the first indigenous women to identify herself publicly as "feminist," according to Ross, working on the issues that all women face, such as equal pay, children's health and welfare, reproductive rights, and domestic violence. But, what made Shanley's work uniquely indigenous was that she also promoted the cause of tribal sovereignty.[83] In an interesting twist on the presumed relationship—from the perspective of many mainstream, Euro-centric feminists—between white women and indigenous women (one of oppressor and oppressed), Paula Gunn Allen noted, in "Who Is Your Mother? Red Roots of White Feminism," that according to Ross, all indigenous peoples are traditionally feminist. If feminists were to acknowledge this fact, great strides could be made toward the goal of decolonization, wrote Ross.[84]

Women of Color Feminisms on the World Stage: Global, Postcolonial, and Transnational Feminisms

Global, postcolonial, and transnational feminisms are all concerned with the problems and challenges faced by women worldwide, but each approach can be understood to entail a distinctive way of thinking about these problems. There is much overlap among the three approaches and the lines between them are by no means clearly drawn. For example, all three approaches engage the question of the extent to which there is a commonality of experience for those who have been identified as embodying the category of "woman" worldwide; all concern themselves with the factual realities of women's daily lives worldwide; all approaches actively address the idea of situated difference; all interrogate the possibility of coalition across cultural and racial boundaries; and all attempt to find solutions to the problems faced by women through attention to the various ways in which women from different cultures, ethnicities, races, and classes experience patriarchy and oppression. However, in our view, it is helpful to feminist theorizing and goals to think about the ways in which global, postcolonial, and transnational feminisms can be understood to represent divergent trends in contemporary feminist theory and in practice as well. Perhaps a general way of understanding these trends—again, where the lines of divergence are drawn in broad, permeable strokes—is in terms of the extent to which historically and culturally situated difference (particularly in terms of the experience of oppression) on the part of differing ethnic, racial, and cultural groups is understood to operate as a factor in the possibility of universal solutions to feminist concerns.

In our view, a representative sampling of the ways in which the approaches of global, postcolonial, and transnational feminisms are divergent are: (1) in terms of the social identity of the theorists, (2) in terms of the kinds of issues addressed by the theorists, and (3) in terms of the degree to which there is a belief in the prospect of universal solutions to feminist concerns. Global feminists are primarily Western (white) women, largely concerned with issues of women's health care and human rights, and for the most part staunch believers in the possibility of universal solutions to what are understood to be universal feminist concerns. In contrast, transnational feminists are almost exclusively women of color, largely concerned with economic issues, and very active, strong opponents of the possibility of universal solutions to feminist concerns. Postcolonial feminists are a breed in between, understood today primarily as a group of feminist theorists—part global, part transnational—that rose up at the end of the twentieth century as part and parcel of the poststructuralism prevalent at the time.[85] At least as regards substantive engagement with the concerns of women of color feminists (e.g., racism and racial oppression, and the role these play in female subordination), postcolonial feminism is sometimes understood as a branch of Third-Wave feminism, which has recently been described as not having "sufficiently shifted the mainstream feminist project to ensure that [the] inclusion of racial difference [is] fundamentally transformative."[86] Although postcolonial feminism makes much of *gesturing* toward addressing the concerns of women of color, particularly through its active inclusion of diversity and diversity concerns into the mainstream (Western) feminist project, at the same time the ultimate result may be what Chela Sandoval calls a "presence/absence" of true diversity,[87] a mere "token inclusion" of the texts of women of color, "without reconceptualizing the whole white, middle-class, gendered knowledge base."[88]

Global Feminism

Seeking Common Ground.   Global feminism stresses the links between the various kinds of oppression women experience throughout the world. The vantage point of many global feminists is expressed well by Charlotte Bunch:

> To make global feminist consciousness a powerful force in the world demands that we make the local, global and the global, local. Such a movement . . . must be centered on a sense of connectedness among women active at the grass roots in various regions. For women in industrialized countries, this connectedness must be based in the authenticity of our struggles at home, in our need to learn from others, and in our efforts to understand the global implications of our actions, not in liberal guilt, condescending charity, or the false imposition of our models on others. Thus, for example, when we fight to have a birth control device banned in the United States because it is unsafe, we must simultaneously demand that it be destroyed rather than dumped on women in the Third World.[89]

Global feminists believe that "the oppression of women in one part of the world is often affected by what happens in another, and . . . no woman is free until the conditions of oppression of women are eliminated everywhere."[90]

They view feminism as the process through which women can discuss their commonalities and differences as honestly as possible in an effort to secure the following two long-term goals:

1. The right of women to freedom of choice, and the power to control our own lives within and outside of the home. Having control over our lives and our bodies is essential to ensure a sense of dignity and autonomy for every woman.
2. The removal of all forms of inequity and oppression through the creation of a more just social and economic order, nationally and internationally. This means the involvement of women in national liberation struggles, in plans for national development, and in local and global struggles for change.[91]

Not surprisingly, areas of particular concern to global feminists are the reproductive-controlling technologies (e.g., contraception, sterilization, and abortion) and the reproduction-aiding technologies (e.g., intrauterine donor insemination and in vitro fertilization). Reflecting on the myriad ways in which government authorities seek to manipulate and control women's reproductive powers worldwide, global feminists note that although many women in developing nations want access to safe and effective contraceptives and abortions so they can control the size of their families, this preference does not necessarily apply to all women in developing nations. In the first place, say global feminists, there are a sizeable number of women who want large families, despite the fact that being responsible for the care of many children may preclude or limit their participation in the paid workforce. In the second place, it is not always in women's best interests to use reproductive technologies—not, for example, if contraceptives are unsafe. It is one thing for women to use potentially harmful contraceptives in a nation such as the United States, where follow-up medical care is generally available to all women. But it is quite another for women to have access to such contraceptives in cultural settings in which no provisions have been made for follow-up care. Specifically, Shawn Meghan Burn compared the distribution of some hormonal contraceptives in different countries:

In most Western countries, the Pill is prescribed by a physician, and a woman must have a Pap smear once a year to get her prescription renewed. This permits screening for . . . side effects . . . and for screening out those women for whom the Pill is contraindicated. . . . However in some countries (including Brazil, Mexico, and Bangladesh), the Pill is sold without a prescription in pharmacies and stores. Depo-Provera is sold over the counter in Nigeria and even along the roadside. Long distances to health-care facilities often preclude the monitoring that increases the safety and effectiveness of contraceptive methods.[92]

Still, Burn's observations withstanding, from the perspective of some global feminists, banning over-the-counter sales of the Pill in non-Western nations might not necessarily best serve the women in them. Ideally, all women should have access to affordable health care. But in the absence of such care, and even with full knowledge that certain contraceptives may be somewhat unsafe, many women may still prefer the convenience, low cost, and privacy of an over-the-counter Pill purchase to a burdensome, relatively expensive, and public visit to a clinic, where health-care givers may chastise them for wanting to practice birth control at all.[93] Similarly, in many developing nations, where men seek to control women's reproductive and sexual lives in particularly harsh ways, a woman may gladly risk using a possibly unsafe contraceptive if that contraceptive is one that she can secure and use without her husband's knowledge.[94]

In the third place, in the same way that having access to contraceptives is not always an unalloyed blessing for women, easy access to sterilization may not always be in women's best interests, either. Worldwide, sterilizations are often less than fully voluntary. For example, during Indira Gandhi's years as prime minister of India, the nation set the world record for vasectomies at ten million in 1974, largely as a result of government policies that gave material goods to poor, illiterate men in exchange for their agreement to be sterilized. Not only did Indian government authorities fail to secure anything approximating genuine informed consent from most of these men prior to their sterilization, but the authorities also often neglected to give the men the promised materials goods after their sterilization. When these facts became known, the public lost confidence in Gandhi's government. Indian citizens protested that poor people should not be seduced with prizes, such as money, food, clothes, and radios, to give up their reproductive rights.[95] Interestingly, the "sterilization scandal" played a key role in Gandhi's overthrow as prime minister. This scandal did not dissuade government authorities in other nations from developing similarly enticing sterilization policies for their people, however. For example, over twenty years later, Bangladesh's sterilization incentive program gave people not only several weeks' wages but also saris for women and *lungis* (pants) for men.[96]

In the fourth place, as with contraception and sterilization, utilization of abortion services is not an unalloyed blessing for women. To be sure, preventing women from having access to safe abortions often has tragic results. Even in nations where contraceptives are available and affordable, women (and men) do not always elect to use them, for any number of reasons. Unwanted pregnancies are sometimes the result of such decisions. Although relatively few nations completely forbid abortion, in 26 percent of a group of seventy-two developing nations, abortion is prohibited with the exception of saving the woman's life.[97] As a result of this state of affairs, many women who want abortions resort to illegal, usually unsafe abortions. Worldwide, about sixty-eight thousand women die as a result of subjecting themselves to an unsafe abortion.[98] The situation for women is particularly perilous in sub-Saharan Africa, Central Asia, Southeast Asia, and Latin America, according to Burn.[99]

Yet abortion is not always in women's overall best interests. According to global feminists, women in the former Soviet Union, for example, have an average of twelve to fourteen abortions during their lifetime because contraceptives, although legal, are extremely difficult to obtain. Apparently, Russian cost-benefit studies concluded it is less expensive for the government to provide multiple abortions to women than to provide safe, effective, and monitored contraceptives to women. Sadly, in its calculations, the government ignored the toll that multiple abortions take on women's bodies and psyches.[100]

Abortion is also readily available in nations that want to control the size of their populations. But policies such as the one-child policy in China have resulted in women's having multiple abortions to make sure their one child is a boy. In China, most people still prefer boys to girls. In the past, Chinese women got pregnant as many times as necessary to produce at least one male offspring. If women produced too many daughters on the way to delivering a son, the mothers sometimes resorted to female infanticide or child abandonment. Nowadays, due to the availability of low-cost, easily accessible sex-selection techniques, such as ultrasound, and to a lesser extent amniocentesis, most Chinese prefer to electively abort their female fetuses over facing the trauma of a female-infanticide or female-abandonment decision.

So effective has the increased use of sex-selection techniques been in China, an enormous sex-ratio imbalance has been created there. In fact, the sex-ratio imbalance in China in 2012 was 1.06 males for every one female.[101] Although a low supply of women in a nation might be thought to increase women's status, instead it seems to increases women's vulnerability. In the rural sections of China, for example, men kidnap women and force their victims to marry them. Even worse, some poor families have resorted to selling their prepubescent daughters to men who want a bride.[102] Realizing that they had a serious "bachelor" problem on their hands, Chinese government officials have relaxed the one-child policy and inaugurated a girls-are-as-good-as-boys

campaign. They have also outlawed such techniques as ultrasound and amniocentesis for purposes of sex selection.[103]

As in China, permissive abortion, sterilization, and contraceptive policies
in India, another nation that prefers male offspring to female offspring, have
resulted in a sex-ratio imbalance of 1.12 males born for every one female.[104]
And, as in China, Indian authorities have decided to ban the use of ultrasound and amniocentesis for sex-selection purposes, in an effort to correct India's sex-ratio imbalance. The ban, however, has not been uniformly enforced.
In addition, many women, particularly in India's rural regions, continue to
engage in female infanticide because daughters are costly in India.[105] Girls'
parents must provide wedding dowries for their daughters. These dowries are
no trivial matter. On the contrary, they can be so large as to threaten the liveli-
hood of the girls' parents.

Exacerbating the situation in India is the fact that when it banned ultrasound and amniocentesis for sex-selection purposes, the Indian government
did not ban all sex-selection techniques. Because of this lacuna in the law,
Gametrics, a US company with clinics in many Third World nations, started
to heavily market a *preconception* sex-selection technology in India. The technology separates Y chromosomes from X chromosomes. Women who want a
baby boy and who can afford the technology are inseminated with andro-
sperm only. Reflecting on this costly technology, Maria Mies commented,
"This example shows clearly that the sexist and racist ideology is closely interwoven with capitalist profit motives, that the logic of selection and elimination has a definite economic base. Patriarchy and racism are not only
ethically rejectable ideologies, they mean *business* indeed."[106]

Global feminists wish to develop a "feminist humanism" that combines
"the respect for differences characteristic of progressive movements since the
1960s with the universalistic aspirations of earlier liberatory traditions."[107] For
example, the late feminist political theorist Susan Moller Okin claimed that
feminists must talk about *women's* needs generically as well as specifically.[108]
Conceding that as a group, women do not experience gender inequality to the
same extent and degree, Okin nonetheless insisted that all women do experience it in some way or another, for the same reasons, and with the same consequences. Because virtually all societies regard women as the "second sex," as
existing to some degree for men's sexual pleasure, reproductive use, and domestic service—and for all of society's care—women throughout the world
tend to have not only less sexual freedom and reproductive choice than men
have, but also worse socioeconomic and health status.

Okin's views and views like hers were voiced beginning in the 1970s at
several International Women's Conferences, including ones in Mexico City
(1975), Copenhagen (1980), Nairobi (1985), and Beijing (1995). At these

conferences, women from both developed and developing nations revealed that their quality of life was diminished simply by virtue of their female sex. They discussed how their respective nations' sex, reproduction, marriage, divorce, child-custody, family-life, and work laws worsened their lot in life, and how women and girls, far more than men and boys, were sexually vulnerable, unhealthy, uneducated, and poor.[109]

Women's Rights as Human Rights.   Global feminists are very concerned with rights on the world stage. In other words, they are concerned with why individuals may lay claim to some social arrangements, goods, and services but not to others. Agreeing with Diane Elson that states must see to it that their citizens' rights are concretized, philosopher Martha Nussbaum specified which social arrangements, goods, and services a state must definitely provide to the individuals who live within its border. As she saw it, individuals may demand as a matter of "right" from the state only those arrangements, goods, and services that will enable them to develop two sets of functional human capabilities: those that, if left undeveloped, render a life not human at all, and those that, if left undeveloped, render a human life less than a good life.[110]

Nussbaum's list of functional human capabilities included noncontroversial ones, such as life, bodily health, and bodily integrity. But her list also included more controversial functional human capabilities, such as the capability to play and to relate to nonhuman animals. Thus, it is not surprising that some global feminists viewed Nussbaum's list as reflecting not the needs of all women but the needs of "highly educated, artistically inclined, self-consciously and voluntarily Western women."[111] To this criticism, Nussbaum responded that she did not wish to impose her "good life" on any woman other than herself; she just wanted other women to have the means they need to choose their own version of the good life.

Many global feminists remained skeptical of Nussbaum's response, however. In an attempt to justify their skepticism, they pointed to passages from Nussbaum's writings, such as the following one:

> The capabilities approach insists that a woman's affiliation with a certain group or culture should not be taken as normative for her unless, on due consideration, with all the capabilities at her disposal, she makes that norm her own. We should take care to extend to each individual full capabilities to pursue the items on the list and then see whether they want to avail themselves of these opportunities. Usually they do, even when tradition says they should not. Martha Chen's work with [Indian] widows . . . reveals that they are already deeply critical of the cultural norms that determine their life quality. One week at a widows' conference

in Bangalore was sufficient to cause these formerly secluded widows to put on forbidden colors and to apply for loans; one elderly woman, "widowed" at the age of seven, danced for the first time in her life, whirling wildly in the center of the floor. . . . Why should women cling to a tradition, indeed, when it is usually not their voice that speaks or their interests that are served?[112]

Nussbaum's suggestion that one week at a conference could undo years of enculturation struck some global feminist critics as fanciful. Although they conceded that Nussbaum's understanding of human rights in terms of capabilities moves from an abstract interpretation to a contextual interpretation of human rights, they nonetheless claimed that it ultimately reverts to type— that is, liberalism as constructed in the Western world. Commented Vivienne Jabri of King's College Centre for International Relations, Department of War Studies:

> The practical implication of Nussbaum's approach . . . is the production of subjects whose emancipation is defined in terms of their full participation in the global liberal order. Apart from the banality of the certainties expressed, there is here a form of "epistemic violence" that astounds. In representing her discourse as a baseline for an international feminism, Nussbaum reiterates a late-modern form of colonial mentality that leaves the subject of its discourse shorn of history and complexity. This subject is hence denied a presence. This form of international feminism is ultimately a form of disciplining biopolitics, where the distribution of female bodies is ultimately what can constitute their freedom as consumers within the global marketplace, where, to use Spivak, "to be" is "to be gainfully employed."[113]

Seemingly, it is not an easy task for global feminists to strike a balance between universalism and relativism. Yet it is a task that remains high on global feminists' to-do list.

Postcolonial Feminism

Postcolonial feminists share with global feminists a concern for feminist issues worldwide, but take pains to include the ideas and texts of non-Western women into the discussion, in a way that global feminism does not *explicitly* do. While global feminism attempts to extend the Western concept of universal human rights to women on the world stage, is primarily concerned with health-care and reproductive issues, and is protective of human rights, postcolonial feminists are more concerned with the economic and political challenges faced by women and members of oppressed groups than with the health-care and reproductive issues they face. In other words, postcolonial feminism is concerned with the political struggles of oppressed women of color worldwide and is suspicious of any pretense in the West that the effects of colonialism have disappeared.

Self-Definition.   Actively engaged in directly combating what are under-stood as the ongoing and deleterious effects of colonialism (including, among other things, Euro-centric cultural hegemony, the codification of colonialist-masculinist dominance, and racism), postcolonial feminists concern them-selves primarily with cautioning formerly colonized peoples against allowing themselves to be defined, controlled, regulated, marginalized, stigmatized, be-littled, or in any other way devalued by what is understood as the constant and perpetual threat of "epistemic violence" and cultural annihilation coming from their former colonizers.[114]

Postcolonial feminists, in other words, refuse to let themselves or their problems be defined or assessed by Euro-centric standards. They take issue with the West's division of nations into First World nations (i.e., heavily in-dustrialized and market-based nations located primarily in the Northern Hemisphere) on the one hand and Third World nations (i.e., economically developing nations located primarily in the Southern Hemisphere) on the other, and examine how this division operates to disempower, delegitimize, and disadvantage formerly colonized people, particularly women. Economic and political issues are the primary concern of postcolonial feminists, who stress that women's oppression as members of formerly colonized peoples is often greater than their oppression as women per se.

Postcolonial feminists proudly adopt the classic feminist standpoint that the personal and the political are one.[115] What goes on in the privacy of one's home, including one's bedroom, affects how men and women relate in the larger social order. Sexual and reproductive freedom should be of no more or less importance to women than economic and political justice. Socialist femi-nist Emily Woo Yamaski made this point most forcefully: "I cannot be an Asian American on Monday, a woman on Tuesday, a lesbian on Wednesday, a worker/student on Thursday, and a political radical on Friday. I am all these things every day."[116]

The World's Proletariat.   As Robin Morgan noted, "Women are the world's proletariat."[117] Even though it constitutes 60 to 80 percent of most na-tions' economies, housework continues to suffer from "gross national product invisibility."[118] To deny that women work, stressed Morgan, is absurd. Women

constitute almost the totality of the world's food producers and are responsible
for most of the world's hand portage of water and fuel. In most nations, hand-
icrafts are largely or solely the products of female labor, and in most nations,
women constitute a large portion of tourist industry workers, including the
notorious sex tourism industry, which caters to businessmen who pay for the
sexual services of women in the nations they visit.[119]

In addition, women are migrant and seasonal workers in agrarian nations
and part-time laborers in industrialized nations. A significant percentage of
the eldercare, childcare, and domestic work done in Western nations is done
by women from developing nations who have left their own families back
home to make money to support them. There is, said Arlie Hochschild, a
"global heart transplant" at work in the exportation of care from poor, developing nations to wealthy, developed nations.[120]

Also of particular significance in developing nations is the large number
of women who work in factories owned by Western multinational companies. Most of the women (and men) who labor in these factories work under
sweatshop conditions. Rosemary Radford Ruether noted that these conditions include the following ones: "Workers receive less than a living wage, are
forced to work long hours (ten to twelve hours a day) without overtime pay,
work in unsafe conditions, are harassed on the job, physically and verbally
abused, and are prevented from organizing unions and bargaining for better
conditions."[121] Examples of the global market at work include Indonesia,
where female factory workers receive about $1.25 a day for ten or even more
hours of work; Vietnam, where female factory workers get about six cents an
hour to assemble the promotional toys US children find in their McDonald's
Happy Meal boxes.[122] And there is Mexico, where female workers laboring in
factories on the Mexican side of the United States–Mexico border receive far
less wages than do female workers laboring in factories on the US side of this
same border.[123]

Postcolonial feminists debate whether women should work under sweatshop conditions. On the one hand, such work has made some women better
off "as members of families who rely on their support, as mothers who want
a better standard of living for their children, as young unmarried women
who want the status that economic independence sometimes brings."[124] On
the other hand, such work has made other women compliant and docile to a
fault, unwilling to defend their human rights for fear of losing their jobs.
Protest seems in order, said Ruether, as long as a Nike worker in Asia earns
less than two dollars a day and Nike CEO Phil Knight owns $4.5 billion in
Nike stock.[125]

Adding to women's total workload is the eight or more hours of unrecognized work (housework, childcare, eldercare, sick care) they do every day.

When governments and businesses do respond to women's complaints about their "double day" (eight or more hours of recognized work outside the home and eight or more hours of unrecognized work inside the home), the response, more often than not, does not substantially improve women's situations. Governments or businesses tell women to work part-time or to get on a "mommy track," strategies that are not feasible for women who need to support their families and that are not desirable for women who want to improve their status and wages at work. Even worse, some governments and businesses fail to understand women's complaints about their "double day" of work at all, recommending sexist solutions. For example, Cuba's Fidel Castro once proposed that "hairdressers remain open during the evening to ease the burden of the woman who is employed during the day but needs to be attractive in her house wifing role at night."[126]

Reflecting on how hard women work and how little government and business has done to ameliorate women's lot, Morgan concluded this state of affairs obtains because "Big Brother's" interests are not served by providing women the same kind of work and economic security it provides men. Whether Big Brother lives in the First World or Third World, said Morgan, "a marginal female labor force is a highly convenient asset: cheap, always available, easily and callously disposed of."[127]

Postcolonial feminists are somewhat critical of developed nations' efforts to improve developing nations' economies in general and women's lot in particular. Specifically, these feminists are skeptical about Western development programs for formerly colonized peoples, owing to a history of those people having been exploited by their former colonizers as sources of cheap labor and valuable resources. These Western nations also dismissed the cultures and traditions of the indigenous peoples they colonized, often rationalizing what amounted to cultural annihilation, in the name of "civilization." As part of the domination that is colonialism, Western nations often forced native peoples to learn and speak European languages and to convert to Christianity.[128]

After World War II, most colonizers pulled out of the lands they had exploited, viewing these territories as an increasing cost rather than benefit. Sadly, and largely because of what the colonizing nations had done to them, many Asians, Africans, and South Americans found themselves incredibly poor. They were then forced to go to their former colonizers to borrow money. In the 1960s, interest rates were relatively low and many formerly colonized nations borrowed large amounts of money from Western nations. The formerly colonized nations assumed that they could boost their economies relatively quickly and pay back their debt swiftly. Unfortunately, most of these nations found it extraordinarily difficult to catch up to the nations that had previously exploited them. By the time the formerly colonized nations realized that development is a slow process, interest rates had risen steeply, and the borrowers were unable to pay the interest on their loans.

To prevent the world economic system from crashing, the International Monetary Fund and the World Bank rescheduled the debts of many formerly colonized nations. As part of this plan, they required the affected nations to adjust the structure of their economies to ease their integration into the global economic system. According to Ruether, the "formula" for so-called Structural Adjustment was harsh. Among other things, it required "devaluation of local currency . . . the removal of trade barriers that protected local industries and agriculture . . . the privatization of public sector enterprises, such as transportation, energy, telephones, and electricity . . . and the removal of minimum wage laws and state subsidies for basic foods, education, and health services for the poor."[129] Moreover, to earn enough foreign currency to finance their rescheduled external debts, formerly colonized nations had to export as many inexpensive goods as possible to Western nations or work for large transnational companies located within their boundaries, or do both. As a result of this state of affairs, most formerly colonized nations were unable to produce their own consumer goods and were forced to import them from the West. Not only did these goods prove to be costly, but they also bore the cultural imprint of the West: Nike sneakers, Camel cigarettes, Coca-Cola, Ford automobiles, Levi Strauss blue jeans, and Dell computers. This so-called McDonaldization of the world is taken by many to have effectively amounted to the recolonization of formerly colonized nations.[130]

Postcolonial feminists claim that women in formerly colonized nations bear the brunt of what Alison Jaggar termed the "Southern debt."[131] Detailing how the Western you-can-catch-up-to-us policies serve the interests of the former colonizers far more than the interests of the formerly colonized, Maria Mies, for example, noted that Western economists make unrealistic promises to formerly colonized peoples. Westerners tell the people that the formerly colonized can attain the same standard of living as people in the West enjoy, while doubting the truth of their predictions about endless progress and limitless growth.[132] Observing that the world's population will swell to 11 billion after the year 2050, Mies stated: "If of these eleven billion people the per capita energy consumption was similar to that of Americans in the mid-1970s, conventional oil resource would be exhausted in 34–74 years."[133]

Because developed nations find it difficult to maintain high standards of living, Mies speculated that whatever the West gives to developing nations in the way of benefits, it extracts in the way of costs. Specifically, she said, industrialized nations pass on to their "partners" in developing nations the economic, social, and ecological costs developed nations cannot pay without dropping from their privileged status to something more akin to the status of developing nations:

> The relationship between colonized and colonizer is based not on any measure of partnership but rather on the latter's coercion and violence in its dealings with the former. This relationship is in fact the secret of un-limited growth in the centers of accumulation. If externalization of all the costs of industrial production were not possible, if they had to be borne by the industrialized countries themselves, that is if they were internal-ized, an immediate end to unlimited growth would be inevitable.[134]

In sum, stressed Mies, "catching-up development" is not *feasible* for two reasons: (1) There are only so many resources to divide among humankind, and they are currently inequitably distributed and consumed; and (2) to maintain its present power, the existing "colonial world order" needs to maintain the economic gap it promises to eliminate. For example, the overall affluence of women in developed nations depends on the overall poverty of women in developing nations:

> Only while women in Asia, Africa, or Latin America can be forced to work for much lower wages than those in affluent societies—and that is made possible through the debt trap—can enough capital be accumu-lated in the rich countries so that even unemployed women are guaran-teed a minimum income; but all unemployed women in the world cannot expect this. Within a world system based on exploitation "some are more equal than others."[135]

In addition to claiming that "catching-up development" schemes are not feasible, Mies noted that, in her estimation, they are also not *desirable*. She observed that the West's "good life" is actually a very *bad* life insofar as human relationships are concerned. People in the West are too busy making money to spend time with one another. They are so strained and stressed they have little sense of selfhood or ultimate meaning. People in the West run the rat race, day after day, until the day they die, said Mies. Their children inherit their considerable material goods, and the cycle continues of meaningless running around until one drops dead.

The point of Mies's critique of the West was not to recommend that be-cause poor people in developing nations had enviable family and friendship relationships and a more appropriate set of life values than those typically dis-played by hard-core Western materialists, the poor should stay dirt poor. Rather, it was that because money and power are limited goods, a relentless and single-minded pursuit of them inevitably leads to discord. In this connection, Mies offered an example that focused on Western women and women in developing nations as one another's competitors:

> It may be in the interest of Third World women working in the garment industry for export, to get higher wages, or even wages equivalent to those paid in the industrialized countries; but if they actually received these wages then the working-class woman in the North could hardly afford to buy those garments, or buy as many of them as she does now. In her interest the price of these garments must remain low. Hence the interests of these two sets of women who are linked through the world market are antagonistic.[136]

As long as the possession of material goods and power is equated with human happiness, said Mies, there will be the kind of competition and antagonism that inevitably leads to conflict and even war. Women will be set against women globally and against their own men nationally.

From the perspective of postcolonial feminists, stressed Mies, developed nations must abandon their view of the "good life" and substitute for it a view predicated not on the *quantity* of one's possessions and power but on the *quality* of one's relationships. In addition, developed nations must confront the material world's limits and vow to live within them. Only then will it be possible to create a new world order, in which divisions such as the politically incorrect "First World–Third World" are incomprehensible. Finally, from the perspective of postcolonial feminists, women should take the lead in devising and implementing the systems, structures, policies, and programs needed to effect this transformation.

A Rejection of Rights Talk.   Interestingly, unlike global feminists who are very much inspired by the language of women's rights as human rights in international documents such as the United Nations Universal Declaration of Human Rights, the Convention on the Elimination of All Forms of Discrimination Against Women, and the United Nations Declaration on the Elimination of Violence Against Women,[137] postcolonial feminists have doubts about a women's rights approach to problems.

One reason some postcolonial feminists lacked enthusiasm for women's rights is that they heard within rights talk a lingering tendency to privilege first-generation civil and political rights over second-generation economic and social rights.[138] Typical first-generation rights include freedom from oppression and from governmental interference with liberty of thought and action, whereas typical second-generation rights include the right to food, clothing, shelter, education, health care, work, rest, and reasonable payment.[139] If women's first-generation rights are honored without equal attention to women's second-generation rights, many women will remain at a real disadvantage, said these feminists. For example, a poor woman's right to have an abortion does not mean much if it simply prevents others from interfering with her decision to abort her fetus. She also needs the funds to pay for an abortion. And even if funding is available, her right to have an abortion will mean but little if, as a result of her abortion decision, she is ostracized from her community or rejected, abused, or divorced by a husband on whom she is financially and socially dependent.

Other postcolonial feminists rejected rights language not so much for the reason just given, but because they think some of the rights that get privileged as *universal human rights* are not as universal as their proponents insist. These postcolonial feminists claim that rights are the creation of Western liberalism. These rights represent only, or primarily, the values and interests that people in such nations as the United States favor. Anne Phillips pointed out that the high value placed on autonomy in statements of universal human rights may be "a central preoccupation of Western cultures" and that many women do not value "personal autonomy and mobility over the ties of family or community."[140] They do not want to be "liberated" from either the constraints of tradition or the obligations and limitations that go with belonging to a community. Phillips's observation was reinforced by Australian feminist Chilla Bulbeck, who described her reaction to a pro-choice rally she attended in Washington, DC:

> I was struck by the anger of many of the speakers and participants. A black and white women's vocal group from Manhattan . . . shouted out the slogan "We are fierce, we are feminist, and we are in your face." Robin Morgan urged us to buy T-shirts proclaiming, "Rage plus women equals power." One placard read "Abort Bush Before His Second Term." Angry arguments erupted between the pro-choice women and the pro-life women who had erected a "cemetery of innocents" nearby (representing aborted fetuses . . .). I went to the United States believing I knew it intimately from the flood of films, television programs, and academic books that pervade Australian popular and intellectual culture. Yet I felt battered and cut adrift by the assertiveness and anger, by the incessant refrain of rights and freedoms. This fashion of feminism was unfamiliar to me.[141]

Still other postcolonial feminists raise even more basic objections to rights talk. They thought it was a mistake to invoke as normative the concept of rights instead of its arguably correlative concept of responsibilities or duties.

As they saw it, my right to at least a subsistence amount of food is dependent on your or someone else's responsibility to provide it for me. One feminist theorist who insisted that rights are best understood in terms of responsibilities was Diane Elson. She presented human rights as claims "to a set of social arrangements—to norms, institutions, laws and an enabling economic environment—that can best secure the enjoyment of these rights."[142]

Moreover, she claimed it is wrong for states to stand idly by as charitable organizations and other nongovernment organizations struggle to maintain society's infrastructures so as to prevent its members from harm.

Transnational Feminism

Transnational feminism is almost entirely crafted by women of color and self-consciously showcases the unique vantage points of what are sometimes called "subaltern" women or women in developing nations. Transnational feminism has been defined as:

> activism of various groups of women, whom mainstream Western feminist theory and practices traditionally marginalized, which directed feminist attention toward power difference rooted in the structures of race, culture, class, histories of colonization and migration, sexuality, and so on. While this challenge to universal feminism has enabled more contextualized analyses of women's lives and opened new spaces for coalition building, it has unsettled traditional feminist demands for gender equality that were based on developmentalist and modernization discourses.[143]

In other words, transnational feminism is concerned with connections between nationhood, race, gender, sexuality and economic exploitation on a world scale in the context of the rise of global capitalism. Transnational feminists, even more than postcolonial feminists, are concerned with imperialism and its social, political, and economic effects; and work to organize resistance to capitalist hegemonies as they interrogate the relationship between those hegemonies and the nation-state. For example, transnational feminisms challenge global feminism's usage and implementation of the concept of the "Third World woman" as if all women in this category share the same cultural experiences or have the same experience of oppression. Chandra Talpade Mohanty wrote, for example, that Western feminism often overlooks the discursive and cultural heterogeneities of the lives of women in the Third World, despite the reality that the experience of oppression is incredibly diverse and contingent on geography, history, and culture. For Mohanty, Western feminism tends to discursively colonize the material and historical heterogeneities of the lives of women in the third world, thereby producing/re-presenting a composite, singular "Third World Woman"—an image which appears arbitrarily constructed, but nevertheless carries with it the authorizing signature of Western humanist discourse.[144]

Mohanty continued:

I argue that assumptions of privilege and ethnocentric universality on the one hand, and inadequate self-consciousness about the effect of Western scholarship on the "third world" in the context of a world system dominated by the West on the other, characterize a sizable extent of Western feminist work on women in the third world. . . . It is in this process of homogenization and systemitization of the oppression of women in the third world that power is exercised in much of recent Western feminist discourse, and this power needs to be defined and named.[145]

From the perspective of many transnational feminists, then, while global feminists may be well intentioned in their attempts to extend to non-Western women what they take to be insights about what women in general need and deserve, the efforts of global feminists in this regard are condescending and ill-informed regarding non-Western cultures and value systems.

Transnational feminism works to build between women the kinds of worldwide alliances that global feminism purportedly seeks, but rather than pursuing what it understands as the utopian ideal of global sisterhood, its aim is more equitable and constructive alliances between women across cultural contexts.

Critiques of Women of Color Feminisms

Critique One: "Of Color" Is an Objectifying Label

For some feminists, the idea of a feminism designed especially for a group of persons called "women of color"—let alone multiple feminisms designed especially for different subsets of "women of color"—is problematic. Many argue, for example, that to identify a group of persons set apart from others on the basis of color or race reifies the concept of biological race that also undermines the (third-wave) project of moving past restrictive, limiting categories regarding race or gender. But, the appropriation of the term *of color* can also be understood as a mechanism to identify those who have been on the receiving end of racially motivated oppression. Additionally, it can reveal a commonality among a multiplicity of women, on the basis of which they might collectively generate political power. In recent years, a compromise has been made between these two positions, so that a feminist identifying herself as "of color" need not be understood as reifying the concept of biological race, but only as acknowledging that one of the axes of oppression she faces is *racialized* oppression.

Critique Two: Intersectionality Is a Limited Concept

Since intersectionality came into being roughly in the early 1990s, the axes of oppression identified at that time have multiplied. Whereas race, gender, class, and sexuality were the primary axes of oppression understood to intersect and shape particular women's experiences at the origin of the concept of intersectionality, recently such factors as religion, nationality, and citizenship status have been added to the list of axes. The critique is often levied that the concept of intersectionality itself is of a bygone era, implying that the categories of race, gender, class, sexuality and even religion or nationality are problematically based in second-wave essentialist notions about clearly defined races, genders, and so on. Race and gender cannot "intersect," on this view, unless the theoretical (and actual) boundaries between different races and genders are fairly clearly defined in the first place.

"Interstitiality" has recently been offered in place of intersectionality as an organizing concept to explain the complex web of socio-historical and socio-legal forces at work in the social creation of identity, particularly as that identity is shaped by oppression. *Interstitiality* means different things for different feminists. For some, the concept is meant to invoke the ill-defined but nevertheless existent space between the existing identity categories of race, gender, and so on. For others, the concept is meant to highlight the unlimited number of identity categories that can overlap and interact in the formation of identity. Perhaps it is the case, however, that intersectionality and interstitialty are not incompatible concepts, and can perhaps be understood as different names for the same phenomenon. What interstitiality does seem to add to intersectionality, however, is an emphasis on the nonessential nature of any singular group identity marker.

Critique Three: No Distinction Between African American/Black Feminism and Mixed Race Feminism

The "races" at work in Mixed Race feminism in the United States as described in this chapter are primarily the so-called black race and the so-called white race.[146] However, many African American/Black feminists argue that the political landscape in America requires that Mixed Race feminists understand themselves primarily as African American/Black feminists and only secondarily as feminists of mixed race. After all, say these thinkers, most African American women are "mixed" (i.e., most are the product of so-called racial mixing). But, for purposes of what the concept of race means in the United States and how it plays out in the lives of those who are assigned a race, adopting a so-called mixed race identity instead of an African American one can be understood as an attempt to distance oneself from one's African heritage in an effort to obtain the benefits of white privilege, say these African American/Black feminists. We are all women of color, say these thinkers, and to the extent that one tries to distance oneself from association with one's African heritage by self-identifying as being of mixed race is to be engaged in an act of self-hatred and even, for some thinkers, an act of hegemonic oppression.

For many Mixed Race feminists, however, while the points of these thinkers are well taken, and it is important to be careful not to eschew or disparage one's African ancestry in the formation of one's self-proclaimed racial identity, many Mixed Race feminists find that it is equally important to acknowledge all aspects of their racial heritage; both because to deny some parts of themselves while accepting others is arguably an act of self-hatred, and because many Mixed Race feminists understand themselves to be living symbols for the promise of racial harmony in the United States. If both (or all "races") can exist harmoniously in the embodiment of the mixed race person, then why can't the "races" exist harmoniously in the world? In this sense, there is an optimism in Mixed Race feminism that makes its vantage point unique, and through which glimpses of the feminist project of a future free from racism, sexism, homophobia, ableism, ageism, and so on, can be seen.

Critique Four: Global Feminism Neglects the Particularity of Women's Experiences

Arguably based in a kind of Kantian ethics that takes for granted the reliability and legitimacy of such things as reason, autonomy, freedom, and universal moral truth, global feminism is understood by some critics as problematically neglectful of the particularity of women's experiences. There is no one "women's experience," these critics charge. Instead, there is a multiplicity of women's experiences. In their pursuit of sweeping solutions to the problems faced by the women of the world, these critics charge that global feminists, while meaning well, unwittingly engage in acts of cultural imperialism and ego-based paternalism. When getting together to decide how women in developing nations can be rendered as "free" and "autonomous" as they are, critics charge, global feminists seldom reflect on the extent to which what counts as "freedom" is culturally determined, or the extent to which "autonomy" is a fiction created by the wealthy and used to justify a failure to consider the effect of one's actions on others. Similarly, all discussion of what is in the "best interests" of women in non-Western countries, discussion of what their "needs" are or of what the basic "functional human capabilities" are, is limited by a lack of firsthand experience with the problems faced by these particular women. The solutions posed by global feminists cannot help but be ineffectual at a minimum and harmful in the worst-case scenario, say critics.

But, global feminists respond that it is part of their project to take proactive steps to understand the problems of the women they wish to help. Through a close examination of the problems faced by these women, global feminists are confident that they are in a position to make decisions about what is best for them, even if what is "best" for these women is usually measured, to varying degrees, in terms of what global feminists understand as what is best for themselves. In other words, key to global feminism is an assumption about the universality of the female experience, and an assumption about certain commonalities in the problems of women worldwide. These problems include violence against women, enforced external control over the female reproduction process, and the denial of a general right to live one's own life and control one's own destiny.

Critique Five: Postcolonial Feminism as Global Feminism

Many critics of postcolonial feminism see little difference between postcolonial feminism and global feminism in terms of the regard given to the unique problems faced by women of color. The primary concern of postcolonial feminism, these critics charge, is capitalist exploitation of the proletariat rather than addressing the specific problems of women of color in developing nations or facilitating the agency of women of color. Rights, these critics charge, are often the only mechanism through which women of color can facilitate their own agency. A third critique of postcolonial feminism is that its inclusion of texts written by persons of color is but a fetishization of the problems of women of color, with the texts understood as a new and exotic toy to make the research of postcolonial feminists (most of whom are white) stand out in the crowd. Meanwhile, the problems of women of color worldwide are left unsolved, say these critics. Postcolonial feminists would likely respond that they are truly concerned with the problems of women of color in formerly colonized nations.

Conclusion

Women of color feminists present a great challenge to mainstream, Western feminism: how to unite women in, through, and despite their differences. In a dialogical essay coauthored with Maria Lugones, Elizabeth Spelman stressed that to develop an adequate (inclusive) feminist theory, a wide variety of women would have to formulate it together. Lugones reacted to Spelman's proposal with some challenging points. She wondered whether women who had previously been marginalized by the recognized authorities in feminist thought would now want to join them to create a better feminist theory. Perhaps these once-marginalized women would prefer to create their own theory, in their own voices, without shouldering the burdens that generally accompany collaborative projects.

Lugones was concerned about the motives behind reigning feminist authorities' sudden interest in the views of "Others." Was the motive a self-interested one, in the sense of "self-growth or self expansion, feeding off the rich 'difference' of the other?" Or, just as bad, was the motive a mere sense of duty, understood as an act of noblesse oblige or as an anemic substitute for true love?[147] Lugones then continued that such motives, if present, would make it impossible for white women/First World women to fully partner with women of color/Third World women in theory making. She stressed that the only motive capable of bringing women together to weave a feminist theory strong enough to withstand the challenges of the twenty-first century is the motive of wanting to be friends. Unless one woman wants to be another woman's friend, she will be unable to summon the psychic energy to travel to that woman's world to imagine or see the other woman living her life there as a self rather than as an "Other." Therefore, according to Lugones as well as Spelman and Morgan, the chief task of women of color feminists and global, postcolonial, and transnational feminists is to help women learn how to be each other's friends.

Disagreeing with Morgan's, Spelman's, and Lugones's views on the essential goal of feminism are a variety of thinkers, including bell hooks, Audre Lorde, and Iris Young. Although hooks and Lorde sometimes employed the language of sisterhood in their writings, for them sisterhood is a political rather than a personal concept. Women can be sisters in the sense of being political comrades, but only if they are willing to truly confront their differences. Imagining, perceiving, tolerating, and welcoming are fine, insofar as they go, but confronting differences requires far more painful activities, such as being enraged and being shamed. There is a difference, hooks emphasized, between "bourgeois-women's-liberation" sisterhood and [inclusive] feminist sisterhood. The former focuses on women's "supporting" one another, where support serves "as a prop or a foundation for a weak structure" and where women, emphasizing their "shared victimization," give each other "unqualified approval."[148] The latter rejects this sentimental brand of sisterhood and offers instead a type of sisterhood that begins with women's confronting and combating one another's differences, and ends with their using these very same differences to "accelerate their positive advance" toward the goals they are presumed to share. As hooks explained, "Women do not need to eradicate difference to feel solidarity. We do not need to share common oppression to fight equally to end oppression. . . . We can be sisters united by shared interests and beliefs, united in our appreciation for diversity, united in our struggle to end sexist oppression, united in political solidarity."[149] Lorde also stressed the importance of maintaining women's differences rather than trying to transcend them. She claimed, for example, that feminists don't have to love one another to be able to work with one another.[150] In the same vein, Young observed that although women should not be enemies, they should not expect to be friends. They should simply be content to be "strangers,"[151] or, we might add, acquaintances.

Rejecting the homogenizing, conformist tendencies of the language of community and family, Young argued that feminists should not try to be "sisters" and "friends" with women whose worlds are radically different than their own. As Nancie Caraway noted, for Young, the "insistence on the ideal of shared subjectivity . . . leads to undesirable political implications."[152] Young repeatedly urged feminists to distrust the desire "for reciprocal recognition and identification with others . . . because it denies differences in the concrete sense of making it difficult for people to respect those with whom they do not identify."[153] Young claimed, said Caraway, that feminists should not want to be sisters or friends, because such desires "thwart our principled calls for heterogeneity in feminism."[154]

Most forms of worldwide, mainstream feminism attempt to extrapolate historically Western feminist concerns onto women in other countries, cultures, and value systems, arguably motivated by a kind of naive, universalist belief that the concerns of Western women are concerns of women all over the world. There is a clear attempt on the part of all mainstream feminists concerned with the problems of women worldwide to understand and sincerely grapple with the unique and culturally situated needs of the various women of color worldwide. However, although it is of course ultimately impossible (for Fernandes Botts) to speak for all women of color, to the degree that doing so is possible, the reader should note that from the perspective of the woman of color, however heartfelt and sincere such efforts are on the part of the mainstream feminist with a worldwide focus, it is simply impossible for the mainstream (white) feminist to fully and properly affect the kind of change women of color need and require. There is an insurmountable barrier of experience between the experiences of the mainstream feminist and the entrenched, systemic, and worldwide problem called racial oppression. So, while the feminist of color can fairly concede that there is some overlap among the concerns of women worldwide (e.g., vague general concerns, such as safety or reproductive issues), as the section on Indigenous feminism in particular highlights, it may be that each embodied experience of patriarchy is significantly affected by membership in the one or more specific racial or ethnic groups of which each woman is a part. This particularly may be the case where the racial or ethnic group in question has a history of having been oppressed in a way that is specific to that group. And how can this not be the case? To the extent that a woman has been racialized, she has been oppressed, and she has been oppressed in a way that is unique to the particular racial classification(s) assigned to her, as well as the experience of being female. In other words, the experiences of patriarchal oppression of each of the groups of women of color in the United States has its own features and challenges, as does the experience of oppression of each of the groups of women (of color or not) all over the world.

Although part of the point of revising this chapter for the fourth edition was to highlight the unique experiences of oppression and patriarchy of various groups of women of color in the United States and to highlight the unique concerns of various women of color worldwide (as well as the pros and cons of ways of approaching worldwide feminist concerns), another motivation was to bring to (Tong's) seminal and classical text on feminist thought the increasingly felt need to let women of color *speak for themselves,* to identify their agency, as well as their right to define their own concerns and to work amongst themselves to find workable solutions to those concerns. The contemporary feminist project is no longer respectably conceivable from the vantage point of the Anglo-European feminists who are responsible for the so-called first and second waves of feminism, although the efforts, challenges, and theoretical schemas of these brave and trailblazing women certainly play an important key role in conceptualizing the worldwide feminist project. But the new project—the project for the future—is one that includes all women, in all of their varied and beautiful and powerful forms. It must necessarily be conceived from and examined through a vantage point that is panoramically opened up to the situated and distinctive perspectives of women of all colors; that is, to women of color feminisms in all of their situated complexities.

Questions for Discussion

1. Discuss the consequences on the formation of personal identity of the black/white binary thought to exist in the United States. Consider the tangible repercussions for individual identity and for society.
2. Is it likely that white feminists will ever forsake "white privilege" for the sake of solidarity with women of color? Why or why not?

3. Does race actually exist? Or is it merely a social construct? If it actually exists, how do we determine one's race? By the "one-drop" rule—or is that arbitrarily established to privilege whites? If race is a social construct, what purposes does it serve?

4. Cite examples of women of color needing to participate in the Western and/or "white" world. Explain why such a necessity inevitably infringes upon the interests and rights of women of color. How might women work together to cherish and include non-Western women and their vantage points into the larger socio-political context?

5. Explain the notion that some women are more equal than others. Is it possible for some women to remain affluent—at the expense of other, marginalized women (or men, for that matter)—and still consider themselves true feminists? Why or why not?

6. How might the language of universal human rights not actually benefit women universally? In your estimation, what is the better approach to ensuring that all women enjoy equal dignity: (1) some form of normative morality, or (2) moral pluralism? How would you implement your approach?

7

Ecofeminism

Ecofeminists focus on human beings' domination of the nonhuman world, or nature. Because women are culturally tied to nature, ecofeminists argue there are conceptual, symbolic, and linguistic connections between feminist and ecological issues. According to Karen J. Warren, the Western world's basic beliefs, values, attitudes, and assumptions about itself and its inhabitants have been shaped by an oppressive patriarchal conceptual framework, the purpose of which is to explain, justify, and maintain relationships of domination and subordination in general and men's domination of women in particular. The most significant features of this framework are:

- *Value-hierarchical thinking:* "up-down" thinking, which places higher value, status, or prestige on what is "up" rather than on what is "down";
- *Value dualisms:* disjunctive pairs in which the disjuncts are seen as oppositional (rather than as complementary) and exclusive (rather than as inclusive) and that place higher value (status, prestige) on one disjunct rather than on the other (e.g., dualisms that give higher value or status to that which has historically been identified as "mind," "reason," and "male" than to that which has historically been identified as "body," "emotion," and "female");
- *Logic of domination:* a structure of argumentation that leads to a justification of subordination.[1]

Patriarchy's hierarchical, dualistic, and oppressive mode of thinking has harmed both women and nature, in Warren's opinion. Indeed, because women have been "naturalized" and nature has been "feminized," it is difficult

255

to know where the oppression of one ends and the other begins. Warren emphasized women are "naturalized" when they are described in animal terms, such as "cows, foxes, chicks, serpents, bitches, beavers, old bats, pussycats, cats, bird-brains, hare-brains."[2] Similarly, nature is "feminized" when "she" is raped, mastered, conquered, controlled, penetrated, subdued, and mined by men, or when "she" is venerated or even worshipped as the grandest mother of all. If man is the lord of nature, if he has been given dominion over it, then he has control not only over nature but also over nature's human analog, woman. Whatever man may do to nature, he may also do to woman.

Similar to the manner in which radical-cultural feminists and radical-libertarian feminists disagree about whether women's association with the work of childbearing and child-rearing is ultimately a source of power or disempowerment for women, "cultural," "nature," or "psychobiologistic" ecofeminists disagree with "social-constructionist" or "social-transformative" ecofeminists about the wisdom of stressing women's association with nature.[3]

Yet despite their sometimes divergent views on women's particular responsibilities to the environment (must we live as simply as possible?), to animals (must we be vegetarians and antivivisectionists?), and to future generations (must we be pacifists and strict population controllers?), all ecofeminists agree with Rosemary Radford Ruether that women's and nature's liberation are a joint project:

> Women must see that there can be no liberation for them and no solution to the ecological aims within a society whose fundamental model of relationships continues to be one of domination. They must unite the demands of the women's movement with those of the ecological movement to envision a radical reshaping of the basic socioeconomic relations and the underlying values of this [modern industrial] society.[4]

Some Roots of Ecofeminism

In her 1962 book, *Silent Spring*, Rachel Carson warned Americans that unless they began to take care of their environment, then "all man's assaults upon the environment [including] the contamination of air, earth, rivers, and sea with dangerous and even lethal materials . . . [will undoubtedly] shatter or alter the very material . . . upon which the shape of the future depends."[5] As ecological concerns about global warming, ozone depletion, waste disposal, factory farming, endangered species, energy conservation, and wilderness preservation grew, an environmental movement took hold in the United States and throughout the world. Although all environmentalists believe human beings should respect nature, and give reasons for doing so, "human-centered" environmentalists provide reasons that are based on furthering human interests, whereas "earth-centered" environmentalists provide reasons that are based on the intrinsic value of the earth itself.

Human-centered environmentalists emphasize that we harm ourselves when we harm the environment. If we exhaust our natural resources or pollute our skies and water, not only we but our progeny will suffer. If we want to have the material goods and lifestyles that industrialization makes possible, we must devise some means to handle the toxic wastes it produces as a by-product. If we want to have the benefit of bountiful and inexpensive energy, we must harness new sources of energy such as the sun and wind, lest we use the entire supply of oil and natural gas currently fueling our economy. If we want to experience the wilderness and see uncultivated vegetation and undomesticated animals, we must prevent commercial enterprises from transforming every piece of wild land into a Disneyland or Club Med. And if we want to preserve the rich diversity of nature and the treasures it might still hold for us, we must safeguard all life-forms, refusing to imperil their existence.

Viewing themselves as realistic or pragmatic about environmental concerns, human-centered environmentalists concede that from time to time, we may have to sacrifice the environment to serve our interests. In other words, sometimes a forest must be cut down so we can use the trees to build homes; sometimes the air must be polluted so we can continue to drive our automobiles; sometimes a predatory species of wild animals must be hunted or relegated to our zoos so our domesticated animals can graze safely. In short, the environment's value is *instrumental;* its meaning, significance, and purpose depends on our needs or wants. The environment exists not for itself but for human beings.

It is not surprising that critics of human-centered environmentalism condemn it as "arrogant anthropomorphism," generally faulting the Judeo-Christian tradition as one of the main players in the devaluation of the environment. They point, for example, to the biblical mandate that instructed *men* to "subdue" the earth and "have dominion over the fish of the sea and over the birds of the air and every living thing that moves upon the earth," as promoting the view that nature has instrumental value only.[6] These same critics also stress how the metaphors and models of mechanistic science, which gained sway during the pre-Enlightenment and Enlightenment periods, reinforced the Bible's anthropomorphic view of nature. They claim that prior to the seventeenth century, we thought of nature organically, as a benevolent female or nurturing mother, as someone who gave freely and generously of *her* bounty to us, her children. After the scientific revolution, however, we reconceived nature mechanistically, as an inert, lifeless machine. As a result of this paradigm shift, we found it easier to justify not only our use but also our misuse and abuse of nature. We reasoned that there is nothing morally wrong with treating a mere "object" in whatever way we wish.

René Descartes's philosophy, which privileged mind over matter, further bolstered the mechanistic conception of nature, according to critics of human-centered environmentalism. His belief that our ability to think ("I think, therefore I am") makes us special led to the view that things that think (*res cogitans,* or human beings) are meant to control things that do not think (animals [as was then believed], trees, and rocks). Gradually, we convinced ourselves that human beings are indeed the highest life-form: the center of the universe. As a result of our exalted self-conception, we took it upon ourselves to decide not only when to protect and preserve the environment for our use but also when to sacrifice it for our greater glory and good.

Human-centered, or anthropomorphic, environmentalism, sometimes termed *shallow ecology,* remained the order of the day until the late 1940s, when a new generation of environmentalists forwarded an earth-centered environmentalism they termed *deep ecology*. This post-Enlightenment view of nature repudiated the modern conception of nature as a machine, reverting to medieval and even ancient conceptions of nature as an organism that has intrinsic as well as instrumental value.

In his much-anthologized essay "The Land Ethic," Aldo Leopold wrote that we should think about the land as "a fountain of energy flowing though a circuit of soils, plants, and animals."[7] Leopold believed the earth is a life system, an intricately interwoven and interdependent intersection of elements that functions as a whole organism. If one element of this system becomes diseased, the whole system is probably sick, and the only way to heal the system is to treat or cure the diseased part, whether that diseased part is an excessively flooded plain, a severely overpopulated herd of deer (or human beings), or a heavily polluted river. To be sure, a treatment or cure for the diseased element will not always be found, but that is to be expected. In fact, the ecosystem's laws of death and decay *require* that its old elements be extinguished: The patterns of regeneration and life continually provide the space necessary for new elements of the ecosystem. It is not important for each particular *part* to continue, said Leopold, but only for the *whole* to continue.

From nature's perspective, as opposed to what Leopold called man's perspective, flows an environmental ethics best termed *biocentric* or *ecocentric*. He claimed "a thing is right when it tends to preserve the integrity, stability, and beauty of the biotic community. It is wrong when it tends to do otherwise."[8] To illustrate his point, Leopold gave the example of a river sandbar, a very particular and small environmental system. Such a system has an identifiable integrity; it is a unity of interdependent elements combining together to make a whole with a unique character. It has a certain stability, not because it does not change but because it changes only gradually. An evolving river sandbar has a particular beauty in its harmonious, well-ordered form: a unity in diversity. When envisioned on a larger scale, this small environmental system interlocks with other small environmental systems, together constituting the very large ecosystem of which human beings are simply a part. This, the largest of all ecosystems, is none other than nature, wherein morality becomes a matter of conscious (or thinking) beings' preserving its integrity, stability, and beauty.

Leopold's thinking was at the forefront of the conceptual revolution that replaced the anthropomorphism of shallow ecology with the biocentrism of deep ecology. Arne Naess and George Sessions articulated the principal tenets of deep ecology:

1. The well-being and flourishing of human and non-human life on earth have value in themselves (synonyms intrinsic value, inherent value). These values are independent of the usefulness of the non-human world for human purposes.
2. Richness and diversity of life forms contribute to the realization of these values and are also values in themselves.
3. Humans have no right to reduce this richness and diversity except to satisfy vital needs.
4. The flourishing of human life and cultures is compatible with a substantial decrease of the human population. The flourishing of non-human life requires such a decrease.
5. Present human interference with the non-human world is excessive, and the situation is rapidly worsening.
6. Policies must therefore be changed. These policies affect basic economic, technological, and ideological structures. The resulting state of affairs will be deeply different from the present.
7. The ideological change is mainly that of appreciating life quality (dwelling in situations of inherent value) rather than adhering to an increasingly higher standard of living. There will be a profound awareness of the difference between big and great.
8. Those who subscribe to the foregoing points have an obligation directly or indirectly to try to implement the necessary changes.[9]

Critics of deep ecology fault both the theory underlying deep ecology and some of its tactics. They demand to know what the *source* of nature's intrinsic value is, rejecting the mere fact of nature's "is-ness" as an inadequate answer to their question. Just because something exists, they say, does not make it intrinsically valuable. In an effort to persuade these critics that nature is indeed intrinsically valuable, Peter Wenz argued there is something intuitively wrong about destroying an ecosystem when there is no good reason to do so. He claimed that if the last surviving human being after a worldwide disaster had a choice between saving or not saving all the remaining plant and animal life on the earth, it would not be "a matter of moral indifference" whether the person chose to save these life-forms.[10] Although critics of deep ecology agree with Wenz that the earth has value independent of us, they do not agree with the view that the earth's interests are equal to or even more important than ours. For example, critic Luc Ferry vehemently objected to a proposal by some deep ecologists that if we fail or refuse to control the size of our population voluntarily, the government should force us to do so, so that *nonhuman* animals have enough food and space. Does this mean, asked Ferry, that to get the ideal human–nonhuman population ratio,[11] our government should do nothing to stop the kind of "massive human die backs" caused by famine, disease, and war?[12] Are we to be handled like an overpopulated herd of deer?

Ecofeminism: New Philosophy or Ancient Wisdom?

Ecofeminism is a relatively new variant of ecological ethics. In fact, the term *ecofeminism* first appeared in 1974 in Françoise d'Eaubonne's *Le Féminisme ou la Mort*. In this work d'Eaubonne expressed the view that there exists a direct link between the oppression of women and the oppression of nature. She claimed the liberation of one cannot be effected apart from the liberation of the other.[13] A decade or so after d'Eaubonne coined the term, Karen J. Warren further specified four core assumptions of ecofeminism:

> (1) There are important connections between the oppression of women and the oppression of nature; (2) understanding the nature of these connections is necessary to any adequate understanding of the oppression of women and the oppression of nature; (3) feminist theory and practice must include an ecological perspective; and (4) solutions to ecological problems must include a feminist perspective.[14]

In many ways, ecofeminism resembles deep ecology, yet ecofeminists generally fault deep ecologists for missing one crucial point. According to ecofeminists, deep ecologists mistakenly oppose anthropocentrism in general when the real problem is not so much or only the Western world's *human*-centeredness, but its *male*-centeredness. Androcentrism, not anthropomorphism, is the chief enemy of nature.

Although she praised deep ecologists' "concerted effort . . . to rethink Western metaphysics, epistemology, and ethics," ecofeminist Ariel Kay Salleh nonetheless found their rethinking "deficient."[15] Noting that most of deep ecology's spokespeople are *men,* Salleh accused them of being afraid to confront the sexism as well as naturism causing our current environmental crisis. The "deep ecology movement will not truly happen," she said, "until men are brave enough to rediscover and to love the woman inside themselves."[16] Salleh's thesis, which is shared by many ecofeminists, is "that the hatred of women, which ipso facto brings about that of nature, is one of the principal mechanisms governing the actions of men (of 'males') and, thus, the whole of Western/patriarchal culture."[17]

Carol Adams perhaps most significantly reshaped the debate between shallow and deep ecology with the publication of her book *The Sexual Politics of Meat,* in which she established a link between patriarchal culture's oppression of both women and animals. One of the ways in which Adams illustrated her feminist vegetarian theory was to remind us of the Greek myth of Zeus and Metis, in which Zeus ("patriarch of patriarchs") lusts after Metis (goddess of knowledge and prudence), pursuing, raping, and ultimately swallowing her alive. After these horrific activities, Zeus explains them by observing that Metis will always remain in his belly, providing him with counsel. According to Adams, this myth demonstrates how "sexual violence and meat eating are collapsed" into each other.[18] Adams stressed that "an essential component of androcentric culture has been built upon these activities of Zeus: viewing the sexually desired object as consumable."[19] Animals, like women, are consumed as objects of pleasure in a cycle of objectification (animals = food), fragmentation (animal carcasses are dismembered so as to be turned into food), and finally consumption (on our dinner plates). Likewise, women are objectified (female body = sexual plaything), fragmented (into fetishized parts, such as breasts, buttocks, and vaginas), and consumed (via conquest, rape, pornography, etc.). In Adam's estimation, the rights of women and animals are inextricably joined, placing vegetarian ecofeminists firmly in the corner of deep ecology.

Tensions in Nature: Ecofeminist Thought

Although ecofeminists agree that the association of women with nature is the root cause of both sexism and naturism, they disagree about whether women's connections to nature are primarily biological and psychological or primarily social and cultural. They also disagree about whether women should deemphasize, emphasize, or reconceive their connections with nature. According to Ynestra King, "The recognition of the connections between women and nature and of women's bridge-like position between nature and culture poses three possible directions of feminism."[20] The first direction is to *sever* the woman-nature connection by totally integrating women into culture and the realm of production. The second is to *reaffirm* the woman-nature connection, proposing that female nature is not only different from, but also somehow better than, male culture. The third is to transform the woman-nature connection by using it to create "a different kind of culture and politics that would integrate intuitive, spiritual, and rational forms of knowledge . . . and create a free, ecological society."[21] Implicit in King's understanding of transformative ecofeminism is the postmodern feminist belief that ultimately all forms of human oppression are rooted in those dichotomous conceptual schemes that privilege one member of a dyad over another (e.g., male over female, nature over culture, science over spirituality).

Severing the Woman-Nature Connection

Simone de Beauvoir.   Among the feminists who have pondered women's association with nature is existentialist feminist Simone de Beauvoir. As we noted in Chapter 5, de Beauvoir urged women to transcend their links to nature so as to overcome their status as the other, or second, sex. She believed woman's identity as the other is derived partly from her biology—especially her reproductive capacity—and partly from her socially imposed child-rearing responsibilities. De Beauvoir did not view woman's body as woman's friend. On the contrary, she viewed woman's body as fundamentally alienating, as an energy drain leaving women too tired to participate in the kind of creative activity men enjoy.[22]

In addition, de Beauvoir stressed that human beings are cast in a *pour-soi/en-soi* dialectic. *Pour-soi* (being-for-itself) entails being a self, consciously aware of the possibilities for self-creation that the future presents; *en-soi* (being-in-itself) entails being the other, a thing without a future and therefore without any possibilities for transformation. Although all human beings are both *pour-soi* and *en-soi*, Western culture tends to view men as more likely to be mainly *pour-soi* and women as *en-soi*.

Sensing that they are as free as men, women nonetheless engage in bad faith by playing the role of the other. De Beauvoir noted that "along with the ethical urge of each individual to affirm his subjective existence, there is also the temptation to forgo liberty and become a thing."[23] If women are ever to be liberated from the status of the second sex, they must, she said, resist the temptation of the "easy way out." By refusing to be the other—the "it," the *en-soi*, the immanent one, the natural one—women will liberate not only themselves but also men. No longer will men be able to hide from their freedom in the bosom of "woman."

Reflecting on de Beauvoir's suggested program for women's liberation, ecofeminist Val Plumwood reproached de Beauvoir for giving women who care about nature the wrong advice:

> For Simone de Beauvoir woman is to become fully human in the same way as man, by joining him in distancing from and in transcending and controlling nature. She opposes male transcendence and conquering of nature to woman's immanence, being identified with and passively immersed in nature and the body. The "full humanity" to be achieved by woman involves becoming part of the superior sphere of the spirit and dominating and transcending nature and physicality, the sphere of freedom and controllability, in contrast to being immersed in nature and in blind uncontrollability. Woman becomes "fully human" by being absorbed in a masculine sphere of freedom and transcendence conceptualized in human-chauvinist terms.[24]

Plumwood feared that by rejecting the *en-soi* realm, the world of immanence, women will gain not true personhood but merely the opportunity to become men's full partners in the campaign to control or dominate nature. The male-female dichotomy will not be bridged or healed into wholeness. Rather, the female member of this long-standing dyad will simply be erased into the male member. Moreover, the culture-nature dichotomy will not be eliminated, but instead will be worsened. Abandoned by woman, nature will find itself utterly defenseless against the forces of culture.

Sherry B. Ortner. According to another feminist, Sherry B. Ortner, it will not be easy for women to disassociate themselves from nature, because virtually all societies believe women are closer to nature than men are. There are, she said, three reasons for the near universality of this belief. First, women's *physiology* is "more involved more of the time with the 'species of life'; it is woman's body that nurtures humanity's future." Second, women's primary *place* remains the domestic sphere, where "animal-like infants" are slowly transformed into cultural beings and where plant and animal products are shaped into food, clothing, and shelter. Third, women's *psyche*, "appropriately molded to mothering functions by her own socialization," tends toward more relational, concrete, and particular modes of thinking than do men's psyche.[25]

In Ortner's opinion, virtually every society's view of women as somehow existing *between* nature and culture has several consequences, each of them inviting a different interpretation of the term *intermediate*. First, *intermediate* can simply mean that women have a "middle status," lower than men's status but higher than nature's status. Second, it can mean that women "mediate," or perform some set of synthesizing or converting functions between nature and culture—for example, the socialization of children. Unless children are properly socialized, no society can survive; it needs its members to conform to its rules and regulations. For this reason, hypothesized Ortner, societies seek to restrict women's sexual, reproductive, educational, and occupational choices. The more conservative women are, the more rule-following they and their children will be. Third, and finally, the term *intermediate* can mean "of greater symbolic ambiguity." Because society cannot quite understand the nature of women, it is not certain whether to associate women with life or death, good or evil, order or chaos.[26] Do women hold society together, or do they chip away at its margins?

Society's view that women are intermediaries between culture and nature is, said Ortner, the product of women's "social actuality"—that is, women's physiology, domestic role, and feminine psyche. Thus, the way to alter this view of women is to change women's social actuality so that women as well as men are viewed as fully cultural persons capable of determining the course of history. Unfortunately, continued Ortner, women's social actuality cannot change unless society's view of women as intermediaries between culture and nature changes. Women will never escape this circular trap unless their situation is simultaneously attacked from both sides: from the social actuality side (women's reproductively special physiology, domestic role, and feminine psyche) *and* the conceptual or ideological side (women as occupying middle status, performing mediating functions between nature and culture, and carrying ambiguous symbolic baggage). Explaining her point at some length, Ortner claimed:

> Efforts directed solely at changing the social institutions—through setting quotas on hiring, for example, or through passing equal-pay-for-equal-work laws—cannot have far-reaching effects if cultural language and imagery continue to purvey a relatively devalued view of women. But at the same time efforts directed solely at changing cultural assumptions—through male and female consciousness-raising groups, for example, or through revision of education materials and mass-media imagery—cannot be successful unless the institutional base of the society is changed to support and reinforce the changed cultural view.[27]

Ortner believed that the effect of this two-pronged attack on women's situation would be to involve both men and women equally "in projects of creativity and transcendence." At last, women as well as men would be seen as "cultural," and women no less than men would participate "in culture's ongoing dialectic with nature."[28]

Like de Beauvoir's line of reasoning, Ortner's led to the conclusion that women can be liberated without nature's being liberated. Had Ortner thought otherwise, she would have argued not only that women are just as "cultural" as men but also that men are just as "natural" as women. In other words, she would have aimed to change men's societal actuality and the ideology that supports it, as much as she aimed to change women's. If society needs to bridge women's "distance" from culture by involving women in "creative" and "transcendent" tasks, then it also needs to bridge men's distance from nature by involving men in "repetitive" and "immanent" tasks.

Reaffirming the Woman-Nature Connection

Mary Daly: *Gyn/Ecology.*   In general, ecofeminists with a radical-cultural feminist background seek to strengthen rather than weaken women's connections to nature. Unlike de Beauvoir and Ortner, nature ecofeminists such as Mary Daly believe the traits traditionally associated with women—for example, caring, nurturing, and intuitiveness—are not so much the result of social constructions as the product of women's actual biological and psychological experiences. The problem is not that women have a closer relationship with nature than men do, but that this relationship is undervalued. Nature ecofeminists reject the assumed inferiority of both women and nature as well as the assumed superiority of both men and culture. Instead, they insist nature/woman is at least equal to and perhaps even better than culture/man, implying that traditional female virtues, not traditional male virtues, can foster improved social relations and less aggressive, more sustainable ways of life.

As Daly moved toward a lesbian separatist feminism perspective, she began to reject male culture as evil and to embrace female culture as good. She speculated that before the establishment of patriarchy, there existed an original matriarchy. In this gynocentric world, women flourished. They controlled their own lives, bonded with one another and with the nonhuman world of animals and nature, and lived both freely and happily. Thus, Daly saw the process of women's liberation as putting women back in touch with women's original "wild" and "lusty" natural world and freeing them from men's "domesticating" and "dispiriting" cultural world.[29]

Daly contrasted women's life-giving powers with men's death-dealing powers. She claimed women have the capacity for a fully human life, a vigorous life lived in dynamic communion with animals, earth, and stars. Men, she maintained, lack this capacity. They are, she said, parasites who feed off women's energy to fuel their destructive activities and constricting thoughts. Because they cannot bring life into the world and are incapable of bonding with nature, men substitute artificial life for flesh-and-blood life and, in acts of envious rage directed against women, seek not only to control and destroy women but also to control and destroy all that is natural. Male culture is everything female nature is not; it is about disease and death rather than health and life, said Daly:

> The products of necrophilic Apollonian male mating are of course the technological "offspring" which pollute the heavens and the earth. Since the passion of necrophiliacs is for the destruction of life and since their attraction is to all that is dead, dying, and purely mechanical, the fathers' fetishized "fetuses" (reproductions/replicas of themselves), with which they passionately identify, are fatal for the future of this planet. Nuclear reactors and the poisons they produce, stockpiles of atomic bombs, ozone-destroying aerosol spray propellants, oil tankers "designed" to self-destruct in the ocean, iatrogenic medications and carcinogenic food additives, refined sugar, mind pollutants of all kinds—these are the multiple fetuses/feces of stale male-mates in love with a dead world that is ultimately co-equal and consubstantial with themselves. The excrement of Exxon is everywhere. It is ominously omnipresent.[30]

Daly linked men's pollution of nature with men's "pollution" of women, contrasting men's *gynecology* with women's *gyn/ecology*. Men's gynecology is about segmenting and specializing reproduction as if it was just another mode of production; it is about substituting the fake for the real, the artificial for the natural; it is about cutting whole into parts. In contrast, women's gyn/ecology is about "dis-covering, de-veloping the complex web of living/loving relationships *of our own kind*. It is about *women* living, loving, creating our Selves, our cosmos."[31] Whereas men's gynecology depends upon "fixation and dismemberment," women's gyn/ecology affirms everything is connected.[32] According to Daly, women must work hard to stop the patriarchal forces of necrophilia—that is, of death. Most women, she claimed, have been seduced into cooperating with the "phallocentric" system of "necrophilia"; they have become men's "fembots," permitting themselves to be drained of their life forces.[33] In the days of matriarchy, Daly said, women reproduced through parthenogenesis, their eggs dividing and developing independently of sperm. Now, in the days of patriarchy, men have persuaded women to exchange natural reproduction for artificial reproduction. Men have invited women to enter a world in which *male* gynecologists snatch women's eggs from women's wombs to hatch them in technology's wombs, or artificial placentae. With this "advance" in science, said Daly, men move closer to achieving what they really seek—death—and unless women refuse to become men's "fembots," men will consume them together with nature.[34]

Susan Griffin.   Although Susan Griffin did not claim there are *biological* connections between women and nature, she did claim there are *ontological* connections between women and nature.[35] Specifically, Griffin wrote, "We know ourselves to be made from this earth. We know this earth is made from our bodies. For we see ourselves. And we are nature. We are nature seeing nature. We are nature with a concept of nature. Nature weeping. Nature speaking of nature to nature."[36] In addition to implying women have a special way of knowing and perceiving reality because of their special connections to nature, Griffin suggested it is women who must help human beings escape the false and destructive dualistic world into which men, particularly male Western philosophers, have led us.

In particular, Griffin used poetry to challenge dualistic thinking, instrumental rationality, and unbridled technology. She countered the objective, dispassionate, and disembodied voice of male culture with the subjective, passionate, embodied voice of female culture. If men can identify with machines and wonder whether machines (e.g., computers and robots) have feelings as well as thoughts, then women can identify with animals and wonder whether animals have thoughts as well as feelings.

Griffin sought to overcome dualism by providing what David Macauley has termed an "antidote to Plato's epistemological hierarchy." In his *Republic,* Plato led Western man out of what the philosopher regarded as an inferior sensory realm, the world of appearances, into what he regarded as a superior intellectual realm, the world of forms. In this latter world supposedly reside such *ideas* as beauty, truth, and goodness. However, in book 1 of *Woman and Nature,* Griffin suggested Plato led us astray by his incorrectly insisting that spirit is superior to matter and by prompting us to view man as mind and woman as body. Plato's dualistic hierarchy, stressed Griffin, is behind Western society's view that women are men's inferiors.[37]

Emphasizing the links between men's ideas about nature and their attitudes toward women, Griffin saw similarities between men's domestication of animals and domestication of women. She also noted ways in which women have either actively participated in or passively accepted their own "taming." For example, in a chapter entitled "Cows: The Way We Yield," Griffin suggested that the words used to describe a cow can be used equally well to describe a woman:

> She is a great cow. She stands in the midst of her own soft flesh, her thighs great wide arches, round columns, her hips wide enough for calving, sturdy, rounded, swaying, stupefied mass, a cradle, a waving field of nipples, her udder brushing the grass, a great cow, who thinks nothing, who waits to be milked, year after year, who delivers up calves, who stands

ready for the bull, who is faithful, always there, yielding at the same hour, day after day, that warm substance, the milk white of her eye, staring, trusting, sluggish, bucolic, inert, bovine mind dozing and dreaming, who lays open her flesh, like a drone, for the use of the world.[38]

Asked why she chose to describe women in terms of domestic rather than wild animals, Griffin responded that her two-year experience as a house-bound wife and mother caused her to identify with domestic animals, whom she viewed as well taken care of but decidedly unfree.[39]

Viewing Western thought's decision to privilege culture (man) over nature (woman) as a disastrous one, Griffin proceeded in book 2 of *Woman and Nature* to discuss all the conceptual rifts that Platonic philosophy generated: mind-body, intellect-emotion, city-wilderness, knower-known. She also critiqued scientific knowledge, ridiculing the importance men attach to numbers, in particular how men quantify everything in the universe and in their possession. Everything is reducible to a sum, a statistic, a cost-benefit ratio, said Griffin. Horrified by the thought of a world ruled by and reduced to numbers, Griffin urged women to journey out of culture—the labyrinth of dualistic thinking—back into nature, the cave where matter and spirit merge into one, the true habitat of human beings who are more than mere "ideas."

Finally, in the third and fourth books of *Woman and Nature,* Griffin claimed we can overcome the kind of thinking that belittles nature, materiality, the body, and women, but only if women learn to speak for themselves and for the natural world. She insisted we need to replace "his certainty"—quantity, probability, and gravity—with "her possibility"; his "land" and "timber" with "this earth" and "the forest"; and his reason with her emotion. Nature has a value that cannot be reduced to its usefulness to culture, and woman has a value that cannot be reduced to her usefulness to man.

In some of her later work, Griffin revisited the nature-culture dichotomy, depicting pornography as culture's revenge against nature as well as men's revenge against women. "We will see," said Griffin, "that the bodies of women in pornography, mastered, bound, silenced, beaten, even murdered, are symbols for natural feeling and the powers of nature which the pornographic mind hates and fears."[40] Commenting on Griffin's analysis of the pornographic mind, David Macauley urged us to ask ourselves

whether there now exists . . . a kind of earth pornography, since the gendered planet, the "mother of life" or "our nurse" as Plato referred to it, is not only violated literally by strip mining, deforestation, and radioactive waste but subjected increasingly to the circulation of a voyeuristic media—as the image of a bounded, blue sphere is re-placed (away from natural context) on billboards or commercials in order to sell computers, hamburgers, or candidate's positions."[41]

Just as women's violated bodies are used to sell all sorts of commodities, such as cars, boats, and designer jeans, so, too, is nature's violated "body" used similarly. Women, implied Griffin, must refuse to let themselves and nature be exploited in such ways. Reform, indeed revolution, begins with saying no to what *is* and instead seeks what *might be.*

Spiritual Ecofeminism

Closely allied to radical-cultural ecofeminists are a variety of so-called spiritual ecofeminists.[42] Inspired by Mary Daly's *Gyn/Ecology* and Rosemary Radford Ruether's *New Woman, New Earth,* they insist that no matter which theology, religion, or spirituality women adopt, it must be an embodied rather than a disembodied way of relating to the ultimate source or deepest wellspring of meaning. Implicit in the thought of most spiritual ecofeminists is the view that unless patriarchal religions, such as Judaism and Christianity, can purge themselves of the idea of an omnipotent, disembodied male spirit, women should abandon the oppressive confines of their synagogues and churches and run to the open spaces of nature, where they can practice any one of several earth-based spiritualities.

Although spiritual ecofeminists draw strength from a variety of earth-based spiritualities, these thinkers tend to gravitate toward ancient goddess worship and nature-oriented Native American ritual. They believe cultures that view the female body as sacred also view nature as sacred, honoring its cycles and rhythms. Spiritual ecofeminists often draw an analogy between the role of women in biological production and the role of an archetypal "Earth Mother" or "birth-mother" (usually referred to as "Gaia") in giving life and creating all that exists.[43] Because women's role is analogous to Gaia's role, women's relationship to nature is privileged over men's relationship to nature, according to spiritual ecofeminists.

Starhawk

Among the best-known spiritual ecofeminists who stress the woman-nature link is Starhawk, a Wiccan priestess, social activist, and psychotherapist. In one of her poems, she wrote that nature's and women's work are one and the same:

Out of the bone, ash
Out of the ash, pain
Out of the pain, the swelling
Out of the swelling, the opening
Out of the opening, the labor
Out of the labor, the birth
Out of the birth, the turning
wheel the turning tide.[44]

Through their uniquely female bodily experiences—their monthly menses, the demanding symbiosis of pregnancy, the pain of childbirth, and the pleasure of breast-feeding their infants—women supposedly come to know, in a way men cannot, that human beings are one with nature.

Starhawk claimed that the kind of earth-based spirituality she practices as a witch—that is, a woman charged with the task and possessing the skill to "bend" and "reshape" Western culture—provides a good deal of the energy in the feminist movement.[45] In her estimation, earth-based spirituality has three core concepts. The first is *immanence.* The Goddess is *in* the living world, in the human, animal, plant, and mineral communities. Therefore, each being has value, and each conscious being also has power. Understood not as power over but as power from within, this power is "the inherent ability . . . to become what we are meant to be—as a seed has within it the inherent power to root, grow, flower, and fruit."[46] We grow in this kind of creative power, claimed Starhawk, when we take on responsibility for everyone and everything to which we are related and also when we strive to achieve personal integrity by prioritizing our needs and those of our entire relational network. Spirituality is not an "opiate"; it is an energizer and stimulus to action. She explained: "When what's going on is the poisoning and destruction of the earth, our own personal development requires that we grapple with that and do something to stop it, to turn the tide and heal the planet."[47]

The second feature of earth-based spirituality is *interconnection* and the expanded view of self it encourages. Not only are our bodies natural, but so, too, are our minds. Starhawk stressed: "Our human capacities of loyalty and love, rage and humor, lust, intuition, intellect, and compassion are as much a part of nature as the lizards and the redwood forests."[48] The more we understand that we are nature, she wrote, the more we will understand our oneness with all that exists: human beings, natural cycles and processes, animals, and plants. We will make the mistake neither of allying ourselves with human beings against nature nor of allying ourselves with nature against human beings, as some environmentalists do when they engage in extreme forms of so-called ecoterrorism. Killing animal-research scientists in the name of animal liberation is no better than killing animals to find cures for the diseases threatening human beings. There is, implied Starhawk, almost always a way to serve the interests of one and all. Our own interests "are linked to black people in South Africa as well as to forest-dwellers in the Amazon, and . . . their interests in turn are not separate from those of the eagle, the whale, and the grizzly bear."[49]

The third and probably most important feature of earth-based spirituality is the kind of *compassionate lifestyle* many women lead. Starhawk claimed that unless all people adopt this type of lifestyle, which requires them to care for one another, we can forget about "reweaving the world" or "healing the wounds." Thus, she faulted deep ecologist Daniel Conner for suggesting "the AIDS virus may be Gaia's tailor-made answer to human overpopulation," as well as deep ecologist Dave Foreman for opposing the provision of famine relief to starving African nations: "When environmentalists applaud the demise of Africans and homosexuals, they ally themselves with the same interests that are killing people of color, gay people, women, and other vulnerable groups. Those same interests are destroying the earth's ecosystems and raping the wilderness."[50] According to Starhawk, spiritual ecofeminists—especially those who regard themselves as witches—bring to the environmental movement a compassionate perspective that permits them "to identify powerlessness and the structures that perpetuate it as the root cause of famine, of overpopulation, of the callous destruction of the natural environment."[51]

The nature-culture dichotomy, indeed all dichotomies, must be dissolved so we can appreciate the "oneness" of reality. Starhawk implied, however, that it is not a matter of indifference how this oneness is achieved. Culture ought to be subsumed into nature rather than vice versa, for unless we all live more simply, masses of people will not be able to live at all. Like Rosemary Radford Ruether, Starhawk viewed the present distribution of the world's wealth among people as shockingly unjust.[52] She urged people committed to world justice and ecological sustainability to engage in direct action movements such as the massive anti–World Trade Organization protests that started in Seattle in November 1999 and have continued to this day. She also recommended that social justice activists use communications media, in particular the Internet and cell phones, to make visible and audible to people the sights and sounds of human poverty.

Starhawk had an ambitious program for achieving social justice. She insisted that, starting in their own local communities, activists must take the five following steps to achieve a sustainable economy: (1) They must shift away from oil and coal to renewable, clean forms of energy (solar and wind); (2) they must stop relying on machines to do their work for them and start relying on their own muscle power; (3) they must get serious about recycling the waste side of consumption and production; (4) they must resist the forces of "monoculture," instead affirming and strengthening different cultures; (5) and they must learn to do more with less resources.[53]

Starhawk admitted that, initially, it would be difficult for people to forsake the creative comforts and luxuries of today's high-end, unsustainable economies. Still, she believed that as people started to lead simpler lives, they would discover there is more to life than possessing things. Starhawk urged women to take the lead in the save-the-earth movement, bringing as many men into it as possible:

> *The labor is hard, the night is long*
> *We are midwives, and men who tend*
> *   the birth and bond with the child*
> *We are birthing, and being born*
> *We are trying to perform an act of*
> *   magic—*
> *To pull a living child out of a near-corpse of the mother we are*
> *   simultaneously poisoning, who is also ourselves.*[54]

With Mary Daly, Starhawk declared her absolute opposition to the forces of death (necrophilia) and her wholehearted affirmation of life.

Carol Christ

Like Starhawk, Carol Christ is a "pagan" spiritual ecofeminist. Christ consistently sought to replace the God of patriarchy (omniscient, omnipotent, and immutable) with a Goddess of humanity (learning, fallible, and constantly changing). She wanted people to practice Goddess religion, that is, the effort to imaginatively reconstruct the egalitarian harmony between humans and nature that existed in supposedly nonhierarchical, prepatriarchal times. For Christ, hierarchical thinking and its alienating dualisms have been our undoing. By tapping into the power of the Goddess in ourselves—a "Goddess" she defined as the lure to goodness—we can help one another overcome the alienated and hostile relations that characterize our power-hungry world.

Interestingly, Christ did not guarantee us success in our efforts to become more egalitarian and loving. She saw the web of good human relationships, including good human relationships with nature, as a fragile one in continual need of repair. But rather than despairing at the thought of people endlessly trying to fix faltering human relationships, Christ embraced this thought as providing us with our meaning and purpose. She suggested we rise each morning with the following greeting to the sun: "As this day dawns in beauty, we pledge ourselves to repair the web."[55]

Like spiritual ecofeminists in general, Christ believed that by connecting to nature—its beauty, mystery, complexity—we can be inspired to be better (i.e., more loving) people. We do not need an all-powerful rule giver, armed with laws and punishments for rule breakers, to force us to be good. On the contrary. We need only the Goddess—that is, the energy of human creativity and transformation within themselves—to want to be good.

Diann Neu

Although most spiritual ecofeminists are pagan, not all are. Diann Neu, co-founder of the Women's Alliance for Theology, Ethics and Ritual (WATER) claimed that even though kyriarchal liturgies (i.e., those that value the domination of some beings over others) are disconcerting to ecofeminists, ecofeminist liturgies are not. She said that "ecofeminist liturgies are designed to reconnect participants with nature, women, and the divine. They invite participants to feel the depth and sacredness of this relationship."[56] For example, the mandate in Ephesians that wives submit to their husbands undermines the purity of worship; whereas praise for the virtuous wife of Proverbs 31, which values and respects women's personal autonomy, conveys an ecofeminist message. Neu outlined seven ecofeminist liturgical principles intended to replace traditional patriarchal systems of worship that tend to subvert the roles of both women and nature:

1. Ecofeminist liturgies value women's bodies and nature as holy vehicles of Divine revelation, and honor women and nature in all their diversity as imagining the Divine and as enjoying Divine activity.
2. Ecofeminist liturgies use symbols and stories, images and words, gestures and dances, along with a variety of art forms that reflect the interconnectedness of creation.
3. Ecofeminist liturgies use language that reflects the inherent goodness of women and the Earth.
4. Ecofeminist liturgies use music that identifies with the Earth community.
5. Ecofeminist liturgies are celebrated in environments that reflect the sacredness of the Earth.
6. Ecofeminist liturgies image the Divine as the source of life that sustains all creation.
7. Ecofeminist liturgies motivate participants to sustain a balanced and diverse Earth community, to resist its oppressors, and to lament the violence and abuse that has been done to it.[57]

Transformative Ecofeminism

Unlike nature ecofeminists and spiritual ecofeminists, transformative or social-constructionist ecofeminists sought to transform the nature-woman connection. They claimed that women's connection to nature is socially constructed and ideologically reinforced. Because this is so, women can help transform the meaning of their connection to both nature and culture.

Dorothy Dinnerstein

Western dichotomous thought, said Dorothy Dinnerstein, must be exploded if there is to be an end to the oppression of everyone and everything currently devalued. This explosion must begin with the deconstruction of the male-female dichotomy, for it is the fundamental source of "the silent hatred of Mother Earth which breathes side by side with our love for her, and which, like the hate we feel for our human mothers, poisons our attachment to life."[58] Dinnerstein claimed that as a result of our nearly exclusively female practice of mothering, all infants (be they male or female) come to view women as responsible for both their most positive *and* their most negative feelings. At times, mothers meet their children's needs immediately and completely, totally satisfying and soothing their offspring. At other times, however, mothers fail to meet their children's needs, thereby discomforting, frustrating, or angering the children. As it is with mothers—that is, women—so it is with nature, the realm of reality with which women are identified. Mother Nature can bestow blessings on human beings, but she can also mete out harms and hardships to them: hurricanes, volcanoes, floods, fires, famines, disease, death. Thus, the only way for human beings—especially men, who do not bodily resemble the mother in the ways women do—to deal with "the mother" or "nature" is to seek to control her, to separate her from all that is male or identified as masculine, including culture.

Dinnerstein asserted, however, that the attempt to exclude women and nature from men and culture has caused us (she includes women as complicit in this psychopathological arrangement) not only to *maim and exploit women, and stunt and deform men*" but also to proceed "*toward the final matricide—the rageful, greedy murder of the planet that spawned us.*"[59] Borrowing an idea from Lewis Mumford, she observed that most of us are firm believers in the "megamachine" myth. This myth espouses the view that human beings can use their mind and tools not only to extend control over nature and everything identified with nature—woman, the body, life, death, and so on—but also to make huge monetary profits in doing so. According to Dinnerstein, this myth will continue to rule our thoughts and actions unless we end the present division of the world into male and female (culture and nature) and the assignments of women to nature (child-rearing as well as childbearing) and men to culture (world building). Women must bring nature into culture (by entering the public world), and men must bring culture into nature (by entering the private world). Then and only then will we see that men and women (culture and nature) are *one* and that it is counterproductive for half of reality to try to dominate the other half. A reality, divided and at war with itself, cannot and will not survive. Thus, Dinnerstein proclaimed, "The core meaning of feminism . . . lies, at this point, in its relations to earthly life's survival."[60] Unless men and women get their act together and start behaving like adults instead of infants, the human species can expect a rapid demise.

Karen J. Warren

Like Dinnerstein, Karen J. Warren emphasized that the dualisms threatening to destroy us are social constructions. In a capitalist, patriarchal society, women and nature, men and culture, have certain meanings, but these meanings are far from necessary. They would be very different in the kind of socialist, non-patriarchal society Marge Piercy posited in *Woman on the Edge of Time,* a work of fiction in which people rejected all dualisms, beginning with the male-female dichotomy (see Chapter 2). Persons are both masculine and feminine; society is both natural and cultural.[61]

Wanting very much to reconceptualize nature and culture as well as man and woman, Warren claimed feminists must be ecofeminists—without insisting, as Piercy did, that women must forsake their special role in biological reproduction.[62] Warren argued that, *logically,* feminism is just as much a movement to end naturism as it is a movement to end sexism:

(C1) Feminism is a movement to end sexism.
(C2) But sexism is conceptually linked with naturism (through an oppressive conceptual framework characterized by a logic of domination).
(C3) Thus, feminism is (also) a movement to end naturism.[63]

All forms of oppression are interlocked and intertwined. Oppression is a many-headed beast that will continue to exist and regenerate itself until human beings manage *completely* to behead it.

Focusing on the kind of ethics currently informing environmentalism, Warren noted there are within it many sexist elements, or male biases, that undermine its ability to "save the earth." Only an ecofeminist ethics—an ethics free of androcentric as well as anthropocentric distortions—can overcome naturism once and for all. Such an ethics, said Warren, must be a "care-sensitive ethics."[64]

In elaborating her preferred ecofeminist ethics, Warren claimed it had eight "necessary" or "boundary" conditions. First, an ecofeminist ethics is a theory-in-process that evolves together with people. Second, an ecofeminist ethics is entirely "opposed to any 'ism' that presupposes or advances a logic of domination."[65] No thread of sexism, racism, classism, naturism, or other ism may be woven into the ecofeminist quilt. Third, and very important, an ecofeminist ethics is a contextualist ethics that invites people to narrate their relationships: to specify *how* they relate to humans, nonhuman animals, and nature. Fourth, if it is anything, said Warren, an ecofeminist ethics is an inclusivist ethics that acknowledges, respects, and welcomes difference. Unlike an exclusivist ethics, an inclusivist ethics is empirically unbiased; that is, it passes the "R-4 test" for *good* generalizations about different sorts of human beings, nonhuman animals, and nature.[66] By making sure that its empirical claims are based on data that is (1) representative, (2) random, (3) the right size, and (4) replicable, continued Warren, an inclusivist ethics avoids the biases that characterize an exclusivist ethics. Fifth, an ecofeminist ethics does not aim to be "objective," even though, as we just noted, it does aim to be unbiased.[67] To be unbiased is not to be neutral. Rather, it is to be eager to incorporate all perspectives, particularly perspectives that might otherwise not get voiced, into its consciousness. Sixth, an ecofeminist ethics, according to Warren, views the values of care, love, friendship, and appropriate trust as the core values of all ethics. Seventh, an ecofeminist ethics aims to redefine both what it means to be a truly human person and what it means to make a decision ethically. Eighth, and most important, an ecofeminist ethics is not based on reason to the exclusion of emotion but on an *intelligence* that requires reason and emotion to work together and to be recognized as equally important in ethical decision making.[68]

By working within the framework of the kind of ethics just described, claimed Warren, ecofeminists can learn to relate to nonhumans in ways that overcome the nature-culture split. In one example, intended to illustrate this type of overcoming, Warren contrasted rock climbers who climb to conquer mountains and rock climbers who climb to know mountains (and therefore themselves) in new ways. When an ecofeminist climbs a mountain, said Warren, the climber assumes he or she has a genuine *relationship* to it. The person's concern is not in showing the mountain who is boss by conquering it but in becoming its friend, someone who cares about it. Thus, an ecofeminist does not look at the mountain with an "arrogant eye," viewing it as a hunk of inert matter trying to exhaust, and thereby get the best of, her or him. Rather, an ecofeminist sees it with a "loving eye," viewing it as a unique reality with much to tell the climber about his or her strengths and weaknesses.[69]

In another example, Warren told the story of a young Sioux boy sent by his father to learn "the old Indian ways" from his grandfather. Among other things, the boy's grandfather taught him how to hunt by instructing him

> to shoot your four-legged brother in his hind area, slowing it down but not killing it. Then, take the four-legged's head in your hands, and look into his eyes. The eyes are where all the suffering is. Look into your brother's eyes and feel his pain. Then, take your knife and cut the four-legged under his chin, here, on his neck, so that he dies quickly. And as you do, ask your brother, the four-legged, for forgiveness for what you do. Offer also a prayer of thanks to your four-legged kin for offering his body to you just now, when you need food to eat and clothing to wear. And promise the four-legged that you will put yourself back into the earth when you die, to become nourishment for the earth, and for the sister flowers, and for the brother deer. It is appropriate that you should offer this blessing for the four-legged and, in due time, reciprocate in turn with your body in this way, as the four-legged gives life to you for your survival.[70]

The lesson the Sioux grandfather taught his grandson about hunting is clearly far more ecofeminist (antinaturist and antisexist) than the lesson the typical "great white hunter" would teach his grandson about hunting for the fun or sport of it, for the pleasure of the kill. The Sioux hunting lesson is one that informs us how people whose conceptual schemes are not oppositional see themselves in *relationship* to nonhuman nature. Nevertheless, the Sioux hunting lesson is not fully ecofeminist, for it does not proceed from a gender analysis. Moreover, it arose in a culture that treats women as less than men's equals. This last observation suggests, contrary to what Warren asserts, that even in a culture where women are no more identified with nature than men are, sexism might still exist.

According to Warren, we need a feminism more comprehensive than all other forms of feminism taken together. We need, she said, an entirely transformative feminism, a feminism that has six features.[71] First, it recognizes and makes explicit the interconnections between all systems of oppression. Second, it stresses the diversity of women's experiences, forsaking the search for "woman" and her unitary experience. Third, it rejects the logic of domination. Fourth, it rethinks what it means to be a human being, courageously reconsidering whether humans should view consciousness (and rationality) as not only that which distinguishes them from nonhumans but which somehow makes them better than nonhumans. Fifth, it relies on an ethic that stresses those traditional feminine virtues that tend to weave, interconnect, and unite people. And sixth, it maintains that science and technology be used only to the extent they preserve the earth.[72]

Given Warren's analysis of transformative feminism, it would seem to constitute a "thinking space" where men and women from all over the world can gather together to mix and match multiple feminist insights.

Global Ecofeminism

Among the ecofeminists who have adopted a global perspective are Maria Mies, a sociologist known for her work on development economics, and Vandana Shiva, a physicist known for her interests in spirituality. Mies and Shiva stressed that because women, more than men, are engaged in the work of sustaining daily life, women, more than men, are concerned about the elements: air, water, earth, fire. To be able to bear and rear healthy children and to provide their families with nourishing food, adequate clothing, and sturdy housing, women need fertile soil, lush plant life, fresh water, and clean air. In addition, Mies and Shiva lamented Western culture's obsession with the idea of "sameness"—the universal "I," the overarching "one." Capitalism and patriarchy, they observed, are systems that stamp out difference, doggedly cloning themselves, their ideas, and their salable goods wherever they go. Finally, like many Marxist and socialist feminists, Mies and Shiva observed how people in capitalist patriarchies tend to be alienated from everything: the products of their labor, nature, each other, and even themselves. As a result, human beings in capitalist patriarchies often engage in some fairly bizarre behavior to reduce their alienation.

In an essay entitled "White Man's Dilemma: His Search for What He Has Destroyed," Mies described in detail some of the mind-boggling ways all people, but particularly white men in capitalist patriarchies, aim to connect with nature—the very nature that their lifestyle and patterns of consumption threaten to destroy.[73] First, she said, the white man attempts to run away from the confines of his urban office "into 'Nature,' the 'wilderness,' the 'underdeveloped' countries of the South, to areas where the white man has not yet 'penetrated.'" Tourist agents in the developed countries promote excursions into undeveloped nations with trip descriptions such as the following one: "European tourists can live in villages in close contact with the 'natives' in African-style huts with minimum comfort, African food, no running water and where European and African children play together. The 'real' Africa to be touched!" Second, continued Mies, rather than trying to unite with the "mundane" nature right in his backyard, the white man seeks to experience a more "exotic" type of nature: nature as "colony, backward, exotic, distant and dangerous, the nature of Asia, Africa, South America."

Those who yearn for this kind of nature do not desire to relate to it productively by working on it or tending to it; rather, by absorbing it or consuming it—by locking it in the chambers of their cameras or by marketing it to others as souvenirs. Third, she says, the white man longs for yet another kind of nature, the space known as a woman's body. It, too, is wild terrain, the "dark continent," so the white man relates to a woman's body as he relates to nature: as object of his gaze, as commodity, as a form of play to liberate him, if only for a moment, from his relentless workday:

> The growing sex-obsessing apparent in all industrial societies is . . . a direct consequence of alienation from nature, the absence of a sensual interacting with nature in people's work life. Sexuality is supposed to be the totally "other" from work: it should not interfere with work, but should be strictly separated from the work life. Sexuality is the "transcendence" of work, the "heaven" after the "valley of tears and sweat" of work, the real essence of leisure. . . . The tragedy is, however, that this "heaven" is also a commodity, to be bought like any other. And like the acquisition of other consumer goods, ultimately, it disappoints. . . . Therefore, the constantly disappointed striving to attain this "heaven" transforms need into an addiction.[74]

Reflecting on Mies's comments, we may find it easy to view Mies and her coauthor, Shiva, as socialist-*transformative* ecofeminists. Shiva, as well as Mies, believed there are enough similarities among women to motivate women to work together against capitalist patriarchy and the destructive isms it spawns. As evidence that all women share similar interests in preserving nature, Mies and Shiva provided numerous examples of Third World and First World women struggling against ecological destruction and deterioration. Women, they noted, have led the battle to preserve the bases of life wherever and whenever military and industrial interests have threatened them.

Among the case studies Shiva presented to demonstrate why, for example, water, is an ecofeminist issue and not simply an ecological issue, is the 2002–2004 women's movement against a Coca-Cola plant in the small village of Plachimada, located in the southern Indian state of Kerala. Commissioned in March 2000, the plant was to produce over 1.2 million bottles of Coca-Cola products daily. The local government issued Coca-Cola a conditional license to install a motorized water pump. However, according to residents, the plant began extracting 1.5 million liters of water daily, causing water levels—initially 150 feet below the ground—to drop to a staggering 500 feet below ground. According to tribals and farmers, the sharp decrease in water was due in part to Coca-Cola's installing haphazardly placed bore wells to tap ground water. The water shortage threatened crop cultivation, drinking water, and waterways. Additionally, what water Coca-Cola wasn't taking, it was polluting, dumping waste material outside the plant, which ran into wells, canals, and fields during the rainy season. Consequently, 260 publicly funded local wells became dry, and by 2003, Plachimada's district medical officer declared the local water unfit for drinking. Meanwhile, in April 2002, the women of Plachimada began a sit-in at the gates of the Coca-Cola plant, an act of nonviolent resistance that stretched into September 2003. In December 2003, the Kerala High Court supported the women's demands and ordered Coca-Cola to stop thieving the local water, stating: "The public trust doctrine primarily rests on the principle that certain resources like air, sea, waters, and the forests have such a great importance to the people as a whole that it would be wholly unjustified to make them a subject of private ownership. The said resources being a gift of nature, they should be made freely available to everyone, irrespective of their status in life."[75] By January 2004, the women of Plachimada had attracted the attention of global activists who arrived in solidarity with the World Water Conference. Ultimately, in February 2004, Kerala's chief minister ordered the closure of the Coca-Cola plant, due to pressure from the burgeoning antihydropiracy movement and the worsening drought crisis. The movement of women against the Coca-Cola plant's water theft and pollution was less about environmental aesthetics or corporate politics and much more about preserving the holistic health of the community by living simply, with respect for the earth, and faulting a business that was taking far more than its fair share of natural resources. The feminist ethics of care, interconnectedness, and sharing resources had prevailed for the citizens of Plachimada.[76]

If life is a theme for socialist-transformative ecofeminists, so, too, is freedom. The freedom to which Mies and Shiva referred is not the kind of Marxist freedom that requires man to master nature and therefore woman's body. Rather, it is the kind of freedom that asks all of us to recognize and accept our naturalness, our physicality and materiality, our carnality and mortality. Because nature is an exhaustible good, we must learn to conserve it by living as simply as possible and by consuming as little as possible. If we care about our descendants' lives, we must develop a so-called subsistence perspective.

It is not surprising that Mies and Shiva proposed a subsistence perspective as the key to dissolving all the practices and systems that threaten to destroy the earth. These women are, after all, *socialist*-transformative ecofeminists for whom transformation must be material as well as spiritual. Mies claimed people in capitalist patriarchies need to take ten steps if they are serious about developing a subsistence lifestyle:

1. People should produce only enough to satisfy fundamental human *needs*, resisting the urge to produce "an ever-growing mountain of commodities and money (wages or profit)" in a futile attempt to still people's endless and insatiable wants.

2. People should use only as much of nature as they need to, treating it as a reality with "her own subjectivity"; and people should use each other not to make money but to create communities capable of meeting people's fundamental needs, especially their need for intimacy.

3. People should replace representative democracy with participatory democracy so each man and woman has the opportunity to express his or her concerns to everyone else.

4. People should develop "multidimensional or synergic" problem-solving approaches, since the problems of contemporary society are interrelated.

5. People should combine contemporary science, technologies, and knowledge with ancient wisdom, traditions, and even magic.

6. People should break down the boundaries between work and play, the sciences and the arts, spirit and matter.

7. People should view water, air, earth, and all natural resources as community goods rather than as private possessions.

8. Men as well as women should adopt the socialist-transformative ecofeminist view, the subsistence perspective. Specifically, men must stop focusing on making as much money as possible and focus instead on making their families as loving as possible.

9. Men as well as women should cultivate traditional feminine virtues (caring, compassion, nurturance) and engage in subsistence production, for "only a society based on a subsistence perspective can afford to live in peace with nature, and uphold peace between nations, generations and men and women."

10. Most important, people should realize that in order for each person to have enough, no person can "have it all."[77]

Kamla Bhasin, an Indian feminist, captured the essences of the "sustainable development" model well:

The standard of living of the North's affluent societies cannot be generalized. This was already clear to Mahatma Gandhi 60 years ago, who, when asked by a British journalist whether he would like India to have the same standard of living as Britain, replied: "To have its standard of living a tiny country like Britain had to exploit half the globe. How many globes will India need to exploit to have the same standard of living?" From an ecological and feminist perspective, moreover, even if there were more globes to be exploited, it is not even desirable that this development paradigm and standard of living was generalized, because it has failed to fulfill its promises of happiness, freedom, dignity and peace, even for those who have profited from it.[78]

Vegetarian Ecofeminism

Although the relationship between vegetarianism and ecofeminism has been mentioned earlier, this relationship deserves more consideration not only because of the large role that animals play in nature, but also because of the amount of suffering and pain inflicted upon animals worldwide. According to Carol Adams, "From the leather in our shoes, the soap we use to cleanse our face, the down in the comforter, the meat we eat, and the dairy products we rely on, our world as we now know it is structures around a dependence on the death of the other animals."[79] Many ecofeminists are vegetarians or vegans. Vegetarians do not eat meat but use animal by-products. For vegans, the abstention from animal flesh is insufficient, because animals used for by-products are also reduced to their instrumental value and are subjects of extreme suffering within, for example, dairy farms, egg hatcheries, and experimentation laboratories. Vegetarian and vegan ecofeminists tend not to be absolutist in their moral stances; rather, they are often contextual moral vegetarians, as opposed to universal moral vegetarians.[80] In general, contextual moral vegetarians concede that there are societies in which using animal flesh or bodily products is necessary for human survival. One of these societies may be the Native American tribe Karen Warren described, which could not survive unless it hunted. Such societies are exceptional, however. According to many contextual vegetarian feminists, eating meat or even eggs or dairy products is not necessary for survival for most people living in developed societies. On the contrary, developed societies have readily available a surplus of economic protein and calcium options, such as beans, whole grains, nut milks, and soy-based cheese and meat alternatives, as well as a variety of synthetic materials for clothing and other commodity needs.

According to Grace Kao, there are three sorts of criteria that vegetarian ecofeminists use to make their case for contextual moral vegetarianism. The first is based on the "moral standing of animals"; the second, on an "ethics of care" toward animals; and the third, on "the larger sociopolitical context of contemporary meat production and consumption."[81]

Two philosophers who have taken the moral standing of animals seriously are Peter Singer (*Animal Liberation,* 1975)[82] and Tom Regan (*The Case for An-*

imal Rights, 1983).[83] According to Singer, utilitarianism demands that the interests of each sentient being (that is, any being able to feel pleasure and pain) must be taken into account in moral decision-making. Reasoning in a different way, Regan posits that the reason we must reject and certainly not kill a sentient being is that the being has the capacity and/or actuality of some form of thinking, calculating, reasoning, and consciousness. Because most non-human animals—especially large mammals, such as whales, dolphins, elephants, and great apes—seem self-aware and to have the ability to engage in some form of thinking and communication, human beings must not violate these animals' most basic rights by abusing or killing them. When critics protest that the interests of nonhuman animals are not as important as human beings' interests or that the kind of thinking nonhuman animals engage in is not as advanced as human thought, Singer and Regan proclaim these critics "speciests," unfairly biased toward members of their own species.

Vegetarian ecofeminists are not entirely happy with Singer's and Regan's arguments on behalf of animals' interests, owing to what they see as Singer's and Regan's "sole reliance on reason and their exclusion of emotion."[84] They stress the importance of sympathy for nonhuman animals, which are to be viewed as individuals with the capacity to feel. Although some feminists may be persuaded to become vegetarian ecofeminists through rationalization alone, many come to vegetarian ecofeminism because they have an intolerance for animal suffering.[85]

An "ethics of care" toward animals is an extension of the sympathy argument in favor of vegetarian ecofeminism, according to Kao.[86] A good way to understand Kao's point here is to reflect on how much some people care about their pet dogs and cats. Many people view their pets as members of the family: They feed them, enjoy recreation with them, tend to their health-care needs, and suffer immense distress upon the death of an animal companion. Moreover, most people cringe at animal cruelty if it involves dogs, cats, horses, great apes, dolphins, or other large, culturally familiar animals. So, the argument goes, if we can and should sympathize with a beaten and starved dog, then why can't we or shouldn't we sympathize with a hen stuffed into a battery cage (unable to spread her wings or enjoy the sunlight), or a beaten and sickly piglet lying forgotten on the concrete floor of a factory farm? It is worth considering that something like Carol Adam's "absent referent" must be at work.[87] Adams explained,

> We live in a culture that has institutionalized the oppression of animals on at least two levels: in formal structures such as slaughterhouses, meat markets, zoos, laboratories, and circuses, and through our language. That

we refer to meat eating rather than to corpse eating is a central example of how our language transmits the dominant culture's approval of this activity.[88]

When we are singing "Old MacDonald Had a Farm" or reading *Charlotte's Web,* we block from our consciousness the individual pigs, cows, chickens, lambs, and so forth, that wind up as so-called meat on our platters. These animals are "absent referents." On this view, the term *meat* hides from us the fact that we are eating a cow or pig we saw last week in a feed lot. If we focus on the individual animal, we become conscious that we are eating a sentient being and not an object. Within the larger sociopolitical context of using animals for food are found two primary concerns: environmental denigration and the impact on human health. Vegetarian ecofeminists find allies in environmentalists because breeding, raising, and slaughtering herds of animals contributes to extreme natural resource depletion. Marti Kheel, author of *Nature Ethics: An Ecofeminist Perspective,* elaborated:

> The livestock industry is "one of the top two or three most significant contributors to the most serious environmental problems, at every scale from local to global. . . . The impact is so significant that it needs to be addressed with urgency."[89]

In other words, for Kheel, the environmental cost of producing and consuming animal products is threatening to the entire natural world that perpetuates a culture of oppression that devalues all life. Vegetarian ecofeminists also find allies in holistic health advocates, believing that meat- and dairy-based products contribute to a variety of ailments, including heart disease, obesity, diabetes, and cancer. According to T. Colin Campbell, author of *The China Study,* for example, "the more animal protein you eat, the more heart disease you have," and likewise, the higher your cholesterol levels.[90] Campbell also points out that vegetarians and vegans are generally "five to thirty pounds slimmer than their fellow citizens," suggesting that a plant-based whole foods diet helps combat obesity.[91] Similarly, both type 1 and type 2 diabetics have shown dramatic improvements in managing and/or reversing their disease when placed on a plant-based diet.[92] Concerning cancer, according to a 2001 Harvard report on prostate cancer research, dairy intake is "one of the most consistent predictors for prostate cancer in the published literature";[93] and increased consumption of animal protein is linked to both breast cancer[94] and colon cancer.[95] These facts suggest to vegetarian ecofeminists that a society in which eating animal products is taken for granted is a society in which our bodies are suffering. Martha Nussbaum has developed perhaps one of the most compelling and robust theoretical strategies in support of vegetarian ecofeminism. Calling animals "beings entitled to a dignified existence," Nussbaum writes:

> Dignified existence would seem at least to include the following: adequate opportunities for nutrition and physical activity; freedom from pain, squalor, and cruelty; freedom to act in ways that are characteristic of the species (rather than to be confined); freedom from fear and opportunities for rewarding interactions with other creatures of the same species and of different species; a chance to enjoy the light and air in tranquility.[96]

Nussbaum suggests the "capabilities approach" she developed in the 1980s with economist Amartya Sen—though initially established for human application—is better suited to address the question of the ethical treatment of animals than is either utilitarianism (e.g., the interests-based approach taken by Singer) or contractarianism (e.g., the rights-based approach taken by Regan). For many vegetarian ecofeminists, Nussbaum's capabilities approach has the added feature of avoiding the anthropocentric tone of most approaches to establishing the moral considerability of animals. For Nussbaum, each animal entity is worthy of moral consideration in itself, and as such, its similarity to the human species is irrelevant. Moreover, for vegetarian and vegan ecofeminists, a political focus on animal capabilities and resulting human responsibilities for care could be the nudge needed to eventually liberate animals from human oppression. Because vegetarian ecofeminists believe all forms of oppression are linked, for these feminists, movement away from an anthropocentric society that subjugates nonhuman species is also a move away from a society that subjugates all.

Critiques of Ecofeminism

Critiques of Nature Ecofeminism

The critiques raised against nature ecofeminism are similar to those raised against radical-cultural feminism. In the estimation of Janet Biehl, nature ecofeminists err when they "biologize women as presumably uniquely ecological beings" who are able to relate to and understand nature in ways men simply cannot, and who are caring and nurturing in ways men, try as they might, can never be.[97] There is, says Biehl, too much willingness among nature ecofeminists either to reduce women into mere bodies or to limit women's potentialities and abilities to those associated with their supposedly "caring nature." As Biehl sees it, nature ecofeminism is reactionary rather than revolutionary. Quoting Simone de Beauvoir, from whom many nature ecofeminists borrow their basic concept of women's and nature's otherness, Biehl stresses that women celebrate the nature-woman connection at their own peril, for "that's the formula used to try and keep women quiet."[98] Biehl insists that nature ecofeminists, such as Mary Daly, misled women by suggesting women can by fiat "reclaim" the meaning of the nature-woman connection as an entirely positive one. In reality, Biehl points out, the nature-woman connection has been "enormously debasing to women," and centuries of negative cultural baggage cannot be cast off by passionate "reclaiming" alone.[99]

Critiques of Spiritual Ecofeminism

Critics fault spiritual ecofeminists for substituting religion for politics and for spending too much time dancing in the moonlight, casting "magic" spells, chanting mantras, doing yoga, "mindfully" meditating, and giving one another massages. Defenders of spiritual ecofeminism concede that some spiritual ecofeminists might have mistaken New Age or "spa" spirituality for genuine ecofeminist spirituality, but they insist such mistakes are the exception, not the rule. Goddess worship is not, according to Mies and Shiva, "luxury spirituality," "the idealist icing on top of the material cake of the West's standard of living."[100] It is not about turning the East's spiritual and cultural treasures into commodities for sale as exotica to privileged and pampered Western people who lack "meaning." Rather, Goddess worship is an attempt to break the culturally constructed dichotomy between spirituality and materiality and to recognize everything and everyone as worthy and deserving of respect. Spiritual ecofeminists, observes Ynestra King, are not otherworldly dreamers; they are this-worldly activists. Spiritual ecofeminists use such "community-building techniques" as performance art, kinesthetic observations (dancing and chanting), and ritual to enable people "to establish and maintain community with one another in contentious and difficult situations of political engagement in the public world."[101] Some spiritual ecofeminists may indeed choose to restrict their political activities to their local communities, insisting "theirs is the politics of everyday life, the transformation of fundamental relationships, even if that takes place only in small communities."[102] They claim so-called everyday politics is "much more effective than countering the power games of men with similar games."[103] But just because some spiritual ecofeminists refuse to play power games with men does not mean these feminists should be dismissed as crystal gazers. Not everyone who cares about the earth and works to safeguard it needs to move to the Women's Peace

Camp at Greenham Commons in England; there is work to be done in one's own backyard as well as in faraway places.

Critiques of Transformative Ecofeminism

Social-constructionist ecofeminists deny that women are naturally caring and nurturing. Instead they claim that women's feminine characteristics are the products of enculturation or socialization. For example, Carolyn Merchant repeatedly emphasizes that "any analysis that times women's supposed special qualities to a biological destiny thwarts the possibility of liberation. A politics grounded in women's culture, experience, and values can be seen as reactionary."[104] Women are no more "natural" than they are "cultural." But critics of social-constructionist ecofeminism point out that it may be a mistake to delink women and nature.

Deemphasizing the connections between women's and nature's life-giving capacities may, these critics say, "somewhat diminish the original ecofeminist passion to reclaim 'nature' in an organic sense—certainly when it comes to women's biology."[105] They further claim that an ecofeminism grounded in women's traditional feminine virtues, maternal roles, and special relationship to nature need not be "reactionary." Such an ecofeminism can be "revolutionary"; it can motivate women to get engaged in political action. For example, Ynestra King, a critic of cultural (nature) ecofeminism, notes that throughout her entire pregnancy, she kept thinking that in the time it took her to gestate one precious human being, eight thousand children in the Persian Gulf had starved to death or died of causes directly attributable to the weapons used by US forces during the Gulf War of 1990–1991. Overwhelmed by this thought, she realized that "thinking like an ecofeminist" requires one to make "abstract connections concrete."[106]

Although they find the perspective of all transformative ecofeminists compelling, critics suspect its demands are too challenging for relatively affluent people to accept. In particular, the critics think the degree of activism and lifestyle change that transformative-socialist ecofeminism requires are commitments that comfortable and complacent citizens are unlikely to embrace. Most people, including most feminists, do not want to radically change the way they live. For example, they do not want to become "card-carrying" vegetarians or pacifists.

In response to this objection, some socialist and transformative ecofeminists simply comment that people's reluctance to make lifestyle changes is not a moral justification for their not doing so. Altruism requires a certain measure of self-sacrifice. Other socialist and transformative ecofeminists soften this response by conceding that moral progress is often incremental. Even if a person is not willing to forsake eating meat altogether, for example, he or she can at least refuse to eat animals that have been factory-farmed or grown under extremely cruel conditions.

Likewise, even if a person is not willing to devote the bulk of his or her time working for environmental causes or feels overwhelmed by them, there is *always* some positive difference, however small, he or she can make. According to Judith Auerbach, Doretta Zemp, creator of the satirical comic strip *Roseanna of the Planet,* commented:

> Too often the environmental issues are bigger than we are, and we feel helpless in the face of their enormity, such as the greenhouse effect, the rape of the rain forests, and the Bhopal pesticide leak, which killed 2,500 people and permanently injured 17,000 more. What can we do about that? But Roseanna, my character, is down to our size. She and her best friend, stuffy old Egmont, wax in passion over concerns that are on our scale: chemicals in the home, neighborhood pollution, and the malathion spraying against our will. They disagree on everything except where to go for solutions. He uses ivory tower rhetoric and blind faith. I see Roseanna as every woman, and I see Egmont as exemplifying conventional wisdom, government, and big business.[107]

While Egmont stands idly by, trusting that Big Brother will save everyone from environmental doom, Roseanna is busy throwing out the ozone-damaging deodorants in her bathroom, the poisonous bug sprays under her kitchen sink, and the herbicide-laden cosmetics on her bureau. Seemingly, there is always something one can do.

Finally, even if a person is not a pacifist, he or she can be antimilitary. To be opposed to the waging of wars—the intention of which is domination by means of destruction of life—is not the same as being opposed to participating in any act of violence whatsoever. Self-defense and wars waged for the purpose of liberating oneself and one's people from the forces of death are not incompatible with socialist and transformative ecofeminist ideals. To be sure, socialist and transformative ecofeminists will try to resolve conflicts creatively (e.g., nonviolently) and peacefully (e.g., through rational destruction). But when they realize their voices will not be heard and the destruction of everything and everyone (especially their children) precious to them will continue, even the most peaceful ecofeminists will fight for *life*.

Critiques of Global Ecofeminism

Critics of global ecofeminism, such as Janet Biehl, find the counterposition of women and nature (on the one hand) against Western culture at large (on the other hand) regressive for the interests of women. Of particular concern for these critics are: (1) the association of the feminine with the irrational; (2) the location of Western women outside of the purview of Western culture; (3) the implied assertion that women have a dominant role in developing a sensibility of "caring" and "nurturing"; and that (4) women are unique in their ability to appreciate humanity's "interconnectedness" with the natural world.[108] Also of concern for these critics is what they see as the lack of consistency in global ecofeminist theorizing:

> Some assert that "All is One," while others argue for particularism and multiciplicity. Some are influenced by social ecology, while others have ties with deep ecology. Some regard ecofeminism as a liberatory concept of nearly unprecedented proportions, while others . . . reject the name "ecofeminism" altogether as insulting to feminist activists.[109]

Even more disturbing for these critics is the way, as they see it, global ecofeminism tends to "celebrate the identification of women with nature as an ontological reality."[110]

> [Global ecofeminists] thereby speciously biologize the personality traits that patricentric society assigns to women. The implication of this position is to confine women to the same regressive social definitions from which feminists have fought long and hard to emancipate women."[111]

Most "embarrassing" about global ecofeminism, say these critics, is that

> [its] sweeping but highly confused cosmology introduces magic, goddesses, witchcraft, privileged quasi-biological traits, irrationalities, Neolithic atavisms, and mysticism into a movement that once tried to gain the best benefits of the Enlightenment and the most valuable features of [Western] civilization for women.[112]

Critiques of Vegetarian Ecofeminism

Most vegetarian ecofeminists are contextual moral vegetarians, as opposed to universal moral vegetarians. Contextual moral vegetarians concede there may be some exceptions to the rule of not using or killing animals for various products, while universal moral vegetarians believe animals should never be utilized as a mere means to an end. According to Karen Warren, however, animal welfarists are at fault for exalting animals "to the status of full-fledged members of the moral club to which humans belong," challenging the traditionally accepted ethical hierarchy.[113] Some feminists may also find that comparing the plight of animals to that of women serves to both degrade and distract from women's interests. For these critics, women's rights should not be linked to the rights of nonhuman species, because so doing suggests a demeaning commonality with so-called lower species. Additionally, animal welfarists elevate sentient individuals (humans and animals) "over and against the rest of nature," while the "ecological 'wholes' (e.g., populations, communities, species, and ecosystems) are inappropriately omitted from moral consideration."[114] In other words, Warren says animals and humans are viewed without any "historical, social, and material contexts and independent of any relationships to other moral subjects."[115] Likewise, Warren says that universal moral vegetarianism is problematic because it rests upon a "male physiological norm" that presupposes everyone can easily and safely abstain from animal products, when in fact some populations would find the lifestyle quite challenging (e.g., "some infants, children, adolescents, gestating and lactating women, Inuit, [and] primal peoples").[116] While some universal moral vegetarians may bring examples to refute Warren's claims that vegetarianism isn't possible for everybody, this particular criticism sheds light on why many vegetarian ecofeminists are not absolutist. Feminist ethicists of care advise empathy with those in all walks of life. Ultimately, Warren suggests that universal moral vegetarianism is guilty of perpetuating "moral arrogance," which ultimately raises the philosophical distinction between "a value judgment" and "being judgmental" of nonsimilarly situated persons.[117]

Marti Kheel says there are three common theoretical challenges to absolutist vegetarian ecofeminism: "(1) cultural practices, (2) predation within ecology, and (3) concern for the suffering of plants."[118] Concerning culture (and related to Warren's comments on judgmentalism), Kheel explains that dietary choices are intensely personal, and meat-eating is often accepted "when it is embedded in cultural traditions and conducted with 'respect,'" suggesting that to condemn meat-eating could be "disrespectful of other cultures and may even smack of racism."[119] Yet Kheel notes that just because an act is "tradition" does not mean that the act is above moral judgment.[120]

Other critics of absolutist vegetarian ecofeminism contend that "meat eating is a *natural* [emphasis hers] predatory activity that is fully consistent with ecology."[121] In other words, they believe humans are simply part of a natural food chain and need animal protein to sustain themselves (similar again to Warren's comments that some people are physically unable to exist without animal protein). Absolutist vegetarian ecofeminists respond that the "need" for animal products has been addressed by the availability of inexpensive protein alternatives. Critics reply, however, that this need has only been addressed in Western nations, leaving the rest of the world without the protein that meat provides and that is required for a healthy diet.

The final theoretical challenge to absolutist vegetarian ecofeminism, according to Kheel, is the potential suffering of plants when used for food or other products. Kheel responds that it is the language of "rights."

> Although it is also tempting to invoke the language of "rights" or concepts such as "inherent value" or "inherent worth" to defend other-than-human animals, these constructs bring one group of beings into the orbit of moral concern by excluding the rest of nature. Animal advocates, for example, routinely invoke the "rights" of "sentient" or "self-conscious" animals, but few argue for the rights of rivers, mountains, and streams. The notion of rights, thus, places a conceptual wedge between the concerns of animal rights proponents and environmentalists.[122]

According to Kheel, such theories as Nussbaum's capability approach may help solve this problem, in that they recognize that different parts of nature have different "needs," which means humans should strive to respect the needs we empathetically are best able to determine as relevant.[123] In being citizens on a planet with finite resources, we will inevitably effectuate some sort of harm to enable us to survive, by utilizing limited supplies of water, soil, clean air, and calories for survival. But according to Kheel, vegans can "find comfort in knowing that [their] diet helps to reduce suffering, since far fewer plants are required to feed a person on a vegan diet than one who eats animal-based foods."[124]

Conclusion

No matter the differences that exist between social-constructionist and nature ecofeminists or between socialist and spiritual ecofeminists, all ecofeminists believe human beings are connected to the nonhuman world: animal, plant, and inert. Unfortunately, we do not always acknowledge our relationship to the nonhuman world. As a result, we do violence to one another and to nature, congratulating ourselves on protecting our self-interests. In reality, each day, we kill ourselves by laying waste to the earth from which we originate and to which we will return.

Given the state of human affairs just described, ecofeminists wonder what it will take for the majority of human beings to realize how irrational as well as unfeeling human systems of oppression and domination are. These systems bring in their wake hate, anger, destruction, and death, yet we cling to our social constructs. Is the solution to this pathological state of affairs to create a culture in which we honor women and nature as some sort of saviors? Or is it instead to follow Dinnerstein's instructions and insist that men and women alike assume equal responsibility for both child-rearing and world building? What will it take for us to stop thinking dichotomously and to realize we are our own worst enemies? Are we wasting time waiting for the saving grace of some Godot when we should instead be using our own heads and hearts to stop destroying what we in fact are: an interdependent whole, a unity that exists in and through, and not despite, its diversity? Ecofeminists, especially transformative-socialist ecofeminists, and vegetarian/vegan ecofeminists, have already made their decision. They stopped waiting for the revolution, the transformation, the miracle to happen a long time ago. They are busy at work (and play), doing what they can to eliminate the blights that brown the earth and kill the human spirit.[125] The question remains, however, whether the rest of us are set to join them. Hopefully, this new millennium will bring the right answer.

Questions for Discussion

1. How has religion contributed to an oppressive culture for both women and nature? Is it correct to posit that oppression is not necessarily embedded within religion, but the result of a selfish misinterpretation of religious texts? Provide examples in which both women and nature are devalued, and consider under what religious reasoning such devaluation occurred.

2. Do you believe women can be liberated without simultaneously liberating nature? Or do you believe there is a larger culture of oppression that must be toppled so as to emancipate all within the grip of injustice?

3. Reflect on connections among the commodification of women, the "sexual politics of meat," and "earth pornography." Consider examples from advertising, entertainment, and recreation. How does the "pornographic mind" convey that women, animals, and nature are only useful in so far as they are useful to man, and to culture writ large?

4. In what ways does Warren's suggestion to erase the nature-culture dichotomy work to liberate both women and men, as well as animals and nature? How does inclusivist ethics provide a voice to the historically voiceless among us (both sentient and nonsentient)?

5. Compare and contrast subsistence cultures with capitalist patriarchies. What steps could Western society begin taking to move toward the subsistence perspective?

6. Are ecofeminists (and feminists, for that matter) morally obligated to adopt some form of vegetarian lifestyle? Why or why not?

Conclusion

The primary purpose of this book has remained constant throughout its four editions: to highlight some of the main approaches to feminist thought, without insisting that feminists must necessarily accept every aspect of an approach to feminist thought to recognize its contribution to feminist thought in general. For example, I am attracted to those feminist modes of thought that stress difference and/or that are most inclusive of those who have suffered from any of our world's many violences: heterosexism, racism, classism, colonialism, ableism, speciesism, and so forth. I am equally attracted to those feminist modes of thought that translate into action, a concretization of one's commitment to fight for those who are oppressed.

There was a time when I thought that Marxist/socialist feminism was the most inclusive form of feminism, because it showed how the forces of sexism and classism interlock in a capitalist patriarchy and how "woman's estate" is determined by both her reproductive and productive role. What I did not really fully notice back then was the extent to which Marxist/socialist feminists glossed over issues related to heterosexism, racism, ableism, and speciesism in particular. For this reason, I now regard ecofeminism, particularly vegetarian ecofeminism, as the most inclusive form of feminism, embracing all of nature, including nonhuman beings in its arms. Will I always maintain this view? Given my track record, my guess is probably not. As society changes in terms of the demographics of women (including the fact that many theorists believe that soon people of color will cease to be the minority and become the majority of people in the United States), what are understood to be legitimate or serious, mainstream feminist concerns will likely also change. Significantly, US society is already increasingly comfortable with people who are mixed race and multiethnic—who have transcended the boundaries of any one race or one ethnicity. Similarly, parents of children whose race or ethnicity is blended are starting to report that their children find white/nonwhite oppositions of little meaning or concern to them. In a *New York Times* article, one mother of three mixed race and diversely ethnic sons commented, "Race takes a backseat to what they listen to . . . , what movies they see. . . . One is into Japanese anime. Another is immersed in rap."[1] The same mother noted that one of her sons has a "hip-hop persona" and has friends whose skin color ranges from very white to very black.

Clearly, being a feminist in a society where a growing number of young people purportedly "choose" their sexual, racial, or ethnic identity is different from being a feminist in my heyday, specifically back when personal identity was largely understood as fixed and worked against anyone who crossed gender lines or was a person of color.

Similarly, the global context in which feminist theorizing currently takes place also seems to require acknowledgment that most women living in developing nations are disadvantaged, as are women in so-called settler societies, such as indigenous women in the United States.[2] Also disadvantaged are migrant and immigrant women who have left their native lands—for example, African women in the United Kingdom.[3] It may be that feminist theorizing in a global context requires the realization of the difficulties of recognizing, acknowledging, respecting, and honoring—let alone meeting—diverse women's needs.

The women of color feminisms described in this book bear out this observation. Each of the various women of color feminisms treated has its own unique set of problems and its own distinctive vantage point that warrants respect and incorporation into the overall understanding of feminist thinking. Additionally, the unique needs of women of color are not just external to feminism itself, but internal to it as well. Yes, African American/Black feminists, Mixed Race feminists, Latina/Latin American feminists, Asian American feminists, Indigenous feminists, and women of color worldwide all have their own unique problems, and it is important to recognize the uniqueness of each of these sets of problems; but even within feminism itself, women of color face the challenge of wishing to have their agency respected; that is, of wanting and needing to be the ones to identify their own problems for themselves rather than having mainstream (white) feminists identify their problems for them.

Self-described "third-wave" feminists understand themselves as responding to the wants and needs of women of color in this regard. Specifically, they understand themselves as striving to be inclusive of the plurality of feminist vantage points available on the world stage and are desirous of shaping a new kind of feminism that is not so much interested in getting women to want what they *should* want, as it is desirous of responding to what women of all colors and ethnicities *say* they *do* want. This desire to be inclusive and responsive on the part of "third-wave" feminists manifests itself, in part, as an intent to be careful to not second-guess or judge whether the wants and desires expressed by women of diverse backgrounds are authentic or not. These feminists describe the context in which they practice feminism as one of "lived messiness."[4] Rebecca Walker speculates, for example, that third-wave feminists are not as judgmental as their second-wave feminist mothers were. Walker stresses that because "the lines between Us and Them are often blurred," third-wave feminists seek to create identities that "accommodate ambiguity" and "multiple positionalities."[5]

So, on the surface it would seem that young ("third-wave") feminists are better equipped than older feminists to deal with women's differences. But, on a deeper level, I am not so sure this is the case. From where I sit, the home of many younger feminists seems so "messy" that not enough pots and pans can be found within it to cook a decent feminist meal. Sometimes these feminists seem to me to be a collection of strongly individual women, expressing one another's different feelings to one another and leaving it at that. As Allison Howry and Julia Wood put it, "Many young women today wear their 'feminism lightly.'"[6]

As I see it, younger feminists need some sort of unitary goal—an agenda that rallies women to go beyond just being oneself, doing what one wants to do, or being a person whose identity is almost overwhelmingly hyphenated. Whereas the challenge for second-wave feminism was to learn to recognize and use women's differences productively so as to overcome the idea that all women are necessarily oppressed in the same sort of way, it also seems to me that the challenge for today's feminists is to recognize that to address the problems that women across the globe still face *as women*, it is necessary to understand women as constitutive of some sort of cohesive social group with something on the order of common goals and interests. It seems to me that today's (mainstream/"third-wave"/younger) feminists need to understand that just because some women are empowered does not mean *all* women are.[7]

Women of color feminisms can help out in this regard. If nothing else, women of color feminisms ask mainstream feminists, third wave or otherwise, to acknowledge that the experience of oppression of women of color is different from the experience of oppression faced by mainstream (white) women. The vast majority of so-called third-wave feminists are white, and while many of these feminists might feel completely emancipated, many women of color feminists do not.

I am particularly concerned by the tendency of some third-wave feminists to describe second-wave feminism as "victim feminism" and third-wave feminism as "power feminism." In the writings of such third-wave feminists as Heywood, Drake, and Walker, power feminism seems fairly benign, but in the hands of other thinkers, best labeled *postfeminists,* "power feminism" can get very mean-spirited. Writers such as Katie Roiphe, Camille Paglia, and Rene Denfeld insist that nowadays women are free to be whoever they want to be and to do whatever they want to do.[8] The implication of these postfeminists is that women's only enemy today is themselves.

But the facts do not support these assertions. *White* women in the United States and many other developed nations may be more equal and free than they were fifty or even twenty-five years ago, but the data available indicate they still earn about seventy-nine cents for every dollar men earn; they still do a disproportionate amount of the housework, childcare, and eldercare; and they still face the glass ceiling. Moreover, violence against women is still a worldwide problem that transcends race, class, and socioeconomic status, as evidenced by the fact that domestic violence is now recognized as the leading cause of injury to women.[9] In addition, women of color in the United States continue to suffer the consequences of institutionalized and intersectional oppression and marginalization; and women worldwide—particularly women of color in developing nations—live in conditions more oppressive than even those conditions that challenged first-wave US feminists at the turn of the nineteenth century.

So, in my estimation, feminist Christine Di Stefano, who has done much to mediate between second-wave and third-wave feminists, is on to something when she points out that to solve these problems feminists must hold on to the belief that, for women,

> Gender is basic in ways that we have to fully understand, . . . it functions as "a difference that makes a difference," even as it can no longer claim the legitimating mantle of the difference. The figure of the shrinking woman may perhaps be best appreciated and utilized as an aporia within contemporary theory: as a recurring paradox, question, dead end, or blind spot to which we must repeatedly return, because to ignore her altogether is to risk forgetting and thereby losing what is left of her.[10]

From my point of view, women exist as *women.* At least I know I exist as a woman (and Tina knows she exists as a woman). And it is this knowledge that requires (Tina and) me to ask contemporary mainstream feminists to see in women's differences—especially their differences in privilege—a call to judgment and for judgment. It "just ain't fair" (and violates the basic feminist call for equality) that some women are so powerful while others remain so powerless. Understood from this perspective, so-called third-wave feminism (particularly the postfeminist form) looks a lot more like simple selfishness and self-absorption and a lot less like feminism to (Tina and) me.

This is not yet the time for postfeminism, for there are far too many vulnerable women (and men, and children, and other sentient beings) who continue to live under conditions of patriarchy, sexism, racism, homophobia, ableism, ageism, speciesism and other forms of oppression. As my generation of feminists slips into the realm of history, it is time to look to this generation's feminists. Perhaps one of them may be the feminist who points to yet another way to think about women, for as far as I can tell, rethinking what has already been thought about women and/or conceiving distinctively new thoughts about women is the hallmark of feminist thought, and the hope of fulfilling its promise of equality for all.

Notes

Introduction: The Diversity of Feminist Thinking

1. Mary Wollstonecraft, *A Vindication of the Rights of Woman,* ed. Carol H. Poston (New York: W. W. Norton, 1975).

2. John Stuart Mill, "The Subjection of Women," in John Stuart Mill and Harriet Taylor Mill, *Essays on Sex Equality,* ed. Alice S. Rossi (Chicago: University of Chicago Press, 1970), 184–185.

3. Catharine A. MacKinnon elaborated upon the sex/gender system in "Feminism, Marxism, Method, and the State: An Agenda for Theory," *Signs: Journal of Women in Culture and Society* 7, no. 3 (Spring 1982): 515–516.

4. Linda Alcoff, "Cultural Feminism Versus Poststructuralism: The Identity Crisis in Feminist Theory," *Signs: Journal of Women in Culture and Society* 13, no. 31 (1988): 408; Ann Ferguson, "The Sex Debate in the Women's Movement: A Socialist-Feminist View," *Against the Current* (September/October 1983): 10–16; Alice Echols, "The New Feminism of Yin and Yang," in *Powers of Desire: The Politics of Sexuality,* ed. Ann Snitow, Christine Stansell, and Sharon Thompson (New York: Monthly Review Press, 1983), 445.

5. See Mary Vetterling-Braggin, ed., *"Femininity," "Masculinity," and "Androgyny"* (Totowa, NJ: Rowman & Littlefield, 1982), 6.

6. Carol S. Vance, ed., *Pleasure and Danger: Exploring Female Sexuality* (Boston: Routledge & Kegan Paul, 1984).

7. Rosemarie Tong, *Women, Sex and the Law* (Totowa, NJ: Rowman & Littlefield, 1984).

8. Mary Daly, *Gyn/Ecology: The Metaethics of Radical Feminism* (Boston: Beacon Press, 1978).

9. Charlotte Bunch, "Lesbians in Revolt," in *Women and Values,* ed. Marilyn Pearsall (Belmont, CA: Wadsworth, 1986), 128–132.

10. Shulamith Firestone, *The Dialectic of Sex* (New York: Bantam Books, 1970).

11. Adrienne Rich, *Of Woman Born* (New York: W. W. Norton, 1976); Sara Ruddick, "Maternal Thinking," in *Mothering: Essays in Feminist Theory,* ed. Joyce Trebilcot (Totowa, NJ: Rowman & Allanheld, 1984).

12. See, for example, Gena Corea, *The Mother Machine: Reproductive Technologies from Artificial Insemination to Artificial Wombs* (New York: Harper & Row, 1985).

13. Friedrich Engels, *The Origin of the Family, Private Property, and the State* (New York: International Publishers, 1972), 103.

14. Juliet Mitchell, *Woman's Estate* (New York: Pantheon Books, 1971).

15. Alison M. Jaggar, *Feminist Politics and Human Nature* (Totowa, NJ: Rowman & Allanheld, 1983), 316–317.

16. Dorothy Dinnerstein, *The Mermaid and the Minotaur: Sexual Arrangements and Human Malaise* (New York: Harper Colophon Books, 1977), 161.

17. Sherry B. Ortner, "Oedipal Father, Mother's Brother, and the Penis: A Review of Juliet Mitchell's *Psychoanalysis and Feminism,*" *Feminist Studies* 2, nos. 2–3 (1975): 179.

18. Nancy Chodorow, *The Reproduction of Mothering* (Berkeley: University of California Press, 1978).

19. Simone de Beauvoir, *The Second Sex,* trans. and ed. H. M. Parshley (New York: Vintage Books, 1974).

20. Ynestra King, "Healing the Wounds: Feminism, Ecology, and Nature/Culture Dualism," in *Feminism and Philosophy,* ed. Nancy Tuana and Rosemarie Tong (Boulder, CO: Westview Press, 1995).

Chapter 1: Liberal Feminism

1. Douglas MacLean and Claudia Mills, eds., *Liberalism Reconsidered* (Totowa, NJ: Rowman & Allanheld, 1983).

2. Susan Wendell, "A (Qualified) Defense of Liberal Feminism," *Hypatia* 2, no. 2 (Summer 1987): 65–94.

3. Alison M. Jaggar, *Feminist Politics and Human Nature* (Totowa, NJ: Rowman & Allanheld, 1983).

4. Ibid., 33.

5. Michael J. Sandel, ed., *Liberalism and Its Critics* (New York: New York University Press, 1984), 4. I owe this reference to Michael Weber, who also clarified for me the distinction between the "right" and the "good."

6. Jaggar, *Feminist Politics and Human Nature,* 31.

7. According to Carole Pateman, the private world is one "of particularism, of subjection, inequality, nature, emotion, love and partiality" (Carole Pateman, *The Problem of Political Obligation: A Critique of Liberal Theory* [Berkeley: University of California Press, 1979], 190).

8. Again according to Pateman, the public world is one "of the individual, or universalism, of impartial rules and laws, of freedom, equality, rights, property, contract, self-interest, justice—and political obligation" (ibid., 198).

9. Sandel employed this terminology in *Liberalism and Its Critics,* 4.

10. Wendell, "A (Qualified) Defense of Liberal Feminism," 66.

11. Ibid., 90.

12. Martha Nussbaum, *Sex and Social Justice* (New York: Oxford University Press, 2000), 62.

13. Zillah Eisenstein, *The Radical Future of Liberal Feminism* (Boston: Northeastern University Press, 1986), 96–99.

14. Mary Wollstonecraft, *A Vindication of the Rights of Woman,* ed. Carol H. Poston (New York: W. W. Norton, 1975).

15. Ibid., 56.

16. Ibid., 23.

17. Jean-Jacques Rousseau, *Emile,* trans. Allan Bloom (New York: Basic Books, 1979).

18. Allan Bloom advanced a contemporary argument in support of sexual dimorphism (Allan Bloom, *The Closing of the American Mind* [New York: Simon & Schuster, 1987], 97–137).

19. Wollstonecraft, *A Vindication of the Rights of Woman,* 61.

20. Ibid.

21. Ibid., 152.

22. Immanuel Kant, *Groundwork of the Metaphysic of Morals,* trans. H. J. Paton (New York: Harper Torchbooks, 1958).

23. Jane Roland Martin, *Reclaiming a Conversation: The Ideal of the Educated Woman* (New Haven, CT: Yale University Press, 1985), 76.

24. Wollstonecraft, *A Vindication of the Rights of Woman,* 152.

25. Judith A. Sabrosky, *From Rationality to Liberation* (Westport, CT: Greenwood Press, 1979), 31.

26. Wollstonecraft, *A Vindication of the Rights of Woman,* 147.

27. Ironically, Wollstonecraft's personal life was driven by emotions. As Eisenstein, *The Radical Future of Liberal Feminism,* 106, described it, Wollstonecraft "tried unsuccessfully to live the life of independence."

28. Wollstonecraft, *A Vindication of the Rights of Woman,* 34.

29. Kant, *Groundwork of the Metaphysic of Morals,* 63–64, 79, 95–98.

30. Alice S. Rossi, "Sentiment and Intellect: The Story of John Stuart Mill and Harriet Taylor Mill," in John Stuart Mill and Harriet Taylor Mill, *Essays on Sex Equality,* ed. Alice S. Rossi (Chicago: University of Chicago Press, 1970), 28.

31. John Stuart Mill and Harriet Taylor Mill, "Early Essays on Marriage and Divorce," in Mill and Taylor Mill, *Essays on Sex Equality,* 75, 81, and 86.

32. Ibid., 75.

33. Harriet Taylor Mill, "Enfranchisement of Women," in Mill and Taylor Mill, *Essays on Sex Equality,* 95.

34. Ibid., 104 (emphasis mine).

35. Ibid., 105.

36. Mill and Taylor Mill, "Early Essays on Marriage and Divorce," 74–75.

37. Taylor Mill, "Enfranchisement of Women," 105.

38. Richard Krouse, "Mill and Marx on Marriage, Divorce, and the Family," *Social Concept* 1, no. 2 (September 1983): 48.

39. Eisenstein, *The Radical Future of Liberal Feminism,* 131.

40. John Stuart Mill, "The Subjection of Women," in Mill and Taylor Mill, *Essays on Sex Equality,* 221.

41. Susan Moller Okin, *Women in Western Political Thought* (Princeton, NJ: Princeton University Press, 1979), 197–232.

42. Wollstonecraft, *A Vindication of the Rights of Woman,* 77.

43. Mill, "The Subjection of Women," 186.

44. Ibid., 154.

45. Ibid., 213.

46. John Stuart Mill, "Periodical Literature 'Edinburgh Review,'" *Westminster Review* 1, no. 2 (April 1824): 526.

47. Wollstonecraft, *A Vindication of the Rights of Woman,* 39.

48. See Mill's description of Harriet Taylor in John Stuart Mill, *Autobiography* (London: Oxford University Press, 1924), 156–160.

49. Mill, "The Subjection of Women," 177.

50. Angela Y. Davis, *Women, Race and Class* (New York: Random House, 1981), 42.

51. Judith Hole and Ellen Levine, *Rebirth of Feminism* (New York: Quadrangle Books, 1971), 3.

52. Ibid., 434.

53. Ibid.

54. Ibid., 435.

55. Quoted in Elizabeth Cady Stanton, Susan B. Anthony, and Matilda Joslyn Gage, *History of Woman Suffrage,* vol. 1 (1848–1861) (New York: Fowler and Wells, 1881), 115–117.

56. Davis, *Women, Race and Class,* 75.

57. Hole and Levine, *Rebirth of Feminism,* 14.

58. Maren Lockwood Carden, *The New Feminist Movement* (New York: Russell Sage Foundation, 1974), 3.

59. Ibid., 16.

60. Caroline Bird, *Born Female* (New York: David McKay Company, 1968), 1.

61. Betty Friedan, "N.O.W.: How It Began," *Women Speaking,* April 1967, 4.

62. "NOW (National Organization for Women) Bill of Rights (Adopted at NOW's first national conference, Washington, D.C., 1967)," in *Sisterhood Is Powerful,* ed. Robin Morgan (New York: Random House, 1970), 513–514.

63. All these issues were addressed in Patricia Tjadens and Nancy Thoenes, *Full Report of the Prevalence, Incidence and Consequences of Violence Against Women* (Washington, DC: National Institute of Justice and Centers for Disease Prevention, 2000).

64. Report of the President, Second National Conference of NOW, Washington, DC, November 18, 1967," cited in Hole and Levine, *Rebirth of Feminism,* 6.

65. Betty Friedan, National Organization for Women, Memorandum, September 22, 1969.

66. Carden, *The New Feminist Movement,* 113.

67. Alice Echols, *Daring to Be Bad: Radical Feminism in America 1967–1975* (Minneapolis: University of Minnesota Press, 1987), 215.

68. National Organization for Women, "1998 Declaration of Sentiments of The National Organization for Women," cited from http://www.now.org/organization/conference/1998/vision98.html, accessed March 16, 2012.

69. Betty Friedan, *The Feminine Mystique* (New York: Dell, 1974).

70. Ibid., 69–70.

71. Ibid., 22–27.

72. Ibid., 380.

73. Ibid., 330.

74. Betty Friedan, *The Second Stage* (New York: Summit Books, 1981).

75. Ibid., 20–21.

76. Ibid., 67.

77. Ibid., 28.

78. Ibid., 27.

79. Eisenstein, *The Radical Future of Liberal Feminism,* 190.

80. Ibid.

81. Friedan, *The Second Stage,* 112.

82. Ibid., 148.

83. James Sterba, "Feminism Has Not Discriminated Against Men," in *Does Feminism Discriminate Against Men?: A Debate,* ed. Warren Farrell and James P. Sterba (Oxford: Oxford University Press, 2007).

84. Friedan, *The Feminine Mystique,* 362, 363.

85. See Judith Stacey, "The New Conservative Feminism," *Feminist Studies* 9, no. 3 (Fall 1983): 562.

86. Friedan, *The Second Stage,* 248, 249.

87. Ibid., 249.

88. Quoted in John Leo, "Are Women 'Male Clones'?" *Time,* August 18, 1986, 63.

89. Quoted in ibid., 64.

90. Betty Friedan, *The Fountain of Age* (New York: Simon & Schuster, 1993), 157.

91. Ibid., 638.

92. Friedan, *The Second Stage,* 342.

93. Ibid., 41.

94. Eisenstein, *The Radical Future of Liberal Feminism,* 176.

95. For a detailed discussion of the distinction between sex and gender, see Ethel Spector Person, "Sexuality as the Mainstay of Identity: Psychoanalytic Perspectives," *Signs: Journal of Women in Culture and Society* 5, no. 4 (Summer 1980): 606.

96. US Census Bureau, "Women's History Month: March 2011," US Census Bureau News (Washington, DC: US Department of Commerce, January 26, 2011): 2.

97. Louise August, "It Isn't Over: The Continuing Under-Representation of Female Faculty," Association for Institutional Research (Ann Arbor, MI: Center for the Education of Women, 2006), 15.

98. Not all liberal feminists agree that women and minority male candidates should be viewed as equally disadvantaged. The more *liberal* a liberal feminist is, the more likely she is to view gender and race or ethnic disadvantages as being on par. The more *feminist* a liberal feminist is, the more likely she is to focus her attention exclusively on women.

99. Jane English, "Sex Roles and Gender: Introduction," in *Feminism and Philosophy,* ed. Mary Vetterling-Braggin, Frederick A. Elliston, and Jane English (Totowa, NJ: Rowman & Littlefield, 1977), 39.

100. There is much debate about how factors such as race, class, and ethnicity affect the social construction of gender. See Carol Stack, *All Our Kin* (New York: Harper & Row, 1974).

101. By no means has the interest in androgyny been confined to liberal feminists. Radical feminists have also explored this notion, expressing, however, more reservations about it.

102. Carolyn G. Heilbrun, *Toward the Promise of Androgyny* (New York: Alfred A. Knopf, 1973), x–xi.

103. Sandra L. Bem, "Probing the Promise of Androgyny," in *Beyond Sex-Role Stereotypes: Reading Toward a Psychology of Androgyny,* ed. Alexandra G. Kaplan and Joan P. Bean (Boston: Little, Brown, 1976), 51ff.

104. Although not a liberal feminist, Joyce Trebilcot has forwarded an analysis of androgyny that liberal feminists have found useful. See Joyce Trebilcot, "Two Forms of Androgynism," in *"Femininity," "Masculinity," and "Androgyny,"* ed. Mary Vetterling-Braggin (Totowa, NJ: Rowman & Littlefield, 1982), 161–170.

105. Jaggar, *Feminist Politics and Human Nature,* 28.

106. Ibid., 40–42.

107. Ibid., 41.

108. Naomi Scheman, "Individualism and the Objects of Psychology," in *Discovering Reality: Feminist Perspectives on Epistemology, Metaphysics, Methodology, and the Philosophy of Science,* ed. Sandra Harding and Merrill B. Hintikka (Dordrecht, Netherlands: D. Reidel, 1983), 225–244.

109. Ibid., 232.

110. Wendell, "A (Qualified) Defense of Liberal Feminism," 66.

111. Ibid.

112. Ibid., 76.

113. Jean Bethke Elshtain, "Feminism, Family and Community," *Dissent* 29 (Fall 1982): 442.

114. Jean Bethke Elshtain, *Public Man, Private Woman* (Princeton, NJ: Princeton University Press, 1981), 252.

115. In the nineteenth century, many of the suffragists waxed eloquently about women's moral superiority. See Ida Husted Harper, ed., *History of Woman Suffrage,* vol. 5 (New York: National American Woman Suffrage Association, 1922), 126. See, for example, the section on feminist ethics in *Women and Values,* ed. Marilyn Pearsall (Belmont, CA.: Wadsworth, 1986), 266–364.

116. Elshtain, *Public Man, Private Woman,* 253.

117. Ibid., 243 (emphasis in original).

118. Ibid., 251.

119. Ibid., 336.

120. Ibid., 237.

121. Barbara Arneil, *Politics and Feminism* (Oxford: Blackwell Press, 1999), 147.

122. Angela Y. Davis, "Reflections on the Black Woman's Role in the Community of Slaves," *Black Scholar* 3 (1971): 7.

123. Ireland, "The State of NOW," 26.

124. Elizabeth Erlich, "Do the Sunset Years Have to Be Gloomy?" *New York Times Book Review,* 1994, 18.

125. Ibid.

126. Quoted in Hole and Levine, *Rebirth of Feminism,* 94.

127. Ellen Willis, "The Conservatism of *Ms.*," in *Feminist Revolution,* ed. Redstockings (New York: Random House, 1975), 170–171.

128. See for example Gaiutra Bahadur, "Should My People Need Me," *Ms.* 22, issue 1 (Winter 2012), 40–42. Bahadur interviews Aung San Suu Kyi, the political leader of Burma.

129. One of these exceptions is Janet Radcliffe Richards, *The Skeptical Feminist* (London: Routledge & Kegan Paul, 1980).

130. Willis, "The Conservatism of *Ms.*," 170.

131. Wendell, "A (Qualified) Defense of Liberal Feminism," 86.

132. Ruth Groenhout, "Essentialist Challenges to Liberal Feminism," *Social Theory and Practice* 28, no. 1 (January 2002): 57.

133. Ibid.

134. Anne Phillips, "Feminism and Liberalism Revisited: Has Martha Nussbaum Got It Right?" *Constellations* 8, no. 2 (2001): 250.

135. Nussbaum, *Sex and Social Justice,* 59.

136. Ibid., 62.

137. Immanuel Kant, *Groundwork of the Metaphysics of Morals* (Cambridge: Cambridge University Press, 1998).

138. Nussbaum, *Sex and Social Justice,* 68.

139. Ibid., 70.

140. Ibid., 71.

141. *Concepts and Definition of Terms Used to Construct the Constitutional Equality Amendment (CEA).* Accessed April 4, 2012, from http://www.now.org/issues/economic/cea /concept.html.

Chapter 2: Radical Feminism: Libertarian and Cultural Perspectives

1. See Judith Hole and Ellen Levine, *Rebirth of Feminism* (New York: Quadrangle, 1971), 108.

2. Linda Napikoski, "New York Radical Women," accessed from http://womens history.about.com/od/feminism/a/new_york_radical_women.htm, April 14, 2012.

3. Ibid.

4. Tasha N. Dubriwny, "Consciousness-Raising as Collective Rhetoric: The Articulation of Experience in the Redstockings' Abortion Speak-Out of 1969," *Quarterly Journal of Speech* 91, no. 4 (November 2005): 395–422.

5. Valerie Bryson, *Feminist Debates: Issues of Theory and Political Practice* (New York: New York University Press, 1999), 27.

6. Alison M. Jaggar and Paula S. Rothenberg, eds., *Feminist Frameworks* (New York: McGraw-Hill, 1984), 186.

7. Joreen Freeman, as quoted in *Radical Feminism,* eds. Anne Koedt, Ellen Levine, and Anita Rapone (New York: Quadrangle, 1973), 52.

8. Alice Echols, "The New Feminism of Yin and Yang," in *Powers of Desire: The Politics of Sexuality,* ed. Ann Snitow, Christine Stansell, and Sharon Thompson (New York: Monthly Review Press, 1983), 445.

9. Ibid.

10. Alison M. Jaggar, "Feminist Ethics," in *Encyclopedia of Ethics,* ed. Lawrence Becker with Charlotte Becker (New York: Garland, 1992), 364.

11. Echols, "The New Feminism of Yin and Yang," 440.

12. Linda Alcoff, "Cultural Feminism Versus Poststructuralism: The Identity Crisis in Feminist Theory," *Signs: Journal of Women in Culture and Society* 13, no. 3 (1988): 408.

13. Gayle Rubin, "The Traffic in Women," in *Toward an Anthropology of Women,* ed. Rayna R. Reiter (New York: Monthly Review Press, 1975), 159.

14. Hester Eisenstein, *Contemporary Feminist Thought* (Boston: G. K. Hall, 1983), 8.

15. Kate Millett, *Sexual Politics* (Garden City, NY: Doubleday, 1970), 25.

16. Ibid., 43–46.

17. Ibid., 178.

18. Herbert Barry III, Margaret K. Bacon, and Irwin L. Child, "A Cross-Cultural Survey of Some Sex Differences in Socialization," in *Selected Studies in Marriage and the Family,* 2nd ed., ed. Robert F. Winch, Robert McGinnis, and Herbert R. Barringer (New York: Holt, Rinehart and Winston, 1962), 267.

19. In the 1970s, Millett asserted that what society needs is a single standard of "sex freedom" for boys and girls and a single standard of parental responsibility for fathers and mothers. Without such unitary standards for sexual and parental behavior, equality between men and women will remain ephemeral (Millett, *Sexual Politics,* 62).

20. Shulamith Firestone, *The Dialectic of Sex* (New York: Bantam Books, 1970), 59.

21. Ibid., 175.

22. Ibid.

23. Ibid., 190.

24. Ibid., 191 and 242.

25. Marilyn French, *Beyond Power: On Women, Men, and Morals* (New York: Summit Books, 1985), 72.

26. Ibid., 25–66.

27. Ibid., 67.

28. Ibid., 69.

29. Ibid., 68.

30. Ibid., 443.

31. Joyce Trebilcot, "Conceiving Wisdom: Notes on the Logic of Feminism," *Sinister Wisdom* 3 (Fall 1979): 46.

32. Alison M. Jaggar, *Feminist Politics and Human Nature* (Totowa, NJ: Rowman & Allanheld, 1983), 252.

33. French, *Beyond Power,* 487–488.

34. Mary Daly, *Beyond God the Father: Toward a Philosophy of Women's Liberation* (Boston: Beacon Press, 1973).

35. Using French's terminology in this context, we may say that an imminent God infuses women with the "power-to-grow" into their own image and likeness, rather than be molded into the image and likeness of a transcendent God interested only in expressing his "power-over" others.

36. Alice Rossi, "Sex Equality: The Beginning of Ideology," in *Masculine/Feminine,* ed. Betty Roszak and Theodore Roszak (New York: Harper & Row, 1969), 173–186.

37. Daly, *Beyond God the Father,* 105.

38. Mary Daly, *Gyn/Ecology: The Metaethics of Radical Feminism* (Boston: Beacon Press, 1978), 59.

39. Ibid., 107–312.

40. Ibid., xi.

41. Ibid., 68.

42. See Ann-Janine Morey-Gaines, "Metaphor and Radical Feminism: Some Cautionary Comments on Mary Daly's *Gyn/Ecology,*" *Soundings* 65, no. 3 (Fall 1982): 347–348.

43. Daly, *Gyn/Ecology,* 334.

44. Ibid., 336.

45. Ibid., 337.

46. Ibid., 14–15.

47. Mary Daly, *Pure Lust: Elemental Feminist Philosophy* (Boston: Beacon Press, 1984), 203.

48. Ibid., 2.

49. Ibid., 2–3.

50. Ibid., 35.

51. Ibid., 204.

52. Betty Friedan, *The Feminine Mystique* (New York: Dell, 1974).

53. Daly, *Pure Lust,* 206.

54. See Carole S. Vance, "Pleasure and Danger: Toward a Politics of Sexuality," in *Pleasure and Danger: Exploring Female Sexuality,* ed. Carole S. Vance (Boston: Routledge & Kegan Paul, 1984), 1–27.

55. Ann Ferguson, "Sex War: The Debate Between Radical and Liberation Feminists," *Signs: Journal of Women in Culture and Society* 10, no. 1 (Autumn 1984): 109.

56. Ibid., 108.

57. Ibid.

58. Ibid., 109.

59. Gayle Rubin, "Thinking Sex: Notes for a Radical Theory of the Politics of Sexuality," in *Pleasure and Danger: Exploring Female Sexuality,* ed. Carole S. Vance (Boston: Routledge & Kegan Paul, 1984), 275–301.

60. Ibid., 275.

61. Ibid., 278.

62. Gayle Rubin, "Samois," in *Encyclopedia of Lesbian, Gay, Bisexual, and Transgender History in America,* ed. Marc Stein (New York: Scribner, 2004), 67–69.

63. Alice Echols, "The Taming of the Id," in *Pleasure and Danger: Exploring Female Sexuality,* ed. Carole S. Vance (Boston: Routledge & Kegan Paul, 1984), 59.

64. Ibid.

65. Ibid.

66. Rubin, "Thinking Sex," 278.

67. Radicalesbians, "The Woman-Identified-Woman," in *Radical Feminism: A Documentary Reader,* ed. Barbara A. Crow (New York: New York University Press, 2000), 236.

68. Deirdre English, Amber Hollibaugh, and Gayle Rubin, "Talking Sex: A Conversation on Sexuality and Feminism," in *Socialist Review* 11, no 4 (July/August 1981): 53.

69. See the debate between Christina Hoff Sommers and Marilyn Friedman in Marilyn Friedman and Jan Narveson, *Political Correctness: For and Against* (Lanham, MD: Rowman & Littlefield, 1995), 36–37.

70. Catharine A. MacKinnon, "Francis Biddle's Sister: Pornography, Civil Rights, and Speech," in *Feminism Unmodified: Disclosures on Life and Law* (Cambridge, Mass.: Harvard University Press, 1987), 176.

71. Catharine A. MacKinnon, "Feminism, Marxism, Method, and the State: An Agenda for Theory," *Signs: Journal of Women in Culture and Society* 7, no. 3 (Spring 1982): 533.

72. Appendix I, Minneapolis, Minn., Code of Ordinances, title 7, ch. 139, 1 amending 39.10.

73. Stuart Taylor Jr., "Pornography Foes Lose New Weapons in Supreme Court," *New York Times,* February 25, 1986, 1.

74. Nan D. Hunter and Sylvia A. Law, Brief Amici Curiae of Feminist Anti-Censorship Task Force et al. to US Court of Appeals for the Seventh Circuit, *American Booksellers Association, Inc. et al. v. William H. Hudnut III et al.* (April 18, 1985): 9–18.

75. Ibid., 11.

76. MacKinnon, "Feminism, Marxism, Method, and the State," 533.

77. KaeLyn, "Feminist Porn: Sex, Consent, and Getting Off," *Feminste* (July 23, 2008), accessed April 10, 2012.

78. Ibid.

79. Ibid.

80. Ibid.

81. Anne Koedt, "The Myth of the Vaginal Orgasm," *Notes from the Second Year: Women's Liberation—Major Writings of the Radical Feminists* (April 1970), 41.

82. Ibid.

83. Adrienne Rich, "Compulsory Heterosexuality and Lesbian Existence," in *Living with Contradictions: Controversies in Feminist Social Ethics,* ed. Alison M. Jaggar (Boulder, CO: Westview Press, 1994), 488.

84. Deirdre English, quoted in Hole and Levine, *Rebirth of Feminism,* 221.

85. English, Hollibaugh, and Rubin, "Talking Sex," 49.

86. Nancy Myron and Charlotte Bunch, eds., *Lesbianism and the Women's Movement* (Baltimore: Diana, 1975), 36.

87. Bat-Ami Bar On, "The Feminist Sexuality Debates and the Transformation of the Political," *Hypatia* 7, no. 4 (Fall 1992), 49.

88. See "Redstockings Manifesto," in *Sisterhood Is Powerful,* ed. Robin Morgan (New York: Random House, 1970), 534.

89. English, Hollibaugh, and Rubin, "Talking Sex," 50.

90. "Redstockings Manifesto," 534.

91. "New York Covens' Leaflet," in *Sisterhood Is Powerful,* ed. Robin Morgan (New York: Random House, 1970), 539–540.

92. Adrienne Rich, "Compulsory Heterosexuality and Lesbian Existence (1980)," *Journal of Women's History* 15, no. 3 (August 2003): 18–19.

93. Friedrich Engels, *Socialism: Utopian or Scientific,* quoted in Firestone, *The Dialectic of Sex,* 1–12.

94. Firestone, *The Dialectic of Sex,* 12.

95. Because the claim that biology is the cause of women's oppression sounds similar to the claim that women's biology is their destiny, it is important to stress the difference between these two claims. Whereas conservatives believe that the constraints of nature exist necessarily, radical feminists insist that it is within women's power to overcome the constraints. For some conservative views, see George Gilder, *Sexual Suicide* (New York: Quadrangle, 1973), and Lionel Tiger, *Men in Groups* (New York: Random House, 1969). For some feminist views, see Mary Vetterling-Braggin, ed., *"Femininity," "Masculinity," and "Androgyny"* (Totowa, NJ: Rowman & Littlefield, 1982).

96. Firestone, *The Dialectic of Sex,* 12.

97. Ibid., 198–199.

98. Marge Piercy, *Woman on the Edge of Time* (New York: Fawcett Crest Books, 1976).

99. Ibid., 102.

100. Ibid., 105–106.

101. Ibid., 183.

102. Azizah al-Hibri, *Research in Philosophy and Technology,* ed. Paul T. Durbin (London: JAL Press, 1984), vol. 7, 266.

103. Anne Donchin, "The Future of Mothering: Reproductive Technology and Feminist Theory," *Hypatia* 1, no. 2 (Fall 1986): 131.

104. Mary O'Brien, *The Politics of Reproduction* (Boston: Routledge & Kegan Paul, 1981).

105. Ibid., 8, 20ff., and 35–36. See also Sara Ann Ketchum, "New Reproductive Technologies and the Definition of Parenthood: A Feminist Perspective" (photocopy, June 18, 1987). Paper given at the Feminism and Legal Theory Conference at the University of Wisconsin–Madison, Summer 1987.

106. Adrienne Rich, *Of Woman Born* (New York: W. W. Norton, 1979), 111.

107. Ibid., 38–39.

108. Firestone, *The Dialectic of Sex,* 199.

109. Andrea Dworkin, *Right-Wing Women* (New York: Coward-McCann, 1983), 187–188.

110. Margaret Atwood, *The Handmaid's Tale* (New York: Fawcett Crest Books, 1985).

111. Ibid., 164.

112. Gena Corea, *The Mother Machine: Reproduction Technologies from Artificial Insemination to Artificial Wombs* (New York: Harper & Row, 1985), 107–119.

113. Gena Corea, "Egg Snatchers," in *Test-Tube Women: What Future for Motherhood?* ed. Rita Arditti, Renate Duelli Klein, and Shelley Minden (London: Pandora Press, 1984), 45.

114. Robyn Rowland, "Reproductive Technologies: The Final Solution to the Woman Question," in *Test-Tube Women: What Future for Motherhood?* ed. Rita Arditti, Renate Duelli Klein, and Shelley Minden (London: Pandora Press, 1984), 365–366.

115. Ibid., 368.

116. Jennifer Parks, "Rethinking Radical Politics in the Context of Assisted Reproductive Technology," *Bioethics* 23, no. 1 (2009): 20–27.

117. Ibid., 21.

118. Christine Overall, "Access to In Vitro Fertilization: Costs, Care and Consent," *Dialogue* 30 (1991): 383–398.

119. Jennifer Ludden, "Egg Freezing Puts the Biological Clock on Hold," *NPR* (May 31, 2011).

120. Alison M. Jaggar, *Feminist Politics and Human Nature* (Totowa, N.J.: Rowman & Allanheld, 1983), 256.

121. Ann Oakley, *Woman's Work: The Housewife, Past and Present* (New York: Pantheon Books, 1974), 186.

122. Ibid., 187, 199.

123. Ibid., 201.

124. Ibid., 201–203.

125. Ibid., 203.

126. The claim that adopted children fare just as well as biological children is more controversial than Oakley believed. See, for example, Betty Reid Mendell, *Where Are the Children? A Close Analysis of Foster Care and Adoption* (Lexington, Mass.: Lexington Books, 1973).

127. The kibbutzim have come under fire, however. See, for example, "The Pathogenic Commune," *Science News* 122, no. 76 (July 3, 1982): 76.

128. Firestone, *The Dialectic of Sex,* 229.

129. Ibid., 228–230.

130. Rich, *Of Woman Born,* 174.

131. Ibid., 13.

132. Ibid., 57.

133. Ibid., 13.

134. Ibid., 57.

135. Because the term *surrogate mother* suggests that such a woman is not a real mother but a substitute mother, many feminists prefer the term *contracted mother.*

136. Corea, *The Mother Machine,* 213–249.

137. "A Surrogate's Story of Loving and Losing," *U.S. News & World Report,* June 6, 1983, 12.

138. *Boston Globe,* October 2, 1987, 1.

139. Ann Ferguson, "The Sex Debate in the Women's Movement: A Socialist-Feminist View," *Against the Current* (September/October 1983): 12.

140. Ibid., 13.

141. Ibid. (emphasis mine).

142. Ibid.

143. Denise Thompson, *Radical Feminism Today* (London: Sage Publishing, 2001), 146.

Chapter 3: Marxist and Socialist Feminism: Classical and Contemporary

1. Karl Marx, *Capital* (New York: International Publishers, 1967), vol. 3, 791.

2. Nancy Holmstrom, "The Socialist Feminist Project," *Monthly Review Press* 54, no. 10 (2002): 1.

3. Richard Schmitt, *Introduction to Marx and Engels* (Boulder, CO: Westview Press, 1987), 7–8.

4. Karl Marx, *A Contribution to the Critique of Political Economy* (New York: International Publishers, 1972), 20–21.

5. Schmitt, *Introduction to Marx and Engels,* 14.

6. Nancy Holmstrom, "A Marxist Theory of Women's Nature," *Ethics* 94, no. 1 (April 1984): 464.

7. Robert L. Heilbroner, *Marxism: For and Against* (New York: W. W. Norton, 1980), 107.

8. Henry Burrows Acton, *What Marx Really Said* (London: MacDonald, 1967), 41.

9. Ernest Mandel, *An Introduction to Marxist Economic Theory* (New York: Pathfinder Press, 1970), 25.

10. Marx's discussion of surplus value and exploitation is found in his three-volume work *Capital,* particularly volumes 1 and 2. For a more detailed introduction to these concepts, see Wallis Arthur Suchting, *Marx: An Introduction* (New York: New York University Press, 1983).

11. Schmitt, *Introduction to Marx and Engels,* 96–97.

12. For an elaboration of these points, see Mandel, *An Introduction to Marxist Economic Theory.*

13. Karl Marx, *The 18th Brumaire of Louis Bonaparte* (New York: International Publishers, 1968), 608.

14. Here the term *class* is being used in a sense that falls short of the technical Marxist sense. As we shall see, it is very debatable that women form a true class. For an excellent

discussion of the phrase *bourgeois feminism,* see Marilyn J. Boxer, "Rethinking the Social-ist Construction and International Career of the Concept 'Bourgeois Feminism,'" *American Historical Review* 112, no. 1 (February 2007): 131–158.

15. Allen W. Wood, *Karl Marx* (London: Routledge & Kegan Paul, 1981), 8.

16. Heilbroner, *Marxism: For and Against,* 72.

17. Karl Marx, "Economic and Philosophic Manuscripts," in *Early Writings,* ed. T. B. Bottomore (New York: McGraw-Hill, 1964), 122. I owe this reference as well as several good analyses of alienation to Michael Weber.

18. Ann Foreman, *Femininity As Alienation: Women and the Family in Marxism and Psychoanalysis* (London: Pluto Press, 1977), 65.

19. Ibid., 101–102.

20. Quoted in David McLellan, *Karl Marx* (New York: Penguin Books, 1975), 33.

21. Karl Marx and Friedrich Engels, *The German Ideology,* in *The Marx-Engels Reader,* ed. Robert C. Tucker (New York: W. W. Norton, 1978), 199.

22. Schmitt, *Introduction to Marx and Engels,* 202.

23. Friedrich Engels, *The Origin of the Family, Private Property and the State* (New York: International Publishers, 1972), 103.

24. Ibid.

25. Notions of hunting and gathering as popularized from anthropological studies are often oversimplified. We should be aware, therefore, of the danger of attributing a rigid sexual division of labor to "hunting and gathering" societies, past and present. Women and children may contribute meat to the diet, just as men may contribute root or grain foods. Noticing Engels's dependence on stereotypical ideas of women's and men's work should lead readers to view Engels's account as less-than-accurate history. I owe this reminder to Antje Haussen Lewis.

26. Engels quoted approvingly the controversial thesis of a now largely discredited anthropologist. The thesis was that women in pairing societies wielded considerable political as well as economic power: "The women were the great power among the clans, [*gentes*], as everywhere else. They did not hesitate, when occasion required 'to knock off the horns,' as it was technically called, from the head of a chief, and send him back to the ranks of the warriors" (Engels, *Origin of the Family,* 113). Apparently, it did not strike Engels as odd that a powerful matriarch would let herself be forcibly seized as a wife by a man whose "horns" she could have had "knocked off."

27. Ibid.

28. Lise Vogel, *Marxism and the Oppression of Women: Towards a Unitary Theory* (New Brunswick, NJ: Rutgers University Press, 1983), 82.

29. Engels, *Origin of the Family,* 117.

30. Jane Flax asked why a group of matriarchs would have let men control the tribe's animals or use the fact of their control to gain power over women (Jane Flax, "Do Feminists Need Marxism?" in *Building Feminist Theory: Essays from "Quest," a Feminist Quarterly* [New York: Longman, 1981], 176).

31. Engels, *Origin of the Family,* 117.

32. Marx and Engels, *German Ideology,* 201.

33. Engels, *Origin of the Family,* 118–119.

34. Ibid., 120.

35. Ibid., 121.

36. Ibid., 137.

37. Ibid., 128.

38. Ibid., 137–139.

39. Ibid., 79.

40. Barrett, *Women's Oppression Today: Problems in Marxist Feminist Analysis* (London: Verso, 1980), 49.

41. Evelyn Reed, "Women: Caste, Class, or Oppressed Sex?" *International Socialist Review* 31, no. 3 (September 1970): 15–17 and 40–41.

42. Ibid., 17.

43. Ibid.

44. Ibid., 40.

45. Ibid.

46. Ibid., 41.

47. Truth be told, much factory work, for example, turned out to be as meaningless for "socialist" workers as it had been for capitalist workers.

48. Olga Voronina, "Soviet Patriarchy: Past and Present," *Hypatia* 8, no. 4 (Fall 1993): 107.

49. Margaret Benston, "The Political Economy of Women's Liberation," *Monthly Review* 21, no. 4 (September 1969): 16.

50. Ibid., 21.

51. Mariarosa Dalla Costa and Selma James, "Women and the Subversion of the Community," in *The Power of Women and the Subversion of Community* (Bristol, England: Falling Wall Press, 1972), 34.

52. In the final analysis, Dalla Costa and James viewed men as the dupes of capital rather than as the wily oppressors of women. Men, they said, appear to be the sole recipients of domestic services, but in fact "the figure of the boss is concealed behind that of the husband" (ibid., 35–36).

53. Wendy Edmond and Suzie Fleming expressed the same conviction in even more forceful terms: "Housewives keep their families in the cheapest way; they nurse the children under the worst circumstances and all the toiling of thousands of housewives enables the possessing classes to increase their riches, and to get the labour-power of men and children in the most profitable way" (Wendy Edmond and Suzie Fleming, "If Women Were Paid for All They Do," in *All Work and No Pay,* ed. Wendy Edmond and Suzie Fleming [London: Power of Women Collective and Falling Wall Press, 1975], 8).

54. See Ann Crittenden Scott, "The Value of Housework for Love or Money?" *Ms.,* June 1972, 56–58.

55. Ibid.

56. See US Department of Labor, Bureau of Labor Statistics, *Household Data, 2011 Annual Averages.*

57. US Department of Labor, *Employment Standards Administration Wage and Hour Division,* May 2011, available at http://www.bls.gov/oes/current/oes372012.htm.

58. Carol Lopate, "Pay for Housework?" *Social Policy* 5, no. 3 (September–October 1974): 28.

59. Ibid., 29–31.

60. Observed in Stevi Jackson, "Marxism and Feminism," in *Marxism and Social Science,* ed. Andrew Gamble, David Marsh, and Tony Tant (Champaign: University of Illinois Press, 1999), 17.

61. Chris Beasley, *What Is Feminism?* (London: Sage Publications, 1999), 62–64.

62. Ibid., 64.

63. Juliet Mitchell, *Woman's Estate* (New York: Pantheon Books, 1971), 100–101 (emphasis mine).

64. Mitchell was convinced that women's limited role in production cannot be explained solely or even primarily by their supposed physical weakness. In the first place, men have forced women to do "women's work," and "women's work in all its varieties requires much physical strength. Second, even if women are not as physically strong as men, and even if their original, limited role in production can be attributed to their gap in strength, this same gap cannot explain women's current, limited role in production" (ibid., 104).

65. Ibid., 107.

66. Ibid.

67. Alison M. Jaggar, *Feminist Politics and Human Nature* (Totowa, NJ: Rowman & Allanheld, 1983), 114–115 and 308.

68. Ibid., 309–310.

69. Ibid., 310–311.

70. Although Jaggar did not make specific points about in vitro fertilization, the points I raise here seem to fit her analysis.

71. "Percentage of women leading medical research studies rises, but still lags behind men," Massachusetts General Hospital news release, July 19, 2006, http://www2.massgeneral.org/news/releases/071906jagsi.html.

72. Jaggar, *Feminist Politics and Human Nature*, 315.

73. Ibid.

74. Ibid., 316.

75. Ibid., 317.

76. Iris Marion Young, "Beyond the Unhappy Marriage: A Critique of the Dual Systems Theory," in *Women and Revolution*, ed. Lydia Sargent (Boston: South End Press, 1981), 58 (emphasis in original).

77. Heidi Hartmann, "The Unhappy Marriage of Marxism and Feminism: Towards a More Progressive Union," in *Women and Revolution*, ed. Lydia Sargent (Boston: South End Press, 1981), 428.

78. Ibid., 428–431.

79. Human Development Report Team 2010, "The Real Wealth of Nations: Pathways to Human Development," *United Nations Development Programme* (2010), 113, available at http://hdr.undp.org/en/media/HDR_2010_EN_Complete_reprint.pdf.

80. National Alliance for Caregiving, "Caregiving in the U.S. 2009," (2009), 22, available at http://www.caregiving.org/data/Caregiving_in_the_US_2009_full_report.pdf.

81. Nancy Holmstrom, ed., introduction to *The Socialist Feminist Project: A Contemporary Reader in Theory and* Politics (New York: Monthly Review Press, 2003), 3.

82. Aki Ito and Toru Fujioka, "Women Beat Men to Jobs as Japan 'Mancession' Spurs Deflation," *Bloomberg Businessweek*, January 5, 2012, available at http://www.businessweek.com/news/2012-01-05/women-beat-men-to-jobs-as-japan-mancession-spurs-deflation.html.

83. Geoff Meade, Gender Pay Gap Across Europe Condemned," *The Independent*, March 5, 2010, available at http://www.independent.co.uk/news/world/europe/gender-pay gap across-europe-condemned-1916862.html.

84. US Department of Labor, Bureau of Labor Statistics, "Women's Earnings as a Percent of Men's in 2010" (January 10, 2012), available at http://www.bls.gov/opub/ted /2012/ted_20120110.htm.

85. Molly Hennessy-Fiske, "Gender Pay Gap Narrows—for Unexpected Reasons," *Los Angeles Times,* December 3, 2006, A23.

86. For example, a US Census Bureau study found that the occupations that are most segregated by gender include heavy vehicle and mobile equipment service technicians and mechanics (99 percent men); brickmasons, blockmasons, and stonemasons (98.9 percent men); bus and truck mechanics and diesel engine specialists (98.8 percent men); preschool and kindergarten teachers (97.8 percent women); dental hygienists (97.7 percent women); and secretaries and administrative assistants (96.5 percent women); G. Scott Thomas, "Where the Men, and Women, Work," *American City Business Journals* (April 19, 2004), available at www.bizjournals.com/edit_special/12.html.

87. See US Department of Labor, Bureau of Labor Statistics, "Employed Persons by Detailed Occupation, Sex, Race, and Hispanic or Latino Ethnicity" (2011): 3, available at http://www.bls.gov/cps/cpsaat11.pdf.

88. Valerie Bryson, *Feminist Debates: Issues of Theory and Political Practice* (New York: New York University, 1999), 137.

89. Laura Petrecca, "Number of Female 'Fortune' 500 CEOs at Record High," *USA Today,* October 26, 2011, available at http://www.usatoday.com/money/companies /management/story/2011–10–26/women-ceos-fortune-500-companies/50933224/1.

90. See US Department of Labor, Bureau of Labor Statistics, "Employed Persons by Detailed Occupation."

91. Ibid., 4.

92. Ibid.

93. Ibid., 3.

94. Ibid., 2.

95. See, for example, Katherine Bowers, "Ruling OKs Class Action Suit Against Wal-Mart," *Women's Wear Daily* 193, no. 29 (February 7, 2007): 39.

96. For example, a 2010 Bureau of Labor Statistics report found that 26 percent of women wage earners work part-time, while 13 percent of men wage earners work part-time. See US Department of Labor, Bureau of Labor Statistics, "Highlights of Women's Earnings in 2009" (June 2010): 2, available at http://www.bls.gov/cps/cpswom2009.pdf.

97. A provocative recent article that suggests that women do not "choose" to leave the paid workforce in droves, but are ambivalent at best about this decision or necessity, is E. J. Graff, "The Opt-Out Myth," *Columbia Journalism Review* (March–April 2007), available at www.cjr.org/issues/2007/2/Graff.asp.

98. See, for example, L. M. Sixel, "EEOC Alleges Unequal Pay for Same Work," *Houston Chronicle,* August 23, 2005, 94.

99. *Equal Pay Act of 1963* (Pub. L. 88–93) (EPA), as amended, as it appears in volume 29 of the United States Code, at section 206(d).

100. Amy Joyce, "Unusual Job Titles a Sign of the Times," *Merced (Calif.) Sun-Star,* December 23, 2006, 1.

101. Roslyn L. Feldberg, "Comparable Worth: Toward Theory and Practice in the United States," *Signs: Journal of Women in Culture and Society* 10, no. 2 (Winter 1984): 311–313.

102. Ibid., 1.

103. Ibid., 3.

104. Helen Remick, "Major Issues in A Priori Applications," in *Comparable Worth and Wage Discrimination: Technical Possibilities and Political Realities,* ed. Helen Remick (Philadelphia: Temple University Press, 1984), 102.

105. Jake Lamar, "A Worthy but Knotty Question," *Time,* February 6, 1984, 30.

106. Teresa Amott and Julie Matthaei, "Comparable Worth, Incomparable Pay," *Radical America* 18, no. 5 (September–October 1984): 25.

107. Kay S. Hymowitz, "The Single-Mom Catastrophe," *Los Angeles Times,* June 2, 2012, available at http://www.latimes.com/news/opinion/commentary/la-oe-hymowitz-unmarried-mothers-20120603,0,1889065.story.

108. Amott and Matthaei, "Comparable Worth, Incomparable Pay," 25.

109. The World Bank Group, "Globalization" Web page, available at http://go.worldbank.org/V7BJE9FD30.

110. Shawn Meghan Burn, *Women Across Cultures: A Global Perspective* (Mountain View, CA: Mayfield Publishing, 2000), 120.

111. Ibid.

112. Ibid.

113. Ricardo Alonso-Zaldivar, "Care Homes Hiring More Foreigners," *Los Angeles Times,* October 20, 2005, available at http://articles.latimes.com/2005/oct/20/nation/na-immig20.

114. Alessio Cangiano, Isabel Shutes, Sarah Spencer, and George Leeson, "Migrant Care Workers in Ageing Societies: Research Findings in the United Kingdom," Report, COMPAS: ESRC Centre on Migration, Policy, and Society, University of Oxford (June 2009), 182.

115. Pei-Chia Lan, "Among Women: Migrant Domestics and Their Taiwanese Employers Across Generations," in *Global Woman: Nannies, Maids, and Sex Workers in the New Economy,* ed. Barbara Ehrenreich and Arlie Russell Hochschild (New York: Holt Paperbacks, 2002), 184.

116. Ibid., 171.

117. Ibid., 188.

118. Ibid., 171.

119. Ibid., 172.

120. Mary K. Zimmerman, Jacqueline S. Litt, and Christine E. Bose, *Global Dimensions of Gender and Carework* (Stanford, CA: Stanford Social Sciences, 2006).

121. Matt McAllester, "America Is Stealing the World's Doctors," *New York Times Magazine,* March 7, 2012, available at http://www.nytimes.com/2012/03/11/magazine/america-is-stealing-foreign-doctors.html?pagewanted=all.

122. Juliet Mitchell, *Psychoanalysis and Feminism* (New York: Vintage Books, 1974), 412 (see also Mitchell, *Woman's Estate,* 100–101).

123. Mitchell, *Psychoanalysis and Feminism,* 416.

124. Although Mitchell's analysis is dated, women still have not come as long a way as they should have by now.

125. Jackson, "Marxism and Feminism," 33.

126. Ibid., 33.

Chapter 4: Psychoanalytic and Care-Focused Feminism

1. Sigmund Freud, *Sexuality and the Psychology of Love* (New York: Collier Books, 1968).

2. Ibid., 192.

3. Ibid., 187–188.

4. Sigmund Freud, "Femininity," in Sigmund Freud, *The Complete Introductory Lectures on Psychoanalysis,* trans. and ed. James Strachey (New York: W. W. Norton, 1966), 542.

5. Ibid., 593–596.

6. Some of Freud's arguments seem to run counter to the case for a shift in female erotogenic zones. Freud claimed that male and female sexual organs develop out of the same embryonic structures and that vestiges of the male reproductive structures are found in the female, and vice versa. Thus, human anatomy would seem to be bisexual. Moreover, Freud observed that although femininity is ordinarily associated with passivity and masculinity with activity, this association is misleading because women can be active and men passive in some directions. It is more precise to say that although feminine persons prefer passive aims and masculine persons active aims, considerable activity is required to achieve any aim whatsoever. When it comes to a sexual aim—switching one's erotogenic zone from the clitoris to the vagina, for example—it takes incredible sexual energy or activity (libido) to accomplish the transition (ibid., 580).

7. Ibid., 596.

8. Freud, *Sexuality and the Psychology of Love,* 191.

9. Betty Friedan, *The Feminine Mystique* (New York: Dell, 1974).

10. Shulamith Firestone, *The Dialectic of Sex* (New York: Bantam Books, 1970).

11. Kate Millett, *Sexual Politics* (Garden City, NY: Doubleday, 1970).

12. Dorothy Dinnerstein, *The Mermaid and the Minotaur: Sexual Arrangements and Human Malaise* (New York: Harper Colophon Books, 1977), 5.

13. Ibid., 40–54.

14. Ibid., 59–66.

15. Ibid., 66.

16. Given that a man cannot enter a symbiotic relationship with a woman without reinvoking painful memories of his total helplessness before the infinite power of the mother, he will use his power, Dinnerstein theorized, to fulfill his basic needs for security, love, and self-esteem. This bid for omnipotence extends to control over both nature and women, two forces that must be kept in check lest their presumably uncontrollable powers be unleashed. In contrast to a man, a woman can safely seek symbiosis with a man as a means to attain the ends of security, love, and self-esteem. She can do this because, for her, symbiosis with a man does not conjure up the specter of the omnipotent mother. However, the *idea* of being or becoming an omnipotent mother does terrify her, and this specter may explain woman's discomfort with female power (ibid., 61).

17. Ibid., 124–134.

18. Ibid.

19. Nancy Chodorow, *The Reproduction of Mothering: Psychoanalysis and the Sociology of Gender* (Berkeley: University of California Press, 1978), 32.

20. Ibid., 107.

21. Ibid., 126.

22. Ibid., 200.

23. Ibid., 135, 187.

24. Ibid., 218.

25. Judith Lorber, "On *The Reproduction of Mothering:* A Methodological Debate," *Signs: Journal of Women in Culture and Society* 6, no. 3 (Spring 1981): 482–486.

26. Jean Bethke Elshtain, *Public Man, Private Woman* (Princeton, NJ: Princeton University Press, 1981), 288.

27. Ibid., 290.

28. Janice Raymond, "Female Friendship: Contra Chodorow and Dinnerstein," *Hypatia* 1, no. 2 (Fall 1986): 44–45.

29. Ibid., 37.

30. Adrienne Rich, "Compulsory Heterosexuality and Lesbian Existence," in *The Signs Reader: Women, Gender, and Scholarship,* ed. E. Abel and E. K. Abel (Chicago: University of Chicago Press, 1983), 182.

31. Juliet Mitchell, *Woman's Estate* (New York: Pantheon Books, 1971), 164–165.

32. Ibid.

33. Ibid., 170.

34. Juliet Mitchell, *Psychoanalysis and Feminism* (New York: Vintage Books, 1974), 370.

35. Ibid., 373.

36. Ibid., 375.

37. Sigmund Freud, "Totem and Taboo," in *The Standard Edition of the Complete Psychological Works of Sigmund Freud,* trans. and ed. James Strachey (New York: W. W. Norton, 1966), 144.

38. Jacques Lacan, *The Language of the Self* (Baltimore: Johns Hopkins University Press, 1968), 271.

39. Mitchell, *Psychoanalysis and Feminism,* 415.

40. Sherry B. Ortner, "Oedipal Father, Mother's Brother, and the Penis: A Review of Juliet Mitchell's *Psychoanalysis and Feminism,*" *Feminist Studies* 2, nos. 2–3 (1975): 179.

41. Ibid.

42. Marge Piercy, *Woman on the Edge of Time* (New York: Fawcett Crest, 1976).

43. Chris Weedon, *Feminist Practice & Poststructuralist Theory* (New York: Basil Blackwell, 1987), 50.

44. Ibid., 51.

45. Jacques Lacan, *Écrits: A Selection,* trans. Alan Sheridan (New York: W. W. Norton, 1977), 64–66.

46. Claire Duchen, *Feminism in France: From May '68 to Mitterrand* (London: Routledge & Kegan Paul, 1986), 78.

47. Lacan, *Écrits: A Selection,* 2.

48. According to Lacan, the original mother-child unity is in some way a metaphor for truth—for an isomorphic relationship between word and object. Ideally, both mother and child, and word and object, would remain united, but society will not stand for such unity. As a result of the castration complex brought on by the arrival of the father, who represents social power symbolized by the phallus, not only mother and child but also word and object must be split.

49. Lacan, *Écrits: A Selection,* 1–7.

50. Luce Irigaray, *This Sex Which Is Not One,* trans. Catherine Porter (Ithaca, NY: Cornell University Press, 1985), 28.

51. According to Claire Duchen, Irigaray believed "that before a 'feminine feminine,' a non-phallic feminine, can even be *thought,* women need to examine the male philosophical and psychoanalytical texts which have contributed to the construction of the 'masculine

feminine,' the phallic feminine, in order to locate and identify it" (Duchen, *Feminism in France,* 87–88).

52. Irigaray, *This Sex Which Is Not One,* 32.

53. Toril Moi, *Sexual/Textual Politics: Feminist Literary Theory* (New York: Methuen, 1985), 132.

54. Irigaray, *This Sex Which Is Not One,* 74.

55. Ibid.

56. Luce Irigaray, "Is the Subject of Science Sexed?" trans. Carol Mastrangelo Bové, *Hypatia* 2, no. 3 (Fall 1987): 66.

57. Irigaray, *This Sex Which Is Not One,* 32.

58. Ibid.

59. Moi, *Sexual/Textual Politics,* 140.

60. In an interview, Irigaray stated that there is nothing other than masculine discourse. When the interviewer said, "I don't understand what 'masculine discourse' means," Irigaray retorted, "Of course not, since there is no other" (Irigaray, *This Sex Which Is Not One,* 140).

61. Ibid., 29.

62. Dorothy Leland, "Lacanian Psychoanalysis and French Feminism: Toward an Adequate Political Psychology," *Hypatia* 3, no. 3 (Winter 1989): 90–99.

63. Kelly Oliver, "Julia Kristeva's Feminist Revolutions," *Hypatia* 8, no. 3 (Summer 1993): 101.

64. Julia Kristeva, "The Novel As Polylogue," in *Desire in Language,* trans. Leon S. Roudiez, and ed. Thomas Gora, Alice Jardine, and Leon S. Roudiez (New York: Columbia University Press, 1990), 159–209.

65. Oliver, "Julia Kristeva's Feminist Revolutions," 98.

66. Julia Kristeva, *Powers of Horror,* trans. Leon Roudiez (New York: Columbia University Press, 1982), 205–206.

67. Leland, "Lacanian Psychoanalysis and French Feminism," 93.

68. Ibid., 94.

69. Ibid.

70. Cited in ibid., 95.

71. Ibid.

72. Ibid.

73. Ibid.

74. Judith Butler, *Gender Trouble: Feminism and the Subversion of Identity* (New York: Routledge, 1990).

75. Carol Gilligan, *In a Different Voice* (Cambridge, MA: Harvard University Press, 1982).

76. Gilligan, *In a Different Voice,* 22–23.

77. Lawrence Kohlberg, "From Is to Ought: How to Commit the Naturalistic Fallacy and Get Away with It in the Study of Moral Development," in *Cognitive Development and Epistemology,* ed. Theodore Mischel (New York: Academic Press, 1971), 164–165.

78. Gilligan, *In a Different Voice,* 74–75.

79. Carol Gilligan, "Adolescent Development Reconsidered," in *Mapping the Moral Domain,* ed. Carol Gilligan, Janie Victoria Ward, and Jill McLean Taylor (Cambridge, MA: Harvard University Press, 1988), xxii.

80. Nel Noddings, *Caring: A Feminine Approach to Ethics and Moral Education* (Berkeley: University of California Press, 1984), 3.

81. Ibid., 96.

82. Ibid., 3–4.

83. Ibid., 83.

84. Ibid., 5.

85. Ibid., 79.

86. Ibid., 80.

87. Ibid., 83.

88. Nel Noddings, *Women and Evil* (Berkeley: University of California Press, 1989), 91.

89. Ibid., 96.

90. Ibid., 206.

91. Ibid., 211.

92. Ibid., 213.

93. Fiona Robinson, *Globalizing Care: Ethics, Feminist Theory and International Relations* (Boulder, CO: Westview Press, 1999), 15–20.

94. Susan Hekman, *Moral Voices, Moral Selves: Carol Gilligan and Feminist Moral Theory* (Cambridge: Polity Press, 1995), 1.

95. Sandra L. Bartky, *Femininity and Domination* (New York: Routledge, 1990), 105.

96. Ibid., 104.

97. Ibid., 109.

98. Bill Puka, "The Liberation of Caring: A Different Voice for Gilligan's 'Different Voice,'" *Hypatia* 5, no. 1 (Spring 1990): 59 and 60.

99. Quoted in Robinson, *Globalizing Care,* 19.

100. Brian Barry, *Justice As Impartiality* (Oxford: Oxford University Press, 1995), 252–256.

101. A related debate emphasizes that Gilligan's readers are frequently left with the impression that a female ethics of care is *better* than a male ethics of justice. Many radical-cultural feminists would gladly applaud Gilligan were she indeed arguing women's moral values are not only different from men's but also better. But Gilligan insisted she was claiming only a difference, not a superiority. Her aim, she stressed, was to ensure that woman's moral voice be taken as seriously as man's. But if Gilligan was not making any superiority claims, then her book may not be normative enough. Critics wonder which is it better to be: just or caring? Should we be like Abraham, who was willing to sacrifice his beloved son Isaac to fulfill God's will? Or should we be like the mother whose baby King Solomon threatened to cut in half? (We will recall that in this biblical story, two women claim to be the same child's mother. When King Solomon threatened to divide the baby in two, he prompted the true mother to forsake her claim, so as to secure her child's survival.) Gilligan resisted answering these questions, although she certainly led many of her readers to view Abraham as a religious fanatic and to view the real mother in the Solomon story as a person who has her values properly ordered.

As Gilligan saw it, the question of which is better—an ethics of care or an ethics of justice—is an apples-and-oranges question. Both an ethics of care and an ethics of justice are good. But to insist one kind of morality is the better is to manifest a nearly pathological need for a unitary, absolute, and universal moral standard that can erase our very real moral tensions as with a magic wand. If we are able to achieve moral maturity, Gilligan implied, we must be willing to vacillate between an ethics of care and an ethics of justice. But even if her critics were willing to concede ethical vacillation is morally acceptable, they were not willing to let Gilligan simply describe an ethics of care on the one hand and an ethics of justice on the other without attempting to translate between these two systems. Her critics believe that such attempts at translation would do much to reinforce Gilligan's later claim that the ethics of care and of justice are ultimately compatible. For more details, see Gilligan, *In a Different Voice,* 151–174.

102. Marilyn Friedman, "Beyond Caring: The De-Moralization of Gender," in *Science, Morality and Feminist Theory,* ed. Marsha Hanen and Kai Nielsen (Calgary: University of Calgary Press, 1987), 100.

103. Friedman, "Beyond Caring," 101–102.

104. Gilligan, *In a Different Voice,* 174.

105. Carol Gilligan, "Moral Orientation and Moral Development," in *Women and Moral Theory,* ed. Eva Feder Kittay and Diana T. Meyers (Totowa, NJ: Rowman & Littlefield, 1987), 25–26.

106. Sarah Lucia Hoagland, "Some Thoughts About *Caring,*" in *Feminist Ethics,* ed. Claudia Card (Lawrence, KS: University Press of Kansas, 1991), 251.

107. Noddings, *Caring,* 73.

108. Ibid., 102.

109. Hoagland, "Some Thoughts About *Caring,*" 256.

110. Nel Noddings, "A Response," *Hypatia* 5, no. 6 (Spring 1990): 125.

111. Ibid.

112. Sara Ruddick, "Maternal Thinking," in *Mothering: Essays in Feminist Theory,* ed. Joyce Trebilcot (Totowa, NJ: Rowman & Allanheld, 1984), 214.

113. Ibid.

114. Ibid., 215.

115. Ibid., 19.

116. Ibid., 67.

117. Ibid., 71, 73, and 74.

118. Ibid., 98.

119. Ibid., 118.

120. Ibid., 123.

121. Virginia Held, *The Ethics of Care* (Oxford: Oxford University Press, 2006), 64.

122. Virginia Held, "Feminism and Moral Theory," in *Women and Moral Theory,* ed. Eva Feder Kittay and Diana Meyers (Savage, MD: Rowman & Littlefield, 1987), 112–113.

123. Held, *The Ethics of Care,* 113.

124. Held, "Feminism and Moral Theory," 116–117.

125. Held, *The Ethics of Care,* 134–135.

126. Virginia Held, "The Obligations of Mothers and Fathers," in *Mothering: Essays in Feminist Theory,* ed. Joyce Trebilcot (Totowa, NJ: Rowman & Allanheld, 1984), 7.

127. Ibid., 11.

128. Ibid., 53 and 54.

129. Eva Feder Kittay, *Love's Labor: Essays on Women, Equality and Dependency* (New York: Routledge, 1999), 19.

130. Ibid., 158.

131. Ibid., 51.

132. Robert Goodin, *Protecting the Vulnerable* (Chicago: University of Chicago Press, 1985).

133. Kittay, *Love's Labor,* 55.

134. Ibid.

135. Ibid., 59.

136. Ibid., 25.

137. Ibid., 68.

138. Ibid., 107.

139. Ibid.

140. Rosemarie Tong, "Love's Labor in the Health Care System: Working Toward Gender Equity," *Hypatia* 17, no. 3 (Summer 2002): 200.

141. John Rawls, *A Theory of Justice* (Cambridge, MA: Harvard University Press, 1971), 60–65.

142. Kittay, *Love's Labor,* 113.

143. Elizabeth Cady Stanton, *The Woman's Bible,* 2 vols. (New York: Arno, 1972; originally published 1895 and 1899).

144. Barbara Houston, "Rescuing Womanly Virtues," in *Science, Morality, and Feminist Theory,* ed. Marsha Hanen and Kai Nielsen (Calgary: University of Calgary Press, 1987), 131.

145. Sheila Mullett, "Shifting Perspectives: A New Approach to Ethics," in *Feminist Perspectives,* ed. Lorraine Code, Sheila Mullett, and Christine Overall (Toronto: University of Toronto Press, 1989), 119.

146. Ibid.

Chapter 5: Existentialist and Postmodern Feminism

1. Margaret A. Simons and Jessica Benjamin, "Simone de Beauvoir: An Interview," *Feminist Studies* 5, no. 2 (Summer 1979): 336.

2. Terry Keefe, *Simone de Beauvoir* (Totowa, NJ: Barnes & Noble, 1983).

3. G. W. F. Hegel, *The Phenomenology of Mind,* trans. J. B. Baille (New York: Harper & Row, 1967).

4. Jean-Paul Sartre, *Being and Nothingness,* trans. Hazel E. Barnes (New York: Philosophical Library, 1956).

5. Jean-Paul Sartre, *Existentialism,* trans. Bernard Frechtman (New York: Philosophical Library, 1947), 115.

6. Sartre, *Being and Nothingness,* 364.

7. I owe this reminder to Michael Weber.

8. Sartre, *Being and Nothingness,* 59–60.

9. Ibid., 55–56.

10. Ibid., 56.

11. Jean-Paul Sartre, *The Emotions: Outline of a Theory,* trans. Bernard Frechtman (New York: Philosophical Library, 1948).

12. Sartre, *Being and Nothingness,* 252–302.

13. Ibid., 378–379.

14. Ibid., 380.

15. Ibid., 381.

16. Ibid., 393.

17. Ibid., 412.

18. Dorothy Kaufmann McCall, "Simone de Beauvoir, *The Second Sex,* and Jean-Paul Sartre," *Signs: Journal of Women in Culture and Society* 5, no. 2 (1979): 210.

19. Simone de Beauvoir, *The Second Sex,* trans. and ed. H. M. Parshley (New York: Vintage Books, 1974), 24.

20. Ibid., 41.

21. Ibid., 51.

22. Ibid., 55.

23. Ibid., 64.

24. Ibid., 72.

25. Ibid., 89–90.

26. Ibid., 284. De Beauvoir reserved special criticism for Montherlant and Lawrence. Unlike Claudel, Breton, and Stendhal, who believed the ideal woman freely chooses to sacrifice herself for man not because she is required to do so but because she wants to, Montherlant and Lawrence made of female self-sacrifice a nearly sacred duty (ibid., 280–285).

27. Ibid., 180–181.

28. Ibid., 256n.

29. According to Marguerite La Caze, de Beauvoir's translator Henry Parshley should have translated "Woman's Life Today" as "Woman's Lived-Experience," thereby showing her work as phenomenological and not merely descriptive. *Beauvoir and* The Second Sex*: Feminism, Race, and the Origins of Existentialism* by Margaret A. Simons (New York: Rowman & Littlefield, 1999) in *Hypatia* 14, no. 4 (Fall 1999): 175.

30. Ibid., 500.

31. Ibid., 502–503.

32. It is no secret that de Beauvoir was not enamored of motherhood as we know it. The following quotation is fairly representative of her view: "As motherhood is today, maternity-slavery, as some feminists call it, does indeed want to be free and independent, for those who want to earn their living, for those who want to think for themselves, and for those who want to have a life of their own" (Simons and Benjamin, "Simone de Beauvoir," 241).

33. De Beauvoir, *The Second Sex,* 571.

34. Ibid., 761–763.

35. Ibid., 630.

36. De Beauvoir's view of the prostitute as an exceptional woman who dares to challenge the sexual mores of her society was rooted in several studies, especially those of ancient Greece describing the *hetaerae.* In these studies, Athens is described as a center for prostitution, where the prostitutes were divided into at least three classes. Lowest on the status ladder were the *pornai,* who were checked over before their services were bought. Of slightly higher status were the *ayletrides,* or players, who entertained guests with their music as well as their bodies. Occupying the highest position were the *hetaerae.* In some ways these intellectually gifted as well as physically endowed women were more privileged than were respectable Athenian wives and mothers. They were able to amass great wealth and exert considerable power in the public domain through the men they entertained—this at a time when these men's wives and mothers were without economic and political power. See Will Durant, *The Life of Greece* (New York: Simon & Schuster, 1939).

37. De Beauvoir, *The Second Sex,* 700.

38. Ibid., 710–711.

39. Ibid., 748.

40. Ibid., 795.

41. Simone de Beauvoir, *The Prime of Life,* trans. Peter Green (Harmondsworth, UK: Penguin Books, 1965), 291–292.

42. De Beauvoir, *The Second Sex,* 791.

43. Sartre, *Being and Nothingness,* 412.

44. Josephine Donovan, *Feminist Theory: The Intellectual Traditions of American Feminism* (New York: Frederick Ungar, 1985), 136.

45. Ibid., 137.

46. Meredith Tax, "Woman and Her Mind: The Story of an Everyday Life," in *Notes from the Second Year: Women's Liberation—Major Writings of the Radical Feminists* (April 1970), 12.

47. Sandra Bartky, "Narcissism, Femininity and Alienation," *Social Theory and Practice* 8, no. 2 (Summer 1982): 137.

48. De Beauvoir, *The Second Sex,* 147.

49. Jean Bethke Elshtain, *Public Man, Private Woman* (Princeton, NJ: Princeton University Press, 1981), 306.

50. Simone de Beauvoir, *Memoirs of a Dutiful Daughter,* trans. James Kirkup (Harmondsworth, England: Penguin Books, 1963), 131.

51. De Beauvoir, *The Second Sex,* 553.

52. For an interesting analysis of de Beauvoir's "linguistic ambivalence" about the terms *brotherhood* and *sisterhood,* see Eléanor Kuykendall, "Linguistic Ambivalence in Simone de Beauvoir's Feminist Theory," in *The Thinking Muse,* ed. Iris Young and Jeffner Allen (Bloomington: Indiana University Press, 1989).

53. See entire issue of *Hypatia* 14, no. 4 (Fall 1999 Special Issue), The Philosophy of Simone de Beauvoir, edited by Margaret A. Simons.

54. Anne Whitmarsh, *Simone de Beauvoir and the Limits of Commitment* (Cambridge: Cambridge University Press, 1981), 151.

55. Ibid.

56. Ibid.

57. De Beauvoir, *The Second Sex,* 34.

58. De Beauvoir, *The Prime of Life,* 109.

59. Simons and Benjamin, "Simone de Beauvoir," 342.

60. Ibid.

61. Judith Butler, "Contingent Foundations: Feminism and the Question of 'Postmodernism,'" in *Feminists Theorize the Political,* ed. Judith Butler and Joan W. Scott (New York: Routledge, 1992), 4.

62. Ibid., 5.

63. Anglo-American feminists initially limited the ranks of postmodern feminists to "French feminists" because so many exponents of postmodern feminism were either French nationals or women living in France (especially Paris). In response to this limitation, many directors of women's studies programs in France protested that US academics have a very narrow conception of who counts as a French feminist or as a postmodern feminist. In a review of Claire Duchen's book *Feminism in France: From May '68 to Mitterrand* (London: Routledge & Kegan Paul, 1986), Elaine Viennot wrote, "To taste the full flavor of these distortions, it is necessary to know that the French feminist movement

is, in certain American universities, an object of study (I assure you right away, you would not recognize it . . .), and that this book has every possibility of being bought by every American library; it is also necessary to know that certain of our compatriots (J. Kristeva, J. Derrida . . .) reign over there as masters of the university enclave" (Eléanor Kuykendall, trans., *Études féministes: bulletin national d'information* 1 [Fall 1987]: 40). Whether the sentiments of this review, published by the Association pour les études féministes and the Centre lyonnais d'études féministes/Association femmes, féminisme et recherché Rhône Alpes and brought to my attention by Eléanor Kuykendall, are widely shared by French academics is a question for debate. In any event, Viennot's criticisms are not idiosyncratic and merit a careful reading.

64. Jane Flax, "Postmodernism and Gender Relations in Feminist Theory," in *Feminism/Postmodernism,* ed. Linda Nicholson (New York: Routledge, 1990), 41–42.

65. Jacques Derrida, *Writing and Difference,* trans. Alan Bass (Chicago: University of Chicago Press, 1978).

66. Toril Moi, *Sexual/Textual Politics: Feminist Literary Theory* (New York: Routledge, 1985), 106.

67. Ibid.

68. Ibid.

69. Ann Rosalind Jones, "Writing the Body: Toward an Understanding of *l'Écriture Féminine,*" *Feminist Studies* 7, no. 1 (Summer 1981): 248.

70. Hélène Cixous and Catherine Clement, "Sorties," in *The Newly Born Woman,* trans. Betsy Wing (Minneapolis: University of Minnesota Press, 1986), 63, 65.

71. Ibid., 65.

72. Hélène Cixous, "The Laugh of the Medusa," in *New French Feminisms,* ed. Elaine Marks and Isabelle de Courtviron (New York: Schocken Books, 1981), 249.

73. Ibid., 245

74. Ibid., 262.

75. Elaine Marks and Isabelle de Courtviron, "Introduction III," in *New French Feminisms,* ed. Elaine Marks and Isabelle de Courtviron (New York: Schocken Books, 1981), 36.

76. Cixous, "The Laugh of the Medusa," 256.

77. Ibid., 251 and 259–260.

78. Ibid., 256.

79. Ibid., 259–260.

80. Madan Sarup, *Post-Structuralism and Postmodernism,* 2nd ed. (Athens: University of Georgia Press, 1993), 74.

81. Michel Foucault, *The History of Sexuality,* vol. 1, *An Introduction,* trans. Robert Hurley (London: Allen Lane, 1979), 93.

82. Philip Barker, *Michel Foucault: An Introduction* (Edinburgh: Edinburgh University Press, 1998), 27.

83. Chris Weedon, *Feminist Practice and Poststructuralist Theory* (New York: Basil Blackwell, 1987), 119.

84. Foucault, *The History of Sexuality,* 25.

85. Sarup, *Post-Structuralism and Postmodernism,* 74.

86. Barker, *Michel Foucault: An Introduction,* 32.

87. Michel Foucault, "The Discourse on Power," in *Remarks on Marx,* trans. R. James Goldstein and James Cascaito (New York: Semiotext(e), Columbia University, 1991), 1174.

88. Kathryn Pauly Morgan, "Women and the Knife: Cosmetic Surgery and the Colonization of Women's Bodies," *Hypatia* 6, no. 3 (Fall 1991): 40.

89. Ibid.

90. Naomi Wolf, *The Beauty Myth: How Images of Beauty Are Used Against Women* (New York: William Morrow, 1991), 13, 14, and 233.

91. Ibid.

92. Debra L. Gimlin, "Cosmetic Surgery: Paying for Your Beauty," in *Body Work: Beauty and Self-Image in American Culture,* ed. Debra L. Gimlin (Berkeley: University of California Press, 2002), 95.

93. Sandra Lee Bartky, "Foucault, Femininity, and the Modernization of Patriarchal Power," in *Femininity and Domination: Studies in the Phenomenology of Oppression* (New York: Routledge, 1990), 81.

94. Judith Butler, *Gender Trouble: Feminism and the Subversion of Identity* (New York: Routledge, 1990), 8.

95. De Beauvoir, *The Second Sex.*

96. Judith Butler, "Variations on Sex and Gender: Beauvoir, Wittig and Foucault," in *Feminism As Critique: Essays on the Politics of Gender in Late-Capitalist Societies,* ed. Seyla Benhabib and Drucilla Cornell (Cambridge: Polity Press, 1987), 131.

97. Sara Salin, *Judith Butler* (New York: Routledge, 2002), 50.

98. J. L. Austin, *How to Do Things with Words* (Cambridge, MA: Harvard University Press, 1962), 6.

99. Salin, *Judith Butler,* 89.

100. Ibid.

101. Martha C. Nussbaum, "The Professor of Parody," *The New Republic,* February 22, 1999, 41.

102. Nussbaum, "The Professor of Parody," 41.

103. Judith Butler, *The Psychic Life of Power: Theories in Subjection* (Stanford, CA: Stanford University Press, 1997).

104. Nussbaum, "The Professor of Parody," 43.

105. Ibid., 44.

106. Judith Butler, *Undoing Gender* (New York: Routledge, 2004), 204.

107. Ibid., 204–205.

108. Nussbaum, "The Professor of Parody," 43.

109. Gary A. Olson and Lynn Worsham, "Changing the Subject: Judith Butler's Politics of Radical Resignification," *JAC: A Journal of Rhetoric, Culture, and Politics* 20, no. 4 (2000): 728.

110. Elizabeth Grosz, "Sexual Difference and the Problem of Essentialism," in *The Essential Difference,* ed. Naomi Schor and Elizabeth Weed (Bloomington: Indiana University Press, 1994), 88.

111. Ibid., 89.

112. Ibid.

113. Ibid., 91.

114. Ibid., 91–92.

115. Ibid., 91.

116. Naomi Schor, "Introduction," in *The Essential Difference,* ed. Schor and Weed, vii.

117. Margaret Whitford, "Luce Irigaray and the Female Imaginary: Speaking as a Woman," *Radical Philosophy* 43 (Summer 1986): 7.

118. Teresa de Lauretis, "The Essence of the Triangle or, Taking the Risks of Essentialism Seriously," in *The Essential Difference,* ed. Schor and Weed, 3.

119. Ibid., 4.

120. Linda Alcoff, "Cultural Feminism Versus Post-Structuralism: The Identity Crisis in Feminist Theory," *Signs: A Journal of Women in Culture and Society* 13, no. 3 (1988): 434–435.

121. De Lauretis, "The Essence of the Triangle," 10.

122. Teresa de Lauretis, *Technologies of Gender* (Bloomington: Indiana University Press, 1987), x.

123. Ibid., 48.

124. Genesis 2:19.

125. Lao-tzu, "The Tao-te-Ching," in *The Texts of Taoism,* ed. James Legge (New York: Dover, 1962).

126. Christine di Stefano, "Dilemmas of Difference," in *Feminism/Postmodernism,* ed. Linda J. Nicholson (New York: Routledge, 1990), 75.

127. Ibid., 78.

128. Olson and Worsham, "Changing the Subject," 743.

129. Ibid.

Chapter 6: Women of Color Feminisms

1. Naomi Zack indicated that she is more comfortable with the description "non-white" than "of color" to describe the organizing quality that defines the group of people meant to be described by these phrases on the theory that "of color" implied the existence of biological races, an existence she famously and appropriately rejects. See Naomi Zack, *Women of Color and Philosophy: A Critical Reader* (Oxford: Blackwell Publishers, 2000), 2.

2. For a definition of *double consciousness,* see note 19 of this chapter.

3. For a good discussion of "white privilege," see Peggy McIntosh, "White Privilege and Male Privilege: A Personal Account of Coming to See Correspondences Through Work in Women's Studies," in *Critical White Studies: Looking Behind the Mirror,* ed. Richard Delgado and Jean Stefanic (Philadelphia: Temple University Press, 1997).

4. Elizabeth V. Spelman, *Inessential Woman: Problems of Exclusion in Feminist Thought* (Boston: Beacon Press, 1998), 11–12.

5. Ibid., 12.

6. Ibid., 13.

7. Angela Davis, *Women, Race, and Class* (New York: Random House, Inc., 1981).

8. Combahee River Collective, "A Black Feminist Statement," in *All the Women Are White, All the Blacks Are Men, But Some of Us Are Brave: Black Women's Studies,* ed. Gloria T. Hull, Patricia Bell Scott, and Barbara Smith (New York: Feminist Press, 1982).

9. Audre Lorde, *Sister Outsider* (Berkeley: The Crossing Press, 1984).

10. Kimberlé Crenshaw, "Mapping the Margins: Intersectionality, Identity, Politics, and Violence against Women of Color, in *Critical Race Theory: The Key Writings That Formed the Movement,* ed. Kimberlé Crenshaw, Neil Gotanda, Gary Peller, and Kendall Thomas (New York: The New Press, 1995), 357–383.

11. Ibid, 360.

12. Patricia Hill Collins, *Black Feminist Thought: Knowledge, Consciousness, and the Politics of Empowerment,* 2nd ed. (New York and London: Routledge, 2000), 18.

13. We have used the term *African American/Black feminism* to designate the theories in this section for two reasons. First, we included *African American* to highlight what we understand as the ultimately *ethnic* nature of category and second, we used the term *Black* because *Black feminist* with a capital *B* is the way many of the feminists in this category describe themselves. Other terms, such as *African American* or *black,* will be used instead of *African American/Black* when not paired with the term *feminism* or *feminist,* as appropriate to the circumstances. For example, if a given thinker herself uses the term *black* in her theorizing we have also used this term; however, *African American* is the default term. We have used the term *Indigenous feminism* instead of *indigenous feminism* for the same reason; in other words, *Indigenous* with a capital *I* is the way many of these feminists self-designate. The term *indigenous* will be used outside of a pairing with the term *feminist* or *feminism.*

14. Anna Julia Cooper, *A Voice from the South: By a Woman from the South* (New York: Oxford University Press, 1988).

15. Ibid.

16. In the third wave, the significance and importance of the idea of African American/Black feminism per se has been most famously treated in the work of Patricia Hill Collins, who both fleshes out and criticizes the idea of a unique African American/Black feminism in her book *Black Feminist Thought.*

17. Speech delivered at the Women's Rights Convention in Akron, Ohio, in 1851. Dictated autobiography, Sojourner Truth, *The Narrative of Sojourner Truth: A Northern Slave* (Boston: J. B. Yerrinton & Son, 1850).

18. Ibid.

19. In the realm of race theory, the idea that African American/black persons in America (regardless of gender) have (at least) two different phenomenological identity experiences is known as "double consciousness," at term originated by W. E. B. DuBois in *The Souls of Black Folk* (New York: Gramercy Books, 1994). DuBois describes the experience of "double-consciousness" as follows: "One ever feels his two-ness—an American, a Negro; two souls, two thoughts, two unreconciled strivings; two warring ideals in one dark body, whose dogged strength alone keeps it from being torn asunder."

20. Carleton Mabee, *Sojourner Truth: Slave, Prophet, Legend* (New York: New York University Press, 1993), 173.

21. Harriet Beecher Stowe, "Sojourner Truth," *Rochester Evening Express,* December 13, 1866.

22. The perception of woman as powerful is later reflected, for example, in Alice Walker's definition of "womanist" (her substitute term for *feminist,* for African American/Black feminists) in *In Search of Our Mothers' Gardens: Womanist Prose* (Orlando: Harcourt Books, 1983): "womanist: 1. From *womanish* (Opposite of 'girlish,' i.e., frivolous, irresponsible, not serious.) A black feminist of color. From the black folk expression of mothers to female children, 'you acting womanish,' i.e., like a woman. Usually referring to outrageous, audacious, courageous or *willful* behavior. Wanting to know more and in greater depth than is considered 'good' for one. Interested in grown up doings. Acting grown up. Being grown up. Interchangeable with another black folk expression, 'You trying to be grown.' Responsible. In charge. *Serious.*"

23. For example, during the formative years of the United States, white men enacted laws according to which white women would lose their citizenship rights if they married men of color. Nancy Leong, "Judicial Erasure of Mixed Race Discrimination," *American University Law Review* 59, no. 3 (February 2010): 469.

24. See, for example, Aida Hurtado, *The Color of Privilege: Three Blasphemies on Race and Feminism* (Ann Arbor, MI: University of Michigan Press, 1996).

25. Ibid., 58.

26. See, for example, Kimberlé Crenshaw, "Mapping the Margins: Intersectionality, Identity Politics, and Violence against Women of Color," *Stanford Law Review* 43, no. 6 (1991): 1241–1299: "Feminist efforts to politicize experiences of women and antiracist efforts to politicize experiences of people of color have frequently proceeded as though the issues and experiences they each detail occur on mutually exclusive terrains. . . . Contemporary feminist and antiracist discourses have failed to consider intersectional identities such as women of color . . . " (1242–1243).

27. bell hooks, *Yearning: Race, Gender and Cultural Politics* (Boston: South End Press, 1990), 59.

28. bell hooks, "Naked Without Shame: A Counter-hegemonic Body Politic," in *Talking Visions: Multicultural Feminism in a Transnational Age,* ed. Ella Shohat (Cambridge, MA: MIT Press, 1998), 69.

29. Audre Lorde, "The Master's Tools Will Never Dismantle the Master's House," in *This Bridge Called My Back: Writings by Radical Women of Color,* ed. Cherríe Moraga and Gloria E. Anzaldúa (New York: Kitchen Table/Women of Color Press, 1984), 112.

30. Ibid., 111.

31. Ibid., 112.

32. Patricia Hill Collins, *Black Feminist Thought: Knowledge, Consciousness, and the Politics of Empowerment* (Boston: Unwin Hyman, 1990), 6.

33. Ibid.

34. Ibid., 67.

35. Adele Clark, "Subtle Forms of Sterilization Abuse: A Reproductive Rights Analysis," in *Test-Tube Women: What Future for Motherhood?,* ed. Rita Arditti, Renate Duelli Klein, and Shelley Minden (London: Pandora Press, 1985), 198.

36. Helen Rodriguez-Treas, "Sterilization Abuse," in *Biological Woman: The Convenient Myth,* ed. Ruth Hubbard, Mary Sue Henifin, and Barbara Fried (Cambridge, MA: Schenkman, 1982), 150.

37. "Contraception Raises Ethical Concerns," *Medical Ethics Advisor* 9, no. 2 (February 1991): 17.

38. See, for example, Donna-Dale Marcano, "The Color of Change in Continental Feminist Philosophy," *Journal of Speculative Philosophy* 26, no. 2, (2012): 211; Donna-Dale Marcano, "Re-Reading Plato's *Symposium* Through the Lens of a Black Woman," in *Reframing the Practice of Philosophy* (Albany: SUNY Press, 2012), 225; Kathryn Gines, "Black Feminism and Intersectional Analyses: A Defense of Intersectionality," *Philosophy Today* 55 (2011 Supplement): 275; Kathryn Gines, "Being a Black Woman Philosopher: Reflections on Founding the Collegium of Black Women Philosophers," *Hypatia* 26, no. 2 (May 2011): 429; Kristie Dotson, "Tracking Epistemic Violence, Tracking Practices of Silencing." *Hypatia* 26, no. 2 (May 2011): 236–257; Kristie Dotson. "Concrete Flowers: Contemplating the Profession of Philosophy," *Hypatia* 26, no. 2 (May 2011): 403–409.

39. For background on this perspective, see, for example, Charles Mills, *The Racial Contract* (Ithaca: Cornell University Press, 1997).

40. For more on the "black/white binary," see, for example, Ronald Sundstrom, *The Browning of America and the Evasion of Social Justice* (Albany: State University of New York, 2008).

41. Adrian Piper, "Passing for White, Passing for Black," in *Talking Visions: Multicultural Feminism in a Transnational Age,* ed. Ella Shohat (Cambridge, MA: MIT Press, 1998), 89.

42. Naomi Zack, "Mixed Black and White Race and Public Policy," *Hypatia* 10, no. 1 (Winter 1995); 123–124.

43. Shohat, *Talking Visions,* 7–8.

44. Linda Martin Alcoff, *Visible Identities: Race, Gender, and the Self* (Oxford: Oxford University Press, 2006), 269.

45. Ibid.

46. Ibid.

47. Ibid., 179.

48. Ibid., 188–189.

49. Tina Fernandes Botts, "Antidiscrimination Law and the Multiracial Experience," *Hastings Race and Poverty Law Journal* 10, no. 2 (April 2013).

50. Tina Fernandes Botts, "Hermeneutics, Race, and Gender," in *The Routledge Companion to Philosophical Hermeneutics,* ed. Jeff Malpas and Hans-Helmuth Gander (New York: Routledge, forthcoming as of April 2013).

51. Jennifer Lisa Vest, "Names," *Canadian Journal of Native Studies* 30, no. 1 (Spring 2010).

52. Ofelia Schutte, "Cultural Alterity," in *Women and Color and Philosophy,* ed. Naomi Zack (Malden, MA: Blackwell Publishers, Ltd., 2000), 46.

53. Ibid., 49.

54. Gloria Anzaldúa, *Borderlands/La Frontera* (San Francisco: Aunt Lute Books, 1999).

55. Maria Lugones and Elizabeth Spelman, "Have We Got a Theory for You! Feminist Theory, Cultural Imperialism, and the Demand for the Woman's Voice," in *Feminist Philosophies,* ed. Janet A. Kourany, James Sterba, and Rosemarie Tong (Englewood Cliffs, NJ: Prentice-Hall, 1992), 388.

56. Leslie Bow, "Racial Interstitiality and the Anxieties of the 'Partly Colored': Representations of Asians under Jim Crow," *Journal of Asian American Studies* 10, no. 1 (February 2007): 1.

57. Ibid.

58. Ibid., 4.

59. Ibid.

60. Ibid.

61. Ibid., 3.

62. Ibid., 4. See James W. Loewen, *The Mississippi Chinese: Between Black and White* (Long Grove, IL: Waveland Press, 1988).

63. Bow, citing Avtar Brah, *Cartoraphies of Diaspora: Contesting Identities* (London: Routledge, 1996), 1.

64. Bow, 26.

65. Mitsuye Yamada, "Asian Pacific American Women and Feminism," in *Feminist Theory: A Reader,* ed. Wendy K. Kolmar and Frances Bartkowski (Boston: McGraw-Hill Higher Education), 366.

66. Ibid., 366.

67. Ibid., 367.

68. Ibid.

69. Ibid.

70. Ibid.

71. Ibid.

72. Donna Hightower Langston, *The Native American World* (Hoboken, NJ: John Wiley & Sons, 2003), 430.

73. Hightower Langston, *The Native American World,* 430.

74. Paula Gunn Allen, "Kochinnenako in Academe: Three Approaches to Interpreting a Keres Indian Tale," in *Feminist Theory: A Reader,* ed. Wendy K. Kolmar and Frances Bartkowski (New York: McGraw-Hill), 395–404.

75. Ibid.

76. Ibid., 401.

77. Ibid.

78. Ibid., 402.

79. Ibid.

80. Ibid.

81. Luana Ross, "From the 'F' Word to Indigenous/Feminisms," *Wicazo Sa Review* 24, no. 2 (Fall 2009, special issue): 39–52.

82. Ibid.

83. Ibid.

84. Ibid., citing Paula Gunn Allen, "Who Is Your Mother? Red Roots of White Feminism," *Sinister Wisdom* 25 (Winter 1984): 34–46.

85. See, for example, Judith Butler, *Gender Trouble: Feminism and the Subversion of Identity* (New York: Routledge, 1990).

86. Rebecca L. Clark Mane, "Transmuting Grammars of Whiteness in Third-Wave Feminism: Interrogating Postrace Histories, Postmodern Abstraction, and the Proliferation of Difference in Third-Wave Texts," *Signs* 38, no. 1 (September 2012): 71–98.

87. Chela Sandoval, *Methodology of the Oppressed* (Minneapolis: University of Minnesota Press, 2000), 95.

88. See M. Jacqui Alexander and Chandra Talpade Mohanty, eds., *Feminist Genealogies, Colonial Legacies, Democratic Futures* (New York: Routledge, 1997).

89. Charlotte Bunch, "Prospects for Global Feminism," in *Feminist Frameworks,* 3rd ed., ed. Alison M. Jaggar and Paula S. Rothenberg (New York: McGraw-Hill, 1993), 249.

90. Bunch, "Prospects," 249.

91. Ibid., 250.

92. Shawn Meghan Burn, *Women Across Cultures: A Global Perspective* (Mountain View, CA: Mayfield Publishing, 2000), 73.

93. Noemi Ehrenfeld Lenkiewicz, "Women's Control over Their Bodies," in *Women in the Third World: An Encyclopedia of Contemporary Issues,* ed. Nelly Stromquist (New York: Garland Publishing, 1998), 197–199.

94. Burn, *Women Across Cultures,* 53.

95. David Warwick, "Ethics and Population Control in Developing Countries," *Hastings Center Report* 4, no. 3 (June 1974): 3.

96. Barbara Hartmann, *Reproductive Rights and Wrongs: The Global Politics of Population Control* (Boston: South End Press, 1995).

97. David A. Grimes, Janie Benson, Susheela Singh, et al., "Unsafe Abortion: The Preventable Pandemic," *World Health Organization* (Geneva: Department of Reproductive Health and Research, 2006): 4.

98. Ibid., 2.

99. Friday E. Okonofua, "Abortion and Maternal Mortality in the Developing World," *Journal of Obstetrics and Gynaecology Canada* 28, no. 11 (November 2006): 974–979.

100. Patricia H. David et al., "Women's Reproductive Health Needs in Russia: What Can We Learn from an Intervention to Improve Post-Abortion Care?" *Health Policy and Planning* 22, no. 2 (February 2007): 83–94.

101. Central Intelligence Agency, "The World Factbook: Sex Ratio," accessed September 30, 2012, http://www.cia.gov.

102. Judith Banister, "Shortage of Girls in China Today: Causes, Consequences, International Comparisons, and Solutions," *Journal of Population Research* (May 2004), available at http://www.prb.org/presentations/ShortageofGirlsinChina.ppt.

103. Associated Press, "World Briefing, Asia," A6.

104. Central Intelligence Agency, "The World Factbook: Sex Ratio," accessed September 30, 2012, http://www.cia.gov.

105. Swapan Seth, "Sex Selective Feticide in India," *Journal of Assisted Reproduction and Genetics* 24, no. 5 (May 2007): 153–154.

106. Maria Mies, "New Reproductive Technologies: Sexist and Racist Implications," in *Ecofeminism,* by Maria Mies and Vandana Shiva (London: Zed, 1993), 194.

107. Nancy Holmstrom, "Human Nature," in *A Companion to Feminist Philosophy,* ed. Alison M. Jaggar and Iris Marion Young (Oxford: Blackwell Publishers, 1998), 288.

108. Susan Moller Okin, "Inequalities Between Sexes in Different Cultural Contexts," in *Women, Culture, and Development,* ed. Martha Nussbaum and Jonathan Glover (Oxford: Clarendon Press, 1995), 294.

109. Susan Moller Okin, "Feminism, Women's Human Rights, and Cultural Differences," *Hypatia* 13, no. 2 (1998): 42.

110. Martha Nussbaum, "Women's Capabilities and Social Justice," in *Gender Justice, Development and Rights,* ed. Maxine Molyneux and Shahra Razavi (Oxford: Oxford University Press, 2002), 60–62.

111. Daniel Engster, "Rethinking Care Theory: The Practice of Caring and the Obligation to Care," *Hypatia* 20, no. 3 (Summer 2005): 52.

112. Martha Nussbaum, *Sex and Social Justice* (New York: Oxford University Press, 1999).

113. Vivienne Jabri, "Feminist Ethics and Hegemonic Global Politics," *Alternatives* 29 (2004): 275.

114. See Gayatri Chakravorty Spivak, "Can the Subaltern Speak?," in *Marxism and the Interpretation of Culture,* ed. Gary Nelson and Lawrence Grossberg (London: Macmillan, 1988), 280–287.

115. See Carol Hanisch, "The Personal Is Political," in *Notes from the Second Year: Women's Liberation: Major Writings of the Radical Feminists,* ed. Shulamith Firestone and Anne Koedt (New York: Radical Feminism, 1970).

116. Quoted in Nellie Wong, "Socialist Feminism: Our Bridge to Freedom," in *Third World Women and the Politics of Feminism,* ed. Chandra Talpads Mohanty, Ann Russo, and Lourde Torres (Bloomington: Indiana University Press, 1991), 293.

117. Robin Morgan, *Sisterhood Is Global* (Garden City, NY: Crossing Press, 1984), 5.

118. Ibid.

119. Ibid., 765.

120. Arlie Russell Hochschild, "Love and Gold," in *Global Economy,* ed. Arlie Russell Hochschild (New York: Henry Holt and Company, 2002).

121. Rosemary Radford Ruether, *Integrating Ecofeminism, Globalization, and World Religions* (Lanham, MD: Rowman & Littlefield, 2005), 146.

122. Joann Lim, "Sweatshops Are Us," in *Rethinking Globalization: Teaching for Justice in an Unjust World,* ed. Bill Bigelow and Bob Peterson (Milwaukee: Rethinking Schools Press, 2002), 158–159.

123. Aurelie Charles, "Fairness and Wages in Mexico's Maquiladora Industry: An Empirical Analysis of Labor Demand and the Gender Wage Gap," *Review of Social Economy* 69, no. 1 (March 2011): 1–28.

124. Fauzia Erfan Ahmed, "The Rise of the Bangladesh Garment Industry: Globalization, Women Workers, and Voice," *NWSA Journal* 16, no. 2 (Summer 2002): 34–45.

125. Ruether, *Integrating Ecofeminism, Globalization, and World Religions,* 146.

126. Morgan, *Sisterhood Is Global,* 16.

127. Ibid.

128. Alison Jaggar, "A Feminist Critique of the Alleged Southern Debt," *Hypatia* 17, no. 4 (Fall 2002): 119–121.

129. Ruether, *Integrating Ecofeminism, Globalization, and World Religions,* 4.

130. See George Ritzer, *The McDonaldization of Society* (Thousand Oaks, CA: Pine Forge Press, 2004).

131. Jaggar, "A Feminist Critique," 2002.

132. Maria Mies, "The Myths of Catching-Up Development," in *Ecofeminism,* ed. Maria Mies and Vandana Shiva (London: Zed, 1993), 58.

133. Ibid., 60.

134. Ibid., 59.

135. Ibid., 66.

136. Ibid., 67.

137. For the first two documents, see Susan Moller Okin, "Recognizing Women's Rights As Human Rights," *APA Newsletters* 97, no. 2 (Spring 1998). For the last document, see United Nations Declaration on the Elimination of Violence Against Women, 85th Plenary Meeting, December 20, 1993, A/RES/48/104, available at http://www.un.org/documents/ga/res/48/a48r104.htm.

138. Spike V. Peterson and Laura Parisi, "Are Women Human? It's Not an Academic Question," in *Human Rights Fifty Years On: A Radical Reappraisal,* ed. Tony Evans (Manchester, UK: Manchester University Press, 1998), 142–153.

139. Seth Faison, "China Turns the Tables, Faulting U.S. on Rights," *New York Times,* March 5, 1997, A8.

140. Anne Phillips, "Multiculturalism, Universalism, and the Claims of Democracy," in *Gender, Justice, Development, and Rights,* ed. Maxine Molyneux and Shahra Razavi (Oxford: Oxford University Press, 2002), 125.

141. Chilla Bulbeck, *Re-Orienting Western Feminisms: Women's Diversity in a Postcolonial World* (Cambridge: Cambridge University Press, 1998), 5.

142. Quoted in "Introduction" in *Gender Justice, Development and Rights,* ed. Maxine Molyneux and Shahra Razavi (Oxford: Oxford University Press, 2002), 13.

143. Deniz Kandiyoti, "Reflections on Gender in Muslim Societies: From Nairobi to Beijing," in *Faith and Freedom: Women's Human Rights in the Muslim World,* ed. Mahnaz Afkhami (Syracuse, NY: Syracuse University Press, 1995), 32.

144. Chandra Talpade Mohanty, "Under Western Eyes" in *Colonial Discourse and Postcolonial Theory* (New York: Columbia University Press, 1994), 334–335.

145. Ibid., 335.

146. As the work of Jennifer Lisa Vest, among others, highlights, however, the mixed race experience in the United States commonly includes ancestry from the so-called Native American or indigenous race as well.

147. Maria Lugones and Elizabeth Spelman, "Have We Got a Theory for You!," 388 and 389.

148. bell hooks, *Feminist Theory: From Margin to Center* (Boston: South End Press, 1984), 404.

149. Ibid.

150. Audre Lorde, *Sister Outsider,* 113.

151. Iris Marion Young, "The Ideal of Community and the Politics of Difference," in *Feminism/Postmodernism,* ed. Linda J. Nicholson (New York: Routledge, 1990), 308.

152. Nancie Caraway, *Segregated Sisterhood: Racism and the Politics of American Feminism* (Knoxville: University of Tennessee Press, 1991).

153. Young, "The Ideal of Community and the Politics of Difference," 311.

154. Caraway, *Segregated Sisterhood,* 206.

Chapter 7: Ecofeminism

1. Karen J. Warren, "The Power and the Promise of Ecological Feminism," in *Ecological Feminist Philosophies*, ed. Karen J. Warren (Bloomington: Indiana University Press, 1996), 20.

2. Karen J. Warren, "Feminism and the Environment: An Overview of the Issues," *APA Newsletter on Feminism and Philosophy* 90, no. 3 (Fall 1991): 110–111.

3. The terms *cultural ecofeminists* and *nature ecofeminists* are from Karen J. Warren, "Feminism and Ecology: Making Connections," in *Readings in Ecology and Feminist Theology,* ed. Mary Heather MacKinnon and Marie McIntyre (Kansas City, KS: Sheed and Ward, 1995), 114. The terms *psychobiologistic ecofeminists* and *social-constructionist ecofeminist* are from Janet Biehl, *Rethinking Feminist Politics* (Boston: South End Press, 1991), 11 and 17.

4. Rosemary Radford Ruether, *New Woman/New Earth: Sexist Ideologies and Human Liberation* (New York: Seabury Press, 1975), 204.

5. Rachel Carson, *Silent Spring* (Boston: Houghton Mifflin, 1962), 16–23.

6. Robert Alter, trans. and comm., *Genesis* (New York: W. W. Norton, 1996).

7. Aldo Leopold, "The Land Ethic," in *A Sand County Almanac* (New York: Oxford University Press, 1987).

8. See John Hospers, *Understanding the Arts* (Englewood Cliffs, NJ: Prentice-Hall, 1982).

9. Arne Naess, "The Deep Ecological Movement: Some Philosophical Aspects," *Philosophical Inquiry* 8 (1986): 10–13.

10. Peter S. Wenz, "Ecology and Morality," in *Ethics and Animals,* ed. Harlan B. Miller and William H. Williams (Clifton, NJ: Humana Press, 1983), 185–191.

11. The optimum human population would be about 500 million, according to James Lovelock; 100 million, according to Arne Naess. See Luc Ferry, *The New Ecological Order,* trans. Carol Volk (Chicago: University of Chicago Press, 1992), 75.

12. William Aiken, "Non-Anthropocentric Ethical Challenges," in *Earthbound: New Introductory Essays in Environmental Ethics,* ed. Tom Regan (New York: Random House, 1984), 269.

13. See George Sessions, "The Deep Ecology Movement: A Review," *Environmental Review* 9 (1987): 115.

14. Karen J. Warren, "Feminism and Ecology," *Environmental Review* 9, no. 1 (Spring 1987): 3–20.

15. Ariel Kay Salleh, "Deeper than Deep Ecology: The Ecofeminist Connection," *Environmental Ethics* 6, no. 1 (1984): 339.

16. Ibid.

17. Ferry, *The New Ecological Order,* 118.

18. Carol J. Adams, *The Sexual Politics of Meat: A Feminist-Vegetarian Critical Theory,* 3rd ed. (New York: The Continuum International Publishing Group, Inc., 1990), 27.

19. Ibid., 75.

20. Ynestra King, "The Ecology of Feminism and the Feminism of Ecology," in *Healing the Wounds: The Promise of Ecofeminism,* ed. Judith Plant (Philadelphia: New Society Publishers, 1989), 22–23.

21. Ibid., 23.

22. Simone de Beauvoir, *The Second Sex,* trans. and ed. H. M. Parshley (New York: Vintage Books, 1952), 19–29.

23. Ibid., xxi.

24. Val Plumwood, "Ecofeminism: An Overview and Discussion of Positions and Arguments," *Australian Journal of Philosophy* 64, supplement (June 1986): 135.

25. Sherry B. Ortner, "Is Female to Male as Nature Is to Culture?" in *Readings in Ecology and Feminist Theory,* ed. Mary Heather MacKinnon and Marie McIntyre (Kansas City, KS: Sheed and Ward, 1995), 40–41 and 51.

26. Ibid., 52–53.

27. Ibid., 54.

28. Ibid., 54–55.

29. Mary Daly, *Pure Lust* (Boston: Beacon Press, 1984), 25.

30. Mary Daly, *Gyn/Ecology* (Boston: Beacon Press, 1978), 63–64.

31. Ibid., 10–11 (emphasis mine).

32. Ibid.

33. Ibid., 12–13.

34. Ibid., 21.

35. See David Macauley, "On Women, Animals and Nature: An Interview with Eco-Feminist Susan Griffin," *APA Newsletter on Feminism* 90, no. 3 (Fall 1991): 118.

36. Susan Griffin, *Woman and Nature: The Roaring Inside Her* (New York: Harper & Row, 1978), 226.

37. Ibid., 83–90.

38. Ibid., 67.

39. Macauley, "An Interview with Eco-Feminist Susan Griffin," 117.

40. Susan Griffin, *Pornography and Silence: Culture's Revenge Against Nature* (New York: Harper & Row, 1981), 2.

41. Macauley, "An Interview with Eco-Feminist Susan Griffin," 117.

42. Deena Metzger, Gloria Orenstein, Dale Colleen Hamilton, Paula Gum Allen, Margot Adler, Dolores LaChapelle, A. K. Salleh, and Radha Bratt are also considered to be spiritual ecofeminists.

43. Riane Eisler, "The Gaia Tradition and the Partnership Future: An Ecofeminist Manifesto," in *Reweaving the World: The Emergence of Ecofeminism,* ed. Irene Diamond and Gloria Feman Orenstein (San Francisco: Sierra Club Books, 1990), 23.

44. Starhawk, "Power, Authority, and Mystery: Ecofeminism and Earth-Based Spirituality," in *Reweaving the World: The Emergence of Ecofeminism,* ed. Irene Diamond and Gloria Feman Orenstein (San Francisco: Sierra Club Books, 1990), 86.

45. Starhawk, "Feminist, Earth-Based Spirituality and Ecofeminism," in *Healing the Wounds: The Promise of Ecofeminism,* ed. Judith Plant (Philadelphia: New Society Publishers, 1989), 176.

46. Ibid., 177.

47. Ibid., 178.

48. Ibid.

49. Ibid.

50. Ibid., 179.

51. Ibid., 180.

52. Rosemary Radford Ruether, *Integrating Ecofeminism, Globalization and World Religions* (Lanham, MD: Rowman & Littlefield, 2005), 8.

53. Starhawk, *Webs of Power: Notes from the Global Uprising* (Gabriol Island, BC: New Society Publishers, 2002), 244–245.

54. Starhawk, "A Story of Beginnings," in *Healing the Wounds: The Promise of Ecofeminism,* ed. Judith Plant, 115.

55. Carol Christ, *She Who Changes: Re-imagining the Divine in the World* (New York: MacMillan Palgrave, 2003), 240.

56. Diann L. Neu, *Return Blessings: Ecofeminist Liturgies Renewing the Earth* (Cleveland: Pilgrim Press, 2002), 5.

57. Ibid., 23–29.

58. Dorothy Dinnerstein, "Survival on Earth: The Meaning of Feminism," in *Healing the Wounds: The Promise of Ecofeminism,* ed. Judith Plant (Philadelphia: New Society Publishers, 1989), 193.

59. Ibid.

60. Ibid., 174.

61. Marge Piercy, *Woman on the Edge of Time* (New York: Fawcett Crest, 1976).

62. Ibid., 105.

63. Warren, "The Power and the Promise of Ecological Feminism," 178.

64. Karen J. Warren, *Ecofeminist Philosophy: A Western Perspective on What It Is and Why It Matters* (Lanham, Md.: Rowman & Littlefield, 2000), 97.

65. Ibid., 99.

66. Ibid., 100.

67. Ibid.

68. Ibid., 101.

69. Ibid., 189–190.

70. Ibid.

71. Warren, "Feminism and Ecology: Making Connections," 118.

72. Ibid.

73. Maria Mies, "White Man's Dilemma: His Search for What He Has Destroyed," in Maria Shiva and Vandana Shiva, *Ecofeminism* (London: Zed, 1993), 132–163.

74. Ibid., 137–138.

75. Vandana Shiva, *Earth Democracy: Justice, Sustainability, and Peace* (Boston: South End Press, 2005), 169.

76. Ibid., 168–170.

77. Maria Mies, "The Need for a New Vision: The Subsistence Perspective," in Mies and Shiva, *Ecofeminism,* 247.

78. Ibid., 322.

79. Carol J. Adams, *The Sexual Politics of Meat: A Feminist Vegetarian Critical Theory,* 3rd ed. (New York: The Continuum International Publishing Group, Inc., 2010), 94.

80. Grace Kao, "Consistency in Ecofeminist Ethics," *The International Journal of the Humanities* 3 (2005/2006), 11.

81. Kao, 12.

82. Peter Singer, *Animal Liberation,* 4th ed. (New York: HarperCollins Publishers, 2009).

83. Tom Regan, *The Case for Animal Rights* (Berkeley: University of California Press, 1983).

84. Greta Gaard, "Vegetarian Ecofeminism: A Review Essay," *Frontiers: A Journal of Women Studies* 23, no. 3 (2002): 122.

85. Ibid., 123.

86. Kao, "Consistency in Ecofeminist Ethics," 15.

87. Adams, *The Sexual Politics of Meat,* 134.

88. Ibid., 94.

89. Marti Kheel, *Nature Ethics: An Ecofeminist Perspective* (Latham, MD: Rowman & Littlefield, 2008), 240.

90. T. Colin Campbell and Thomas M. Campbell II, *The China Study: Startling Implications for Diet, Weight Loss and Long-term Health* (Dallas: BenBella Books, 2006), 119.

91. Ibid., 139.

92. Ibid., 151–153.

93. Ibid., 178.

94. Ibid., 65.

95. Ibid., 170.

96. Martha C. Nussbaum, *Frontiers of Justice: Disability, Nationality, Species Membership* (Cambridge: Harvard University, 2006), 325–326.

97. Janet Biehl, *Rethinking Ecofeminist Politics* (Boston: South End Press, 1991), 14.

98. Ibid., 16 (quoting Simone de Beauvoir).

99. Ibid.

100. Mies and Shiva, *Ecofeminism,* 19.

101. Ynestra King, "Engendering a Peaceful Planet: Ecology, Economy, and Ecofeminism in Contemporary Context," *Women Studies Quarterly* 23 (Fall/Winter 1995): 19.

102. Mies and Shiva, *Ecofeminism*, 18.

103. Ibid.

104. Carolyn Merchant, *Radical Ecology: The Search for a Livable World* (New York: Routledge, 1992).

105. Biehl, *Rethinking Feminist Politics*, 118.

106. King, "Engendering a Peaceful Planet," 16–17.

107. Quoted in Judith Auerbach, "The Intersection of Feminism and the Environmental Movement, or What Is Feminist About the Feminist Perspective on the Environment?," *American Behavioral Scientist* 37, no. 8 (August 1994): 1095.

108. Biehl, *Rethinking Ecofeminist Politics*, 1–27.

109. Ibid.

110. Ibid.

111. Ibid.

112. Ibid.

113. Warren, *Ecofeminist Philosophy*, 127.

114. Ibid.

115. Ibid.

116. Ibid., 130.

117. Ibid., 129.

118. Kheel, *Nature Ethics*, 236.

119. Ibid.

120. Ibid.

121. Ibid., 237.

122. Ibid., 238.

123. Ibid., 238–239.

124. Ibid., 239.

125. Editors of the International Forum on Globalization, "From Bretton Woods to Alternatives," in *Alternatives to Economic Globalization*, ed. The International Forum on Globalization (San Francisco: Berrett–Koehler, 2002), 228–238.

Conclusion

1. Mireya Navarro, "Going Beyond Black and White, Hispanics in Census Pick 'Other,'" *New York Times*, November 9, 2003, late edition, East Coast, A1, A21.

2. Ibid.

3. Eileen O'Keefe and Martha Chinouya, "Global Migrants, Gendered Tradition, and Human Rights: Africans and HIV in the United Kingdom," in *Feminist Bioethics, Human Rights, and the Developing World: Integrating Global and Local Perspectives*, ed. Susan Dodds, Anne Donchin, and Rosemarie Tong (Lanham, MD: Rowman & Littlefield, 2004).

4. Leslie Heywood and Jennifer Drake, *Third Wave Agenda: Being Feminist, Doing Feminism* (Minneapolis: University of Minnesota Press, 1997), 8.

5. Rebecca Walker, ed., "Being Real: An Introduction," in *To Be Real: Telling the Truth and Changing the Face of Feminism* (New York: Anchor Books, 1995), xxxiii–xxxiv.

6. Allison L. Howry and Julia T. Wood, "Something Old, Something New, Something Borrowed: Themes in the Voices of a New Generation of Feminists," *Southern Communication Journal* 4, no. 66 (Summer 2001): 324.

7. Ann Ferguson, "Sex and Work: Women as a New Revolutionary Class," in *An Anthology of Western Marxism: From Lukács and Gramsci to Socialist Feminism,* ed. Robert S. Gottlieb (Oxford: Oxford University Press, 1989), 352.

8. Katie Roiphe, *The Morning After: Sex, Fear, and Feminism on Campus* (New York: Little & Brown, 1993); Camille Paglia, *Sex, Art, and American Culture: Essays* (New York: Random House, 1992); and Rene Denfeld, *The New Victorians: A Young Woman's Challenge to the Old Feminist Order* (New York: Routledge, 1995).

9. *United States v. Morrison*, 529 US 598, 631 (2000).

10. Christine Di Stefano, "Dilemmas of Difference," in *Feminism/Postmodernism,* ed. Linda J. Nicholson (New York: Routledge, 1990), 63–82.

Bibliography

Introduction

Alcoff, Linda. "Culture Feminism Versus Poststructuralism: The Identity Crisis in Feminist Theory." *Signs: Journal of Women in Culture and Society* 13, no. 31 (1988): 408.

Bunch, Charlotte. "Lesbians in Revolt." In *Women and Values,* edited by Marilyn Pearsall. Belmont, CA: Wadsworth, 1986.

Chodorow, Nancy. *The Reproduction of Mothering.* Berkeley: University of California Press, 1978.

Corea, Gena. *The Mother Machine: Reproductive Technologies from Artificial Insemination to Artificial Wombs.* New York: Harper & Row, 1985.

Daly, Mary. *Gyn/Ecology: The Metaethics of Radical Feminism.* Boston: Beacon Press, 1978.

de Beauvoir, Simone. *The Second Sex,* translated and edited by H. M. Parshley. New York: Vintage Books, 1974.

Dinnerstein, Dorothy. *The Mermaid and the Minotaur: Sexual Arrangements and Human Malaise.* New York: Harper Colophon Books, 1977.

Echols, Alice. "The New Feminism of Yin and Yang." In *Powers of Desire: The Politics of Sexuality,* edited by Ann Snitow, Christine Stansell, and Sharon Thompson. New York: Monthly Review Press, 1983.

Engels, Friedrich. *The Origin of the Family, Private Property, and the State.* New York: International Publishers, 1972.

Ferguson, Ann. "The Sex Debate in the Women's Movement: A Socialist-Feminist View." *Against the Current* (September/October 1983): 10–16.

Firestone, Shulamith. *The Dialectic of Sex.* New York: Bantam Books, 1970.

Jaggar, Alison M. *Feminist Politics and Human Nature.* Totowa, NJ: Rowman & Allanheld, 1983.

King, Ynestra. "Healing the Wounds: Feminism, Ecology, and Nature/Culture Dualism." In *Feminism and Philosophy,* edited by Nancy Tuana and Rosemarie Tong. Boulder, CO: Westview Press, 1995.

MacKinnon, Catharine A. "Feminism, Marxism, Method, and the State: An Agenda for Theory." *Signs: Journal of Women in Culture and Society* 7, no. 3 (Spring 1982): 515–516.

Mill, John Stuart. "The Subjection of Women." In John Stuart Mill and Harriet Taylor Mill, *Essays on Sex Equality,* edited by Alice S. Rossi. Chicago: University of Chicago Press, 1970.

Mitchell, Juliet. *Woman's Estate.* New York: Pantheon Books, 1971.

Ortner, Sherry B. "Oedipal Father, Mother's Brother, and the Penis: A Review of Juliet Mitchell's *Psychoanalysis and Feminism.*" *Feminist Studies* 2, nos. 2–3 (1975): 179.

Rich, Adrienne. *Of Woman Born.* New York: W. W. Norton, 1976.

Ruddick, Sara. "Maternal Thinking." In *Mothering: Essays in Feminist Theory,* edited by Joyce Trebilcot. Totowa, NJ: Rowman & Allanheld, 1984.

Tong, Rosemarie. *Women, Sex and the Law.* Totowa, NJ: Rowman & Littlefield, 1984.

Vance, Carol S. ed. *Pleasure and Danger: Exploring Female Sexuality.* Boston: Routledge & Kegan Paul, 1984.

Vetterling-Braggin, Mary, ed. *"Femininity," "Masculinity," and "Androgyny."* Totowa, NJ: Rowman & Littlefield, 1982.

Wollstonecraft, Mary. *A Vindication of the Rights of Woman,* edited by Carol H. Poston. New York: W. W. Norton, 1975.

Chapter 1: Liberal Feminism

MacLean, Douglas, and Claudia Mills, eds. *Liberalism Reconsidered.* Totowa, NJ: Rowman & Allanheld, 1983.

Wendell, Susan. "A (Qualified) Defense of Liberal Feminism." *Hypatia* 2, no. 2 (Summer 1987): 65–94.

Conceptual Roots of Liberal Feminist Thought and Action

Arneil, Barbara. *Politics and Feminism.* Reading, MA: Blackwell, 1999.

Bailey, Alison, and Chris Cuomo. *The Feminist Philosophy Reader.* Columbus, OH: McGraw-Hill, 2007.

Banner, Lois. *Women in Modern America.* New York: Harcourt Brace, 1995.

Bentham, Jeremy. *The Principles of Morals and Legislation.* New York: Hafner, 1965.

Berg, Barbara. *The Remembered Gate: Origins of American Feminism.* New York: Oxford University Press, 1979.

Berlin, Isaiah. *Two Concepts of Liberty.* Oxford: Clarendon Press, 1961.

Brennan, Teresa, and Carole Pateman. "'Mere Auxiliaries to the Commonwealth': Women and the Origins of Liberalism." *Political Studies* 27, no. 2 (June 1979): 183–200.

Bridenthal, Renate, Claudia Koonz, and Susan Stuard, eds. *Becoming Visible: Women in European History.* Boston: Houghton Mifflin, 1977.

Brockett, L. P. *Woman: Her Rights, Wrongs, Privileges, and Responsibilities.* 1869. Freeport, NY: Books for Libraries Press, 1970.

Butler, Judith, and Joan W. Scott. *Feminists Theorize the Political.* New York: Routledge, 1992.

Butler, Melissa A. "Early Liberal Roots of Feminism: John Locke and the Attack on Patriarchy." *American Political Science Review* 72, no. 1, 1978: 135–150.

Carroll, Berenice A., ed. *Liberating Women's History: Theoretical and Critical Essays.* Urbana: University of Illinois Press, 1976.

Clark, Lorenne M. G. "Women and Locke: Who Owns the Apples in the Garden of Eden?" In *The Sexism of Social and Political Theory,* edited by Lorenne M. B. Clark and Lydia Lange. Toronto: University of Toronto Press, 1979.

Collins, Gail. *America's Women: Four Hundred Years of Dolls, Drudges, Helpmates, and Heroines.* New York: William Morrow, 2003.

Dahlberg, Frances, ed. *Woman the Gatherer.* New Haven, CT: Yale University Press, 1981.

Davis, Angela Y. *Women, Race and Class.* New York: Random House, 1981.

Dicker, Rory C. *A History of U.S. Feminisms.* Berkeley: Seal Press, 2008.

Donovan, Josephine. *Feminist Theory: The Intellectual Traditions.* 4th ed. New York: Continuum International Publishing Group, 2012.

Dworkin, Ronald. "Liberalism." In *Public and Private Morality,* edited by Stuart Hampshire. Cambridge: Cambridge University Press, 1978.

————. *Taking Rights Seriously.* Cambridge, MA: Harvard University Press, 1977.

Epstein, Barbara. *The Success and Failures of Feminism.* Indianapolis: Indiana University Press, 2002, 118–125.

Evans, Judith. *Feminist Theory Today: An Introduction to Second-Wave Feminism.* London: Sage, 1995.

Flexner, Eleanor, and Ellen Fitzpatrick. *A Century of Struggle.* Cambridge, MA: Harvard University Press, 1996.

Freedman, Estelle. *The Essential Feminist Reader.* New York: Modern Library, 2007.

Fuller, Margaret. *Woman in the Nineteenth Century.* New York: W. W. Norton, 1971.

Gerson, Gal. "Liberal Feminism: Individuality and Oppositions in Wollstonecraft and Mill." *Political Studies* 50 (2002): 794–810.

Gilman, Charlotte Perkins. *Women and Economics.* New York: Harper & Row, 1966.

Grimké, Sarah. *Letters on "The Equality of the Sexes" and "The Condition of Woman."* New York: Burt Franklin, 1970.

Gutmann, Amy. *Liberal Equality.* New York: Cambridge University Press, 1980.

Hobbes, Thomas. *Leviathan.* New York: E. Dutton, 1950.

Hole, Judith, and Ellen Levine. *Rebirth of Feminism.* New York: Quadrangle, 1971.

Jaggar, Alison M. *Feminist Politics and Human Nature.* Totowa, NJ: Rowman & Allanheld, 1983.

Krouse, Richard. "Mill and Marx on Marriage, Divorce, and the Family." *Social Concept* 1, no. 2 (September 1983): 36–75.

————. "Patriarchal Liberalism and Beyond: From John Stuart Mill to Harriet Taylor." In *The Family in Political Thought,* edited by Jean Bethke Elshtain. Amherst: University of Massachusetts Press, 1981.

Kvam, Kristen E., Linda S. Schearing, and Valarie H. Ziegler. *Eve and Adam: Jewish, Christian, and Muslim Readings on Genesis and Gender.* Bloomington: Indiana University Press, 1999.

MacLean, Douglas, and Claudia Mills, eds. *Liberalism Reconsidered.* Totowa, NJ: Rowman & Allanheld, 1983.

Nussbaum, Martha. *Sex and Social Justice.* New York: Oxford University Press, 2000.

Okin, Susan Moller. *Justice, Gender, and the Family.* New York: Basic Books, 1989.

Pateman, Carole. *The Problem of Political Obligation: A Critique of Liberal Theory.* Berkeley: University of California Press, 1979.

Pearsall, Marilyn, ed. *Women and Values: Readings in Recent Feminist Philosophy.* Belmont, CA: Wadsworth, 1986.

Rawls, John. *A Theory of Justice.* Cambridge, MA: Harvard University Press, 1971.

Rendall, Jane. *The Origins of Modern Feminism: Women in Britain, France, and the United States, 1780–1850.* New York: Schocken, 1984.

Rossi, Alice S. *The Feminist Papers: From Adams to De Beauvoir.* New York: Columbia University Press, 1973.

Sabrosky, Judith A. *From Rationality to Liberation.* Westport, CT: Greenwood Press, 1979.

Sandel, Michael J. *Liberalism and Its Critics.* New York: New York University Press, 1984.

———. *Liberalism and the Limits of Justice.* New York: Cambridge University Press, 1982.

Sapiro, Virginia. *Women in American Society.* 4th ed. Mountain View, CA: Mayfield, 1994.

Scott, Joan W. "Feminism's History." *Journal of Women's History* 16, no. 2 (2004): 10–28.

"Seneca Falls Declaration of Sentiments and Resolutions (1848)." In *Feminism: The Essential Historical Writings,* edited by Miriam Schneir. New York: Random House, 1972.

Stansell, Christine. *The Feminist Promise: 1792 to the Present.* New York: Modern Library, 2010.

Strauss, Leo. *Liberalism: Ancient and Modern.* New York: Basic Books, 1968.

Wendell, Susan. "A (Qualified) Defense of Liberal Feminism." *Hypatia* 2, no. 2 (Summer 1987): 65–93.

Wright, Frances. *Life, Letters and Lectures, 1834/44.* New York: Arno Press, 1972.

Eighteenth-Century Thought: Equal Education

Botting, Eileen Hunt. *Family Feuds: Wollstonecraft, Burke, and Rousseau on the Transformation of the Family.* Albany: State University of New York Press, 2006.

Eisenstein, Zillah. *The Radical Future of Liberal Feminism.* Boston: Northeastern University Press, 1986.

Godwin, William. *Memoirs of Mary Wollstonecraft.* Edited by W. Clark Durant. New York: Gordon Press, 1972.

Kant, Immanuel. *Groundwork of the Metaphysic of Moral.* Translated by H. J. Paton. New York: Harper Torchbooks, 1958.

Kohli, Wendy R., and Nicholas C. Burbules. *Feminisms and Educational Research.* Lanham, MD: Rowman & Littlefield, 2012.

Martin, Jane Roland. *Reclaiming a Conversation: The Ideal of the Educated Woman.* New Haven, CT: Yale University Press, 1985.

Rousseau, Jean-Jacques. *Emile.* Translated by Allan Bloom. New York: Basic Books, 1979.

Sabrosky, Judith A. *From Rationality to Liberation.* Westport, CT: Greenwood Press, 1979.

Wollstonecraft, Mary. *A Vindication of the Rights of Woman.* Edited by Carol H. Poston. New York: W. W. Norton, 1975.

Nineteenth-Century Thought: Equal Liberty

Dowling, Colette. *The Cinderella Syndrome: Women's Hidden Fear of Independence.* New York: Summit Books, 1981.

Jacobs, Jo Ellen. *The Voice of Harriet Taylor Mill.* Bloomington: Indiana University Press, 2002.

————, ed. *The Complete Works of Harriet Taylor Mill.* Bloomington: Indiana University Press, 1998.

Mill, John Stuart. *Autobiography.* London: Oxford University Press, 1924.

————. "Periodical Literature 'Edinburgh Review.'" *Westminster Review* 1, no. 2 (April 1824).

————. "The Subjection of Women." In *Essays on Sex Equality,* edited by Alice S. Rossi. Chicago: University of Chicago Press, 1970.

————. *Utilitarianism, Liberty, and Representative Government.* New York: E. Dutton, 1910.

Rossi, Alice S. "Sentiment and Intellect: The Story of John Stuart Mill and Harriet Taylor Mill." In *Essays on Sex Equality,* by John Stuart Mill and Harriet Taylor Mill; edited by Alice S. Rossi. Chicago: University of Chicago Press, 1970.

Stafford, William. "Is Mill's 'Liberal' Feminism 'Masculinist'?" *Journal of Political Ideologies* 9, no. 2 (June 2004): 159–179.

Nineteenth-Century Action: The Suffrage

Adams, Katherine H., and Michael L. Keene. *Alice Paul and the American Suffrage Campaign.* Chicago: University of Illinois Press, 2008.

Baker, Jean H. *Sisters: The Lives of America's Suffragists.* New York: Hill and Wang, 2006.

Davis, Angela Y. *Women, Race and Class.* New York: Random House, 1981.

DuBois, Ellen Carol, ed. *Elizabeth Cady Stanton, Susan B. Anthony: Correspondence, Writings, Speeches.* New York: Schocken Books, 1981.

Harper, Ida Husted, ed. *History of Woman Suffrage.* Vol. 5. New York: National American Woman Suffrage Association, 1922.

Hole, Judith, and Ellen Levine, *Rebirth of Feminism.* New York: Quadrangle Books, 1971.

Stanton, Elizabeth Cady, Susan B. Anthony, and Matilda Joslyn Gage. *History of Woman Suffrage.* Vol. 1, *1848–1861.* New York: Fowler and Wells, 1881. Reprint New York: Arno Press, 1969.

Walton, Mary. *A Woman's Crusade: Alice Paul and the Battle for the Ballot.* New York: Palgrave Macmillan, 2010.

Twentieth-Century Action: Equal Rights

Ackerman, Bruce. "Political Liberalisms." *Journal of Philosophy* 91, no. 7 (1994): 364–386.

Amnesty International. *Human Rights Are Women's Right.* New York: Amnesty International Publications, 1995.

————. *Women in the Front Line.* New York: Amnesty International Publications, 1991.

Arneil, Barbara. *Politics and Feminism.* Oxford: Blackwell Press, 1999.

Bachman, Ronet, and Linda Salzman. *Violence Against Women.* Washington, DC: US Department of Justice, Bureau of Justice Statistics, 2001.

Boyd, Susan. *Child Custody Law, and Women's Work.* New York: Oxford, 2003.

Brownmiller, Susan. *Against Our Will.* New York: Simon & Schuster, 1975.

Carden, Maren Lockwood. *The New Feminist Movement.* New York: Russell Sage Foundation, 1974.

Collins, Gail. *When Everything Changed: The Amazing Journey of American Women from 1960 to the Present.* New York: Little, Brown and Company, 2009.

Echols, Alice. *Daring to Be Bad: Radical Feminism in America, 1967–1975.* Minneapolis: University of Minnesota Press, 1987.

Elshtain, Jean Bethke. *Meditations on Modern Political Thought: Masculine/Feminine Themes from Luther to Prendt.* New York: Praeger, 1986.

———. *Public Man, Private Woman.* Princeton, NJ: Princeton University Press, 1981.

Frazer, Elizabeth, and Nicola Lacey. *The Politics of Community: A Feminist Critique of the Liberal Communitarian Debate.* Toronto: University of Toronto Press, 1993.

Friedan, Betty. "Betty Friedan Critiques Feminism and Calls for New Directions." *New York Times Magazine,* July 5, 1981.

———. "Feminism Takes a New Turn." *New York Times Magazine,* November 18, 1979.

———. "N.O.W.: How It Began." *Women Speaking,* April 1967.

Gilbert, Neil. *The Transformation of the Welfare State.* New York: Oxford, 2002.

Gornick, Janet, and Marcia Meyers. *Families That Work.* New York: Russell Sage, 2003.

Hewitt, Nancy, ed. *No Permanent Waves: Recasting Histories of U.S. Feminism.* Piscataway, NJ: Rutgers University Press, 2010.

Hochschild, Arlie. *Second Shift.* Updated edition. New York: Penguin, 2003.

Ireland, Patricia. "The State of NOW." *Ms.,* July/August 1992.

Kanowitz, Leo. *Women and the Law: The Unfinished Revolution.* Albuquerque: University of New Mexico Press, 1969.

Koss, Mary, et al. "The Scope of Rape: Incidence and Prevalence of Sexual Aggression and Victimization in a National Sample of Higher Education Students." *Journal of Counseling and Clinical Psychology* 24 (1988): 68–72.

Leivick, Sarah. "Use of Battered Woman Syndrome to Defend the Abused and Prosecute the Abuser." *Georgetown Journal of Gender and Law* 6 (2005): 391ff.

MacLean, Nancy. *The American Women's Movement, 1945–2000: A Brief History with Documents.* Boston: Bedford/St. Martin's, 2008.

Martin, Del. *Battered Wives.* Revised edition. Volcano, CA: Volcano, 1981.

Mayeri, Serena. *Reasoning from Race: Feminism, Law, and the Civil Rights Revolution.* Cambridge: Harvard University Press, 2011.

Mendes, Kaitlynn. *Feminism in the News: Representations of the Women's Movement Since the 1960s.* New York: Palgrave Macmillan, 2011.

NOW Bill of Rights. In *Sisterhood Is Powerful,* edited by Robin Morgan. New York: Random House, 1970.

Peters, Julia, and Andrea Wolper, eds. *Women's Rights, Human Rights: International Feminist Perspectives.* New York: Routledge, 1995.

Rosser, Sue. *Women's Health: Missing from U.S. Medicine.* Bloomington: Indiana University Press, 1994.

Rossi, Alice. "Equality Between the Sexes: An Immodest Proposal." *Daedalus* 93, no. 2 (1964): 607–652.

Schiebinger, Londa. "Women's Health and Clinical Trials." *Journal of Clinical Investigations* 112 (2003): 973–977.

Schneider, Elizabeth M. and Stephanie M. Wildman. *Women and the Law: Stories.* New York: Thompson Reuters/Foundation Press, 2011.

Schreiber, Ronnee. *Righting Feminism: Conservative Women and American Politics.* New York: Oxford University Press, 2008.

Schwartzman, Lisa H. *Challenging Liberalism: Feminism as Political Critique.* University Park: Pennsylvania State University Press, 2006.

Stacey, Judith. *Brave New Families: Stories of Domestic Upheaval in Late Twentieth Century America.* New York: Basic Books, 1990.

———. "The New Conservative Feminism." *Feminist Studies* 9, no. 3 (Fall 1983).

Steinem, Gloria. "Now That It's Reagan." *Ms.*, January 1981, 28–33.

Sterba, James. "Feminism Has Not Discriminated Against Men." In *Does Feminism Discriminate Against Men?,* edited by Warren Farrell and James Sterba. New York: Oxford University Press, 2007.

Sterba, James P., and Linda LeMoncheck. *Sexual Harassment: Issues and Answers.* New York: Oxford, 2001.

Stopler, Gila. "Gender Construction and the Limits of Liberal Equality." *Texas Journal of Women and the Law* 15 (2005): 44–78.

Straus, Murray. "The Controversy over Domestic Violence by Women." In *Violence and Intimate Relationships,* edited by Ximena B. Arriaga and Stuart Oskamp. Thousand Oaks, CA: Sage, 1999, 29.

Thomas, Tracy A., and Tracey Jean Boisseau, eds. *Feminist Legal History: Essays on Women and the Law.* New York: New York University Press, 2011.

Tjadens, Patricia, and Nancy Thoennes. *Full Report of the Prevalence, Incidence and Consequences of Violence Against Women.* Washington, DC: National Institute of Justice and Centers for Disease Prevention, 2000.

Valk, Anne M. *Radical Sisters: Second-Wave Feminism and Black Liberation in Washington, D.C.* Chicago: University of Illinois Press, 2008.

Venker, Suzanne, and Phyllis Schlafly. *The Flipside of Feminism: What Conservative Women Know—and Men Can't Say.* Washington, DC: WND Books, 2011.

Wagner DeCew, Judith. "The Combat Exclusion and the Role of Women in the Military." *Hypatia* 10 (Winter 1995): 56–73.

Warrior, Betsy, and Lisa Leghorn. *Houseworker's Handbook.* 3rd expanded ed. Cambridge, MA: Women's Center, 1995.

Weisberg, D. Kelly. *Applications of Feminist Legal Theory to Women's Lives: Sex, Violence, Work, and Reproduction.* Philadelphia: Temple University Press, 1996.

Weitzman, Lenore. *Divorce Revolution.* New York: Free Press, 1985.

Twentieth-Century Thought: Sameness Versus Difference

Benatar, David. "The Second Sexism." *Social Theory and Practice* 29 (2003): 177–210.

Bird, Caroline. *Born Female.* New York: David McKay Company, 1968.

Crittenden, Ann. *The Price of Motherhood.* New York: Henry Holt, 2001.

Eisenstein, Zillah. *The Radical Future of Liberal Feminism.* Boston: Northeastern University Press, 1986.

Feldman, Gayle. "Women Are Different." *Self,* July 1997, 105–108, 154.

Friedan, Betty. *The Feminine Mystique.* New York: Dell, 1974.

———. *The Fountain of Age.* New York: Simon & Schuster, 1993.

———. *The Second Stage.* New York: Summit Books, 1981.

Groenhout, Ruth. "Essentialist Challenges to Liberal Feminism." *Social Theory and Practice* 28, no. 1 (January 2002): 57.

Lee, Valerie, et al. *The Influence of School Climate on Gender Differences in the Achievement and Engagement of Young Adolescents.* Washington, DC: AAUW Educational Foundation, 1996.

Nye, Andrea. *Feminist Theory and the Philosophies of Man.* New York: Routledge, 1989.

Richards, Janet Radcliffe. *The Skeptical Feminist.* London: Routledge & Kegan Paul, 1980.

Stacey, Judith. "The New Conservative Feminism." *Feminist Studies* 9, no. 3 (Fall 1983): 562.

Sterba, James. "Feminism Has Not Discriminated Against Men." In *Does Feminism Discriminate Against Men?: A Debate,* edited by Warren Farrell and James P. Sterba. Oxford: Oxford University Press, 2007.

Contemporary Directions in Liberal Feminism

August, Louise. "It Isn't Over: The Continuing Under-Representation of Female Faculty." Association for Institutional Research. Ann Arbor, MI: Center for the Education of Women, 2006.

Baehr, Amy R. "Toward a New Feminist Liberalism: Okin, Rawls, and Habermas." *Hypatia* 11, no. 1 (Winter 1996): 49–66.

Bem, Sandra L. "Probing the Promise of Androgyny." In *Beyond Sex-Role Stereotypes: Reading Toward a Psychology of Androgyny,* edited by Alexandra G. Kaplan and Joan Bean. Boston: Little, Brown, 1976.

Brooks, Ann. *Post-feminisms: Feminism, Cultural Theory, and Cultural Forms.* New York: Routledge, 1997.

Bryson, Valerie. *Feminist Debates: Issues of Theory and Political Practice.* New York: New York University Press, 1999.

Bumiller, Kristin. *In an Abusive State: How Neoliberalism Appropriated the Feminist Movement Against Sexual Violence.* Durham, Duke University Press, 2008.

Card, Claudia. "The L Word and the F Word." *Hypatia* 21, no. 2 (2006): 223–229.

———, ed. *On Feminist Ethics and Politics.* Lawrence: University Press of Kansas, 1999.

Carroll, Susan J., and Richard L. Fox. *Gender and Elections: Shaping the Future of American Politics.* 2nd ed. New York: Cambridge University Press, 2010.

Code, Lorraine. *What Can She Know? Feminist Theory and the Construction of Knowledge.* Ithaca, NY: Cornell University Press, 1991.

Eisenstein, Zillah R. *The Radical Future of Liberal Feminism.* New York: Longman, 1981.

English, Jane. "Sex Roles and Gender: Introduction." In *Feminism and Philosophy,* edited by Mary Vetterling-Braggin, Frederick A. Elliston, and Jane English. Totowa, NJ: Rowman & Littlefield, 1977.

Ford, Lynne E. *Women and Politics: The Pursuit of Equality.* 3rd ed. Boston: Wadsworth, 2011.

Galston, William A. *Liberal Purposes: Goods, Virtues, and Diversity in the Liberal State.* Cambridge: Cambridge University Press, 1991.

Groenhout, Ruth E. "Essentialist Challenges to Liberal Feminism." *Social Theory and Practice* 28, no. 1 (January 2002): 51–75.

Heilbrun, Carolyn G. *Toward the Promise of Androgyny.* New York: Alfred A. Knopf, 1973.

Hunter College Women's Studies Collective. *Women's Realities, Women's Choices: An Introduction to Women's Studies.* New York: Oxford University Press, 1983.

Klausen, Jytte, and Charles S. Maier, eds. *Has Liberalism Failed Women? Assuring Equal Representation in Europe and the United States.* New York: Palgrave, 2001.

Kornblut, Anne E. *Notes from the Cracked Ceiling: Hillary Clinton, Sarah Palin, and What It Will Take for a Woman to Win.* New York: Crown Publishers, 2009.

Krook, Mona Lena, and Sarah Childs, eds. *Women, Gender, and Politics: A Reader.* New York: Oxford University Press, 2010.

Labaton, Vivien, and Dawn Lundy Martin, eds. *The Fire This Time: Young Activists and the New Feminism.* New York: Anchor Books, 2004.

Lawless, Jennifer L., and Richard L. Fox. *It Still Takes a Candidate: Why Women Don't Run for Office.* 2nd ed. New York: Cambridge University Press, 2010.

Molyneux, Maxine, and Shahra Razavi, eds. *Gender Justice, Development, and Rights.* Oxford: Oxford University Press, 2002.

Okin, Susan Moller. *Women in Western Political Thought.* Princeton, NJ: Princeton University Press, 1979.

Saul, Jennifer Mather. *Feminism: Issues and Arguments.* Oxford: Oxford University Press, 2003.

Schwarzenbach, Sibyl. *On Civic Friendship: Including Women in the State.* New York: Columbia University Press, 2009.

Shildrick, Margrit. *Leaky Bodies and Boundaries: Feminism, Postmodernism, and (Bio)ethics.* New York: Routledge, 1997.

Stack, Carol. *All Our Kin.* New York: Harper & Row, 1974.

Steinem, Gloria. *Outrageous Acts and Everyday Rebellions.* New York: Holt, Rinehart and Winston, 1983.

Trebilcot, Joyce. "Two Forms of Androgynism." In *"Femininity," "Masculinity," and "Androgyny,"* edited by Mary Vetterling-Braggin. Totowa, NJ: Rowman & Littlefield, 1982.

Critiques of Liberal Feminism

Arneil, Barbara. *Politics and Feminism.* Oxford: Blackwell Press, 1999.

Davis, Angela Y. "Reflections on the Black Woman's Role in the Community of Slaves." *Black Scholar* 3 (1971).

Elshtain, Jean Bethke. "Feminism, Family and Community." *Dissent* 29 (Fall 1982): 442.

———. *Public Man, Private Woman.* Princeton, NJ: Princeton University Press, 1981, 252.

Erlich, Elizabeth. "Do the Sunset Years Have to Be Gloomy?" *New York Times Book Review.*

Harper, Ida Husted, ed. *History of Woman Suffrage.* Vol. 5. New York: National American Woman Suffrage Association, 1922.

Hole, Judith, and Ellen Levine. *Rebirth of Feminism.* New York: Quadrangle Books, 1971.

Jaggar, Alison M. *Feminist Politics and Human Nature.* Totowa, NJ: Rowman & Allanheld, 1983.

Pearsall, Marilyn, ed. *Women and Values.* Belmont, CA.: Wadsworth, 1986.

Scheman, Naomi. "Individualism and the Objects of Psychology." In *Discovering Reality: Feminist Perspectives on Epistemology, Metaphysics, Methodology, and the Philosophy of Science,* edited by Sandra Harding and Merrill B. Hintikka. Dordrecht, Netherlands: D. Reidel, 1983.

Wendell, Susan. "A (Qualified) Defense of Liberal Feminism." *Hypatia* 2, no. 2 (Summer 1987): 66.

Conclusion

Bahadur, Gaiutra. "Should My People Need Me." *Ms.* 22, issue 1 (Winter 2012), 40–42.

Groenhout, Ruth. "Essentialist Challenges to Liberal Feminism." *Social Theory and Practice* 28, no. 1 (January 2002): 57.

Kant, Immanuel. *Groundwork of the Metaphysics of Morals.* Cambridge: Cambridge University Press, 1998.

Nussbaum, Martha. *Sex and Social Justice.* New York: Oxford University Press, 2000.

Phillips, Anne. "Feminism and Liberalism Revisited: Has Martha Nussbaum Got It Right?" *Constellations* 8, no. 2 (2001), 250.

Richards, Janet Radcliffe. *The Skeptical Feminist.* London: Routledge & Kegan Paul, 1980.

Wendell, Susan. "A (Qualified) Defense of Liberal Feminism." *Hypatia* 2, no. 2 (Summer 1987): 86.

Ellen Willis, "The Conservatism of *Ms.*" In *Feminist Revolution,* edited by Redstockings. New York: Random House, 1975.

Chapter 2: Radical Feminism: Libertarian and Cultural Perspectives

Alcoff, Linda. "Cultural Feminism Versus Poststructuralism: The Identity Crisis in Feminist Theory." *Signs: Journal of Women in Culture and Society* 13, no. 3 (1988): 408.

Bell, Diane, and Renate Klein. *Radically Speaking: Feminism Reclaimed.* North Melbourne, Australia: Spinifex, 1996.

Calhoun, Cheshire. "Taking Seriously Dual Systems and Sex." *Hypatia* 13, no. 1 (1998): 224–231.

Card, Claudia. "Radicalesbianfeminist Theory." *Hypatia* 13, no. 1 (1998): 206–213.

Coote, Anna, and Beatrix Campbell. *Sweet Freedom: The Movement for Women's Liberation.* Boston: Blackwell Publishers, 1987.

Corrin, Chris. *Desperately Seeking Sisterhood: Still Challenging and Building.* Oxford: Taylor & Francis, 1997.

Crow, Barbara A. *Radical Feminism: A Documentary Reader.* New York: New York University Press, 2000.

Dubriwny, Tasha N. "Consciousness-Raising as Collective Rhetoric: The Articulation of Experience in the Redstockings' Abortion Speak-Out of 1969." *Quarterly Journal of Speech* 91, no. 4 (November 2005): 395–422.

Echols, Alice. "The New Feminism of Yin and Yang." In *Powers of Desire: The Politics of Sexuality,* edited by Ann Snitow, Christine Stansell, and Sharon Thompson. New York: Monthly Review Press, 1983.

Ferguson, Ann. "Sex War: The Debate between Radical and Liberation Feminists." *Signs: Journal of Women in Culture and Society* 10, no. 1 (Autumn 1984): 106–135.

Freeman, Joreen. In *Radical Feminism,* edited by Anne Koedt, Ellen Levine, and Anita Rapone. New York: Quadrangle, 1973.

Giovanni, Nikki. *My House.* New York: William Morrow, 1972.

Hirsch, Marianne, and Evelyn Fox Keller. *Conflicts in Feminism.* New York: Routledge, 1990.

Hole, Judith, and Ellen Levine. *Rebirth of Feminism.* New York: Quadrangle, 1971.

Jaggar, Alison M., and Paula S. Rothenberg, eds. *Feminist Frameworks.* New York: McGraw-Hill, 1984.

Klein, Renate, and Deborah Lynn Steinberg. *Radical Voices: A Decade of Feminist Resistance from Women's Studies International Forum.* New York: Pergamon Press, 1989.

Koedt, Anne, Ellen Levine, and Anita Rapone, eds. *Radical Feminism.* New York: Quadrangle, 1973.

Laclau, Ernesto, and Chantal Mouffe. *Hegemony and Socialist Strategy: Towards a Radical Democratic Politics.* London: Verso, 1989.

Mandell, Nancy. *Feminist Issues: Race, Class, and Sexuality.* Scarborough, Ontario: Prentice-Hall, 1995.

Mantilla, Karla. "Backlash and a *Feminism* That Is Contrary to *Feminism.*" *Off Our Backs* 37, no. 1 (2007): 58–61.

Napikoski, Linda. "New York Radical Women." Accessed April 14, 2012, http://womens history.about.com/od/feminism/a/new_york_radical_women.htm.

Rhodes, Jacqueline. *Radical Feminism, Writing, and Critical Agency.* New York: State University of New York Press, 2005.

Rowland, Robyn, and Renate D. Klein. "Radical Feminism: Critique and Construct." In *Feminist Knowledge: Critique and Construct,* edited by Sneja Guner. New York: Routledge, 1990.

Stanton, Elizabeth Cady. *The Woman's Bible.* 2 vols. 1895 and 1899. New York: Arno Press, 1972.

Stein, Arlene. *Shameless: Sexual Dissidence in American Culture.* New York: New York University Press, 2006.

Trebilcot, Joyce. "Conceiving Wisdom: Notes on the Logic of Feminism." *Sinister Wisdom* 3 (Fall 1979).

Whittier, Nancy. *Feminist Generations: The Persistence of the Radical Feminist Movement.* Philadelphia: Temple University Press, 1995.

Libertarian and Cultural Views on the Sex/Gender System

Azzoni, Elena. *A Year Straight: Confessions of a Boy-Crazy Lesbian Beauty Queen.* Berkeley: Seal Press, 2011.

Bartlett, Katherine T., and Rosanne Kennedy, eds. *Feminist Legal Theory: Readings in Law and Gender.* Oxford: Westview Press, 1991.

Calhoun, Cheshire. "Taking Seriously Dual Systems and Sex." *Hypatia* 13, no. 1 (Winter 1998): 224–231.

Daly, Mary. *Beyond God the Father: Toward a Philosophy of Women's Liberation.* Boston: Beacon Press, 1973.

———. *Gyn/Ecology: The Metaethics of Radical Feminism.* Boston: Beacon Press, 1978.

———. *Pure Lust: Elemental Feminist Philosophy.* Boston: Beacon Press, 1984.

Diamond, Morty, ed. *Trans/Love: Radical Sex, Love & Relationships Beyond the Gender Binary.* San Francisco: Manic D Press, 2011.

Dinnerstein, Dorothy. *The Mermaid and the Minotaur: Sexual Arrangements and Human Malaise.* New York: Harper Colophon Books, 1977.

Eisenstein, Hester. *Contemporary Feminist Thought.* Boston: G. K. Hall, 1983.

Eliot, Lise. *Pink Brain, Blue Brain: How Small Differences Grow into Troublesome Gaps—And What We Can Do About It.* New York: Houghton Mifflin Harcourt, 2009.

Firestone, Shulamith. *The Dialectic of Sex.* New York: Bantam Books, 1970.

French, Marilyn. *Beyond Power: On Women, Men, and Morals.* New York: Summit Books, 1985.

Friedan, Betty. *The Feminine Mystique.* New York: Dell, 1974.

Gilder, George. *Sexual Suicide.* New York: Quadrangle, 1973.

Halberstam, J. Jack. *Gaga Feminism: Sex, Gender, and the End of Normal.* Boston: Beacon Press, 2012.

Hoff Sommers, Christina. *The War Against Boys: How Misguided Feminism Is Harming Our Young Men.* New York: Simon & Schuster, 2001.

———. *Who Stole Feminism? How Women Have Betrayed Women.* New York: Simon & Schuster, 1995.

Jaggar, Alison M. *Feminist Politics and Human Nature.* Totowa, NJ: Rowman & Allanheld, 1983.

Miller, Henry. *Sexus.* New York: Grove Press, 1965.

Millett, Kate. *Sexual Politics.* Garden City, NY: Doubleday, 1970.

Nietzsche, Friedrich. *On the Genealogy of Morals.* Translated by Walter Kaufmann and R. Hollingdale. New York: Vintage Books, 1969.

O'Toole, Laura L., Jessica R. Schiffman, and Margie L. Kiter Edwards, eds. *Gender Violence: Interdisciplinary Perspectives.* New York: New York University Press, 2007.

Reeser, Todd. *Masculinities in Theory: An Introduction.* Chichester, UK: Wiley-Blackwell, 2010.

Roiphe, Katie. *The Morning After: Sex, Fear and Feminism.* Boston: Back Bay Books, 1994.

Rubin, Gayle. "The Traffic in Women." In *Toward an Anthropology of Women,* edited by Rayna R. Reiter. New York: Monthly Review Press, 1975.

Serano, Julia. *Whipping Girl: A Transsexual Woman on Sexism and the Scapegoating of Femininity.* Emeryville: Seal Press, 2007.

Soper, Kate. "Feminism, Humanism, and Postmodernism." *Radical Philosophy* 55 (Summer 1990): 11–17.

Vetterling-Braggin, Mary, ed., *"Femininity," "Masculinity," and "Androgyny."* Totowa, NJ: Rowman & Littlefield, 1982.

Women, Gender, and Philosophy. Special issue of *Radical Philosophy* 34 (Summer 1983).

Some Cultural Views on Gender

Daly, Mary. *Beyond God the Father: Toward a Philosophy of Women's Liberation.* Boston: Beacon Press, 1973.

———. *Gyn/Ecology: The Metaethics of Radical Feminism.* Boston: Beacon Press, 1978.

———. *Pure Lust: Elemental Feminist Philosophy.* Boston: Beacon Press, 1984.

French, Marilyn. *Beyond Power: On Women, Men and Morals.* New York: Summit Books, 1985.

Friedan, Betty. *The Feminine Mystique.* New York: Dell, 1974.

Jaggar, Alison M. *Feminist Politics and Human Nature.* Totowa, NJ: Rowman & Allanheld, 1983.

Morey-Gaines, Ann-Janine. "Metaphor and Radical Feminism: Some Cautionary Comments on Mary Daly's *Gyn/Ecology.*" *Soundings* 65, no. 3 (Fall 1982): 347–348.

Rossi, Alice. "Sex Equality: The Beginning of Ideology." In *Masculine/Feminine,* edited by Betty Roszak and Theodore Roszak. New York: Harper & Row, 1969.

Trebilcot, Joyce. "Conceiving Wisdom: Notes on the Logic of Feminism." *Sinister Wisdom* 3 (Fall 1979): 46.

Sexuality, Male Domination, and Female Subordination

Bacchi, Carol Lee. *Same Difference, Feminism and Sexual Difference.* North Sydney, NSW: Allen and Unwin, 1990.

Blumstein, Philip, and Pepper Schwartz. *American Couples.* New York: William Morrow, 1983.

Bushnell, Dana E., ed. *"Nagging" Questions: Feminist Ethics in Everyday Life.* Lanham, MD: Rowman & Littlefield, 1995.

Coward, Rosalind. *Patriarchal Precedents: Sexuality and Social Relations.* London: Routledge and Kegan Paul, 1983.

Dworkin, Andrea. *Letters from a War Zone.* Brooklyn, NY: Lawrence Hill Books, 1993.

———. *Our Blood: Prophecies and Discourses on Sexual Politics.* New York: G. Putnam, 1981.

———. *Right-Wing Women.* New York: Coward-McCann, 1983.

———. *Woman Hating: A Radical Look at Sexuality.* New York: E. Dutton, 1974.

Echols, Alice. "The Taming of the Id." In *Pleasure and Danger: Exploring Female Sexuality,* edited by Carole S. Vance. Boston: Routledge & Kegan Paul, 1984.

Epstein, Cynthia Fuchs. *A Woman's Place.* Berkeley: University of California Press, 1971.

Fahs, Breanne. *Performing Sex: The Making and Unmaking of Women's Erotic Lives.* Albany: State University of New York Press, 2011.

Fairchilds, Cissie. "Female Sexual Attitudes and the Rise of Illegitimacy: A Case Study." *Journal of Interdisciplinary History* 8, no. 4 (Spring 1978): 627–667.

Ferguson, Ann. "Sex War: The Debate Between Radical and Liberation Feminists." *Signs: Journal of Women in Culture and Society* 10, no. 1 (Autumn 1984): 109.

Frye, Marilyn. *The Politics of Reality: Essays in Feminist Theory.* Trumansburg, NY: Crossing Press, 1983.

Hegarty, Marilyn, E. *Victory Girls, Khaki-Wackies, and Patriotutes: The Regulation of Female Sexuality during World War II.* New York: New York University Press, 2008.

Herbst Lewis, Carolyn. *Prescription for Heterosexuality: Sexual Citizenship in the Cold War Era.* Chapel Hill: University of North Carolina Press, 2010.

Lee, Patrick C., and Robert Sussman Stewart, eds. *Sex Differences: Cultural and Developmental Dimensions.* New York: Urizen, 1976.

Linden, Robin Ruth, et al., eds. *Against Sadomasochism: A Radical Feminist Analysis.* East Palo Alto, CA: Frog in the Well Press, 1982.

Maccoby, Eleanor, ed. *The Development of Sex Differences.* Stanford, CA: Stanford University Press, 1966.

MacKinnon, Catharine A., ed. *Women's Lives, Men's Laws.* Cambridge, MA: Belknap Press of Harvard University Press, 2005.

Martin, Del. *Battered Wives.* New York: Pocket Books, 1976.

Parker, Katherine, and Lisa Leghorn. *Woman's Worth: Sexual Economics and the World of Women.* London: Routledge & Kegan Paul, 1981.

Redstockings, ed. *Feminist Revolution.* New York: Random House, 1975.

Rubin, Gayle. "Thinking Sex: Notes for a Radical Theory of the Politics of Sexuality." In *Pleasure and Danger: Exploring Female Sexuality,* Carole S. Vance. Boston: Routledge & Kegan Paul, 1984.

Schechter, Susan. *Women and Male Violence.* Boston: South End Press, 1982.

Shafer, Carolyn M., and Marilyn Frye. "Rape and Respect." In *Women and Values: Readings in Recent Feminist Philosophy,* edited by Marilyn Pearsall. Belmont, CA: Wadsworth, 1986.

Shulman, Alix Kates. "Sex and Power: Sexual Bases of Radical Feminism." *Signs: Journal of Women in Culture and Society* 5, no. 4 (Summer 1980): 590–604.

Smart, Carol, and Barry Smart, eds. *Women, Sexuality, and Social Control.* London: Routledge and Kegan Paul, 1978.

Spender, Dale. *Man Made Language.* Boston: Routledge & Kegan Paul, 1980.

Strossen, Nadine, ed. *Defending Pornography: Free Speech, Sex, and the Fight for Women's Rights.* New York: New York University Press, 2000.

Valenti, Jessica. *He's a Stud, She's a Slut, and 49 Other Double Standards Every Woman Should Know.* Berkeley: Seal Press, 2008.

———. *The Purity Myth: How America's Obsession with Virginity Is Hurting Young Women.* Berkeley: Seal Press, 2010.

Vance, Carole S., ed. *Pleasure and Danger: Exploring Female Sexuality.* Boston: Routledge & Kegan Paul, 1984.

Wakoski, Diane. *The Motorcycle Betrayal Poems.* New York: Simon & Schuster, 1971.

Weitz, Rose, ed. *The Politics of Women's Bodies: Sexuality, Appearance and Behavior.* New York: Oxford University Press, 1998.

The Pornography Debate

Assiter, Alison. *Pornography, Feminism, and the Individual.* London: Pluto Press, 1991.

Attwood, Feona. "Pornography and Objectification." *Feminist Media Studies* 4, no. 1 (March 2004): 7–19.

Berger, Ronald J., Patricia Searles, and Charles E. Cottle. *Feminism and Pornography.* New York: Praeger Publishers, 1991.

Blakely, Mary Kay. "Is One Woman's Sexuality Another Woman's Pornography?" *Ms.,* April 1985, 37–47.

Bronstein, Carolyn. *Battling Pornography: The American Feminist Anti-Pornography Movement, 1976–1986.* New York: Cambridge University Press, 2011.

Chancer, Lynn S. *Reconcilable Differences: Confronting Beauty, Pornography, and the Future of Feminism.* Berkeley: University of California Press, 1998.

Ciclitira, Karen. "Pornography, Women and Feminism: Between Pleasure and Politics." *Sexualities* 7, no. 3 (August 2004): 281–301.

Cornell, Drucilla. *Feminism and Pornography.* Oxford: Oxford University Press, 2000.

Donnerstein, Edward. *The Question of Pornography: Research Findings and Policy Implications.* New York: Free Press, 1987.

Dworkin, Andrea. "'Pornography's Exquisite Volunteers.'" *Ms.,* March 1981.

———. *Pornography: Men Possessing Women.* New York: Perigee Books, 1981.

English, Deirdre. "The Politics of Porn: Can Feminists Walk the Line?" *Mother Jones,* April 1980.

Griffin, Susan. *Pornography and Silence.* New York: Harper & Row, 1981.

———. *Rape: The Power of Consciousness.* San Francisco: Harper & Row, 1979.

Itzin, Catherine, ed. *Pornography: Women, Violence, and Civil Liberties.* Oxford: Oxford University Press, 1993.

KaeLyn. "Feminist Porn: Sex, Consent, and Getting Off." *Feminste* (July 23, 2008), accessed April 10, 2012.

Lederer, Laura, ed. *Take Back the Night: Women on Pornography.* New York: William Morrow, 1980.

Long, Julia. *Anti-Porn: The Resurgence of Anti-Pornography Feminism.* London: Zed Books, 2012.

MacKinnon, Catharine A. "Feminism, Marxism, Method, and the State: An Agenda for Theory." *Signs: Journal of Women in Culture and Society* 7, no. 3 (Spring 1982): 533.

———. "Francis Biddle's Sister: Pornography, Civil Rights, and Speech." In *Feminism Unmodified: Disclosures on Life and Law.* Cambridge: Harvard University Press, 1987.

Malamuth, Neil, and Edward Donnerstein. *Pornography and Sexual Aggression.* New York: Academic Press, 1984.

McCarthy, Sarah J. "Pornography, Rape, and the Cult of Macho." *Humanist* 40, no. 5 (September–October 1980): 11–20.

Newland, Laura. "Not for Sale: Feminists Resisting Prostitution and Pornography." *Off Our Backs* 35, no. 7 (August 2005): 30.

Rodgerson, Gillian, and Elizabeth Wilson, eds. *Pornography and Feminism: The Case Against Censorship.* London: Lawrence & Wishart, 1991.

Sabo, Anne. *After Pornified: How Women Are Transforming Pornography & Why It Really Matters.* Alresford, UK: Zero Books, 2012.

Segal, Lynne. *Sex Exposed: Sexuality and the Pornography Debate.* Piscataway, NJ: Rutgers University Press, 1993.

Soble, Alan. *Pornography: Marxism, Feminism, and the Future of Sexuality.* New Haven, CT: Yale University Press, 1986.

———. *Pornography, Sex, and Feminism.* Amherst, NY: Prometheus Books, 2002.

Strossen, Nadine. *Defending Pornography: Free Speech, Sex, and the Fight for Women's Rights.* New York: New York University Press, 2000.

Taylor, Stuart Jr. "Pornography Foes Lose New Weapons in Supreme Court." *New York Times,* February 25, 1986, 1.

Tyler, Meagan. *Selling Sex Short: The Pornographic and Sexological Construction of Women's Sexuality in the West.* Newcastle upon Tyne, UK: Cambridge Scholars Publishing, 2011.

The Lesbianism Controversy

Allen, Jeffner. *Lesbian Philosophy: Explorations.* Palo Alto: Institute of Lesbian Studies, 1986.

Atkinson, Ti-Grace. *Amazon Odyssey.* New York: Links, 1974.

———. "Lesbianism and Feminism." In *Amazon Expedition: A Lesbian-Feminist Anthology,* edited by Phyllis Birkby et al. Washington, NJ: Times Change Press, 1973.

———. "Radical Feminism: A Declaration of War." In *Women and Values: Readings in Recent Feminist Philosophy,* edited by Marilyn Pearsall. Belmont, CA: Wadsworth, 1986.

Bar On, Bat-Ami. "The Feminist Sexuality Debates and the Transformation of the Political." *Hypatia* 7, no. 4 (Fall 1992): 49.

Beck, Evelyn Torton, ed. *Nice Jewish Girls: A Lesbian Anthology.* Watertown, MA: Persephone Press, 1982.

Brandt, Eric, ed. *Dangerous Liaisons: Blacks, Gays, and the Struggle for Equality.* New York: New Press, 1999.

Bulkin, Elly, Minnie Bruce Pratt, and Barbara Smith. *Yours in Struggle: Three Feminist Perspectives on Anti-Semitism and Racism.* New York: Long Haul Press, 1984.

Califia, Pat. "Feminism and Sadomasochism." *Co-evolution Quarterly* 33 (Spring 1981).

———. *Sapphistry: The Book of Lesbian Sexuality.* Tallahassee, FL: Naiad Press, 1983.

Card, Claudia, ed. *Adventures in Lesbian Philosophy.* Bloomington: Indiana University Press, 1994.

———. "Radicalesbianfeminist Theory." *Hypatia* 13, no. 1 (1998): 206–213.

Ciasullo, Ann M. "Making Her (In)Visible: Cultural Representations of Lesbianism and the Lesbian Body in the 1990s." *Feminist Studies* 27, no. 3 (Fall 2001): 577.

Clarke, Cheryl. "Being Pro-Gay and Pro-Lesbian in Straight Institutions." *Journal of Gay and Lesbian Social Services* 3, no. 2. (1995): 95–100.

———. "Knowing the Danger and Going There Anyway." *Sojourner: The Women's Forum* 16, no. 1 (1990): 14–15.

Cole, Johnnetta Betsch, and Beverly Guy-Sheftall. "Black, Lesbian, and Gay: Speaking the Unspeakable." In *Gender Talk: The Struggle for Women's Equality in African American Communities.* New York: One World Ballantine Books, 2003.

Cuomo, Chris J. "Thoughts on Lesbian Differences." *Hypatia* 13, no. 1 (1998): 198–205.

Daly, Meg. *Surface Tension: Love, Sex, and Politics Between Lesbians and Straight Women.* New York: Simon & Schuster, 1996.

Ettorre, E. M. *Lesbians, Women, and Society.* London: Routledge and Kegan Paul, 1980.

Faderman, Lillian. *Odd Girls and Twilight Lovers: A History of Lesbian Life in Twentieth-Century America.* New York: Columbia University Press, 1991.

Frye, Marilyn. "Do You Have to Be a Lesbian to Be a Feminist?" *Off Our Backs* 20, no. 8 (September 30, 1990): 21.

———. *Willful Virgin: Essays in Feminism, 1976–1992.* Freedom, CA: Crossing Press, 1992.

Fuss, Diane, ed. *Inside/Out: Lesbian Theories, Gay Theories.* London: Routledge, 1991.

Goodman, Gerre, et al. *No Turning Back: Lesbian and Gay Liberation for the '80s.* Philadelphia: New Society Publishers, 1983.

Grier, Barbara, and Coletta Reid, eds. *The Lavender Herring: Lesbian Essays from "The Ladder."* Baltimore: Diana Press, 1976.

Harne, Lynne, and Elaine Miller, eds., *All the Rage: Reasserting Radical Lesbian Feminism.* London: Women's Press, 1996.

Harris, Laura, and Elizabeth Crocker, eds. *Femme: Feminists, Lesbians, and Bad Girls.* New York: Routledge, 1997.

Hawthorne, Susan. "The Depoliticising of Lesbian Culture." *Hecate* 29, no. 2 (2003): 235.

Heller, Dana, ed. *Cross-Purposes: Lesbians, Feminists, and the Limits of Alliance.* Bloomington: Indiana University Press, 1997.

Jeffreys, Sheila. *The Lesbian Heresy: A Feminist Perspective on the Lesbian Sexual Revolution.* North Melbourne, Australia: Spinifex, 1993.

Johnston, Jill. *Lesbian Nation: The Feminist Solution.* New York: Simon & Schuster, 1974.

Kleindienst, Kris, ed. *This Is What a Lesbian Looks Like.* Ithaca, NY: Firebrand Books, 1999.

Koedt, Anne. "The Myth of the Vaginal Orgasm." *Notes from the Second Year: Women's Liberation—Major Writings of the Radical Feminists,* April 1970. Available at many websites, including http://www.uic.edu/orgs/cwluherstory/CWLUArchive/vaginal myth.html.

Laner, Mary R., and Roy H. Laner. "Sexual Preference or Personal Style? Why Lesbians Are Disliked." *Journal of Homosexuality* 5, no. 4 (1980): 339–356.

Law, Sylvia. "Homosexuality and the Social Meaning of Gender." *Wisconsin Law Review* 2 (1988): 187–235.

Marinucci, Mimi. *Feminism Is Queer: The Intimate Connection Between Queer and Feminist Theory.* London: Zed Books, 2010.

Mohin, Lilian, ed. *An Intimacy of Equals: Lesbian Feminist Ethics.* New York: Harrington Park Press, 1996.

Morland, Iain, and Annabelle Willox, eds. *Queer Theory.* Houndmills, Basingstoke, Hampshire, UK; New York: Palgrave Macmillan, 2005.

Myron, Nancy, and Charlotte Bunch, eds. *Lesbianism and the Women's Movement.* Baltimore: Diana, 1975.

Nestle, Joan. *Persistent Desire: A Butch-Femme Reader.* Boston: Alyson Publications, 1992.

"New York Covens' Leaflet." In *Sisterhood Is Powerful,* edited by Robin Morgan. New York: Random House, 1970.

Phelan, Shane. *Identity Politics: Lesbian Feminism and the Limits of Community.* Philadelphia: Temple University Press, 1989.

Redstockings Manifesto. In *Sisterhood Is Powerful,* edited by Robin Morgan. New York: Random House, 1970.

Rich, Adrienne. "Compulsory Heterosexuality and Lesbian Existence." In *Living with Contradictions: Controversies in Feminist Social Ethics,* edited by Alison M. Jaggar. Boulder, CO: Westview Press, 1994.

Rule, Jane. *Lesbian Images.* Trumansburg, NY: Crossing Press, 1982.

Samois. *Coming to Power: Writings and Graphics on Lesbian S/M.* Palo Alto: Up Press, 1981.

Shugar, Dana R. *Separatism and Women's Community.* Lincoln: University of Nebraska Press, 1995.

Stein, Arlene. *Shameless: Sexual Dissidence in American Culture.* New York: New York University Press, 2006.

———, ed. *Sisters, Sexperts, Queers: Beyond the Lesbian Nation.* New York: Plume, 1993.

Tanner, Donna K. *The Lesbian Couple.* Lexington, MA: Lexington Books, 1978.

Valk, Anne M. "Living a Feminist Lifestyle: The Intersection of Theory and Action in a Lesbian Feminist Collective." *Feminist Studies* 28, no. 2 (2002): 303.

Weed, Elizabeth, and Naomi Schor, eds. *Feminism Meets Queer Theory.* Bloomington: Indiana University Press, 1997.

Weise, Elizabeth Reba, ed. *Closer to Home: Bisexuality & Feminism.* Seattle: Seal Press, 1992.

Wolf, Sherry. *Sexuality and Socialism: History, Politics, and Theory of LGBT Liberation.* Chicago: Haymarket Books, 2009.

Reproduction, Men, and Women

Adams, Alice. *Reproducing the Womb: Images of Childbirth in Science, Feminist Theory, and Literature.* Ithaca and London: Cornell University Press, 1994.

Atwood, Margaret. *The Handmaid's Tale.* New York: Fawcett Crest Books, 1985.

Baruch, Elaine, Amadeo D'Adamo, and Joni Seager, eds. *Embryos, Ethics and Women's Rights: Exploring the New Reproductive Technologies.* New York: Harrington Park Press, 1988.

Cohen, Cynthia B. "'Give Me Children or I Shall Die!' New Reproductive Technologies and Harm to Children." *The Hastings Center Report* 26 (1996).

Colb, Sherry F. *When Sex Counts: Making Babies and Making Law.* Lanham, MD: Rowman & Littlefield, 2007.

Corea, Gena. "Egg Snatchers." In *Test-Tube Women: What Future for Motherhood?*, edited by Rita Arditti, Renate Duelli Klein, and Shelley Minden. London: Pandora Press, 1984.

———. *The Mother Machine: Reproduction Technologies from Artificial Insemination to Artificial Wombs.* New York: Harper & Row, 1985.

Craven, Christa. *Pushing for Midwives: Homebirth Mothers and the Reproductive Rights Movement.* Philadelphia: Temple University Press, 2010.

Crossley, Mary. "Dimensions of Equality in Regulating Assisted Reproductive Technologies." *Journal of Gender, Race, and Justice* 9, no. 2 (Winter 2005): 273.

Donchin, Anne. "The Future of Mothering: Reproductive Technology and Feminist Theory." *Hypatia* 1, no. 2 (Fall 1986): 131.

Dresser, Rebecca. "Regulating Assisted Reproduction." *The Hastings Center Report* 30 (2000).

Dworkin, Andrea. *Right-Wing Women.* New York: Coward-McCann, 1983.

Firestone, Shulamith. *The Dialectic of Sex.* New York: Bantam Books, 1970.

Goldberg, Michelle. *The Means of Reproduction: Sex, Power, and the Future of the World.* New York: Penguin Press, 2009.

Goodwin, Michele. "Assisted Reproductive Technology and the Double Bind: The Illusory Choice of Motherhood." *Journal of Gender, Race, and Justice* 9, no. 1 (Fall 2005): 1–55.

Goslinga-Roy, Gillian M. "Body Boundaries, Fiction of the Female Self: An Ethnographic Perspective on Power, Feminism, and the Reproductive Technologies." *Feminist Studies* 26, no. 1 (Spring 2000): 113–141.

Ketchum, Sara Ann. "Selling Babies and Selling Bodies." In *Feminist Perspectives in Medical Ethics*, edited by Helen Holmes and Laura M. Purdy. Bloomington: Indiana University Press, 1992.

Makus, Ingrid. *Women, Politics, and Reproduction: The Liberal Legacy.* Toronto: University of Toronto Press, 1996.

Mellown, Mary Ruth. "An Incomplete Picture: The Debate About Surrogate Motherhood." *Harvard Women's Law Journal* 8 (Spring 1985): 231–246.

Moore, Lisa Jean. *Sperm Counts: Overcome by Man's Most Precious Fluid.* New York: New York University Press, 2007.

Mundy, Liza. *Everything Conceivable: How Assisted Reproduction Is Changing Men, Women, and the World.* New York: Alfred Knopf, 2007.

Naff, Clay Farris, ed. *Reproductive Technology.* Farmington Hills, MI: Greenhaven Press, 2006.

O'Brien, Mary. *The Politics of Reproduction.* Boston: Routledge & Kegan Paul, 1981.

Overall, Christine. "Access to In Vitro Fertilization: Costs, Care and Consent." *Dialogue* 30 (1991): 383–398.

———. *Ethics and Human Reproduction: A Feminist Analysis.* Boston: Allen & Unwin, 1987.

———. *Feminist Perspectives: Philosophical Essays on Method and Morals.* Toronto: University of Toronto Press, 1988.

———. *Human Reproduction: Principles, Practices, Policies.* New York: Oxford University Press, 1993.

Parks, Jennifer. "Rethinking Radical Politics in the Context of Assisted Reproductive Technology." *Bioethics* 23, no. 1 (2009): 20–27.

Purdy, Laura. *Reproducing Persons: Issues in Feminist Bioethics.* Ithaca, NY: Cornell University Press, 1996.

Raymond, Janice. *Women as Wombs: Reproductive Technologies and the Battle over Women's Freedom.* San Francisco: Harper & Row, 1993.

Rodin, Judith, and Aila Collins, eds. *Women and New Reproductive Technologies: Medical, Psychosocial, Legal and Ethical Dilemmas.* Hillside, NJ: Lawrence Erlbaum Associates, 1991.

Rowland, Robyn. "Reproductive Technologies: The Final Solution to the Woman Question." In *Test-Tube Women: What Future for Motherhood?,* edited by Rita Arditti, Renate Duelli Klein, and Shelley Minden. London: Pandora Press, 1984.

Sherwin, Susan. *No Longer Patient: Feminist Ethics and Health Care.* Philadelphia: Temple University Press, 1992.

Solinger, Rickie. *Pregnancy and Power: A Short History of Reproductive Politics in America.* New York: New York University Press, 2005.

"A Surrogate's Story of Loving and Losing." *U.S. News & World Report,* June 6, 1983, 12.

Tong, Rosemarie. *Feminist Approaches to Bioethics.* Boulder, CO: Westview Press, 1997.

Wolf, Susan, ed. *Feminism and Bioethics: Beyond Reproduction.* Oxford: Oxford University Press, 1996.

Radical-Libertarian and Radical-Cultural Views on Mothering

Allen, Jeffner. "Motherhood: The Annihilation of Women." In *Women and Values: Readings in Recent Feminist Philosophy,* edited by Marilyn Pearsall. Belmont, CA: Wadsworth, 1986.

Alpert, Jane. "Mother Right: A New Feminist Theory." *Ms.,* August 1973.

Atwood, Margaret. *The Handmaid's Tale.* New York: Fawcett Crest Books, 1985.

Badinter, Elisabeth. *The Conflict: How Modern Motherhood Undermines the Status of Women.* New York: Metropolitan Books, 2010.

Blades, Joan, and Kristin Rowe-Finkbeiner. *The Motherhood Manifesto: What American Moms Want—And What to Do About It.* New York: Nation Books, 2006.

Blank, Robert H. *Mother and Fetus: Changing Notions of Maternal Responsibility.* New York: Greenwood Press, 1992.

Brakman, Sarah-Vaughan, and Sally J. Scholz. "Adoption, ART, and a Re-Conception of the Maternal Body: Toward Embodied Maternity." *Hypatia* 21, no. 1 (Winter 2006): 54–77.

Brison, Susan J. "Contentious Freedom: Sex Work and Social Construction." *Hypatia* 21, no. 4 (Fall 2006): 192–200.

Brown, Ivana. "Mommy Memoirs: Feminism, Gender and Motherhood in Popular Literature." *Journal of the Association for Research on Mothering* 8, nos. 1 and 2 (September 2006).

Cahill, Susan, ed. *Motherhood.* New York: Avon Books, 1982.

Chesler, Phyllis. *Sacred Bond: The Legacy of Baby M.* New York: Times Books, 1988.

Chodorow, Nancy. *The Reproduction of Mothering.* Berkeley: University of California Press, 1978.

Crittenden, Anne. *The Price of Motherhood: Why the Most Important Job in the World Is the Least Valued.* London: Metropolitan Books, 2001.

DiQuinzio, Patrice. *The Impossibility of Motherhood: Feminism, Individualism, and the Problem of Mothering.* New York: Routledge, 1999.

———. "The Politics of the Mothers' Movement in the United States: Possibilities and Pitfalls." *Journal of the Association for Research on Mothering* 8, nos. 1 and 2 (September 2006).

———. "Reconceiving Pregnancy and Childcare: Ethics, Experience, and Reproductive Labor." *Hypatia* 22, no. 3 (Summer 2007): 204.

Dworkin, Andrea. *Right-Wing Women.* New York: Coward-McCann, 1983.

Ehrenreich, Barbara, and Deirdre English. *For Her Own Good.* New York: Anchor/Doubleday, 1979.

Ferguson, Ann. *Blood at the Root: Motherhood, Sexuality, and Male Dominance.* London: Pandora Press, 1989.

———. "Motherhood and Sexuality: Some Feminist Questions." *Hypatia* 1, no. 2 (Fall 1986): 3–22.

Folbre, Nancy. *The Invisible Heart: Economics and Family Values.* New York: New Press, 2001.

Green, Fiona Joy. "Developing a Feminist Motherline: Reflections on a Decade of Feminist Parenting." *Journal of the Association for Research on Mothering* 8, nos. 1 and 2 (September 2006).

Hattery, Angela. *Women, Work and Family: Balancing and Weaving.* Thousand Oaks, CA: Sage Publications, 2001.

Hewett, Heather. "Talkin' Bout a Revolution: Building a Mothers' Movement in the Third World." *Journal of the Association for Research on Mothering* 8, nos. 1 and 2 (September 2006).

Jaggar, Alison M. *Feminist Politics and Human Nature.* Totowa, NJ: Rowman & Allanheld, 1983.

Kinser, Amber E. *Feminism and Mothering.* Berkeley: Seal Press, 2010.

Lintott, Sheila, and Maureen Sander-Staudt, eds. *Philosophical Inquiries into Pregnancy, Childbirth, and Mothering: Maternal Subjects.* New York: Routledge, 2012.

Mahowald, Mary Briody. *Women and Children in Health Care: An Unequal Majority.* New York: Oxford University Press, 1993.

Mendell, Betty Reid. *Where Are the Children? A Close Analysis of Foster Care and Adoption.* Lexington, MA: Lexington Books, 1973.

Middleton, Amy. "Mothering Under Duress: Examining the Inclusiveness of Feminist Mothering Theory." *The Journal of the Association for Research on Mothering* 8, nos. 1 and 2 (September 2006).

Oakley, Ann. *Woman's Work: The Housewife, Past and Present.* New York: Pantheon Books, 1974.

O'Beirne, Kate. *Women Who Make the World Worse: And How Their Radical Feminist Assault Is Ruining Our Families, Military, Schools, and Sports.* New York: Sentinel, 2006.

Piercy, Marge. *Woman on the Edge of Time.* New York: Fawcett Crest Books, 1976.

Purdy, Laura. *In Their Best Interest? The Case Against Equal Rights for Children.* Ithaca, NY: Cornell University Press, 1992.

Rich, Adrienne. *Of Woman Born.* New York: W. W. Norton, 1979.

Ruddick, Sara. "Maternal Thinking." In *Mothering,* edited by Joyce Trebilcot. Totowa, NJ: Rowman & Allanheld, 1984.

Trebilcot, Joyce, ed. *Mothering: Essays in Feminist Theory.* Totowa, NJ: Rowman & Allanheld, 1984.

Wilson, Leslie, et al. "'She Could Be Anything She Wants to Be': Mothers and Daughters and Feminist Theory." *Journal of the Association for Research on Mothering* 8, nos. 1 and 2 (September 2006).

Critiques of Radical-Libertarian and Radical-Cultural Feminism: Beyond Polarization

Ferguson, Ann. "The Sex Debate in the Women's Movement: A Socialist-Feminist View." *Against the Current* (September/October 1983): 12.

Conclusion

Thompson, Denise. *Radical Feminism Today.* London: Sage Publishing, 2001.

Chapter 3: Marxist and Socialist Feminism: Classical and Contemporary

Holmstrom, Nancy. "The Socialist Feminist Project." *Monthly Review Press* 54, no. 10 (2002): 1.

Marx, Karl. *Capital.* Vol. 3. New York: International Publishers, 1967.

Some Marxist Concepts and Theories

Acton, Henry Burrows. *What Marx Really Said.* London: MacDonald, 1967.

Anderson, Kevin. *Marx at the Margins: On Nationalism, Ethnicity, and Non-Western Societies.* Chicago: University of Chicago Press, 2010.

Benston, Margaret. "The Political Economy of Women's Liberation." *Monthly Review* 21, no. 4 (September 1969): 13–27.

Buchanan, Allen. *Marx and Justice: The Radical Critique of Liberalism.* Totowa, NJ: Littlefield, Adams, 1972.

Engels, Friedrich. *The Origin of the Family, Private Property and the State.* New York: International Publishers, 1972.

Fine, Ben, Alfredo Saad-Filho, and Marco Buffo, eds. *The Elgar Companion to Marxist Economics.* Elgar Original Reference. Cheltenham, UK: Edward Elgar Publishing Limited, 2012.

Flax, Jane. "Do Feminists Need Marxism?" In *Building Feminist Theory: Essays from "Quest," a Feminist Quarterly.* New York: Longman, 1981.

Foreman, Ann. *Femininity as Alienation: Women and the Family in Marxism and Psychoanalysis.* London: Pluto Press, 1977.

Harding, Sandra. "Two Influential Theories of Ignorance and Philosophy's Interests in Ignoring Them." *Hypatia* 21, no. 3 (Summer 2006): 20–36.

Harvey, David. *A Companion to Marx's* Capital. London: Verso, 2010.

Heilbroner, Robert L. *Marxism: For and Against.* New York: W. W. Norton, 1980.

Holmstrom, Nancy. "A Marxist Theory of Women's Nature." *Ethics* 94, no. 1 (April 1984): 464.

Kruks, Sonia. *Situation and Human Existence: Freedom, Subjectivity and Society.* New York: Routledge, 1990.

Kuhn, Annette, and Ann Marie Wolpe, eds. *Feminism and Materialism: Women and Modes of Production.* Boston: Routledge & Kegan Paul, 1978.

Lane, Ann J. "Woman in Society: A Critique of Friedrich Engels." In *Liberating Women's History,* edited by Berenice A. Carroll. Champaign: University of Illinois Press, 1976.

Mandel, Ernest. *An Introduction to Marxist Economic Theory.* New York: Pathfinder Press, 1970.

Marx, Karl. *The 18th Brumaire of Louis Bonaparte.* New York: International Publishers, 1968.

———. *Capital.* Vol. 3. New York: International Publishers, 1967.

———. *A Contribution to the Critique of Political Economy.* New York: International Publishers, 1972.

———. "Economic and Philosophic Manuscripts." In *Early Writings,* translated and edited by T. B. Bottomore. New York: McGraw-Hill, 1964.

———. *Grundrisse: Foundations of the Critique of Political Economy,* translated and edited by T. B. Bottomore. New York: Vintage Books, 1973.

Marx, Karl, and Friedrich Engels. *The German Ideology.* In *The Marx-Engels Reader,* translated and edited by Robert C. Tucker. New York: W. W. Norton, 1978.

McLellan, David. *Karl Marx.* New York: Penguin Books, 1975.

Millett, Kate. *Sexual Politics.* New York: Ballantine Books, 1969.

Oakley, Ann. *Sex, Gender, and Society.* London: Temple Smith, 1972.

Quick, Paddy. "The Class Nature of Women's Oppression." *Review of Radical Political Economics* 9, no. 3 (Winter 1977): 42–53.

Reed, Evelyn. *Problems of Woman's Liberation.* New York: Pathfinder Press, 1970.

Sacks, Karen. "Engels Revisited: Women, the Organization of Production and Private Property." In *Toward an Anthropology of Women,* edited by Rayna R. Reiter. New York: Monthly Review Press, 1975.

Saffiote, Heleieth I. B. *Women in Class Society.* Translated by Michael Vale. New York: Monthly Review Press, 1978.

Schmitt, Richard. *Introduction to Marx and Engels.* Boulder, CO: Westview Press, 1987.

Slaughter, Cliff. *Marx and Marxism: An Introduction.* New York: Longman, 1985.

Suchting, Wallis Arthur. *Marx: An Introduction.* New York: New York University Press, 1983.

Tabak, Mehmet. *Dialectics of Human Nature in Marx's Philosophy.* New York: Palgrave Macmillan, 2012.

Vogel, Lise. *Marxism and the Oppression of Women: Towards a Unitary Theory.* New Brunswick, NJ: Rutgers University Press, 1983.

Wood, Allen W. *Karl Marx.* London: Routledge & Kegan Paul, 1981.

Classical Marxist Feminism: General Reflections

Barrett, Michèle, and Mary McIntosh. "The Family Wage: Some Problems for Socialists and Feminists." *Capital and Class* 2 (1980): 51–57.

Beechey, Veronica. "Some Notes on Female Wage Labour in Capitalist Production." *Capital and Class* 3 (Autumn 1977): 45–66.

Bergmann, Barbara. *The Economic Emergence of Women.* New York: Basic Books, 1986: 212.

Boserup, Ester. *Women's Role in Economic Development.* London: George Allen and Unwin, 1970.

Boxer, Marilyn J. "Rethinking the Socialist Construction and International Career of the Concept 'Bourgeois Feminism.'" *American Historical Review* 112, no. 1 (February 2007): 131–158.

Braudel, Fernand. *Capitalism and Material Life 1400–1800.* Translated by Miriam Kochan. New York: Harper & Row, 1973.

Collins, Jane L., and Victoria Mayer. *Both Hands Tied: Welfare Reform and the Race to the Bottom in the Low-Wage Labor Market.* Chicago: University of Chicago Press, 2012.

Coulson, Margaret, Branka Magaš, and Hilary Wainwright. "'The Housewife and Her Labour Under Capitalism': A Critique." *New Left Review* 89 (January–February 1975): 59–71.

Cowan, Ruth Schwartz. "The 'Industrial Revolution' in the Home: Household Technology and Social Change in the Twentieth Century." *Technology and Culture* 17, no. 1 (1976): 1–23.

Dalla Costa, Mariarosa. "A General Strike." In *All Work and No Pay,* edited by Wendy Edmond and Suzie Fleming. London: Power of Women Collective and Falling Wall Press, 1975.

Dalla Costa, Mariarosa, and Selma James. *The Power of Women and the Subversion of Community.* Bristol, England: Falling Wall Press, 1972.

Davin, Delia. *Woman-Work: Women and the Party in Revolutionary China.* Oxford: Clarendon Press, 1976.

Edmond, Wendy, and Suzie Fleming. "If Women Were Paid for All They Do." In *All Work and No Pay,* edited by Wendy Edmond and Suzie Fleming. London: Power of Women Collective and Falling Wall Press, 1975.

Ferguson, Ann. "The Che-Lumumba School: Creating a Revolutionary Family-Community." *Quest* 5, no. 3 (February–March 1980).

Freedman, Estelle. *No Turning Back: The History of Feminism and the Future of Women.* New York: Ballantine Books, 2002.

Garson, Barbara. *All the Livelong Day: The Meaning and Demeaning of Routine Work.* New York: Penguin Books, 1975.

Gerstein, Ira. "Domestic Work and Capitalism." *Radical America* 7, nos. 4–5 (July–October 1973): 101–128.

Glazer-Malbin, Nona. "Housework." *Signs: Journal of Women in Culture and Society* 1, no. 4 (1976): 905–922.

Gordon, David M., Richard Edwards, and Michael Reich. *Segmented Work, Divided Workers.* New York: Cambridge University Press, 1982.

Gottfried, Paul Edward. *The Strange Death of Marxism.* Columbia: University of Missouri Press, 2005.

Guettel, Charnie. *Marxism and Feminism.* Toronto: Women's Education Press, 1974.

Hartmann, Heidi I. "The Family as the Locus of Gender, Class, and Political Struggle: The Example of Housework." *Signs: Journal of Women in Culture and Society* 6, no. 3 (1981): 366–394.

Jackson, Stevi. "Marxism and Feminism." In *Marxism and Social Science,* edited by Andrew Gamble, David Marsh, and Tony Tant, 17. Champaign: University of Illinois Press, 1999.

———. "Towards a Historical Sociology of Housework." *Women's Studies International Forum* 15, no. 2 (1992): 153–172.

Kaluzynska, Eva. "Wiping the Floor with Theory: A Survey of Writings on Housework." *Feminist Review* 6 (1980): 27–54.

Lenin, V. I. *The Emancipation of Women: From the Writings of V. I. Lenin.* New York: International Publishers, 1934.

Levine, Rhonda, ed. *Social Class and Stratification: Classic Statements and Theoretical Debates.* Lanham, MD: Rowman and Littlefield, 2006.

MacKinnon, Catharine A. "Feminism, Marxism, Method, and the State: An Agenda for Theory." *Signs: Journal of Women in Culture and Society* 7, no. 3 (Spring 1982): 515–545.

Malos, Ellen, ed. *The Politics of Housework.* London: Allison & Busby, 1980.

McDuffie, Eric. *Sojourning for Freedom: Black Women, American Communism, and the Making of Black Left Feminism.* Durham: Duke University Press, 2011.

Mitterauer, Michael, and Reinhard Sieder. *The European Family: Patriarchy to Partnership from the Middle Ages to the Present.* Translated by Karla Oosterveen and Manfred Horzinger. Oxford: Blackwell, 1982.

Molyneux, Maxine. "Beyond the Domestic Labour Debate." *New Left Review* 116 (July–August 1979): 3–27.

Nicholson, Linda J. *Gender and History: The Limits of Social Theory in the Age of the Family.* New York: Columbia University Press, 1986.

Reed, Evelyn. "Women: Caste, Class, or Oppressed Sex?" *International Socialist Review* 31, no. 3 (September 1970): 15–17 and 40–41.

Rosenberg, Charles E., ed. *The Family in History.* Philadelphia: University of Pennsylvania Press, 1975.

Scott, Anne Crittenden. "The Value of Housework for Love or Money?" *Ms.,* June 1972, 56–58.

Scott, Linda M. "Market Feminism: The Case for a Paradigm Shift." *Advertising & Society Review* 7, no. 2 (2006).

Secombe, Wally. "The Housewife and Her Labour Under Capitalism." *New Left Review* 83 (January–February 1973): 3–24.

Sharpless, Rebecca. *Cooking in Other Women's Kitchens: Domestic Workers in the South, 1865–1960.* Durham: University of North Carolina Press, 2010.

Tilly, Louise A., and Joan W. Scott. *Women, Work, and Family.* New York: Holt, Rinehart and Winston, 1978.

US Department of Labor. *Employment Standards Administration Wage and Hour Division.* January 1, 2007. Available at http://www.dol.gov/esa/minwage/america.htm#content.

Voronina, Olga. "Soviet Patriarchy: Past and Present." *Hypatia* 8, no. 4 (Fall 1993): 107.

Walby, Sylvia. *Patriarchy at Work.* Cambridge: Polity Press, 1986.

———. "Policy Developments for Workplace Gender Equity in a Global Era: The Importance of the EU in the UK." *Review of Policy Research* 20, no. 1 (Spring 2003): 45.

Waters, Mary-Alice. *Feminism and the Marxist Movement.* New York: Pathfinder Press, 1994.

Webster, Bruce H. Jr., and Alemayehu Bishaw. *Income, Earnings, and Poverty Data from the 2005 American Community Survey: American Community Survey Reports.* US Census Bureau, American Community Survey Reports, ACS–02. Washington, DC: US Government Printing Office, August 2006. Available at htto://www.census.gov/prod/2006pubs/acs-02.pdf, 7.

Weeks, Kathi. *The Problem with Work: Feminism, Marxism, Antiwork Politics, and Postwork Imaginaries.* Durham: Duke University Press, 2011.

Weigand, Kate. *Red Feminism: American Communism and the Making of Women's Liberation.* Baltimore: Johns Hopkins University Press, 2001.

Wolton, Suke, ed. *Marxism, Mysticism, and Modern Theory.* New York: St. Martin's Press, 1996.

Wright, Erik Olin. "Explanation and Emancipation in Marxism and Feminism." *Sociological Theory* 11, no. 1 (March 1993): 39–54.

Contemporary Socialist Feminism: General Reflections

Alaimo, Stacy, and Susan Hekman, eds. *Material Feminisms.* Bloomington: Indiana University Press, 2008.

Anyon, Jean. "The Retread of Marxism and Socialist Feminism: Postmodern and Poststructural Theories in Education." *Curriculum Inquiry* 24, no. 2 (Summer 1994): 115–133.

Barrett, Michèle. *Women's Oppression Today: Problems in Marxist Feminist Analysis.* London: Verso and New Left Books, 1980.

———. "Words and Things: Materialism and Method in Contemporary Feminist Analysis." In *Destabilizing Theory: Contemporary Feminist Debates,* edited by Michèle Barrett and Anne Phillips. Cambridge: Polity Press, 1992.

Bartky, Sandra L. *Femininity and Domination.* New York: Routledge, 1990.

———. "Narcissism, Femininity and Alienation." *Social Theory and Practice* 8, no. 2 (Summer 1982): 127–144.

———. "On Psychological Oppression." In *Philosophy and Women,* edited by Sharon Bishop and Marjorie Weinzweig. Belmont, CA: Wadsworth, 1979.

Beasley, Chris. *What Is Feminism?* London: Sage Publications, 1999.

Beneria, Lourdes. "Capitalism and Socialism: Some Feminist Questions." In *The Women, Gender, and Development Reader,* edited by Visanthan Nalini et al. Atlantic Highlands, NJ: Zed Books, 1997.

Bennett, Judith M. *History Matters: Patriarchy and the Challenge of Feminism.* Philadelphia: University of Pennsylvania Press, 2006.

Berch, Bettina. *The Endless Day: The Political Economy of Women and Work.* New York: Harcourt Brace Jovanovich, 1982.

Bureau of Labor Statistics, US Department of Labor. "Median Weekly Earnings of Full-Time Wage and Salary Workers by Detailed Occupation and Sex." January 2006. Available at ftp://ftp.bls.gov/pub/special.requests/lf/aat39.txt.

Coward, Rosalind, and John Ellis. *Language and Materialism.* London: Routledge & Kegan Paul, 1977.

Delphy, Christine. *Close to Home: A Materialist Analysis of Women's Oppression,* translated and edited by Diana Leonard. London: Hutchinson, 1984.

Delphy, Christine, and Diana Leonard. *Familiar Exploitation: A New Analysis of Marriage in Contemporary Western Societies.* Cambridge: Polity Press, 1992.

Eisenstein, Zillah, ed. *Capitalist Patriarchy and the Case for Socialist Feminism.* New York: Monthly Review Press, 1979.

Ferree, Myra Marx. "Patriarchies and Feminisms: Two Women's Movements in Post-Unification Germany." *Social Politics* (Spring 1995): 10–24.

———. *Varieties of Feminism: German Gender Politics in Global Perspective.* Stanford: Stanford University Press, 2012.

Friedman, Marilyn. "Nancy J. Hirschmann on the Social Construction of Women's Freedom." *Hypatia* 21, no. 4 (Fall 2006): 182–191.

Funk, Nanette, and Magda Mueller, eds. *Gender Politics and Post Communism.* New York: Routledge, 1993.

Gal, Susan, and Gail, Kligman. *The Politics of Gender after Socialism.* Princeton, NJ: Princeton University Press, 2000.

———, eds. *Reproducing Gender: Politics, Publics, and Everyday Life After Socialism.* Princeton, NJ: Princeton University Press, 2000.

Gimenez, Martha E. "What's Material About Materialist Feminism? A Marxist Feminist Critique." *Radical Philosophy* (May/June 2000).

Goertz, Gary. *Politics, Gender, and Concepts: Theory and Methodology.* Cambridge: Cambridge University Press, 2008.

Graff, E. J. "The Opt-Out Myth." *Columbia Journalism Review* (March/April 2007). Available at http://www.cjr.org/essay/the_optout_myth.php?page-all.

Guenther, Katja M. "'A Bastion of Sanity in a Crazy World:' A Local Feminist Movement and the Reconstitution of Scale, Space, and Place in an Eastern German City." *Advance Access* (Winter 2006): 551–575.

Hartmann, Heidi I. "Capitalism, Patriarchy, and Job Segregation by Sex." In *Capitalist Patriarchy and the Case for Socialist Feminism,* edited by Zillah Eisenstein. New York: Monthly Review Press, 1979.

———. "The Unhappy Marriage of Marxism and Feminism: Towards a More Progressive Union." In *Women and Revolution: A Discussion of the Unhappy Marriage of Marxism and Feminism,* edited by Lydia Sargent. Boston: South End Press, 1981.

Hartmann, Heidi, and Ann R. Markusen. "Contemporary Marxist Theory and Practice: A Feminist Critique." *Review of Radical Political Economics* 12, no. 2 (Summer 1980): 87–93.

Holmstrom, Nancy, ed. *The Socialist Feminist Project: A Contemporary Reader in Theory and Politics.* New York: Monthly Review Press, 2002.

Jackson, Stevi. "Marxism and Feminism." In *Marxism and Social Science,* edited by Andrew Gamble, David Marsh, and Tony Tant. Champaign: University of Illinois Press, 1999.

Jaggar, Alison. *Feminist Politics and Human Nature.* Totowa, NJ: Rowman & Allanheld, 1983.

———. "Prostitution." In *Women and Values: Readings in Recent Feminist Philosophy,* edited by Marilyn Pearsall. Belmont, CA: Wadsworth, 1986.

Martin, Gloria. *Socialist Feminism: The First Decade, 1966–1976.* Seattle: Freedom Socialist Publications, 1978.

Mitchell, Juliet. *Psychoanalysis and Feminism.* New York: Vintage Books, 1974.

———. *Woman's Estate.* New York: Pantheon Books, 1971.

———. "Women: The Longest Revolution." *New Left Review* 40 (November–December 1966): 11–37.

Nicholson, Linda J. *Gender and History: The Limits of Social Theory in the Age of the Family.* New York: Columbia University Press, 1986.

Page, Margaret. "Socialist Feminism: A Political Alternative." *m/f* 2 (1978).

"Part-Time Programs Do Help Firms Hold on to Women Lawyers." *Law Office Management & Administration Report* 7, no. 5 (May 2007): 3.

Penny, Laurie. *Meat Market: Female Flesh Under Capitalism.* Alresford, UK: Zero Books, 2011.

Phelps, Linda. "Patriarchy and Capitalism." *Quest* 2, no. 2 (Fall 1975): 35–48.

Power, Nina. *One Dimensional Woman.* Alresford, UK: Zero Books, 2009.

Radical Women's 23rd Anniversary Conference General Membership. *The Radical Women Manifesto: Socialist Feminist Theory, Program and Organizational Structure.* Seattle: Red Letter Press, 2001.

Rowbotham, Sheila. *Woman's Consciousness, Man's World.* Baltimore: Penguin Books, 1973.

Rowbotham, Sheila, Lynne Segal, and Hilary Wainwright. *Beyond the Fragments: Feminism and the Making of Socialism.* London: Merlin Press, 1979.

Sargent, Lydia, ed. *Women and Revolution: A Discussion of the Unhappy Marriage of Marxism and Feminism.* Boston: South End Press, 1981.

Smith, Sharon. *Women and Socialism: Essays on Women's Liberation.* Chicago: Haymarket Books, 2005.

Spivak, Gayatri Chakravorty. *In Other Worlds.* New York: Routledge, 1988.

Stone, Pamela. *Opting Out?: Why Women Really Quit Careers and Head Home.* Berkeley: University of California Press, 2007.

Taylor, Barbara. "Lords of Creation: Marxism, Feminism and 'Utopian Socialism.'" In *Reader in Feminist Knowledge,* edited by Sneja Gunew, 360–365. New York: Routledge, 1991.

Weinbaum, Batya. *The Curious Courtship of Women's Liberation and Socialism.* Boston: South End Press, 1978.

Young, Iris. "Beyond the Unhappy Marriage: A Critique of the Dual Systems Theory" In *Women and Revolution: A Discussion of the Unhappy Marriage of Marxism and Feminism,* edited by Lydia Sargent, 428. Boston: South End Press, 1981.

———. "The Ideal of Community and the Politics of Difference." In *Feminism/Postmodernism,* edited by Linda J. Nicholson. New York: Routledge, 1990.

Women's Labor Issues

Alonso-Zaldivar, Ricardo. "Care Homes Hiring More Foreigners." *Los Angeles Times,* October 20, 2005. Available at http://articles.latimes.com/2005/oct/20/nation/na-immig20.

Amott, Teresa, and Julie Matthaei. "Comparable Worth, Incomparable Pay." *Radical America* 18, no. 5 (September–October 1984): 25.

Bar-Lev, Abby. "Equal Pay Still Unequal." *Minnesota Daily,* November 30, 2006. Available at http://www.mndaily.com/2006/11/30/equal-pay-still-unqual.

Bergmann, Barbara. *The Economic Emergence of Women.* New York: Basic Books, 1986.

Bettio, Francesca, and Alina Verashchagina, eds. *Frontiers in the Economics of Gender.* New York: Routledge, 2008.

Bowers, Katherine. "Ruling OKs Class Action Suit Against Wal-Mart." *Women's Wear Daily* 193, no. 29 (February 7, 2007): 39.

Bryson, Valerie. *Feminist Debates: Issues of Theory and Political Practice.* New York: New York University, 1999.

Burn, Shawn Meghan. *Women Across Cultures: A Global Perspective.* Mountain View, CA: Mayfield Publishing Company, 2000.

Caraway, Teri L. *Assembling Women: The Feminization of Global Manufacturing.* Ithaca, NY: Cornell University Press, 2007.

Clarke, Simon. *Keynesianism, Monetarism and the Crisis of the State.* Aldershot, UK: Edward Elgar, 1988, 177.

Eisenstein, Hester. *Feminism Seduced: How Global Elites Use Women's Labor and Ideas to Exploit the World.* Boulder, CO: Paradigm Publishers, 2010.

Equal Pay Act of 1963 (Pub. L. 88–93) (EPA), as amended, as it appears in volume 29 of the United States Code, at section 206(d).

Feldberg, Roslyn L. "Comparable Worth: Toward Theory and Practice in the United States." *Signs: Journal of Women in Culture and Society,* 10, no. 2 (Winter 1984): 311–313.

Friedman, Jonathan. "Global System, Globalization and the Parameters of Modernity." In *Global Modernities,* edited by Mike Featherstone et al., 77. London: Sage, 1995.

Giddens, Anthony. *Consequences of Modernity.* Cambridge: Polity Press, 1990, 64.

Goodman, Jacqueline. *Global Perspectives on Gender and Work: Readings and Interpretations.* Lanham, MD: Rowman & Littlefield, 2010.

Harley, Sharon, ed. *Women's Labor in the Global Economy: Speaking in Multiple Voices.* Piscataway, NJ: Rutgers University Press, 2011.

Hennessy-Fiske, Molly. "Gender Pay Gap Narrows—for Unexpected Reasons." *Los Angeles Times,* December 3, 2006, A23.

Hymowitz, Kay S. "The Single-Mom Catastrophe." *Los Angeles Times,* June 2, 2012, available at http://www.latimes.com/news/opinion/commentary/la-oe-hymowitz-unmarried-mothers-20120603,0,1889065.story.

Joyce, Amy. "Unusual Job Titles a Sign of the Times." *Merced (Calif.) Sun-Star,* December 23, 2006, 1.

Lamar, Jake. "A Worthy but Knotty Question." *Time,* February 6, 1984, 30.

Lash, Scott, and John Urry, *Economies of Signs and Space.* London: Sage, 1994.

Ledbetter, Lilly, and Lanier Scott Isom. *Grace and Grit: My Fight for Equal Pay and Fairness at Goodyear and Beyond.* New York: Crown Archetype, 2012.

Luxemburg, Rosa. "The National Question and Autonomy." In *The National Question: Selected Writings by Rosa Luxemburg,* edited by Horace B. Davis. New York: Monthly Review Press, 1976.

Matt McAllester, "America Is Stealing the World's Doctors." *New York Times Magazine,* March 7, 2012. Available at http://www.nytimes.com/2012/03/11/magazine/america-is-stealing-foreign-doctors.html?pagewanted=all.

Murphy, Evelyn. *Getting Even: Why Women Don't Get Paid Like Men—And What to Do About It.* New York: Touchstone, 2005.

Nussbaum, Karen. "Women Clerical Workers." *Socialist Review* 10, no. 1 (January–February 1980): 151–159.

"Paying Women What They're Worth." *QQ Report from the Center for Philosophy and Public Policy* 3, no. 2 (Spring 1983).

Pfister, Bonnie. "It's National Equal Pay Day—and U.S. Women Earn 77 Cents to a Man's Dollar." *San Antonia Express-News,* April 20, 2004.

Remick, Helen. "Major Issues in A Priori Applications." In *Comparable Worth and Wage Discrimination: Technical Possibilities and Political Realities,* edited by Helen Remick. Philadelphia: Temple University Press, 1984.

Robertson, Roland. *Globalization.* London: Sage, 1992.

———. "Globalization: Time-Space and Homogeneity-Heterogeneity." In *Global Modernities,* edited by Mike Featherstone et al., 27. London: Sage, 1995.

Rosenberg, Justin. *The Empire of Civil Society.* London: Verso, 1994.

Scott, Hilda. *Working Your Way to the Bottom.* London: Pandora Press, 1984.

Scott, Linda M. "Market Feminism: The Case for a Paradigm Shift." *Advertising and Society Review* 7, no. 2 (2006).

Shaw, Martin. *Global Society and International Relations.* Cambridge: Polity Press, 1994.

Sixel, L. M. "EEOC Alleges Unequal Pay for Same Work." *Houston Chronicle.* August 23, 2005, 94.

Smart, Barry. *Postmodernism.* London: Routledge, 1993, 173.

Thomas, G. Scott. "Where the Men, and Women, Work." *American City Business Journals,* April 19, 2004. Available at http://www.bizjournals.com/edit_special/12/html.

Tsutsui, Kiyoteru. "Redressing Past Human Rights Violations: Global Dimensions of Contemporary Social Movements." *Social Forces* 85, no. 1 (2006): 331–354.

Wallerstein, Immanuel. *The Modern World System I: Capitalist Agriculture and the Origins of the European World-Economy in the Sixteenth Century.* New York: Academic Press, 1974.

———. *The Modern World System II: Mercantilism and the Consolidation of the European World-Economy, 1600–1750.* New York: Academic Press, 1980.

———. *The Modern World System III: The Second Era of Great Expansion of the Capitalist World-Economy, 1730–1840s.* New York: Academic Press, 1989.

World Bank Group. "Globalization." Web page of World Bank Group, 2001. Available at http://go.worldbank.org/V7BJE9FD30.

Critiques of Marxist and Socialist Feminism

Jackson, Stevi. "Marxism and Feminism." In *Marxism and Social Science,* ed. Andrew Gamble, David Marsh, and Tony Tant. Champaign: University of Illinois Press, 1999.

Mitchell, Juliet. *Psychoanalysis and Feminism.* New York: Vintage Books, 1974.

Conclusion

Jackson, Stevi. "Marxism and Feminism." In *Marxism and Social Science,* ed. Andrew Gamble, David Marsh, and Tony Tant. Champaign: University of Illinois Press, 1999.

Chapter 4: Psychoanalytic and Care-Focused Feminisms

Psychoanalytic Feminism: Focus on Freud

Bernstein, Anne E., and Gloria Marmar Warner. *An Introduction to Contemporary Psychoanalysis.* New York: J. Aronson, 1981.

Chesler, Phyllis. *Women and Madness.* Garden City, NY: Doubleday, 1972.

Cohen, Ira H. *Ideology and Unconscious: Reich, Freud, and Marx.* New York: New York University Press, 1982.

Erdelyi, Matthew Hugh. *Psychoanalysis: Freud's Cognitive Psychology.* New York: W. H. Freeman, 1984.

Freud, Sigmund. *Civilization and Its Discontents.* Translated by James Strachey. New York: W. W. Norton, 1962.

———. "Femininity." In Sigmund Freud, *The Complete Introductory Lectures on Psychoanalysis,* translated and edited by James Strachey. New York: W. W. Norton, 1966.

———. *Sexuality and the Psychology of Love.* New York: Collier Books, 1968.

———. *The Standard Edition of the Complete Psychological Works of Sigmund Freud.* Vol. 12. London: Hogarth Press, 1971.

———. "Totem and Taboo." In *The Standard Edition of the Complete Psychological Works of Sigmund Freud,* translated and edited by James Strachey. New York: W. W. Norton, 1966.

Gay, Peter. *Freud: A Life for Our Time.* New York: W. W. Norton, 1988.

Hall, Calvin Springer. *A Primer of Freudian Psychology.* New York: New American Library, 1954.

Jones, Ernest. *The Life and Work of Sigmund Freud.* New York: Basic Books, 1961.

Laplanche, Jean. *The Language of Psychoanalysis.* New York: W. W. Norton, 1973.

Lichtman, Richard. *The Production of Desire: The Integration of Psychoanalysis into Marxist Theory.* New York: Free Press, 1982.

Reppen, Joseph, ed. *Beyond Freud: A Study of Modern Psychoanalytic Theorists.* Hillsdale, NJ: Analytic Press, 1985.

Roazen, Paul. *Freud: Political and Social Thought.* New York: Alfred A. Knopf, 1968.

Schoenewolf, Gerald. *Forbidden Psychoanalysis: Collected Papers of a Psychoanalytic Centrist.* New York: Living Center Press, 2010.

Feminist Critiques and Appropriations of Freud

Adler, Alfred. *Understanding Human Nature.* New York: Greenberg, 1927.

Beauvoir, Simone de. *The Second Sex,* translated and edited by H. M. Parshley. New York: Vintage Books, 1974.

Chodorow, Nancy. *The Reproduction of Mothering: Psychoanalysis and the Sociology of Gender.* Berkeley: University of California Press, 1978.

Deutsch, Helene. *The Psychology of Women: A Psychoanalytic Interpretation.* New York: Grune & Stratten, 1944.

Dinnerstein, Dorothy. *The Mermaid and the Minotaur: Sexual Arrangements and Human Malaise.* New York: Harper Colophon Books, 1977.

Elshtain, Jean Bethke. *Public Man, Private Woman.* Princeton, NJ: Princeton University Press, 1981.

Fiorini, Leticia Glocer, and Graciela Abelin-Sas Rose, eds. *On Freud's "Femininity."* London: Karnac Books, 2010.

Firestone, Shulamith. *The Dialectic of Sex.* New York: Bantam Books, 1970.

Freud, Sigmund. *Dora: An Analysis of a Case of Hysteria,* edited by Philip Rieff. New York: Collier Books, 1963.

Friedan, Betty. *The Feminine Mystique.* New York: Dell, 1974.

Garrison, Dee. "Karen Horney and Feminism." *Signs: Journal of Women in Culture and Society* 6, no. 4 (1981): 672–691.

Groenhout, Ruth E. *Philosophy, Feminism, and Faith.* Bloomington: Indiana University Press, 2003.

Horney, Karen. "The Flight from Womanhood." In *Feminine Psychology.* New York: W. W. Norton, 1973.

Izenberg, Gerald N. *The Existentialist Critique of Freud: The Crisis of Autonomy.* Princeton, NJ: Princeton University Press, 1976.

Klein, Viola. *The Feminine Character.* London: Routledge & Kegan Paul, 1971.

Kofman, Sarah. *The Enigma of Woman: Woman in Freud's Writings.* Ithaca, NY: Cornell University Press, 1985.

Lorber, Judith. "On *The Reproduction of Mothering:* A Methodological Debate." *Signs: Journal of Women in Culture and Society* 6, no. 3 (Spring 1981): 482–486.

Miller, Jean Baker, ed. *Psychoanalysis and Women.* Baltimore: Penguin Books, 1974.

Millett, Kate. *Sexual Politics.* New York: Ballantine Books, 1969.

Mitchell, Juliet. *Psychoanalysis and Feminism.* New York: Vintage Books, 1974.

———. *Woman's Estate.* New York: Pantheon Books, 1971.

Ortner, Sherry B. "Oedipal Father, Mother's Brother, and the Penis: A Review of Juliet Mitchell's *Psychoanalysis and Feminism.*" *Feminist Studies* 2, nos. 2–3 (1975): 179.

Piercy, Marge. *Woman on the Edge of Time.* New York: Fawcett Crest, 1976.

Rich, Adrienne. "Compulsory Heterosexuality and Lesbian Existence." In *The Signs Reader: Women, Gender, and Scholarship,* edited by Elizabeth Abel and Emily K. Abel, 182. Chicago: University of Chicago Press, 1983.

Ryle, Robyn. *Questioning Gender: A Sociological Exploration.* Thousand Oaks, CA: Pine Forge Press, 2012.

Scott, Joan Wallach. *The Fantasy of Feminist History.* Durham, NC: Duke University Press, 2011.

Stone, Alison. *Feminism, Psychoanalysis, and Maternal Subjectivity.* New York: Routledge, 2012.

Thompson, Clara. "Problems of Womanhood." In *Interpersonal Psychoanalysis: The Selected Papers of Clara Thompson,* edited by M. Green. New York: Basic Books, 1964.

Van Herik, Judith. *Freud on Femininity and Faith.* Berkeley: University of California Press, 1982.

Vetterling-Braggin, Mary, ed. *"Femininity," "Masculinity," and "Androgyny."* Totowa, NJ: Rowman & Littlefield, 1982.

Voloshinov, V. N. *Freudianism: A Marxist Critique.* New York: Academic Press, 1976.

Williams, Juanita. *Psychology of Women: Behavior in a Biosocial Context.* New York: W. W. Norton, 1977.

Wurmser, Léon, and Heidrun Jarass. *Jealousy and Envy: New Views about Two Powerful Feelings.* New York: The Analytic Press, 2008.

Psychoanalytic Feminism: Focus on Lacan

Beardsworth, Sara. "Freud's Oedipus and Kristeva's Narcissus: Three Heterogeneities." *Hypatia* 20, no. 1 (Winter 2005): 54–77.

———. *Julia Kristeva: Psychoanalyses and Modernity.* Albany: SUNY Press, 2004.

Brennan, Teresa, ed. *Between Feminism and Psychoanalysis.* New York: Routledge, 1989.

Burke, Carolyn, et al., eds. *Engaging with Irigaray: Feminist Philosophy and Modern European Thought.* New York: Columbus University Press, 1995.

Butler, Judith. "The Body Politics of Julia Kristeva." In *Revaluing French Feminism,* edited by Nancy Fraser and Sandra Lee Bartky. Bloomington: Indiana University Press, 1992.

Chanter, Tina. *Ethics of Eros: Irigaray's Re-Writing of the Philosophers.* New York: Routledge, 1995.

Chodorow, Nancy. "Toward a Relational Individualism: The Mediation of Self Through Psychoanalysis." In *Reconstructing Individualism: Autonomy, Individuality, and the Self in Western Thought,* edited by Thomas C. Heller, Morton Sosna, and David E. Wellbury. Stanford, CA: Stanford University Press, 1986.

Derrida, Jacques. "The Ends of Man." In *Margins of Philosophy,* translated by Alan Bass. Sussex, UK: Harvester, 1982.

Duchen, Claire. *Feminism in France: From May '68 to Mitterrand.* London: Routledge & Kegan Paul, 1986.

Engel, Stephanie. "Femininity as Tragedy: Re-examining the 'New Narcissism.'" *Socialist Review* 10, no. 5 (September–October 1980): 77–104.

Fuss, Diana J. "'Essentially Speaking': Luce Irigaray's Language of Essence." In *Revaluing French Feminism,* edited by Nancy Fraser and Sandra Lee Bartky, 94–112. Bloomington: Indiana University Press, 1992.

Gallop, Jane. *The Daughter's Seduction: Feminism and Psychoanalysis.* Ithaca, NY: Cornell University Press, 1982.

———. *Reading Lacan.* Ithaca, NY, and London: Cornell University Press, 1985.

Gilligan, Carol. "Adolescent Development Reconsidered." In *Mapping the Moral Domain,* ed. Carol Gilligan, Janie Victoria Ward, and Jill McLean Taylor. Cambridge, MA: Harvard University Press, 1988.

———. *In a Different Voice.* Cambridge, MA: Harvard University Press, 1982.

Irigaray, Luce. "Is the Subject of Science Sexed?" Translated by Carol Mastrangelo Bové. *Hypatia* 2, no. 3 (Fall 1987): 65–87.

———. "Sorcerer Love: A Reading of Plato's Symposium, Diotima's Speech." In *Revaluing French Feminism,* edited by Nancy Fraser and Sandra Lee Bartky, 64–76. Bloomington: Indiana University Press, 1992.

———. *Speculum of the Other Woman.* Translated by Gillian C. Gill. Ithaca, NY: Cornell University Press, 1985.

———. *This Sex Which Is Not One.* Translated by Catherine Porter. Ithaca, NY: Cornell University Press, 1985.

Kozel, Susan. "The Diabolical Strategy of Mimesis: Luce Irigaray's Reading of Maurice Merleau-Ponty." *Hypatia* 11, no. 3 (Summer 1996): 114–129.

Kristeva, Julia. "Cillation du 'Pouvoir' au Refus." Interview by Xavière Gauthier for *Tel Quel* 58 (Summer 1974). In *New French Feminisms,* edited by Elaine Marks and Isabelle de Courtivron. New York: Schocken Classics, 1981.

————. *In the Beginning Was Love: Psychoanalysis and Faith.* New York: Columbia University Press, 1987.

————. "The Novel as Polylogue." In *Desire in Language,* translated by Leon S. Roudiez and edited by Thomas Gora, Alice Jardine, and Leon S. Roudiez. New York: Columbia University Press, 1990.

————. *Powers of Horror.* Translated by Leon Roudiez. New York: Columbia University Press, 1982.

————. *The Sense and Non-Sense of Revolt: The Powers and Limitations of Psychoanalysis.* Vol. 1. Translated by Janine Herman. New York: Columbia University Press, 2000.

Kuykendall, Eléanor H. "Introduction to *Sorcerer Love* by Luce Irigaray." In *Revaluing French Feminism,* edited by Nancy Fraser and Sandra Lee Bartky, 60–63. Bloomington: Indiana University Press, 1992.

Lacan, Jacques. *Écrits: A Selection.* Translated by Alan Sheridan. New York: W. W. Norton, 1977.

————. *The Language of the Self.* Baltimore: Johns Hopkins University Press, 1968.

Leland, Dorothy. "Lacanian Psychoanalysis and French Feminism: Toward an Adequate Political Psychology." *Hypatia* 3, no. 3 (Winter 1989).

Margaroni, Maria. "'The Lost Foundation': Kristeva's Semiotic Chora and Its Ambiguous Legacy." *Hypatia* 20, no. 1 (Winter 2005): 78–98.

Meyers, Diana T. "The Subversion of Women's Agency in Psychoanalytic Feminism: Chodorow, Flox, Kristeva." In *Revaluing French Feminism,* edited by Nancy Fraser and Sandra Lee Bartky, 136–161. Bloomington: Indiana University Press, 1992.

Mitchell, Juliet, and Jacqueline Rose. *Feminine Sexuality: Jacques Lacan and the École Freudienne.* New York: W. W. Norton, 1982.

Moi, Toril. *Sexual/Textual Politics: Feminist Literary Theory.* New York: Methuen, 1985.

Nye, Andrea. "The Hidden Host: Irigaray and Diotima at Plato's Symposium." In *Revaluing French Feminism,* edited by Nancy Fraser and Sandra Lee Bartky, 77–93. Bloomington: Indiana University Press, 1992.

Oliver, Kelly. "Julia Kristeva's Feminist Revolutions." *Hypatia* 8, no. 3 (Summer 1993): 94–114.

Ragland-Sullivan, Ellie. *Jacques Lacan and the Philosophy of Psychoanalyses.* Chicago: University of Illinois Press, 1986.

Ragland-Sullivan, Ellie, and Mark Bracher. *Lacan and the Subject of Language.* New York: Routledge, 1991.

Roudinesco, Elisabeth. *Jacques Lacan.* Translated by Barbara Bray. New York: Columbia University Press, 1999.

Sandford, Stella. *Plato and Sex.* Cambridge: Polity Press, 2010.

Schmitz, Bettina. "Homelessness or Symbolic Castration? Subjectivity, Language Acquisition, and Sociality in Julia Kristeva and Jacques Lacan." Translated by Julia Jansen. *Hypatia* 20, no. 2 (Spring 2005): 69–87.

Udovicki, Jasminka. "Justice and Care in Close Associations." *Hypatia* 8, no. 3 (Summer 1993): 48–60.

Weedon, Chris. *Feminist Practice & Poststructuralist Theory.* New York: Basil Blackwell, 1987.

Whitford, Margaret. *Luce Irigaray: Philosophy in the Feminine.* New York and London: Routledge, 1991.

Wiseman, Mary. "Renaissance Madonna and the Fantasies of Freud." *Hypatia* 8, no. 3 (Summer 1993): 115–135.

Bridges Between Psychoanalytic and Care-Focused Feminists

Meyers, Diana T. *Subjection and Subjectivity: Psychoanalytic Feminism and Moral Philosophy.* New York: Routledge, 1994.

The Roots of Care-Focused Feminism:
Carol Gilligan and Nel Noddings

Baier, Annette C. "Caring About Caring." In *Postures of the Mind: Essays on Mind and Morals.* Minneapolis: University of Minnesota Press, 1985.

Barry, Brian. *Justice As Impartiality.* Oxford: Oxford University Press, 1995.

Bartky, Sandra Lee. "Feeding Egos and Tending Wounds: Deference and Disaffection in Women's Emotional Labor." In *Femininity and Domination,* edited by Sandra Lee Bartky, 99–119. New York: Routledge, 1990.

———. *Femininity and Domination.* New York: Routledge, 1990, 105.

Benhabib, Seyla. "The Generalized and Concrete Other: The Kohlberg-Gilligan Controversy and Moral Theory." In *Women and Moral Theory,* edited by Eva Feder Kittay and Diana T. Meyers. Totowa, NJ: Rowman & Littlefield, 1987.

Bowden, Peta. *Caring: Gender Sensitive Ethics.* London: Routledge, 1997.

Bubeck, Diemut. *Care, Gender, and Justice.* Oxford: Claredon Press, 1995.

Card, Claudia. "Caring and Evil." *Hypatia* 5, no. 1 (Spring 1990): 106.

Clement, Grace. *Care, Autonomy and Justice: Feminism and the Ethic of Care.* Boulder, CO: Westview Press, 1996.

Davis, Kathy. "Toward a Feminist Rhetoric: The Gilligan Debate Revisited." *Women's Studies International Forum* 15, no. 2 (1992): 219–231.

Dinnerstein, Dorothy. *The Mermaid and the Minotaur: Sexual Arrangements and Human Malaise.* New York: Harper and Row, 1977.

Faludi, Susan. *Caregiving: Readings in Knowledge, Practice, Ethics, and Politics.* Philadelphia: University of Pennsylvania Press, 1996, 276.

Fisher, Berenice, and Joan Tronto. "Toward a Feminist Theory of Caring." In *Circles of Care,* edited by Emily Abel and Margaret Nelson. Albany: SUNY Press, 1990.

Friedman, Marilyn. *Autonomy, Gender, Politics.* New York: Oxford University Press, 2003.

Gilligan, Carol. "Adolescent Development Reconsidered." In *Mapping the Moral Domain,* edited by Carol Gilligan, Janie Victoria Ward, and Jill McLean Taylor, xxii. Cambridge, MA: Harvard University Press, 1988.

———. *In a Different Voice.* Cambridge, MA: Harvard University Press, 1982.

———. "Moral Orientation and Moral Development." In *Women and Moral Theory,* edited by Eva Feder Kittay and Diana T. Meyers, 25–26. Totowa, NJ: Rowman & Littlefield, 1987.

Gilligan, Carol, and Grant Wiggins. "The Origins of Morality in Early Childhood Relationships." In *The Emergence of Morality in Young Children,* edited by Jerome Kagan and Sharon Lamb, 279. Chicago: University of Chicago Press, 1987.

Gordon, Suzanne, Patricia Benner, and Nel Nodding, eds. *Caregiving: Readings in Knowledge, Practice, Ethics, and Politics.* Philadelphia: University of Pennsylvania Press, 1996.

Halwani, Raja. "Care Ethics and Virtue Ethics." *Hypatia* 18, no. 3 (Fall 2003): 161–192.

Hekman, Susan J. *Moral Voices, Moral Selves: Carol Gilligan and Feminist Moral Theory.* University Park: Pennsylvania State University Press, 1995.

Hoagland, Sarah Lucia. "Some Concerns About Nel Noddings' *Caring.*" *Hypatia* 5, no. 1 (Spring 1990): 114.

———. "Some Thoughts About *Caring.*" In *Feminist Ethics,* edited by Claudia Card, 250. Lawrence: University Press of Kansas, 1991.

Jaggar, Alison M. "Caring as a Feminist Practice of Moral Reason." In *Justice and Care: Essential Readings in Feminist Ethics,* edited by Virginia Held. Boulder, CO: Westview Press, 1995.

Koehn, Daryl. *Rethinking Feminist Ethics: Care, Trust, and Empathy.* London: Routledge, 1998.

Kohlberg, Lawrence. "From Is to Ought: How to Commit the Naturalistic Fallacy and Get Away with It in the Study of Moral Development." In *Cognitive Development and Epistemology,* edited by Theodore Mischel. New York: Academic Press, 1971.

Kroeger-Mappes, Joy. "The Ethic of Care vis-à-vis the Ethic of Rights: A Problem for Contemporary Moral Theory." *Hypatia* 9, no. 3 (Summer 1994): 108–131.

Larrabee, Mary Jeanne, ed. *An Ethic of Care: Feminist and Interdisciplinary Perspectives.* New York: Routledge, 1993.

Li, Chenyang. "The Confucian Concepts of *Jen* and the Feminist Ethics of Care: A Comparative Study." *Hypatia* 9, no. 1 (1994): 70–89.

———. "Revisiting Confucian *Jen* Ethics and Feminist Care Ethics: A Reply to Daniel Star and Lijun Yuan." *Hypatia* 17, no. 1 (2002): 130–140.

Little, Margaret. "Seeing and Caring: The Role of Affect in Feminist Moral Epistemology." *Hypatia* 10, no. 3 (1995): 117–137.

McLaren, Margaret A. "Feminist Ethics: Care as a Virtue." In *Feminists Doing Ethics,* edited by Peggy DesAutels and Joanne Waugh. Lanham, MD: Rowman & Littlefield, 2001.

Miller, Sarah Clark. *The Ethics of Need: Agency, Dignity, and Obligation.* New York: Routledge, 2012.

———. "A Kantian Ethic of Care?" In *Feminist Interventions in Ethics and Politics: Feminist Ethics and Social Theory,* edited by Barbara S. Andrew, 111–127. Lanham, MD: Rowman & Littlefield, 2005.

Moody-Adams, Michele M. "Gender and the Complexity of Moral Voices." In *Feminist Ethics,* edited by Claudia Card, 193–198. Kansas: University Press of Kansas, 1991.

———. "The Social Construction and Reconstruction of Care." In *Sex, Preference, and Family: Essays on Law and Nature,* edited by David Estlund and Martha Nussbaum, 3–17. New York: Oxford University Press, 1997.

Noddings, Nel. *Caring: A Feminine Approach to Ethics and Moral Education.* Berkeley: University of California Press, 1984, 3.

———, ed. *Educating Citizens for Global Awareness.* New York: Teachers College Press, 2005.

———. *Happiness and Education.* New York: Cambridge University Press, 2003.

———. *The Maternal Factor: Two Paths to Morality.* Berkeley: University of California Press, 2010.

———. *Peace Education: How We Come to Love and Hate War.* New York: Cambridge University Press, 2012.

———. *Starting at Home: Caring and Social Policy.* Berkeley: University of California Press, 2002.

———. *When School Reform Goes Wrong.* New York: Teachers College Press, 2007.

———. *Women and Evil.* Berkeley: University of California Press, 1989, 91.

Puka, Bill. "The Liberation of Caring: A Different Voice for Gilligan's 'Different Voice.'" *Hypatia* 5, no. 1 (Spring 1990): 59.

Robinson, Fiona. *Globalizing Care: Ethics, Feminist Theory and International Relations.* Boulder, CO: Westview Press, 1999.

Sander-Staudt, Maureen. "The Unhappy Marriage of Care Ethics and Virtue Ethics." *Hypatia* 21, no. 4 (Fall 2006): 21–39.

Scher, George. "Other Voices, Other Rooms? Women's Psychology and Moral Theory." In *Women and Moral Theory,* edited by Eva Feder Kittay and Diana T. Meyers, 188. Totowa, NJ: Rowman & Littlefield, 1987.

Simons, Margaret A. "Two Interviews with Simone de Beauvoir." *Hypatia* 3, no. 3 (Winter 1989): 11–27.

Simson, Rosalind S. "Feminine Thinking." *Social Theory & Practice* 31, no. 1 (January 2005): 1–26.

Slicer, Deborah. "Teaching with a Different Ear: Teaching Ethics after Reading Carol Gilligan." *Journal of Value Inquiry* 24 (1990): 55–65.

Slote, Michael. "Caring in the Balance." In *Norms and Values,* edited by Joram G. Haber and Mark S. Hatfon. Lanham, MD: Rowman & Littlefield, 1998.

Star, Daniel. "Do Confucians Really Care? A Defense of the Distinctiveness of Care Ethics: A Reply to Chenyang Li." *Hypatia* 17, no. 1 (2002): 77–106.

Yuan, Lijun. "Ethics of Care and Concept of *Jen:* A Reply to Chenyang Li." *Hypatia* 17, no. 1 (2002): 107–129.

Maternal Ethics and the Ethics of Care

Allmark, Peter. "Is Caring a Virtue?" *Journal of Advanced Nursing* 28, no. 3 (1998): 466–472.

Aronow, Ina. "Doulas Step in When Mothers Need a Hand." *New York Times,* August 1, 1993, 1, Westchester Section.

Badinter, Elisabeth. *Mother Love: Myth and Reality.* New York: Macmillan, 1980.

Baraitser, Lisa. *Maternal Encounters: The Ethics of Interruption.* New York: Routledge, 2009.

Behuniak, Susan M. *A Caring Jurisprudence.* Lanham, MD: Rowman & Littlefield, 1999.

Belenky, Mary Field, Lynne A. Bond, and Jacqueline S. Weinstock. *The Tradition That Has No Name: Nurturing the Development of People, Families, and Communities.* New York: Basic Books, 1997.

Blustein, Jeffrey. *Care and Commitment.* Oxford: Oxford University Press, 1991.

Brender, Natalie. "Political Care and Humanitarian Response." In *Feminists Doing Ethics,* edited by Peggy DesAutels and Joanne Waugh. Lanham, MD: Rowman & Littlefield, 2001.

Botes, Annatjie. "A Comparison between the Ethics of Justice and the Ethics of Care." *Journal of Advanced Nursing* 32, no. 5 (2000): 1071–1075.

Chodorow, Nancy. *The Reproduction of Mothering: Psychoanalysis and the Sociology of Gender.* Berkeley: University of California, 1978.

Clement, Grace. *Care, Autonomy, and Justice: Feminism and the Ethic of Care.* Boulder, CO: Westview, 1996.

Daniel, Norman. *Am I My Parents' Keeper? An Essay on Justice Between the Younger and the Older.* New York: Oxford University Press, 1988.

Davion, Victoria. "Pacifism and Care." *Hypatia* 5 (1990): 90–100.

Deveaux, Monique. "Shifting Paradigms: Theorizing Care and Justice in Political Theory." *Hypatia* 10, no. 2 (Spring 1995): 115–119.

England, Paula, and Nancy Folbre. "The Cost of Caring." *Annals of the American Academy of Political and Social Science* 561 (January 1999): 39–51.

Engster, Daniel. "Care Ethics and Natural Law Theory: Toward an Institutional Political Theory of Caring." *Journal of Politics* 66, no. 1 (February 2004): 113–135.

———. "Rethinking Care Theory: The Practice of Caring and the Obligation to Care." *Hypatia* 20, no. 3 (Summer 2005): 51–74.

Ferguson, Ann. "Motherhood and Sexuality: Some Feminist Questions." *Hypatia* 1, no. 2 (Fall 1986): 3–22.

Goodin, Robert. *Protecting the Vulnerable.* Chicago: University of Chicago Press, 1985.

Gottlieb, Roger S. "The Tasks of Embodied Love: Moral Problems in Caring for Children with Disabilities." *Hypatia* 17, no. 3 (Summer 2002): 225–236.

Gould, Carol, ed. *Beyond Domination: New Perspectives on Women and Philosophy.* Totowa, NJ: Rowman & Allanheld, 1983.

Halfon, Mark S., and Joram G. Haber, eds. *Norms and Values: Essays on the Work of Virginia Held.* Lanham, MD: Rowman & Littlefield, 1998.

Hamington, Maurice, and Dorothy C. Miller, eds. *Socializing Care: Feminist Ethics and Public Issues.* Lanham, MD: Rowman & Littlefield, 2006.

Hanisberg, Julia, and Sara Ruddick, eds. *On Behalf of Mothers: Legal Theorists, Philosophers, and Theologians Reflect on Dilemmas of Parenting.* New York: Beacon Press, 1999.

Hankivsky, Olena. "Imagining Ethical Globalization: The Contributions of a Care Ethics." *Hypatia* 2, no. 1 (June 2006): 91–110.

———, eds. *Mother Troubles: Rethinking Contemporary Maternal Dilemmas.* Boston: Beacon Press, 1999.

Harrington, Mona. *Care and Equality: Inventing a New Family Politics.* New York: Knopf, 1999.

Held, Virginia. "Care and the Extension of Markets." *Hypatia* 17, no. 2 (Spring 2002): 19–33.

———. *The Ethics of Care: Personal, Political and Global.* New York: Oxford University Press, 2006.

———. "Feminism and Moral Theory." In *Women and Moral Theory,* edited by Eva Feder Kittay and Diana Meyers, 112. Savage, MD: Rowman & Littlefield, 1987.

———. *Feminist Morality: Transforming Culture, Society, and Politics.* Chicago: University of Chicago Press, 1993.

———. "The Meshing of Care and Justice." *Hypatia* 10, no. 2 (Spring 1995): 128–132.

———. "The Obligation of Mothers and Fathers." In *Mothering: Essays in Feminist Theory,* edited by Joyce Trebilcot, 1. Totowa, NJ: Rowman & Allanheld, 1984.

Held, Virginia, and Alison Jaggar, eds. *Justice and Care: Essential Readings in Feminist Ethics.* Boulder, CO: Westview, 1995.

Houston, Barbara. "Rescuing Womanly Virtues." In *Science, Morality, and Feminist Theory,* edited by Marsha Hanen and Kai Nielsen. Calgary: University of Calgary Press, 1987.

Kittay, Eva Feder. "At the Margins of Moral Personhood." *Ethics* 116 (October 2005): 100–131.

———. "A Feminist Public Ethic of Care Meets the New Communitarian Family Policy." *Ethics* 111 (April 2001): 523–547.

———. "Human Dependency and Rawlsian Equality." In *Feminists Rethink the Self,* edited by Diana T. Meyers. Boulder, CO: Westview Press, 1996.

———. *Love's Labor: Essays on Women, Equality and Dependency.* New York: Routledge, 1999, 19.

———. "Taking Dependency Seriously." *Hypatia* 10 (Winter 1995): 29.

Kittay, Eva Feder, and Diana T. Meyers, eds. *Women and Moral Theory.* Totowa, NJ: Rowman & Littlefield, 1987.

Kittay, Eva Feder, and Licia Carlson, eds. *Cognitive Disability and Its Challenge to Moral Philosophy.* Malden: Wiley-Blackwell, 2010.

Kramer, Betty J., and Edward H. Thompson, Jr. *Men as Caregivers: Theory, Research, and Service Implications.* New York: Springer, 2002.

Kuhse, Helga. *Caring: Nurses, Women and Ethics.* Oxford: Blackwell, 1997.

Lorber, Judith. "On *The Reproduction of Mothering*: A Methodological Debate." *Signs: Journal of Women in Culture and Society* 6, no. 3 (Spring 1981): 482–486.

MacIntyre, Alasdair. *After Virtue.* Notre Dame, IN: University of Notre Dame Press, 1981, 177.

Manning, Rita C. *Speaking from the Heart: A Feminist Perspective on Ethics.* Lanham, MD: Rowman & Littlefield, 1992.

Morris, Jenny. "Impairment and Disability: Constructing an Ethics of Care That Promotes Human Rights." *Hypatia* 16, no. 4 (Fall 2001): 1–16.

Mullett, Sheila. "Shifting Perspectives: A New Approach to Ethics." In *Feminist Perspectives,* edited by Lorraine Code, Sheila Mullett, and Christine Overall. Toronto: University of Toronto Press, 1989.

Nagel, Thomas. *The View from Nowhere.* Oxford: Oxford University Press, 1986.

Nicholson, Linda J. *Gender and History: The Limits of Social Theory in the Age of the Family.* New York: Columbia University Press, 1986.

Nietzsche, Friedrich. *On the Genealogy of Morals,* translated by Walter Kaufmann and R. Hollingdale. New York: Vintage, 1969.

Nussbaum, Martha. *Creating Capabilities: The Human Development Approach.* Cambridge: Belknap Press of Harvard University Press, 2011.

Okin, Susan. *Justice, Gender and the Family.* New York: Basic Books, 1989.

Porter, Elisabeth. "Can Politics Practice Compassion?" *Hypatia* 21, no. 4 (Fall 2006): 97–123.

Purdy, Laura M. *Reproducing Persons: Issues in Feminist Bioethics.* Ithaca, NY: Cornell University Press, 1996.

Rawls, John. *A Theory of Justice.* Cambridge, MA: Harvard University Press, 1971.

Raymond, Janice. "Female Friendship: Contra Chodorow and Dinnerstein." *Hypatia* 1, no. 2 (Fall 1986): 44–45.

Reverby, Susan. *Ordered to Care.* Cambridge: Cambridge University Press, 1987.

Robinson, Fiona. "Care, Gender and Global Social Justice: Rethinking 'Ethical Globalization.'" *Hypatia* 2, no. 1 (June 2006): 5–25.

———. *Globalizing Care: Ethics, Feminist Theory, and International Relations.* Boulder, CO: Westview, 1999.

Romero, Mary. "Who's Taking Care of the Maid's Children?" In *Feminism and Families,* edited by Hilde Lind. New York: Routledge, 1997.

Rossi, Alice. "On *The Reproduction of Mothering:* A Methodological Debate." *Signs: Journal of Women in Culture and Society* 6, no. 3 (Spring 1981): 497–500.

Ruddick, Sara. "Care as Labor and Relationship." In *Norms and Values: Essays on the Work of Virginia Held,* edited by Mark S. Halfon and Joram C. Haber. Lanham, MD: Rowman & Littlefield, 1998.

———. "Injustice in Families: Assault and Domination." In *Justice and Care: Essential Readings in Feminist Ethics,* edited by Virginia Held, 203–223. Boulder, CO: Westview Press, 1995.

———. "Maternal Thinking." In *Mothering: Essays in Feminist Theory,* edited by Joyce Trebilcot, 214. Totowa, NJ: Rowman & Allanheld, 1984.

Ruddick, William. "Parenthood: Three Concepts and a Principle." In *Family Values: Issues in Ethics, Society and the Family,* edited by Laurence D. Houlgate. Belmont, CA: Wadsworth, 1998.

Sevenhuijsen, Selma. *Citizenship and the Ethics of Care: Feminist Considerations on Justice, Morality and Politics.* London: Routledge, 1998.

———. "Feminist Ethics and Public Health Care Policies." In *Feminist Ethics and Social Policy,* edited by Patrice DiQuinzio and Iris Marion Young. Bloomington: Indiana University Press, 1996.

Shanley, Mary Lyndon. "Public Policy and the Ethics of Care." *Hypatia* 16, no. 3 (Summer 2001): 157–160.

Sherwin, Susan. *No Longer Patient: Feminist Ethics and Health Care.* Philadelphia: Temple University Press, 1992.

Slote, Michael. *Education and Human Values.* New York: Routledge, 2012.

Sommers, Christina Hoff. "Filial Morality." In *Women and Moral Theory,* edited by Eva F. Kittay and Diana T. Meyers. Totowa, NJ: Rowman & Littlefield, 1987.

Stephens, Julie. *Confronting Postmaternal Thinking: Feminism, Memory, and Care.* New York and Chichester, UK: Columbia University Press, 2011.

Stone, Deborah. "Why We Need a Care Movement." *The Nation,* March 12, 2000, 13–15.

Tessman, Lisa, ed. *Feminist Ethics and Social and Political Philosophy: Theorizing the Non-Ideal.* New York: Springer, 2009.

Tong, Rosemarie. "The Ethics of Care: A Feminist Virtue of Care for Healthcare Practitioners." *Journal of Medicine and Philosophy* 23, no. 2 (1998): 131–52.

———. *Feminine and Feminist Ethics.* Belmont, CA: Wadsworth, 1993.

———. "Gender-Based Disparities East/West: Rethinking the Burden of Care in the United States and Taiwan." *Bioethics* 21, no. 9 (2007): 488–499.

———. "Gender Justice for Women: An Elusive Goal." In *Medicine and Social Justice: Essays on the Distribution of Health Care,* edited by Rosamond Rhodes, Margaret P. Battin, and Anita Silvers. Oxford: Oxford University Press, 2012.

———. "Global Perspectives on Health Care: Some Feminist Visions." In *Globalizing Feminist Bioethics: Crosscultural Perspectives,* edited by Rosemarie Tong with Gwen Anderson and Aida Santos. Boulder, CO: Westview Press, 2001.

———. "Love's Labor in the Health Care System: Working Toward Gender Equiaty." *Hypatia* 17, no. 3 (Summer 2002): 200–213.

———. "Long-Term Care for the Elderly: Whose Responsibility Is It?" *International Journal of Feminist Approaches to Bioethics* 2, no. 2 (2009): 5–30.

Tong, Rosemarie, with Nancy Williams. "Gender Justice in the Health Care System: Past Experiences, Present Realities, and Future Hopes." In *Medicine and Social Justice,* edited by Rosamond Rhodes, Margaret Battin, and Anita Silvers. Oxford: Oxford University Press, 2002.

Treblicot, Joyce, ed. *Mothering: New Essays in Feminist Theory.* Totowa, NJ: Rowman & Littlefield, 1987.

Tronto, Joan. "Care as a Political Concept." In *Revisioning the Political: Feminist Reconstructions of Traditional Concepts in Western Political Theory,* edited by Nancy J. Hirschmann and Christine Di Stefano. New York: Free Press, 1996.

——. *Moral Boundaries: A Political Argument for an Ethic of Care.* London: Routledge, 1993.

——. "The 'Nanny' Question in Feminism." *Hypatia* 17, no. 2 (Spring 2002): 34–51.

——. "Woman and Caring: What Can Feminists Learn about Morality from Caring?" In *Justice and Care: Essential Readings in Feminist Ethics,* edited by Virginia Held, 101–115. Boulder, CO: Westview Press, 1995.

Walker, Margaret Urban, ed. *Mother Time: Women, Aging, and Ethics.* Lanham, MD: Rowman & Littlefield, 1998.

West, Robin. "The Right to Care." In *The Subject of Care: Feminist Perspectives on Dependency,* edited by Eva Feder Kittay and Ellen Feder. Lanham, MD: Rowman & Littlefield, 2002.

White, Julie Anne. *Democracy, Justice, and The Welfare State: Reconstructing Public Care.* University Park: Pennsylvania State Press, 2000.

Willett, Cynthia. *Maternal Ethics and Other Slave Moralities.* New York: Routledge, 1995.

Wilson, Richard Ashby, and Richard D. Brown, eds. *Humanitarianism and Suffering: The Mobilization of Empathy.* New York: Cambridge University Press, 2009.

Wong, Sau-ling C. "Diverted Mothering: Representations of Caregivers of Color in the Age of Multiculturalism." In *Mothering: Ideology, Experience and Agency,* edited by Evelyn Nakano Glenn, Grace Chang, and Linda Rennie Forcey. New York: Routledge, 1994.

Yuval-Davis, Nira. *The Politics of Belonging: Intersectional Contestations.* London: Sage Publications, 2011.

Conclusion

Houston, Barbara. "Rescuing Womanly Virtues." In *Science, Morality, and Feminist Theory,* edited by Marsha Hanen and Kai Nielsen. Calgary: University of Calgary Press, 1987.

Mullett, Sheila. "Shifting Perspectives: A New Approach to Ethics." In *Feminist Perspectives,* edited by Lorraine Code, Sheila Mullett, and Christine Overall. Toronto: University of Toronto Press, 1989.

Chapter 5: Existentialist and Postmodern Feminism

Keefe, Terry. *Simone de Beauvoir.* Totowa, NJ: Barnes & Noble, 1983.

Simons, Margaret A., and Jessica Benjamin. "Simone de Beauvoir: An Interview." *Feminist Studies* 5, no. 2 (Summer 1979): 336.

Sartre's Being and Nothingness:
A Backdrop to The Second Sex

Aron, Raymond. *Marxism and the Existentialists*. New York: Harper & Row, 1969.

Barrett, William. *Irrational Man: A Study in Existential Philosophy*. Garden City: Doubleday, 1958.

Caws, Peter. *Sartre*. Boston: Routledge & Kegan Paul, 1979.

Chiodi, Pietro. *Sartre and Marxism*. Atlantic Highlands: Humanities Press, 1976.

Grene, Marjorie. *Dreadful Freedom: A Critique of Existentialism*. Chicago: University of Chicago Press, 1948.

———. *Sartre*. New York: New Viewpoints, 1973.

Heidegger, Martin. *Basic Writings*. New York: HarperCollins, 1993.

Kaufmann, Walter Arnold, ed. *Existentialism from Dostoevsky to Sartre*. New York: New American Library, 1975.

Marino, Gordon. *Basic Writings of Existentialism*. New York: Modern Library, 2004.

Merleau-Ponty, Maurice. *Phenomenology of Perception*. Translated by Colin Smith. New York: Routledge and Kegan Paul, 1962.

Murphy, Julien S., ed. *Feminist Interpretations of Jean-Paul Sartre*. University Park, PA: Pennsylvania State University Press, 1999.

Nietzsche, Friedrich. *Basic Writings of Nietzsche*. Translated by Walter Kaufmann. New York: Random House, 2000.

Oaklander, Nathan L. *Existentialist Philosophy: An Introduction*. 2nd ed. Saddle River, NJ: Prentice Hall, 1995.

Sartre, Jean-Paul. *Being and Nothingness*. Translated by Hazel E. Barnes. New York: Philosophical Library, 1943.

———. *The Emotions: Outline of a Theory*. New York: Philosophical Library, 1948.

———. *Existentialism*. Translated by Bernard Frechtman. New York: Philosophical Library, 1947.

———. *Existentialism Is a Humanism*. Translated by Carol Macomber. New Haven, NJ: Yale University Press, 2007.

Solomon, Robert C., ed. *Existentialism*. 2nd ed. New York: Oxford University Press, 2004.

Simone de Beauvoir's Existentialism for Women

Arp, Kristana. *The Bonds of Freedom: Simone de Beauvoir's Existentialist Ethics*. Peru, IL: Carus Publishing Company, 2001.

Ascher, Carol. *Simone de Beauvoir: A Life of Freedom*. Boston: Beacon Press, 1981.

Bartky, Sandra Lee. *Femininity and Domination: Studies in the Phenomenology of Oppression*. New York: Routledge, 1990.

Beauvoir, Simone de. *Adieux: A Farewell to Sartre*. New York: Pantheon Books, 1984.

———. *The Ethics of Ambiguity*. New York: Citadel Press, 1967.

———. *Letters to Sartre*. Translated and edited by Quinton Hoare. New York: Arcade Publishing, 1990.

———. *Memoirs of a Dutiful Daughter*. Translated by James Kirkup. Harmondsworth, UK: Penguin Books, 1963.

———. *The Prime of Life.* Translated by Peter Green. Harmondsworth, UK: Penguin Books, 1965.

———. *The Second Sex.* Translated and edited by H. M. Parshley. New York: Vintage Books, 1952.

Bergoffen, Debra B. "Simone de Beauvoir and Jean Paul Sartre: Woman, Man and the Desire to Be God." *Constellations* 9 no. 3 (2002): 406–418.

Card, Claudia. *The Cambridge Companion to Simone de Beauvoir.* Cambridge: Cambridge University Press, 2003.

Cohen Shabot, Sara. "On the Question of Woman: Illuminating de Beauvoir through Kantian Epistemology." *Philosophy Today* 51 no. 4 (2007): 369–382.

Fullbrook, Kate and Edward Fullbrook. *Simone de Beauvoir and Jean-Paul Sartre: The Remaking of a Twentieth-Century Legend.* New York: Basic Books, 1994.

Heinamaa, Sara. "What Is a Woman? Butler and Beauvoir on the Foundations of the Sexual Difference." *Hypatia* 12 no. 1 (1997): 20–39.

Jardine, Alice. "An Interview with Simone de Beauvoir." *Signs: Journal of Women in Culture and Society* 5 no. 2 (1979): 224–236.

Keefe, Terry. *Simone de Beauvoir.* Totowa, NJ: Barnes & Noble, 1983.

Kuykendall, Eléanor H. "Linguistic Ambivalence in Simone de Beauvoir's Feminist Theory." In *The Thinking Muse,* edited by Iris Young and Jenniver Allan, 1–30. Bloomington: Indiana University Press, 1989.

Mahon, Joseph. *Existentialism, Feminism and Simone de Beauvoir.* New York: Palgrave Macmillian, 1997.

McCall, Dorothy Kaufmann. "Simone de Beauvoir, *The Second Sex*, and Jean-Paul Sartre." *Signs: Journal of Women in Culture and Society* 5 no. 2 (1979–1980): 209–223.

Noudelmann, François. "What Do Jean-Paul Sartre and Simone de Beauvoir Have to Say to Us Today?" *Diogenes* 54 no. 216 (2007): 35–39.

O'Brien, Wendy, and Lester Embree, eds. *The Existential Phenomenology of Simone de Beauvoir.* Dordrecht, Netherlands: Kluwer Academic Publishers, 2001.

Rowley, Hazel. *Tête-à-Tête: Simone de Beauvoir and Jean-Paul Sartre.* New York: HarperCollins Publishers, 2005.

Schües, Christina, Dorothea E. Olkowski, and Helen A. Fielding, eds. *Time in Feminist Phenomenology.* Bloomington: Indiana University Press, 2011.

Simons, Margaret A. *Hypatia: Special Issue: The Philosophy of Simone de Beauvoir* 14, no. 4 (Fall 1999).

———. "Sexism and the Philosophical Cannon: On reading Beauvoir's *Second Sex.*" *Journal of the History of Ideas* 51 (1990): 487–504.

Simons, Margaret A., and Jessica Benjamin. "Simone de Beauvoir: An Interview." *Feminist Studies* 5, no. 2 (Summer 1979): 330–345.

Warren, Karen J. *An Unconventional History of Western Philosophy: Conversations Between Men and Women Philosophers.* Lanham, MD: Rowman & Littlefield, 2009.

Whitmarsh, Anne. *Simone de Beauvoir and the Limits of Commitment.* Cambridge: Cambridge University Press, 1981.

Wittig, Monique. *The Straight Mind and Other Essays.* Boston: Beacon Press. 1992.

Zerilli, Linda M. G. "A Process Without a Subject: Simone de Beauvoir and Julia Kristeva on Maternity." *Signs: Journal of Women in Culture and Society* 8, no. 1 (1982): 111–135.

Critiques of Existentialist Feminism:
A Communitarian Critique of Existentialist Feminism

Ascher, Carol. *Simone de Beauvoir: A Life of Freedom.* Boston: Beacon Press, 1981.

Beauvoir, Simone de. *Memoirs of a Dutiful Daughter.* Translated by James Kirkup. Harmondsworth, England: Penguin Books, 1963.

Bertozzi, Alberto. "A Critique of Simone de Beauvoir's Existential Ethics." *Philosophy Today* 51 no. 3 (2007): 303–311.

Dietz, Mary G. "Introduction: Debating Simone de Beauvoir." *Signs: Journal of Women in Culture and Society* 18, no. 1 (1983): 74–88.

Elshtain, Jean Bethke. *Public Man, Private Woman.* Princeton, NJ: Princeton University Press, 1981.

Kuykendall, Eléanor H. "Linguistic Ambivalence in Simone de Beauvoir's Feminist Theory." In *The Thinking Muse,* edited by Iris Young and Jeffner Allen. Bloomington: Indiana University Press, 1989.

Lloyd, Genevieve. *The Man of Reason: "Male" and "Female" in Western Philosophy.* Minneapolis: University of Minnesota Press, 1984.

Schutte, Ofelia. "A Critique of Normative Heterosexuality: Identity, Embodiment, and Sexual Difference in Beauvoir and Irigaray." *Hypatia* 12, no. 1 (Winter 1997): 40.

Schwarzer, Alice. *After the Second Sex.* New York: Pantheon Books, 1984.

Whitmarsh, Anne. *Simone de Beauvoir and the Limits of Commitment.* Cambridge: Cambridge University Press, 1981.

Postmodern Feminism

Agger, Ben. *Gender, Culture, and Power: Toward a Feminist Postmodern Critical Theory.* New York: Praeger Publishers, 1993.

Alcoff, Linda Martín. "Cultural Feminism Versus Post-Structuralism: The Identity Crisis in Feminist Theory." In *Feminism and Philosophy: Essential Readings,* edited by Nancy Tuana and Rosemarie Tong. Boulder, CO: Westview Press, 1995.

———. "Philosophy Matters: A Review of Recent Work in Feminist Philosophy." *Signs: Journal of Women in Culture and Society* 25 (2000): 841–882.

Assiter, Alison. *Enlightened Women: Modernist Feminism in a Postmodern Age.* London: Routledge, 1996.

Benhabib, Seyla. *Situating the Self: Gender, Community, and Postmodernism in Contemporary Ethics.* London: Routledge, 1992.

Bree, Germaine. *Women Writers in France.* New Brunswick, NJ: Rutgers University Press, 1973.

Brown, Wendy. "Feminist Hesitations, Postmodern Exposures." *Differences* 3, no. 1 (1991): 63–84.

Butler, Judith. "The Body Politics of Julia Kristeva." *Hypatia* 3, no. 3 (Winter 1989): 104–118.

Cahill, Ann J., and Jennifer Hansen. *Continental Feminism Reader.* Lanham, MD: Rowman & Littlefield, 2003.

Chanter, Tina. *Ethics of Eros: Irigaray's Rewriting of the Philosophers.* New York: Routledge, 1995.

Code, Lorraine. "Feminist Epistemology." In *A Companion to Epistemology,* edited by Jonathan Dancy and Ernst Sosa, 138–142. Oxford: Blackwell, 1992.

Di Stefano, Christine. "Dilemmas of Difference." In *Feminism/Postmodernism,* edited by Linda J. Nicholson, 63–82. New York: Routledge, 1990.

Fauré, Christine. "Absent from History." *Signs: Journal of Women in Culture and Society* 7, no. 1 (1981): 71–80.

Fisher, Linda, and Lester Embree, eds. *Feminist Phenomenology.* Dordrecht, Netherlands: Kluwer Academic Publishers, 2010.

Flax, Jane. "Postmodernism and Gender Relations in Feminist Theory." In *Feminism/Postmodernism,* edited by Linda J. Nicholson. New York: Routledge, 1990.

———. *Thinking Fragments: Psychoanalysis, Feminism, and Postmodernism in the Contemporary West.* Berkeley: University of California Press, 1989.

Fraser, Nancy. *Unruly Practices: Power, Gender and Discourse in Contemporary Critical Theory.* Minneapolis: University of Minnesota Press, 1989.

Fraser, Nancy, and Linda J. Nicholson. "Social Criticism Without Philosophy: An Encounter Between Feminism and Postmodernism." In *Feminism/Postmodernism,* edited by Linda J. Nicholson. New York: Routledge, 1990.

Grosz, Elizabeth. *Sexual Subversions: Three French Feminists.* Sydney, Australia: Allen & Unwin, 1989.

Grosz, Elizabeth, with Pheng Cheah. *Irigary and the Political Future of Sexual Difference.* Baltimore: Johns Hopkins University Press, 1998.

Hekman, Susan. *Gender and Knowledge: Elements of a Postmodern Feminism.* Cambridge: Polity Press, 1990.

———. *The Material of Knowledge: Feminist Disclosures.* Bloomington: Indiana University Press, 2010.

Hemmings, Clare. *Why Stories Matter: The Political Grammar of Feminist Theory.* Durham, NC: Duke University Press, 2011.

Irigaray, Luce. *An Ethics of Difference.* Translated by Carolyn Burke and Gillian Gill. Ithaca, NY: Cornell University Press, 1993.

———. "Is the Subject of Science Sexed?" Translated by Carol Mastrangelo Bové. *Hypatia* 2, no. 3 (Fall 1987): 66.

———. *Speculum of the Other Woman.* Translated by Gillian C. Gill. Ithaca, NY: Cornell University Press, 1985.

———. *This Sex Which Is Not One.* Translated by Catherine Porter. Ithaca, NY: Cornell University Press, 1985.

Ives, Kelly. *Cixous, Irigaray, Kristeva: The Jouissance of French Feminism.* Kent, UK: Crescent Moon Publishing, 2010.

Jardine, Alice, and Hester Eisenstein, eds. *The Future of Difference.* New Brunswick, NJ: Rutgers University Press, 1985.

Jones, Ann Rosalind. "Writing the Body: Toward an Understanding of *l'Écriture Féminine.*" *Feminist Studies* 7, no. 1 (Summer 1981): 248.

Kolmar, Wendy, and Frances Bartkowski, eds. *Feminist Theory: A Reader.* New York: Routledge, 2000.

Kristeva, Julia. *About Chinese Women.* Translated by Anita Barrows. New York: Marion Boyars, 1977.

———. *Desire in Language.* Translated by Leon Roudiez. New York: Columbia University Press, 1982.

————. *Powers of Horror.* Translated by Leon Roudiez. New York: Columbia University Press, 1982.

————. "Women's Time." *Signs: Journal of Women in Culture and Society* 7, no. 1 (Summer 1981): 13–35.

Kuykendall, Eléanor H. "Toward an Ethic of Nurturance: Luce Irigaray on Mothering and Power." In *Mothering: Essays in Feminist Theory,* edited by Joyce Trebilcot. Totowa, NJ: Rowman & Allanheld, 1984.

Mann, Susan. *Doing Feminist Theory: From Modernity to Postmodernity.* New York: Oxford University Press, 2012.

Marchand, Marianne H., and Jane Parpart, eds. *Feminism/Postmodernism/Development.* New York: Routledge, 1994.

Marks, Elaine. "Review Essay: Women and Literature in France." *Signs: Journal of Women in Culture and Society* 3, no. 4 (Summer 1978): 832–842.

Messer-Davidow, Ellen. *Disciplining Feminism: From Social Activism to Academic Discourse.* Durham, NC: Duke University Press, 2002.

Moi, Toril. *The Kristeva Reader.* New York: Columbia University Press, 1986.

Nicholson, Linda, ed. *Feminism/Postmodernism.* London: Routledge, 1989.

Oliver, Kelly, *French Feminism Reader.* Lanham, MD: Rowman & Littlefield, 2000.

————. *French Feminist Thought: A Reader.* New York: Blackwell, 1987.

————. "Julia Kristeva's Feminist Revolutions." *Hypatia* 8, no. 3 (Summer 1993).

————. *Witnessing: Beyond Recognition.* Minneapolis: University of Minnesota Press, 2001.

Oliver, Kelly, with Lisa Walsh, eds. *Contemporary French Feminism.* New York: Oxford University Press, 2005.

Orr, Catherine M., Ann Braithwaite, and Diane Lichtenstein, eds. *Rethinking Womens' and Gender Studies.* New York: Routledge, 2012.

Spivak, Gayatri Chakravorty. *Identity: Further Essays on Culture as Politics.* New York: Routledge, 2000.

Weedon, Chris. *Feminist Practice and Poststructuralist Theory.* Cambridge: Blackwell, 1987.

Whitford, Margaret, ed. *The Irigaray Reader.* Cambridge: Blackwell, 1991.

————. "Luce Irigaray and the Female Imaginary: Speaking as a Woman." *Radical Philosophy* 43 (Summer 1986): 7.

————. *Luce Irigaray: Philosophy in the Feminine.* New York: Routledge, 1991.

Wittig, Monique. *The Lesbian Body.* New York: William Morrow, 1975.

————. *Les Guérillères.* New York: Viking, 1971.

————. *The Opoponax.* New York: Simon & Schuster, 1966.

————. *The Straight Mind and Other Essays.* Boston: Beacon Press, 1992.

Postmodernism/Postmodern Feminism: Keynotes

Brennan, Teresa, ed. *History after Lacan.* London: Routledge, 1993.

Clément, Catherine. *The Lives and Legends of Jacques Lacan.* New York: Columbia University Press, 1983.

Grosz, Elizabeth. *Jacques Lacan: A Feminist Introduction.* New York: Routledge, 1990.

Hicks, Stephen R. C. *Exploring Postmodernism: Skepticism and Socialism from Rousseau to Foucault.* Tempe, AZ: Scholarly Publishing, 2004.

Lacan, Jacques. *Écrits: A Selection.* Translated by Alan Sheridan. New York: W. W. Norton, 1977.

———. "The Meaning of the Phallus." In *Feminine Sexuality,* edited by Juliet Mitchell and Jacqueline Rose. New York: W. W. Norton, 1982.

Lyotard, Jean-François. *The Postmodern Condition: A Report on Knowledge.* Minneapolis: University of Minnesota Press, 1984.

Smart, Barry. *Postmodernity: Key Ideas.* New York: Routledge, 1993.

Sturrock, John. Introduction to *Structuralism and Since: From Lévi-Strauss to Derrida.* New York: Oxford University Press, 1979.

Wolin, Richard. "Modernism vs. Postmodernism." *Telos* 62 (1984–1985): 9–29.

Jacques Derrida

Derrida, Jacques. *Margins of Philosophy.* Translated by Alan Bass. Chicago: University of Chicago Press, 1982.

———. *Of Grammatology.* Translated by Gayatri Chakravorty Spivak. Baltimore: Johns Hopkins University Press, 1974.

———. *Positions.* Translated by Alan Bass. Chicago: University of Chicago Press, 1982.

———. *The Post Card: From Socrates to Freud and Beyond.* Translated by Alan Bass. Chicago: University of Chicago Press, 1987.

———. *Spurs: Nietzsche's Styles.* Translated by Barbara Harlow. Chicago: University of Chicago Press, 1978.

———. *Writing and Difference.* Translated by Alan Bass. Chicago: University of Chicago Press, 1978.

Feder, Ellen K., Mary C. Rawlinson, and Emily Zakin, eds. *Derrida and Feminism.* New York: Routledge, 1997.

Jones, Irwin. *Derrida and the Writing of the Body.* Surrey, UK: Ashgate Publishing, 2010.

Hélène Cixous

Cixous, Hélène. *The Book of Promethea.* Translated by Betsy Wing. Lincoln: University of Nebraska Press, 1991.

———. "Castration or Decapitation?" *Signs: Journal of Women in Culture and Society* 7, no. 1 (Summer 1981): 41–55.

———. *"Coming to Writing" and Other Essays.* Translated by Sarah Cornell et al. Cambridge, MA: Harvard University Press, 1991.

———. "The Laugh of the Medusa." In *New French Feminisms,* edited by Elaine Marks and Isabelle de Courtivron. New York: Schocken Books, 1981.

Cixous, Hélène, and Catherine Clément. "Sorties." In *The Newly Born Woman.* Translated by Betsy Wing. Minneapolis: University of Minnesota Press, 1986.

Cixous, Hélène, with Mireille Calle-Gruber. *Hélène Cixous, Rootprints: Memory and Life Writings.* Translated by Eric Prenowitz. New York: Routledge, 1997.

Duchen, Claire. *Feminism in France: From May '68 to Mitterrand.* London: Routledge & Kegan Paul, 1986.

Sellers, Susan, ed. *The Hélène Cixous Reader.* New York: Routledge, 1994.

Michel Foucault

Christmas, Simon. "Michel Foucault." In *An Introduction to Modern European Philosophy,* edited by Jenny Teichman and Graham White. New York: Palgrave MacMillan, 1995.

Connolly, William. "Taylor, Foucault, and Otherness." *Political Theory* 13, no. 3 (1985): 365–376.

Diamond, Irene, and Lee Quinby, eds. *Feminism and Foucault: Reflections on Resistance.* Boston: Northeastern University Press, 1988.

Dudrick, David. "Foucault, Butler, and the Body." *European Journal of Philosophy* 13, no. 2 (2005): 226–246.

Eribon, Didier. *Michel Foucault.* Translated by Betsy Wing. Cambridge, MA: Harvard University Press, 1991.

Foucault, Michel. *Archeology of Knowledge.* Translated by A. Sheridan Smith. New York: Harper & Row, 1972.

———. *The Birth of the Clinic.* Translated by A. Sheridan Smith. New York: Pantheon, 1973.

———. *Discipline and Punish: The Birth of the Prison.* London: Allen Lane, 1977.

———. *The History of Sexuality.* Vol. 1, *An Introduction.* London: Penguin, 1984.

———. *The History of Sexuality.* Volumes 1–3, *Introduction, The Uses of Pleasure, and Care of the Self.* Translated by Robert Hurley. New York: Vintage, 1988–1990.

———. *Madness and Civilization.* Translated by Richard Howard. New York: Pantheon, 1965.

———. *The Order of Things.* New York: Vintage, 1973.

———. *Power/Knowledge.* Edited by Colin Gordon. New York: Random House, 1981.

McHoul, Alec, and Wendy Grace. *A Foucault Primer: Discourse, Power and the Subject.* New York: New York University Press, 1993.

McNay, Lois. *Foucault and Feminism and the Self.* Boston: Northeastern University Press, 1993.

Mitchell, Juliet, and Jacqueline Rose, eds. *Feminine Sexuality: Jacques Lacan and the École Freudienne,* translated by Jacqueline Rose. New York: W. W. Norton, 1982.

Ramazanoglu, Caroline, ed. *Up Against Foucault: Exploration of Some Tensions Between Foucault and Feminism.* New York: Routledge, 1993.

Rawlinson, Mary C., Sabrina L. Horn, and Serene J. Khader. *Thinking with Irigaray.* Albany: State University Press of New York, 2011.

Sawicki, Jana. *Disciplining Foucault: Feminism, Power, and the Body.* New York: Routledge, 1991.

Taylor, Dianna, and Karen Vintges, eds. *Feminism and the Final Foucault.* Urbana: University of Illinois Press, 2004.

Judith Butler

Allen, Amy. "Dependency, Subordination, and Recognition: On Judith Butler's Theory of Subjection." *Continental Philosophy Review* 38 (2006): 199–222.

Butler, Judith. *Bodies That Matter: On the Discursive Limits of "Sex."* New York: Routledge, 1993.

———. *Excitable Speech: A Politics of the Performative.* New York: Routledge, 1997.

———. *Gender Trouble: Feminism and the Subversion of Identity.* New York: Routledge, 1990.

———. *The Psychic Life of Power: Theories in Subjection.* Stanford, CA: Stanford University Press, 1997.

———. *Subjects of Desire: Hegelian Reflections in Twentieth Century France.* New York: Columbia University Press, 1987.

———. *Undoing Gender.* New York: Routledge, 2004.

Butler, Judith, Elisabeth Beck-Gernsheim, and Lidia Puigvert. *Women and Social Transformation.* New York: Routledge, 2003.

Magnus, Kathy Dow. "The Unaccountable Subject: Judith Butler and the Social Conditions of Intersubjective Agency." *Hypatia* 21, no. 2 (Spring 2006): 81–103.

McNay, Lois. "Subject, Psyche, and Agency: The Work of Judith Butler." *Theory, Culture & Society* 16, no. 2 (1999): 175–193.

Mills, Catherine. "Contesting the Political: Butler and Foucault on Power and Resistance." *Journal of Political Philosophy* 11, no. 3 (2003): 253–272.

———. "Efficacy and Vulnerability: Judith Butler on Reiteration and Resistance." *Australian Feminist Studies* 159, no. 32 (2000): 265–279.

Salih, Sara. *Judith Butler.* New York: Routledge, 2002.

Critiques of Postmodern Feminism

Belenky, Mary Field, Blythe McVicker Clinchy, Nancy Rule Goldberger, and Jill Mattuck Tarule. *Women's Ways of Knowing: The Development of Self, Voice, and Mind.* New York: Basic Books, 1986.

Benhabib, Seyla. "Feminism and Postmodernism." In *Feminist Contentions: A Philosophical Exchange,* edited by Seyla Benhabib et al., 17–34. New York and London: Routledge, 1994.

Bordo, Susan. "Feminism, Postmodernism, and Gender-Scepticism." In *Feminism/Postmodernism,* edited by Linda J. Nicholson, 133–156. New York: Routledge, 1990.

Di Stefano, Christine. "Dilemmas of Difference." In *Feminism/Postmodernism,* edited by Linda J. Nicholson. New York: Routledge, 1990.

Fausto-Sterling, Anne. *Myths of Gender: Biological Theories About Women and Men.* New York: Basic Books, 1985.

Flax, Jane. "Postmodernism and Gender Relations in Feminist Theory." In *Feminism/Postmodernism,* edited by Linda J. Nicholson. New York: Routledge, 1990.

———. *Thinking Fragments: Psychoanalysis, Feminism, and Postmodernism in the Contemporary West.* Berkeley: University of California Press, 1990.

Foucault, Michel. *Power/Knowledge.* Edited by Colin Gordon. New York: Random House, 1981.

Moi, Toril. *Sexual/Textual Politics: Feminist Literary Theory.* New York: Methuen, 1985.

Nussbaum, Martha C. "The Professor of Parody: The Hip Defeatism of Judith Butler." *The New Republic,* February 22, 1999, 37–45.

Shildrick, Margrit. *Leaky Bodies and Boundaries: Feminism, Postmodernism and (Bio)Ethics.* New York: Routledge, 1997.

Webster, Fiona. "The Politics of Sex and Gender: Benhabib and Butler Debate Subjectivity." *Hypatia* 15, no. 1 (Winter 2000): 1–22.

Whitford, Margaret. "Luce Irigaray and the Female Imaginary: Speaking as a Woman." *Radical Philosophy* 43 (Summer 1986): 7.

Chapter 6: Women of Color Feminisms

Albrecht, Lisa, and Rose M. Brewer, eds. *Bridges of Power: Women's Multicultural Alliances.* Philadelphia: New Society Publishers, 1990.

Alcoff, Linda Martín. *Visible Identities: Race, Gender, and the Self.* Oxford: Oxford University Press, 2006.

———. "What Should White People Do?" *Hypatia* 13, no. 3 (Summer 1998): 6–26.

Bailey, Alison, and Jacquelyn Zita. "The Reproduction of Whiteness: Race and the Regulation of the Gendered Body." *Hypatia* 22, no. 2 (Spring 2007): vii–xv.

Beemyn, Brett, and Mickey Eliason, eds. *Queer Studies: A Lesbian, Gay, Bisexual and Transgender Anthology.* New York and London: New York University Press, 1996.

Bulkin, Elly, Minnie Bruce Pratt, and Barbara Smith, eds. *Yours in Struggle: Three Feminist Perspectives on Anti-Semitism and Racism.* Ithaca, NY: Firebrand Books, 1984.

Chock, Phyllis Pease. "Culturalism: Pluralism, Culture, and Race in the *Harvard Encyclopedia of American Ethnic Groups.*" In *(Multi)Culturalism and the Baggage of "Race."* Special Issue. *Identities: Global Studies in Culture and Power* 1, no. 4 (April 1985): 301–324.

Cooper, Anna Julia. *A Voice from the South: By a Woman from the South.* New York: Oxford University Press, 1988.

Crenshaw, Kimberlé, Neil Gotanda, and Gary Peller, eds. *Critical Race Theory: The Key Writings That Formed the Movement.* New York: New Press, 1996.

Davies, Miranda. *Third World—Second Sex.* London: Zed Books, 1983.

Davis, Angela Y. *Angela Davis: An Autobiography.* New York: International Publishers, 1988.

———. *Women, Culture, and Politics.* New York: Vintage Books, 1990.

———. *Women, Race, and Class.* New York: Vintage Books/Random House, 1981.

Dicker, Susan. *Languages in America: A Pluralist View.* Philadelphia: Multilingual Matters Limited, 1966.

DuBois, Ellen Carol, and Vicki L. Ruiz, eds. *Unequal Sisters: A Multicultural Reader in U.S. Women's History.* New York: Routledge, 1990.

Eisenstein, Zillah R. *Hatreds: Racialized and Sexualized Conflicts in the 21st Century.* New York: Routledge, 1996.

Essed, Philomena, and Rita Gircour. *Diversity: Gender, Color, and Culture.* Amherst: University of Massachusetts Press, 1996.

Eze, Emmanuel Chukwudi. *Achieving Our Humanity: The Idea of a Postracial Future.* New York: Routledge, 2001.

Ferguson, Russell, et al., eds. *Out There: Marginalizations and Contemporary Cultures.* New York: New Museum of Contemporary Art; Cambridge, MA: MIT Press, 1991.

Fernandes Botts, Tina. "Antidiscrimination Law and the Multiracial Experience." *Hastings Race and Poverty Law Journal* 10, no. 2 (April 2013).

———. "Hermeneutics, Race, and Gender." In *The Routledge Companion to Philosophical Hermeneutics,* edited by Jeff Malpas and Hans-Helmuth Gander. New York: Routledge, forthcoming as of April 2013.

Fernandez, Carlos. "La Raza and the Melting Pot: A Comparative Look at Multiethnicity." In *Racially Mixed People in America,* edited by Maria P. Root. Newbury Park, CA: Sage, 1992.

Fowers, Blaine J., and Frank C. Richardson. "Why Is Multiculturalism Good?" *American Psychologist* 51, no. 6 (June 1996): 609.

Frankenberg, Ruth. *White Women, Race Matters.* Minneapolis: University of Minnesota Press, 1993.

Fraser, Nancy, and Axel Honneth. *Redistribution or Recognition? A Political-Philosophical Exchange.* Translated by Joel Golb, James Ingram, and Christiane Wilke. London: Verso, 2003.

Fusco, Coco. *English Is Broken Here: Notes on Cultural Fusion in the Americas.* New York: New Press, 1995.

Glazer, Nathan, and Daniel Patrick Moynihan. *Beyond the Melting Pot: The Negroes, Puerto Ricans, Jews, Italian, and Irish of New York City.* 2nd ed. Cambridge, MA: MIT Press, 1970.

Gunew, Sneja, and Anna Yeatman. *Feminism and the Politics of Difference.* St. Leonards, NSW: Allen and Unwin, 1993.

Haraway, Donna J. *Private Visions: Gender, Race, and Nature in the World of Modern Science.* New York: Routledge, 1989.

Harris, Cheryl I. "Whiteness as Property." In *Critical Race Theory: The Key Writings That Formed the Movement,* edited by Kimberlé Crenshaw et al. New York: New Press, 1995.

Henderson, Sarah, and Alana Jeydel. *Women and Politics in a Global World.* 2nd ed. New York: Oxford University Press, 2009.

Herr, Ranjoo Seodu. "A Third World Feminist Defense of Multiculturalism." *Social Theory and Practice* 30, no. 1 (January 2004): 73–103.

Hochschild, Jennifer. *Facing Up to the American Dream: Race, Class and the Soul of the Nation.* Princeton, NJ: Princeton University Press, 1995.

Hollinger, David A. *Post-ethnic America: Beyond Multiculturalism.* New York: Harper Collins, 1995.

Holmstrom, Nancy. "Human Nature." In *A Comparison to Feminist Philosophy,* edited by Alison M. Jaggar and Iris Marion Young. Oxford: Blackwell, 1998.

Hull, Gloria T., Patricia Bell Scott, and Barbara Smith, eds. *All the Women Are White, All the Blacks Are Men, But Some of Us Are Brave: Black Women's Studies.* New York: Feminist Press, 1982.

Katz, Judith. *White Awareness: Handbook for Anti-Racism Training.* Norman: University of Oklahoma Press, 1978.

King, Katie. *Theory in Its Feminist Travels: Conversations in U.S. Women's Movements.* Indianapolis: Indiana University Press, 1994.

Kirk, Gwyn. *Women's Lives: Multicultural Perspectives.* New York: McGraw Hill, 2009.

Lamphere, Louise, Helena Ragoné, and Patricia Zavella, eds. *Situated Lives: Gender and Culture in Everyday Life.* New York and London: Routledge, 1997.

Lee, Jung Young. *Marginality: The Key to Multicultural Theology.* Minneapolis: Fortress Press, 1995.

MacKinnon, Catherine A. *Are Women Human?: And Other International Dialogues.* Cambridge: Belknap Press of Harvard University Press, 2007.

Matisons, Michelle Renee. "Feminism and Multiculturalism: The Dialogue Continues." *Social Theory and Practice* 29, no. 4 (October 2003): 655–664.

Mookherjee, Monica. "Review Article: Feminism and Multiculturalism—Putting Okin and Shachar in Question." *Journal of Moral Philosophy* 2, no. 2 (2005): 237–241.

———. *Women's Rights as Multicultural Claims: Reconfiguring Gender and Diversity in Political Philosophy.* Edinburgh, Scotland: Edinburgh University Press, 2009.

Moraga, Cherríe, and Gloria Anzaldúa, eds. *This Bridge Called My Back: Writings by Radical Women of Color.* Latham, NY: Kitchen Table/Women of Color Press, 1981.

Moya, Paula M. L. *Learning from Experience: Minority Identities, Multicultural Struggles.* Berkeley: University of California Press, 2002.

Newman, Louise Michele. *White Women's Rights: The Racial Origins of Feminism in the United States.* New York: Oxford University Press, 1999.

Okin, Susan M. *Is Multiculturalism Bad for Women?* Princeton, NJ: Princeton University Press, 1999.

Phillips, Anne. "Multiculturalism, Universalism, and the Claims of Democracy." In *Gender, Justice, Development, and Rights,* edited by Maxine Molyneux and Shahra Razavi. Oxford: Oxford University Press, 2002.

Powell, Timothy B. "All Colors Flow into Rainbows and Nooses: The Struggle to Define Academic Multiculturalism." *Cultural Critique* 55 (Fall 2003): 152–181.

Pratt, Geraldine, and Victoria Rosner, eds. *The Global and the Intimate: Feminism in Our Time.* New York and Chichester, UK: Columbia University Press, 2012.

Ramazanoglu, Caroline. *Feminism and the Contradictions of Oppression.* London and New York: Routledge, 1989.

Raz, Joseph. "Multiculturalism: A Liberal Perspective." *Dissent* (Winter 1994): 74.

Rojas, Maythee. *Women of Color and Feminism: Seal Studies.* Berkeley: Seal Press, 2009.

Rutherford, Alexandra, Rose Capdevila, Vindhya Undurti, and Ingrid Palmary, eds. *Handbook of International Feminisms: Perspectives on Psychology, Women, Culture, and Rights (International and Cultural Psychology).* New York: Springer Science+ Business Media, 2011.

Scheman, Naomi. *Engendering: Construction of Knowledge, Authority, and Privilege.* New York: Routledge, 1993.

Schlesinger, Arthur M. Jr. *The Disuniting of America.* Knoxville, TN: Whittle Books, 1990.

Schueller, Malini Johar. "Analogy and (White) Feminist Theory: Thinking Race and the Color of the Cyborg Body." *Signs: Journal of Women in Culture and Society* 31, no. 1 (Autumn 2005): 63–92.

Shachar, Ayelet. *Multicultural Jurisdictions: Cultural Differences and Women's Rights.* Cambridge: Cambridge University Press, 2001.

Spelman, Elizabeth V. *Inessential Woman: Problems of Exclusion in Feminist Thought.* Boston: Beacon Press, 1988.

Spillers, Hortense J. *Comparative American Identities: Race, Sex and Nationality in Modern Text.* New York: Routledge, 1991.

Spinner-Halev, Jeff. "Feminism, Multiculturalism, Oppression, and the State." *Ethics* 112 (October 2001): 84–113.

Takaki, Ronald. *A Different Mirror: A History of Multicultural America.* New York: Oxford University Press, 1993.

———. *From Different Shores: Perspectives on Race and Ethnicity in America.* 2nd ed. New York: Oxford University Press, 1994.

———. *Iron Cages: Race and Culture in 19th Century America.* New York: Oxford University Press, 1990.

Tickner, J. Ann, and Laura Sjoberg, eds. *Feminism and International Relations: Conversations about the Past, Present and Future.* New York: Routledge, 2011.

Vest, Jennifer Lisa. "Names." *Canadian Journal of Native Studies* 30, no. 1 (Spring 2010).

Ware, Vron. *Beyond the Pale: White Women, Racism and History.* New York and London: Verso, 1992.

Warnke, Georgia. "Race, Gender, and Antiessentialist Politics." *Signs: Journal of Women in Culture and Society* 31, no. 1 (Autumn 2005): 93–116.

Wayne, Tiffany, ed. *Feminist Writings from Ancient Times to the Modern World: A Global Sourcebook and History.* 2 vols. Santa Barbara, CA: Greenwood, 2011.

Wiegman, Robyn. *American Anatomies: Theorizing Race and Gender.* Durham, NC: Duke University Press, 1995.

Wing, Adrien Katherine, ed. *Critical Race Feminism: A Reader.* New York and London: New York University Press, 1997.

Zack, Naomi. "Mixed Black and White Race and Public Policy." *Hypatia* 10, no. 1 (Winter 1995): 120–132.

Zinn, Maxine Baca, and Bonnie Thornton Dill, eds. *Women of Color in U.S. Society.* Philadelphia: Temple University Press, 1994.

From Multiculturalism to Intersectionality

Collins, Patricia Hill. *Black Feminist Thought: Knowledge, Consciousness, and the Politics of Empowerment,* 2nd ed. New York and London: Routledge, 2000.

Combahee River Collective. "A Black Feminist Statement." In *All the Women Are White, All the Blacks Are Men, But Some of Us Are Brave: Black Women's Studies,* edited by Gloria T. Hull, Patricia Bell Scott, and Barbara Smith. New York: Feminist Press, 1982.

Crenshaw, Kimberlé. "Mapping the Margins: Intersectionality, Identity, Politics, and Violence against Women of Color." In *Critical Race Theory: The Key Writings that Formed the Movement,* edited by Kimberlé Crenshaw, Neil Gotanda, Gary Peller, and Kendall Thomas. New York: The New Press, 1995.

Davis, Angela. *Women, Race, and Class.* New York: Random House, Inc., 1981.

Lorde, Audre. *Sister Outsider.* Berkeley: The Crossing Press, 1984.

McIntosh, Peggy. "White Privilege and Male Privilege: A Personal Account of Coming to See Correspondences Through Work in Women's Studies." In *Critical White Studies: Looking Behind the Mirror,* edited by Richard Delgado and Jean Stefanic. Philadelphia: Temple University Press, 1997.

Spelman, Elizabeth V. *Inessential Woman: Problems of Exclusion in Feminist Thought.* Boston: Beacon Press, 1998.

Zack, Naomi. *Women of Color and Philosophy: A Critical Reader.* Oxford: Blackwell Publishers, 2000.

Women of Color Feminisms in the United States

African American/Black Feminism

Bobo, Jacqueline. *Black Women as Cultural Readers.* New York: Columbia University Press, 1995.

Carby, Hazel. *Reconstructing Womanhood: The Emergence of the Afro-American Woman Novelist.* New York: Oxford University Press, 1987.

Collins, Patricia Hill. *Black Feminist Thought: Knowledge, Consciousness, and the Politics of Empowerment.* Boston: Unwin and Hyman, 1990.

———. "Learning from the Outsider Within: The Sociological Significance of Black Feminist Thought." In *Feminist Approaches to Theory and Methodology: An Interdisciplinary Reader,* edited by Sharlene Hesse-Biber, Christina Gilmartin, and Robin Lydenberg. New York: Oxford, 1999.

Davis, Angela Y. "Gender, Class, and Multiculturalism: Rethinking 'Race' Politics." In *Mapping Multiculturalism,* edited by Avery R. Gordon and Christopher Newfield, 40–48. Minneapolis: University of Minnesota Press, 1996.

DuBois, W. E. B. *Black Reconstruction in America, 1860–1880.* New York: Free Press, 1999.

Giddings, Paula. *When and Where I Enter: The Impact of Black Women on Race and Sex in America.* New York: Bantam Books, 1984.

Higashida, Cheryl. *Black Internationalist Feminism: Women Writers of the Black Left, 1945–1995.* Champaign: University of Illinois Press, 2011.

hooks, bell. *Ain't I a Woman: Black Women and Feminism.* Boston: South End Press, 1984.

———. *Black Looks: Race and Representation.* Boston: South End Press, 1992.

———. *Feminist Theory: From Margin to Center.* Boston: South End Press, 1984.

———. "Naked Without Shame: A Counter-Hegemonic Body Politic." In *Talking Visions: Multicultural Feminism in a Transnational Age,* edited by Ella Shohat. Cambridge, MA: The MIT Press, 1998.

———. *Talking Back: Thinking Feminist, Thinking Black.* Boston: South End Press, 1989.

———. *Yearning: Race, Gender and Cultural Politics.* Boston: South End Press, 1990.

James, Stanlie M., and Abena P. A. Busia, eds. *Theorizing Black Feminisms: The Visionary Pragmatism of Black Women.* New York and London: Routledge, 1993.

King, Deborah. "Multiple Jeopardy: The Context of a Black Feminist Ideology." In *Feminist Frameworks,* edited by Alison M. Jaggar and Paula S. Rothenberg. 3rd edition. New York: McGraw-Hill, 1993.

Lorde, Audre. "Age, Race, Class, and Sex: Women Redefining Difference." In *Race, Class, and Gender,* edited by Margaret L. Andersen and Patricia Hill Collins. 2nd edition. Belmont, CA: Wadsworth, 1995.

———. *The Cancer Journals.* San Francisco: Spinster/Aunt Lute, 1980.

———. *I Am Your Sister: Black Women Organizing Across Sexualities.* New York: Kitchen Table/Women of Color Press, 1985.

———. *Sister Outsider.* Freedom, CA: Crossing Press, 1984.

———. *Zami, A New Spelling of My Name: A Biomythography.* Freedom, CA: The Crossing Press, 1982.

Mabee, Carleton. *Sojourner Truth: Slave, Prophet, Legend.* New York: New York University Press, 1993.

Mosley, Albert G. "Negritude, Nationalism, and Nativism: Racists or Racialists?" In *Racism,* edited by Leonard Harris. Amherst, NY: Humanity Books, 1999.

Pearson, Jonna Lian. "Multicultural Feminism and Sisterhood Among Women of Color in Social Change Dialogue." *Howard Journal of Communications* 18 (2007): 88.

Piper, Adrian. "Passing for White, Passing for Black." In *Talking Visions: Multicultural Feminism in a Transitional Age,* edited by Ella Shohat. Cambridge, MA: MIT Press, 1998.

Smith, Barbara, ed. *Home Girls: A Black Feminist Anthology.* Latham, NY: Kitchen Table/Women of Color Press, 1983.

White, Aaronette M. *African Americans Doing Feminism: Putting Theory into Everyday Practice.* Albany: State University of New York Press, 2010.

———. *Ain't I a Feminist? African American Men Speak Out on Fatherhood, Friendship, Forgiveness, and Freedom.* Albany: State University of New York Press, 2008.

Zack, Naomi. "Mixed Black and White Race and Public Policy." *Hypatia* 10, no. 1 (Winter 1995): 123–124.

Zackodnik, Teresa C. *"We Must Be Up and Doing": A Reader in Early African American Feminisms.* Peterborough, Ontario: Broadview Press, 2010.

Mixed Race Feminism

Bettez, Silvia Cristina. *But Don't Call Me White: Mixed Race Women Exposing Nuances of Privilege and Oppression Politics*. Rotterdam: Sense Publishers, 2011.

Cross, June. *Secret Daughter: A Mixed-Race Daughter and the Mother Who Gave Her Away*. New York: Penguin Group, 2006.

DeRango-Adem, Adebe, and Andrea Thompson. *Other Tongues: Mixed-Race Women Speak Out*. Toronto: Ianna Publications, 2010.

Dewan, Indra Angeli. *Recasting Race: Women of Mixed Heritage in Further Education*. Stoke-on-Trent, UK: Trentham Books, 2008.

Fernandes Botts, Tina. "Antidiscrimination Law and the Multiracial Experience." *Hastings Race and Poverty Law Journal* 10, no. 2 (April 2013).

————. "Hermeneutics, Race, and Gender." In *The Routledge Companion to Philosophical Hermeneutics,* edited by Jeff Malpas and Hans-Helmuth Gander. New York: Routledge, forthcoming as of April 2013.

Sundstrom, Ronald R. *The Browning of America and the Evasion of Social Justice*. Albany: State University Press of New York, 2008.

Vest, Jennifer Lisa. "Names." *Canadian Journal of Native Studies* 30, no. 1 (Spring 2010).

Wright, Marguerite. *I'm Chocolate, You're Vanilla: Raising Healthy Black and White Children in a Race-Conscious World*. San Francisco: Jossey-Bass Publishers, 1998.

Zack, Naomi. "Mixed Black and White Race and Public Policy." *Hypatia* 10, no. 1 (Winter 1995): 123–124.

————. *Women of Color and Philosophy: A Critical Reader*. Oxford: Blackwell Publishers, 2000.

Latin American/Latina Feminism

Alcoff, Linda Martin. *Visible Identities: Race, Gender, and the Self*. New York: Oxford University Press, 2006.

Anzaldúa, Gloria. *Borderlands/La Frontera: The New Mestiza*. San Francisco: Spinsters/Aunt Lute, 1987.

————, ed. *Making Face, Making Soul/Haciendo Caras: Creative and Critical Perspectives by Women of Color*. San Francisco: Aunt Lute Books, 1990.

Arredondo, Gabriela F., Aída Hurtado, Norma Klahn, Olga Nájera-Ramírez, and Patricia Zavella, eds. *Chicana Feminisms: A Critical Reader*. Durham, NC: Duke University Press, 2003.

Asencio, Marysol, and Katie Acosta. "Macho Men and Passive Women." *Conscience: The News Journal of Catholic Opinion* 28, no. 2 (Summer 2007).

Blea, Irene I. *La Chicana and the Intersection of Race, Class, and Gender*. Westport, CT, and London: Praeger, 1992.

Dávila, Arlene. *Latinos, Inc.: The Marketing and Making of a People*. Berkeley: University of California Press, 2001.

Flores, William V., and Rina Benmayor. *Latino Cultural Citizenship: Claiming Identity, Space and Rights*. Boston: Beacon Press, 1997.

Haney López, Ian F. "Race and Erasure: The Salience of Race to Latinos/as." In *The Latino Condition,* edited by Richard Delgado and Jean Stefancic. New York: New York University Press, 1998.

Lugones, Maria, and Elisabeth Spelman. "Have We Got a Theory for You! Feminist Theory, Cultural Imperialism, and the Demand for the Woman's Voice." In *Femi-*

nist Philosophies, edited by Janet A. Kourany, James Sterba, and Rosemarie Tong. Englewood Cliffs, NJ: Prentice-Hall, 1992.

Moraga, Cherríe. *Loving in the War Years: Lo que nunca pasó por sus labios.* Boston: South End Press, 1983.

Oboler, Suzanne. *Ethnic Labels, Latino Lives: Identity and the Politics of (Re)Presentation in the United States.* Minneapolis: University of Minnesota Press, 1995.

Ramirez, Deborah A. "It's Not Just Black and White Anymore." In *The Latino Condition,* edited by Richard Delgado and Jean Stefancic. New York: New York University Press, 1998.

Ramos, Juanita, ed. *Compañeras: Latina Lesbians.* New York: Latina Lesbian History Project, 1987.

Rosaldo, Renato. "Identity Politics: An Ethnography by a Participant." In *Identity Politics Reconsidered,* edited by Linda M. Alcoff et al. New York: Palgrave Macmillan, 2006.

Saldívar-Hull, Sonia. *Feminism on the Border: Chicana Gender Politics and Literature.* Berkeley: University of California Press, 2000.

Schutte, Ofelia. "Cultural Alterity: Cross-Cultural Communication and Feminist Theory in North-South Contexts." In *Decentering the Center: Philosophy for a Multicultural, Postcolonial, and Feminist World,* edited by Uma Narayan and Sandra Harding. Bloomington: Indiana University Press, 2000. First published in *Hypatia* 13, no. 2 (Spring 1998).

———. *Cultural Identity and Social Liberation in Latin American Thought.* Albany: State University of New York Press, 1993.

Trujillo, Carla, ed. *Chicana Lesbians: The Girls Our Mothers Warned Us About.* Berkeley: Third Woman Press, 1991.

Zea, Leopoldo. "Identity: A Latin American Philosophical Problem." *Philosophical Forum* 20 (Fall–Winter 1988–1989): 33–42.

Asian American Feminism

Asian Women United of California, eds. *Making Waves: An Anthology of Writings by and About Asian American Women.* Boston: Beacon Press, 1989.

Cha, Theresa Hak Kyung. *Dictee.* New York: Tanam Press, 1982.

Chen, Ya-chen. *The Many Dimensions of Chinese Feminism.* New York: Palgrave Macmillan, 2011.

Hongo, Garrett, ed. *Under Western Eyes: Personal Essays from Asian-Americans.* New York: Anchor Books, 1995.

Katjasungkana, Nursyahbani, and Saskia E. Wieringa, eds. *The Future of Asian Feminisms: Confronting Fundamentalisms, Conflicts and Neo-liberalism.* Newcastle upon Tyne, UK: Cambridge Scholars Publishing, 2012.

Kim, Elaine H. *Asian American Literature: An Introduction to the Writings and Their Social Context.* Philadelphia: Temple University Press, 1984.

Kim, Elaine H., and Lilia V. Villanueva, eds. *Making More Waves: New Asian American Writing by Asian Women.* Boston: Beacon Press, 1997.

Kim, Elaine H., and Eui-Young Yu. *East to America: Korean American Life Stories.* New York: New Press, 1995.

Klasen, Stephan, and Claudia Wink. "A Turning Point in Gender Bias in Mortality? An Update on the Number of Missing Women." *Population and Development Review* 28, no. 2 (January 2002): 285–312.

Loomba, Ania, and Ritty A. Lukose, eds. *South Asian Feminisms.* Durham, NC: Duke University Press, 2012.

Lowe, Lisa. "Heterogeneity, Hybridity, Multiplicity: Making Asian American Difference." *Diaspora* 1 (1991): 24–44.

Marchetti, Gina. *Romance and the "Yellow Peril": Race, Sex, and Discursive Strategies in Hollywood Fiction.* Los Angeles and Berkeley: University of California Press, 1994.

Okihiro, Gary. *Margins to Mainstreams: Asians in American History and Culture.* Seattle: University of Washington Press, 1994.

Sen, Amartya. "More than 100 Million Women Are Missing." *The New York Review of Books* 37, no. 20 (December 20, 1990).

Takagi, Dana Y. *The Retreat from Race: Asian-American Admissions and Racial Politics.* New Brunswick, NJ: Rutgers University Press, 1992.

Wong, Diane Yen-Mei. *Dear Diane: Letters from Our Daughters.* San Francisco: San Francisco Study Center, 1983.

Wu, Frank. *Yellow: Race in America beyond Black and White.* New York: Basic Books, 2002.

Indigenous Feminism

Allen, Paula Gunn. "Kochinnenako in Academe: Three Approaches to Interpreting a Keres Indian Tale." In *Feminist Theory: A Reader,* edited by Wendy K. Kolmar and Frances Bartkowski. New York: McGraw-Hill.

————. *The Sacred Hoop: Recovering the Feminine in American Indian Traditions.* Boston: Beacon Press, 1986.

————, ed. *Spider Woman's Granddaughters: Traditional Tales and Contemporary Writing by Native American Women.* Boston: Beacon Press, 1986.

Bataille, Gretchen, and Kathleen Mullen Sands. *American Indian Women: Telling Their Lives.* Lincoln: University of Nebraska Press, 1984.

Dearborn, Mary V. *Pocahontas's Daughters: Gender and Ethnicity in American Culture.* New York: Oxford University Press, 1986.

Green, Rayna. *Indians of North America: Women in American Indian Society.* New York and Philadelphia: Chelsea House Publishers, 1992.

————. *Native American Women: A Contextual Bibliography.* Bloomington: Indiana University Press, 1983.

Jaimes, M. Annette, ed. *The State of Native America: Genocide, Colonization and Resistance.* Boston: South End Press, 1992.

Kailo, Kaarina. *Wo(Men) and Bears: The Gifts of Nature, Culture and Gender Revisited.* Toronto: Ianna Publications, 2008.

Lawrence, Bonita. "Gender, Race, and the Regulation of Native Identity in Canada and the United States: An Overview." *Hypatia* 18, no. 2 (Spring 2003): 3–31.

Mihesuah, Devon Abbott. *Indigenous American Women: Decolonization, Empowerment, Activism.* Lincoln: University of Nebraska Press, 2003.

Pillow, Wanda. "Searching for Sacajawea: Whitened Reproductions and Endarkened Representations." *Hypatia* 22, no. 2 (Spring 2007): 1–19.

Poupart, Lisa. "The Familiar Face of Genocide: Internalized Oppression Among American Indians." *Hypatia* 18, no. 2 (Spring 2003): 86–100.

Sarris, Greg. *Keeping Slug Women Alive: A Holistic Approach to American Indian Texts.* Berkeley, Los Angeles, and Oxford: University of California Press, 1993.

Sellers, Stephanie A. *Native American Women's Studies: A Primer*. New York: Peter Lang Publishing, 2008.

Silko, Leslie Marmon. *Yellow Woman and a Beauty of Spirit: Essays on Native American Life Today*. New York: Touchstone/Simon & Schuster, 1997.

Smith, Andy. "Not an Indian Tradition: The Sexual Colonization of Native Peoples." *Hypatia* 18, no. 2 (Spring 2003): 70–85.

Waters, Anne. "Introduction: Indigenous Women in the Americas." *Hypatia* 18, no. 2 (Spring 2003): ix–xx.

Women of Color Feminisms on the World Stage: Global, Postcolonial, and Transnational Feminisms

Global Feminism

Abdulhadi, Rabab, Evelyn Alsultany, and Nadine Naber, eds. *Arab & Arab American Feminisms: Gender, Violence, & Belonging (Gender, Culture, and Politics in the Middle East)*. Syracuse, NY: Syracuse University Press, 2011.

Barber, Benjamin. *Jihad vs. McWorld: How Globalism and Tribalism Are Reshaping the World*. New York: Ballantine, 1995.

Barry, Kathleen. *The Prostitution of Sexuality: The Global Exploitation of Women*. New York and London: New York University Press, 1995.

Benhabib, Seyla. *Claims of Culture: Equality and Diversity in the Global Era*. Princeton, NJ: Princeton University Press, 2002.

Burn, Shawn Meghan. *Women Across Cultures: A Global Perspective*. Mountain View, CA: Mayfield Publishing, 2000.

Cohen, Colleen Ballerino, Richard Wilk, and Beverly Stoeltje. *Beauty Queens on the Global Stage: Gender, Contests, and Power*. New York and London: Routledge, 1996.

Crystal, David. *English as a Global Language*. Cambridge: Cambridge University Press, 1997.

Ehrenrich, Barbara, and Annette Fuentes. *Women in Global Factory*. Boston: South End Press, 1983.

Enloe, Cynthia. *Bananas, Beaches, and Bases: Making Feminist Sense of International Politics*. Berkeley: University of California Press, 1989.

Eschle, Catherine, and Bice Maiguascha. *Making Feminist Sense of the Global Justice Movement*. Lanham, MD: Rowan & Littlefield Publishers, 2010.

Ferguson, Ann. "Resisting the Veil of Privilege: Building Bridge Identities as an Ethico-Politics of Global Feminisms." *Hypatia* 13, no. 3 (Summer 1998): 95–113.

Ferree, Myra Marx. *Varieties of Feminism: German Gender Politics in Global Perspective*. Stanford, CA: Stanford University Press, 2012.

Ginsburg, Faye, and Rayna Rapp, eds. *Conceiving the New World Order: The Global Politics of Reproduction*. Berkeley, Los Angeles, and London: University of California Press, 1995.

Hartman, Tova. *Feminism Encounters Traditional Judaism: Resistance and Accommodation (HBI Series on Jewish Women)*. Lebanon, NH: University Press of New England, 2007.

Hellsten, Sirrku Kristiina. "From Human Wrongs to Universal Rights: Communication and Feminist Challenges for the Promotion of Women's Health in the Third World." *Developing World Bioethics* 1, no. 2 (2001): 108–109.

Jabri, Vivienne. "Feminist Ethics and Hegemonic Global Politics." *Alternatives* 29 (2004): 275.

Jaggar, Alison. "Globalizing Feminist Ethics." *Hypatia* 13 (1998): 7–31.

King, Anthony D., ed. *Culture, Globalization and the World-System: Contemporary Conditions for the Representation of Identity.* Minneapolis: University of Minnesota Press, 2000.

Mohanty, Chandra Talpade, Ann Russo, and Lourdes Torres, eds. *Third World Women and the Politics of Feminism.* Bloomington and Indianapolis: Indiana University Press, 1991.

Nash, June, and María Patricia Fernández-Kelly. *Women, Men, and the International Division of Labor.* Albany: State University of New York Press, 1983.

Nussbaum, Martha. "Women's Capabilities and Social Justice." In *Gender, Justice, Development, and Rights,* edited by Maxine Molyneux and Shahra Razavi. Oxford: Oxford University Press, 2002.

Okin, Susan Moller. "Feminism, Women's Human Rights, and Cultural Differences." *Hypatia* 13, no. 2 (1998): 42.

———. "Inequalities Between Sexes in Different Cultural Contexts." In *Women, Culture, and Development,* edited by Martha Nussbaum and Jonathan Glover, 294. Oxford: Clarendon Press, 1995.

———. "Recognizing Women's Rights as Human Rights." *APA Newsletters* 97, no. 2 (Spring 1998).

Paxton, Pamela M., and Melanie M. Hughes. *Women, Politics, and Power: A Global Perspective.* Thousand Oaks, CA: Pine Ford Press, 2007.

Peterson, Spike V., and Laura Parisi. "Are Women Human? It's Not an Academic Question." In *Human Rights Fifty Years On: A Radical Reappraisal,* edited by Tony Evans. Manchester, UK: Manchester University Press, 1998.

Sinclair, M. Thea, ed. *Gender, Work, and Tourism.* London and New York: Routledge, 1997.

Towns, Ann E. *Women and States: Norms and Hierarchies in International Society.* New York: Cambridge University Press, 2010.

United Nations Declaration on the Elimination of Violence Against Women. 85th Plenary Meeting. December 20, 1993. A/RES/48/104. Available at http://www.un.org/documents/ga/res/48/a48r104.htm.

Postcolonial Feminism

Abu-Lughod, Lila. *Writing Women's Worlds: Bedouin Stories.* Berkeley and Los Angeles: University of California Press, 1993.

Afkhami, Mahnaz. *Women in Exile.* Charlottesville and London: University Press of Virginia, 1994.

Ahmed, Leila. *Women and Gender in Islam: Historical Roots of a Modern Debate.* New Haven, CT: Yale University Press, 1992.

Alexander, M. Jacqui, and Chandra Talpade Mohanty, eds. *Feminist Genealogies, Colonial Legacies, Democratic Futures.* New York: Routledge, 1996.

Alexander, Meena. *The Shock of Arrival: Reflections on Postcolonial Experience.* Boston: South End Press, 1996.

Alloula, Malek. *The Colonial Harem.* Minneapolis: University of Minnesota Press, 1986.

Bartkowski, Frances. *Travelers, Immigrants, Inmates: Essays in Estrangement.* Minneapolis: University of Minnesota Press, 1995.

Bulbeck, Chilla. *Re-Orienting Western Feminisms: Women's Diversity in a Postcolonial World.* Cambridge: Cambridge University Press, 1998.

Chaudhuri, Nupur, and Margaret Strobel, eds. *Western Women and Imperialism: Complicity and Resistance.* Bloomington and Indianapolis: Indiana University Press, 1992.

Donaldson, Laura E. *Decolonizing Feminisms: Race, Gender and Empire Building.* Chapel Hill: University of North Carolina Press, 1992.

Etienne, Mona, ed. *Women and Colonization: Anthropological Perspectives.* New York: Bergin & Garvey Publishers, 1980.

Green, Mary Jean, et al., eds. *Post-Colonial Subjects: Francophone Women Writers.* Minneapolis and London: University of Minnesota Press, 1996.

Guerrero, M. A. Jaimes. "'Patriarchal Colonialism' and Indigenism: Implications for Native Feminist Spirituality and Native Womanism." *Hypatia* 18, no. 2 (Spring 2003): 58–69.

Harding, Sandra. *Sciences from Below: Feminisms, Postcolonialities, and Modernities.* Durham, NC: Duke University Press, 2008.

Jayawardena, Kumari. *Feminism and Nationalism in the Third World.* London and Atlantic Highlands, NJ: Zed Books, 1986.

Loomba, Ania. *Colonialism/Postcolonialism.* London: Routledge, 1998.

McClintock, Anne. *Imperial Leather: Race, Gender and Sexuality in the Colonial Contest.* New York and London: Routledge, 1995.

McClintock, Anne, Aamir Mufti, and Ella Shohat, eds. *Dangerous Liaisons: Gender, Nation, and Post-Colonial Perspectives.* Minneapolis: University of Minnesota Press, 1997.

Mohanty, Chandra Talpade. "Under Western Eyes Revisited: Feminist Solidarity through Anticapitalist Struggles." *Signs: Journal of Women in Culture and Society* 28, no. 2 (2003): 499–535.

Mohanty, Chandra Talpade, Minnie Bruce Pratt, and Robin L. Riley, eds. *Feminism and War.* New York: Zed Books, 2008.

Molyneux, Maxine, and Shahra Razavi, eds. "Introduction." In *Gender Justice, Development and Rights.* Oxford: Oxford University Press, 2002.

Narayan, Uma. *Dislocating Cultures: Identities, Traditions, and Third-World Feminisms.* New York: Routledge, 1997.

Narayan, Uma, and Sandra Harding. "Introduction. Border Crossings: Multicultural and Postcolonial Feminist Challenges to Philosophy (Part I)." *Hypatia* 13, no. 2 (Spring 1998): 86–106.

———. "Introduction. Border Crossings: Multicultural and Postcolonial Feminist Challenges to Philosophy (Part II)." *Hypatia* 13, no. 3 (Summer 1998): 1–5.

Seshadri-Crooks, Kalpana. "At the Margins of Postcolonial Studies." In *The Pre-Occupation of Postcolonial Studies,* edited by Fawzia Azfal-Khan and Kalpana Seshadri-Crooks. Durham, NC: Duke University Press, 2000.

Sharpe, Jenny. *Allegories of Empire: The Figure of Woman in the Colonial Text.* Minneapolis: University of Minnesota Press, 1993.

Spivak, Gayatri Chakravorty. *A Critique of Postcolonial Reason: Toward a History of the Vanishing Present.* Cambridge, MA: Harvard University Press, 1999.

Suzack, Cheryl, Shari M. Huhndorf, Jeanne Perreault, and Jean Barman, eds. *Indigenous Women and Feminism: Politics, Activism, Culture.* Vancouver: UBC Press, 2011.

Waller, Marquerite, and Sylvia Marcos, eds. *Dialogue and Difference: Feminisms Challenge Globalization.* New York: Palgrave Macmillan, 2005.

Transnational Feminism

Ferree, Myra Marx, and Aili Mari Tripp, eds. *Global Feminism: Transnational Women's Activism, Organizing, and Human Rights*. New York: New York University Press, 2006.

Grewal, Inderpal. *Transnational America: Feminisms, Diasporas, Neoliberalisms*. Durham, NC: Duke University Press, 2005.

Kaplan, Karen, Norma Alarcon, and Minoo Moallem, eds. *Between Woman and Nation: Nationalisms, Transnational Feminisms, and the State*. Durham, NC: Duke University Press, 1999.

Marciniak, Katarzyna, Anikó Imre, and Áine O'Healy, eds. *Transnational Feminism in Film and Media*. New York: Palgrave Macmillan, 2007.

Moghadam, Valentine M. *Globalizing Women: Transnational Feminist Networks*. Baltimore: The Johns Hopkins University Press, 2005.

Mohanty, Chandra Talpade. *Feminism Without Borders: Decolonizing Theory, Practicing Solidarity*. Durham, NC: Duke University Press, 2003.

Roces, Mina, and Louise Edwards. *Women's Movements in Asia: Feminisms and Transnational Activism*. New York: Routledge, 2010.

Shohat, Ella, ed. "Area Studies, Transnationalism, and the Feminist Production of Knowledge." *Signs: Journal of Women in Culture and Society* 26, no. 4 (2001): 1269–1272.

———. *Talking Visions: Multicultural Feminism in a Transitional Age*. Cambridge, MA: MIT Press, 1998.

Swarr, Amanda Lock, and Richa Nagar. *Critical Transnational Feminist Praxis*. Albany: State University of New York Press, 2010.

Thayer, Millie. *Making Transnational Feminism: Rural Women, NGO Activists, and Northern Donors in Brazil*. New York: Routledge, 2010.

Conclusion

Caraway, Nancie. *Segregated Sisterhood: Racism and the Politics of American Feminism*. Knoxville: University of Tennessee Press, 1991.

hooks, bell. *Feminist Theory: From Margin to Center*. Boston: South End Press, 1984.

Lorde, Audre. *Sister Outsider*. Berkeley: The Crossing Press, 1984.

Young, Iris Marion. "The Ideal of Community and the Politics of Difference." In *Feminism/Postmodernism*, edited by Linda J. Nicholson. New York: Routledge, 1990.

Chapter 7: Ecofeminism

Biehl, Janet. *Rethinking Feminist Politics*. Boston: South End Press, 1991.

Ruether, Rosemary Radford. *New Woman/New Earth: Sexist Ideologies and Human Liberation*. New York: Seabury Press, 1975.

Warren, Karen J., ed. "Feminism and Ecology: Making Connections." In *Readings in Ecology and Feminist Theology*, edited by Mary Heather MacKinnon and Marie McIntyre. Kansas City, KS: Sheed and Ward, 1995.

———. "Feminism and the Environment: An Overview of the Issues." *APA Newsletter on Feminism and Philosophy* 90, no. 3 (Fall 1991): 110–111.

———. "The Power and the Promise of Ecological Feminism." In *Ecological Feminist Philosophies*. Bloomington: Indiana University Press, 1996.

Some Roots of Ecofeminism

Abram, David. *Becoming Animal: An Earthly Cosmology.* New York: Vintage, 2011.

————. *The Spell of the Sensuous: Perception and Language in a More-Than-Human World.* New York: Vintage, 1996.

Adorno, Theodor W. *Minima Moralia: Reflections from Damaged Life.* Translated by E. F. N. Jephcott. London: New Left Books, 1974.

Aiken, William. "Non-Anthropocentric Ethical Challenges." In *Earthbound: New Introductory Essays in Environmental Ethics,* edited by Tom Regan. New York: Random House, 1984.

Brown, Charles S., and Ted Toadvine, eds. *Eco-Phenomenology: Back to the Earth Itself.* Albany: State University of New York Press, 2003.

Caldecott, Leonie, and Stephanie Leland, eds. *Reclaim the Earth.* London: Women's Press, 1983.

Callicott, J. Baird. "Do Deconstructive Ecology and Sociobiology Undermine Leopold's Land Ethic?" In *Environmental Philosophy,* edited by Michael E. Zimmerman et al., 145–164. 2nd ed. Upper Saddle River, NJ: Prentice-Hall, 1998.

Carson, Rachel. *Silent Spring.* Boston: Houghton Mifflin, 1962.

Code, Lorraine. *Epistemic Responsibility.* Hanover, NH: University Press of New England, 1987.

Collard, Andrée, with Joyce Contrucci. *Rape of the Wild: Man's Violence Against Animals and the Earth.* Bloomington: Indiana University Press, 1988.

Curry, Patrick. *Ecological Ethics: An Introduction.* Cambridge: Polity Press, 2011.

Ferry, Luc. *The New Ecological Order.* Translated by Carol Volk. Chicago: University of Chicago Press, 1992.

Gebara, Ivone. *Longing for Running Water: Ecofeminism and Liberation.* Minneapolis: Fortress Press, 1999.

Harding, Sandra. *The Science Question in Feminism.* Ithaca, NY: Cornell University Press, 1986.

Kheel, Marti. *Nature Ethics: An Ecofeminist Perspective.* Lanham, MD: Rowman & Littlefield, 2008.

Kohák, Erazim. *The Embers and the Stars: A Philosophical Inquiry into the Moral Sense of Nature.* Chicago: University of Chicago Press, 1984.

Leopold, Aldo. "The Land Ethic." In *A Sand County Almanac: With Other Essays on Conservation from Round River.* New York: Oxford University Press, 1987.

McDaniel, Jay B. *Earth, Sky, God, and Mortals: Developing an Ecological Spirituality.* Mystic, CT: Twenty-Third Publications, 1990.

Munroe, Jennifer, and Rebecca Laroche, eds. *Ecofeminist Approaches to Early Modernity: Literatures, Cultures, and the Environment.* New York: Palgrave Macmillan, 2011.

Naess, Arne. "The Deep Ecological Movement: Some Philosophical Aspects." *Philosophical Inquiry* 8 (1986): 10–13.

Salleh, Ariel Kay. "Deeper Than Deep Ecology: The Ecofeminist Connection." *Environmental Ethics* 6, no. 1 (1984): 339.

Sarkar, Sahotra. *Environmental Philosophy: from Theory to Practice.* West Sussex, UK: John Wiley & Sons, 2012.

Scully, Matthew. *Dominion: The Power of Man, the Suffering of Animals, and the Call to Mercy.* New York: St. Martin's Press, 2002.

Stibbe, Arran. *Animals Erased: Discourse, Ecology, and Reconnection with the Natural World.* Middletown, CT: Wesleyan University Press, 2012.

Taylor, Paul W. *Respect for Nature: A Theory of Environmental Ethics.* Princeton, NJ: Princeton University Press, 1986, 2011.

Vakoch, Douglas A., ed. *Feminist Ecocriticism: Environment, Women, and Literature.* Plymouth, UK: Lexington Books, 2012.

Warren, Karen J., ed. *Ecofeminism: Women, Culture, Nature.* Bloomington: Indiana University Press, 1997.

Wenz, Peter S. "Ecology and Morality." In *Ethics and Animals,* edited by Harlan B. Miller and William H. Williams. Clifton, NJ: Humana Press, 1983.

Ecofeminism: New Philosophy or Ancient Wisdom?

Alaimo, Stacy. "Cyborg and Ecofeminist Interventions: Challenges for an Environmental Feminism." *Feminist Studies* 20, no. 1 (Spring 1994): 133–152.

Allen, Paula Gunn. "The Woman I Love Is a Planet; the Planet I Love Is a Tree." In *Reweaving the World: The Emergence of Ecofeminism,* edited by Irene Diamond and Gloria Feman Orenstein. San Francisco: Sierra Club Books, 1990.

Auerbach, Judith. "The Intersection of Feminism and the Environmental Movement, or What Is Feminist About the Feminist Perspective on the Environment?" *American Behavioral Scientist* 37, no. 8 (August 1994): 1095.

Beauvoir, Simone de. *The Second Sex.* Translated and edited by H. M. Parshley. New York: Vintage Books, 1952.

Biehl, Janet. *Rethinking Feminist Politics.* Boston: South End Press, 1991.

Cook, Julie. "The Philosophical Colonization of Ecofeminism." *Environmental Ethics* 20, no. 3 (Fall 1998): 227–246.

Diamond, Irene, and Gloria Feman Orenstein, eds. *Reweaving the World: The Emergence of Ecofeminism.* San Francisco: Sierra Club Books, 1990.

Gaard, Greta. *Ecological Politics: Ecofeminists and the Greens.* Philadelphia: Temple University Press, 1993.

King, Ynestra. "The Ecology of Feminism and the Feminism of Ecology." In *Healing the Wounds: The Promise of Ecofeminism,* edited by Judith Plant. Santa Cruz, CA: New Society Publishers, 1989.

———. "Engendering a Peaceful Planet: Ecology, Economy, and Ecofeminism in Contemporary Context." *Women's Studies Quarterly* 23 (Fall–Winter 1995): 19.

Mellor, Mary. *Feminism and Ecology.* New York: New York University Press, 1997.

Merchant, Carolyn. *The Death of Nature: Women, Ecology, and the Scientific Revolution.* San Francisco: Harper & Row, 1980.

Nordquist, Joan. "Ecofeminist Theory: A Bibliography." In *Social Theory: A Bibliographic Series* 36. Santa Cruz, CA: Reference and Research Services, 1994.

Ortner, Sherry B. "Is Female to Male as Nature Is to Culture?" In *Readings in Ecology and Feminist Theory,* edited by Mary Heather MacKinnon and Marie McIntyre. Kansas City, KS: Sheed and Ward, 1995.

Plumwood, Val. *Feminism and the Mastery of Nature (Opening Out: Feminism for Today).* London: Routledge, 1993.

Roach, Catherine. "Loving Your Mother: On the Woman-Nature Connection." In *Ecological Feminist Philosophies,* edited by Karen J. Warren, 52–65. Bloomington: Indiana University Press, 1996.

Salleh, Ariel Kay. "Deeper Than Deep Ecology: The Ecofeminist Connection." *Environmental Ethics* 6, no. 1 (1984): 339.

Sessions, George. "The Deep Ecology Movement: A Review." *Environmental Review* 9 (1987): 115.

Spretnak, Charlene. "Feminism and Ecology: Making Connections." In *Readings in Ecology and Feminist Theology,* edited by Mary Heather MacKinnon and Marie McIntyre. Kansas City, KS: Sheed and Ward, 1995.

Sturgeon, Noël. *Ecofeminist Natures: Race, Gender, Feminist Theory and Political Action.* New York: Routledge, 1997.

———. *Environmentalism in Popular Culture: Gender, Race, Sexuality, and the Politics of the Natural.* Tuscon: University of Arizona Press, 2008.

Warren, Karen J. "Feminism and Ecology." *Environmental Review* 9, no. 1 (Spring 1987): 3–20.

Zabinski, Catherine. "Scientific Ecology and Ecological Feminism: The Potential for Dialogue." In *Ecofeminism: Women, Culture, Nature,* edited by Karen J. Warren, 314–324. Bloomington: Indiana University Press, 1997.

Tensions in Nature: Ecofeminist Thought

Anderlini-D'Onofrio, Serena. *Gaia and the New Politics of Love: Notes for a Poly Planet.* Berkeley: North Atlantic Books, 2009.

Corrigan, Theresa, and Stephanie Hoppe. *With a Fly's Eye, Whale's Wit, and Woman's Heart: Animals and Women.* Pittsburgh: Cleis Press, 1989.

Crittenden, Chris. "Subordinate and Oppressive Conceptual Frameworks: A Defense of Ecofeminist Perspectives." *Environmental Ethics* 20, no. 3 (Fall 1998): 247–263.

Cuomo, Christine. "Toward Thoughtful Ecofeminist Activism." In *Ecological Feminist Philosophies,* edited by Karen J. Warren, 42–51. Bloomington: Indiana University Press, 1996.

———. "Unravelling the Problems in Ecofeminism." *Environmental Ethics* 14, no. 4 (Winter 1992): 351–363.

Curtin, Deane. "Toward an Ecological Ethic of Care." In *Ecological Feminist Philosophies,* edited by Karen J. Warren, 129–143. Bloomington: Indiana University Press, 1996.

Dalton, Anne Marie. *Ecotheology and the Practice of Hope.* Albany: State University of New York Press, 2010.

Daly, Mary. *Gyn/Ecology.* Boston: Beacon Press, 1978.

———. *Pure Lust.* Boston: Beacon Press, 1984.

Datar, Chhaya. *Ecofeminism Revisited: Introduction to the Discourse.* Jaipur, India: Rawat Publications, 2011.

Eisler, Riane. "The Gaia Tradition and the Partnership Future: An Ecofeminist Manifesto." In *Reweaving the World: The Emergence of Ecofeminism,* edited by Irene Diamond and Gloria Feman Orenstein. San Francisco: Sierra Club Books, 1990.

Estés, Clarissa Pinkola. *Women Who Run with the Wolves.* New York: Random House Publishing Group, 1992.

Gaard, Greta. *The Nature of Home: Taking Root in a Place.* Tucson: University of Arizona Press, 2007.

Gebara, Ivone. *Longing for Running Water: Ecofeminism and Liberation.* Minneapolis: Fortress Press, 1999.

Gray, Elizabeth Dodson. *Green Paradise Lost.* Wellesley, MA: Roundtable Press, 1981.

———. *Sacred Dimensions of Women's Experience.* Wellesley, MA: Roundtable Press, 1988.

Grey, Mary C. *Sacred Longings: The Ecological Spirit and Global Culture.* Minneapolis: Fortress Press, 2001.

Griffin, Susan. *Pornography and Silence: Culture's Revenge Against Nature.* New York: Harper & Row, 1981.

———. *Woman and Nature: The Roaring Inside Her.* New York: Harper & Row, 1978.

Gruen, Lori. "Toward an Ecofeminist Moral Epistemology." In *Ecological Feminism,* edited by Karen J. Warren, 120–138. New York: Routledge, 1994.

Hyner, Bernadette H., and Precious McKenzie Stearns. *Forces of Nature: Natural(-izing) Gender and Gender(-ing) Nature in the Discourses of Western Culture.* Newcastle upon Tyne, UK: Cambridge Scholars Publishing, 2009.

Kheel, Marti. "The Liberation of Nature: A Circular Affair." *Environmental Ethics* 7, no. 2 (1985): 135–149.

King, Roger J. H. "Caring About Nature: Feminist Ethics and the Environment." In *Ecological Feminist Philosophies,* edited by Karen J. Warren, 82–96. Bloomington: Indiana University Press, 1996.

King, Ynestra. "The Ecology of Feminism and the Feminism of Ecology." In *Healing the Wounds: The Promise of Ecofeminism,* edited by Judith Plant. Philadelphia: New Society Publishers, 1989.

Kordecki, Lesley. *Ecofeminist Subjectivities: Chaucer's Talking Birds (New Middle Ages).* New York: Palgrave Macmillan, 2011.

Kremmerer, Lisa, and Anthony J. Nocella II, eds. *Call to Compassion: Religious Perspectives on Animal Advocacy.* Brooklyn, NY: Lantern Books, 2011.

Lahar, Stephanie. "Ecofeminist Theory and Grassroots Politics." In *Ecological Feminist Philosophies,* edited by Karen J. Warren, 1–18. Bloomington: Indiana University Press, 1996.

McElroy, Susan Chernak. *All My Relations: Living with Animals as Teachers and Healers.* Novato, CA: New World Library, 2004.

Merchant, Carolyn. *Reinventing Eden: The Fate of Nature in Western Culture.* New York: Routledge, 2003.

Murphy, Patrick D. "Ground, Pivot, Motion: Ecofeminist Theory, Dialogics, and Literary Practice." In *Ecological Feminist Philosophies,* edited by Karen J. Warren, 228–243. Bloomington: Indiana University Press, 1996.

Ortner, Sherry B. "Is Female to Male as Nature Is to Culture?" In *Readings in Ecology and Feminist Theory,* edited by Mary Heather MacKinnon and Marie McIntyre. Kansas City, KS: Sheed and Ward, 1995.

Piercy, Marge. *Woman on the Edge of Time.* New York: Fawcett Crest Books, 1976.

Plant, Judith, ed. *Healing the Wounds: The Promise of Ecofeminism.* Santa Cruz, CA: New Society Publishers, 1989.

Plumwood, Val. "Ecofeminism: An Overview and Discussion of Positions and Arguments." *Australian Journal of Philosophy* 64, supplement (June 1986): 135.

Ruether, Rosemary Radford. *Ecofeminism: Symbolic and Social Connections Between the Oppression of Women and the Domination of Nature.* Charlotte: University of North Carolina, 1991.

———. *New Woman/New Earth: Sexist Ideologies and Human Liberation.* New York: Seabury Press, 1975.

———, ed. *Women Healing Earth: Third World Women on Ecology, Feminism and Religion.* Maryknoll, NY: Orbis Books, 1996.

Salleh, Ariel Kay. *Ecofeminism as Politics: Nature, Marx and the Postmodern.* New York: Zed Books, 1997.

Sandilands, Catriona. *The Good-Natured Feminist: Ecofeminism and the Quest for Democracy.* Minneapolis: University of Minnesota Press, 1999.

Vakoch, Douglas A., ed. *Ecofeminism and Rhetoric: Critical Perspectives in Sex, Technology and Discourse.* New York: Berghahn Books, 2011.

Spiritual Ecofeminism

Adams, Carol J., ed. *Ecofeminism and the Sacred.* New York: Continuum, 1994.

Christ, Carol. *She Who Changes: Re-imagining the Divine in the World.* New York: Macmillan Palgrave, 2003.

Eaton, Heather. *Introducing Ecofeminist Theologies.* London: T&T Clark International, 2005.

Eisler, Riane. "The Gaia Tradition and the Partnership Future: An Ecofeminist Manifesto." In *Reweaving the World: The Emergence of Ecofeminism,* edited by Irene Diamond and Gloria Feman Orenstein. San Francisco: Sierra Club Books, 1990.

McDaniel, Jay B. *Of God and Pelicans: A Theology of Reverence for Life.* Louisville, KY: Westminster/John Knox Press, 1989.

Neu, Diann L. *Return Blessings: Ecofeminist Liturgies Renewing the Earth.* Cleveland: Pilgrim Press, 2002.

Ruether, Rosemary Radford. *Integrating Ecofeminism, Globalization and World Religions.* Lanham, MD: Rowman & Littlefield, 2005.

Spretnak, Charlene, ed. *The Politics of Women's Spirituality.* Garden City, NY: Anchor, 1982.

Starhawk. *Dreaming in the Dark: Magic, Sex and Politics.* Boston: Beacon, 1982.

———. *Rebirth of the Goddess: Finding Meaning in Feminist Spirituality.* New York: Routledge, 1997.

———. *She Who Changes: Re-imagining the Divine in the World.* New York: Macmillan Palgrave, 2003.

———. *The Spiral Dance: A Rebirth of the Ancient Religion of the Great Goddess.* San Francisco: HarperSanFrancisco, 1979.

———. *Truth or Dare: Encounters with Power, Authority and Mystery.* San Francisco: Harper and Row, 1987.

Tompkins, Ptolemy. *The Divine Life of Animals.* New York: Three Rivers Press. 2010.

Transformative Ecofeminism

Dinnerstein, Dorothy. "Survival on Earth: The Meaning of Feminism." In *Healing the Wounds: The Promise of Ecofeminism,* edited by Judith Plant. Santa Cruz, CA: New Society Publishers, 1989.

Piercy, Marge. *Woman on the Edge of Time.* New York: Fawcett Crest, 1976.

Warren, Karen J. "Care-Sensitive Ethics and Situated Universalism." In *Global Environmental Ethics,* edited by Nicholas Low, 131–145. London: Routledge, 1999.

———. "Deep Ecology and Ecofeminism." In *Philosophical Dialogues: Arne Naess and the Progress of Ecophilosophy,* edited by Nina Witoszek and Andrew Brennan, 255–269. Lanham, MD: Rowman & Littlefield, 1999.

———. *Ecofeminist Philosophy: A Western Perspective on What It Is and Why It Matters.* Lanham, MD: Rowman & Littlefield, 2000, 970.

Global Ecofeminism

Chua, Amy. *World on Fire: How Exploring Free Market Democracy Breeds Ethnic Hatred and Global Instability.* New York: Anchor, 2003, 123–145; 163–175.

Cibreiro, Estrella, and Francisca López, eds. *Global Issues in Contemporary Hispanic Women Writers: Shaping Gender, the Environment, and Politics* (Routledge Studies in Contemporary Literature). New York: Routledge, 2012.

Cuomo, Christine. "Ecofeminism, Deep Ecology, and Human Population." In *Ecological Feminism,* edited by Karen J. Warren, 88–105. New York: Routledge, 1994.

Eaton, Heather, and Lois Ann Lorentzen. *Ecofeminism and Globalization: Exploring Culture, Context and Religion.* Lanham, MD: Rowman & Littlefield, 2003.

"From Bretton Woods to Alternatives." In *Alternatives to Economic Globalization,* edited by International Forum on Globalization, 228–238. San Francisco: Berrett-Koehler, 2002.

LaChapelle, Dolores. *Earth Wisdom.* Silverton, CO: Way of the Mountain Learning Center and International College, 1978.

Mellor, Mary. *Feminism and Ecology.* New York: New York University Press, 1997.

Merchant, Carolyn. *Radical Ecology: The Search for a Livable World.* New York: Routledge, 1992.

Mies, Maria, and Vandana Shiva. *Ecofeminism.* London: Zed Books, 1993.

Moe-Lobeda, Cynthia. *Globalization and God: Healing a Broken World.* Minneapolis: Fortress Press, 2002.

Nhanenge, Jytte. *Ecofeminism: Towards Integrating the Concerns of Women, Poor People, and Nature into Development.* Lanham, MD: University Press of America, 2011.

Ress, Mary Judith. *Ecofeminism in Latin America (Women from the Margins).* Maryknoll, NY: Orbis Books, 2006.

Rich, Bruce. *Mortgaging the Earth: The World Bank, Environmental Impoverishment and the Crisis of Development.* Boston: Beacon, 1994, 49–106.

Rocheleau, Dianne, Barbara Thomas-Slayter, and Esther Wangari, eds. *Feminist Political Ecology: Global Issues and Local Experiences.* New York: Routledge, 1996.

Ruether, Rosemary Radford. "Culture and Women's Rights." *Conscience* 16, no. 4 (Winter, 1995–1996): 13–15.

———, ed. *Women Healing Earth: Third World Women on Ecology, Feminism and Religion.* Maryknoll, NY: Orbis Books, 1996.

Salleh, Ariel. *Eco-Sufficiency and Global Justice: Women Write Political Ecology.* London: Pluto Press, 2009.

Seager, Joni. *Earth Follies: Coming to Feminist Terms with the Global Environmental Crisis.* New York: Routledge, 1993.

Shiva, Vandana. *Biopiracy: The Plunder of Nature and Knowledge.* Boston: South End Press, 1997.

———. *Earth Democracy: Justice, Sustainability, and Peace.* Brooklyn, NY: South End Press, 2005.

———. *Staying Alive: Women, Ecology and Development.* Second Edition. Brooklyn, NY: South End Press, 2010.

———. *Stolen Harvest: The Hijacking of the Global Food Supply.* Cambridge: South End Press, 2000.

———. "Taking Empirical Data Seriously: An Ecofeminist Philosophy Perspective." In *Living with Contradictions: Controversies in Feminist Social Ethics,* edited by Alison M. Jaggar, 642–643. Boulder, CO: Westview Press, 1994.

Starhawk. *Webs of Power: Notes from the Global Uprising.* Gabriola Island, BC: New Society Publishers, 2002.

Sutcliffe, Bob. *100 Ways of Seeing an Unequal World.* London: Zed Books, 2001, sections 23, 33.

Vegetarian Ecofeminism

Adams, Carol J. *The Sexual Politics of Meat: A Feminist Vegetarian Critical Theory.* 3rd ed. New York: The Continuum International Publishing Group Inc, 2010.

Adams, Carol J., and Josephine Donovan, eds. *The Feminist Care Tradition in Animal Ethics.* New York: Columbia University Press, 2007.

Armstrong, Susan. *The Animal Ethics Reader.* 2nd ed. New York: Routledge, 2008.

Beauchamp, Tom L., and Frey, R. G. eds. *The Oxford Handbook of Animal Ethics.* Oxford: Oxford University Press, 2011.

Bekoff, Marc, ed. *Encyclopedia of Animal Rights and Welfare.* 2nd ed. 2 vols. Santa Barbara, CA: Greenwood Press, 2010.

DeMello, Margo. *Animals and Society: An Introductino to Human-Animal Studies.* New York: Columbia University Press, 2012.

Dunayer, Joan. *Animal Equality: Language and Liberation.* Derwood, MD: Ryce Publishing, 2001.

Francione, Gary L. *Animals as Persons: Essays on the Abolition of Animal Exploitation.* Chichester, UK: Columbia University Press, 2008.

Gaard, Greta. "Vegetarian Ecofeminism: A Review Essay." *Frontiers: A Journal of Women Studies* 23, no. 3 (2002): 117–146.

Gaarder, Emily. *Women and the Animal Rights Movement.* Piscataway, NJ: Rutgers University Press, 2011.

Gruen, Lori, and Kari Weil, eds. *Hypatia: Special Issue, Animal Others* 27, no. 3 (Summer 2012).

Imhoff, Daniel, ed. *The CAFO Reader: The Tragedy of Industrial Animal Factories.* Berkley and Los Angeles: University of California Press, 2010.

Joy, Melanie. *Why We Love Dogs, Eat Pigs, and Wear Cows: An Introduction to Carnism.* San Francisco: Conari Press, 2010.

Kao, Grace. "Consistency in Ecofeminist Ethics." *The International Journal of the Humanities* 3 (2005/2006).

Kemmerer, Lisa, ed. *Animals and World Religions*. New York: Oxford University Press, 2011.

————. *Sister Species: Women, Animals and Social Justice*. Chicago: University of Illinois Press, 2011.

Kheel, Marti. *Nature Ethics: An Ecofeminist Perspective*. Latham, MD: Rowman & Littlefield, 2008.

Nussbaum, Martha C. *Frontiers of Justice: Disability, Nationality, Species Membership*. Cambridge: Harvard University Press, 2006.

Regan, Tom. *The Case for Animal Rights*. 2nd ed. Berkeley: University of California Press, 2004.

Sanbonmatsu, John, ed. *Critical Theory and Animal Liberation*. Lanham, MD: Rowman & Littlefield, 2011.

Shevelow, Kathryn. *For the Love of Animals: The Rise of the Animal Protection Movement*. New York: Holt Paperbacks, 2008.

Singer, Peter. *Animal Liberation*. 4th ed. New York: HarperCollins Publishers, 2009.

Singer, Peter, and Jim Mason, eds. *The Ethics of What We Eat*. Emmaus, PA: Rodale, 2006.

Socha, Kim. *Women, Destruction, and the Avant-Garde: A Paradigm for Animal Liberation*. New York: Rodopi, 2011.

Steeves, H. Peter, and Tom Regan, eds. *Animal Others: On Ethics, Ontology and Animal Life*. Albany: State University of New York Press, 1999.

Sunstein, Cass R., and Martha C. Nussbaum, eds. *Animal Rights: Current Debates and New Directions*. Oxford: Oxford University Press, 2004.

Critiques of Ecofeminism

Critiques of Nature Ecofeminism

Biehl, Janet. *Rethinking Ecofeminist Politics*. Boston: South End Press, 1991.

Critiques of Spiritual Ecofeminism

King, Ynestra. "Engendering a Peaceful Planet: Ecology, Economy, and Ecofeminism in Contemporary Context." *Women Studies Quarterly* 23 (Fall/Winter 1995): 19.

Mies, Maria. "White Man's Dilemma: His Search for What He Has Destroyed." In *Ecofeminism*, edited by Maria Shiva and Vandana Shiva. London: Zed, 1993.

Critiques of Transformative Ecofeminism

Auerbach, Judith. "The Intersection of Feminism and the Environmental Movement, or What Is Feminist About the Feminist Perspective on the Environment?" *American Behavioral Scientist* 37, no. 8 (August 1994): 1095.

Biehl, Janet. *Rethinking Ecofeminist Politics*. Boston: South End Press, 1991.

King, Ynestra. "Engendering a Peaceful Planet: Ecology, Economy, and Ecofeminism in Contemporary Context." *Women Studies Quarterly* 23 (Fall/Winter 1995): 16–17.

Merchant, Carolyn. *Radical Ecology: The Search for a Livable World*. New York: Routledge, 1992.

Critiques of Global Ecofeminism

Biehl, Janet. *Rethinking Ecofeminist Politics.* Boston: South End Press, 1991.

Critiques of Vegetarian Ecofeminism

Kheel, Marti. *Nature Ethics: An Ecofeminist Perspective.* Latham, MD: Rowman & Littlefield, 2008.

Warren, Karen J. *Ecofeminist Philosophy: A Western Perspective on What It Is and Why It Matters.* Latham, MD: Rowman & Littlefield, 2000.

Conclusion

Alfonso, Rita, and Jo Trigilio. "Surfing the Third Wave: A Dialogue Between Two Third Wave Feminists." *Hypatia* 12, no. 3 (Summer 1997): 8–16.

Berger, Melody. *We Don't Need Another Wave: Dispatches from the Next Generation of Feminists.* Emeryville, CA: Seal Press, 2006.

Breines, Wini. "What's Love Got to Do with It? White Women, Black Women, and Feminism in the Movement Years." *Signs: Journal of Women in Culture and Society* 27, no. 4 (Summer 2002): 1095–1133.

Bruns, Cindy M., and Colleen Trimble. "Rising Tide: Taking Our Place as Young Feminist Psychologists." In *The Newest Generation: Third Wave Psychotherapy,* edited by Ellen Kaschak, 19–36. Binghamton, NY: Haworth Press, 2001.

Cashen, Jeanne. "The Revolution Is Mine: Grrrl Resistance in a Commodity Culture." Unpublished manuscript. University of New Orleans, 2002.

Denfeld, Rene. *The New Victorians: A Young Woman's Challenge to the Old Feminist Order.* New York: Routledge, 1995.

Dicker, Rory, and Alison Piepmeier, eds. *Catching a Wave: Reclaiming Feminism for the 21st Century.* Boston: Northeastern University Press, 2003.

Di Stefano, Christine. "Dilemmas of Difference." In *Feminism/Postmodernism,* edited by Linda J. Nicholson. New York: Routledge, 1990.

Edut, Ophira, ed. *Adios Barbie: Young Women Write about Body Image and Identity.* Seattle: Seal Press, 1998.

Ensler, Eve. *The Vagina Monologues.* London: Virago Press, 2001.

Ferguson, Ann. "Sex and Work: Women as a New Revolutionary Class." In *An Anthology of Western Marxism: From Lukács and Gramsci to Socialist Feminism,* edited by Robert S. Gottlieb. Oxford: Oxford University Press, 1989.

Findlen, Barbara, ed. *Listen Up! Voices from the Next Feminist Generations.* Berkeley, CA: Seal Press, 1995.

Genz, Stephanie, and Benjamin A. Brabon. *Postfeminism: Cultural Texts and Theories.* Edinburgh, Scotland: Edinburgh University Press, 2009.

Gillis, Stacy, Gillian Howie, and Rebecca Munford. *Third Wave Feminism: A Critical Exploration.* New York: Palgrave, 2007.

Halstead, Ted. "A Politics for Generation X." *Atlantic Monthly* 284, no. 2 (August 1999): 33–42.

Henry, Astrid. "Feminism's Family Problem: Feminist Generations and the Mother-Daughter Trope." In *Catching a Wave: Reclaiming Feminism for the 21st Century,* edited by Rory Dicker and Alison Piepmeier, 209–231. Boston: Northeastern University Press, 2003.

————. *Not My Mother's Sister: Generational Conflict and Third-Wave Feminism.* Bloomington: Indiana University Press, 2004.

Hernández, Daisy, and Bushra Reman, eds. *Colonize This! Young Women of Color and Today's Feminism.* Berkeley, CA: Seal Press, 2002.

Heywood, Leslie, and Jennifer Drake, eds. *Third Wave Agenda: Being Feminist, Doing Feminism.* Minneapolis: University of Minnesota Press, 1997.

Howry, Allison L., and Julia T. Wood. "Something Old, Something New, Something-Borrowed: Themes in the Voices of a New Generation of Feminists." *SouthernCommunication Journal* 4, no. 66 (Summer 2001): 324.

Huffman, D. J. "Making Sense of Third Wave Feminism." MA thesis. University of New Orleans, 2002.

Jervis, Lisa, and Andi Zeisler, eds. *Bitchfest.* New York: Farrar, Straus, and Giroux, 2006.

Johnson, Merri Lisa. *Third Wave Feminism and Television: Jane Puts It in a Box.* London: I. B. Tauris & Co. Ltd, 2007.

Kinser, Amber. "Negotiating Space For/Through Third-Wave Feminism." *NWSA Journal* 16, no. 3 (2005): 124–153.

Koyama, Emi. "The Transfeminist Manifesto." In *Catching a Wave: Reclaiming Feminism for the 21st Century,* edited by Rory Dicker and Alison Piepmeier, 244–259. Boston: Northeastern University Press, 2003.

Kunin, Madeleine M. *The New Feminist Agenda: Defining the Next Revolution for Women, Work, and Family.* White River Junction, VT: Chelsea Green Publishing, 2012.

Levy, Ariel. *Female Chauvinist Pigs: Women and the Rise of Raunch Culture.* New York: Free Press, 2005.

McRobbie, Angela. *The Aftermath of Feminism: Gender, Culture and Social Change.* London: Sage Publications, 2009.

Musico, Inga. *Cunt: A Declaration of Independence.* Berkeley: Seal Press, 2002.

Navarro, Mireya. "Going Beyond Black and White, Hispanics in Census Pick 'Other.'" *New York Times,* November 9, 2003, late edition, East Coast, A1, A21.

O'Keefe, Eileen, and Martha Chinouya. "Global Migrants, Gendered Tradition, and Human Rights: Africans and HIV in the United Kingdom." In *Feminist Bioethics, Human Rights, and the Developing World: Integrating Global and Local Perspectives,* edited by Susan Dodds, Anne Donchin, and Rosemarie Tong. Lanham, MD: Rowman & Littlefield, 2004.

Paglia, Camille. *Sex, Art, and American Culture: Essays.* New York: Random House, 1992.

Quinn, Rebecca. "An Open Letter to Institutional Mothers." In *Generations: Academic Feminists in Dialogue,* edited by Devoney Looser and Ann Kaplan. Minneapolis: University of Minnesota Press, 1997.

Roiphe, Katie. *The Morning After: Sex, Fear, and Feminism on Campus.* New York: Little & Brown, 1993.

Rowe-Finkbeiner, Kristin. *The F-Word.* New York: Avalon Publishing Group, 2004.

Siegel, Deborah L. "The Legacy of the Personal: Generating Theory in Feminism's Third Wave." *Hypatia* 12, no. 3 (1997): 46–75.

————. *Sisterhood, Interrupted: From Radical Women to Grrls Gone Wild.* New York: Palgrave Macmillan, 2007.

Springer, Kimberly. "Third Wave Black Feminism?" *Signs: Journal of Women in Culture and Society* 27, no. 4 (2002): 1059–1082.

United States v. Morrison, 529 US 598, 2000.

Walker, Rebecca, ed. *To Be Real: Telling the Truth and Changing the Face of Feminism.* New York: Anchor Books, 1995.

Whittier, Nancy. Feminist Generations: The Persistence of the Radical Women's Movement. Philadelphia: Temple University Press, 1995.

Wlodarczyk, Justyna. *Ungrateful Daughters: Third Wave Feminist Writings.* Newcastle upon Tyne, UK: Cambridge Scholars Publishing, 2010.

Zaslow, Emilie. *Feminism, Inc.: Coming of Age in Girl Power Media Culture.* New York: Palgrave Macmillan, 2009.

Zeilinger, Julie. *A Little F'd Up: Why Feminism Is Not a Dirty Word.* Berkeley: Seal Press, 2012.

Index

twentieth-century, 23

welfare, 35

Wollstonecraft, Mary and, 1, 13–16, 18, 19, 28

women's liberation and, 4, 18, 36

women's oppression and, 2

women's rights groups and, 23–27

women's suffrage and, 13, 15, 20–23

Liberalism, 1–2

capitalism and, 95

classical, 11, 12

freedom and, 174

human nature and, 94

liberal feminism and, 11

reason and, 11

welfare, 11, 12–13, 97

Liberation. *See* Women's lilberation

Liberty. *See* Freedom

Lopate, Carol, 106

Lorde, Audre, 214, 216, 218, 219

Lugones, Maria, 225, 251

Macauley, David, 267, 268–269

MacKinnon, Catharien, 68, 69

MacKinnon, Catharine, 67

Mailer, Norman, 55

Mainstream feminism, 296

goals of, 216

indigenous feminism and, 229–230

women of color feminism and, 213, 250–251

women's oppression and, 218–220

Mansfield, Katherine, 187

Mao Zedong, 123

Mapping the Moral Domain (Gilligan), 154

Marcano, Donna-Dale, 221

Marriage, 17, 20, 21, 27, 29, 101, 102–103, 183–184, 273

Martin, Jane Roland, 15

Marx, Karl, 74, 75, 93, 95, 96, 100, 101, 103

Marxism

alienation and, 125

class and, 96–99

economics, theory of and, 95–96

family relations, theory of and, 101–103

freedom and, 174, 280

human nature and, 94, 100

politics, theory of and, 99–101

power and, 96

society, theory of and, 96–99

women as a class and, 125

Marxist feminism

alienation and, 98–99

capitalism and, 4, 95–96

class and, 96–99

classical, 103–107

concepts and theories of, 94–103

critiques of, 123–124

general reflections on, 103–107

Marxism, concepts and theories of and, 94–103

radical feminism and, 5

theory of economics and, 95–96

wages-for-housework campaign and, 106–107

women's labor and, 104–105

women's oppression and, 4, 95, 96, 103–104, 123

Masculinity

care-focused feminism and, 7

cultural, 31

definition of, 36

patriarchy and, 59, 62

psychosexual development and, 128

radical-cultural feminism and, 60

radical-libertarian feminism and, 2, 52

Masochism, 177–178

McCall, Dorothy Kaufmann, 179

Medicine, Beatrice, 230

Men

abolition and, 21, 22

child-rearing and, 167

evil, understanding of and, 156–158

female sexuality and, 3

intellectual capability of, 19

moral development of, 152–153

moral reasoning and, 158

reason and, 7, 14

reproductive role of, 179–180

sexual division of labor and, 125

sexuality and, 66

traditional roles, liberation from of, 49